Curriculum and Instructional Methods for the Elementary and Middle School

FOURTH EDITION

Curriculum and Instructional Methods for the Elementary and Middle School

FOURTH EDITION

Johanna Kasin Lemlech
University of Southern California

Merrill,
an imprint of Prentice Hall
Upper Saddle River, New Jersey   Columbus, Ohio

Library of Congress Cataloging-in-Publication Data

Lemlech, Johanna Kasin
    Curriculum and instructional methods for the elementary and middle
school / Johanna Kasin Lemlech. – 4th ed.
        p.   cm.
    Includes bibliographical/references and indexes.
    ISBN 0-13-262130-4

     1. Elementary school teaching—United States–Handbooks, manuals,
etc. 2. Middle school teaching–United States–Handbooks, manuals,
etc. 3. Classroom management–United States–Handbooks, manuals,
etc. 4. Education, elementary–United States–Handbooks, manuals,
etc. I. Title
LB1570.L453   1998
372.1102–dc21   97-21783

                  CIP

Cover Photo: John S. Bunker/SuperStock
Editor: Debra A. Stollenwerk
Production Editor: Mary M. Irvin
Design Coordinator: Karrie M. Converse
Text Designer and Production Coordination: Custom Editorial Productions, Inc.
Cover Designer: Brian Deep
Production Manager: Laura Messerly
Director of Marketing: Kevin Flanagan
Marketing Manager: Suzanne Stanton
Advertising/Marketing Coordinator: Julie Shough

This book was set in Janson Text by Custom Editorial Productions, Inc., and was printed and bound by
Courier/Kendalville. The cover was printed by Phoenix Color Corp.

Earlier edition, © 1994 by Macmillan College Publishing Company, Inc. Earlier editions, entitled
Curriculum and Instructional Methods for the Elementary School © by Macmillan Publishing Company, and ©
1984 by Johanna Kasin Lemlech.

Photo Credits: Culver Pictures, Inc., 17; Scott Cunningham/Merrill, 80, 114, 295; Paula Goldman, 107, 136, 171, 177, 192,
218, 271, 290, 307, 356; Lloyd Lemerman/Merrill, 250; Johanna Kasin Lemlech, 3, 37, 40, 44, 53, 62, 75, 125, 153, 160,
167, 181, 186, 201, 209, 227, 254, 259, 281, 303, 318, 323, 327, 345, 348, 369; Anne Vega/Merrill, 105, 379

Printed in the United States of America

10 9 8 7 6 5 4 3 2

ISBN 0-13-262130-4

Prentice-Hall International (UK) Limited, *London*
Prentice-Hall of Australia Pty. Limited, *Sydney*
Prentice-Hall Canada Inc., *Toronto*
Prentice-Hall Hispanoamericana, S. A., *Mexico*
Prentice-Hall of India Private Limited, *New Delhi*
Prentice-Hall of Japan, Inc., *Tokyo*
Simon & Schuster Asia Pte. Ltd., *Singapore*
Editora Prentice-Hall do Brasil, Ltda., *Rio de Janeiro*

This book is dedicated to my husband Bernard Lemlech

and

to the memory of my parents Mollie and Henry Kasin, who helped me realize that teachers *can* improve society.

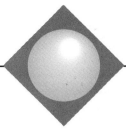

Preface

Teaching in elementary and middle school classrooms is not what it used to be. It is *not* what you remember about your own early school experiences. Schools in the twenty-first century will respond to competition in the marketplace. By this I mean that changes will include the possible advent of vouchers, the charter school movement, specialized schools in the public school sector, and increasing numbers of private schools. Teachers will need to speak out, be more savvy about communicating their own expertise, and be more willing to explain about the curriculum, pedagogy, and the school environment.

As schools become less bureaucratic and teachers more involved in making the critical decisions that govern schools, the school will become more democratic and more of a learning and professional community. This will mean that teachers understand (and accept) the inherent responsibilities of leadership and professionalism. Teachers will take control not only of the curriculum, instructional processes, and student assessment, but also of their own professional growth.

Better understanding of how students learn and how to aid the learning process is changing the way schools look, and the ways that teachers teach. Constructivist learning necessitates that students are perceived as active partners in framing the learning process. New understandings about how we learn have emphasized that knowledge is individually constructed and reconstructed. Students need personal experiences (and need to use their prior experiences) to produce knowledge.

It is clear that the teacher's role has changed. No longer can teachers expect to be fountains of wisdom and convey knowledge to passive students. Rote learning of skills and total reliance on the textbook are out of step with the information age, an interdisciplinary curriculum, and higher-order thinking.

As I write this introduction to the fourth edition, I realize that it is the changing roles of teachers that have influenced me most throughout the text. Teachers need to know about historical traditions in education (Chapters 2 and 3 of the text) in order to understand the purpose of democratic schools. Our diverse society and current social problems require teachers who take charge of schooling, respect diversity, understand how individuals learn, and know how to work collaboratively with colleagues (Chapters 1, 3, 5, and 18).

Constructivist teaching is emphasized throughout the text, but Part II focuses on the delivery of instruction. The emphasis is on student interaction, teaching as guiding (instead of disseminating), and teacher modeling inquiry and learning.

Though teachers do not pour knowledge into passive students, as teachers we need to know the curriculum (subject fields) and know how to integrate instruction, use time wisely, accept responsibility for meeting standards, and employ authentic measures of assessment. Assessment is discussed in Chapter 11, and Part III of the text provides a comprehensive introduction to each subject field.

The new teacher professional also recognizes that part of being a member of a learning community means carrying out a researcher's role. To improve instruction and to improve the quality of life in classrooms, teachers need to dialogue with colleagues and take part in creating research studies. Finding out what students know and don't know, comparing and contrasting learning resources, and recognizing the effect of environments on learning signify other ways that teachers are taking control of their professional lives and the classrooms in which they work. Teacher research is highlighted in many of the chapters in this fourth edition and discussed in Chapter 18.

This text is for teachers in all phases of a professional career. It is intended as a reference and to raise critical questions about professional practice and provide dialogue about professional concerns. The text should be helpful to individuals in graduate and undergraduate studies, for preservice and inservice, and for those who study and plan curriculum and instructional processes.

NEW IN THIS EDITION

Several features of the fourth edition are different. Each chapter begins with a brief synopsis that serves as an advance organizer. Because the language of teaching has changed dramatically in the last several years, I have included also at the beginning of each chapter a section entitled Professional Lexicon. The terms in the lexicon correspond to the content of each chapter.

The chapter summaries in this edition have changed. Summary statements are grouped under headings that relate to the main ideas of the chapter. The summary statements are numbered and provide the key ideas included in the chapter.

This fourth edition continues the practice of using boxes to alert the reader to research findings and research applications. However, I have extended the boxes to include teaching hints, and also new to this edition are research citations from classroom teachers entitled *Teacher Research*.

Certain aspects of teaching are of particular importance to new teachers. Classroom management suggestions are emphasized throughout the text. Sections about *inclusion* are included in the curriculum chapters and the subject is fully discussed in Chapter 1. Integration of subject fields is discussed in Chapter 9 and applications are discussed in the curriculum chapters. Special emphasis on integration occurs in the chapter on the arts, Chapter 17.

ACKNOWLEDGMENTS

A special thank you to the many teachers and principals who provided me with opportunities to observe and participate in their classrooms with bright and interested students. I want to thank the principals, teachers, and students (and their parents) who gave permission for the picture-taking sessions. First let me compliment photographer Paula Goldman for her patience and outstanding photographs. The pictures and participants were from the following schools: Edison Elementary School, Glendale Unified School District (principal Joanna Junge and teachers Misa Dugally, Michelle Noble, Sonia Sogge, Kevin Reilly, Arda Derian, and very special thank you to Caitlin Rabanera, who coordinated the picture taking); Euclid Elementary School, Los Angeles Unified School District (teachers Geraldine Allen and Melanie Crawford); Brentwood Elementary School, Los Angeles Unified School District (teachers Lillian Walker and JoAnn Lopez); and Lincoln Middle School, Santa Monica Unified School District, (principal Ilene Straus and teachers Eileen Hiss, Bonnie Schwartz, and Kenneth Vander Veen).

I am indebted to a number of people who critiqued chapters in the text and provided significant feedback for this fourth edition. These individuals are Hillary Hertzog, Joy Morin, Sandra Kaplan, and Margo Pensavalle. I am also indebted to Lou Ann Evans and Eileen Swartz, USC coordinators who work with the student teachers, for their insightful suggestions.

A special thank you to editor Debbie Stollenwerk, editorial assistant Penny Burleson, and production editors Mary Irvin and JaNoel Lowe.

I am grateful for the assistance of many readers of prior editions who have sent comments and contributed ideas. I also need to thank many of my doctoral students and colleagues who have faithfully read this edition and contributed reflections, research, and insight.

Several colleagues painstakingly reviewed the text in its entirety and contributed very relevant and meaningful assistance. These individuals are Anita Baker, Baylor University; Adrianna H. Francis, Eastern Kentucky University; Maureen Gillette, College of St. Rose; Susan Hahn, Dominican College of San Rafael; William D. Smith, Monmouth College; and Patti Trietsch, Sul Ross State University.

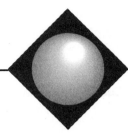

Brief Contents

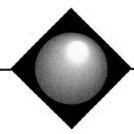

Contents

◆ PART III
UNDERSTANDING THE CURRICULUM   225

CHAPTER 12
Teaching English Language Arts   227

CHAPTER 13
Social Experiences: The Nature of the Social Studies   259

PART I

CHALLENGE, CHOICE, AND RESPONSIBILITY OF ELEMENTARY AND MIDDLE SCHOOL TEACHERS

Teaching in elementary and middle schools requires knowledge of U.S. society in the past, present, and future. Teachers face many challenges and increasing responsibilities because they influence the lives of students and the quality of future life. Curriculum decisions are based on understanding developmental needs and interests of children, the learning process, our society, our history, and the possibilities for the future. The first three chapters of Part I focus on societal needs, tensions, goals, and traditions. Chapter 4 focuses on the children we teach, how they differ, and how they learn. The four chapters of Part I set the stage for the study of curriculum, instructional methods, and professional responsibilities.

INTRODUCTION: TEACHERS' LEADERSHIP ROLES

Mary Hogan, Greg Thomas, and Karen Adazzio are three fictitious teachers you will encounter from time to time throughout this text. The brief sketches of the teachers that follow highlight their experiences, attitudes, and beliefs about teaching. Each, in his or her own way, is a teacher-leader.

MARY HOGAN

Mary Hogan is in her second year of teaching. She teaches second grade at a large urban elementary school. There are 1,300 students at the school and 85 percent of them are native Spanish speakers. Her school district, located in the western United States, enrolls 625,000 students.

Hogan was educated at a private university in a collegial teacher preparation program. In her student teaching experience she was paired with another student teacher, and together they practiced in the same classroom. The two student teachers planned lessons together and often taught side by side. They were responsible for observing each other teach and for providing each other with feedback. As a consequence of this experience, Hogan is quite comfortable with having colleagues come into the classroom to observe. She continues to keep in close touch with her student teaching colleague, and they talk frequently about teaching.

Hogan's preparation program emphasized several models of teaching, and she became expert at applying a variety of approaches to accomplish her instructional purposes. She considers the classroom environment extremely important for motivating students, and she frequently uses learning centers to differentiate curriculum content and skill activities. Hogan believes that it is the teacher's responsibility to help students learn *how* to learn. She works hard to generate the kinds of questions that will provoke students' thinking.

As a second-year teacher, Hogan is not totally comfortable with her own classroom management skills, but she believes in helping students become responsible for their own behavior. Her classroom rules were set by the students and are extremely simple. ("We are responsible for our own behavior. We respect others.")

Because Hogan is so skilled in her use of teaching models, she was asked by her principal to demonstrate lessons for other teachers. She gained considerable respect from the other teachers at her school for what they consider innovative approaches and for her willingness to allow others to observe in her classroom.

GREG THOMAS

Greg Thomas teaches fifth grade in a southern rural school. His school district enrolls 3,200 students. The school where he teaches has an enrollment of 475 students. He has been a teacher for seven years, five of which have been at his present teaching assignment.

Thomas likes to use the project method for teaching. He involves students in choosing in-depth investigations, such as the study of ecological problems in their rural community and how these problems differ from or are similar to problems in the past and expectations for the future. His class may study a topic for several days or weeks with individuals or small groups responsible for different aspects of the study. The project method facilitates both an interdisciplinary conceptual focus and the integration of skills across subject fields. Thomas believes that teachers have opportunities to improve society through their curriculum and instructional decisions.

Students in Thomas's classroom are highly motivated due to the nature of his projects and their own involvement in curriculum decision making. As a result parents are always anxious to see that their children are placed in Thomas's class.

Greg Thomas is considered a curriculum innovator. Recently his principal suggested to the superintendent that Thomas work with other teachers to develop new curricular approaches. As a consequence, he is relieved from teaching responsibilities two days per month for district curricular planning and for working with other teachers. He also has developed a special parent workshop program to inform parents about the curriculum and to enlist parental assistance in obtaining special funds for resource materials and field trips for students.

Think about your own beliefs about teaching and teachers' responsibilities. What do you want to emphasize as you choose what to teach and how to teach it?

KAREN ADAZZIO

Karen Adazzio teaches seventh grade in a middle school in the northeastern United States. The school district has a school population of 32,075 students and has just recently reorganized the schools in the district, changing from the concept of grades K–6, 7–9, and 10–12 to grades K–5 in the elementary schools, 6–8 in middle schools, and 9–12 in the high schools.

Adazzio is a very unusual teacher. She began her teaching career as an elementary teacher. Then she obtained a secondary credential and taught at the senior high school level. Recently, after 17 years of teaching, she asked to be assigned to one of the new middle schools. Because Adazzio believes that adolescents often feel displaced and unconnected in the departmentalized structure of junior high schools, she was active in convincing other teachers to experiment with her in a new structure, sometimes referred to as a *house*, that groups teachers and students together as a team.

This new approach, popularized by Ted Sizer's Coalition of Essential Schools, has cast Adazzio in the role of the instructional leader for her team. She works with five other teachers, 160 students, and parents. Two periods a day she is released to help improve curriculum, instructional approaches, and the counseling of students.

Adazzio is eclectic in her educational beliefs. She believes that middle school children need to be involved in problem solving and that teachers need to focus on problem situations to generate students' interests. She also believes that her students must learn to fit in to their community so her choice of problematic situations tends to emphasize teen-age dilemmas and community problems.

C H A P T E R

Teachers, Schools, and Society

School is an institution created by society to socialize and democratize the young. But in a diverse society, people differ about goals, standards, and what they want taught in the curriculum. This chapter focuses on differing expectations and the ensuing challenges that confront schools.

After you study this chapter, you should be able to accomplish the following:

1. Identify national education goals and explain the controversies associated with those goals.
2. Identify several school programs created to assist low-income families.
3. Suggest ways that teachers can help to reduce school and community violence.
4. Explain the role of teachers in identifying child abuse.
5. Explain why some individuals favor a health literacy curriculum and others believe it is a family concern.
6. Discuss what teachers can do to ensure equal educational opportunity.
7. Contrast the differing approaches to gender equity and gender equality.
8. Identify at-risk students and the steps the school can take to assist these students.
9. Identify the controversy related to the inclusive school and classroom. Why do some teachers favor it and others oppose it?
10. Discuss the differing beliefs about including multicultural education in the curriculum.
11. Contrast the different beliefs about bilingual education.
12. Explain why it is important to identify and develop programs for gifted and talented students.
13. Suggest ways to involve parents in the education of their children.

Professional Lexicon

at-risk students   Students whom schools can anticipate will have difficulty completing high school education because of associated problems.

content standards   Measures used to judge what is to be taught to students at varied levels of education.

English as a second language (ESL)   Instruction of nonnative English speakers to teach fluency in reading, writing, and understanding the English language.

exceptional learners   Students who are gifted, talented, or have disabilities; any individual whose performance differs from the average group of students.

full-service schools   A school that coordinates health and social services for school community families.

gender bias   Bias related to sex-role stereotyping that leads to different classroom practices for girls and boys.

gender equality   The concept that everyone starts out on the same rung of the ladder and has equal access.

gender equity   The concept that teachers are aware of traditional biases and act to enhance opportunity for the target group.

inclusive school and classroom   A school and classroom that teaches (includes) students with disabilities.

individualized educational program (IEP)   An instructional plan that identifies the needs and capacities of the subject individual.

limited English proficiency (LEP)   Used to describe a student who is learning English as a second language.

multicultural education   The conscious inclusion in the curriculum of the experiences and culture of all students.

performance standards   Measures used to judge what has been learned through application.

SOCIETAL EXPECTATIONS FOR SCHOOLS

Schools are social institutions consciously developed by society to control the education of children. Schools can differ markedly by deliberately providing unique environmental experiences. People in the United States expect schools to teach basic fundamentals, transmit selected social customs, develop civility in the young, and foster the development of individual talents.

These expectations have been prevalent throughout our history, but the United States had no formally stated national goals until 1989. In 1989 at an education summit, six national goals were set, and in 1994, Congress adopted the goals and created two additional goals. It was Congress's intent that by the year 2000 progress would be achieved toward accomplishing each of the following goals:

1. All children in America will start school ready to learn.
2. The high school graduation rate will increase to at least 90 percent.
3. All students will leave grades 4, 8, and 12 having demonstrated competency over challenging subject matter including English, mathematics, science, foreign languages, civics and government, economics, arts, history, and geography; and every school in America will ensure that all students learn to use their minds well, so they may be prepared for responsible citizenship, further learning, and productive employment in our Nation's modern economy.
4. The Nation's teaching force will have access to programs for the continued improvement of their professional skills and the opportunity to acquire the knowledge and skills needed to instruct and prepare all American students for the next century.
5. United States students will be first in the world in mathematics and science achievement.
6. Every adult American will be literate and will possess the knowledge and skills necessary to compete in a global economy and exercise the rights and responsibilities of citizenship.
7. Every school in the United States will be free of drugs, violence, and the unauthorized presence of firearms and alcohol and will offer a disciplined environment conducive to learning.
8. Every school will promote partnerships that will increase parental involvement and participation in promoting the social, emotional, and academic growth of children (National Goals Report, 1994, pp. 13–14).

Some educators believe that the setting of national goals was motivated by individuals and organizations who desired to stimulate the national economy, making the United States more competitive in the global marketplace (Howe, 1995). Educators question whether schools do in fact affect the national economy. The RAND Institute on Education and Training (April 1994) reported that only about 14 percent of U.S. economic growth could be affected by education and training. Few educators doubt, however, that school reform is needed. Most believe that reform should be accomplished because of a commitment to the democratic purposes of education and belief that all Americans should have equality of opportunity.

Blythe Clinchy (1995) expresses concern that the national goals treat students as objects, passive receptacles to be filled with content standards, and then evaluated to check performance standards. This concept of the student affects not only what is taught, but how it is taught, and Clinchy believes that this conflicts with current research in developmental psychology (see Chapter 4).

Concurrent with the setting of national goals has been the movement to set content and performance standards. **Content standards** focus on what students should learn in the subject fields. (The curriculum chapters will feature some of those standards.) **Performance standards** are intended to allow students to demonstrate the application of what they know. The controversy over standards has to do with questions such as "Who sets the standards?" and "Who decides if the standards are appropriate?"

Harold Howe II (1995) calls attention to the shift in federal policy from *interest* in the schools to *control* of the schools. He warns that the Goals 2000 plan means that Uncle Sam is sitting in the back of every public classroom and that a new bureaucratic structure affects teachers and the learning process.

Eisner (1995) questions the wisdom of uniformity in a nation with 45 million students and 2.5 million teachers. Uniformity of content and performance negates understanding of individual differences and differences related to geographic regions, interests, and community preferences.

While the education community debates the viability of national standards, the public expects schools to address social problems including health and safety, socioeconomic problems, child abuse and neglect, compensatory education, and education of all students in a diverse society. Clearly, schools (and teachers) are asked to accomplish goals that go far beyond their capabilities. This occurs because the public is more familiar with the schools as a social institution than with other social institutions (such as cultural centers, recreational facilities, social welfare facilities, and health facilities).

SOCIAL PROBLEMS AFFECTING SCHOOLS

POVERTY

In Greg Thomas's rural community, more than one-third of the students suffer the effects of poverty. Poverty is more prevalent in rural communities than in urban areas. Thomas knows that there is a relationship between socioeconomic status and achievement in school. Sociologists study socioeconomic status by relating information about an individual's occupation, education, and income. Most sociologists also accept that there are identifiable value, attitude, and belief differences related to socioeconomic status. Low socioeconomic status or poverty conditions have been related to poor attendance and failure in schools and can be a determinant of I.Q. at age five (Cohen, 1993, p. 4).

Poverty rates are particularly high for minority groups. Approximately 20 percent of the total United States population is at the poverty level. During periods of economic recession all classes of people can experience adversities, but for those individuals without education and considered unskilled, the experience of poverty is quite different. Children growing up poor may feel little control over their lives, and they are often frightened, and resigned.

In a Los Angeles elementary school a principal told the story of a kindergarten boy sent to her office by the teacher because the child was so restless, angry, sour, and mean to others. The teacher's note said, "We need a little rest from Eduardo; please keep him for a while." The principal asked the child to accompany her to the cafeteria so that she could have a late breakfast. The cafeteria manager gave the principal a grilled cheese sandwich and coffee. She and the child sat down, and the principal asked the boy if he would like to help her with the sandwich. Eduardo devoured half of the sandwich, and when the principal offered the other half, quickly ate that, too. Asked if he wanted more, the child responded affirmatively. Later the child was sent back to class and the teacher asked the principal, "What did you say to Eduardo? He came back to class and for the first time took part in a group activity."

Breakfast and lunch programs in many inner-city schools do help children from low-income families, but sometimes the mechanism for obtaining the help is not in place. Helping children from low-income families requires the collaborative efforts of several social agencies. It is often the responsibility of the school nurse or counselor to recognize those children with special needs and contact appropriate help organizations. School personnel clearly recognize the need for more social services for the poor. Studies by the Carnegie Corporation indicate that the United States provides less health care for the children of the poor than most other industrialized nations.

Head Start and other early childhood programs were created (1965) as intervention programs for preschoolers from low-income families to provide health care, nutrition, and nurturing environments and experiences before the children entered school. These programs are intended to equalize opportunity for poor children.

FULL-SERVICE SCHOOL PROGRAMS

The **full-service school** is a concept taking root in some urban areas. Child care and family services are coordinated by a school-based social service counselor. The counselor has access to those social agencies that help the poor. Health agencies and university-based medical and dental care programs are often included in a network of family care providers. The school counselor refers families to the different agencies for care. The counselor may be involved with parent education and screening programs.

HOMELESSNESS

The number of homeless children throughout the United States is growing. For schools this means that there is a growing transient population that needs to be served. Transferring students' records from school to school and district to district sometimes means that school records never catch up to the child. Homeless children typically lag two to three years behind in reading and mathematics ability.

In working with homeless children, teachers need to be particularly sensitive to their problems and when possible, facilitate their educational experience by providing the following advantages:

- Provide a means for the students to do homework assignments by giving them the resources they need and finding a place for them to do the work

- Encourage school parent groups to help the homeless by providing clothing and school work tools
- Encourage another child to act as a buddy and tutor for the homeless child to ensure that he or she is aware of school facilities and school rules

VIOLENCE

We live in a violent society, and the schools are not immune to the problems of the community. Many urban schools lock the gates either to keep the community out, or close the children in. Children's daily personal experiences include knowledge of violence—in the home, on television, on the streets, in the movies they watch, and in the games they play.

Young elementary students who experience bullying, abuse, neglect, and harsh or erratic discipline are more likely to display aggressive and violent behavior. There is some evidence that violent behavior is learned. To help students deal with aggression and violence, schools are implementing curricula that teaches students how to deal with anger and conflict.

Role-playing is an effective teaching strategy with students of all ages. By acting out different roles and perspectives, students gain insight into the causes of conflict. Problem solving culminates the role-playing activity as students discuss how the conflict situation could have been avoided. Role-playing techniques and ideas are presented in Chapter 8.

Perhaps the greatest contribution the schools can make to prevent violent behavior is to focus on communication skills. Learning to express anger and dissatisfaction in ways other than through physical violence has the potential to curb disorderly behavior. Although schools cannot rid society of violence, perceptive and sensitive teachers can be role models and demonstrate caring behavior to students from all social classes who may lack parental support.

Teaching Hints:
Diminishing Violent Behavior

- Introduce and practice cooperative work groups
- Insist that students talk out disagreements emphasizing communication skills
- Role-play conflict situations
- Teach conflict resolution through the use of compromise and negotiation skills
- Help to mediate conflicts among students.

CHILD ABUSE

Child abuse occurs among all social classes. The Child Abuse Prevention and Treatment Act was passed by Congress in 1974 to assist states in implementing programs for preventing, identifying, and treating victims of child abuse and neglect.

In Mary Hogan's second-grade classroom, she was introduced to a new female student who appeared shy, withdrawn, and not too alert during instruction. The child's school records were not immediately available, but Hogan kept a watchful eye on the child to see how she interacted with other students. When the records did arrive, Hogan saw that her school work was not remarkable, but what she would describe as average; however, the child's attendance record was poor.

About three weeks after entering the class, the child came to school after an absence of four days with dark circles around her eyes and black and blue marks on her upper arms. Hogan decided to request a parent conference. At the conference, the mother said the child had fallen off her bicycle; she said the child was poorly coordinated and fell frequently.

At no time during physical activities at school did Hogan observe the child to fall or to have coordination problems. Hogan suspected maltreatment and reported the case to her principal who began the process of notification, adhering to school district policy.

Child abuse and neglect is a societal problem and teachers are frequently the "first to know." Because teachers see their students every day, they are more likely to note evidence of abuse. Teachers are responsible for reporting incidents of abuse. (See the discussion about instruction of child abuse in Chapter 16.)

HEALTH EDUCATION

Karen Adazzio, our seventh-grade teacher, has realized that health education represents a prime example of the societal problems that affect the schools. At her middle school she sees daily evidence of students using drugs, alcohol, and tobacco. She has counseled pregnant 13-year-old students; she is aware of students with acquired immune deficiency syndrome (AIDS).

Adazzio is aware that many critics of the schools do not believe that these problems should be represented in the school curriculum. She would respond with a John Dewey tenet: the school is a social institution and schools are extensions of the community. She believes that the school must educate the community's children; therefore, the school is responsible for adjusting to the needs of the community.

Most educators believe that high-risk sexual behavior should be discussed in classrooms beginning in grade five. School districts need to work with members of the community to develop appropriate curriculum in these sensitive areas. The health education curriculum is discussed in Chapter 16.

CHALLENGES SCHOOLS CONFRONT AND THE CHOICES THEY MAKE

EQUAL OPPORTUNITY FOR EDUCATION

Equal educational opportunity implies equal access to every facet of education. This includes the following types of opportunities:

- interact with the best teachers
- use the best facilities, including equipment and materials
- share the wealth of school support
- interact with other students
- study all subjects
- prepare for all vocations

All students have not always had equal access to an education in the United States. Students with disabilities were often denied schooling because schools did not accommodate people with special needs. Non-English-speaking students are still often denied appropriate instruction because bilingual specialist teachers are not available. Prior to 1954 (*Brown v. Topeka Board of Education*), southern schools were segregated, and students were denied equal access to public schooling.

Despite the fact that all students are compelled to attend school, and in this postmodern era have free access to the public schools, inequality exists. Rural and inner-city children lack many of the advantages of suburban and middle-class children. For example, the poor child probably has not had the preschool experiences that build readiness for schooling (travel, books, problem-solving toys, visits to cultural events, learning-oriented nursery school, in-depth conversations, good nutrition, medical attention).

Equal educational opportunity also is limited by certain school practices. For example, schools may limit access by the way they treat students based on academic performance. If students need a specific grade point average to take part in the school chorus or band or special community activities, then access is denied to most students. If the math laboratory or the computer is only available to those with special talents or those who finish their math assignment early, then other students are denied these enrichment activities. Tracking and ability grouping may be used to limit access to special subjects and enrichment activities. Frequently, students who are academically below average spend all of their school day in remedial activities in the very subjects they dislike most instead of in activities that they enjoy and in which they demonstrate success.

GENDER EQUITY

Streitmatter (1994) distinguishes among three concepts: **gender bias, gender equality** of opportunity, and **gender equity.** Sex role bias has been documented in the curriculum, in materials of instruction, and in the ways teachers treat children. For example, girls engage in fewer interactions with teachers and receive less attention than do boys, and African-American girls have even fewer interactions with teachers than do white girls (AAUW, 1992). Gender bias is based on the notion that there are innate differences between males and females, such as in thinking processes, learning processes, and emotional behavior. There is a great deal of research demonstrating differences in the ways boys and girls are socialized (toys, responsibilities, career choice opportunities). Socialization practices often have led to assumptions about the sexes (males are more competitive; females are more emotional). When these practices persist in school practices and in the workplace, gender bias occurs.

Equality of opportunity for the sexes means that everyone starts out on the same rung of the ladder and receives the same treatment. Streitmatter notes that this means that all students read the same materials, are subject to the same curriculum, and receive the same instruction.

The concept of equity in education means that teachers are aware of traditional biases and make an effort to "enhance opportunities for the at-risk group" (Streitmatter, 1994, p. 9). Karen Adazzio attempts to use both the concept of opportunity and equity. In advising girls, she insists that they take algebra in the middle school; she asks the algebra teacher to be sure that girls receive many opportunities to discuss algebraic theories and to raise questions. Thus Adazzio is assuring girls of the opportunity to take advanced mathematics and because they are **at-risk students,** she asks that they receive special treatment.

Research Findings: *Gender Play*

Thorne (1994), a sociologist, has studied gender play in schools and notes that boys usually dominate play areas, but she has observed that Spanish-speaking children of both sexes play together, speaking Spanish. She concluded that the children were more comfortable speaking Spanish with each other in an alien environment; for this reason they did not observe traditional gender-based rules of play.

Recognizing traditional biases, teachers are faced with the challenge of balancing opportunity and providing special treatment. In Mary Hogan's second-grade classroom, she makes a special effort to see that her "helper" responsibilities are not based on traditional sexual practices. For example, girls get to carry things and empty the trash; boys get to clean the sink and be an office monitor.

In Greg Thomas's fifth-grade classroom, he is aware that girls seldom participate in the annual school science fair. As a consequence he makes a special effort to encourage his girls to become involved. He does this by specifically telling girls that he expects them to participate in the fair and that he will provide assistance as needed.

If you are already teaching in a classroom, you may want to think about the students in your classroom and the ways you encourage them. Using Figure 1.1 as a checklist, consider equity issues such as sex, race, social class, and high and low achievers.

AT-RISK STUDENTS

Who are the students at risk? The category includes students who have difficulty completing their high school education because they have limited English speaking skills; are special education students; are subject to poverty, homelessness, drugs, violence, life-threatening illness, and teen-age pregnancy; and have a history of failing school grades and frequent absences.

Schools have a difficult time helping these students because their problems require the assistance of other social institutions and parental involvement. Academic assistance can be provided through school-based mentoring

Figure 1.1 Equity Checklist for Working with Students in Your Classroom.

	Yes	No
1. Are all children encouraged to set personal goals?		
2. Do all children have the opportunity to choose some work and leisure activities?		
3. Are all children allowed to assist one another?		
4. In seating children in the classroom are all children favored?		
5. Are all students praised as frequently and for the same purposes?		
6. Are all students provided with nonverbal behavioral clues, such as smiles, eye contact, friendly pats, and understanding looks?		
7. When misbehavior occurs, are all students subject to the same amount and type of criticism?		
8. When asking students questions, are all students provided with content clues if they fail to respond?		
9. Is student-to-student interaction encouraged?		
10. Is group placement in your classroom changed frequently?		
11. Does group placement reflect a variety of teaching purposes?		
12. Are different instructional strategies used when a child has failed to learn?		
13. In planning an instructional strategy, have you focused on the individual in the group?		
14. During a discussion, are all students called upon?		
15. During a discussion, are all students given time to respond?		
16. During a discussion, are all students encouraged to initiate a new line of thinking or to ask a question?		
17. In small group work, do all children have an opportunity to be both leader and participant?		

Research Readings

Roderick (1995) studied retention rates and school policy. She concluded that repeating a grade did not provide remediational benefits and may cause students to drop out of school.

and tutoring programs. Through the use of a buddy system and cross-age tutoring, some schools have made a difference in the drop-out rate. At-risk students often need counseling programs to enhance their self-esteem.

In one Los Angeles middle school the performing arts teacher purposefully asked several at-risk students to participate in a forthcoming musical program. The close association with other students and recognition that they were needed if the musical production was to be successful served as motivation to encourage attendance of the at-risk students. Participation in the high-visibility program developed the self-esteem of this target group.

Some states try to penalize school drop-outs and/or the parents of drop-outs. This is done by revoking driver's licenses for senior high school students or reducing welfare payments to parents of children with poor attendance patterns. However, there is no evidence that harsh programs that invoke penalties are successful.

Linking parents to their child's education has the potential to assist the at-risk student. For parents who are unaware of their child's problems, communication between teacher and parent may provide the key to attendance and support. However, for some parents, school involvement may be out of the question because of working hours or traditional fear of schools and teachers.

Some success has been achieved by having parent advisory groups communicate with the larger parent population. Involvement in school decision making such as school uniform requirements and after-school program decisions seem to motivate parental interest.

A joint project of the National Parent Teacher Association and the Los Angeles County Office of Education involved parents of young children in a national mathematics education program aimed at helping parents teach math to their children at home. The parents attended a meeting at their local school and viewed a math education video. The distance education pro-

gram was offered in both English and Spanish, and although it was aimed at parents, many people brought their children with them. Participation in programs such as this helps to link parents and the school and makes parents less hesitant to come to the school with a problem.

THE INCLUSIVE CLASSROOM

Students with disabilities are typically described as **exceptional learners.** Included in this designation are students with a variety of physical or learning disabilities. Special education programs were designed to meet their needs. These programs attempted to provide a basic education in an environment free from academic competition and the discriminatory behavior of peers.

In the late 1960s special education teachers and educational researchers began to question the effectiveness of special education placement, and minority parents questioned the validity of I.Q. tests that labeled their children retarded. Many children whose primary language was not English appeared to have learning problems when placed in a monolingual immersion situation. Teachers unable to distinguish non-English-speaking children from children with genuine learning disabilities placed them in special education classrooms. Mercer (1971) verified that special education classrooms were populated with a disproportionate number of children from minority groups and low economic backgrounds, all labeled mentally retarded.

FULL EDUCATIONAL OPPORTUNITIES

In 1974 Congress passed the Education Amendments (PL 93-380) to the 1968 Education of the Handicapped Act (PL 90-247), which specified criteria for funding special education programs. The act established a goal to provide full educational opportunities to all children with disabilities. Provisions specified that "to the maximum extent appropriate, handicapped children in public or private institutions or other care facilities are educated with children who are not handicapped and that removal from the regular classroom occurs only when the handicap is of such severity that educational services cannot be achieved satisfactorily" (Education Amendments, 1974).

Should all students regardless of disabilities (learning, behavioral, cognitive, or physical) be integrated into the regular classroom?

In addition, PL 93-380 specified that testing and evaluation materials used for the purpose of classifying and placing children with disabilities be "selected and administered so as not to be racially or culturally discriminatory."

INDIVIDUALIZED EDUCATIONAL PROGRAM

Public Law 94-142, the Individuals with Disabilities Education Act (1975), has been cited as a "bill of rights" for children with disabilities. The law (originally the Education for All Handicapped Children Act, amended in 1990 and renamed) has implications for all children, both with and without disabilities, because it specifies the use of an **individualized education program (IEP)** to identify individual needs and capacities. The act guarantees that children with disabilities receive free and appropriate special education and related services, conforming to the nature of their disability.

In accordance with PL 94-142, the IEP must specify the following information:

- The student's present educational achievement level
- Appropriate annual and short-range educational goals
- Special services to achieve or implement the goals
- The extent to which the student with disabilities can be placed in a regular classroom
- Annual review of instructional goals, progress, and implementation plans

The IEP plan must be signed by the student's parent or guardian to indicate that the parent or guardian participated in the planning conference and agreed with the proposed program.

Proponents of the **inclusive school and classroom** believe that all children regardless of disability should be educated in a regular classroom *(mainstreamed)* with his or her peer group. These educators are concerned that self-contained special education classrooms separate learners and label them learning disabled and low-achieving, yet offer no special curriculum (Wang, Reynolds, and Walberg, 1995).

Albert Shanker, the late president of the American Federation of Teachers (1995), was concerned that full inclusion in mainstream classrooms is not appropriate for all children with disabilities. He believed that inclusion may be used by local and state boards of education as a device to save money by cutting back on special education services. Shanker advocated placement

Do you believe that in the regular classroom students can receive appropriate instruction to meet their special needs? Does labeling a student put him or her at a disadvantage?

in the mainstream classroom dependent on necessary support services to child and regular classroom teacher. His proposal included special training for all teachers who work with students who are disabled.

DIVERSITY AND MULTICULTURAL EDUCATION

When content and learning experiences are selected for teaching, state, district, or individual perspective influences choice. This perspective is never neutral. Opinions, criteria, and beliefs about what is appropriate can provide a framework for curriculum choices. When a teacher or school district chooses to teach one thing, something else is omitted. The public (or educator) that yearns for the "good old days" may well be asking for content and learning experiences that in the past were oriented to western civilization, Christians, and white males.

United States society is diverse in race, ethnicity, religion, social class, culture, and exceptionality. Add to this our regional-geographic differences and we see a society that must be served by schools that are open to many perspectives and competing viewpoints.

Multicultural education means that all students are represented in the curriculum; no group is omitted or alienated. Multicultural education does *not* mean a special social studies unit. (This week will be devoted to African-American history.) Nelson, Carlson, and Palonsky (1996, p. 227) comment that "Multiculturalism should find its way into every corner of the curriculum and at every grade level . . ." These authors point out that immigrants in the nineteenth century primarily came from European countries. Americanization through schooling was not perceived as antagonistic, dysfunctional, or frustrating to those immigrants. However, many of the immigrants in the late twentieth century come from the Orient and South America; these immigrants cannot embrace the Anglo-American heritage that is frequently taught.

Critics of multicultural education counter that schools are responsible for developing (and socializing students for) a common culture. That we are different in many ways is not the issue in this perspective. This viewpoint stresses that the public schools must prepare citizens for democratic participation and teach

Research Readings

Davidman and Davidman (1994) suggest the following ways to improve multicultural education:

- Involve parents of all cultures in an advisory team.
- Encourage students to study in small groups and provide support to each other.
- Recognize how each student is unique; help students appreciate their own uniqueness.
- Select content and learning experiences that encourage student participation.
- Help students recognize historical racism and gender and cultural exploitation.

American values and traditions. They believe that the culture of the United States represents a composite of many cultures including European, Asian, and South American, and that the schools are a vehicle for unifying the country by teaching the immigrants about the "common" democratic culture. Proponents of the common culture argue that particular beliefs, ethnic pride, and religious orientations should be taught after school or on weekends; these ideas are not the job of the public school.

BILINGUALISM: TEACHING LANGUAGE-MINORITY STUDENTS

The role of native language instruction in the public schools has been debated for decades. Educators, as well as society as a whole, appear to be divided between those who view bilingualism as an asset and those who believe it negatively affects a child's academic development. The debate focuses on whether **limited-English-proficiency (LEP)** students, sometimes called English learners, should be taught content in their native language or taught in **English as a Second Language (ESL)**.

Landmark Decisions

In 1968 Congress passed the Bilingual Education Act as Title VII of the Elementary/Secondary Education Act. Since that time, over half a billion dollars has been provided for bilingual education.

In 1974 the United States Supreme Court ruled that the San Francisco Unified School District had to provide equal educational opportunities for all stu-

dents. In *Lau v. Nichols* the Court required the San Francisco school district to provide bilingual education to the Chinese-speaking students of the district. The decision required school districts to rectify those English language deficiencies that excluded students from effective participation in educational programs.

Later that same year, Congress extended bilingual education to include bicultural education. Congress stated that bilingual education must exhibit an appreciation of the cultural heritage of the target group. The expansion of the Title VII Act recognized the intimate relationship of language, culture, and ethnic identity.

Transition Versus Maintenance

The goal of bilingual education, as it was originally conceived, was to teach limited-English-speaking and non-English-speaking children the basic skills in their native language so they would not fall behind academically. At the same time, the children would be given some English language experiences. Only when their oral language development in English was sophisticated enough were they to receive basic skills instruction in English. The transition stage refers to the period when the limited-English speaker or the non-English speaker receives instruction in basic skills in a language other than English.

The concept of bilingual maintenance was conceived out of a concern that the native speaker of languages other than English would lose his or her native identity. Maintenance programs reinforce the worth and dignity of the student's native heritage even after that student has acquired English-speaking ability.

Teachers often voice concern that they do not know precisely when to discontinue native language instruction. Most agree that the original intent of Congress was that native language instruction should last for about two years and that at the end of that period the students should be ready to resume their education in English. Continued support and maintenance of linguistic abilities for students who speak a different native language have not had federal support.

The ability to express oneself in a second language develops slowly. Most individuals, regardless of age, go through an extended silent period, listening to the new language before risking speech. Current research on language learning reveals that fluency increases gradually as the individual learns to integrate listening, speaking, reading, and writing. Initial speech in the new language is strictly functional, related to surroundings and needs. As fluency increases, syntax becomes more complex and sentence structures demonstrate causal, sequential, comparative, or other relationships. Refined and abstract language occurs over time as the language learner gains mastery and confidence.

Since most individuals will learn functional language as need arises, the task of the school is to go beyond basic skills to develop students' thinking processes. It is important that students continue to learn language skills and thinking processes in their primary language (since most typically that is the language that is reinforced in the home) and the skills can then be applied to English.

Concurrent with primary language instruction, students need opportunities to acquire English through the presentation of understandable and meaningful messages. The primary language instruction should prepare students with knowledge and experiences that can be applied to the context of instruction in the new language.

In Mary Hogan's second grade there are a number of LEP students. Hogan uses a variety of concrete materials to foster student understanding. While reading a book about Curious George, Mary used puppets and miniature toys to illustrate the action as she slowly read the story. She uses techniques that are described as S̲pecially D̲esigned A̲cademic I̲nstruction in E̲nglish (SDAIE).

When asking questions, Hogan provides plenty of time for her LEP students to respond. She makes it a point to accept the student's response without making corrections, but she may repeat the response in her own words. When explaining concepts to her students she will use simple language and provide many examples to help students comprehend. She tends to use a lot of body language to convey her messages. She exaggerates emotions and tries to provide sensory activities for her children. Whenever possible she will encourage her students to explain what she has taught in their own words. At the end of the school day she asks her stu-

---

Research Findings:
Transferring Language Skills

Teachers may not speak students' native language, but they can still assist their second-language learners through the following means:

- Encouraging use of native language skills to learn to read and write in English
- Building students' self-esteem by respecting students' primary language and culture (Au, 1993, p. 148)

---

dents to: "Tell me what you learned today." In this way she prepares them to tell their parents about school.

Mary Hogan's students receive some of their instruction in their native language, and she believes that this has a positive effect on their self-esteem. Whenever possible Hogan uses the students' own language and culture in her lessons. (This is described as an "additive" approach to language instruction.) However, in some classrooms students speak so many different languages that primary language instruction is impossible. As a consequence teachers need to use the SDAIE techniques and provide many opportunities for students to work in small groups with native English speakers to learn English from their peers.

TEACHING GIFTED AND TALENTED STUDENTS

Exceptional children status is conferred also on gifted and talented students. The Marland Report (1972) identified the population of gifted and talented students as those children capable of high performance with demonstrated and/or potential ability in the following six areas:

1. General intellectual ability
2. Specific academic aptitude
3. Creative or productive thinking
4. Leadership ability
5. Visual and performing arts
6. Psychomotor ability

The report served as a federal policy statement assisting in the identification of this target population for the purpose of providing differentiated educational programs and/or services so that gifted and talented students would realize their potential and contribute to

Teaching Hints:
Helping English Learners

- Language skills acquired in the primary language will transfer to the second language.
- Significant concepts should be taught in the primary language; students' stored knowledge then can be used to apply and extend ideas in English.

society. However, many parents and educators have raised questions about the six categories. For example, most specialists in gifted education recognize that the six categories do not operate independently of each other, yet there is a tendency to use separate identification procedures with each of the six categories.

In addition, Renzulli (1978) pointed out the significance and effect on performance of the individual's motivation and persistence. Renzulli does not recommend using cognitive factors as a primary measure of giftedness; instead, he proposes giving equal attention to three factors: general ability (not necessarily "superior"), task commitment (a motivational factor), and creativity. Renzulli portrays the three clusters graphically as overlapping factors brought to bear upon general performance areas such as mathematics, visual arts, physical sciences, and so on, and specific performance areas such as cartooning, astronomy, map making, choreography, city planning, play writing, sculpture, how animals learn, and so on. Renzulli's three factors emphasize the interaction of cognitive and affective components.

Gallagher (1995) emphasizes that environment and sequential experiences are extremely important for the fruition of native ability. He believes that many talented children go unrecognized because they lack opportunity, developmental practice, and motivation. He raises the question of whether the education of gifted students is a civil rights issue.

Minority students are under represented in classes for the gifted and talented. Many educators believe this is a consequence of lack of encouragement and opportunity to build the necessary knowledge structure. Just as females have not been encouraged to pursue higher math and science course work, there is a shortage of African-American and Hispanic students in elementary and middle school gifted programs. Interestingly, Asian children are over represented. Many educators believe this has occurred because Asian parents emphasize academic performance. It appears that differential representation among the gifted and talented population is another example of equity due to an imbalance of opportunity and environmental experiences.

Gifted and talented children provide yet another challenge for teachers to develop differentiated programs and services that go beyond the regular school program. These programs should encompass both content acceleration and content enrichment. These will be discussed in Chapter 4 along with the characteristics of this population.

THE ELASTIC CURRICULUM

What should the curriculum contain? Some educators believe that the curriculum is "stuffed." Earlier in this chapter you learned about societal problems affecting schools. Should schools deal with these problems through the curriculum? For example, should the schools develop a curriculum related to life problems? The content could include personal and community health, substance abuse prevention, human sexuality, and HIV/AIDS prevention. In addition, should the curriculum deal with issues related to inequality and intercultural relations, overpopulation, poverty and homelessness, consumer education, violence, and crime? Dewey (1916, 1944, p. 99) believed that social institutions need to adjust to social times and the needs of the people.

> A society which makes provision for participation in its good of all its members on equal terms and which secures flexible readjustment of its institutions through interaction of the different forms of associated life is in so far democratic. Such a society must have a type of education which gives individuals a personal interest in social relationships and control, and the habits of mind which secure social changes without introducing disorder.

But significant life problems are not considered "basic" or "core" curriculum. Some individuals think that the school has become a dumping ground and has forgotten the purpose of education (Nelson, Carlson, and Palonsky, 1996). They ask, how far can the curriculum be stretched?

Noddings (1992) believes that instruction in the basics is not the main task of schools. She states that "if the school has one main goal, a goal that guides the establishment and priority of all others, it should be to promote the growth of students as healthy, competent, moral people (p. 10)." If schools take responsibility to teach about social problems, what should be left out? Should people in the United States expect their schools to solve sociopolitical problems?

PUBLIC SUPPORT AND INVOLVEMENT IN THE SCHOOLS

There is a great deal of evidence that parental support and involvement in schools help children succeed academically. Traditional involvement patterns had parents working as room mothers, chauffeurs, chaperons, and in organizing tasks such as Halloween festivals and bake sales. In this postmodern era, there are many interpretations of parent involvement. For example, in some regions of the country, parents select their school principal. In some schools, parents serve as special resource instructors and come to school to teach in a club program or serve as guest speakers.

Parental participation in advisory councils is now a common occurrence. Advisory councils can become involved in making decisions about school priorities. In a low-income school in Los Angeles, the parents took part in deciding whether or not the school should join with other neighborhood schools in a full-service network. In a charter school, the parents decided to donate their time and skills to repair and improve school buildings, plumbing, and property. As a consequence the money saved was used to upgrade computers in each classroom.

Parental involvement in schools can be aimed at preventing problems. Families living in close proximity of the school can serve as neighborhood watch members to protect the school from vandalism.

In Greg Thomas's rural community, he contacts each child's family and invites them to visit in the classroom. In Mary Hogan's urban school, she recognizes that school visitations during the day may be a luxury most parents cannot afford. She greets parents at an open house in the evening and solicits home-based involvement. Karen Adazzio communicates to parents with a newsletter that she and her students compose.

There is no single pattern of parent involvement. Adult education programs for parents can be used to motivate parent interest in the schools. Giving parents some decision-making responsibilities helps to generate participation and build a real school community.

SUMMARY

Teachers, Schools, and Societal Problems

1. The school is a social institution, and as such it is affected by societal problems and social forces within local communities and society at large.
2. Some of the problems affecting school programs and curriculum include helping students from poverty conditions, whether schools should coordinate social services for families, helping the homeless, dealing with violence, identifying child abuse, and teaching about drug and substance abuse and HIV/AIDS.
3. Some of the challenges confronting schools, curriculum choices, and teaching processes include ensuring equality of opportunity for all students—

those with disabilities, minority students, and students identified as at-risk, as well as minimizing problems related to gender stereotyping.
4. Another challenge affecting teachers is whether or not they should integrate students with disabilities in the classroom thereby intensifying the instructional range of educational needs.
5. Controversy about multicultural education and bilingual education affect the development of curriculum and the way students who are English learners are taught.
6. Gifted and talented children provide yet another challenge for teachers to develop differentiated programs and services.
7. Schools are asked to solve many of society's problems. To make decisions about programs and curriculum, teachers need parental involvement in the schools.

DISCUSSION QUESTIONS AND APPLICATION EXERCISES

1. Do you agree or disagree with each of the following statements? Working in small groups, discuss your beliefs and expectations concerning school programs and teachers' responsibilities.
   - Teachers should teach children with disabilities in the regular classroom.
   - Teachers should develop a curriculum for sex education.
   - Teachers should be conscious of equity issues in the classroom and consider affected groups.
   - Schools should provide breakfast and lunch programs for children of poverty.
   - Teachers need to help students learn conflict management techniques to reduce school and community violence.
   - The school should develop bilingual maintenance and transition programs.
2. How does cultural identity affect school success? Discuss how teachers can integrate multicultural education in all subject fields.
3. Identify school practices that stereotype students by gender. How can teachers change these practices?
4. Why is it important to recognize and provide special curricula for gifted and talented students?
5. Why is stuffing the curriculum a problem?
6. Do you believe there should be national goals and standards for curriculum and students' performance?

Teachers, Schools, and Curriculum in Historical Perspective

A brief perspective of the history of U.S. schools is presented chronologically in this chapter. It is common to categorize and label periods of history, but the ensuing events do not cease when a period ends. So you will find that beliefs conflict and events overlap and are recycled throughout our school history. As you read this chapter think about these questions: What kind of schools did society need during each period of history? In what ways did beliefs about how children learn affect the content of the curriculum and the ways students were taught? How did national and international political, economic, and sociologic forces and technologic changes affect schools, teachers, and the curriculum?

After you study this chapter, you should be able to accomplish the following:

1. Trace the development of the school curriculum from colonial to modern times, explaining how social and political forces affected the development of the curriculum.
2. Identify changes in teaching methodology through time by distinguishing among different theories of child development and explaining how these theories affected teaching methodologies.
3. Trace the federal government's interest in education throughout U.S. history.
4. Identify ways in which schools differed in the varied regions of the country in earlier American times.
5. Identify changes in the education of girls and minorities throughout U.S. history.
6. Discuss the conflicts associated with "Americanizing" or assimilating students.
7. Trace the development of textbooks, instructional materials, and media used throughout our history.
8. Explain why education is considered the great equalizer.
9. Identify early leaders in U.S. education and explain how their beliefs shaped the U.S. school.
10. Identify several European educators whose beliefs influenced the U.S. school.
11. Using historical time periods, identify the changing role of teachers.

Professional Lexicon

academy   A private school for middle class children created during the colonial period of history.

apprentice schools   Schools designed to teach a skill and occupation.

common schools   Schools established during the nationalist period to teach basic skills to all elementary children.

constructivist approach   An approach that encourages students to structure personal understanding through an active learning experience.

dame schools   Schools that taught ABCs and basic reading in the homes of women in the colonial community.

Latin grammar school   A school designed to prepare boys for higher education; taught by college educated schoolmasters.

monitorial system   A system in which bright students were selected as monitors and were

taught by teachers; the monitors taught the other students.

normal school   A school for the preparation of elementary teachers.

parochial schools   Sectarian schools established by religious groups to preserve language and religious beliefs.

progressive education   A movement characterized by active teaching and learning focused on the needs and interests of students.

scientific management   An approach that viewed the school as a factory and teachers as workers; the school was to be managed to increase productivity (achievement) and efficiency.

town schools   Schools established by people in the New England colonies who shared similar ideas and beliefs.

In looking back over the development of schools and the curriculum, there are four time periods that distinguish the development of the American school:

- The Colonial Period, 1600–1776
- The Nationalist Period, 1776–1876
- The Expanding United States, 1876–1930
- The Modern Era, 1930–present

THE COLONIAL PERIOD

Most of our early settlers came from western Europe. In adjusting to life in a new country, the new Americans began by transplanting the educational practices they were accustomed to from the Old World. For some of the new settlers this meant a classical education; for others, it meant reading, ciphering, and religion.

Religion was the dominating influence on the education of the young in colonial America. The first teachers in the colonies were preachers. The Puritans in New England believed that children should learn to read the Bible to help them frustrate the devil! The Puritans' religious zeal influenced the course of schooling from the start. In 1647 the Massachusetts Bay Colony enacted the "Old Deluder Satan" Act, which required towns of 50 or more families to employ a teacher to teach reading and writing, and towns of 100 or more families to employ a Latin teacher to prepare students to enter Harvard College (established 1636). Children were to be educated at the expense of the community, and the actual building of the schools, levying of taxes, and hiring of teachers were responsibilities of the towns. We can see that the precedent of federal interest in education and state responsibility for education was set at this early date. Different types of schools were built in the New England colonies: dame schools, town schools, apprentice schools, Latin grammar schools, and parochial schools.

NEW ENGLAND COLONIES

The Puritans

The Puritans were harsh disciplinarians. They believed that children were naturally sinful and depraved. Children needed to be taught to be useful to society. Schooling was supposed to impart knowledge that would help the child be socially and economically useful. Play was considered worthless, causing children to become lazy. The Puritans did not recognize childish behavior or child talk. Children were viewed as miniature adults and needed to be disciplined in order to become productive adults.

The **dame schools** were taught by women in the community who needed extra money and were willing to relieve other parents of their responsibility to teach their children to read. The dame typically listened to the children read aloud, recite their ABCs, and practice spelling while she knitted, sewed, or worked at the spinning wheel. The schoolroom was the living room of the woman's house (Johnson, 1963).

New England Town Schools

The New England **town schools,** or charity schools, were for poor children. The curriculum included reading, writing, arithmetic, spelling, catechism, and the singing of religious hymns. The schoolmasters used the New England Primer. Used for more than 100 years, this book contained an illustrated alphabet with religious jingles such as "In Adam's Fall We sinned all"; "Zacheas, he Did climb the Tree, His Lord to see"; "Peter deny'd His Lord and cry'd" (Johnson, 1963, pp. 80-81). Reading and religion were integrated in this manner. In arithmetic the students learned to count, add, and subtract.

The schoolhouse typically consisted of just one room. The teacher's desk was centered in the front of the room and students sat on benches at desks arranged on the other three sides. One wall had pegs to hold the children's coats, and usually there was a bench under the pegs for the children's dinner baskets. Quite frequently the younger children sat at the front or center of the room near the stove, and the older children sat at the rear.

Schoolmasters

Schoolmasters in the early days had to prove themselves as taskmasters and disciplinarians. Behind the schoolmaster's desk were switches. A whipping post about five feet tall and set into the floor was typical in colonial schools, as was a dunce stool. Students were frequently whipped and embarrassed in front of their classmates. They were expected to memorize what was in their primer and recite (standing up toeing a crack on the schoolroom floor) what they had learned to the schoolmaster. Drill, rote learning, and corporal punishment characterized the teaching methodology of the colonial schoolmaster.

Upper-class boys were prepared by tutors for the **Latin grammar school,** which mirrored the European classical school. Upper-class girls were also taught by tutors, but they were not allowed to attend the grammar school. Students at the Latin grammar school were taught Latin and Greek and read Latin and Greek authors. The boys studied Latin grammar and composition and, to a lesser degree, mathematics, science, and history.

Unlike the schoolmasters of the Latin grammar school, who had college degrees, the schoolmasters of the town schools may have mastered just elementary education. They usually had not selected teaching as an occupation but rather taught during the winter to supplement farming income. These schoolmasters were certified by the selectmen of the community, who examined an applicant and decided if he was capable of handling the students and smart enough to be a teacher.

In colonial days children only attended school when they were not needed at home or on the farm. The custom of summer vacation is related to the closing of the colonial school so that boys could work on the farm and girls could help their mothers with sewing and cooking. Since many of the schoolmasters also worked during the harvest season or had other jobs during the summer, schoolmarms were sometimes employed to teach the younger children, girls, and sometimes boys who needed extra help. The "marms," as the younger children often called their female teachers, taught manners, the ABCs, ciphering, and sewing.

Schoolmasters were usually paid $10.00 to $12.00 a month. Schoolmarms earned about $1.75 per week. The schoolmaster was expected to board in the students' homes, often spending about a week with each family. Johnson (1963, p. 127) relates the story of one schoolmaster who kept a diary of his boarding experience in Vermont. The family fed the teacher some form of baked gander, hot or cold, every day of the week. The schoolmaster became ill and lost considerable weight! Schoolmasters were treated as indentured servants.

MIDDLE ATLANTIC COLONIES

The New England colonies were characterized by a common language, religion, and Puritan value structure. This was not true in the New York, New Jersey, Pennsylvania, and Delaware regions. The Germans settled in Pennsylvania, the Dutch in New York, and the Swedish in Delaware. The Middle Atlantic colonies were diverse in religion, language, and values. These colonies had Lutheran, Baptist, Jewish, and

Roman Catholic populations, as well as Quakers and Dutch Reformed Church members. Both independent schools and parochial schools were established in these colonies.

In New York the Dutch **parochial schools** taught reading, writing, and religion. The Church of England also established a number of charity schools. **Apprentice schools** in New York taught specific skills and trades. Some of the private schools taught navigation skills, surveying, geography, the French and Spanish languages, and bookkeeping. The influence of New York as a commercial port obviously affected the curriculum.

Benjamin Franklin's Influence

Some of the private schools in New York were what Benjamin Franklin called academies. An **academy** served middle-class children whose parents paid tuition. The most famous academy was the Academy of Pennsylvania, which Franklin established himself in Philadelphia in 1751. (Franklin's academy later became the University of Pennsylvania.) Unlike other colonial leaders, Franklin believed that students should enjoy school and that education should be practical.

Franklin organized the curriculum sequentially to make sense to students and to prepare them for life. In modern curriculum language, in his academy subject fields were integrated and sequenced. He used history as the integrating core for students to study geography, government, logic, languages, literature, ancient history, religion, and oratory. Franklin was not impressed with either tradition or religion. He did not consider the study of Latin and Greek terribly important, but he realized that students might need the languages to study the classics. He did not want curriculum decisions based on what was traditionally taught in schools. Similarly, he did not hold with the Puritan concept of the child as inherently sinful; therefore, religion was not important to him as a school subject. However, Franklin had a strong moral sense and expected teachers to develop students' moral habits.

In Pennsylvania, all children attended school, including African-Americans and Native Americans. The Quakers did not consider the child innately wicked, and they did not practice corporal punishment. Their curriculum included reading, arithmetic, writing, and religion, and more practical studies needed by society, such as handicrafts, domestic science, and agriculture.

SOUTHERN COLONIES

Colonial education in the South was quite different from that in the New England and Middle Atlantic colonies. Families lived far apart, making it difficult to establish schools to serve a community. Most upper-class families had private tutors for their children. The tutor lived with a family on its plantation for a period of time, perhaps a month, and then moved on to another family. The slave population was not allowed to become literate, although there were some exceptions. Also, lower-class whites in the South did not have access to formal schooling.

FOUNDATIONS OF AMERICAN EDUCATION

Although the colonies differed in the ways they educated their children, there were some similarities:

- Religion was a dominating influence and considered a priority in colonial America.
- Except at Benjamin Franklin's academy, subjects were taught separately (not integrated).
- There was a definite social class structure evident in the way children were educated.

- The classroom contained children of many ages, and the schoolmasters managed ungraded classrooms.
- Teaching methods were limited to drill, memorization, and recitation.

Table 2.1 summarizes the social forces that influenced the development of schools during the colonial period.

THE NATIONALIST PERIOD

If Greg Thomas, Mary Hogan, and Karen Adazzio had been teachers (schoolmaster and schoolmarms) 200 years ago, their classrooms would look somewhat different from classrooms of today. In fact, curriculum content, curriculum organization, and teaching methods would be dissimilar. However, the teacher's responsibilities, surprisingly, would be much the same. For example, a schoolmaster during the nationalistic period of U.S. history (1776–1876) agreed to the following contract terms:

- The schoolmaster must teach 25 students for 80 days.
- The school term will begin the first week after Thanksgiving.
- The schoolmaster must be honest and of high moral character.
- Each child must be taught as much as he is capable of learning.
- At the end of the term, a report identifying student progress in each subject must be submitted to the trustee (Lemlech and Marks, 1976, p. 8).

Nationalism influenced not only the development of the school and the curriculum in the United States,

Table 2.1 Society and Schools in the Colonial Period

Societal Needs	Societal Beliefs	Social Forces
Field workers for an agrarian society	Children inherently bad, lazy	Economic needs: raw materials for export
For a limited few, a classical education	Strict discipline	Sociology: class society, dichotomy rich/poor
Reading the Bible; religion a priority value	Boys should be educated	
	Classical education for some	
	Girls should be homemakers	
	Exercise the mind through drill and memorization	

but during this period teacher contracts also specified the number of children to be taught and the fact that the children were expected to learn as much as they were capable of learning. The roots of the accountability movement can be traced to this period in U.S. history.

The young country's new Congress passed the first land grant legislation affecting education when they divided the Northwest Territory into six-square-mile townships composed of 36 sections. The Northwest Ordinance of 1785 stipulated that the sixteenth section of every township was to be used for education. The Tenth Amendment to the United States Constitution gave the power and responsibility for education to the states. The Northwest Ordinance demonstrated the federal government's intent to continue the colonial tradition of showing interest in education through legislation. Federal financial assistance to education was initiated through this act.

Debates about educational ideology began immediately after the Revolution, because the country's political leaders were concerned with how to develop children's loyalty to the new nation. The writings of Thomas Jefferson, Benjamin Rush, and Noah Webster provided evidence that our leaders expected schools to develop loyalty and patriotism.

These great patriots wanted homogeneous, patriotic Americans trained to be critical thinkers. This conflict in aims continues today. Education in the United States was to be distinctly American, not European. Education should be practical not classical, and education should meet the needs of a new nation that had to develop its industry, commerce, and agriculture. Benjamin Franklin advocated the practical curriculum. The academy system he established during the colonial years continued into this period. There were approximately 6,000 academies of varying sizes in the 1800s. Franklin's academy offered such practical skill subjects as printing, engraving, cabinet making, shipbuilding, and farming. The focal point of the curriculum, however, was history. The academy also taught English grammar, composition, rhetoric, classics, and mathematics.

In the South, schoolhouses were built on fallow fields. Most of the teachers were local clergymen, who boarded with families in the community and received a small amount of salary based on the number of students they taught. Schoolmasters in the South were considered more harsh and strict than their New England counterparts.

There is very little information about the education of African-Americans after the Revolution. In 1808, John Chavis, an African-American Presbyterian preacher from Lexington, Virginia, opened a school in Raleigh, North Carolina. He taught both African-American and white students from sundown until 10:00 P.M. White parents paid him $2.50 per child, and African-American parents paid $1.75 per child. Chavis promised to attend to the students' moral development and education. Apparently the school was in operation for a number of years, because in 1830 the Raleigh Register commended Chavis for the behavior and scholarship of his students. Schools for African-American students also existed in Boston, the District of Columbia, New York, and Philadelphia (Lemlech and Marks, 1976).

TEXTBOOKS FOR THE NEW NATION

Textbooks in early American schools had been English works. One of the first concerns of the new nation was that students no longer be required to use books from England. Noah Webster was intent on creating the nation's cultural identity. His *Blue-Backed Speller* (1783) contained moral lessons and fables, standardized pronunciation of words to be used for spelling, and historical and geographical names from the United States. Tens of millions of copies of his spelling book were published.

Also widely used were Nicholas Pike's *Arithmetic* (1778) and Lindley Murray's *English Grammar* (1795). Pike's book was not available for students; the schoolmaster recited problems aloud, and the students wrote them on their slates.

In geography, Jedediah Morse's *Elements of Geography* (1795) was used. This text was extremely important in the development of patriotism. The book was 144 pages long, but contained only two maps and no other illustrations. Johnson (1963, p. 330) describes Morse's geography text and includes text samples in the original script. The following, abstracted from Johnson and minus the script, is an illustration of Morse's information about Washington, DC:

> The city of Washington stands at the junction of the rivers Patomak and the Eastern Branch. The situation of this metropolis is upon the great post road, equidistant from the northern and southern extremities of the Union. The public offices were removed to this city in the summer of 1800, and here in future Congress will hold their sessions.

The *McGuffey Eclectic Readers* represented the first set of graded textbooks. More than 120 million copies were sold between 1840 and 1920. It is generally assumed that this set of books influenced the development of the graded school. The McGuffey readers were supposed to be more interesting for children than the earlier readers.

Children's supplies also increased during this period. Children were expected to bring to school a copy book constructed of unlined paper sewn into a cover of brown paper or newspaper. The copy book was used for dictation, solving problems, and practice exercises. The children were also required to bring a ruler and a *plummet*, which was a homemade pencil. Older children brought quill pens and ink to school.

Teaching methods during this period also changed slightly. Since more students were attending school, schoolmasters developed the **monitor system,** which they believed was an efficient means to deal with increased class size. The monitorial, or Lancastrian school, developed by Joseph Lancaster and Andrew Bell, was established about 1800, and had bright students teaching and supervising ten other students. The monitor was first instructed by the schoolmaster and then placed in charge of a row of students. The monitors helped out the schoolmaster by teaching what they had learned and listening to recitations, taking attendance, and testing their rows of students. Students vied for the monitor position; however, this teaching method lost favor due to its reliance on children as teachers. Monitorial schools existed until about 1850 in the United States.

The Education of Females

After the Revolution, academies were established for females. In the main, girls received only an elementary education. In some towns, girls were only allowed to attend school during the summer months when the boys worked in the fields. Typically, girls were expected to prepare themselves for marriage and motherhood. Boys, however, were expected to be more worldly in their interests. Jedediah Morse, the author of the geography text, taught in a school for girls in New Haven, Connecticut. Joseph Emerson established an academy for girls in Byfield and another one in Saugus, Massachusetts.

Many schools were established by women. Sarah Pierce was the founder and principal of a school for girls in Litchfield, Connecticut. Harriet Beecher Stowe, author of *Uncle Tom's Cabin* and a graduate of Pierce's school, opened an academy for girls in Cincinnati, Ohio. Other academies for girls were established in New Hampshire and New York; the academies offered a broader education for girls. According to Walsh (1995, p. 70), the girls from wealthy families attended private schools and learned to read, write, do simple arithmetic, embroider, play music, paint, and speak French. Greek and Latin were considered too difficult for women.

Common School Revival

Common schools, providing free elementary education, were first established in New England between 1820 and 1850. Prior to the common school, poor parents had to declare their poverty in order for their children to attend school at public expense. Common schools were responsible for basic skill instruction and socialization. Ornstein and Levine (1981, p. 180) identify three legislative stages that affected the establishment of elementary public school systems. In the first stage, legislatures permitted the organization of local school districts, subject to the approval of the majority of voters in the district. In the second stage, the development of school districts was encouraged, as were the election of school boards and the raising of revenues to support the schools. State support was provided in stage two to encourage the establishment of common schools. In the third stage, legislatures compelled the establishment of common schools. Districts were required to elect a school board and set a minimum tax rate. In some states there were additional requirements such as minimum curriculum requirements, school maintenance, and building requirements.

Education, the Great Equalizer

Horace Mann became the superintendent of schools for the State of Massachusetts. In his Fifth Annual Report to the Board of Education of Massachusetts (1842), he implored the board to recognize that education was the great equalizer of the conditions of men. Universal education would counteract "the domination of capital and the servility of labor." Mann envisioned a just society where there was equal opportunity for all people to earn a living and to experience security. Mann was probably the first educator to talk about equality of opportunity.

The common school revival awakened Americans to the need to educate all children. During this period (1826–1876) state boards of education were established, the curriculum was broadened, legislatures increased revenues for schools, and the normal school developed.

Henry Barnard was another early champion of the common school. Barnard was secretary of the Connecticut Board of Education, a state commissioner of the public schools in Rhode Island, and United States commissioner of education from 1867 to 1870. Barnard wanted the public schools to teach English, basic skills, and civic education. He was an advocate for the development of formalized teacher education and believed that teachers should be well paid in order to motivate prospective teachers.

TEACHER EDUCATION

The Normal School

Horace Mann wanted to improve schools by improving teacher education. He studied teaching methods in Europe and then lectured and wrote about how to improve teaching. In 1839, he established the first **normal school,** or school for preparing elementary teachers, in the United States.

Young teachers in the normal school founded by Mann in Lexington, Massachusetts, often kept journals of their experiences. One teacher recorded that she read from Abbott's *The Teacher* and studied philosophy, physiology, political economy, history, pronunciation, orthography, and music. The principal of the school was Cyrus Peirce, who initiated role-playing to help his students prepare for teaching. Peirce was concerned that teachers taught too few subjects in the common school, failed to understand the true nature of children, did not understand the subject matter, and did not have appropriate skills to teach and manage classrooms (Lemlech and Marks, 1976). It is hard to believe that Peirce was complaining about teachers in the 1840s!

Education in the normal school included lectures, modeling of teaching procedures, peer teaching (which was supervised by Peirce), teaching in a model school, and practicing skills and school management. A normal school education was considered to be just slightly above a high school education. Women were encouraged to attend the normal schools because a university education still was not readily available for women. Twelve state preparatory schools for teachers

Research Readings

Walsh (1995, p. 72) reports that in 1865 there were 22 normal schools to prepare teachers for a nation of 35,000,000. However, most school officials believed that teacher education was a waste of resources.

existed in the United States by 1860. The normal schools granted teaching certificates.

Teacher Institutes

Teachers began to be concerned about their own education. In 1839, Henry Barnard arranged the first state teachers' institute in Connecticut. By 1860, 15 states required teachers to attend the state institute. Often teachers traveled to the institute during a spring recess. In California the custom of attendance at "institutes" persisted into the 1960s. The Los Angeles Unified School District refused to pay teachers for their spring vacation unless they had attended 10 institute meetings prior to the vacation period each year.

Institutes did not change much through the years. At the early institutes, teachers were presented with Hall's *Lectures on Schoolkeeping* (1829), David Page's *Theory and Practice of Teaching* (1847), and Abbott's *The Teacher* (1833). Institutes in the 1960s included lectures by specialists and seminars on teaching methods, new ideas, and new materials.

The institutes encouraged teachers to discuss common problems. From these discussions evolved professional teacher organizations, the first of which formed in 1845 in New York, Massachusetts, and Rhode Island. The National Teachers Association, which became the National Education Association (NEA), was organized in Philadelphia by teachers and for teachers in 1957. The NEA's purpose was "to elevate the character and advance the interests of the profession of teaching, and to promote the cause of popular education in the United States" (Lemlech and Marks, 1976, p. 19).

FREE PUBLIC EDUCATION

By the end of the nationalist era, free public school education was a reality. The first compulsory education law was enacted in 1853 in Massachusetts. Millions of immigrants came to the United States from

Eastern Europe. The new immigrants settled in the cities; they lived in poverty and were willing to work for substandard wages. As the cities grew, so did school enrollments. Besag and Nelson (1984) report that Chicago's population grew from 4,500 in 1840 to 1 million in 1890. The immigrants needed English classes, and in fact night classes were established in Chicago for children who could not attend during the day. Schools became more standardized and centralized. District boards consolidated and school systems developed.

Francis Adams, an Englishman, visited the United States in 1875 and described the school system he observed. He wrote that Americans were proud of their schools and had personal interest, as well as patriotic interest, in the schools. He noted that local government gave people control over their schools and that the people prized this responsibility. He believed that the decentralization of U.S. schools was excessive and inefficient, but he did not foresee any change in the system. He was amazed at the popularity of the schools and the large percentage of children in attendance. He attributed this to the fact that schools were free and that parents did not have to ask for charity or patronage.

At the time of Adam's visit, compulsory attendance laws were being considered by many states. Adams wrote that seven or eight states had passed laws, but were having difficulty enforcing compulsory attendance. (The early laws were concerned with enforcing a set number of days of attendance.) Adams was also interested in what he called the "religious difficulty." Most of the schools sought to provide a satisfactory secular education; religion was to be left to the church schools and Sunday schools. Many of the schools began the day with reading a selection from the Bible or singing a hymn, but Adams felt this practice would be challenged in the near future. He foresaw the common school as a secular institution. Adams also mentioned that teacher salaries were so low that the teaching profession was below its appropriate level. In 1875 women were attracted to teaching, and Adams noted that women were extensively employed in education. He felt they were more qualified for elementary teaching than men.

CONCEPTS OF CHILD DEVELOPMENT

Interesting changes in the concept of child development affected both the content and method of education during the nineteenth century. Faculty psychologists believed that the mind was divided into various powers such as will, reason, and instinct. They believed that each mental power depended on the vigor of the others. There was interaction among the powers, and if one area was underdeveloped, then the others would suffer. As a consequence, psychologists suggested that certain subjects in the curriculum would develop the intellect. They recommended the study of natural history and sciences. Generally, the emphasis on rote learning has been attributed to the influence of the faculty psychologists.

In England, preschoolers were placed in infant schools to give them firsthand educational experiences; the children were kept active singing and dancing and experiencing some formalized book learning. The idea of infant schools was adopted in Boston in 1816 by educational theorists who did not agree with the faculty psychologists. They believed that the emphasis on memory lessons and recitation repressed the child, made learning mechanical, and developed poor intellectual habits. In contrast, the infant schools focused on children enjoying such activities as listening to stories, singing, admiring pictures, and asking questions. The educational theorists wanted to cultivate children's natural curiosity. Natural science, drawing, and singing were added to the curriculum.

The English philosopher/sociologist Herbert Spencer (1820–1903) also influenced the development of the curriculum. Spencer expected schools to prepare a child for living and believed the way to do this was to determine the important activities of life and include these activities in educational programs. In the text *Education: Intellectual, Moral, and Physical* (1860), Spencer's famous essay "What Knowledge Is of Most Worth?" classified life activities in terms of their importance. Spencer favored the teaching of science in the curriculum, and he wanted children to learn via the discovery method.

Throughout the nineteenth century there was a reconsideration of what the child can and should learn, based on ideas about how children develop and mature. The faculty psychologists wanted a balanced curriculum to develop all of the brain's powers, which they considered interdependent. An important question of the time was whether a child could learn everything about an academic subject. Many educators believed that the young child could not learn with the same thoroughness as an older child and that there was no way to complete one subject before attempting another, which was what some psychologists advocated.

Educational theorists were convinced that subjects needed to be simplified for the young and become increasingly complex as the child matured (shades of the twentieth century!).

CHANGES IN THE SCHOOLS

As the United States wakened and expanded after the Revolution, great changes in the school occurred:

- The development of the nation replaced religion as the dominating influence and priority.
- In cities, graded schools replaced the ungraded one-room schoolhouse.
- The curriculum expanded beyond reading, writing, arithmetic, and spelling to include history, geography, physiology, grammar, composition, agriculture, music, and drawing. In the academies a variety of practical courses were offered.
- Kindergartens were established, as were academies for girls.
- Classes to teach English to immigrants were offered.
- Normal schools were established to prepare teachers; female students predominated in these schools.
- Teachers' associations developed.
- Institutes for in-service education were organized.
- Textbooks produced in the United States were used.
- In addition to memorization and drill, the monitor system was developed, and group instruction began in some classrooms.
- Ideas of faculty psychologists predominated, but educational theorists also became influential. The child was no longer considered inherently bad.

The needs and beliefs of United States society in the nationalist period gave rise to many changes in the country's education system (Table 2.2).

THE EXPANDING UNITED STATES

INFLUENCES ON EDUCATIONAL THOUGHT AND PRACTICES

Throughout our early history, U.S. educational thought was shaped by English and European educators. Three educational leaders were particularly influential: Johann Heinrich Pestalozzi, Friedrich Froebel, and Johann Friedrich Herbart.

John Heinrich Pestalozzi (1746–1827), a Swiss educator, believed that children learned through their senses and that the natural development of the child should be used to guide education. In 1801 he wrote *How Gertrude Teaches Her Children*, one of the great classics in education. Pestalozzi's ideas guided the development of the modern elementary school. He affected teaching practices and influenced Hall's thoughts as he wrote *Lectures on School Keeping* (1829).

Friedrich Froebel (1782–1852), a German educator, is considered the father of the kindergarten (which translates directly to *garden where children grow*). He wanted children to begin school at age three or four. Froebel's method of education was play; he believed that through constructive play, children developed and learned. In the kindergarten he emphasized using manipulative objects and helping children explore and express themselves.

The German psychologist **Johann Friedrich Herbart** (1776–1841) believed that education should develop the individual's personal character and prepare the individual to be socially useful. Herbart advocated the teaching of history, literature, and science at all grade levels for character development. He did not believe that the mechanical nature of skill subjects (the three Rs) contributed to character development or that they could be used to develop interest in learning. He wanted history, literature, or science to

Table 2.2 Society and Schools in the Nationalist Period

Societal Needs	Societal Beliefs	Social Forces
Loyalty to new nation	Faculty psychology	Economic needs: industry, commerce, agriculture
Patriotism	Mind divided into compartments	Industrial Revolution
Practical education	Need to exercise and train the mind through the teaching of science and history	Sociology: equal opportunity
Teaching of the English language		Growth of urban centers
American textbooks	Rote learning; recitation	Westward Movement
Universal education		

be used as an integrating core with other subjects correlated to the area of concentration.

Followers of Herbart formalized a five-step classroom teaching method based on the assumption that the teacher was well acquainted with the learner and the learner's prior knowledge. The five steps were preparation (the teacher used the students' prior learning as a starting point), presentation (new information and materials), association (comparison of new and existing knowledge for students), generalization (rules and principles based on the new information), and application (generalizations are applied). Madeline Hunter's formula lesson plan, the rage of the 1980s, was based on Herbart's five step method.

Francis W. Parker (1837–1902) was the superintendent of schools in Quincy, Massachusetts, from 1875 to 1880. Influenced by Pestalozzi and Froebel, he changed the way children were taught to read and speak in school. Parker's methods were called the *Quincy system.* He believed that teaching should be consistent with the natural ways in which children learn. Parker eliminated the study of grammar and introduced natural conversation into the curriculum. Children wrote about their experiences, activities, and feelings. Spelling was taught as the children needed assistance during writing. Parker introduced the idea of field trips, and the geography of the community was related to the field trips.

John Dewey (1859–1952) was very much influenced by Parker and the Quincy system. In 1896, Dewey and his wife opened the Laboratory School at the University of Chicago. The purpose of the school was to test Dewey's theories and provide an arena to demonstrate new teaching methods. In 1897, Dewey published *My Pedagogic Creed*, which expressed his philosophy about schools, the curriculum, and children. Dewey believed that the school was an extension of the community and thus should represent real life, and that activities that are familiar to the child should be the focus of school studies. Dewey regarded the individual as a social being and education as a social process that should stimulate the child's natural interests. The process of education should begin with psychological insight into the individual's capacities, interests, and habits. True education uses the children's experiences and provides group interaction so that the children understand themselves as members of the group and perceive themselves through the responses of others.

Dewey conceived education as the continuing reconstruction of experience. In discussing his ideas about the curriculum, Dewey maintained that the child's own social activities should be used to correlate school subjects. He did not believe that any one subject should be used as the focal point to integrate other subject fields. According to Dewey, "the only way to make the child conscious of his social heritage is to enable him to perform those fundamental types of activity which make civilization what it is" (1897, p. 9).

Dewey (1916, 1944, p. 139) wrote about the significance of experience in thinking:

> The nature of experience can be understood only by noting that it includes an active and a passive element. On the active hand, experience is *trying* a meaning which is made explicit in the connecter term experiment. On the passive, it is *undergoing*. When we experience something we act upon it, we do something with it; then we suffer or undergo the consequences. The connection of these two phases of experience measures the fruitfulness or value of the experience. Mere activity does not constitute experience.

Dewey's method of education was to cultivate the active side of the child before the passive and to observe and use the child's interests. The child's natural interest was not to be repressed nor simply humored. The teacher's task was to penetrate the surface to detect genuine interest and to select worthwhile experiences and appropriate subject matter.

Dewey analyzed the thinking process and differentiated between mere thinking and reflective thinking. He outlined the theory and methodology of reflective thinking. His work on the relationship of reflective thinking to the educative process served as a theoretical foundation to later researchers. Dewey's analysis of the thinking process is discussed in Chapter 7.

Dewey believed that teachers cannot train children to think but can create the desire and set the proper conditions in the classroom to motivate thinking. The teacher can help students develop curiosity, sensitivity, and habits of subjecting ideas to the test of rationality in order to cultivate the method of inquiry. Dewey warned that teachers must be aware of both the formal and informal aspects of the school situation that affect the student. The teacher's every act, overt and covert, influences the student.

Whereas Dewey was the philosopher-educator, **William Heard Kilpatrick** (1871–1965) was the methodologist. Kilpatrick wanted to develop pedagogical theory using Dewey's educational ideas and the psychology of the time. Kilpatrick believed that student activity was essential to learning. Educative activity needed to stress continuity or relatedness to prior activity, a desired goal (purpose), and new patterns of behavior to attain the goal. Activities needed to be congruent with students' interests and capacities so there would be an appropriate beginning to the activity. It was essential that students recognized the goal of the activity. Kilpatrick identified four phases of what he called the "Purposeful Act":

1. *Purposing*—originating an idea, deciding, determining to act
2. *Planning*—deciding on the course of action
3. *Executing*—carrying out the plan of action
4. *Judging*—determining the extent of success or failure (Litsinger, 1965, p. 17)

In 1951, Kilpatrick (p.314) contrasted what he termed the old curriculum and the new:

> The old consists of a systematically arranged *content of formulated knowledge* which the learner is to acquire. The new consists of *the total living of the child* so far as the school can affect it, living of a kind to build the desired character.

But Kilpatrick was misinterpreted as being totally child-centered. The emphasis on purposeful activity as the critical element in the learning process was not understood. Purposeful activities are those that engage the learner in expressing an idea, enjoying an aesthetic experience, solving a problem, or practicing a skill.

PROGRESSIVE EDUCATORS

The **progressive education** movement (1920–1950) embraced the philosophy of John Dewey, although Dewey himself was never a progressive educator. The progressive educators took issue with the old curriculum and methodology. They were concerned with students' needs, interests, and development. They wanted materials of instruction that would be interesting to children. They favored the use of concrete learning materials, and they wanted children to have diverse experiences with a variety of people and places. Progressive educators advocated purposeful activities focused on individual and group goals.

The Progressive Education Association, founded in 1919, recognized the contributions of Pestalozzi, Froebel, and Herbart, as well as those of the U.S. educators Mann, Parker, Dewey, Kilpatrick, Bode, and

Counts. The association's journal, *Progressive Education*, featured articles and research about curriculum and instruction in schools in which the newer philosophy and principles were followed.

The Progressive Education Association, and the progressive movement in general, contributed to our modern perspective of the curriculum and the teaching and learning process. Progressive educators believed that education should be focused on real-life problems and situations. They denounced authoritarian teachers and the use of corporal punishment in the classroom. They criticized teaching methods that focused primarily on the use of the textbook and rote learning, advocating motivation to stimulate students' interests. Progressive educators wanted the teacher to be a guide and counselor in the learning process; they wanted students, whenever possible, to have direct experiences, purposeful activities, and opportunities for problem solving. Education was to focus on the learner not the subject, and activities were to be cooperative not competitive.

EFFICIENCY IN EDUCATION, 1913–1930s

By the late 1800s, school districts had consolidated and become larger. School boards were no longer representative of the population; instead, business people and professionals predominated. School boards wanted schools to be efficient like factories; values such as punctuality, rigor, attention, and standards were espoused. Graded schools and graded textbooks resulted in standardized instruction.

In 1912, John Franklin Bobbitt, an education instructor at the University of Chicago, wrote "The Elimination of Waste in Education." Bobbitt described the problems related to enormous growth in Gary, Indiana. Property taxes, used to support the Gary school system, were assessed based on property valuation two years earlier, when the population was one-quarter as great. The school system was faced with inadequate facilities to accommodate the students.

Bobbitt said the choices were to build inferior facilities and provide two shifts (double time) for students, or to embrace **scientific management** and build a modern school plant. Gary chose the latter. The educational engineer developed a plan to operate the schools in Gary at 100 percent efficiency. The basic plan included classrooms and special facilities (basement, garden, attic, auditorium, shops, workrooms, laboratories, and playground). While half the students used the classrooms, the other half would use the special facilities.

Curriculum Division

The educational program was divided into regular and special studies. The regular studies included arithmetic, history, geography, reading, writing, spelling, and composition. Nature study, manual activities, drawing, literature, music, and play made up the special studies. Each teacher was responsible for three hours in the classroom or three hours of special activities. Teachers were supposed to use their nonteaching time to plan lessons or grade papers; at the end of the day they were expected to go home, "like other classes of workers," and leave their papers and books at school.

Gary's superintendent of schools was not satisfied with this plan because it only used the schools six hours per day. The children—no longer having extensive chores to do at home—spent much of their day playing in the streets and alleys. The superintendent of schools decided to open the schools on Saturdays for voluntary attendance. Next, he unsuccessfully sought to keep the schools open during the summer and create an all-year school system, with students free to choose to attend three quarters of the year.

There was concern about other types of waste in the Gary system as well. Students who were doing poorly in school were a major concern. Teachers were supposed to help the "laggards" during study time by teaching study techniques. Sometimes the students received double doses of the subject in which they were weak. This, however, was not true if a student was poor in the special subjects. On occasion, a student who was sickly and lacking physical vitality was assigned to the special subjects for the entire day until the student's physician declared him or her to be well.

Another principle of scientific management used in the Gary schools was to educate each individual to his or her capabilities. The program was supposed to be flexible to meet the needs of all students in the community. Bobbitt equated this with using the raw materials appropriately to ensure the finished product is as good as it can be!

Bobbitt probably took his cue from Frederick Taylor, who formulated time and motion studies. Taylor raised the consciousness of factory owners to the specification of workers' time and efforts, thereby making factories more efficient. Since Taylor's discovery was based on "scientific" inquiry, it was perceived as creditable. From that moment on schools have been plagued by the concept of improving education through specification of tasks and efficient teaching. Understanding that schools are not factories and neither teaching nor learning are routine escapes many modern educators just as it did in Bobbitt's era.

Creation of School Administration

Scientific management established the role of specialist teachers hired for specific purposes. The separate roles of teachers and administrators were also initiated during this era. In large school districts many administrative positions were created, but in smaller districts affected by consolidation, jobs were eliminated. Because of their traditional, subservient roles, women typically did not become administrators.

IMMIGRANT EDUCATION

To escape poverty and persecution in their native lands, more than 35 million immigrants came to the United States between 1815 and 1915 (Tyack, 1967). They sought a higher standard of living, freedom, and tolerance. They were enormously diverse in their cultural and linguistic backgrounds. The immigrants settled in the large cities and sought out their own cultural groups, family, and friends. They clung together for economic support and physical security in what became known as ghetto areas.

The schools accepted responsibility to help the immigrants assimilate to life in the United States. The assimilation process included teaching the immigrants certain habits of neatness, cleanliness, and punctuality along with loyalty and patriotism. Countless tales by immigrants chronicle their experiences in the United States during a period when becoming part of the melting pot was considered the only choice.

 Point to Ponder

L.Q. Ross (1937, p.5) provides an amusing account of American Night Preparatory School for Adults (an "Americanization" class):

> Further encouragement revealed that in Mr. Kaplan's literary Valhalla the "most famous tree American wriders" were Jeck Laundon, Valt Viterman, and the author of "Hawk L. Barry-Feen," one Mocktvain. Mr. Kaplan took pains to point out that he did not mention Relfvaldo Amerson because "He is a poyet, an' I'm talkink about wriders."

APPROACHING THE MODERN ERA

Our fictitious teachers, Greg Thomas, Mary Hogan, and Karen Adazzio, could begin to recognize elementary and secondary schools during this period because they began to resemble the modern schools of today in form, in philosophy, and in focus.

- Educational theorists began to experiment with teaching methods more closely matched to the natural development of children.
- John Dewey influenced educators' concepts of the school, the curriculum, and the child. He opened his Laboratory School for the demonstration of teaching methods at the University of Chicago.
- Dewey's reflective thinking process and Kilpatrick's purposeful act affected research and teaching methods.
- The progressive education movement focused attention on real-life problems as appropriate areas of study in the curriculum. The movement influenced methodology by advocating motivation to stimulate students' interests. Education began to focus more on the learner than on the subject.
- The role of the teacher in some schools changed from authoritarian to guide.
- Distinct roles developed for teachers and administrators.
- Advocates of scientific management emphasized factory-like values: efficiency, punctuality, neatness, utilization of resources, focus on product.

Table 2.3 provides an overview of the social forces that influenced the growth of the education system as the United States moved toward the modern era.

THE MODERN ERA

During World War I, more women were employed as teachers, but when the men returned home from the war, the women often lost their jobs. Some school districts refused to hire married women for fear they would become pregnant. This attitude persisted into the late 1940s. Salaries for teachers were depressed, primarily because the profession attracted females. Most school districts paid secondary teachers more than elementary teachers, mainly because male teachers predominated in the high schools. The double salary schedule in school districts was a reality until the 1950s.

The Depression years (1929–1930s) made many educators critical of the factory system and the efficiency cult; the child-centered school of the 1920s gave way to the social-centered school of the 1930s. George Counts wrote "Dare the Schools Build a New Social Order?" in 1932, imploring teachers to take control of the schools and the curriculum in order to influence social attitudes, ideals, and behaviors. Progressive educators urged the teaching of social issues and problems, social studies, and global issues; their recommendations were not adopted because the United States was in a very conservative, isolationist stage.

World War II (1941) ended the Depression and U.S. isolationism. Once again men were no longer available to teach and to supervise, and women stepped in and took over until the end of the war, when once again they were forced out. During the Cold War years (early 1950s) the United States fell behind Russia in science and technology, and there was a pressing need to prepare scientists and engineers. The federal government responded with funds, distributed through the National Science Foundation, to upgrade science and math programs in the schools.

In 1954 the historic Supreme Court decision *Brown v. Topeka Board of Education* made racial segregation unconstitutional. However, schools—both in the North and the South—were extremely slow in complying with the necessary changes. In northern cities, busing was implemented to desegregate the schools, and bitter community feelings developed in both African-American and white neighborhoods.

Table 2.3 Society and Schools in the Expanding United States

Societal Needs	Societal Beliefs	Social Forces
Practical education	Behaviorism	Economics: Factory system, efficiency
Focus on real-life problems	Child-centered curriculum beginning	Psychology: Behaviorism
Secondary education	Factory-like values	Sociology: Rise of Middle Class
School facilities		
Immigrant education		Movement from rural to urban centers

CHANGES IN THE CURRICULUM AND SCHOOL

In the years between the end of World War II and the Soviet launching of Sputnik (1957), the elementary curriculum in the United States consolidated into broad fields of study. Social studies replaced the teaching of history, geography, and civics. Language arts unified the teaching of reading, writing, speaking, and listening. Health education often encompassed physical education and health. Fine arts included music and art education. Science and mathematics were taught separately.

Elementary schools became larger during this period. The average school housed 600 students. Kindergarten enrollments increased. Most new school buildings were one story, instead of the older pattern of two- and three-story buildings. Consideration of the activities of students affected the changes.

School libraries become commonplace and teachers had a variety of textbooks to use. No longer was the teacher forced to use a single text in a subject field; many teachers, however, did seem to be wedded to the single textbook.

The National Science Foundation funded curriculum projects in science and programs to teach teachers new math. This agency also funded projects in social studies, which influenced social studies teaching and became known as the new social studies. Both the science and the social studies projects emphasized inquiry learning and understanding the underlying disciplines in the physical and social sciences.

President Lyndon Johnson's Great Society programs in the mid-1960s focused on education to help the culturally disadvantaged. Programs to train unemployed youth were developed. Head Start and other early childhood programs were created for preschoolers from culturally disadvantaged families; these programs were expected to make up for the lack of stimulating experiences in the home. The programs focused on reading-readiness activities, health, and nutrition. The preschool programs were seen as an opportunity to put the disadvantaged youth on a par with middle- and upper-class students when they entered school. (The controversy over equal educational opportunity begun by Horace Mann and exacerbated in the 1960s and 1970s was discussed in Chapter 1.)

Throughout the 1960s, 1970s, and early 1980s, the schools benefitted from federally supported special programs, including programs for students with disabilities and the disadvantaged, bilingual programs, vocational programs, school lunch programs, and gifted programs. But funding for special purposes also brought about regulations and control, and there were times when some educators felt the schools were stifled by too many federal regulations. Because of funding cuts during the mid-1980s, schools in the 1990s were hurting for monies to support school lunch programs, remedial programs, medical assistance programs, and gifted programs.

Special national projects in mathematics, science, social studies, and the humanities brought about major curriculum reform. But conflicts among educational theorists, educational researchers, and the public at large during the late 1970s and 1980s moved the curriculum, once again, into a conservative back-to-basics direction. The Madeline Hunter lesson plan design attracted policy makers and teacher supervisors who viewed it as a means to standardize and routinize teaching (and evaluate teachers). But the rigidity of the design robbed teachers of creativity and failed to foster student learning.

EMERGENCE OF MIDDLE SCHOOLS

The first middle school originated in Berkeley, California, in 1910. Its purpose was to provide a smoother transition into the high school by meeting the special needs of 12- and 13-year-old students. Organizational plans for schools differed in various parts of the country. In some states elementary education was conceived as kindergarten through grade eight. High schools were structured from grade nine through twelve. The years in the middle were sometimes called intermediate grades. The predominant pattern by the 1940s divided schooling into K–6, 7–9, and 10–12 institutions. As a consequence, the years in the middle became junior high schools and were taught by secondary teachers. The early intent of meeting the special developmental needs of young adolescents was forgotten. Not until the mid–1980s was there real concern that adolescents were dropping out of school before ever getting to the high schools, and this was occurring because the junior high schools were not meeting the intellectual, social, emotional, and physical needs of the age group served by the junior high school. For a discussion of the organizational structure of middle schools, see Chapter 3.

TEACHER EDUCATION

By 1930, schools of education had replaced the normal schools for teachers. Teachers continued to

Research Findings: The Changing Classroom

Larry Cuban (1984, p. 238) studied *How Teachers Taught—Constancy and Change in American Classrooms 1890-1980.* He noted that some elementary teachers created their own versions of child-centered classrooms. But a larger number of teachers initiated student-centered practices just part of the time. He found that by 1980 classrooms were less formal places than they had been in 1890.

specialize in subject areas, in elementary and secondary education, and in working with special populations. All public schools required teaching credentials, and schools of education initiated standards for accreditation. Teacher education included clinical preparation (student teaching) in classrooms prior to the granting of a credential. Teacher education programs vary across the country. Many preparation programs include five full years of study and culminate in a master's degree.

TEXTBOOKS AND MATERIALS

The variety of textbooks published for school use has increased dramatically over the years. Audio-visual materials and hardware developed, and by the 1960s films, filmstrips, cassettes, and other supplementary materials were commonplace in the classroom. By the 1970s teachers were developing learning centers and special laboratories for the use of audio-visual and other supplementary materials. Simulation games, also developed during this period, were used frequently with older elementary and secondary students.

Computers have been used in classrooms since the mid-1980s. Awareness of the significance of computers led to the realization that students need to be computer literate. Heinich et al., (1996, p. 230) identify five broad classes of computer applications for the classroom:

- As an object of instruction
- As a tool
- As an instructional device
- As a catalyst for school restructuring
- As a means of teaching logical thinking

New technology in the classroom will bring about dramatic change in the postmodern school.

METHODOLOGY

From Kilpatrick, teachers learned about the project method of teaching, and teaching units were developed to provide appropriate sequence and integration of learning. Group work was typical in most classrooms during the 1950s. The special curriculum projects of the 1960s and 1970s focused on inquiry learning and concept learning. Inquiry methodology can be traced to Dewey's reflective thinking process. (Inquiry-oriented teaching methodology will be discussed in Chapter 7.) Humanistic teaching strategies and values strategies were also typical in the classrooms of the 1960s and 1970s. Individualized instruction and programmed instruction occurred in many classrooms. Peer teaching was used particularly for skill instruction. Studies of effective teaching techniques and behaviorism influenced methodology in the classrooms of the 1970s and 1980s. As Cuban noted (1984, p. 244) in explaining how teachers taught between 1890 and 1980, instructional practices tend to remain stable over time.

THE POSTMODERN ERA

PERCEPTIONS OF THE LEARNER

New developments in cognitive psychology have changed educational practice in the late 1980s and the 1990s. Rejecting the idea that the mind was made up of compartments that needed to be exercised and rewarded, cognitive theorists have begun to take a **constructivist perspective** of learning. Learning becomes an active process and the learner a seeking organism.

Research Findings: Class Size

- Reductions in class size yield gains in all subject fields, and that gain is maintained over time.
- As the percentage of minority students increases in school districts, the ratio of students to teacher also increases. High-minority districts spend less than low-minority districts hiring and employing teachers (Bracey, 1995).

Postmodern goals focus on a thinking curriculum that engage students in integrated, complex reasoning and problem solving. In the colonial school, students engaged in rote learning and recitation; in the modern school, students are guided to transform information into new understanding that helps them rethink their prior ideas.

In addition to changes in teaching methodology and theories of learning, four challenges permeate schooling in the postmodern era. Two were discussed in Chapter 1, but are significant enough to reiterate here:

1. Concern about multicultural education
2. The viability of national standards

The other two represent changes in thinking about schools and teaching:

3. Restructuring of schools that is more responsive to the needs of learners and communities
4. Attention to the information age

MULTICULTURAL CONCERNS

The United States has always had a so-called "immigrant problem." Through most of our history, immigrants were either ignored or considered marginal characters unworthy of consideration. The schools assumed that their goal was assimilating the immigrants and stirring the melting pot. Textbooks described and legitimatized an homogenous culture.

Cultural literacy as interpreted by E. D. Hirsch, Diane Ravitch, Allan Bloom, and others assumes that people living in the same geographic area have a common culture, a common purpose, and therefore need to understand their (common) cultural heritage. Nineteenth-century schools, in the main, agreed and interpreted their mission as helping the immigrant population fit in socially, politically, and economically. That the schools were not always successful is typically ignored in the rhetoric of the common culture.

Schools in the 1980s and 1990s frequently have had students from more than 40 different countries and speaking more than 40 languages. Though bilingual teachers are sought where there are language majorities, generally schools must cope with cultural and language differences. Ravitch and others who argue for common-culture teaching suggest that after-school and weekend programs should address the needs of ethnic and cultural minorities thereby leaving school

time for the central mission of transmitting the "common" cultural heritage.

Multiculturalists would argue that students bring to the classroom diverse experiences and knowledge and the teacher must draw upon these experiences to build curriculum. This constructivist concept of learning fits with the Dewey notion of experience and thinking and emphasizes the contributions to the society of the United States by its culturally diverse population.

By limiting school experiences to those shared by European-American Protestants, the multiculturalists believe that too many children have grave difficulties in classrooms, and as a consequence, schooling fails them. However, there is widespread agreement that the aim of schooling is to facilitate participation in the mainstream of the culture of the United States. Mainstream values include the following examples:

- Personal liberty
- Equal opportunity and protection
- Social mobility through achievement and hard work
- The rule of law

The challenge confronting schools and teachers is to facilitate biculturalism so that students can participate both in their own culture and mainstream culture.

THE CHALLENGE OF NATIONAL STANDARDS

The purpose of setting standards is to impose change. The ramifications of national standards have not yet become apparent. Many teachers, as well as the public, have felt left out of the debate on standards. Both teachers and the public ask: What are the effects of standards on the diversity of the U.S. population? How will national standards affect teaching methodologies? How do standards affect teaching materials/textbooks? What do teachers need to learn (and believe) in order to implement standards?

It is uncertain whether standards will improve education in the twenty-first century or if those standards are another manifestation of the business community attempting to tell the schools what and how to teach. Nelson, Carlson, and Palonsky (1996) voice concern that "teacher and student freedom to study diverse views of American society, economics, politics, and history could be severely curtailed" by the imposition of national standards (p. 287). These authors note that the schools have been affected by business and industry since the beginning of the twentieth century.

Research Findings: Public School Employment

In 1992, 60 percent of principals and assistant principals were male and 40 percent were female. Among elementary teachers, 13 percent were male and 87 percent were female, and among secondary teachers, 45 percent were male and 55 percent were female (Statistical Abstract of the United States 1995).

Noddings (1995) asks: What do we as a society want for our children in the twenty-first century? She believes that we do not need a national curriculum, new academic standards, and national assessment. What we do need, she states, is to produce caring people who will be concerned for self, others, associates, acquaintances, animals, plants, physical environment, objects, instruments, and ideas (p. 366). Noddings wants to see the schools of the future organized around themes of care, such as teaching students that caring in every domain implies competence.

RESTRUCTURING AND REDESIGNING SCHOOLS

During the 1960s and 1970s the reform of schools was on everyone's agenda. But in the late 1990s it is the *redesign* of schools and the focus on teachers that is of significant concern. Earlier reform efforts focused on changing the bureaucracy of school districts, changing course requirements, setting new testing requirements, and "teacher-proofing" the curriculum.

In preparing for the twenty-first century, school change needs to focus on teacher leadership and professionalism. (See Chapter 18 for more about professional development.) Opportunities for teachers to engage in dialogue about the problems they confront need to be built into the school day. Dewey said it in 1916 (p. 4) and it is still applicable:

> Society not only continues to exist *by* transmission, *by* communication, but it may fairly be said to exist *in* communication. There is more than a verbal tie between the words common, community, and communication. Men live in a community in virtue of the things which they have in common; and communication is the way in which they come to possess things in common. What they have in common in order to form a community or society are aims, beliefs, aspirations, knowledge—a common understanding-like-mindedness as the sociologists say.

The redesign of schools depends on communities of teachers communicating with parents in local school settings to develop the shared purpose Dewey recognized almost 90 years ago.

THE INFORMATION AGE

The roles of teachers and students are changing as a result of media, computers, telephones, cellular networks, satellites, and other means of communication. Table 2.4 relates the goals and beliefs of modern society to the most recent changes in the country's education system.

In the twenty-first century teachers and students will use texts, pictures, voices, data, and two-way video

Table 2.4   Schools and Society in the Modern Era

Societal Needs	Societal Beliefs	Social Forces
Minority and immigrant education	Isolationism	Economics: criticism of the factory system
Bilingual education	Behaviorism	Depression, consolidation of schools and districts
Teachers	Child-centered movement	Sociology: immigration, crime, poverty, homelessness, racial problems, changes in the family
Teacher Education	Attention to the "whole" child	
Life adjustment classes	Cognitive psychology	
Attention to health, poverty, and homelessness	Cooperative learning	
Equal opportunity	Civil rights	Political: global society and democratic movements
Technology	Sexual freedom	
	Accountability	
	Standards	

(Heinich et al., 1996, p. 347). Through technology the access to information will be instantly available. Students and teachers can communicate with other students and teachers around the world. Modem pals may replace pen pals!

Technology has the potential to change the role of the teacher and the structure and design of schools. Chapter 10 discusses in depth the changing role of the teacher from presenter to technologic guide and facilitator. Distance learning programs, already in use by many teachers, provide the opportunity to use the expertise of other teachers and to schedule instruction at a convenient time and place. Learning through the use of telecommunications will be commonplace in the schools of the future.

SUMMARY

The Colonial Period

1. Religion dominated colonial schooling.
2. Children believed to be inherently bad and lazy.
3. Social class-oriented society.
4. Colonies had diverse populations.
5. Upper-class boys received a classical education; girls were expected to be homemakers.

The Nationalist Period

6. After the Revolution, loyalty and patriotism were taught through history and geography.
7. Textbooks and instructional materials were developed for the new nation.
8. Horace Mann and Henry Barnard championed the common school and compulsory education.
9. Normal schools were established for the preparation of teachers.
10. Faculty psychology affected the content and method of teaching.

The Expanding United States

11. United States schools were influenced by European educators.
12. Dewey and Kilpatrick influenced curriculum, teaching methods, and perceptions of children.

13. Efficiency ethic and factory system affected perceptions of schools and teachers.
14. Population shifted from rural areas to urban centers.

The Modern Era

15. School districts hired greater numbers of unmarried female teachers.
16. Educators criticized the factory system when applied to schools.
17. Federal government funded science, math, and early childhood programs.
18. Middle schools are created.
19. Behaviorists influenced teaching methodology and the evaluation of teachers.
20. Child-centered movement gained attention.
21. Cognitive psychology influenced constructivist perspective of learning.
22. Cultural literacy and multicultural education engaged educators in debate.
23. Introduction of national standards concern and many people.
24. Technology began to affect the role of teachers and the design of schools.

DISCUSSION QUESTIONS AND APPLICATION EXERCISES

1. How does your concept of child development affect the content and methodology of education?
2. How have historical events affected curriculum and methods of instruction?
3. Predict what the schools will be like in the year 2015.
4. Visit an elementary and/or middle school. In what ways is the school "factory-like"? Explain.
5. Think back to the days of schoolmasters and schoolmarms. What present-day practices mirror the experiences of those early teachers?
6. How does the federal government affect school programs and teachers' work?
7. In small groups, debate this question: Should the schools transmit the common cultural heritage *or* include diverse cultural experiences in the curriculum?

3

Organizing Patterns:
Schools, Classrooms, and Curricula

Schools, classrooms, and curricula can be organized in a variety of ways to accomplish sought-after goals. The public, educators, and school districts all make decisions affecting patterns of organization. Sometimes these decisions are made by advisory groups that represent the community and teachers. In this chapter you will learn about historical and contemporary organizing patterns for schools, classrooms, and curricula.

Schools differ in the goals they undertake to achieve and the ways they are organized to accomplish those goals. Classrooms, too, can differ in the way they are structured for teaching purposes. The organization of the curricula is influenced by educators' beliefs about the purpose of education and their beliefs about how children learn.

After you study this chapter, you should be able to accomplish the following:

1. Explain why schools are organized by grade levels.
2. Contrast different organizing plans for schools.
3. Discuss how the organizational plan for the school and the classroom affects how teachers teach.
4. Explain how the restructuring of the school affects what teachers do.
5. Discuss the features and purposes of schools of choice and how different teacher and student populations may be accommodated.
6. Discuss how teachers' curriculum conception affects teaching processes and student outcomes.
7. Identify your own curriculum conception and the educational purposes you want to achieve.
8. Contrast grouping plans, the purposes of each, and for what purposes you would use each plan.

Professional Lexicon

academic rationalism   A curriculum concept that includes the study of "Great Books" and certain disciplines such as mathematics, literature, and language to transmit cultural heritage.

alternative schools   Schools that offer curriculum and organizational choices that differ from standard schools.

broad fields   Interdisciplinary approaches that are synthesized or integrated.

career path schools   A type of magnet school oriented to older students that focuses on a specific occupation or profession.

charter schools   Public schools that are publicly funded but operated independently.

cognitive processing   A curricular concept designed to develop students' intellectual processes by generating problems and asking questions.

correlated curriculum   A concept that relates learning experiences in two or more subjects for teaching purposes.

departmentalization   A school organization system that maintains distinct subject boundaries.

fusion   Interdisciplinary approach that cuts across subject field lines.

graded school   A school organized by grade levels.

heterogeneous grouping   Grouping together dissimilar students.

homogeneous grouping   Grouping together students with similar skills.

humanism   A teaching method that focuses on the needs of the individual and provides a caring environment.

magnet school   Schools of choice with areas of specialization to attract students from diverse backgrounds.

multigrade and multiage classes   Classroom organization that mixes students by grade and age for administrative or educational reasons.

nongraded school   A school of choice without grade labels.

---

platoon system   A system designed to maximize school facilities and teacher specializations.

school restructuring   Reorganizing schools to improve student achievement and develop a professional environment for teachers.

self-contained classroom   A classroom with one teacher who is responsible for teaching students all subject fields.

separate subject   A curriculum organized into separate subject fields for teaching.

social reconstruction/adaptation   A curriculum concept that aims to improve society and/or prepare students for living in society.

team teaching   A way of combining the instructional efforts of two or more teachers to use their abilities to best advantage.

technology curriculum   An orientation that focuses on systematic and efficient teaching and learning.

THE STRUCTURAL ORGANIZATION OF SCHOOLS

GRADE-LEVEL ORGANIZATION

The first school to be organized by grade levels was the Quincy Grammar School near Boston. The idea of organizing students by grade levels based on chronological age, is a concept borrowed from European schools to standardize what is taught. The *McGuffey Readers* facilitated teaching by grade levels. Graded structure was easily accepted because skills were emphasized in our early schools. The graded structure was further promoted by the introduction of the monitorial system. With the introduction of U.S. textbooks in reading, arithmetic, spelling, and geography, the graded structure was set. As more textbooks were written and books began to appear in series, schools ordered them by grade levels.

Graded structure makes it relatively easy for a teacher to manage many students by grouping them for instructional purposes. But in fact, in the nineteenth century, students were not grouped for instruction; instead the teacher prepared a single lesson for the whole class. Gradedness provided a factory-like situation. It was economical in terms of materials of instruction and it was efficient. It allowed a whole school to operate with children segregated by grade level. Students were placed in the proper classroom according to the chronological age of each child.

The **graded school** allowed educators to make arbitrary decisions about what should be taught at each grade level. Both subject matter content and skills were sequenced. As students grow older, it is expected that they also grow smarter. Consideration of promotion from one grade to the next was made at the end of each school year. (Variations of this occurred at different times and places, and promotion sometimes happened at the end of a semester.) It began to be assumed that a

student in third grade had completed, with relative success, all of the skills and content designated appropriate for grades one and two, or the student would not have been promoted. If a student could not complete with relative success the skills, subject matter content, and textbooks assigned to a specific grade level, then the student was retained. As time went on, the graded school took some consideration of the student's social maturity. But generally the graded school is thought of as a *lockstep* system of organization.

DISSATISFACTION WITH THE GRADED SYSTEM

Contemporary elementary and middle schools have found a number of ways to improve the system. The discussion of classroom and curricula patterns will highlight some of the ways teachers have found to break the lockstep tradition of the graded school. First let us look at some plans developed as a consequence of dissatisfaction with the graded school.

Alternatives for Groups

In 1965, the superintendent of schools in St. Louis, W. T. Harris, regrouped students at six-week intervals to counteract the apparent rigidity in the graded system. His intent was to provide for children of different ability levels. Students who did exceptionally well moved into a different classroom with other students who were doing advanced work, and students who needed to be retained worked with students at their level. However, students were still taught as a complete class.

The Cambridge Plan, in operation in the early 1900s, was considered a multitrack program. Bright students progressed through the system in less time than the majority of students in the elementary school.

In the Santa Barbara Plan, in the early 1900s, students were divided into three tracks. This plan was the

Access to recreational reading and research support is available in the modern school library.

first to manipulate the content of education. Bright students studied topics in greater depth than average or poor students. All of the students, however, studied the same topics.

Probably the most famous organizational plan was the XYZ Detroit Plan, created in the 1920s. This plan expected bright students to study topics in greater depth and cover the material in less time than students who were less able.

Alternatives for Individuals

None of these plans focused on the individual in the classroom. Students were placed with a particular group of students, and the whole group was treated in the same manner. Students progressed with their groups without consideration of individual differences.

The Pueblo Plan, developed by Preston Search for schools in Pueblo, Colorado, during the 1880s, represented a real attempt to break the lockstep tradition. The plan focused on the individual student and expected the individual to work at his or her own ability level and rate. Search's plan was the first to consider nongraded instruction.

Using Search's ideas, Carleton Washburne introduced the concept of a **nongraded school** to the Winnetka, Illinois, public schools in 1919. Students were expected to progress at their own rate and ability level in this system. During reading and mathematics, students used what we now call programmed materials, with topics arranged sequentially for individual progress. Group activities were conducted in

social studies, music, art, and science. Washburne did not use the term *nongraded* when he referred to his plan, yet it clearly was one of the first models of nongraded instruction.

NONGRADED SCHOOLS

Organizing schools by grades is convenient. It helps to define the teacher work load and has been accepted by the public as policy, custom, and law. It is frequently written into school district contracts with teachers (Schlechty, 1990). However, graded school organization plans do not necessarily meet the needs of students. (This may be a good time to review the contract of early schoolmasters in Chapter 2.)

Grade barriers impose a structure and label students in ways that determine how much students can learn and how much teachers should teach. In contrast to the graded school, the nongraded organizational plan allows continuous progress for students. In nongraded plans, which were first introduced in the 1930s but were not popular until the 1950s, some students may progress five months in a semester; others may progress three months or eight months. Progress may be irregular, slow at times and rapid at other times. A given student is not equally capable in all subject fields. In some subjects the student may surge ahead, and in others lag behind. In a nongraded plan, this is permissible. Neither double

---

What are the advantages and/or disadvantages of teaching in a nongraded school?

promotions nor retention are requirements of the structure. Bright students can be encouraged both in depth and in scope. Slow progress can be permitted in necessary subject fields without denigration of a student's feelings and status. At any time students may change work groups or classrooms to meet specific needs.

Teachers do not have to be concerned that they are offering material that belongs to another teacher. They are not encroaching on another teacher's grade level! Instructional materials may be selected to meet students' needs and the instructional purpose; materials are not restricted to a specific grade level. Teachers are free to be creative.

The nongraded school of the 1960s attempted to break the lockstep of the graded school, but it too had difficulty in placing students at the appropriate starting level. Most nongraded schools used standardized achievement test scores to determine reading and mathematics placement; these skill subjects generally determined in which classroom the student began his or her studies. The advantages of nongradedness are just as dependent on teacher effectiveness as the graded organizational arrangement.

SCHOOLS OF CHOICE

Magnet Schools

Magnet schools are designed to be schools of choice. Their purpose is to attract students from across ethnic groups and geographic regions of a city. Hence they feature a specific curriculum. The school is organized to build its curriculum around the featured magnet attraction. For example, a school for the performing arts would undertake varied public performances that integrate social studies, science, math, and literature around the performing arts production. Students might study literary style and a historical period of time; then they write their own play, create costumes, learn stage design, and study appropriate dance and song to fit the historical setting.

Career Path Schools

The **career path school** is similar to a magnet school, but is more oriented to older students, grades 8–12. Often the career path school is focused on specific occupations or professions. A visual arts school attracts students interested in art design and communication using visual experiences. Schools focused on the health care industry help students prepare for medical

Do you have a teaching passion? Suggest a new magnet school that would allow you to teach in your area of expertise.

careers in laboratories, hospitals, and higher education studies. Some career path schools are modern versions of vocational schools, but oriented to the intermediate and high school student.

Alternative Schools

Alternative schools are schools of choice designed, most typically, for a particular population with a specific need. Most alternative schools attempt to be different in one or more ways from the standard school. Open education is sometimes featured. Parents (and children) choosing an open education school may be choosing a school with less structure and fewer routines. Team teaching may occur. The school may be graded or nongraded. The curriculum may focus on specific subject fields. The program may emphasize science and mathematics or the creative arts. There even are classical education schools, where young children learn foreign languages and read the classics.

During the 1970s and 1980s, the "fundamental" school was popular in many school districts. The fundamental school emphasized basic skill instruction, discipline, deference to authority, drill, rote learning, and recitation. Almost a complete opposite to the "open" school in philosophy, the fundamental school was another school of choice.

Raywid (1994, p. 27) identifies three types of alternative school programs: popular innovations, last-chance programs, and remedial focused programs.

Popular innovations: The magnet school is an example of this alternative. The school may be nontraditional in its organization, administration, curriculum, and instructional processes.

Last-chance programs: These are schools created to hold a captive group of students who face expulsion from their regular school and are really not schools of choice. The programs typically use behavior modification strategies.

Remedial schools: These schools are designed to care for students who need academic and/or social and emotional rehabilitation.

According to Raywid (p. 30), "A good alternative school represents a carefully built community, an engaging instructional program, and a synchronized set of organizational arrangements."

Research Findings:
Teachers and Decision Making

In a study of teachers engaged in school decision making, Griffin (1995) found that changes occurred in student assessment, curriculum frameworks, use of technology, and work with students who do not conform to school norms, but there was little change in classroom practices.

Many alternative schools began as schools-within-schools. They capitalized on the strengths and interests of teachers who created them. Frequently they are directed or administered by a teacher, and they tend to have autonomy from outside regulations. Since the teachers choose to teach in the alternative school they are characterized by the continuity of their faculty.

CHARTER SCHOOLS

A number of states have approved the idea of **charter schools** (California, Colorado, Georgia, Massachusetts, Michigan, Minnesota, New Mexico, and Wisconsin). Under the charter system, certified teachers may create a new and distinctive school. In some states the teachers apply to the school district for the right to reorganize their school and become "chartered." In other states the teachers apply directly to the state. The chartered school is an independent public school that is supported by the state and/or charitable institutions and released from observing the typical school district regulations.

In Los Angeles, charter schools contract for all of their own services. For example, if the school needs plumbing, gardening, or electrical work, the teachers and/or the principal contract for the services as an independent group. Often the community is alerted to the school's need and may donate services to assist the school. Parents are expected to be involved participants. It is for this reason that many charter schools are able to do more for their student population than the traditional school.

TIME AND THE ORGANIZATION OF SCHOOLS

Recall (Chapter 2) that in our early schools both the schoolmaster and male students needed time to work in the fields harvesting crops. Vacations from school were planned around the seasons. Teachers did not get paid for vacation periods because they were expected to hold other jobs, such as working in the fields, during the vacation time.

Sometimes teachers' in-service education was planned for vacation time. Schlechty (1990) notes that in Louisville, Kentucky, teachers' in-service education days are planned around the Kentucky Derby and that schools reopen according to a schedule that does not impact traffic at Derby time.

Teacher recruitment for many years was tied to the vacation concept. Female teachers attracted to the idea of being home with their children during vacation time sought teaching positions. Teacher and parent animosity concerning year-round schooling has been a result of the habit of summer vacation time.

When school districts make time planning decisions, they need to involve teachers. Should teachers work beyond the school day? Should teachers work during so-called vacation periods? In many schools, time is so rigidly structured that teachers and their school districts have little flexibility to engage in planning and governance decisions. Let us now look at how time affects the restructuring of school organization.

SCHOOL RESTRUCTURING

School restructuring is the term used to describe organizational changes in schools. In an effort to improve student achievement and develop a professional environment for teachers, some schools may restructure teacher roles, decision-making procedures, curricula, grouping practices, and evaluation practices for teachers. Fred Newmann (1995, p. 71), director of the Center on Organization and Restructuring of Schools, defines a restructured school as "a school that made major departures from conventional practice in numerous ways." In his study of restructuring schools he found that most of these schools made organizational changes affecting authentic instruction and student achievement, the development of a professional community, and teacher accountability.

The major constraint to successful restructuring is time. Changing the ways that schools deliver instruction involves innovative practices dependent on teacher

How do restructured schools enhance teacher professionalism?

involvement. Restructuring efforts include *site-based management* that gives teachers extensive decision-making responsibility, *team teaching* that requires a great deal of teacher planning time, *cooperative and "hands-on" learning* that may require extensive professional development, and *alternative scheduling* of the school day. These terms will be discussed further as we consider classroom and curricula organizational patterns and professional development in Chapter 18.

PATTERNS OF CLASSROOM ORGANIZATION

THE SELF-CONTAINED CLASSROOM

Advantages

In the **self-contained classroom,** students are placed with one teacher, typically for the entire day. The teacher has the opportunity to become acquainted with students over a long period of time in all subject fields. The teacher in the self-contained classroom is responsible for instruction in all subject fields.

Time management is the responsibility of the teacher in the self-contained classroom; it is also an advantage of the self-contained classroom. Teachers do not have to adhere rigidly to time schedules. If a given activity takes longer than anticipated or if students' learning interests and needs seem to require a longer period of time on any given day, then the teacher has the freedom to manipulate the scheduled plans.

Control over all subjects in the elementary curriculum also allows the teacher to integrate subject fields. Skills taught during reading instruction can be practiced during social studies. Mathematics concepts can be tested during science. When students have the wiggles, teachers can intersperse music or physical education. The teacher also has the flexibility to schedule field trips or guest speakers.

Disadvantages

Disadvantages of the self-contained classroom are rooted primarily in the possible professional and academic weaknesses of the teacher. Because the teacher is responsible for teaching all subject fields, if the teacher lacks expertise or is weak in certain subjects, instruction in those fields suffers. Also, if a teacher prefers one subject over others and spends too much time with the preferred content area, there will be an imbalance in the curriculum. Additionally, if the

teacher lacks insight into growth and development of children, professional performance may be hampered.

Another potential problem focuses on student and teacher isolation. Students may suffer from a lack of interaction with other adult models. A teacher's professional potential may be limited because of a lack of interaction with colleagues. There are means available to alleviate this problem which will be discussed in depth in Chapter 18.

THE DEPARTMENTALIZED CLASSROOM

Advantages

Departmentalized classroom organization compensates for teachers' academic weaknesses. In this plan, teachers instruct in their area or areas of specialization. For a given period of time the specialist provides instruction in one or more subjects. Students are rotated among the teachers in the departmentalized plan. In traditional middle schools, **departmentalization** is the norm. When it is used in elementary education, the students generally are in grades 4–6. The middle school most typically provides the transition point between the self-contained classroom and departmentalization.

Departmentalization is attractive to teachers who want to specialize in a subject field and teach elementary or middle school students. When teachers have to teach all the subjects in the elementary curriculum, it is difficult to be current in certain fields such as science, social studies, and mathematics. These fields in particular require knowledge of the underlying disciplines, and it is unusual for most elementary teachers to be fully competent in all of these subjects.

Another advantage to departmentalization is the opportunity to equip a classroom with specialized materials and equipment for teaching in a subject field. The teacher can keep hands-on materials ready for student use and exhibit special displays in the classroom. As a consequence, material and equipment costs may be reduced, since all classrooms will not need the specialized materials.

Middle schools involved in restructuring, including Karen Adazzio's school, try to use the advantages of both self-contained classrooms and departmentalization. Adazzio teaches and provides leadership in a

Should middle school teachers hold elementary or secondary credentials?

middle school that embraces a team approach. Several teachers work together with a designated group of students, usually about 150 students. The group is sometimes called a *house* or a *team*.

The teachers work to become better acquainted with their team of students. One or more of the teachers serve as teacher generalist, and the others are specialists. A quasi-homeroom environment is established so that students develop a sense of belonging. The generalist teacher selects a core curriculum to teach over an extended block of instructional time. This enables the teacher to be better acquainted with the students. The specialist teachers instruct the elective and other subject fields using interdisciplinary content designs. Thus the middle school student experiences both the coherence of elementary education and the novelty of the secondary pattern of school organization without being overwhelmed by it.

Advantages of this transition plan include allowing students to develop identity with the same group of students and an adviser teacher for the three years of the program. Another advantage is the concept of extending the block of instructional time, thereby providing opportunity for the integration of knowledge and skills across subject fields. In Karen Adazzio's team, the teachers collaborate in long-range unit plans and enjoy teaming for instruction.

Disadvantages

The disadvantages of departmentalization relate to the strengths of the self-contained classroom. In the self-contained classroom teachers are well acquainted with their students. This may not occur as easily in a departmentalized plan. In addition, whenever students are rotated among a group of teachers, attendance and other routines need to be repeated, resulting in some loss of time.

Still another very important consideration relates to the integration of subject fields. In the self-contained classroom the teacher plans lessons for the entire day, week, and month. Most teachers make unit plans in subject fields. The teacher is aware of what needs to be taught in all subjects, and can integrate skills, topics, and concepts so students can interrelate understandings and skills. Time cannot be used as effectively in the departmentalized plan.

LEARNING CENTERS AND LABORATORIES

In some elementary and middle schools, specific rooms are equipped as centers for special studies. Many schools have mathematics laboratories, computer centers, science laboratories, and music and art rooms. These special rooms may be scheduled for teachers to use with their students. The teacher brings his or her

Teachers bring students to the computer learning center to learn how to use the computer and to work on special projects.

class to the laboratory at a specified time. In this way only the laboratory or center needs the specialized equipment and materials. The classroom teacher does the teaching in the center.

In some schools, resource teachers are employed to staff these centers. The self-contained classroom teacher brings the students to the center or laboratory and stays with the class while the resource teacher provides instruction. In schools with resource teachers or music teachers, classroom teachers are often responsible for a greater number of children in their classrooms. In this way the special teacher is released for specialized instruction.

TEAM TEACHING

Team teaching is a way of combining the instructional efforts of two or more teachers in order to use their abilities to best advantage. Teacher aides or assistants may also be included in the teaming arrangement. Teaming can be particularly advantageous at the elementary level because of the diversity of subjects that are taught. For example, if several fourth-grade teachers at a school teamed, each might be a *team leader* for a different subject of the curriculum. The team leader accepts greater responsibility for planning and teaching in the area of his or her expertise. The other members of the team serve as assistants during instruction and help with reinforcement.

Group planning time is extremely important when working in a team situation. Members of the team need to share plans and objectives and receive feedback about whether a lesson accomplished its purpose. Team teaching provides a system whereby new and inexperienced teachers can learn teaching methodologies from more experienced colleagues and receive feedback about their own teaching performance.

Implementation of teaming is different in each situation. In some schools an experienced teacher called the *lead teacher* is responsible for most of the planning. However, the professional reason for teaming should be to refine instructional techniques and provide students with instruction from teachers who are motivated and superior in each subject field. Teaming provides a built-in system for staff development.

Team teaching may also be used in nongraded and multigraded classrooms. Since teachers pool their respective classes in team teaching, this organizational system allows students to be grouped by need rather than by grade. Students move from one group to another depending on the subject and the student's ability and interests. Nongraded teaching teams from primary, middle, or upper grades are popular among teachers in many schools.

THE PLATOON SYSTEM

The **platoon system** maximizes the availability of school facilities to alternate groups and uses teachers' specializations to the utmost. It is related to the old Gary Plan discussed in Chapter 2. Students are divided into two platoons. While one platoon is instructed by the homeroom teacher in language arts or mathematics, the other platoon studies social studies, science, music, art, or physical education with specialized teachers in designated subject-area classrooms. For half of the school day students stay in their homerooms, and during the other half they move among the special teachers. Sometimes the program is divided by days of the week. Perhaps on Monday, Wednesday, and Friday the students will have science and art for their special studies, and on Tuesday and Thursday they will have other special classes. The platoon system enables homeroom teachers to get to know their students well and to perform advisement. At the same time, students have the advantage of interacting with a number of adults.

The platoon system represents a modification of the departmentalized plan, yet it retains many of the shortcomings of departmentalization. Teachers find it difficult to integrate subject fields in the platoon system, and time is lost while students rotate from one class to another and while the special teachers perform routine procedures.

Because of the platoon plan's shortcomings, elementary schools rarely use it today; however, some middle schools (grades 6–8) find the plan advantageous.

EXTENDING THE CLASS PERIOD

At some middle schools the teachers are breaking the lockstep of the traditional 50-minute period by extending some class periods to 90 minutes. The longer time period allows teachers to approach some topics with more depth and gives students the opportunity to become involved in research and hands-on activities. The longer class period affects teacher planning, methodology, instructional materials, and assessment of students.

Planning for the longer period provides more options for the teacher to approach content in depth versus the more typical superficial coverage of content areas.

Methodology is affected by the longer class period because the teacher can now work to develop students' critical thinking skills and provide more opportunities for building communication skills. Greater use of group work and longer assignments is possible.

Textbooks can be treated as resources for students to use for their projects instead of using the text as a structured class assignment. Students are expected to select more text materials and utilize other sources of data to complete project assignments.

Assessment is affected by the greater involvement of students in project work. Rubrics need to be established to set criteria for grading. Students can be enlisted to help set these standards.

Since not all subject fields and classes will enjoy the longer class periods, school programs and scheduling are affected. This means that teachers need to work together to make decisions affecting the school culture in order to make the extended class period work advantageously.

GROUPING AND CLASSROOM ORGANIZATION

Within classrooms students may be organized in a variety of ways. For example, students may be grouped informally using their interests as a basis for group assignment. Students may be grouped by ability or achievement for specific skill needs. Students also may be grouped socially, dependent on degree of independence and maturity.

HOMOGENEOUS GROUPS

Students are sometimes grouped in classrooms to study similar content and to meet similar learning needs. To do this, the teacher needs to select criteria to use to subdivide the classroom group. Most typically students are grouped homogeneously for teaching a specific skill in reading, mathematics, or physical education. Grouping by skill needs in reading or mathematics allows instruction to be differentiated, which is efficient for the teacher and gives students more individualized attention. However, since individual students may differ in achievement in various subjects, it would be detrimental to students for the teacher to use the same ability group throughout the school day.

School principals or teacher advisory groups are usually responsible for arranging classes of students. Sometimes there is an effort to arrange whole classes by levels to decrease the range of ability levels within the classroom. There are a number of problems with doing this. First, since a student rarely tests at the same level in all subjects, it is necessary to select one subject as the criterion for assignment. Because reading is usually the criterion selected, some teachers may have an entire classroom of students reading below grade level. Most teachers tend to favor students who perform at grade level or above grade level. With an entire class of poor readers, other classroom activities may be affected because students will not be able to help each other with reading. (This shortcoming is amplified in the discussion of heterogeneous grouping.)

Another problem associated with **homogeneous grouping** has to do with teacher expectations. Students soon detect how teachers label them. Research indicates that students labeled *low ability* usually perform according to what is expected of them. In addition, there seems to be a tendency to assign low-social-class and minority students to low-ability groups, thus increasing problems associated with equal educational opportunity.

A more advantageous way to arrange whole classroom groups is to select students who are below grade level in skill areas and place them with students who are at grade level. This arrangement allows students to work together and interact in a positive manner. High-ability groups should also be placed with average peers at the same grade level. Under no circumstances should above-average students be placed with older low-ability students at a higher grade level; the high-ability students will surpass the older students and affect the self-concept of those low-ability students.

 Teacher Research

Studying the extended class period, Brett (1996, p. 78) discovered:

- Planning was harder and consumed more time.
- Class time flew by.
- Students worked well and improved their skills.
- Student-teacher relations improved grades and built trust.
- Absenteeism had a greater impact on students.

HETEROGENEOUS GROUPS

By not locking students into a set group throughout the school day, the teacher is able to utilize students' diverse interests and abilities in the different subject fields. **Heterogeneous grouping** means dissimilar grouping. It allows students to develop unique competencies and leadership skills and gives them the opportunity to interact with a greater variety of individuals. It is often desirable to group students in science and social studies. In heterogeneous groups, students may benefit from the experiences of others. If students need to read information during science or social studies, the small group facilitates good readers helping others.

Heterogeneous grouping improves the self-concept of low-ability students, influences their motivation, makes them work harder, and helps them to be accepted by their peer group. Heterogeneous class grouping approximates the community outside the classroom, where there are real-life differences. As a consequence, students' social maturity, moral, and cognitive development are influenced. The importance of grouping and how to begin small group work using heterogeneous grouping will be discussed in Chapter 4.

MULTIAGE AND MULTIGRADE ORGANIZATIONAL PLANS

Multiage classes purposefully mix students of different grade levels for a variety of educational reasons:

- To assist students develop natural relationships with older and younger classmates
- To encourage older students to tutor and mentor younger students, and encourage younger students to emulate older students
- To help students and teachers become better acquainted by keeping the student with the same teacher for a longer period of time
- To minimize competitive behavior and encourage social growth
- To stimulate both cognitive and affective growth

Multigrade classes are typically formed to satisfy administrative needs rather than for educational reasons. In most multigrade classrooms the students are deliberately kept separate through different assignments and curricula.

Multiage and multigrade classes are formed for different reasons, but the end results are much the same.

Both parents and teachers usually object to the multi-grade organization; parents object because they believe students will learn less, and teachers believe that it will be more work. However, Veenman (1995), in a review of 11 studies of multiage/multigrade classes, found that students do not learn more or less than single age/grade classes. The studies also revealed that students in the multiage/multigrade classes had a better attitude towards school, and better personal adjustment and self-concept.

CURRICULUM ORGANIZATIONAL PATTERNS

The historical study of the curriculum in Chapter 2 provided insight on how sociopolitical events and the concept of child development affected the addition of subject fields. As each new subject was added, teachers approached it as a **separate subject** to be organized; that is, they viewed each subject as being independent of all other subjects.

SEPARATE SUBJECTS ORGANIZATION

Utilizing the disciplinary base of a subject field, knowledge is organized to teach the subjects in the curriculum. The curriculum is composed of many separate disciplines. The disciplines often vie with each other for prominence in the school program. Historically, the addition of each new subject field in the elementary school made the teacher's job more difficult. Traditional treatment of separate subjects meant that the teacher was responsible for teaching all about a subject field, and when students learned all about the subject, they were expected to regurgitate it back.

As knowledge expands, the teacher's choice of content becomes more difficult. In the social sciences

Research Findings:
Multigraded and Multiaged Classrooms

Veenman (1995) concluded that student learning in multigraded and multiaged classes are affected by the quality of the instructional practices of the teacher rather than by the organizational structure of the classroom.

alone, the teacher may have to teach anthropology, economics, history, geography, sociology, political science, and psychology. Similarly, the physical sciences contribute to congestion in the elementary curriculum. In addition to these discipline-based subjects, the elementary teacher is providing skill instruction in reading, spelling, grammar, and handwriting, not to mention literature, oral language, mathematics, health, and physical education. To cope with the problem, some teachers began to teach certain subjects every other day.

In addition to the problem of utilization of time to teach the separate disciplines, many teachers and educational critics were concerned that the emphasis on separate disciplines left no time to consider societal problems or even the interests of students. Students were not given opportunity to engage in problem solving, and there was evidence that students could not integrate the knowledge from the various subject fields.

CORRELATED SUBJECTS ORGANIZATION

Many disciplinarians (historians, for example) believe that students should study a subject field the way the scholar does, that is, by using the unique concepts of the discipline and inquiring as the disciplinarian would. However, educators began to realize that students needed integrated learning experiences. To accomplish this, some curriculum specialists advocated organizing key subjects together in a **correlated curriculum.** For example, in the junior high school one sometimes found a course called "Social Living," which in fact was the study of U. S. history and literature. Sometimes one teacher taught this class, and sometimes two teachers cooperated together. Health and science, and sometimes science and mathematics, classes were correlated.

When subjects are correlated, each maintains its own identity, but certain topics are used to tie the subjects together. Correlated subject fields can occur in an open school, a nongraded school, or a graded school. The courses may be team taught, one teacher may teach the subjects, or teachers may jointly plan for the correlation, with each teacher providing instruction in his or her area of expertise.

Schools should be learning environments. Why do teachers need to collaborate to create and model these environments?

FUSION AND BROAD FIELDS AS ORGANIZING PATTERNS

When related subjects are put together into a brand new course they are considered fused. For example, the history of the Renaissance and a historical view of art during the Renaissance period might be fused into a course called art history. **Fusion** may also occur when subjects from the same discipline are put together into a more general subject field course. Illustrative of this would be a course called life science, which fuses biology, botany, and ecology. (Biology itself often represents the process of fusion because it includes botany, zoology, and physiology.) Another example is a high school course called marine biology, which fuses biology and oceanography. Sixth graders often study world history, which combines various history courses.

The **broad fields** organizational scheme is similar to fusion. But in broad fields there is more of an attempt to synthesize the fused subject fields. The modern elementary school curriculum represents this organizational pattern. Social studies includes the study of history, geography, economics, and political science. Quite frequently other social sciences are included as well (anthropology, sociology, and psychology). Language arts comprises the study of oral and written language (reading, writing, spelling, listening, literature, and speech). Science in the elementary school consists of biology, physiology, botany, zoology, entomology, and astronomy. Art includes painting, drawing, sculpture, and possibly art history and appreciation.

The broad fields approach is not intended to be a survey-level approach to a field of study. The approach does allow depth studies that interrelate subject matters. For example, social studies is not just an amalgamation of the various social sciences; studies may focus on a region, or a period of time, or a social problem. In addition, disciplines are not studied in a pure form, but selected knowledge is drawn from the different disciplines.

TEACHERS' BELIEFS AFFECT CURRICULUM

Sometimes consciously, more often unconsciously, teachers make decisions about what to teach, when to teach it, how to teach, and how often and to what extent to teach specific content. These decisions constitute the curriculum of the classroom. The decisions teachers make relate to their own experiences in schools, their beliefs about "What Knowledge Is of

Table 3.1 Teacher's and Students' Roles in Curriculum Conception

Curriculum Conception	Teacher's Role	Students' Role
Academic rationalism	Director Presenter	Acquire knowledge Appreciate knowledge
Social reconstruction/ adaptation	Sensitive leader Guide Foster interaction Research leader	Interact with others in groups Engage in social problem solving
Humanism	Provocateur	Self-actualization Discovery Choosing what to learn
Technology as a curriculum orientation	Sequence learning from part to whole Programmer	Acquire basic skill
Cognitive processing	Generate problems Encourage inquiry	Search for understanding Develop thinking processes

Most Worth?" (Herbert Spencer) and their beliefs about how children learn.

These (sometimes) tenuously constructed beliefs have been aptly described as curriculum conceptions by Eisner and Vallance (1974) and Eisner (1979, 1985). These authors identified five conceptions that are frequently translated into curriculum decisions that affect what teachers do and teach in the classroom, what students do and learn, and how the classroom environment relates to the curriculum. Table 3.1 applies the five conceptions and contrasts teacher and student roles.

1. **Academic rationalism:** The academic rationalist teacher selects "classical" liberal arts content to transmit cultural heritage. The teacher believes that students need to participate in Western society and to do so they must study the classic disciplines. Mathematics, languages and literature (the "Great Books"), and pure science (not general science) constitute the most important content to be taught. Therefore these subjects assume the highest priority in the classroom. Practical subjects, such as vocational and health education, are often slighted.

Adhering to this approach, teachers rarely integrate subject fields, but instead use a separate subject approach and traditional methodology because students are expected to respond to lectures and assigned readings. Students are trained in the liberal arts and expected to understand the leading ideas of Western civilization.

2. **Social reconstruction:** This curriculum conception is the direct opposite of the academic ration-

alist conception. Teachers holding this belief assume a responsibility to make the world a better place to live. Their emphases are the social environment of the community and the needs of the students they teach. They will choose societal themes (such as change) and/or societal problems (such as poverty or homelessness) and build curriculum by integrating subject fields. The goal of social reconstructionists is social reform and developing citizens' responsibility. They believe strongly in the role of education as a means of social mobility.

The classroom environment is arranged to motivate and instruct. Classroom rules reflect democratic procedures, responsibilities, and needs of citizens. Methodology emphasizes cooperative group work, learning by doing, and the scientific method.

Social adaptation: Instead of a focus on making society better in the future, teachers who believe in social adaptation are concerned about adjusting to present-day problems. Their interpretation of the social curriculum conception is to help their students adjust to society by "fitting in." They too look to society for curriculum, but instead of trying to reform the community, they work toward solving everyday problems.

The reconstructionists are more aggressive in their search for ways to reform education and society. The adaptors seek ways to help their students survive in present society. Both groups focus on the social side of teaching and learning.

3. **Humanism:** Most teachers believe they are humanists, but few actually subscribe to this curriculum orientation. The humanistic teacher creates

opportunities for students to achieve self-actualization. Like the social reconstructionist and adaptation orientation, the humanists use the environment of the classroom to motivate and provoke students' interests and studies. The humanist teacher wants students to embark upon self-study and discovery. Curriculum content is personal and focused on the individual child. School and classroom environment and the content of the curriculum are used to influence the student's search for personal integration.

Humanist teachers often teach in alternative schools. They like small classes because the time investment is greater to develop curricula for each student. Students in the humanistic classroom often work alone, choosing what to study and how to study it. They are not bound by time or by strict curriculum goals.

4. **Technology curriculum** orientation: The technologist teacher approaches curriculum with a behavioral orientation. Objectives are clearly written and teaching is to be efficient and focused. The teacher seeks a "system" to communicate learning to the student. The teacher believes that the method of teaching is based on learning and can be defined by specific procedures. The method of teaching is related to the efficiency ethic and scientific management movement (see the discussion of Bobbit's theories in Chapter 2).

The teacher's approach is to break what is to be learned into small bite-size pieces. Students learn step-by-step through drill and practice. The technology-oriented teacher believes in part in whole learning (not wholistic learning). The Hunter lesson plan for teachers captures this orientation. If what is to be learned cannot be written in behavioral terms, then it is not worth teaching. As a consequence the curriculum is skill oriented and emphasizes lower levels of thinking (knowledge, comprehension).

5. **Cognitive processing:** The aim of the teacher is to help students develop cognitive skills—to learn how to learn. Process skills are more important than content. Since society is characterized by change, it is important to enable students to learn on their own. In mathematics the teacher asks students to describe their thinking processes while trying to solve a problem. By listening to other students, the teacher emphasizes that there are many ways to solve problems, but some ways are more efficient than others. Metacognitive thinking is a significant concept in the cognitive processing classroom.

Believing that thinking processes can be taught and that cognitive abilities are developmental, the teacher seeks a problem-oriented curriculum to motivate students' work. Like the social orientation, the teacher tends to group students for projects and experiments so that students learn from their peers and work cooperatively with others.

EXAMPLE TEACHERS' BELIEFS ABOUT CURRICULUM

Mary Hogan emphasizes the cognitive processing approach to learning. She tries to ask questions that stimulate thinking. She chooses learning experiences that motivate students to try out their ideas, and she uses a lot of manipulatives in the classroom. She combines this teaching approach with a social orientation for classroom management by having students set classroom rules and helping them abide by them.

Greg Thomas is a social reconstructionist. He uses the project method of teaching, chooses interdisciplinary content, and integrates skills through the project method. Students work frequently in small groups. His topics are generated by the needs of his students and the community in which they live. He uses time flexibly, allowing content to be explored in depth and students to work at their own pace. Resource materials include a wide range of texts, community field trips, computer data, and expert consultants.

Karen Adazzio is somewhat eclectic in her educational beliefs. She believes that middle school students like to be told what they are responsible for learning; however, she tries to involve the students in problem solving and she tends to select community-oriented problems or dilemmas as departure points for her studies. She is more of a social adaptor than a reconstructionist. She also tends to focus on thinking processes.

How teachers' beliefs affect what happens in their classrooms will be apparent in the successive chapters on instructional processes and the curriculum.

SUMMARY

School Organization

1. In our early schools skills were emphasized; the *McGuffey Readers*, organized by grade levels, encouraged the development of graded schools.
2. Dissatisfaction with graded schools led to experimentation with different organizing plans.

3. The nongraded school is an attempt to break the lockstep of the graded school.
4. Magnet schools, career path schools, and alternative schools are considered schools of choice.
5. School organization, teachers' work, and compensation are all affected by how time is used.
6. School restructuring may affect teacher roles, decision making, the curricula, grouping practices, and evaluation procedures.

Classroom Organization

7. In self-contained classrooms, students stay with the same teacher the entire day, and the teacher teaches all subject fields.
8. In departmentalized classrooms, teachers instruct in their area(s) of specialization and students move from one class to another.
9. Some schools provide special laboratories and learning centers for instruction.
10. Team teaching is a means to combine the instructional efforts of two or more teachers who collaborate for planning and teaching.

Grouping

11. Students with similar needs may be grouped homogeneously to teach specific skills.
12. When grouping heterogeneously, teachers draw upon students' diverse interests and abilities.
13. Multiage classrooms are created to purposefully mix students for educational reasons.
14. Multigrade classrooms are created to purposefully mix students for administrative reasons.

Curriculum Organizational Patterns

15. The most familiar pattern is the separate subject organization in which each subject is treated distinctly.
16. Correlated subjects organization integrates learning experiences but each subject maintains its own identity.
17. Fusion and broad fields relate subjects to each other for synthesis, depth study, and integrative learning experiences.

Teachers' Curriculum Beliefs

18. Teachers' philosophic beliefs influence content, pedagogy, priority for teaching, teacher and students' roles, and the classroom environment.

DISCUSSION QUESTIONS AND APPLICATION EXERCISES

1. Contrast the separate subject approach and the broad fields approach by comparing students' textbooks in sixth-grade and eighth-grade science and social studies. Contrast teaching plans in a self-contained classroom and a departmentalized classroom.
2. Visit a classroom and see if you can identify the teacher's curriculum beliefs by observing the classroom environment and how students are taught. Reflect on a subject that interests you. How would you like to teach it? What would be your role and students' roles? Which curriculum conception would you emphasize?
3. Visit a magnet or career path school and compare it to a traditional school.
4. Teach a lesson with another person. Describe how collaboration with another person affects planning and teaching.
5. Do teachers who teach in nontraditional schools have different characteristics and competencies than those who teach in traditional schools? Explain your thoughts.
6. Think about the concept of *time*. How does the clock control the school calendar, subject priorities, learning experiences, and student assessment?
7. Visit a multiage/multigrade classroom. How does the teacher provide for individual differences? How does the teacher integrate subject fields and students' experiences? How does the classroom differ from a traditional graded classroom?

How Children Learn:
Similarities and Differences

In this chapter you will examine theories about how children differ as they develop socially and cognitively, in their use of language, moral outlook, and sex role. Since theories of development and students' learning styles influence teaching, teachers need to understand the applications of these theories. Social factors controlled by the family also affect students' learning, and these factors are identified. The chapter concludes with a discussion of motivation and its effect on learning. To apply chapter content, a special section on the differentiation of instruction focuses on the means teachers can use to facilitate learning.

After you study this chapter, you should be able to accomplish the following:

1. Explain how a teacher's beliefs about child development affect the teacher's classroom performance.
2. Describe how the theories of Kohlberg, Piaget, Maslow, and Vygotsky may affect the classroom environment and instructional processes.
3. Provide examples of how the family influences motivation and learning.
4. Discuss differences in students' learning perceptions distinguishing between a mastery and performance goal perspective and explain how the student's self-concept affects motivation.
5. Suggest ways to learn about students' preferred learning style and how to use that information in the classroom.
6. Provide examples of how socialization experiences affect learning. Relate your examples to gender experiences.
7. Provide examples of how teachers can apply the theory of multiple intelligences.

Professional Lexicon

adaptive motivation pattern Changing or adjusting behavior to meet the challenge of a task and the environment.

attribution Believing that oneself or others are responsible for success or failure; related to concept of locus of control.

differentiation Individualizing and personalizing the teaching-learning process by distinguishing or modifying content, process, products, and environment.

egocentrism The concept of an individual who cannot see other's viewpoint, Piaget's preoperational learner.

extrinsic motivation Using rewards, prizes, and grades to influence the learner to behave, or to achieve or complete an assignment.

field-dependent learner An individual who prefers interaction with others and the social context of learning.

field-independent learner An individual who has more success in formal teaching-learning situations that stress rewards and competition.

intrinsic motivation Striving to achieve for personal satisfaction and pleasure.

learning style The approach to learning that a particular individual favors; for example, a visual learner or an auditory learner.

locus of control The belief about who or what controls events affecting the individual's life.

mastery goal Motivation for learning is self-improvement.

performance goal Motivation for learning is to outperform others; comparing performance to the accomplishments of others.

proclivity A predisposition (capacity) related to specific content.

self-actualization Maslow's highest personal goal to enhance potential.

socialization The process by which an individual acquires habits, beliefs, and patterns of behavior.

stereotype An exaggerated belief or fixed idea associated with a group of people for the purpose of justifying personal conduct.

teacher expectations Present and future achievement standards based on the teacher's beliefs about the student's performance.

"I know," said the boy as he stood up and raised his fist; "It's this big." Again he emphasized his fist. Mary Hogan laughed. "Yes, Barry, you're right. Everyone raise your fist. Good, now you all know the size of your heart." The teacher continued the lesson, demonstrating by using a plastic model of the heart. While most of the class was as excited and animated as Barry, there were several children in the room who appeared bored. One youngster was staring out of the window. Another student was reading a comic book hidden inside a science textbook.

Individuals differ in a variety of ways. We all have cognitive, affective, and psychomotor abilities. These aptitudes are influenced by social class, cultural group, age, sex, prior experiences, and places of residence. Our interests, motivation to learn, readiness to learn, and efficiency in learning are affected by our characteristics. In the school setting there are other factors that also influence learning, such as the teacher's characteristics and teaching style, the nature of the learning task, the classroom environment, and the student's peer group. Each of these forces affects the individual in unique ways, and so it is not surprising that while some of Barry's classmates were enthusiastic and attentive, others found the learning task less interesting and perhaps even dull.

HOW STUDENTS DIFFER: DEVELOPMENTAL PATTERNS

Knowledge of developmental patterns enables the teacher to match subject matter and teaching methods, with a child's conceptual level. All the students in a fifth-grade classroom are not at the same conceptual level, and the children's ability to handle different subject fields may depend upon the particular subject that is being taught. Barry, in the example above, might work at a high level in science and health, but he may have a great deal of difficulty with mathematics.

Mary Hogan, Barry's teacher, needs to know whether Barry needs concrete materials to work with or whether he can handle abstract symbols. Greg Thomas, a fifth-grade teacher, needs to know whether his students can understand abstract concepts such as freedom, democracy, and Manifest Destiny and use them appropriately, or whether these concepts need to be acted out.

Does Barry, the second grader, understand the concept of time—immediate, past, and future?

PIAGET'S STAGES

Jean Piaget (1896–1980), a Swiss psychologist, developed a framework for understanding age-level changes or developmental stages as children mature. Since all children pass through these stages, it may seem peculiar that these developmental stages are included in a section about individual differences; however, since students mature at different rates it is important to recognize that all students in a given classroom are not at the same cognitive developmental stage at the same time.

Piaget studied developmental patterns of intellectual growth. He found that each of the patterns identified general behavioral characteristics. The four stages he identified are as follows:

1. Sensorimotor (0–2 years)
2. Preoperational (2–7 years)
3. Concrete operations (7–11 years)
4. Formal operations (11–16 years)

Sensorimotor Stage

The sensorimotor stage is the prelanguage stage, and it is vital to the development of thought. During this stage the infant and toddler demonstrate intelligence prior to speech. A baby loses interest in any object that is not in sight, but by the end of the first year the baby will search for a vanished object. Before leaving this stage the baby learns through experience the rudimentary concepts of space, time, causality, and intentionality.

Preoperational Stage

True language begins during the preoperational stage. In the beginning all vehicles that move may be cars to a child, who differentiates them by using the words *big* or *little*. All four-legged animals may be dogs, but as the child structures reality and participates in imitation and symbolic play, he or she begins to conceptualize more accurately by breaking down classes into subclasses through the process of categorization. The child in this stage needs concrete objects to manipulate.

The preoperational child has difficulty managing the concept of reversibility. A typical problem in a second-grade classroom may have to do with understanding the concept of conservation. For example, the teacher has two pint containers on the demonstration table: a tall, skinny one and a short, squat one. The teacher asks the children whether the liquid in one of the containers (the tall, skinny one) will fit into the other container (the short, squat one). Invariably the children will respond that the liquid will not fit into the squat container because the tall, skinny container is higher and bigger! The preoperational student has difficulty focusing on several details at the same time, perhaps because of the need for concrete representation, and this accounts for the inattention to the similarity of size of the two containers.

The concept of **egocentrism** is particularly important in order to understand the preoperational student. During this stage the student is unable to perceive viewpoints other than his or her own, as Flavell (1963, p. 60) explains:

> Egocentrism . . . denotes a cognitive state in which the cognizer sees the world from a single point of view only—his own—but without knowledge of the existence of viewpoints or perspectives and, *a fortiori* without awareness that he is the prisoner of his own.

The student is not role-oriented to others or reflective because of the lack of consciousness and awareness of others' ideas. Since it is so vital that a student be able to perceive his or her own illogical thought in order to progress beyond egocentrism, the student must encounter others and be forced to accommodate his or her thinking process to that of others. Only through repeated and forced social interaction does the child learn to be reflective and to relinquish egocentric thought.

Concrete Operations Stage

During the concrete operations stage the child resolves most of the prior problems with conservation and can think logically about concrete problems. For example, if the teacher told the child that the two containers in the conservation problem were of the same size (a pint) and then asked whether the liquid could be transferred from one to the other, the child in this stage would reason logically and reply "yes," even though he or she might not perceive the two containers as being equal. However, during this stage the student is dependent upon personal experience; therefore, experiences must be appropriately arranged and must be concrete. For instance, an urban child can understand the concept of a rural environment better by seeing a picture depicting farms, tractors, and barns, rather than by hearing a verbal definition only.

Formal Operations Stage

During the formal operations stage the child is no longer tied to concrete reasoning about objects. The child begins abstract thought; skill in scientific reasoning increases. Data can be organized by classifying, seriating, and corresponding. The results of these oper-

How might egocentrism affect discipline in the primary classroom?

ations facilitate logical thinking and allow students to subject thought to inference, implication, identity, conjunction, and disjunction. The student can now reason hypothetically and enjoys "if-then" types of problems.

APPLYING PIAGET'S THEORIES IN THE CLASSROOM

Developmental models assist teachers in deciding what to teach, when to teach it, the sequence of teaching, and the scope of teaching. Using the Piagetian stages, teachers have an indication of the child's conceptual development and can relate the complexity of subject matter to the appropriate readiness level. For example, for a kindergarten or first-grade child, block play provides a means to acquire information, but for a fifth grader or seventh grader, the teacher expects that the child can learn by listening and observing. (Though that may not be the *best* way for the child to learn.)

Also, Piaget has contributed to our understanding of children's need for active learning experiences. Through active participation students discover meaning in their experiences. In Greg Thomas's classroom, the students did not understand that a magnetic field is produced whenever current flows through a wire. Nor did they know how to increase the strength of the magnetic field. Thomas provided the students with iron nails, insulated copper, batteries, and materials for experimentation. Through experimentation the students discovered that by increasing the windings of the wire around the nail, they increased the strength of the electromagnet. Thomas was using what is often called *constructivist* learning. Constructivist learning will be discussed in Chapter 7.

VYGOTSKY'S THEORIES

Lev Vygotsky (1897–1934), a Russian psychologist interested in developmental patterns, differed in some ways from Piaget. Piaget believed that egocentric speech in the preoperational child occurs because the child only focuses on self. As children become less egocentric, they tend to talk more to others and less to themselves. Vygotsky (1962) believed that there is a relationship between language development and concept development. Vygotsky viewed egocentric talk in the preoperational child as the way the child learned language. As the child becomes more operational, speech

---

Can you contrast Vygotsky's concept of egocentrism with Piaget's interpretation?

---

changes and is inner directed. Vygotsky proposed that children begin speech by talking to themselves. Their inner speech is in a sense reflective; they are telling themselves how to perform the activities in which they are engaged. Myers (1987) states that this inner speech takes the form of a conversation, lecture, sermon, or graduation speech, dependent upon the functional activity and context.

For Vygotsky, language development was critical to learning and development. Piaget believed that social development precedes language development; Vygotsky believed that learning precedes development, and that in fact children can often complete tasks with assistance from others prior to independent task completion. This assistance factor helps children internalize learning. Vygotsky called this level of development the *zone of proximal development.*

Vygotsky's theories have implications for the teaching of reading and writing. Practical application of his theory of language and development means that classroom teachers need to encourage social interaction particularly between older and younger students, par-

ents and children, more capable and less capable students. The focus of the tutoring process should be on enabling the learner to gain insight and skills so that scaffolding occurs and the learning is internalized.

KOHLBERG'S STAGES

Lawrence Kohlberg (1927–1987), a Harvard psychologist, developed the theory of moral development. It is a cognitive-developmental theory and, like Piaget's theory of development, proceeds through a series of qualitatively distinct stages. Kohlberg believed that the structure of thought can be separated from the content and that development proceeds in a universal sequence. However, individuals of the same age may differ in their level of development and, ultimately, in their final level of development. Unlike Piaget's stages of development, Kohlberg's stages extend into the middle or late twenties before the individual achieves full moral maturity. According to Kohlberg, many individuals never reach the highest stages of development.

Kohlberg identified three levels of reasoning about moral issues. Within each level there are two stages, thus making a total of six stages of moral reasoning (Table 4.1).

Table 4.1 The Six Moral Judgment Stages

	CONTENT OF STAGE		
Level and Stage	*What Is Right*	*Reasons for Doing Right*	*Social Perspective of Stage*
LEVEL I— PRECONVENTIONAL Stage I—Heteronomous Morality	To avoid breaking rules backed by punishment, obedience for its own sake, and avoiding physical damage to persons and property.	Avoidance of punishment, and the superior power of authorities.	*Egocentric point of view:* Doesn't consider the interests of others or recognize that they differ from the actor's; doesn't relate two points of view. Actions are considered physically rather than in terms of psychological interests of others. Confusion of authority's perspective with one's own.
Stage 2—Individualism, Instrumental Purpose, and Exchange	Following rules only when it is to someone's immediate interest: acting to meet one's own interests and needs and letting others do the same; right is also what's fair, what's an equal exchange, a deal, an agreement.	To serve one's own needs or interests in a world where you have to recognize that other people have their interests, too.	*Concrete individualistic perspective:* Aware that everybody has his own interest to pursue and these conflict, so that right is relative (in the concrete individualistic sense).

(continued on next page)

Table 4.1   *(continued)*

Level and Stage	CONTENT OF STAGE		
	What Is Right	*Reasons for Doing Right*	*Social Perspective of Stage*
LEVEL II— CONVENTIONAL Stage 3—Mutual Interpersonal Expectations, Relationships, and Interpersonal Conformity	Living up to what is expected by people close to you or what people generally expect of people in your role as son, brother, friend, etc. "Being good" is important and means having good motives, showing concern about others. It also means keeping mutual relationships, such as trust, loyalty, respect, and gratitude.	The need to be a good person in your own eyes and those of others; your caring for others; belief in the Golden Rule; desire to maintain rules and authority which support stereotypical good behavior.	*Perspective of the individual in relationships with other individuals:* Aware of shared feelings, agreements, and expectations which take primacy over individual interests; relates points of view through the concrete Golden Rule, putting yourself in the other guy's shoes; does not yet consider generalized system perspective.
Stage 4—Social System and Conscience	Fulfilling the actual duties to which you have agreed. Laws are to be upheld except in extreme cases where they conflict with other fixed social duties. Right is also contributing to society, the group, or institution.	To keep the institution going as a whole, to avoid the breakdown in the system "if everyone did it," or the imperative of conscience to meet one's defined obligations (easily confused with Stage 3 belief in rules and authority; see text).	*Differentiates societal point of view from interpersonal agreement or motives:* Takes the point of view of the system that defines roles and rules; considers individual relations in terms of place in the system.
LEVEL III— POSTCONVENTIONAL OR PRINCIPLED Stage 5— Social Contract or Utility and Individual Rights	Being aware that people hold a variety of values and opinions, that most values and rules are relative to your group. These relative rules should usually be upheld, however, in the interest of impartiality and because they are the social contract. Some nonrelative values and rights like life and liberty, however, must be upheld in any society and regardless of majority opinion.	A sense of obligation to law because of one's social contract to make and abide by laws for the welfare of all and for the protection of all people's rights; a feeling of contractual commitment, freely entered upon, to family, friendship, trust, and work obligations; concern that laws and duties be based on rational calculation of overall utility, "the greatest good for the greatest number."	*Prior-to-society perspective:* Perspective of a rational individual aware of values and rights prior to social attachments and contracts; integrates perspectives by formal mechanisms of agreement, contract, objective impartiality, and due process; considers moral and legal points of view; recognizes that they sometimes conflict and finds it difficult to integrate them.
Stage 6—Universal Ethical Principles	Following self-chosen ethical principles. Particular laws or social agreements are usually valid because they rest on such principles. When laws violate these principles, one acts in accordance with the principle. Principles are universal principles of justice: the equality of human rights and respect for the dignity of human beings as individual persons.	The belief as a rational person in the validity of universal moral principles, and a sense of personal commitment to them.	*Perspective of a moral point of view* from which social arrangements derive. Perspective is that of any rational individual recognizing the nature of morality or the fact that persons are ends in themselves and must be treated as such.

Source: L. Kohlberg, "Moral Stages and Moralization: The Cognitive-Developmental Approach," in *Moral Development and Behavior: Theory, Research, and Social Issues,* edited by Thomas Lickona (Copyright © 1976 by Holt, Rinehart and Winston. Reprinted by permission of Thomas Lickona), pp. 34–35.

Preconventional Level

The individual at the preconventional level typically is a preadolescent. At this level the individual is characterized by a concern for the consequences of rules and behaviors. "Right" behavior serves one's own interest or the interests of someone close. One behaves in the "right" way to avoid punishment, as a deference to power, to serve oneself, or in exchange for a favor. The child is obedient because he or she is afraid of the consequences. Within the preconventional level, the stage 1 individual is sensitive to obedience and punishment; stage 2 individuals are instrumental-relativists and may be responsible to others if being so will ultimately affect their own needs. At this level of moral development, loyalty, gratitude, and justice are not considered, and fairness, quality, and reciprocity are considered only when practical.

Conventional Level

Chronologically, the individual at the conventional level is an adolescent. At this level the individual is capable of moral reasoning that considers family or peers. The stage 3 adolescent at the conventional level aspires to please others in order to achieve their approval. The individual at this stage judges others in terms of whether or not they are perceived as meaning well. The stage 4 individual is concerned with upholding societal rules, expectations, and roles. Right behavior is performed because the individual is motivated to act in a manner approved and expected by society rather than arising out of a concern for punishment.

Postconventional, Autonomous, or Principled Level

The individual at this level is of adult age; however, less than 20 percent of adult society act at the principled level. Universal principles guide the individual's orientation. The stage 5 individual critically examines laws and acknowledges that they can be changed. Rights are determined by the society of which the individual is a member. The individual considers that he or she has a social contract with society to uphold the rights of others and that the individual should act in accordance with ethical values. Arbuthnot and Faust (1981, p. 50) note that stage 5 and stage 6 individuals base their actions on morality rather than social practices. Arbuthnot and Faust related a typical dilemma used to assess one's moral reasoning stage:

> In Europe, a woman was near death from a very bad disease, a special kind of cancer. There was one drug that the

doctors thought might save her. It was a form of radium that a druggist in the same town had recently discovered. The drug was expensive to make but the druggist was charging ten times what the drug cost him to make. He paid \$42 for the radium and charged \$2,000 for a small dose of the drug. The sick woman's husband, Heinz, went to everyone he knew to borrow the money, but he could only get together about \$1,000, which was half of what it cost. He told the druggist that his wife was dying, and asked him to sell it cheaper or let him pay later. But the druggist said, "No, I discovered the drug, and I'm going to make money from it." So Heinz got desperate and broke into the man's store to steal the drug for his wife.

The preconventional child (age eight) responds to this dilemma by stating that it was all right to steal the drug because otherwise the wife would die and there would be nobody to take care of the children. Also, if the husband didn't love his wife he wouldn't take the chance of getting caught. At this stage of development the child is not concerned with the welfare of others. The wife is important because she is needed to take care of the children.

The conventional-level child (age 10) responds that the husband should steal the drug because he "would want to take care of her. He would be a bad husband if he didn't. It'd be okay to steal it because he's doing something good, but the druggist is being mean and selfish" (p. 60). At this level the child recognizes the marital contract; thus the husband acts in the "right" way even though stealing is prohibited.

At the principled level (age 17) the individual responds that the husband should steal the drug though he is breaking the law. At this stage the individual acknowledges that the law was not appropriate because it was "protecting property at the expense of a human life. The value of human life takes precedence over that of property." The individual also concedes that laws should be based on the values of fairness and justice. "I'm sure that a judge and jury would understand Heinz's decision in this case, even though in general they would not condone stealing. Whether he loved her or not is irrelevant; a human life has value apart from personal relationship" (p. 51).

The principled response is based on the universal right to life because in this case the law did not serve its function. Therefore, it was acceptable to disobey it, and the community would accept the rightfulness of the act.

APPLYING MORAL EDUCATION IN THE CLASSROOM

Arbuthnot and Faust (1981) identify three basic goals of moral education:

1. Movement from a lower stage to a higher stage of development

2. Application of more advanced reasoning
3. Implementation of more advanced reasoning in everyday behavior

The first goal can be achieved by having students confront other students who are one stage in advance of their own level. Blatt and Kohlberg (1974) report the successful use of moral dilemma discussions on junior high school–aged children in ghetto schools, suburban schools, and working-class white schools. In each of the classrooms students were identified at three developmental stages. The classroom discussions yielded moral development change to a higher stage of development.

To achieve the second goal, students identify dilemmas that occur in their daily lives. Newspapers, radio and television news, or existing community problems can be used as a basis for discussion. After identifying the dilemma, students are asked how to apply their newly acquired reasoning in order to achieve the goal.

The third goal is achieved when students identify dilemmas in their everyday lives and suggest appropriate personal action. The third goal cannot be directed by the teacher. It occurs because students understand and accept social responsibility. Actual teaching strategies for moral development can be found in Part II of this text.

BRAIN RESEARCH

Brain research supports the Piagetian concept of cognitive development. Interaction with the environment, critical people, and objects in the environment affect experience and the connections the brain makes in the process of learning. Brain development cannot be separated from the individual's life experiences (Caine and Caine, 1991).

The brain, according to Caine and Caine, develops at its own rate; thus there are wide rates of divergence in development among individuals. These authors contend that brain development occurs throughout our lifetime, and they believe strongly in the saying "use it or lose it." The authors also note that brains need rest as well as activity. Sleep and rest periods at school are beneficial to healthy functioning.

Implications of brain-based teaching in Greg Thomas's and Mary Hogan's classrooms would be the use of thematic teaching to organize their learning experiences and help students make connections among the subject fields. In Karen Adazzio's classroom she tries

Research Findings:
Emotions and Intelligence

Gibbs (1995) reports that new brain research indicates that emotions may be the true measure of intelligence (EQ). The term was coined by Peter Salovey and described by Daniel Goleman in a new a book titled *Emotional Intelligence.* The researchers have concluded that EQ is the ability to regulate the emotions to enhance living.

to use everyday experiences, familiar to the students, to introduce new concepts in a subject field discipline.

MULTIPLE INTELLIGENCES

The traditional view of intelligence relies on a quantification of human potential based on the individual's score on an IQ test. For example, the Scholastic Aptitude Test and the Graduate Record Examination are used to measure the individual's verbal and math ability. The scores are used to admit or deny admission to university programs.

Howard Gardner (1993) presents a multifaceted view of intelligence that challenges the traditional model. By looking at different populations, such as children with learning disabilities and adults who suffered brain damage, Gardner identifies seven different intelligences that affect human behavior. He believes that all seven of the intelligences are equal in impact although the first two have traditionally been valued more in our society.

Linguistic intelligence helps the individual detect sounds, rhythms, and meanings of words. Gardner believes that poets exhibit this intelligence.

Logical-mathematical intelligence is demonstrated by the scientist and the mathematician who have the capacity to detect logical and/or numerical patterns. Both the Scholastic Aptitude Test and the Graduate Record Examination are based on measuring linguistic and logical-mathematical intelligences.

Spatial intelligence is demonstrated by engineers, surgeons, sculptors, painters, sailors (and others) who are able to think about a spatial model and use that model to solve problems. For example, spatial problem solving is used for navigation. Artists demonstrate spatial intelligence in the way they integrate space in artwork.

Musical intelligence is demonstrated by the ability to produce, appreciate, and express rhythm, pitch, and timbre.

Bodily-Kinesthetic intelligence is demonstrated by athletes dancers, craftspeople, and surgeons who use their bodies to express an emotion, participate in an athletic event, or demonstrate skill in handling tools. This intelligence requires coordination, balance, and dexterity.

Interpersonal intelligence is the ability to detect the moods, meanings, intentions, and desires of others. Politicians, teachers, therapists, and parents typically demonstrate this intelligence.

Intrapersonal intelligence is the ability to access one's own personal needs, understandings, strengths, and weaknesses and use them to guide personal behavior.

Armstrong (1994, p. 11–12) identifies four major points about Gardner's theory:

1. Individuals possess all seven intelligences though some people may demonstrate greater functioning in a specific area.

2. Most individuals have the capacity to develop the seven intelligences with appropriate encouragement and instruction.

3. The seven intelligences typically work together. For example, the golfer needs dexterity to putt, must possess spatial knowledge to determine the speed and distance of the putt, and requires linguistic intelligence to fabricate his or her score!

4. Within each intelligence there are a variety of ways to demonstrate ability. Musical intelligence may be demonstrated through appreciation of the talents of others or ability to produce music. The storyteller may demonstrate linguistic talent yet be deficient in reading skills.

Applying Multiple Intelligences in the Classroom

Teaching strategies that hit the mark with some students may fail dismally with others. We attribute this to individual differences in favored means to learn and in proclivities. For example, the button bar graphic symbols used in computer programs may work well with spatially inclined computer users, but they fail to inform and assist this author. Teachers need to use a variety of teaching methods to appeal to natural differences among students.

Each of the intelligences has a variety of means that teachers can use to help students learn; however, selecting a learning experience to appeal to one specific intelligence is both time consuming and inappropriate. It is far better to select experiences that allow students to respond in preferred ways.

In Greg Thomas's classroom, when the students worked on science experiments, they had several options for presenting their studies. They could draw the experiment, construct a model of it and demonstrate it, write or tape record a story about its use.

Studying a community problem in Karen Adazzio's classroom involved working in a small investigative group. In the group activity students negotiated with each other to determine how to go about their inquiry tasks. Some students interviewed key people involved in the problem; others took pictures using a camera; still others read about the problem or developed a chain of critical events that affected the problem. Each student chose how he or she could contribute to the group study.

Note that in choosing how to take part in an activity students demonstrate intrapersonal intelligence as well as their inclination. But Gardner (1995, p. 202–203) emphasizes that learning style is not the same as an intelligence. The decision to engage in reading about a social problem instead of interviewing others affected by the problem may relate to the tasks within the subject field, not the student's **proclivity.** The student might make a different decision if faced with a mathematical problem instead of a social problem.

> The concept of *style* designates a general approach that an individual can apply equally to every conceivable content. In contrast, an *intelligence* is a capacity, with its component processes, that is geared to a specific content in the world (such as musical sounds or spatial patterns).

Differentiating Instruction

Applying the theory of multiple intelligences requires an understanding of **differentiation.** When teachers individualize or personalize instruction, they are applying the concept of differentiation. It is possible to differentiate what is taught (content), how it is taught (process), what students are expected to produce (product), and the environment that motivates students.

Content is differentiated by modifying the complexity, depth, and pacing (how quickly students accelerate or are exposed to information) of what is taught. Content can be changed by varying the point of departure and the focus.

Learning to work together cooperatively may be more importatnt than learning subject field content.

Process (instructional means) is differentiated through novelty, by changing the purpose and model of instruction and helping students construct meaning in a variety of ways using varied skill options (critical thinking, problem solving, or research skills).

Products are differentiated by providing choices for students to demonstrate learning (writing stories, performing experiments, or creating in the visual arts).

The *environment* for learning can be differentiated by providing different resources and tools for students to use and by modifying learning centers and work stations.

Teachers use differentiated instruction to provide equal access of developmentally appropriate learning experiences through multiple pathways to a common goal. Students may work individually or in small groups that can be homogeneous or heterogeneous. Differentiation provides a means to challenge all children at appropriate readiness levels, but it requires that teachers also change their expectations of what students will produce.

DIFFERENCES RELATED TO LEARNING STYLE

Learning styles emanate from natural, inborn inclinations. The individual's **learning style** manifests itself through preferred senses and personality characteristics. Learning styles have implications for classroom environments and teaching methods. It is important that teachers recognize the value of a teaching repertoire and that they vary teaching methods and learning options to accommodate students with different styles of learning.

Dunn and Dunn (1978) studied how children and adults learn using educational, industrial, and psychological research. They isolated 18 elements that encompass learning style. Their investigation indicated that learners are affected by their immediate environment, their own emotionality, sociological preferences, and physical needs. Elements related to each of these preferred ways of learning include the following:

Environment: sound, light, temperature, physical design
Emotionality: motivational need for structure or flexibility, persistence, responsibility

Physical Needs: perceptual strengths (sound, sight, touch), mobility (need to move around, ability to sit still), intake (food, drink), time of day (morning, afternoon)

Sociological Preferences: works best alone, works best paired with someone else, works best with peers, works best with adults

REFLECTION VERSUS IMPULSIVITY

Teacher: Boys and girls, why do you think we have laws? Jerry, what do you think?

Jerry: Uh, uh, I don't know.

Mildred: I know, Miss Henry.

Teacher: All right, Mildred, tell us.

Mildred: Because we would get into fights without them.

Ron: Laws don't stop us from getting into fights.

Teacher: Jerry, would you like to tell us now what you were thinking?

Jerry: Well, I think we have laws to help us settle our disputes.

Teacher: Boys and girls, Mildred said we have laws so that we will not fight; Jerry said we have laws to settle disputes. Are they both right?

Yando and Kagan (1968) studied the psychological dimension of reflection versus impulsivity. During classroom discussion and during the reading process, some children tend to respond quickly or impulsively, and others like to reflect and take their time. In the example above, Jerry is a reflective responder, whereas Mildred is impulsive. Teachers can help both Jerry and Mildred improve their thinking processes. For example, the teacher should have stayed with Jerry by giving him more time to answer and even cuing him with another question if necessary. A nonverbal look or hand motion may have slowed Mildred down and helped her think a little more about what she wanted to contribute.

Field Dependency

Learning style has been described in still another way by cognitive researchers who identify the extent to which individuals respond to relevant elements or are distracted by irrelevant components in a given event or situation.

How does cooperative learning affect field-dependent and field-independent learners?

An individual who has difficulty with distracting factors is considered to be a **field-dependent learner.** These individuals prefer interaction with others and opportunities for discussion. They enjoy the social context of situations and respond to verbal praise.

An individual described as a **field-independent learner** prefers lectures and more formal teaching-learning situations. They tend to be more competitive and respond to external rewards, such as grades. In the past, schools have been more oriented to the field-independent learner. Many teachers today believe that competition in the classroom affects learning in a negative way.

SOCIAL FACTORS INFLUENCE LEARNING

FAMILY INFLUENCES

The family is the primary agency for the **socialization** of the child. The family transmits religious identity, cultural identity, occupational identity, race, social class, family name, nationality, and ethnic affiliation.

The early years of family life are crucial for the child because it is believed that 50 percent of the child's potential intelligence is developed from birth to age four and another 30 percent from ages four to eight. The experiences the child is exposed to during these early years no doubt affect the child's later proclivities. The richness of the family environment (books, pictures, colors, objects, music, games, furniture, and people), rewards, and punishments may influence temperament, personality, and general behavior.

Whether the child is punished physically, by eye contact, by restraint, or by verbal abuse affects social behavior and the child's ability in later years to accept criticism. Status expectations and ultimately educational aspiration are learned in the family group. Experiences with siblings affect the child's expectations. The middle child has a different experience from the oldest child or the youngest. The only child has a significantly different experience than the child who has five siblings. The mother's responsibilities in the home and community (cleaning, fixing the television, working outside the home, socializing with neighbors, or playing tennis) provide status expectations. The father's work and activities (handling the finances, working with tools, dressing the children, playing bridge, cooking or not cooking) provide a role model. The interactions between a child and every other family member influence future behavior.

How does the family influence children's motivation?

The stability of the family affects academic achievement. If there is a lack of role models in the home, the child does not learn the social behaviors and attitudes needed to develop self-discipline, training, maturity, and self-control. As a consequence, experience in school is dull and uninteresting. The child may become anxious and frustrated, or even experience cultural shock. However, children of one-parent families who are not economically depressed do not have the same problems as those whose economic status is low. The problems of a low-income family affect how children learn more than differences in family structure.

RACE AND CULTURAL DIFFERENCES

Some behavioral differences in the classroom can be attributed to racial and cultural orientations. For example, teachers in Fresno, California, report that Hmong parents often do not accept the responsibility to visit school and talk to the teachers about their children. Collaborative relationships with the school are not valued. Many Vietnamese parents value education for their sons, but not for their daughters. In addition, some Vietnamese parents resent it if teachers look them in the eye while talking to them.

A Korean middle school student had hurt feelings when his teacher rested his feet on a chair facing the student during a conference. Some Navaho children are taught that a direct look implies anger. Mexican and African-American children will often look down-

cast when spoken to because they are taught that it is disrespectful for a child to look directly at an adult. Cultural differences between school and home affect the relations between teacher and students and teachers and parents. As a consequence, teachers must carefully plan verbal and nonverbal communication.

SEX ROLES AND SOCIALIZATION

Sociologists have consistently observed differences in the ways families socialize boys and girls. Socialization of the girl to assume domestic chores and child-bearing responsibilities and socialization of the boy to assume job responsibilities has been the typical pattern. Agencies such as school, church, scouts, Ys, media, and other societal groups also reinforce sex roles.

Learning a sex role was considered important in order to emancipate the boy from a dependent relationship with his family, particularly with his mother. Sex-role identity and role behavior were also considered important for the female. Girls typically had a role model in the home, but boys rarely saw their fathers at work. Thus, the socialization of the male was more crucial.

Many people are currently questioning the wisdom of sex-role socialization. Changing sex-role patterns and an awareness of the limitations of sex-role social-

---

Research Findings: Family Influences

Watts-Warren (1994–95) studied the links between family life and minority student achievement. She recommended that teachers study curriculum materials and classroom practices to ensure that the white Eurocentric voice is not the only voice in the classroom and to select more appropriate culturally sensitive material. In addition, she cautioned that teacher expectations are critical to the success of all students; therefore, teachers need to identify the underlying assumptions that shape their expectations and classroom decisions. She recommended a classroom environment that embraced democratic pedagogy.

Teacher Research

Stroeher (1994) studied eight of her kindergarten students from upper-middle-class families and eight students from lower-middle to lower-class families. Using interview questions and follow-up questions about gender beliefs and attitudes and pictures of faceless individuals representing seven occupations, students were asked to select gender cards for each occupation. (Choices included male, female, or both genders.) Finally the children were asked to draw themselves in a future career choice. Both the higher and the lower SES groups chose traditional gender roles for career choices; the lower SES group was the more traditional. To counter traditional biases, Stroeher recommends that all teachers survey their students, provide time for nontraditional gender role discussions in the classroom, and expose students to examples and pictures of men and women in nontraditional careers.

ization have led to an understanding of the harmfulness of what in fact was sex-role stereotyping. Stereotyping is an oversimplified or generalized opinion about a group of people. Sex stereotyping made the following types of uncritical judgments:

- Women are emotional, flighty, and domestic.
- Men are aggressive and strong, capable of managing any situation.

Past images of the female characterized her in roles of nurse, teacher, secretary, and social worker, whereas the male had a full range of occupational and professional choices. The school reinforced these **stereotypes** through differential treatment of boys and girls. (Refer to the discussion of gender equity in Chapter 1.)

SOCIAL CLASS AND CHILDREN'S EXPERIENCES

Family and community experiences affect a child's interpretation of his or her world and self-concept. Children are conditioned by interactions with peers, siblings, parents, and important others. Children of poverty (lower-lower class) who wait to be fed beyond the time when they feel hunger have a different feeling about food than children who are fed whenever they ask or who know when breakfast, lunch, and dinner will be served.

Children who have responsive adults nearby have a different perspective than those who are cared for by an older sibling or no one at all. Children perceive their physical and social environment quite accurately. They know when adults cannot pay the bills, cannot find a job, or cannot face reality.

Research Findings: The Gender Gap

Stipp (1992) studied the gender gap and found that schools make it hard for girls to pursue math and science course work. Women who "beat the system" and take two or more college-level mathematics courses earn more money than women who do not. For women, he concluded, "more math means more money." He believes that the first step to achieve equity and erase the gender gap is to overcome ingrained stereotypes, such as that females have lower aptitudes for math and science than males.

The family's economic situation affects the child's daily experiences. The amount and quality of food the child eats, the clothes and personal possessions the child has, supervision and role models, physical comforts and social enrichment, recreation and hobbies, health care and other social services all influence how a child relates to the world. Children who lack social experiences and opportunities to explore and wonder do not accumulate stories to tell about self and others, and are not able to draw upon experiences for motivation and school tasks.

The poverty child's experience may include pessimism and hopelessness as a consequence of observing and listening to the adults in the home. Children learn despair from parents who do not want to transmit optimism or hope that the future will be better than the present. They do this to prepare their children for the hard reality of existence.

MOTIVATION AND ITS EFFECT ON LEARNING

When teachers talk about student motivation they are usually referring to the way students approach learning tasks and how intently they perform each task. Other ways to describe student motivation include whether or not the student demonstrates interest in learning tasks and the goals the student sets for him or herself.

THEORIES OF MOTIVATION

There are several theories of motivation that influence the way teachers teach. These include a behavioral view, personality theory, humanistic interpretation, and cognitive perspective. For many years behavioral psychologists directed teachers to stimulate appropriate behavior through a system of classroom rewards. This is considered the use of external stimuli to reinforce behavior.

An opposing view of motivation holds that students achieve satisfaction from learning and from appropriate behavior. This perspective emphasizes intrinsic forces as sources of motivation. Personality theories of motivation suggest that the need for achievement varies among people, perhaps dependent upon how badly the individual fears failure.

Should teachers promise rewards for the completion of work?

Locus of Control

The social learning theory of Rotter (1966) contributes to the perspective of individual personality differences. Some individuals hold others to blame if they fail an examination, forget their homework, or are late to school. These individuals have what psychologists call an *external* **locus of control.** Other individuals believe that if they fail an examination, it is their own fault; if they are successful in an endeavor, they credit themselves with working to be successful. These individuals have an *internal* locus of control.

Individuals with an internal locus of control view themselves as having control over their environment and fate. They perceive a relationship between personal behavior and consequences.

The individual with an external locus of control is just the opposite. This individual believes that he or she has no control over consequences and views others as responsible and controlling events and circumstances.

Some research indicates that locus of control is influenced by parental behavior. Parents who are continually critical of their children may develop children with an external locus of control, whereas parents who are accepting and approving may develop the internal factor in locus of control.

A *humanistic* interpretation explains behavior as motivated by individual needs. For example, Maslow classifies human needs as either deficiency or growth needs. Deficiency needs are dependent upon others; growth needs are dependent upon the self. Deficiency needs must be satisfied before the individual can enhance personal growth.

Visualize a triangle. Maslow describes the top of the triangle as **self-actualization.** After the individual has satisfied all other needs, he or she is motivated to self-actualize.

Another theory concerning motivation focuses on the student's thought processes (a *cognitive* approach). The essence of this explanation of motivation is that the individual is affected by past experiences with success and failure.

Success and Failure

Weiner and colleagues (1974) have developed an **attribution** model of achievement motivation. They identify four causal attributes that affect the individual's perceived reasons for success and failure. They theorize that the individual believes in personal

---

How does fear of failure affect motivation?

success or failure, and predicts future success or failure, as a consequence of four elements: ability, effort, task difficulty, and luck.

Ability and effort are *internal elements* that the individual can control. Task difficulty and luck are beyond the control of the individual; thus, they are *external elements*. In addition, ability and task difficulty are *stable* or invariant dimensions, whereas luck and effort are elements of change and therefore *unstable*. Using the Weiner model, a student who successfully performs a science experiment could explain the achievement by saying either it was the result of personal ability or it was the result of luck. If the student believes it was ability, his or her confidence will increase; but if the student calls it luck, then success will be less meaningful and probably will not gain self-confidence that could enhance future efforts. The self-confident, success- oriented individual believes that future success is positively related to personal effort and ability.

Mastery and Performance

More recently, in reviewing the research on achievement motivation, Ames (1992) also views motivation through a cognitive lens and finds that positive and negative patterns of response may be elicited by different reasons for task engagement. For example, individuals who view a task as an opportunity to learn new skills, master a skill, or gain a competence based on internalized standards will be more involved and participate for personal satisfaction. These individuals believe that their personal effort will bring them mastery (success) and satisfaction. These individuals develop a pattern of positive achievement motivation. They are also more likely to be risk-takers. It is important here to differentiate between mastery learning and a mastery goal. A mastery goal orientation emphasizes learning as a process of self-improvement; the individual is not in competition with others. Mastery learning is a behavioral orientation that uses principles of operant conditioning.

Individuals with a negative achievement motivation pattern focus on ability to perform as compared to others. Interpersonal competition and normative standards guide their behavior, and as a consequence, these individuals are concerned with protecting their self-worth or ego involvement. Since these students are concerned with avoiding failure, risk-taking activities are unlikely.

Ames describes these two goal orientations as mastery and performance. Ames ties the **mastery goal** orientation to **intrinsic motivation** and task-related cognitive behavior, such as problem solving. When individuals are guided by extrinsic rewards, she believes their efforts are not focused on the activity itself, but are guided by concerns related to the judgments of others.

Student motivation for learning is influenced by a variety of classroom factors including interaction patterns, rewards, instructional strategies, and even the classroom environment. Researchers have determined that two different types of perception affect students' motivation for performing and completing task assignments. For some students, classroom tasks are perceived as a means to improve, participate, and progress. These students have a mastery goal orientation; they view learning as satisfying, fun, and challenging. They recognize that errors are part of learning and, in fact, a means to learn. They enjoy the process of learning, and know that working hard not only provides satisfaction, but ensures success.

Another perception of learning has been called a **performance goal** orientation. Students who perceive goals as performance tasks tend to be concerned with how well they perform in comparison to others. As a consequence, they are often anxious about their assignments, overly concerned with grades, and primarily concerned with completing tasks instead of enjoying the process of learning.

Ames (1992) suggests that a mastery goal orientation motivates effort and helps students achieve success and personal satisfaction; the students are intrinsically motivated. But with a performance goal orientation, students look for **extrinsic** motivation and are concerned about being judged.

TEACHERS' ROLES AND PRACTICES AFFECT MOTIVATION

In classrooms where students are given little opportunity to choose what they learn, how they learn, and the way in which they are evaluated for learning, there is a greater likelihood that the classroom is structured through extrinsic rewards, incentive programs, and normative evaluation. As a consequence, learning becomes joyless. There is also a tendency in these classrooms to overemphasize repetition, drill, and commer-

Teacher Research

In a study of African-American and Hispanic students enrolled in academically rigorous high school courses, Bronkhurst (1995) interviewed the students to study their motivation related to achievement goals; self-perception of ability; role of effort in academic success; influence of parents, teachers, and peers; influence of race and ethnicity; and use of learning strategies.

He learned that successful students:

- recognize the relationship of effort to academic success
- adopt middle-class school values
- develop an **adaptive motivation pattern**
- develop a "raceless persona"
- are less likely to be negatively influenced by peers

Bronkhurst concluded that elementary, middle school, and high school teachers should facilitate the development of an adaptive motivational pattern (mastery oriented and challenging) as part of a school-wide effort focused on culturally diverse students.

cially produced dittoes for practice materials. Some believe this to be prevalent in low socioeconomic and low-achieving classrooms, and as a consequence it may be a cause of negative motivation patterns.

Ames (1992) describes a classroom intervention program called TARGET designed to stimulate positive patterns of motivation. The TARGET dimensions include: tasks, authority, recognition, grouping, evaluation, and time. Emphasis for each of these dimensions is briefly synthesized below.

Tasks or activities for students should be challenging, provide variety, appeal to students' curiosity, and provide for students' personal control (decision making).

Authority suggests that activities foster personal responsibility for learning through real choices in tasks and in leadership roles.

Recognition has to do with classroom rewards. The TARGET program recommends recognition of individual student effort, accomplishments, and improvement. It is important that all students have opportunities to receive recognition.

Grouping strategies should provide opportunities for a variety of interactive patterns, group learning, and student choice.

Figure 4.1   Equitable
Treatment Checklist

	Always	Sometimes
1. Are all children favored indiscriminately when instructional materials are dispensed?		
2. Are all students encouraged to express themselves when they are angry or unhappy?		
3. Are all students "cued" when they cannot respond to discussion questions?		
4. Are all students encouraged to ask questions when they are uncertain or puzzled?		
5. Are all students in the classroom encouraged to initiate a class discussion?		
6. Are assignments differentially made to challenge the capabilities of each child?		
7. Are the talents and interests of all children considered?		
8. Are the classroom rules predictable and fair for all? (Are they equitably enforced?)		
9. Are all students treated equitably and talked to individually?		

Evaluation practices in the classroom should convey to students that it is OK to make mistakes and take risks, and the importance of effort in the learning process. Evaluation should be individual and private rather than normative.

Time should accommodate individual differences and help students control their own pacing by adjusting tasks to fit students' needs.

MOTIVATION AND TEACHER EXPECTATIONS

Since Rosenthal and Jacobson's (1968) study of how **teacher expectations** can affect students' motivation and academic growth, educators have been aware that teacher-student interactions are critical to the learning process. If some students are consistently encouraged over time to pursue thinking tasks, while others are not, in time, students' achievement will closely resemble the teacher's expectations. For this reason it is recognized that teachers should not behave differentially toward students in their classrooms.

The teacher's reaction (earlier in the chapter) to Mildred, the impulsive responder, and to Jerry, the reflective responder, was an example of how teachers can unconsciously reinforce inappropriate behavior. In responding to the need for differentiation of content, process, output, and environments, teachers must be sure that they are equitable in setting appropriate goals and standards for all students. All students need to be encouraged to achieve to the best of their ability.

Figure 4.1 is a checklist that offers examples of what teachers can do to treat students equitably.

INDIVIDUAL DIFFERENCES

There is a wide range of individual differences in every classroom. These differences may be a consequence of developmental patterns; cognitive, affective, and psychomotor differences; socialization experiences; and personality attributes. Teachers need to be sensitive to differences without being overwhelmed by them. Teachers should be able to recognize when students have special needs that require referral to other education consultants (such as a psychologist, speech therapist, or medical doctor). Often students' special problems can be easily identified through careful observation and private conversation with the student. The needs of children with physical disabilities must be met through sensitive academic planning, understanding, and acceptance. Identifying the needs of other exceptional children including the gifted and talented is an important professional task.

SUMMARY
Developmental Patterns

1. Knowledge of developmental patterns enables teachers to match instruction to students' conceptual levels.
2. Piaget's stages of cognitive growth help teachers understand age-level changes.

3. Vygotsky's developmental patterns help teachers understand the relationship between language and concept development.
4. Kohlberg's stages of moral development help teachers plan appropriate social interactions in the classroom.
5. Gardner challenges traditional views of intelligence; he suggests that teachers use a wide variety of teaching strategies.

Learning Styles

6. Learning styles are natural, inborn inclinations manifested through the senses and personality characteristics.
7. Students who respond to learning situations impulsively need to be cautioned to rethink and reconsider.
8. Students easily distracted in formal learning situations may be field dependent in their learning style. These students may prefer interaction with others.
9. Some learners are considered field independent and prefer formal learning environments.

Social Factors Influence Learning

10. The family environment, including economic condition and socialization practices, influence the child's temperament, personality, and general behavior.
11. Cultural differences between the home and school affect teacher-parent and teacher-student relationships.

Motivation and Effect on Learning

12. Teachers' beliefs about students' motivation have been influenced by behavioral, humanistic, and cognitive psychology.
13. Maslow classifies human needs as hierarchical and motivated by deficiency or growth needs.
14. Four causal attributes affect the individual's perceived reasons for success and failure: ability, effort, task difficulty, and luck.
15. Self-confident individuals attribute their success to ability and effort, not luck.
16. When students associate learning tasks as personal needs, they are more likely to participate to achieve personal satisfaction.

DISCUSSION QUESTIONS AND APPLICATION EXERCISES

1. View several TV commercials. Using the information related to social class differences, decide:
   • Which social group is the target audience?
   • Why was this group chosen?
   • What are the underlying value assumptions made about the target group?
2. Observe one or more students you consider to be successful and other students you consider to be unsuccessful. In what ways are their responses and attitudes different? Report on the following factors:
   • Do they work independently and appear involved in their tasks?
   • Do they ask the teacher questions?
   • Do they appear concerned about others?
3. Identify appropriate experiences for kinesthetic, visual, and auditory learners.
4. Plan a learning experience for preoperational students to help them understand viewpoints other than their own.
5. Explain why you should or should not have the same instructional expectations for all primary children.
6. Study physical education activities in several classrooms. Do the activities reinforce sex-role differences?
7. Try Piaget's conservation experiment using a liquid with both a preoperational child and a child whom you believe to be in the concrete operations stage.
8. Suggest ways teachers could help impulsive students become more reflective, and performance-oriented students become mastery oriented.
9. Observe another classroom teacher. Describe how the teacher:
   • encourages students
   • differentiates teaching and learning
   • disciplines in the classroom
   Judge student motivation in this classroom.
10. Compare the differentiation of instruction to cooking the family dinner when family members have different likes, dislikes, and needs.

PART II

DELIVERY OF INSTRUCTION: HOW TEACHERS TEACH

INTRODUCTION

Chapters 5 through 11 are organized to help you understand how teachers manage their classrooms, plan for teaching, and develop a repertoire of teaching techniques.

- Chapter 5 begins with a discussion of classroom management and how it affects planning and organizing for teaching. The chapter then focuses on the planning tasks teachers perform in preparation for the first day of school.
- Chapter 6 examines expository and discussion teaching strategies, research on questioning, and what students' questions mean. The direct instruction model of teaching, cooperative learning, the advance organizer model of teaching, and the comprehension model are featured in this chapter.
- Chapter 7 gives examples of inquiry, constructivist teaching, and problem-solving techniques, and features several models of teaching, including the group investigation model and backward problem solving. In addition, this chapter provides a classroom example of students performing research and case study methods for the classroom.
- Chapter 8 features the social model of role-playing and illustrates gaming and simulations. In addition, instructions are provided for how to develop your own simulation model.
- Chapter 9 explains curriculum development concepts and how to develop a teaching unit. Suggestions and examples for theme teaching and the integration of subject fields are included.

- Chapter 10 discusses the use of instructional media and technology in the classroom, including laser discs, computers, CD/ROMs, videos, and a discussion of distance learning.
- Chapter 11 completes the section by focusing on strategies for performance assessment, the use of rubrics, evaluation, and communication of learning progress. The importance of evaluation as a factor in learning is emphasized.

Before you begin Part II of the text, a general understanding of instructional methods and the author's perspective will facilitate your reading. This introduction to Part II is designed as an advance organizer to prepare you for what is to come.

If you were asked to think about your favorite (and best) school teacher, what would you remember? Do you recall a project that you participated in under the direction of that favored teacher? Is it the teacher's professional competencies that you remember? Are you thinking about the teacher's personal characteristics? The author asked these questions to a group of experienced teachers and was surprised by the number of responses that dealt with the personal dimension. Although we know a great deal about the teaching process and professional competencies, it is obvious that there is little agreement about what is good teaching. Good teaching is so subjective it appears to depend on who is doing the describing and who is doing the teaching.

However, we do know that most experienced, "expert" teachers use a variety of teaching methods. They do not rely on a single, multipurpose teaching strategy. Even though we cannot predict with certainty what will always work, we do know that certain methods of teaching are associated with specific learning outcomes. Before we examine specific instructional techniques, let us review some of the human and situational variables that affect instruction.

DEFINING INSTRUCTION

Instruction is defined as the activity that occurs in the classroom setting, encompassing the resources or materials used and teacher and student variables. The human variables include the following:

- *Student characteristics:* age, sex, developmental level, social class, language, academic and achievement motivation, intellectual development, cognitive style, and self-concept
- *Teacher characteristics:* teaching style, age, sex, social class background, preparatory experiences, warmth, enthusiasm, openness, and management skills

Organizational and content variables also need to be considered for instructional planning. These variables include the following:

- *Organizational considerations:* size of class, space in classroom, time, and class composition
- *Content considerations:* subject grade level, objectives, sequence, resources, and materials

Both human and situational variables affect instruction. The teacher who is cognizant of the variables will use them positively as a guide to planning and implementing instruction. Consider these examples:

- If a first-grade teacher wants to have block work, the teacher needs to consider floor space (which may necessitate the moving of tables and chairs), the equipment (blocks and accessories), and specific lesson objectives.
- 1:00 P.M. on Friday afternoon before Christmas vacation may be a very poor time to have a science experiment. Probably a structured lesson would fit students and teacher better at that particular time.

In other words, the teacher must use common sense in choosing a teaching method. If the amount of time required for a given lesson is not available or other context variables are wrong, then the teacher must make an alternate decision. Human and situational variables should be considered for instructional decisions.

ASSUMPTIONS ABOUT TEACHING

This section of the textbook makes three basic assumptions about teaching. The first assumption addresses the wide spectrum of instructional approaches:

1. *A variety of approaches to instruction is appropriate.* If an open-ended science experiment is inappropriate on a Friday afternoon before vacation, there is probably another strategy that will be quite effective.

This text classifies instructional approaches as either *expository* or *inquiry-problem solving*. To accomplish expository goals, teachers must typically use lecture and direct instruction with appropriate questioning techniques. The advance organizer teaching model is also considered an expository teaching approach.

To accomplish inquiry and problem-solving goals, teachers most typically use teaching models in which students must be involved in constructing meaning. These approaches require both inductive and deductive thinking and may involve group investigation, concept attainment, role-playing, and gaming. This leads us to a second assumption about teaching:

2. *The method of instruction affects the learning process.* This means that although several approaches may be appropriate, each will contribute something quite different. The open-ended science experiment contributes toward self-development, problem-solving skills, social participation (if it is a group project), and understanding of science concepts. Reading out of a science textbook fosters science concepts, but does not foster discovery learning or affect social participation. The important thing to remember is that students will not become reflective problem solvers without the opportunity to practice problem-solving skills.

When instructional approaches, teaching strategies, or models of teaching are discussed in this text, it is likely that the conditions of the classroom will be discussed as well. To describe classroom conditions, instructional specialists typically use words like *environment* or *structure* of the classroom. This refers to how the teacher controls the classroom, the teacher's behavior toward students, and if students' behaviors are encouraged or discouraged.

Perhaps it may surprise you, but different teaching strategies require distinct teacher behaviors. Think about what you do during a lecture. Now think about the expectations of the person delivering the lecture.

Table II.1 Interaction of Learning Environment and Teacher Behavior

Environment	Teacher Behavior
Controlled environment, high structure	Teacher controls the dialog; teacher sets the stage and controls student responses. Limited instructional materials are needed.
Controlled environment, moderate to high structure	Teacher initiates discussions and programs questions to elicit desired responses; teacher controls student interaction to fit discussion. Some supportive instructional materials are needed.
Open environment, moderate structure	Teacher initiates problem or conflict situation; teacher often guides the problem resolution as it moves from stage to stage. A great deal of student interaction is encouraged; students are expected to accept responsibility for problem solving. A variety of instructional materials are needed.
Open environment, low structure	Teacher facilitates democratic processes; students define problems and initiate methods for solving them. Teacher provides many resources and encourages students to use resources out of the classroom.

During the lecture, the classroom or hall is quiet, attention is focused on teacher, and interaction is teacher controlled, usually from teacher-to-student-to-teacher. Table II.1 exhibits the relationship between teacher behavior and the conditions in the classroom.

The third assumption is based on the interaction of learning environment and teacher behavior:

3. *Students react differentially to the instructional process.* Some students learn more effectively with some approaches than with others. The student who is visually oriented does not appreciate the teacher who reads test questions orally to the class. This same student tires listening to a lecture. A student's characteristics affect what is learned.

Table II.2 depicts the relationship between the choice of teaching strategy and the way the classroom is controlled.

STUDENT BEHAVIOR DURING EXPOSITION AND INQUIRY: PROBLEM-SOLVING STRATEGIES

Visualize a balance scale like the one shown in Figure II.1. Learning experiences that accomplish input goals are on one side of the scale. These experiences are planned so students consume information and learn specific skills. Experiences may include a museum visit, a lecture, films and slides, textbooks, television, records and tapes, workbooks, an exhibit, or demonstrations. Student behavior during input includes observation, listening, reading, responding, questioning, and note taking. Students may appear to be passive during input experiences, but in fact, they are using their senses to collect information.

On the other side of the balance scale are learning experiences that accomplish output goals. These experiences are planned so that students produce knowledge. Output strategies require the student to perform in some way. Experiences are extremely diverse and may include some of the following:

- Reports (oral and written)
- Projects
- Map making
- Dramatics, performance, singing
- Role-playing, simulations, gaming
- Experiments
- Discussions, debates

Table II.2 Interplay of Strategy Choice and Learning Environment

Strategy	Learning Environment
Lecture, film, direct instruction	Controlled environment, high structure important
Guided discussions, questioning, analysis	Controlled environment, moderate to high structure
Role-playing, simulations, gaming, dramatizations	Open environment, moderate structure
Discovery, problem solving, group investigations	Open environment, low structure

Figure II.1   Balancing Input
Goals and Output Goals

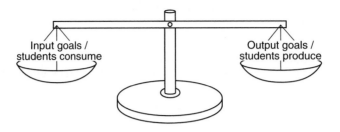

- Construction artwork, hands-on activities
- Interviewing
- Committee work

Student behaviors during output experiences may be independent, in pairs, or in groups, and include some of the following:

- Research skill activity, problem solving
- Exploration, experimentation
- Speaking, writing, acting out
- Manipulative, building

- Questioning, planning, creating
- Valuing, decision making

When students are required to produce something, they process information to develop new meanings. There is a reciprocal relationship between input and output teaching strategies. Think about the teacher's objectives in assigning tasks, and compare the tasks and objectives in Figure II.2. Output strategies are dependent on prior input; thus the teacher balances teaching approaches to maximize learning.

Figure II.2   Contrast the
Teacher's Objectives

Decide whether the teacher wants the student to consume or produce when tasks are prefaced with the following objectives:

Recite _____	Sumarize _____
Imagine _____	Label _____
Measure _____	Contrast _____
Hypothesize _____	Recall _____

Comments: Probably the teacher wants students to consume information or ideas when the following objectives are written: *recite, label, recall, measure.* For students to produce, objectives would probably begin with the following words: *imagine, hypothesize, summarize, contrast.*

5

Classroom Management: Planning and Guiding Learning Experiences

This chapter covers two major aspects of successful teaching: classroom management and initiating instruction. You will learn about the key components of classroom management and look at examples of each, and compare and contrast classroom management and discipline. Because the use of classroom groups is so important during teaching, both large and small group instruction (the hows, whys, and potential traps) are discussed in depth. The chapter provides both scheduling and lesson plan examples, and concludes with a review of the teacher's daily tasks.

After you study this chapter, you should be able to accomplish the following:

1. Define classroom management by identifying the key components.
2. Explain how each of the components affects teacher and student success.
3. Explain the classroom management behaviors of *with-it-ness, overlapping, transition smoothness,* and *ripple effect.*
4. Identify the advantages and disadvantages of small and large group instruction.
5. Suggest classroom activities to develop a sense of belonging and to foster democratic behaviors.
6. Anticipate potential classroom management problems during small and large group instruction by identifying the problems and suggesting means to avoid or alleviate them.
7. Explain why it is important to allow time for both content and group work evaluation.
8. Discuss why teachers should concern themselves with learning about their school community.
9. Select any grade level or subject field and identify how to prepare for the first day of school.
10. Write a lesson plan for a specific learning experience.
11. Identify the daily tasks of the teacher using the headings *management* and *instruction.*

Professional Lexicon

academic feedback   The process of detecting and responding to students' needs for meaning related to content and task assignments.

assessment   Appraisal of what students know and do not know using established procedures.

classroom management   A comprehensive definition of this term is given in the first section of this chapter.

discipline   The process of moderating student behavior with others and motivating students to be personally responsible for self-behavior.

formative evaluation   Measurement of achievement during instruction to facilitate future planning.

integration of instruction   Using the teachable moment to teach skills as needed; utilizing knowledge and skills from one subject field to reinforce or extend instruction in another subject field.

interdisciplinary instruction   Linking subject fields through the use of similar concepts.

monitoring   Observing and responding to behavioral problems and instructional problems.

overlapping   Attending to more than one incident in the classroom simultaneously.

ripple effect   An outbreak of contagious misbehavior often caused by the teacher through public discipline that embarrasses other students.

summative evaluation   Measurement of student achievement (performance) at the end of a learning experience or an instructional unit.

task engagement   The degree of involvement the student demonstrates while performing a task.

transition smoothness   The ability of the teacher to change learning experiences and/or subject fields without causing undue lags of time (and misbehavior).

with-it-ness   A teacher's ability to demonstrate to students his or her awareness of and alertness to student behavior and task engagement.

CLASSROOM MANAGEMENT

Classroom management is the linchpin that makes teaching and learning achievable. The author defines **classroom management** using the key components that affect success in the classroom (Lemlech, 1988, p. 3):

> Classroom management is the orchestration of classroom life: planning curriculum, organizing procedures and resources, arranging the environment to maximize efficiency, monitoring student progress, anticipating potential problems.

The key components of classroom management are planning, organizing, arranging, monitoring, and anticipating. You will learn more about the importance of each of these components in the following sections. Teachers who are successful classroom managers have mastered techniques for planning activities and maintaining high levels of student involvement in those activities, enriching the classroom environment, anticipating organizational and behavioral problems, and monitoring students' progress.

PLANNING INSTRUCTIONAL ACTIVITIES

Significant insight about classroom management originated with the work of Jacob Kounin (1970). Kounin (p. 63) defined *successful* classroom management as "producing a high rate of work involvement and a low rate of deviancy in academic settings." Kounin studied teacher behaviors that produced high and low work involvement of students. He noted the importance of motivation before teachers change activities and the need for variety and challenge in the tasks demanded of students.

Studies of classroom management among experienced teachers and student teachers reveal that certain classroom conditions, teacher planning antecedent to instruction, and teacher behaviors result in a smooth working classroom and high involvement of students. Let's look at a classroom episode to identify some of these significant elements.

It was literature time in Greg Thomas's classroom, and his students were going to read historical novels. Thomas selected novels that depict the life and times of pioneers as they traveled westward. Thomas began the lesson by asking the students, "Suppose we are pioneers living in the Midwest during the 1840s. How would you feel if you were told that tomorrow your family would begin an adventure that would take you across the country?"

By evoking student interest and discussion, Thomas motivated the students to read about the lives of early pioneers. Next he gave the students a short synopsis of several novels and urged the students to select a book to read. Thomas wrote the names of the books on the chalkboard and each student signed his or her name underneath the selected book. The choice of novel determined each student's literary group.

Before the students joined their groups, Thomas told the students they would have to decide how their group would communicate their pioneer story with the rest of the class. He displayed a chart with the possible choices: skits, simulation games, cartoon strips, dioramas, letters from pioneers to friends.

Thomas told the students they would have all week to read and create during their language arts time. Monitors distributed the books and Thomas gave each group a designated place to work; the students formed small groups to begin their reading and group discussions. Thomas circulated, listening and helping when students needed vocabulary or clarification of concepts.

ANALYSIS OF THE TEACHING EPISODE

Steps in Planning

1. Selection of historical novels
2. Question to motivate interest
3. Time for student reaction and discussion
4. Synopsis of novels to stimulate interest
5. Names of novels written on chalkboard
6. Chart of possible student activities
7. Selection of monitors to distribute books
8. Designation of places for groups to work

These activities represent the teacher's prethinking (antecedent planning) needed to move the lesson along. Some of these same activities could be listed for other classroom management components. Had he not performed these planning tasks, there would be time lags while he gathered the novels, framed a motivating question, decided on how to group students, and distributed books.

When time lags while a teacher gets organized or thinks out learning activities, deviant student behavior is more likely (Kounin and Doyle, 1975). Classrooms are virulent settings! When Tom talks and gestures to Dan,

If misbehavior is contagious, consider appropriate behavior. Can it be contagious in a classroom, too?

Mary decides she, too, can engage in play, and before long, the teacher has a whole class to bring to order.

ORGANIZING PROCEDURES

Experienced teachers typically consider the first three weeks of the school year as the most important. During this time, elementary teachers socialize their students to conform to the rules and procedures of the classroom. Evertson and Anderson (1979) confirmed that more effective classroom managers develop specific procedures and communicate them to the children. Examples of such procedures are how to obtain assistance, how to line up at the door, how to work in a group, options for free time, correcting homework, standards for seatwork, and where to put seatwork. These procedures are taught just as if they were part of the content.

Researchers who have studied effective teachers also note that these teachers are precise and clear in their directions to students; they communicate well, listen intently, and express feelings to students. Perhaps the most striking difference between effective and ineffective classroom managers is the knack for anticipating potential problems. The effective teacher anticipates resource and material needs, physical space needs, individual and group needs, noise constraints, traffic flow problems, and affective and cognitive student reactions. Having anticipated these possible problems, the effective teacher preplans to avoid pitfalls.

Another characteristic of effective managers is the ability to set clear expectations. Emmer and Evertson (1981) found that junior high school teachers typically set expectations for behavior, standards for students' academic work, and classroom procedures.

Reviewing Greg Thomas's literature lesson, we can identify some of his organizing tasks.

Steps in Organizing a Lesson

1. Gathering historical novels appropriate for his class
2. Deciding how he would distribute the novels
3. Deciding on reading the novels in small groups and the means for organizing the students into groups
4. Planning the work space
5. Making the chart of activities; deciding that students would select their activity in the small group

MONITORING STUDENTS' PROGRESS AND BEHAVIOR

Kounin (1970) described a number of teacher behaviors related to managerial success. Experienced teachers are able to communicate to students that, as teachers, they are aware of what is going on. Sometimes they do this with a special look or a raised eyebrow, or by standing up, or touching, or walking over to a student. In these ways the teacher conveys the message to desist—or else! Kounin called this awareness behavior **with-it-ness.**

Another behavior that successful teachers manage is paying attention to more than one event at a time, or what Kounin calls **overlapping.** For instance, the teacher may be working with a small reading group; someone walks into the room with a message just as a child raises his hand at his seat for assistance. The teacher leaves the reading group very quietly without disturbing the students, examines the message, whispers a response, helps the child having difficulty, and continues directing the reading lesson without skipping a beat!

Another characteristic related to managerial success is knowing when an activity needs to be changed and managing the change so smoothly, disregarding any irrelevancies, that students continue in the same manner without the lesson's losing momentum. Kounin called this **transition smoothness.** Arlin (1979) also studied transitions between activities and found that off-task behaviors were reduced if teachers monitored what was happening in the classroom and provided clear directions so the transition was structured.

Kounin (1970) concluded that there are a number of consequences related to a teacher's behavior that are often not anticipated. When a teacher disciplines a child in front of other children, there is a **ripple effect.** The ripple effect is influenced by the type of desist the teacher uses. An angry desist produces emotional conflict—sometimes embarrassment—and does not produce conformity by other members of the class.

It is interesting to note that in his 1970 research with kindergarten children, Kounin discovered that by increasing repetition of an activity, the activity changed from being liked to being disliked, and **task engagement** diminished. He concluded that variety and challenge, initiating and maintaining movement, smoothness, and momentum were very important in classrooms.

Kounin's kindergarten study also found that when teachers clarified their meanings by providing information (feedback) to the deviant child along with the desist, the result was more conformity from other children. Firmness, the "I mean it" factor, also produced more conformity than nonconformity in witnesses.

Studies of successful and less successful teachers have determined that the successful teachers maximized their teaching time with students by monitoring individual effort and providing immediate feedback information to the students. These successful teachers appeared to accept personal responsibility for their students' achievement.

Thomas's classroom episode does not give us the student dialogue so we do not know about the teacher-student and student-to-student interaction, but we do know that Thomas monitored his students' small group work and engaged in anticipatory thinking about student behavior.

Anticipatory Thinking in the Classroom

- Telling students to select means to communicate story with others in their small groups
- Communicating a timeframe for reading and completing work

Monitoring Student Needs

- Circulating among groups
- Providing assistance with vocabulary and concepts

THE LEARNING ENVIRONMENT

The classroom environment influences students' behavior. This should not be a surprise to any college student who has sat in a lecture hall and automatically whipped out a notebook and pencil. Seating arrangements in rows, in small groups, in a circle, in the front of the room or the back all influence the interaction of students with each other and with the teacher. When seated in an auditorium or a library, in a gymnasium or a cooperative group, the environmental setting affects students' behavior and the resultant expectations.

The management of the classroom is similarly affected by the environmental setting. Kounin and Sherman (1979) described the fit between preschoolers' behavior and the environmental setting. Preschoolers, who did not have adult structure imposed on them, used a free-play setting and played without dawdling, wandering, crying, or fighting 95 percent of the time. The author has similarly observed preschoolers in a free-play setting, not constrained by adult pressure, acting totally involved. Kounin and Sherman concluded that the preschoolers exhibit "schoolish" behavior and act appropriately when the setting fits the activities.

Teaching Hints: *Managing the Learning Experience*

Successful teachers know how to apply classroom management skills:

- Maximize teaching time with students
- Monitor student effort and behavior
- Provide immediate academic feedback
- Accept responsibility for students' achievements

When the classroom environment does not support the activities a teacher chooses, management problems arise. For example, in a classroom where the tables are in straight rows, it is difficult to develop student discussion skills. If students do not face each other when they talk, interaction becomes a back-and-forth process from student to teacher. As a consequence, the students are not listening to each other; they are waiting for the teacher to call on them. This type of lesson is really a recitation period rather than a class discussion. The effects of this lesson are student boredom, lags between responses, off-task behavior (horseplay), and teacher frustration. In another example, a science classroom without lab space and equipment curtails learning experiences and defines both teaching and learning.

If Thomas did not have space for students to work in small groups to read their novels and create group projects, students would not be able to select their own groups, and he would have had to impose a rigid learning experience.

CLASSROOM MANAGEMENT AND DISCIPLINE

Classroom management and **discipline** are *not* synonymous. The definition given previously (Lemlech, 1988, p. 3), does not even refer to classroom discipline; yet discipline in the classroom is dependent on good classroom management. Chaotic classrooms unstructured by group standards restrict the ability of the teacher to teach and students to learn. Dewey (1915, 1944, p. 22) talks about the social environment of the classroom and its influence on the development of attitudes and dispositions.

> The social environment consists of all the activities of fellow beings that are bound up in the carrying on of the activities of any one of its members. It is truly educative in its effect in the degree in which an individual shares or participates in some conjoint activity.

By circulating among classroom groups, the teacher can monitor student effort and behavior and provide immediate academic feedback.

In many classrooms teachers set the rules, require students (and their parents) to sign classroom rules, provide rewards to students for following the rules (free time, early lunch dismissal, no homework), and punishment to students who do not abide by them (compositions, detention, extra drill work, no recess, no free time). The problem here is that students in these classrooms take no responsibility for helping to set classroom standards and are not motivated to maintain them.

To respond to ongoing classroom discipline problems, teachers often embrace various discipline systems to treat the problem. Bestowing rewards, as in the *token economy* system, is a means whereby teachers try to reinforce appropriate behavior through tokens. When students misbehave, they have to return the tokens, when students accrue enough tokens they can exchange them for rewards and privileges.

Assertive discipline (Canter, 1976) is another such system that emphasizes teachers' rights to impose classroom rules and establish preset consequences. The system is said to be teacher-friendly and by definition, student-unfriendly. The teacher establishes a classroom environment to ensure obedience of the teacher's rules.

I messages (Gordon, 1974) attempt to define for the teacher who "owns" a classroom discipline problem.

According to this system, knowing the "ownership" will improve classroom communication. So if the problem is a student problem, then the teacher presumably can say, "This isn't my problem; you need to deal with it." How knowing this will improve the classroom environment is mind-boggling.

As an experienced classroom teacher, the author believes that these systems, and there are many more, do not attack the root of the problem. Discipline problems are symptomatic of a classroom environment that lacks respect, guidance, and responsibility. In Chapter 4, motivation was discussed and related to the individual's beliefs about who or what controls events affecting the individual's life. Researchers have concluded that success in school depends on the student's recognition that ability and effort are student controlled and they are critical elements for school success.

Teachers can address discipline problems by insisting on student participation in setting classroom rules and standards, and then monitoring classroom happenings by referring back to those rules and standards when misbehavior occurs. It is time well spent when the teacher stops activities and asks students, "What shall we do? We have some friends who are not . . ." Then the teacher guides students to use *their own* standards to explain to the abusers that they have

Point to Ponder: What Would You Do If . . .?

Unbeknown to its captor, the small lizard escaped from its cardboard prison and slithered across the room toward the learning center. Charlie, the lizard's owner, had placed the cardboard box on the floor under his seat. Charlie was what his teacher described as "hyper," and he kicked the lid off the box without being aware that he did so. Charlie had not bothered to tell his teacher that the lizard was visiting the classroom.

It was 10:10 A.M. and many of the students began to close their books (noisily) in anticipation of recess. The teacher ignored the disturbance, but noted the time and began to give directions to prepare for recess. At the same time, Bonnie saw the lizard and screamed; Erik fell over as he tried to capture it; and Charlie came running. "It's mine," he screamed. The teacher was also screaming, "Everyone stop right now! Don't move." What can you infer from this incident about the teacher's classroom management skills? Think about some of the key management components you have learned:

- Classroom organization and rules
- Student responsibility and discipline
- Teacher behavior: "with-it-ness," clarity, firmness

If you were this teacher, would you discuss the problem with the whole class or just with Charlie? What would you say to Bonnie and Erik? Would you do anything about the students who noisily anticipated recess? If so, what?

not been respectful of others' rights, and that they all have participated in setting the rules.

Clearly it is the teacher's responsibility to establish a democratic classroom community. We must transmit our democratic heritage by communicating appropriate habits, values, and ideals of our social life, and we do this by having students experience democracy in action in the classroom.

GROUPING FOR INSTRUCTION

Every moment of classroom life is a learning experience. Students work in the whole class group and in smaller class groups. The grouping experience contributes to each student's understanding of citizenship and inherent responsibility. Whole group instruction is typically associated with formal, traditional classroom teaching and small group instruction with flexible, more open teaching approaches. But in fact, the effective classroom teacher uses both approaches throughout the school day. The skills involved in managing group behavior are basic to classroom management and effective instruction.

WHY GROUP?

Students attending my college classes are often surprised when I group them in clusters of five to seven students on the first or second day of class and present the groups with a problem or an issue for discussion.

During the 15 or 20 minutes that the groups meet (out on the lawn, in adjoining rooms, and in our lecture room), I tour the groups to listen to their discussion, to observe them, and to make suggestions if necessary.

The groups have a designated time to come back and meet as a whole class, and I return to the classroom to await their entrance.

The change in their behavior is remarkable. They leave the room as individuals; straggling out, wary and a little apprehensive about doing something that is not typically done in a college classroom. But their return is different. They come in noisily and companionably, and invariably they sit together as comrades.

The debriefing of the activity occurs in two stages. Stage 1 is substantive. Whenever possible I try to motivate a little bit of conflict among the groups so the reports are not really group reports but, in actuality, a whole class discussion.

As voices rise and adults forget their discussion manners and begin interrupting each other, I nonchalantly ask, "By the way, is there anyone who did not talk in their small group discussion?"

They look around and sheepishly acknowledge that everyone contributed. This initiates Stage 2, in which we discuss my behavior as teacher and their behaviors as learners.

I usually end this session by asking the students, "What did you learn from working in a small group that was valuable?" They invariably will respond with some of the advantages of grouping:

- They felt less inhibited about talking out.
- They learned from their classmates.
- They felt involved.

What decisions does a teacher need to make before students work in small groups?

Table 5.1   Large Group Instruction

Advantages	Disadvantages (possible)
Efficient means for input: lectures, films, guests, demonstrations	Reduces individual responsibility
Develops sense of belonging	Subordinates individual needs to whole group needs
Facilitates teaching of new skills	Impedes differentiation of instruction
Promotes teacher-centered authority	Impedes social participation
Provides single continuous signal source	Increases physical problems (vision, hearing)
	Increases impersonality of teaching and learning
	Reduces task involvement
	Tempts teacher to make an example of disruptive students

Every teaching approach has advantages and disadvantages. The effective teacher chooses the teaching strategy that best meets the needs of the teaching situation in order to accomplish the desired outcomes. Before reading the discussion of group work, study the charts of specified advantages and disadvantages for small and large group instruction (Table 5.1 and Table 5.2).

DISCUSSION: LARGE GROUP INSTRUCTION

Careful study of the two tables reveals that each strategy has both conflicting and contradictory values. For example, Table 5.1 states that advantages of large group instruction include teacher-centered authority and a single continuous signal source; this means that control should be facilitated. Yet, at the same time, the table states that task involvement may be reduced and that the teacher may be tempted to make an example of disruptive students. What is the explanation of this?

According to Kounin and Sherman (1979), certain environmental settings have more holding power than others. Large group settings have the potential to decrease socially ineffective behavior; therefore, if the teacher can hold students' attention, the teacher will be the sole and continuing signal source. If the lesson does not lag and the teacher can manage the disparate interests of the group, high involvement can be achieved.

Large group instruction is potentially efficient because the teacher can introduce a new skill to all students at the same time. The teacher models the skill, and controlled practice occurs under the teacher's watchful eyes. Proper implementation of this approach facilitates keeping the students "on task," thereby increasing academically engaged time.

So why are control problems often more difficult during large group instruction? The discussion in Chapter 4 on the ways in which children differ provided some insight into why this approach is not always successful. Hearing and vision problems or the physical size of some students may be a factor. When students cannot hear or see, they cause problems. Learning-style differences are not provided for when all students must attend in the same way. As a conse-

Table 5.2   Small Group Instruction

Advantages	Disadvantages (possible)
Facilitates communication	Excites students
Promotes interaction	Wastes time if students' group skills are poor
Motivates involvement	Wastes time when introducing new skills
Encourages assisting others, accepting responsibility	Subordinates high and low achiever needs to accomplish group goals
Teaches bargaining, negotiation	Subordinates academic content for group process skills
Promotes decision making	Extroverted, aggressive students may overrule and subordinate introverted students
Necessitates listening to others' viewpoints	
Necessitates sharing own values	
Promotes cooperation, group production, and group learning	
Allows differentiation of instruction	
Frees teacher to observe, listen, and diagnose	

quence, some students will be disinterested. (Think back to Barry's classmates studying the anatomy of the human heart at the beginning of Chapter 4.) Large group instruction assumes that all students need the same lesson, but this may not be true. Because large group instruction is impersonal, it can decrease involvement. Finally, the spatial arrangement of the students during instruction may cause problems. If students are too far away from the teacher, they can pursue their own interests due to lack of monitoring; or, if students are seated too close together, the result may be disruptive behavior. A typical mistake of the beginning teacher is to get upset when students begin to fidget. In an uncontrolled burst of temper, the teacher may lash out at the disruptive student—or at the student the teacher thinks is disruptive. This behavior results in embarrassment for others as well as for the target of the outburst and is known to decrease students' achievement.

Sense of Belonging

It is very important for students to feel a sense of identity with their classmates and their teacher. A sense of belonging motivates attendance at school, encourages cooperative behavior, and enhances the ability to learn. Classroom management is facilitated when students learn to care about others and about their own role in the group. At the beginning of the school year, the teacher must cultivate this sense of belonging and work to develop pride in group identity. Both schoolwide and classroom activities are used to develop ego-satisfying behavior.

Large group activities have the potential to develop this important characteristic. Experienced teachers develop it in a variety of ways as the following example will illustrate.

Greg Thomas has his students create a class song at the beginning of each school year. The students select a popular, classic, or folk tune, and then write lyrics to fit the song. Last year his students selected "Puff the Magic Dragon" and wrote a song called, "We're the Greatest Students." Using harmonicas, autoharps, and rhythm sticks, they orchestrated the song. This activity helped the students develop a class identity and what human relations specialists call *oneness*.

Choral speaking and rhythmic and physical activities performed in a group also have the potential to develop strong group feeling. Activities should be chosen on the basis of their potential to develop group cooperation, responsibility, respect, and dependence

on classmates. More sophisticated activities of longer duration are also appropriate. For example, an activity that takes students out into the community to perform a service in their own neighborhood has the potential for developing group solidarity and oneness.

Discussion: Small Group Instruction

Large group direct instruction tends to be formal and impersonal; as a consequence it can make the classroom a very grim place. It is apparent from the research on teaching strategies that to accomplish creative goals, intuitive thinking, discovery, exploration, and inquiry, small group instruction with less structure is more suitable.

Small groups can take advantage of student diversity as well as homogeneous needs. Teachers can arrange the heterogeneous groups to take advantage of students' special abilities (thereby increasing the likelihood of peer modeling and assistance), or on some occasions the students can choose their own group arrangement (affecting student motivation to participate). For teaching and monitoring specific skill development, arrange the groups homogeneously, but in social studies, science, health, art, music, or physical education, heterogeneous groups are appropriate.

Small group work facilitates the differentiation of instruction. It is more difficult for teachers to manage whole group behavior and individualize instruction; by utilizing small groups teachers can match instruction with the precise needs of the individual. Small groups also enable students to learn from each other and to develop respect for classmates.

Sometimes in the modern classroom we lose sight of the fact that a major purpose of the school is to foster democratic behaviors. If we expect young adults to participate meaningfully in our society, then they need appropriate experiences that teach social participatory skills. Students can learn these skills only when they are confronted by each other and forced to work together. Young children who always get their own way become unsocialized beings. The moment that they are forced to relate to others they must identify areas of agreement and disagreement with others. This in turn motivates confrontation (see the discussion of the theories of Piaget and Kohlberg in Chapter 4) and the use of persuasion, negotiation, and cooperation. They learn self-control in the process, but it is a developmental process.

Research Findings: Cooperation Versus Competition

Studies of cooperative and competitive efforts in problem solving between the years 1929–1993 revealed that cooperative efforts resulted in better problem solving than competitive efforts. This occurred particularly when cooperative groups generated problem-solving strategies in mathematical problems and visuospatial problems (Qin, Johnson, and Johnson, 1995).

MANAGING SMALL AND LARGE GROUP INSTRUCTION

Preplanning (anticipating potential problems) will alleviate most of the difficulties involved in either instructional approach (see Table 5.3 and Table 5.4).

HOW TO BEGIN SMALL GROUP INSTRUCTION

Regardless of the subject, small group instruction necessitates specific teacher and learner behaviors. The next classroom episode should provide you with some ideas about how to begin small group instruction.

Mary Hogan had some of her second graders on the floor in front of her; the rest were seated on chairs behind the group on the floor. On a low table in front of the group, Hogan had a large horseshoe magnet and a number of objects with it; including paper, a pencil, scissors, a crayon, rubber bands, a penny, nails, an eraser, paper clips, a ball, and string.

MOTIVATION

Teacher: Who can tell us what this is? (She holds up the magnet. Many hands go up, and the teacher chooses one student to respond.)

Sue: I bet it's a magnet.

Teacher: What does a magnet do?

Sue: It picks things up.

Teacher: How could we find out?

Bert: See if it will pick those things up that you have on the table.

Teacher: Good idea, Bert. (She uses the magnet to try to pick up the string.)

Jean: Magnets won't pick up string; only certain things.

Teacher: What do you mean, Jean?

Jean: Well, I know string won't work.

Teacher: Come show us what will. (Jean uses magnet and picks up a pin, a nail, and a paper clip.) All right, we can see that Jean made the magnet pick up three items. We also know that it did not pick up the string. In what way are these three items alike? (She holds up the magnet with the pin, the nail, and the paper clip.)

William: I think they must all be made of metal.

Teacher: What kind of metal will magnets pick up? (The teacher looks around, and students appear to be unsure.)

ASSIGNMENT

Teacher: Today, I thought you might be like to be scientists and explore a problem. I am going to ask you to work in small groups. Each group will have some magnets and a bag of objects. Your job is to find out what the magnet will pull and to make a rule about the objects that magnets will pull. If your group makes its rule before the other groups are ready, I will come over and suggest another problem to investigate. When you think your group is ready, or if your group has a problem, have your group leader raise his or her hand, and I will come over and listen to your rule or give you some help.

ORGANIZATION

Mary Hogan distributed magnets and bags of materials to six different locations in the room. The bags contained a penny, nails, wire, screws, pins, and hair curlers.

Teacher: We will need to work together cooperatively. I think we had better make some group work rules. What should they be?

Joe: I think we better have a captain or a leader.

Teacher: Good idea, Joe; I will write the rules on the board. What else?

Mary: We need someone to write down our ideas.

Teacher: Yes, but since writing may be a problem, how about if each group chooses a group reporter for our discussion? (Students nod, and teacher writes another rule. Next, she asks:) How will you decide what to do when you are in your group?

Table 5.3 Management of Small Group Instruction

Potential Problems	Means to Avoid the Problem
Need for structure	Appoint or direct students to choose a leader, recorder, and/or reporter.
Need to communicate group problems	Define appropriate behavior; define operating procedures; chart the rules.
Need to communicate group problems	Ensure that students know how to get your assistance.
Need to share problems and accomplishments	Provide evaluation time at the end of each work period.
Content should not be subordinate to process	Evaluate substantive findings, then group process; do not focus on individual behavior.
Group size	Uneven number of students facilitates compromise; the optimal group size is five to seven.
Materials and resource needs	Anticipate, monitor, and provide necessary materials.
Groups fail to "get started"	If it is a continuing activity, begin by asking all of the groups to identify what they intend to accomplish. If it is a one-time or new activity, verify that each group understands what is expected.
Physical space	Provide and designate a working space for each group so groups do not intrude upon each other.
Deviant behavior (individual)	If behavior cannot be corrected with a reminder, decide what you will do: (a) Have the disruptive student watch another group and report during the evaluation period on what makes groups function smoothly, and what inhibits effective group work. (b) Assign the deviant an individual project; monitor its completion. (c) Share information with and ask for assistance from the parents.
Deviant behavior (group)	Assess whether the problem is a consequence of misunderstanding about the objective. If so, clarify and provide information to refocus group thinking. If there is a nonacademic reason, confer with the group using your best "I mean it" expression; let them know what you expect of them and then monitor their adherence to class rules. Assess whether or not the combination of students in the group should be changed.

Table 5.4 Management of Large Group Instruction

Potential Problems	Means to Avoid the Problem
General disinterest	Choose lesson needed by most students; motivate interest.
High or low achievers' disinterest	Provide special information to interest the highs; comfort the lows by stating that you will be available to give additional assistance after the lesson.
Deviant behavior due to space problems (crowding)	Direct the less mature students to places where they will not be trouble to others. Arrange the room to accommodate this type of instruction.
Inattention due to space problems (class too spread out)	This happens most frequently when students are at tables or desks and the teacher does not establish eye contact. Have students arrange chairs in a three-sided square to face you, or seat students on floor in front of the chalkboard. Do not start the lesson until all students have directed their eyes on you.
Deviant behavior as a consequence of physical problems	Provide for individual needs. Seat students with physical disabilities appropriately.
Impersonality of instruction	Involve students by using short and frequent questions. Wait and encourage responses.

Ben: I guess we better plan.

Teacher: Good point, Ben. We need to plan the experiment. Suppose I write, "Plan the experiment."

Sam: Then we need to do the experiment.

Teacher: OK, so number 4 should be, "Perform the experiment." What will number 5 be?

Terry: We better discuss what we found out.

Teacher: OK, number 5 should be, "Talk about the experiment," and number 6 better be, "Prepare for class discussion." Is there anything else?

Midge: Clean up?

Teacher: Yes, indeed. Let's read our group work rules together.

Group Work Rules

1. Choose a group leader.
2. Choose a group reporter.
3. Plan the experiment.
4. Perform the experiment.
5. Talk about the experiment.
6. Prepare for class discussion.
7. Clean up.

Teacher: Now, boys and girls, when I call your names, please go to the area I designate for your group. Remember to move quietly so that the students who are waiting can hear their names called. If I need your attention, I will flash the lights. (Each group is quietly dismissed to go to work.)

Hogan walked around and observed the progress of the groups while they worked (see Figure 5.1). Each group had several different types of magnets as well as their bag of materials. As Hogan observed each group, she suggested to them: "Arrange the objects in two groups, those that the magnet will pull and those that the magnet will not pull. Find out if all magnets pull the same things."

When the groups thought they were finished, Mary Hogan listened to their rules. Sometimes the rules were not quite accurate, and that would lead to her telling them the names of the metals in the objects that they were testing.

For the groups that were right on target, Hogan had prepared an additional experiment. She asked them to find out if magnets call pull objects through other materials. She suggested that they find out by using books, paper, cardboard, and anything else that was not too thick.

Figure 5.1   Group Work Behaviors

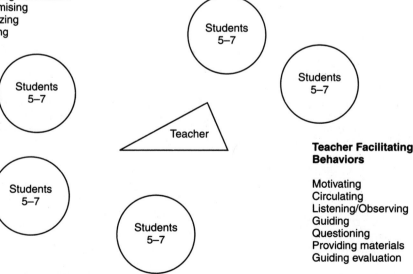

Student Process/Product– Oriented Behaviors

Choosing a group leader
Planning
Searching
Exchanging information
Compromising
Generalizing
Evaluating

Teacher Facilitating Behaviors

Motivating
Circulating
Listening/Observing
Guiding
Questioning
Providing materials
Guiding evaluation

EVALUATION

After about 10 minutes, the students appeared to have concluded their work. Hogan flashed the lights, and all students looked up expectantly. Next she suggested that they leave their magnets and bags on the tables, and she invited each group back to the front of the room to discuss their experiments.

Teacher: Did you test all of your materials and all of your magnets? Sharon, I know you are the reporter for your group; tell us how your group planned its work. (Each group contributes its planning steps.) What did you do next? (Several groups mention her suggestion that they arrange their objects into two groups, those that pulled and those that did not.) Well, what did you find out? Which objects belonged together? (She writes two headings on the board: *Objects Magnet Pulled* and *Objects Magnet Did Not Pull.* The students complete the list by classifying the objects they had tested.)

Teacher: Did all the magnets pull the same objects?

Students: Yes!

Teacher: Well, then, it's time to find out what we learned.

Elena: (Tentatively raising her hand) Magnets pull metals.

Teacher: (Writing the names of the metals or metal alloys next to each object in the first list) Will magnets pull all metals?

William: No. Magnets only pull objects that have iron or steel in them.*

GROUP WORK EVALUATION

Hogan smiled and said, "By golly, you have stated a good rule about magnets," and she wrote it on the board. "Now, boys and girls, what did you think about your first experience working in small groups during science? Let's talk about it." Hogan led the discussion so that students responded to the following questions:

- When you do group work, should everyone get to talk? (Yes.)
- Is it possible for all members of the group to agree? (No.)

---

*Content for this lesson was based on information from Peter C. Gega, *Science in Elementary Education*, 6th ed. (New York: Macmillan, 1990).

- How did you decide what to do when you did not agree?
- Why was it a good idea to try the experiment in different ways?
- Why is it important to listen to all members of the group?
- What was most difficult about group work?
- What was easiest?
- In what ways was your group successful?
- If you work in groups tomorrow, what will you want to remember?

Reviewing the components of Mary Hogan's lesson using small group instruction, we note that there were definite steps involved in the process:

1. Large group instruction and motivation
2. Communication of the assignment
3. Organizing for work
   - Standards for group work
   - Providing materials
   - What to do if the group needs help
   - How the teacher can get students' attention, if needed
   - Time constraints (if any)
   - Assigning work settings
4. Small group instructional process
5. Evaluation
   - Content evaluation
   - Group work evaluation

WHAT DO CHILDREN LEARN?

This section relates student success to the achievement motivation goals discussed in Chapter 4.

LEARNING THROUGH SUCCESS

Among all the other things that the school teaches, children learn to recognize success and failure. The student who has difficulty learning to read experiences failure. After repeated failures in reading or in other areas of the curriculum, everything the child does is affected. Lack of success affects motivation and after a period of time, peers and teacher recognize the student as a loser. If the child perceives this conception by others, he or she learns to play the role of a loser and accepts and anticipates extended failure.

Effective, conscientious teachers can avert the disaster of recurring failure by de-emphasizing areas of weakness. This is not to suggest that reading or other skill areas lack importance, merely that appropriate goals can be set, and legitimate, private rewards bestowed so all children can earn praise from peers and teacher and experience success. Table 5.5 identifies four sets of behavior needed by children to feel successful at school. If a teacher develops activities to promote each of the behavioral goals, students will have the opportunity to be successful at one or more activities throughout the school day. Activities should focus on doing and reasoning. It is important to provide a wide range of activities so every student can be good at something in the course of the day.

It is especially important that students rotate leadership roles. Billy should not always be a group leader or a demonstrator of skills. Mabel should not always

be the one being tutored. If students are to feel successful, they must perceive that others are aware of their strengths. This will only occur through peer interaction, and it must be programmed by the teacher.

In Karen Adazzio's seventh-grade classroom, she noted that although Bert was able to observe every detail in a picture, he read poorly. Bert was often aggressive, and she recognized that he had a very low self-concept. It occurred to her that it might be possible to use Bert's visual strengths to build his self-confidence and ultimately develop his reading skills. She asked Bert if he owned a camera. He said yes, and she suggested that the two of them confer about a project. (Before the conference, Adazzio contacted Bert's mother to obtain her permission to initiate a visual literacy program for Bert.) Bert developed a project that

Table 5.5   School Success-Oriented Behaviors

| Emergent Behaviors | MEANS TO ACHIEVE | | |
	Behavioral Goals	Teacher Behavior	Learner Behavior
Ego-satisfying behaviors	Self-confidence Self-respect Optimism Security Status	Defines class organization, structure, requirements, constraints. Provides motivation, acceptance, clarification, reinforcement, evaluative procedures. Provides appropriate learning and responsibilities.	With knowledge of class organization, structure, requirements, and constraints, develops personal goals for work, companionship, leisure. Chooses both independent and group activities. Acts as a leader and a participant.
Learner-assertive behaviors	Questing Seeking Searching Defining Analyzing Conceptualizing Evaluating	Develops challenging tasks for independent and group inquiry. Develops problem-solving skills and social conscience skills utilizing conflict situations.	Utilizes vocational research, value clarification skills in large and small groups, and independent tasks. Participates in buzz groups, dramatics, construction, exhibits, debates, interview, panels, reporting.
Independence-oriented behaviors	Initiating Decision making Individuality Creativity Dependability	Provides time, space, materials for independent projects (environmental, creative, and skill-oriented).	Defines goal, decides means, develops project or specific task. Participates in cartooning, crossword puzzles, cooking, modeling, sewing, reading, picturemaking hobbies.
Group-satisfying behaviors	Cooperation Rationality Responsibility Respectfulness	Develops group projects and tasks: research, conflict problems, art projects, music making, science experiments, group roles in simulations.	Participates as both leader and group member in small group projects, discussions, games, simulations, art and music works, experiments, choral speaking, listening activities, puppeteering, plays, service projects.

Source: Johanna K. Lemlech, *Handbook for Successful Urban Teaching* (New York: Harper, 1977), p. 58.

involved photographing the community around the school and interviewing homeowners and business people that he knew. He presented the project to his classmates. Using a camera and a tape recorder, Bert learned about the community. Other members of the class learned about the community by reading and utilizing resource materials. Bert's activities were developed with Adazzio's assistance. The behaviors she was focusing on and the activities used to achieve the performance components are outlined in Table 5.6.

When Bert and other members of his class engaged in small group work, they had to listen to each other and take turns talking. Group work in Bert's classroom was practiced almost daily. Students rotated roles of group leader and recorder. Adazzio taught them to participate. As a result of repeated experiences with group work, the students were actively engaged in constructive reasoning.

By changing the typical projects in this classroom, Adazzio manipulated the evaluative feedback that each child received. Bert was perceived by his classmates as a conscientious, creative, rational person, and he began to look at himself as a leader. In time, Adazzio will encourage Bert to talk about his pictures and write stories about them. The stories will be typed, and Bert will develop reading skills by using his own instructional materials.

GROUPING: FROM LARGE TO SMALL

On another occasion, Karen Adazzio's seventh graders were studying world geography and related issues. They had just observed that the area of the Middle East called Israel was in fact the size of about the state of New Jersey. "How come," asked a student named Hank, "both the Arabs and the Jews claim they own the same land?"

Table 5.6 Applying Success-Oriented Behaviors	*Ego-Satisfying Behavior*	*Activities to Achieve*
	Self-confidence	Chooses to take neighborhood pictures with own camera.
	Self-responsibility	
	Optimism	Pursues task and completes pictures.
	Security	Plans and sets goals.
	Status	Communicates plan to classmates.
		Demonstrates how to take pictures, use a light meter, focus on center of interest.
	Learner-Assertive Behavior	
	Questing	Interviews homeowners and businesspeople.
	Seeking	Tapes interviews.
	Searching	Edits tapes and pictures.
	Defining	Prepares tapes and pictures for classroom demonstration.
	Analyzing	
	Conceptualizing	
	Evaluating	
	Independence-Oriented Behaviors	
	Initiating	Mounts pictures on poster board.
	Decision making	Develops a second tape of background music.
	Creativity	Coordinates interviews with background music;
	Individuality	sequences pictures.
	Dependability	Presents project to class and answers questions about it.
	Group-Satisfying Behaviors	
	Cooperation,	Works as a small group leader to discuss community problems and to plan a community service project.
	Rationality	
	Responsibility	
	Respectfulness	

"That's a good question, Hank," Adazzio responded, "let's all consider it. What do you think are the bases for the Arab-Israeli dispute over the land? Mona, what do you think?"

Mona:	I think Jewish and Arab groups both believe their religious roots are in Jerusalem.
Shelly:	Don't both groups call Israel the Promised Land?
John:	Those are both related to their religious claims.
Teacher:	Um, interesting point. Are there other issues besides religious concerns that affect this area and their relationships?
Bill:	Didn't the United Nations give the land to the Jews after World War II? Who did the land belong to before the Jewish people set up a government?
Angie:	Can the United Nations just give away land whenever they want to?
Sal:	I think it was important that the Jewish people have a homeland, and Israel is considered the natural home for them.
Teacher:	So far we have considered religious reasons affecting both the Jewish people and Arab people; Bill, Angie, and Sal raised another set of questions. What are they focusing on? Bill, what did you have in mind when you asked the question about the United Nations?
Bill:	I guess what is puzzling me are the legal issues. I don't know who the land belonged to, and what right the U.N. had to make the decision.
Teacher:	OK, and Sal, what did you mean by "natural" home for the Jewish people?
Sal:	It was tied to Bill's and Angie's questions about legal rights, but I seem to remember that maybe there is something about historical rights to the land.
Jerry:	All people need a national homeland. Shouldn't that affect their relationships, and is that connected to historical rights?
Jean:	What about talking about how Israel has had to defend its homeland against Arab attacks, and also the Arab people who have been displaced because of those wars?
Teacher:	You are doing so well, I can barely keep up with you. Let me see if you can help me identify the issues. First, we identified conflicting religious claims; then we raised the issue of legal rights.
Sal:	And I said there were historical issues.
Jerry:	Yeah, and I think you need to consider nationalism as a need or issue.
Teacher:	All right. I have written five categories on the board: religious claims, legal claims, historical claims, nationalist claims, other claims. Consider what you are most interested in. When I name the category, you raise your hand if you want to research that particular question. We will take time today and tomorrow for some group research. We'll have a short discussion today after you have worked for about 25 minutes, and tomorrow you will present your conclusions to the class. Remember, once in your groups, you should decide who will chair the group, how you will take notes, what each person's responsibility will be, and how you will present your conclusions to the class. All right, who wants to study . . .?

ANALYSIS OF CLASSROOM EPISODE

We do not know what preceded this discussion or much about what the students are studying and the cultural milieu of the classroom, yet certain patterns of behavior are evident:

- The students appear to feel comfortable with initiating questions. (See Hank's first question.)
- It is evident that Adazzio feels no need to have co-action (conversation to and from herself with a single student). The students listen to each other and respond to each other.
- Group research appears to be a regular means of learning in the classroom. (No big deal was made of moving from large to small group activity.)
- Adazzio was grouping by student interest and student choice. Again, the students appeared to be accustomed to this.
- Leadership and task responsibilities are left to the students to identify and make decisions about.
- Adazzio communicates task and time constraints so that students can make pacing decisions.

In reviewing the interaction among students in Adazzio's classroom, it is obvious that the students were interested in thinking about the Israeli-Arab issues;

they were involved and challenged. As a teacher, Adazzio provided interactive support in the form of her questions. She did not offer her opinion or try to lead the students' exploration of the issues.

PLANNING FOR THE BEGINNING OF SCHOOL

School districts often schedule a "pupil-free" day before school starts to provide the staff with an opportunity to plan schedules, agree on committee and whole faculty meeting times, and most importantly, give the teachers time to ready their classrooms for students. In Mary Hogan's year-round school, she vacations only three weeks at a time. Greg Thomas still enjoys a summer vacation, and Karen Adazzio has a somewhat modified year-round schedule.

When Mary Hogan was "off-track" (vacation time), her classroom was used by another teacher. In this way classroom space was never wasted. The school was always open. Arriving in her classroom after a vacation break, Hogan found the tables stacked in the middle of the room. There were four bookcases and two tall display tables. She also located a television, a tape recorder, a computer and printer, and an old record player. On top of one of the cupboards she found her chart rack, and in the closet area there was a chart box on wheels apparently available for her use. Hogan decided to go to the teacher's room and change into work clothes so she could begin the task of moving furniture.

Hogan arranged the furniture first, putting the bookcases under the windows and setting several tables under bulletin boards to serve as interest centers. Using an "E" formation, she organized the tables to accommodate the 31 children. Figure 5.2 illustrates Hogan's room plan. Her plan encourages some social interaction among the children. She knew that at times this might be a disadvantage. (The importance of the physical arrangement of the classroom for class discussion is emphasized in Chapter 6. Hogan situated her desk so it would not impede the traffic pattern in the classroom, nor would it be a focal point.

With the room somewhat organized, Hogan began the task of reading the students' cumulative records. She wanted to find out which literature books the children had used last semester, so she would have a guide in the choice of appropriate books for this semester. The cumulative card in some school districts provides information about students' past experiences in school, such as achievement test scores, textbooks used, and past social studies units. Although Hogan knew that she would do diagnostic testing during the first week of school to pinpoint the children's precise ability levels, she felt it was important that the students begin to read on the first day of school.

Slowly Hogan determined her textbook needs. She conferred with a colleague next door, and then began the laborious task of carrying the different books into the classroom. She reviewed pencil, crayon, and paper needs for the room and brought in chart paper and other supplies for herself. As the room began to take shape, she turned her attention to the bulletin boards.

ROOM ENVIRONMENT

Mary Hogan recognized the value of a cheerful and thought-provoking environment. She wanted to establish interest centers that would support and encourage students to explore and discover, and she hoped that the centers would provide for individual differences. As she surveyed her classroom, she decided that she needed a science center, an art and music center, a social studies center, and a library center. The library center was the easiest. Hogan hung a beautiful poster of children reading books on the bulletin board. Then, in the bookcase below, she put out some of her own books. On top of the bookcase, using book stands, she opened several books to display a picture. She put a small round rug and a beanbag cushion on the floor next to the bookcase. She knew that such furnishings would attract the students (see Table 5.7).

Science Center

Hogan perused the science text to see if any of the units corresponded to some of her own interests and to see if she had supportive materials to set up a center. She decided to begin with a unit about rocks and minerals because she had done a similar unit in student teaching, and she knew she could encourage the children to bring in their favorite rocks. She placed several baskets on a table by the bulletin board. In one basket she placed rocks with different textures, and next to it she put a sign asking the students, *How Do These Rocks Feel?* In another basket she placed rocks that were unusual in color, and near this basket she put another sign, *How Many Colors Do You See?* She would plan lessons to encourage the students to categorize the rocks by both texture and shape.

Figure 5.2   Hogan's Room Plan

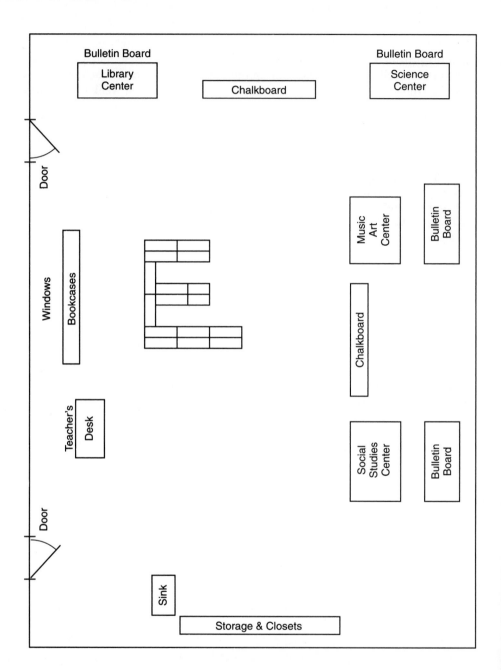

Art and Music Center

On the bulletin board Hogan hung a painting of children dancing. She displayed the second-grade music books and her own autoharp below the picture. She anticipated that she would also display other instruments, but she felt it might be better to develop room standards before she put out too many temptations.

Social Studies Center

Hogan decided that she wanted to display a series of pictures depicting people's basic needs. She had some pictures of her own, and she decided take a look at the school's resource center to see if there were some pictures that she could borrow. Ultimately she decided on one picture of a shelter in New Guinea, another picture of farmers irrigating a field, and a third picture of a

Table 5.7   Teacher Checklist for Beginning of Semester

Room Environment	*Need to Obtain?*
Student Furniture	
Traffic Lanes	
Display Tables, Cabinets, Bookcases	
Bulletin Boards	
Storage Facilities	

Equipment/Resources	*Need to Obtain?*
Computer, Printer	
Television Monitor	
VCR	
Overhead Projector	
Chart Rack	
Map Rack	
Textbooks	
Maps	
Manipulatives	
Student Supplies (pencils, paper)	
Subject Field Specialty Materials	

Procedures, School, and Classroom	*Plans Completed?*
Fire Drill, Exits, Area for Class	
Earthquake Drill	
Bell Schedule	
Physical Education Schedule	
Recess, Lunch, Dismissal Schedule	
Lavatory Facilities (location)	
School-Related Teacher Responsibilities	
Seating Chart, Name Cards	
Class List	
System for Checking out Texts to Students	
How can I reach office personnel, if needed?	
School-wide Rules	
Availability of Nurse	
Monitor/Helper Chart	

Instructional Planning for First Day of School	*Plans Completed?*
How shall I introduce myself?	
How shall I have students get acquainted?	
How shall I become acquainted with students?	
How will I motivate students about our semester activities?	
How shall the students and I decide on classroom standards?	
Have I planned adequately for content and activity blocks with appropriate time allotments for the entire school day?	
Do I have extra activities to serve as "sponges" for unplanned time?	

home vegetable garden. Underneath the pictures appeared the caption, *What Do All People Need?* She placed a small picture file near the bulletin board so the students could browse through the file for other pictures that would help them answer the bulletin board question. Social studies books were also displayed.

Learning Centers

The learning center is designed to motivate, reinforce, and support students' learning needs. A center approach enables the teacher to differentiate instruction to meet individual ability levels and learning-style needs. The center attempts to lure students, coax them, and appeal to their natural inquisitiveness.

ARRANGING SEATING

Although it was getting late and Mary Hogan was rapidly becoming exhausted, she had to establish a seating chart before she left school that first day. The chart would help her learn to identify the students quickly.

Using her class list and her health cards, Hogan began the task of establishing a seating chart. First she sorted through the health cards to identify students with special problems. She noted that she had one child with a partial hearing loss and another student with a limp. She decided on their placement in the classroom and then she began to cluster the rest of the children. The principal had told her earlier that she had one student who sometimes had difficulty working with others; she seated this student so he had a neighbor only on one side. She did not seat students by ability levels, having decided that this practice often had a negative effect on motivation to learn.

THE DAILY SCHEDULE

Finally, Hogan tackled the important task of developing her daily schedule. She studied the elementary curriculum and divided the subjects into major time blocks for teaching purposes.

Language Arts included reading, speaking skills, written skills, spelling, listening skills, handwriting, and literature.

Social Studies/Science included geography, history, political science, economics, psychology, anthropology, sociology, the science of living things, the study of matter and energy, the study of the earth, and the study of the universe.

Physical Education/Health included physical fitness, motor skills, and rhythmic experiences, along with personal and community health.

One of Hogan's main concerns was to intermix active and concentrated experiences so students would not be sitting too long without the opportunity to move around and stretch. First and second graders were at school for $5^1/2$ hours; Hogan was aware that this was a little longer than was customary, requiring her to make a special effort to interweave activities carefully. She also intended to use the longer periods of time for integrating subject fields. She knew that there would be occasions when she would want to use the period after recess or lunch for special projects. Hogan developed the following schedule for her second graders:

Lower Elementary Schedule

8:30–8:40	Class Business/Sharing
8:40–9:40	Language Arts
9:40–10:00	Lower-Grade Recess
10:00–10:45	Language Arts
10:45–11:10	Physical Education/Health
11:10–11:40	Mathematics
11:40–12:40	Lunch
12:40–12:55	Literature/Music
12:55–1:55	Social Studies/Science/Art
1:55–2:00	Cleanup/Sharing/Dismissal

Greg Thomas's schedule provides a contrast. Remember that his students were fifth graders in a southern rural school, and they attended school from 8:30 A.M. to 2:30 P.M. He, too, used broad subject areas to designate his time periods. His daily schedule looked like this:

Upper Elementary Schedule

8:30–8:35	Class Business
8:35–10:00	Language Arts
10:00–10:20	Upper-Grade Recess
10:20–11:20	Social Studies
11:20–12:00	Visual and Performing Arts
12:00–1:00	Lunch
1:00–1:40	Mathematics
1:40–2:10	Physical Education
2:10–3:00	Science/Health

Karen Adazzio's middle school schedule provides still another variation on how to allocate time during the school day. Adazzio's schedule had to be worked out with five other teachers who share responsibility for 160 students. The schedule below demonstrates

Teaching Hints: Scheduling

Plan instruction in 90 minute blocks of time:

- Language arts
- Mathematics
- Social studies and science rotate in a block
- Music and art and physical education

Schedule recess periods prior to a new subject block rather than in the middle of instruction.

how one group of 32 students moves through the daily schedule.

Middle School Schedule

8:30–10:10	Humanities Core, Social Studies
10:10–10:25	Recess
10:25–12:05	Math/Science/Health
12:05–1:00	Lunch
1:00–2:00	Elective Modules: Practical and Fine Arts, Foreign Language
2:05–2:55	Physical Education/Health
2:55	Dismissal (three times per week)
3:00–3:30	House Meetings (twice weekly)

All three teachers are conscious of the need to integrate subject fields to maximize both time and learning. In Adazzio's humanities core, she teaches reading, literature, language arts, history, and geography. The elective modules run for six weeks at a time with students choosing a foreign language class that meets twice weekly for the entire semester and another module that meets three times per week for six weeks. The elective modules for seventh graders include visual and performing arts, food preparation, photography, sculpture, and print shop.

MAINSTREAMED STUDENTS

Mary Hogan has two children with disabilities in her classroom part of each school day. As she planned her daily schedule, she thought they would be able to participate during recess, physical education/health, lunch, and the afternoon program, which included literature, music, and social studies. It might even be possible for the special education children to join the second graders for mathematics. Hogan knew that she would have to consult with the special education teacher.

Greg Thomas also had several students with disabilities. He anticipated that these students would join the rest of his group beginning at recess time and probably spend the rest of the day with his class.

THE FIRST DAY OF SCHOOL

Mary Hogan knew that it was likely there would be a number of new pupils enrolling the first day of the new session. Therefore, she planned academic tasks of a review nature so she could monitor how well students were working and yet be free to give attention to a new student if necessary.

Hogan planned to begin language arts by reading several of Aesop's fables to the class. Then she would group the students heterogeneously and have them read a story about an animal in their literature book. She would ask the students to decide in their groups how the fables differed from the story in their book.

While the students were reading, she would walk around the room, observing the children and offering assistance when needed. She expected that the good readers would help others in their group read the story. The groups would then share their ideas with the whole class.

After the groups discussed the story in their book and how it was different from the fables, Hogan would ask them to draw pictures about either the fables or the story they had read. Then they would be asked to write their own story about their picture. In this way Hogan would begin the writing process. Both spelling and manuscript writing would be informal activities and part of the editing stage of the writing process.

Hogan planned to talk to the students about the bulletin boards. She would help them read the captions and ask them to identify what interested them. Her intent was to begin the science unit that first day by asking children to name the colors they saw in the rocks. She would also ask the students to describe how the rocks felt, and then introduce the concept of texture. She hoped that they would identify the words *smooth*, *rough*, *slippery*, and *jagged*.

For physical education Hogan would play the game Around the World, in which the children are organized into two concentric circles. To play the game, the inside circle sits down on the playground, while the outside circle stands behind a seated player. The teacher gives a direction (skip) and the outside group follows the direction (skips) around the circle until the teacher blows a whistle. Then the outside circle must scamper to stand behind one of the seated players. Several children stand in the center of the circle, and when the whistle blows they, too, try to find a place behind a seated player. After a few minutes the two circles change places. Hogan remembered that this was a very active and exciting game for second graders, and she hoped that it would extract some of their wiggles!

SETTING STANDARDS

With most of her plans made for the first day of school, Mary Hogan turned her attention to classroom management details. She thought about her room arrangement and pondered the traffic pattern. She would discuss exiting and entering patterns with the students. She was also concerned about the need for classroom monitors, so she prepared a pocket chart for that purpose. She expected the students to be able to handle classroom routines without her direction. The following monitoring jobs would have to be performed by the students: door, lights, play equipment, office, window, lunch count, library, art, paper, attendance, books, flag, and centers. Some of the jobs would require more than one person.

Since control problems would be less likely if she could name students quickly, she decided to make name cards to place in front of each student.

She anticipated classroom problems that could be alleviated if the students were encouraged to develop class standards or rules. She decided that the following problem areas should be discussed:

- Walking in the classroom
- The use of quiet voices
- Respecting classmates' right to work
- Putting work aside when the teacher has something important to share
- Maintaining a clean and neat environment
- Pencil sharpening
- Use of the classroom fountain
- Sharing materials (books, games, equipment)
- Listening to others' viewpoints

She anticipated that she would discuss these problems with her students as the need arose. For example, before recess would be an appropriate time to discuss the traffic pattern for leaving the classroom. Also, sometime during the morning she ought to talk to the students about fire drill routines.

Hogan would discuss quiet voices and most of the other routines with the students when they began formal classroom instruction. The class rules would be recorded on the chalkboard until the end of the day, at which time Hogan would transfer them to a chart.

GETTING ACQUAINTED

Mary Hogan recognized that the cumulative records and the health cards provided her with just a bare outline of information about each child. In order to personalize her teaching technique for each student, she wanted to become better acquainted with the interests, attitudes, and personality of each of her students. To begin this task she would read a story to her students about hobbies. After motivating the students to talk about their personal interests, she would have each student write and illustrate a book called *All About Me.* This project would initiate an integrated language and art program.

Other Get-Acquainted Techniques

As Mary Hogan observed her students playing at recess and lunchtime, she would learn about their capacity for cooperative play and teamwork. During the first couple of weeks, she would test their physical skills through skill-related tasks at physical education time (see Chapter 16).

She planned get-acquainted sessions and would invite small groups of children to eat lunch with her in the classroom. The informality of the small group lunch session would provide her with new insights about each student.

She would introduce a puppet family to the students and have different students role-play family decisions related to specific problems:

- Maya was not doing her homework.
- Benjy was ill. Who would stay with him if he could not go to school?

They would also role-play family celebrations: Susan's birthday, Dad's commendation from the police department for bravery, Mom's new job. Hogan would use a variety of diagnostic tests to assess students' ability levels, but she was just as concerned with learning about students' self-reliance, social skills, and sense of belonging. For these capacities she would need to rely on her own observation skills and some sociometric measures (see Chapter 12).

GETTING ACQUAINTED WITH THE COMMUNITY

Karen Adazzio planned to take one of her team members, a new teacher, on a drive around the school community. To understand the students they were to teach, Karen recognized the importance of visiting the community in order to learn about the problems, interests, services, and cultural priorities of the residents. She had prepared a list of 14 questions they would use to facilitate their observation.

COMMUNITY QUESTIONS*

1. Who lives in the community?
2. What is the residential pattern (apartments, single homes)?
3. How does the natural and manmade environment contribute to or detract from the community?
4. What businesses appear to flourish in the community? What businesses appear to flounder?
5. Are there social services within the community available to assist residents (hospitals, clinics, police, fire, legal aid)?
6. Do recreational facilities exist within the community (for children, for adults)?
7. Are distinctive culture characteristics apparent (specialty shops, restaurants, cultural sites, unique patterns, or environmental characteristics)?
8. Are there businesses, places of interest, or sites for field trips?
9. Are resource people available in the community to assist in the classroom?
10. What kinds of work opportunities exist in the community?
11. What special problems are apparent in the community?
12. If there are businesses in the community, does any one type predominate?
13. What special interests are obvious in the community? Do these interests relate to cultural priorities?
14. How might your own interests and talents assist the community?

DAILY TASKS OF THE TEACHER

Most of the tasks of the teacher can be subsumed into two major headings of teacher responsibility: *instruc-*

tion and *management*. (Instruction is the major focus of Chapters 6–8.) A third area of responsibility, not yet discussed, is the teacher's *leadership* role, which is emphasized in Chapter 18.

INSTRUCTIONAL ROLE DECISIONS

Lesson Planning

Upon completion of student teaching, most teacher candidates comment, "Hurrah—no more lesson plans!" In reality, the effective (and experienced) teacher continues to use a lesson plan, but one that is less detailed than a student teacher's plan. In this section we will take a look at the lesson plan of a student teacher, the lesson plan notes of two experienced teachers, and a teacher's weekly plan. You will learn about long-term planning in Chapter 9.

As teachers become more experienced, they are able to anticipate what students will say and their own responses as well. Therefore, the experienced teacher does not have to write these things into the lesson plan procedures. Provision for interaction, discussion, and the thinking process for problem solving no longer appear under procedures, as they do in the student teacher's lesson plan in Figure 5.3 because the experienced teacher automatically provides time for these things to happen. Look at the experienced teacher's lesson plan in Figure 5.4 and you will notice how succinct the plan is compared to the student teacher's plan. For discussion to be effective, however, even experienced teachers have to plan their questioning approach prior to instruction and have cue cards ready for use. Figure 5.5 gives examples of some prompts used by an experienced teacher to keep a lesson moving ahead.

Some teachers like to file their lesson plans into a loose-leaf notebook or a four-by-six-inch box. The advantage of doing this is that it is easy to refer to when a student returns from absence or when a parent comes in for a conference.

Figure 5.6 shows Mary Hogan's weekly planning schedule. She found this form in a special booklet entitled *Weekly Planning Forms* that was given to her by the principal at the first faculty meeting. Hogan still needs lesson planning notes for some subjects, but the weekly plan helps her remember special events and document subject matter preparation through the course of the semester. It is also a handy guide for the substitute teacher if Hogan is absent.

---

*Adapted from J. K. Lemlech, *Handbook for Successful Urban Teaching* (New York: Harper, 1977), pp. 100–101.

Figure 5.3 A Student Teacher's Lesson Plan

Subject: Mathematics—Fifth Grade
Objectives: Students will measure the perimeter of a rectangle.
   Students will use a formula to find the perimeter of a rectangle.
   Students will draw a square.
   Students will define perimeter, rectangle, square.
Materials: Ruler, paper, cardboard shapes, guinea pig, and cage
Procedures:

1. *Motivation:* Display a guinea pig in a cage. Comment that cage is too small, but tell the students, "I did not know what size to buy since I didn't know the size of this cage. How can I find out the size of this cage?" (Students will respond, "Measure it.")
2. Allow several students to measure cage.
3. Have students draw size of cage on board.
4. Have students label *length* and *width.*
5. Have all students draw a small cage on their own paper.
6. Observe students' work.
7. Ask "Do you know the shape of the cage?" (Introduce word *rectangle* and define it.)
8. Ask "Do you know another shape in which all four sides are the same?" (Introduce concept of square as a rectangle with equal sides.)

9. Have children draw a square and label it. (Observe students.)
10. Ask: "If I want to know the distance around the guinea pig's cage, how can I find out?"
11. (Students respond, "Add the lengths and widths.')
12. Have students do this with the chalkboard example.
13. Explain that the word *perimeter* means the distance around the outside of a geometric shape.
14. Ask "Can you think of a shortcut to find the perimeter of a shape?" (Give clues if they cannot.)
15. "Let's see if the shortcut works. Let's use the size of the cage to experiment." (Cage size = 12″ × 18″. 2 × 12 = ? 2 × 18 = ? "Now what do we do?") Pause for suggestions. ("Yes, add them together.")
16. Give students formula: $(2 \times L) + (2 \times W) = $ Perimeter.
17. Hand out cardboard geometric shapes to students.
18. Have students practice measuring and using formula to find perimeter.
19. Students trace shapes on their own paper, measure and label widths and lengths, and use formula to solve the question.
20. *Evaluation:*
    a. Review meaning of perimeter.
    b. Ask students for formula for finding perimeter.
    c. Ask students for definition of *square* and rectangle.
    d. Have students report on perimeter of the card-board shapes.

Integration of Subject Fields and Interdisciplinary Teaching

These two concepts are discussed in depth in Chapter 9, but Mary Hogan needs to consider both concepts as she does her lesson planning. Hogan thinks about **integration of instruction** when she considers the skills students need to read out of the science book and when she uses science and social studies concepts during spelling. Integrating subject fields applies the principle of what Ausubel (1969) called *integrative reconciliation.* Students'

Figure 5.4 An Experienced Teacher's Lesson Plan

Subject: Math
Objectives: Measure, draw, define rectangle, square, perimeter. Use formula to find perimeter.
Materials: Guinea pig cage (for motivation), ruler, shapes
Procedure:

1. *Motivation:* Use cage with guinea pig!
2. Introduce L., W. Use cage.
3. Have students draw; observe.
4. Define rectangle, square.
5. Have students find P. of cage.
6. Explain formula.
7. Have students practice using shapes.
8. Evaluate objectives.

Figure 5.5 An Experienced Teacher's Lesson Plan Notes and Question Prompts

1. Display picture of partial environment.
2. Are you familiar with what picture shows?
3. Does it show everything that is around it?
4. What seems to be missing?
5. What evidence do you have? How do you know something is missing?
6. How do you suppose we could find out what is missing?
7. Do you know what these (resources) are?
8. How do you use these resources?
9. How would a scientist, mathematician, or judge obtain proof?
10. Today you're going to be a research explorer. You are going to collect evidence that will help you decide what is missing in the picture. Let's talk about what you will need.

Adapted with permission from planning notes of Lillian Walker, teacher in the Los Angeles Unified School District.

Figure 5.6 Weekly Planning Schedule

	Monday	Tuesday	Wednesday	Thursday	Friday	Special Notes
Reading	Predict endings to stories Read in literature books	Use science book, Chapter 2	Identify central problem in stories	Read about fossils in science book, pp. 110–114	Free choice reading Read orally	Use centers
Writing	Write new endings for stories Share endings	Choose topic Begin own story	Revise stories	Edit stories	Share stories	
Spelling and handwriting	Use words from rock center	Teach patterns in words; Slippery, jagged Practice writing	Use words in sentences and stories →	→	Spelling test	
Physical education/ health	Teach side throw Play Caboose Dodge Ball	←	Play Circle Relay ←	Rhythms: Teach Hokey-Pokey* Practice skipping	Nutrition: Use health book—Chapter 1	*Borrow record from Miss Smith
Math	Use flannel board for story of 5; use sticks; draw story of 5	Practice addition facts through 5	Tell number stories Use flannel board	Teach hours; use individual clocks; use practice sheets on clocks →		
Literature and music	Teach Grey Squirrel Sing old favorites	← ←	Read: *Horton Hatches an Egg*	Teach *America* Review songs	Read poetry from speech book	
Science, social studies (SS), art	Science: Work in groups to classify rocks; discuss properties of rocks	Science: Use tools to change shape of rocks; discuss	SS: Initiate unit (use arranged environment), "What do all people need"	SS: Research "Basic Needs" Use picture file, filmstrip, chart, books	Art: Finger painting	
Special Notes	Send note home with Billy M. for parent conference			Remind children to bring aprons for art lesson		

99

prior experiences are utilized as new ideas are integrated with previously learned knowledge. Instead of gaining knowledge in a fragmented or compartmentalized single subject approach (like a textbook), ideas are broadly related across subject fields. This permits the elementary and middle school teacher to develop a balanced curriculum. The daily schedule, defined by broad subject fields, is designed to facilitate integrative and interdisciplinary teaching. The daily schedule should not be interpreted so strictly that it hinders the integration of subject fields or reflects an unbalanced curriculum.

Interdisciplinary instruction helps students make connections between subject fields. For example, one might take the concept of *role* and explore its meaning in different disciplines. Consider playing the role of Peter Pan in a musical production and studying roles in feudal society. Interdisciplinary teaching emphasizes the linkages among disciplines. Teachers must consider both integrative opportunities and interdisciplinary instruction when planning curriculum.

DATA GATHERING

A student's success in school is dependent on the teacher's accurate **assessment** of cognitive and affective learner needs. Assessment occurs in a variety of ways. First the teacher must decide what it is she or he needs to know about students. Specify skills, concepts, attitudes, and values. Once this is done, decide what techniques or procedures to use for the assessment.

Assessment

Use simple checklists to evaluate skill sequences, specific behaviors, or interests and concepts. (See Chapter 11 for examples.) Record your observations of students' interests, skill performance, and on-task behavior on observation cards. Anecdotal records, conferences, and diaries contribute to the assessment process. Tests you prepare as well as standardized achievement tests provide data for interpretation. Once you have gathered the data, diagnose needs. An accurate diagnosis is the *sine qua non* for appropriate instructional planning.

Diagnosis

The term *diagnosis* is often used in education the same way it is used in medicine. Assessment provides the data, the symptoms, and the signs. You use the data to interpret the condition of learning and the situation most likely to facilitate the learning process. You can

Teaching Hints:
Instructional Planning

When faced with problems of "what works," expert teachers use creative ideas, advice of colleagues, and professional lore (Sykes, 1996, p. 466).

record technical descriptions based on the data, although it is not always necessary to do so.

Prescription

Diagnosis is the interpretation of the data, but prescription refers to the plan the teacher uses to carry out instruction. Mary Hogan, our fictitious second-grade teacher, decided that Charlie was continually frustrated trying to complete classroom assignments. She decided to change Charlie's assignments to what she and Charlie thought would be manageable for him. The result was that Charlie expressed delight in his own progress and began to make great strides in several subject fields. Hogan's prescription was obviously accurate and appropriate for Charlie.

Classroom grouping decisions should always be based on a careful analysis of the school and grade level data. For example, at one school, teachers were told to move five students from an all fifth-grade classroom to a fourth/fifth-grade combination room and to move five fourth-grade students to a third/fourth-grade combination room. The teachers made their choices without any data about the students. In both cases the consequences were atypical; third-grade students were superior in achievement to the fourth-grade students in the third/fourth-grade combination class, and the fourth-grade students were superior in achievement to the fifth-grade students in the fourth/fifth-grade combination room. As a result, there were a lot of highly frustrated students whose egos were affected negatively, and there were also control problems for the teachers.

If the teachers had reviewed the evidence before making their decisions, they would have placed average fourth graders with low-to-average third graders and average fifth graders with low-to-average fourth graders. An appropriate prescription is one that provides for a reasonable instructional program corresponding to students' needs. Selection of the appropriate learning experiences is also based on the prescription. Instruction is based on the assessment, the diagnosis, and the prescription. These three components make up the planning stage for instruction.

INSTRUCTIONAL PLANNING

Presentation

The term *prescription* was used broadly in the previous section to signify the plan for teaching. That plan should also include methodological decisions about teaching strategy and instructional materials. The *presentation* can include actual direct instruction by the teacher or indirect instruction through discovery approaches. Teachers base presentation decisions on grouping needs, individual skill levels, the nature of the learning task, and the appropriateness of the instructional materials. In the classroom the teacher mediates instruction using the plan that was conceived before the beginning of the school day. The greater the teacher's skill in the presentation of instruction, the greater will be the engagement rate of students. (In other words, the students will pay attention!) A carefully planned and structured lesson facilitates students' understanding of what they are expected to learn and how they should go about it. Discovery approaches need to be planned and structured just as carefully as a direct instructional lesson in reading or mathematics.

Monitoring

Monitoring is an instructional task component. During instruction the teacher must keep track of student progress. By checking student progress, the teacher knows whether to deviate from the plan or to carry on. Monitoring is closely related to assessment. If the original assessment provided inaccurate data, then the diagnosis and the prescription will be wrong. The teacher monitors instruction by circulating around the room during practice periods or while students are working in small groups. During a direct instructional episode, teachers frequently monitor progress by asking questions.

Reinforcement

As the teacher monitors instruction, he or she gives feedback to the students. Students' engagement rate is higher when teachers let them know whether they are right, wrong, or on the right track. **Academic feedback** has been closely related to students' achievement by researchers.

Teachers reinforce the purpose of instruction and good study habits by providing time to correct seatwork or homework. At learning centers, you can provide reinforcement by developing a system whereby students can correct their own work or find out if their work is on target. Some curriculum materials and programmed textbooks also provide immediate feedback to the student.

Evaluation

Formative (ongoing) **evaluation** need not be distinguished from monitoring and reinforcement because an ongoing type of evaluation helps keep students on task and provides immediate feedback so the students know if they are progressing. **Summative evaluation** is also a progress report to both teacher and student (as well as parents), but it does not monitor instruction in the same interactive way.

MANAGEMENT DECISIONS

The three components of teacher responsibility—management, instruction, and leadership—should not be separated as if they were distinct entities. The teacher who is not an effective classroom manager will not be an effective instructor, nor will this individual be able to provide leadership. It is only for the purpose of opening up and viewing the varied tasks of the classroom teacher that these three components are isolated as if they were distinct occurrences. The following seven items should provide some insight into teachers' daily management decisions.

1. *Classroom business:* Taking attendance, collecting milk money, handing out notices, collecting parent responses—these are but a few of the daily tasks that teachers perform under the heading of classroom business.

2. *Scheduling:* Coordinating the work of other teachers, such as the music teacher, the special reading teacher, and the special educator, may fall under the heading of arranging the daily schedule. Facilitating the work of these professionals and coordinating their work with your own existing schedule is an important but sometimes wearing task.

3. *Arranging the environment:* Another management task that must be attended to daily is arranging seating for special instructional strategies. How should children be seated during a classroom discussion? What should you do with the tables for a construction lesson?

Should the chairs be stacked during finger painting so students will not touch them? How can you make a learning center more attractive? Should you change the bulletin board display? These and countless other questions are attended to as teachers make environmental decisions.

4. *Anticipating instructional and organizational problems:* One of the most important decisions that teachers make on a daily basis has to do with grouping students for instructional activities. In physical education, how can you ensure that there will be balanced teams and that less-skilled students will not end up with hurt feelings? For small group project or planning experiences, students should be grouped heterogeneously. Should you, the teacher, choose the group that is to work together, or will you allow students to choose? How will you group for the science experiment and the social studies research lesson?

Today is Rhythms day, but the auditorium is not available. Should you rearrange the classroom, or have rhythms outside, or change the activity?

Yesterday it appeared that the students did not understand the math concepts that you taught. Should you reteach or continue on and hope for the best?

Your students have written a class play and will perform it for the other third-grade classrooms, but Billy, the star performer, has a temperature. Should you let him stay and perform, reschedule the play, or attempt it without him?

5. *Supplies:* One of the most frustrating but typical problems of the new teacher is the failure to anticipate material needs. Paper for writing or math work, pencils, art supplies, colored paper, and tagboard for charts all need to be surveyed before instructional time. The teacher who constantly bothers classroom neighbors to borrow materials becomes very unpopular. The need for reference books, such as dictionaries or textbooks, also must be anticipated before class time. Audio-visual equipment is another common supply item that is forgotten until needed. Successful teachers have the right equipment and supplies on hand at the right time.

6. *Routines:* Many classroom routines can be set on a weekly or monthly basis (monitors, group leaders), but you may need to plan some procedures almost on a daily basis. For example, a learning center for language arts and art experiences provided the opportunity for children to make masks. This activity required the use of colored paper, scissors, and paste. The teacher needed to anticipate where the students would put their wastepaper and how they would clean their hands after using paste. A simple paper bag, tacked to the bulletin board, served as a waste container, and because the classroom had no sink, the teacher brought in a pail of water and placed paper towels next to it.

Routines concerned with collecting seatwork, self-correcting center work, or handing out paper and other supplies need to be reinforced daily by the classroom teacher.

7. *Monitoring behavior:* Monitoring instruction has been cited as an instructional component; monitoring behavior is specified as a management component. The line is fine between these two classifications. A key task during instruction is to maintain academic interest and involvement of the students. Research indicates that the higher the engagement rate, the higher the achievement. Substantive feedback is important in instructional monitoring, but just as important is the teacher's expression of with-it-ness. The teacher who communicates awareness of what is happening in the classroom knows precisely when to stand by a student and demand attention, when to smile or make eye contact with a student, when to nod approval or disapproval, and when to change activities.

The seven management tasks discussed above are daily responsibilities, and each needs to be carried out in an efficient manner.

SUMMARY

Classroom Management

1. Classroom management encompasses the teacher's planning, organizing, and monitoring tasks to achieve success in the classroom.
2. Successful classroom management helps students maintain high task involvement.
3. Discipline and classroom management are not synonymous.
4. Discipline problems are symptomatic of a classroom environment that lacks respect, guidance, and responsibility.
5. In democratic environments, students accept responsibility for their behavior because they have had the opportunity to define classroom rules and standards.

Grouping

6. Students should work in both large and small groups throughout the school day.

7. By fostering a sense of belonging to the classroom group, cooperative behavior is encouraged and learning enhanced.
8. Small groups encourage student participation and facilitate differentiation of instruction.
9. To improve students' small group work, evaluation should focus on the substantive accomplishments of the group and group process skills.

Teachers' Daily Tasks

10. Teachers engage in planning, instruction, and management tasks throughout the school day.
11. Planning tasks include organizing the classroom environment, attending to supplies, and short- and long-range instructional planning.
12. Instructional tasks include diagnosing and interpreting students' needs, making methodological decisions, monitoring students' work, and reinforcing and evaluating instruction and learning.
13. Teachers' management tasks include the daily business of the classroom, scheduling, establishing routines, and supervising the work of other adults who may assist in the classroom.

DISCUSSION QUESTIONS AND APPLICATION EXERCISES

1. Students were crowded at lunch tables with about 16 children at each table. They ate their bagged lunches and banged elbows with each other. Some spilled milk; some exchanged sandwiches and desserts. Papers and lunches were flying through the air. The lunch area was dirty and excessively noisy.

   The lunch supervisors blew their whistles. One of the supervisors threatened, "Unless you stop talking and clean up, we will not excuse you to play on the playground." Do you think the supervisors were right to ask the students to be quiet? How would adults act in the same setting? Suggest some alternative ways of handling the lunch problem.
2. Review the *What Would You Do If...?* incident in this chapter and respond to the questions at the end of it.
3. Plan a first day of school using your choice of subject field(s) and grade level.
4. Explain how you will integrate several mainstreamed children into your program.
5. Explain why scheduling longer blocks of time facilitates a thinking curriculum.
6. Why are behavioral approaches to classroom discipline considered quick fix strategies that do not treat the underlying problems? (Should students be "paid" for appropriate behavior? Why or why not?)
7. Suggest some classroom standards that encourage good citizenship and participation in the classroom.
8. How does small group work improve students' social skills?
9. Plan a group activity to develop group identity and a sense of belonging.

CHAPTER

6

Exposition and Discussion Strategies

In this chapter two modes of instruction are explored: expository and discussion. The *expository* mode focuses on the teacher. The teacher's task is to communicate information to students. The teacher may do this through lecturing or sometimes through the use of a combination technique of lecture, question, and short-answer response. Expository teaching is an efficient means to communicate a great deal of information to a large group of students simultaneously. But lecturing and reading are not the only means for expository teaching; direct instruction and comprehension models help to vary the transmission process. *Discussion* techniques, also discussed in this chapter, provide an opportunity for students to share knowledge and gain information from peers. Good discussions require stimulating questions. Both discussion and question strategies are demonstrated in the chapter.

After you study this chapter, you should be able to accomplish the following:

1. Identify the teaching sequence for direct instruction of specific concepts and skills.
2. Differentiate among the three types of practices used in direct instruction.
3. Contrast the comprehension model with the direct instruction mode.
4. Use the advance organizer model of teaching.
5. Explain the use of guided discussion during direct instruction.
6. Identify the characteristics of oral discussions and explain the use of the classroom environment and discussion roles.
7. Identify and define the three types of discussion and corresponding teacher behavior.
8. Identify the characteristics of good questions.
9. Write questions in a cluster sequence to achieve specific purposes.

The main purpose of **expository teaching** is to transmit knowledge. There is very little interaction among students during expository teaching. The classroom environment is controlled, and there is moderate to high structure. The teacher controls discussion by initiating questions and eliciting short-answer responses.

In contrast to transmitting knowledge from teacher to students, the class discussion shares knowledge.

Professional Lexicon

advance organizer A framework for organizing and structuring new knowledge, to facilitate meaningful acquisition of information via presentations and readings.

co-action A back-and-forth conversation between two individuals such as the teacher and a student.

direct instruction A means to teach specific knowledge or skills efficiently using three major processes: presentation, practice, and feedback.

expository teaching Communicating knowledge by controlling the input process. The learner's task is to consume the knowledge using visual and auditory means.

guided practice Engagement of students in acquiring knowledge or skills using practice material while the teacher monitors and provides feedback.

independent practice Students work independently to apply what they have learned by using the skill or knowledge in a new way.

interaction Communication among several individuals involving more than one-way discussion; may be cooperative or combative.

refocusing Reestablishing purpose by reiterating the assignment and clarifying meanings when students go off in the wrong direction or are off-task.

structured practice Controlled practice sessions in which the teacher uses short-answer questions and elicits responses to verify student understanding of what is to be learned.

Students may take equal responsibility with the teacher for stimulating and maintaining a meaningful discussion.

Direct instruction is a type of expository teaching. Direct instruction usually conforms to the following format:

- Diagnosis
- Prescription
- Modeling (presentation, lecture)
- Practice
- Monitoring
- Feedback

DIRECT INSTRUCTION

EFFECTIVE TEACHING OF CONCEPTS AND SKILLS

In the 1970s and early 1980s, a number of researchers confirmed that when teachers maintain a highly structured environment for teaching specific concepts and skills, they are able to maximize student engagement and time on-task. Teaching in this manner is characterized by large group instruction, teacher direction, the academic focus, and the preponderance of practice.

Group Instruction

Though direct instruction may occur when the teacher is working with a small group of students, most typically the teacher is directing the class as a whole. Student performance during instruction is closely monitored to verify understanding and academic engagement.

Teacher-Directed Instruction

The most successful teachers (those whose students achieve highest gains) are strong classroom leaders. They plan their teaching objectives, teach to them in a businesslike way, ask meaningful short-answer questions directed to the students, listen to the student responses, and give immediate feedback.

Academic Focus

During direct instruction the teacher relates what is to be learned to what students already know and communicates to students the purpose of the lesson. The new knowledge or skill is introduced using concrete objects or pictures to assist students learn through both oral and visual means. The teacher models what is to be learned and through sharply focused questions, verifies student understanding by eliciting responses.

Practice

The most important aspect of direct instruction is the focus on practice. After the presentation and modeling, the teacher observes and assists student practice. It is important to provide immediate feedback, telling students what is correct and what is incorrect. Confident that students are gaining competence and understanding, the teacher assigns a second practice time. During this **guided practice** the students receive less assistance, but the teacher monitors the practice and continues to provide feedback. The concept or skill is

During direct instruction, the teacher's task is to communicate information to students

reinforced through **independent practice** as students apply the new knowledge or skill. This may take the form of a homework assignment or an in-class project at a higher cognitive level.

During **structured practice,** it is essential that the teacher ask specific factual questions and elicit student response. The teacher should provide academic feedback during this time. Several studies of low-achieving students verify that convergent questions with single answers should be asked during the practice and drill period and that students should be provided with immediate feedback. Rosenshine and Stevens (1986) note that in most of the studies reviewed, the frequency of direct factual teacher questions and the frequency of accurate student responses were positively associated with high achievement.

Success Is Important. A number of studies emphasize that when students work alone and when they work during the controlled practice period, they need to be successful. Correct answers should be possible at least 80 percent of the time for low socioeconomic students and at least 70 percent of the time for students of high socioeconomic status.

During skill instruction, students need to experience both fact questions and higher cognitive questions. Students also need to participate in recitation immediately after reading textbook content. Recitation serves the dual purpose of providing students with practice recalling content and enabling the teacher to provide students with immediate feedback.

**Teaching Hints:
Designated Instructional Practices**

The research concerning successful skill instruction is specific. The most efficient method appears to be a four-step process:

1. The teacher demonstrates or models the skill objective, and/or presents new information.
2. Students practice the skill, with the teacher observing and providing immediate feedback (structured practice).
3. Students practice the skill with less teacher assistance but with continued teacher monitoring (guided practice).
4. Students apply what has been learned in a different way (independent practice).

Monitoring Independent Practice. The independent practice period usually takes the form of follow-up seatwork during reading instruction or practicing a small number of examples of the skill during mathematics. Since success is so important, the exercises that students do should be relatively easy. As students practice, the teacher monitors the students' work and provides immediate feedback in the form of positive reinforcement or a short explanation when a student needs assistance. The feedback provided to the student should not take more than 30 seconds of the teacher's time; if it takes longer, the teacher can assume that the original explanation was faulty.

IS DIRECT INSTRUCTION EVER INAPPROPRIATE?

Peterson (1979) used the work of Horwitz (1979) to compare the effects of open versus traditional approaches on student achievement. She concluded that students who experience direct instruction do slightly better on achievement tests but slightly worse on tests of abstract thinking that validate creativity and problem-solving ability. Open teaching approaches facilitate creative thinking and problem solving. They also improve students' attitudes toward school and the teacher and increase students' independence and curiosity.

The research cited in Chapter 4 tells us that students who feel that they have personal control of their successes and failures do better (achieve more) when the teacher uses an open approach to teaching. The student whose style is self-directed (having an internal locus of control) is frustrated during direct instruction. Students who feel that others control their successes and failures do equally well in either direct or open teaching approaches. However, students who have an external locus of control seem to prefer direct instruction because their learning style matches the controlled setting of direct instruction.

The effectiveness of direct instruction often depends on the ability of the students. High-achieving, task-oriented students appear to do worse in direct instruction. Peterson and Janicki (1979) found that high-ability students did better when the teacher used small group instruction as opposed to large group instruction. The low-ability students did better when the teacher used large group instruction.

It is apparent from the research on direct teaching and open teaching approaches that if the teacher's objective is inquiry teaching/problem solving, analysis, synthesis, evaluation, or judgment, then open approaches are superior. If, on the other hand, the teaching objective is essential skill instruction, learning facts, or simple comprehension of information, then direct instruction should be used. However, the choice of a teaching approach should also be based on the students. High-ability students may be frustrated with direct instruction, whereas low-ability students appear to need the structured environment that accompanies direct instruction.

GUIDED DISCUSSION AND DIRECT INSTRUCTION

Direct instruction depends on students' on-task behaviors. To facilitate students' understanding, involvement, and success, teachers question students during skill instruction. The strategy is really a mixture of expository teaching and guided discussion. The questions are oriented to factual and comprehension information. Short answer responses are required from students. The teacher calls on a student during instruction to verify that he or she understands. If the student makes a mistake, the teacher corrects it, thereby providing instant feedback. Small group reading instruction may be guided by the following sequence:

- Group question to cue silent reading
- Teacher question to an individual related to the silent reading
- Response
- Teacher question to another student
- Response
- Repeat sequence

During instruction of a new skill, the format is similar. The teacher may *present* or *model* the new skill or concept. Next the teacher questions students about the presentation, providing them with structured practice. The questions are factual and require short answers. To verify that others understand, the teacher may continue the question/answer format. **Co-action** rather than **interaction** occurs between teacher and student. When using this format, students must understand the purpose of the lesson so they can concentrate on the essential elements. Next, students engage in another practice opportunity with the teacher monitoring their work. This is called guided practice. Finally, students may be given an assignment to apply what they have learned in a new way to see if they have really mastered the skill, providing independent practice.

MARY HOGAN PRESENTS A LESSON USING DIRECT INSTRUCTION

Let us suppose that in Mary Hogan's second-grade classroom, she had determined that several of her youngsters did not understand the use of context clues. She planned a lesson using a short story in a literature book, *The Very Hungry Caterpillar* by Eric Carle. First she told the story using only the pictures. (In this way, she modeled the comprehension skill of using context clues.)

Next Hogan introduced the lesson, announcing, "Boys and girls, today we are going to see if we can play the game of detective. I am going to show some pictures to you, and you try to guess what is happening in the story from these pictures."

Hogan showed the pictures in sequence to the students. Then she asked specific questions about the action in each of the pictures: Who do we see in this picture? What is Ramon doing? How can you tell? Why do you think Ramon is crying? (Hogan was providing the students with structured practice.)

She then guided the students through the story using the pictures. Then she said, "Let's find out if we were good detectives."

This time the students read the story in the usual manner with silent reading cued by an appropriate question, but once again the questions related to the sequence of the pictures.

When the students recognized their success as detectives, Hogan provided them with another opportunity to practice. She had prepared short, simple stories. The students worked with a partner. One student

Research Findings: Using Feedback

Students working in cooperative learning groups in a seventh-grade math class were given a self-assessment instrument to appraise their group processes. Ross (1996) found that the feedback procedure increased students' skill in asking for and giving help to each other. Students' self-efficacy was enhanced by the process.

told the story using the pictures that were provided, and the other student confirmed the story by reading it. Then they exchanged roles with new stories. Hogan watched, listened, and provided feedback. (This time students were engaged semi-independently in guided practice.)

Next Hogan brought out a number of literature books and asked the students to select what interested them. She told them to see if they could use their detective skills to read the books. In this way she provided independent practice at the application level. Later she would provide time for the students to tell others their stories.

If you analyze Hogan's lesson, you can clearly see it had several stages:

1. Planning (diagnosis and prescription)
2. Instruction (presentation/modeling)
3. Practice (structured, guided, and application level)

GREG THOMAS PRESENTS A LESSON USING DIRECT INSTRUCTION

Greg Thomas's fifth-grade class is back at work on the social studies lesson introduced in Chapter 5. Thomas begins the session by displaying a newsprint chart. "These are the questions you raised yesterday," he tells the class. "Before you select which group you want to work with, we need to organize a way for you to take your notes. Simple outlines provide a means to organize what you read so that you can use it and amplify it at a later time. I'm going to demonstrate outlining using the information we read yesterday." Thomas displays a second chart showing a simple outline (Figure 6.1).

Teacher and students engage in talk about how the outline touches on key ideas of their reading and how they can use the outline to help them remember important information. Then, Thomas tells the students, "We need to practice outlining. Let's all read these

Figure 6.1   Thomas's Outline Chart

> I. Great Trails West
>   A. Jumping-off Places
>   B. Organization for Travel
>   C. Rendezvous Points
> II. Leaders
>   A. Scouting
>   B. Settlers

Why is Greg Thomas teaching outlining during social studies time? Should he do this?

two paragraphs and see if we can identify the main idea."

He passes out the reading. Students work individually. When Thomas is satisfied that students have had ample time, he asks them to identify the main idea. He jots down several responses, but it is apparent that most of the students agree that the selection is about the Oregon Trail.

Now Thomas asks the students to identify other ideas in the passage. Together they develop a simple outline that Thomas writes on the chalkboard. When it appears that the students are comfortable with their joint work, Thomas directs them to read another passage in their text and practice on their own. While they do this, he walks around, assists, and offers suggestions. He reminds them, "If you need help, raise your hand or nod at me as I walk around the room."

After about 10 minutes, Thomas has the students share their efforts. "OK, you seem to have the idea about how to use outlining to help you take notes. Now we will choose our research groups to study the Great Trails West and when you need to take notes for your investigation, I want you to use the outlining technique we have just studied."

An analysis of Thomas's lesson using direct instruction is as follows:

1. Orientation: Thomas related what needed to be learned (outlining) to what students had read the previous day and their group research tasks.

2. Presentation: Thomas demonstrated simple outlining and discussed with the students how the outline fit what they had read.

3. Structured practice: Thomas gave the students a short passage to read and had them contribute to the development of an outline that he wrote on the chalkboard. Questions and discussion contributed to this task.

4. Guided practice: Students were given another passage to read out of their texts and asked to develop an outline individually. Thomas monitored and assisted. Students raised hands or caught Thomas's eye if they needed help.

5. Independent practice: Students selected groups for research on the Great Trails West. Groups outline their findings, and in this way they apply the new skill they have learned.

CLASSROOM MANAGEMENT NOTES: DIRECT INSTRUCTION

Planning

Thomas related new learning to prior learning. He had prepared a chart for his presentation and had additional reading passages ready to use for his structured practice. He made decisions about using the text for guided practice and how he would group students.

Environment

Thomas used the whole class as a group to orient the students about what they were to learn and for structured and guided practice. It was obvious that students would move into small groups later in the lesson. He used the chalkboard and a chart for his lesson.

Organizing Procedures and Resources

His decisions that involved first large group teaching, and then individual work, and then group work required organizational skills. His use of the chart, a separate reading passage, and then texts demonstrated his organization of resources.

Monitoring

Thomas had to monitor student understanding during the presentation and structured practice. Then he monitored individual work during the guided practice while students worked out of their texts.

Anticipating Problems

By having his materials ready, Thomas had no lag time and no misbehavior. He directed learning throughout the lesson. He communicated task instructions clearly, and monitored both whole group and independent work. Students knew what was expected of them throughout the lesson, and how to obtain help.

THE COMPREHENSION MODEL: A VARIATION OF DIRECT INSTRUCTION

Students need to learn and practice comprehension strategies. During reading, comprehension is facilitated when the learner is asked to do the following tasks:

- Summarize what he or she has read
- Identify the main idea of what was read

- Transform the reading into his/her own words by telling others
- Predict future events or applications of the content

As you read about Karen Adazzio's lesson in the next section, pay attention to the students' tasks and the questions she asks them. You may want to classify the tasks and questions into the four categories identified above.

KAREN ADAZZIO'S COMPREHENSION MODEL LESSON

In Karen Adazzio's seventh-grade classroom, the students are reading Daniel Davis's *Behind Barbed Wire: The Imprisonment of Japanese Americans During World War II*. Adazzio begins the day's reading, asking the students to look at the pictures and captions on certain pages. She asks, "How do you think the little girl feels as she sees all her family's belongings packed in crates and duffel bags?" After several responses, Adazzio asks another question, "What do you think happened to Japanese-American stores and businesses that were sealed and padlocked by the government?"

Using the pictures to obtain context information and their own experiences, the students respond. After this initial discussion, Adazzio asks the students to read and identify what actions the United States government took against Japanese-Americans during World War II. The students read silently and Adazzio observes them carefully. Sometimes a student raises a hand when he or she finds a word that is difficult to read; usually Adazzio can detect when a student has a problem. If Adazzio sees that many students are having a problem with a word or expression, she will stop the reading, explain the word, and have students give examples of the word in different sentences.

When the students appear to be ready, Adazzio asks, "Who can identify some of the government actions?" Several students respond, and Adazzio makes a list on the board. Next Adazzio asks, "In what ways were civil rights denied to the Japanese-Americans?" The students return to their books, once again reading about the government's actions.

When the students appear to be ready, Adazzio engages them in a discussion of civil rights and this period of American history. Then she asks them, "What were the effects of the internment on the lives of Japanese-Americans?" This question requires students to once again look at some of the pictures in the book and make some assumptions about what they were reading because the question is not fully answered in

---
**Why is it important for students to tell
what happened in their own words?**

---

the book. Finally, Adazzio asks the students, "Do you think this could happen today? Why or why not?"

Some of the students continue to read; others are reflecting. Adazzio provides considerable time before she begins the discussion and continues to focus on the likelihood of similar actions today.

REVIEWING THE STEPS IN THE COMPREHENSION MODEL

1. Direct silent reading with a comprehension question. Help students use context clues. Students read . . . to find out . . .

2. Monitor silent reading and provide vocabulary assistance as needed. If many students have the same or similar problems, then provide whole group assistance; otherwise help the individual.

3. Increase the complexity of the questions, but begin with questions that ask students to demonstrate their understanding of the main idea. Next ask questions that require students to interpret meaning by reading between the lines. Finally ask questions that require analysis, synthesis, evaluation, and characterization by asking students to use personal experiences and to construct meaning that goes beyond the given information.

THE ADVANCE ORGANIZER MODEL OF TEACHING

Greg Thomas's students are reading about immigrants to the United States. The students are using a variety of textbooks and teacher-prepared material based on their reading abilities. Thomas wants to be sure that his students understand the ideas and information they encounter in their reading. It is important to the lesson that they all search out the same concepts.

Thomas announces to the students, "Today we are going to read about immigrant groups who came to the United States between 1890 and 1920." He told them that when they had finished reading, they should be able to answer the following questions:

- Why did people leave their native countries and come to the United States?
- Where did many immigrant groups settle in the United States?

- How did the different immigrant groups help the people in the United States?

"Who can tell me what the word *immigrant* means?" (Students respond, and Thomas agrees.)

Thomas then asks, "What does the word *migration* mean?" (Thomas helps the students define the concept.)

Thomas suggests to the class that they may want to take notes from their readings to verify the answers to the questions. He intends to follow up with a class discussion.

During the discussion, Thomas has the students prove their responses by referring to the material they have read. He will evaluate the lesson by asking the class these questions:

- Who came to the United States?
- What was their native land?
- Why did they migrate?
- Where did they settle?
- How did they earn a living in the United States?
- How did they help the United States?

Thomas helps his students integrate the information by having them identify three reasons why groups immigrate and asking them how immigrant groups affect their new country.

Thomas's approach represents the **advance organizer** model of teaching. The syntax for the advance organizer model comes from the work of Joyce and Weil (1996, pp. 265–278). The model is derived from the theories of David Ausubel (1963), an educational psychologist who believes that knowledge can be organized and presented by teachers in an orderly manner to help students process new information. The model is useful in all subject fields.

The advance organizer model has three phases. In phase one, students are told the purpose of the lesson and the organizer is presented. In our fictitious fifth-grade classroom, Thomas told the students what they were to read, presented them with organizing questions, and helped them to define key terms they would encounter in their reading.

In phase two, the material is presented; the lesson proceeds. In Thomas' lesson, the students do their reading and take notes.

In phase three, the lesson is integrated (principle of integrative reconciliation). Thomas used a discussion to elicit the responses to the questions and integrate the lesson.

An example of the advance organizer model in a lower grade classroom is a music lesson Mary Hogan carefully planned.*

Hogan told her second graders that they were going to learn to read music notation and study rhythm. On the board she wrote the words *rhythm, beat, meter,* and *tempo.* She also drew a staff, a meter signature, and notes of different values.

Next Hogan told the students that rhythm is composed of different components, which include beat, meter, and tempo. She explained, "We are going to experience these different components today, and at the end of the lesson we will see if you can describe or demonstrate these rhythmic components."

Hogan proceeded to have students feel their own heartbeat. Then she had them tap out the beat of a familiar popular song. Next she brought out a metronome, and the students clapped to the steady beat.

After the students understood the concept of beat, Hogan played two versions of another familiar song. One version was brisk and the other slow. In this way she taught about tempo. Then she taught about note values and rests and introduced the concept of meter. With each concept she had the students participate by singing or clapping.

Hogan concluded her lesson by saying, "We have experienced rhythm today. Who thinks they can explain what rhythm is?" The students talked about how rhythm was the overall, ongoing movement of the music. Hogan used each of the components introduced in the lesson to help the students talk about what they had learned about rhythm.

THE ADVANCE ORGANIZER AND CLASSROOM MANAGEMENT

The purpose of the advance organizer model is to clarify and organize meaningful information and ideas to facilitate students' processing skills. It is for this reason that the teacher preplans the lesson and presents the organizer to the students and then verifies that students understand the structure of the lesson. The teacher controls the presentation and helps students see its relationship to what they are going to learn.

The lesson should be evaluated using the same organizing structure presented at the beginning of the lesson. In this way the teacher ensures integrative rec-

onciliation of knowledge. Although the advance organizer model is a structured teaching model, the teacher needs to facilitate ample class interaction during the discussion. Throughout the lesson, students are encouraged to ask questions and clarify ideas.

DISCUSSION STRATEGIES
CHARACTERISTICS OF ORAL DISCUSSIONS

A true *discussion* involves the sharing of ideas, thoughts, and feelings. An oral discussion is not a soliloquy; it is a conversation in which two or more individuals participate. During most classroom discussions, it is expected that students will participate equally, and depending on the type of discussion, the teacher may play an equal role, adopt a leadership role, or choose not to participate at all.

Participants in a discussion use background information and experiences or data from recently acquired research or study. Although it is possible to participate silently by listening, the individual who does not express ideas, thoughts, and feelings is probably not involved in the discussion.

Classroom discussions may involve the whole class or a small group of students. The discussion may have a discussion leader, who may or may not be the teacher. The leader may ask questions to focus the discussion and increase participation, or the leader may act as a moderator.

A classroom discussion should have a purpose. Students are assembled in a group to talk in a meaningful way. This underlying purpose differentiates the classroom discussion from an idle conversation. Discussions progress through a series of steps; however, the steps are not necessarily sequentially accomplished. A discussion usually begins with a get-acquainted-with-the-topic stage; it then generally proceeds to a problem-definition stage in which the participants focus on the purpose. The discussion may have a data-gathering stage, and ultimately the discussion terminates with a conclusion or summing up.

DISCUSSION MANNERS

Discussion manners and skills are crucial to the success of the teaching strategy. If participants in a discussion

*Based on suggestions in M. L. Hoffer and C. R. Hoffer, *Music in the Elementary Classroom* (New York: Harcourt Brace Jovanovich, 1987).

What are some of the things teachers can learn about students by observing them during a class discussion?

To participate in a large group discussion, students need to be able to see each other.

are equal, then the flow of conversation moves around the group and encourages individual responses and contributions. But if the discussion is characterized by a back-and-forth exchange between teacher and student *(co-action)*, then group *interaction* is discouraged, the flow of ideas is limited, the sense of group belonging diminishes, and positive social attitudes are not developed.

Discussion manners are as important for the teacher as they are for the students, and most are a matter of good sense. However, the manners and skills need to be taught, modeled, and practiced. Good discussions do not happen automatically. Taking turns—not monopolizing the conversation—is one of the first things that needs to be taught and modeled. For students to grasp this idea, it is important to call attention to it during the evaluation. Although this is just common sense, it cannot be taken for granted.

Listening to others is another common-sense item, but it entails attending to the discussion. The importance of careful listening is not meaningful to students until they realize that some discussion contributions are repetitious and irrelevant.

The importance of not making conversation asides to a neighbor or to a limited few needs to be constantly reiterated, or the discussion will deteriorate into many small purposeless conversations.

That contributions should be meaningful and focus on the topic or purpose hardly needs to be mentioned except that this is a most difficult task for young students.

The hardest skill to learn is the ability to synthesize the discussion or develop a conclusion based on the discussion. The capacity to do this comes through practice. Even adults tend to allow the discussion leader to assume this responsibility; yet, in fact, every discussion participant should be developing the conclusion or synthesis and be ready to challenge and contribute to the culmination of the discussion.

CLASSROOM ENVIRONMENT AND DISCUSSION ROLES

The classroom environment affects the success of the discussion, and the size of the discussion group influences the skills needed by teacher and students. In a discussion group, students' faces are close together. They see each other easily; they know when someone is about to speak. If the students are motivated by their discussion, they will not be distracted easily. In small discussion groups the teacher's role is supportive and facilitative. The teacher walks among the groups, observing and providing assistance when needed.

In large discussion groups, students sometimes cannot see each other. This may occur because the need to see each other was not anticipated in the planning of the discussion formation. "Eyeballing" is crucial, however; in a large group, how else do you know when a classmate is about to speak? We learn a great deal about each other by watching eyes, hands, posture, and facial expressions. If students cannot see each other, they may not focus in on the discussion or become involved.

The teacher's role during the large group discussion depends both on the purpose of the discussion and on the teacher's own personality needs. If the classroom climate is highly structured and the teacher demands rigid control, the discussion is limited to a select few students. The interaction pattern is from teacher to student and back to teacher again. However, if the teacher creates an open, warm, encouraging climate for discussion, the flow of ideas moves among the students, and students learn to listen to classmates and take turns. Try to achieve a moderate environment; the teacher who is too rigid or too permissive will have a limited discussion monopolized by aggressive students. Taba (1967) states that the teacher who is too permissive and abandons the discussion totally to the students will have a limited and chaotic discussion period.

Leadership Role

All group discussions need a leader. The leadership role may be assumed by either teacher or students. Typically in a small discussion group, a student is designated as the leader. Ultimately, all students should learn to assume the leadership role.

The basic purpose of a discussion is to encourage students to gather and process information by sharing with others and listening to others. This objective helps to define the role of the discussion leader. The leader's attitude influences the discussion. Facilitative behaviors are important to encourage participation. These include the following behaviors:

- Accepting all responses by assuming a nonjudgmental attitude
- Encouraging spontaneity by not injecting personal statements or evaluative responses
- Soliciting feelings and value responses through questioning and asking for clarification
- Extending thinking through summative statements

These behaviors are thoroughly discussed in the *Teaching Tasks and Behaviors* section later in this chapter.

Students can learn to assume the leadership role when they are provided with practice situations and given an evaluation of their leadership performance. A checklist for evaluating discussions is included in Chapter 11.

Participatory Role

This role is assumed by most of the students (and occasionally by the teacher). It needs a great deal of practice. The very young, egocentric child has difficulty sharing and listening to others. Until the child learns group participatory behaviors, discussions are difficult. Acceptance of group responsibility is a developmental process. Behaviors include the following:

- Sensitivity to others' viewpoints
- Listening to others and asking questions of others
- Assuming responsibility to contribute ideas, thoughts, and feelings

It is important to remember that these behaviors are only learned if they are practiced, and they can be learned at any grade level.

Recorder's Role

This role is important in most discussions. It is the recorder's job to log the discussion and be ready to recount it during the evaluative period. Group members assist the recorder in keeping an accurate chronicle of the meeting. Verbatim minutes are unnecessary; it is more important to note the trends in the discussion and the decisions that are made. The recorder may also assist the group leader by recounting the discussion and summarizing it at different times in order to keep the group on target.

DISCUSSION PROBLEMS

Some teachers complain that students never stop talking. However, sometimes these same teachers complain that their students do not participate in class discussions. Why does this apparent incongruity occur? What happens may be related to several factors:

- Students have been successfully inhibited and feel that participation is undesired by the teacher.
- Students feel that they are in a fishbowl during a discussion, and they become shy.
- The teacher or discussion leader or several aggressive students monopolize the discussion, causing others not to participate.
- Students are disinterested in the topic/problem/question posed for discussion.

If the lack of participation is related to the first factor, inhibition, there is very little that can be suggested to remedy the problem. The teacher needs to remember that at school, students are supposed to use language; the teacher's professional expertise should be used to find as many constructive means as possible to develop language usage. Students who have been turned off to talking can be helped quickly by eliminating the negative influences and by reinforcing positive speech behaviors.

It is relevant to consider the different types of discussions when dealing with the second factor, shyness. Students of all ages are frequently intimidated by the large class discussion. Shyness can be dealt with through the use of the small group discussion. In groups of no more than seven students, everyone participates, and students' discussion skills can be developed.

If the third problem, aggressiveness, affects participation, the teacher must develop questioning and involvement strategies to guide the discussion and to encourage interaction.

The fourth factor, disinterest, simply means that the students need to participate in the planning process and help identify meaningful topics or problems.

The Aggressive, Overtalkative Student

If the overtalkative student could hear himself as others do, there would be no problem! The trick is to help this student develop an accurate self-perception. One of the most effective means of accomplishing this is to have the student observe another student who has a similar problem.

For example, when Greg Thomas had this problem in his classroom, he suggested that Ginger, an aggressive talker, observe another group of students during the discussion lesson. Ginger's task was to provide feedback to the group she was observing concerning participation and progress toward the group objective. Thomas cautioned Ginger not to hurt anyone's feelings. Specifically, Ginger was asked to answer the following questions:

- Did everyone contribute and participate?
- Did the group accomplish its purpose?
- Who helped the group most to accomplish its purpose?
- What problems did the group have?
- What suggestions would you make to the group?

Ginger was flattered to be the group observer. When she reported to the group, she observed that one person (Sylvia) had monopolized the conversation on several occasions with the result that the group did not have time to reach a conclusion.

Thomas talked with Ginger about her findings and asked her if she recalled performing in a similar fashion. Ginger recognized that she, too, had often monopolized the conversation. Although Ginger still needed to be reminded during successive sessions, her awareness of the problem improved her own performance.

If Thomas had not had two aggressive talkers in his classroom, he could have accomplished the same objective by taping a small group session and asking Ginger to listen and evaluate using the tape recorder.

The Shy Student

A teacher can best help the introverted student by providing experiences to talk in a small group situation. The shy student is usually overwhelmed by whole class participation. Careful group placement with an unselfish group of students will facilitate the shy child's participation. It should be considered extremely unusual if a child does not participate in the small group. If this occurs, the teacher needs to seek assistance from the parents and colleagues.

In the large group it may be possible to encourage participation of the shy child by providing opportunities prefaced with questions directed to the student. "Sally, what do you think about this?" "Rob, do you agree with that statement?" "Helen, how would you handle this problem?" However, this tactic must be done cautiously because direct questions to the shy student may complicate the problem.

Another thing to remember with the shy child is to provide plenty of response time. Sometimes children anticipate that the teacher will not wait for them to respond; thus, the shy child becomes more inhibited because of the expectation of being cut off before a full response has been made.

TYPES OF DISCUSSIONS

Unstructured or "Free" Discussion

The sharing discussion of kindergarten and first-grade classrooms is an example of an unstructured meeting time in which students simply practice talking, listening, and questioning each other. This type of free discussion has no set purpose other than language usage, the expression of personal feelings, and learning to talk to an audience. The teacher usually refrains from contributing to this discussion in order to encourage spontaneity. The sharing discussion can be made more relevant by suggesting to students that they bring important items to class for the sharing period. These items might include "a book I like," "my hobby," "my collection," "an experiment I performed," "something I made."

The unstructured discussion is also used to initiate new topics or areas of study, such as a social studies unit. The purpose of the free discussion in this situation is to encourage students to identify interests and problems to find out what students really know about the new topic. The free discussion is typically a large group activity, although it does not need to be.

Semistructured Discussion

In this type of discussion, students are usually reporting progress toward a specific purpose, or exchanging information as a result of a research/problem-solving lesson, or contributing information gained from a field trip or a special experience. The discussion has been structured by the prior activity or by specific instructions. For an example of the semistructured discussion, review Mary Hogan's problem-solving assignment concerning magnets in Chapter 5. These primary students were asked to find out what magnets pull and were asked to make a rule about what magnets pull. Their small group discussions and their large group evaluative discussion are characteristic of the semistructured type of discussion.

Structured Discussion

This is a guided discussion that has been preplanned to accomplish specific cognitive functions. The structured discussion depends on a sequenced questioning strategy. The purpose is to facilitate the development of cognitive skills by beginning with a lower-level cognitive skill and moving to the generalization level. The structured discussion can help students develop concepts, make decisions, and learn to solve problems. During the course of the discussion, students contribute information (data), and as they listen to others and to the questions, they process the data in order to arrive at the concept, a generalization, a prediction, or a decision.

TEACHING TASKS AND BEHAVIORS

There are two basic ideas to keep in mind when using discussion as an instructional approach. The first is that the students need to learn *how* to discuss, which means that there are skills they need to master in order to discuss well. The second point is that there is a purpose related to academic content to be accomplished through use of the discussion technique. Thus, at the end of a discussion, the evaluation should focus on both the discussion process and on the sub-stantive nature of the subject for discussion. Teacher tasks relate to those two purposes. For example, students learn discussion skills more easily if they practice the skills in a small group situation. Therefore, the teacher needs to consider the composition of the small group. In Chapter 5, you learned that small groups are better if they are composed of five to seven students. Discussion will be facilitated if the group members are different rather than alike. Students' natural differences may be related to dialect, sex, socioeconomic status, verbal ability, and intelligence. Some studies indicate that students' speech develops best when the student has to explain and clarify meanings. So one of the first tasks of the teacher is to consider the size and composition of small groups when assigning students to a discussion activity.

Discussion Rules and Roles

Another teacher task is the presentation, teaching, and follow-up of discussion rules and roles. Conversing in a group is a difficult cognitive activity. The first thing that students need to learn is how to recognize when another speaker has finished talking. Students can be asked, "How do you think you can tell when your friend has concluded speaking?" The basic response is "when they stop." But the next question is the real key, "How can you tell when a friend is ready to speak?" The students' response should be, "I can tell by the eyes or when the person begins to . . ." The bottom line in rule making for discussion is that students must learn to take turns without hand-raising. Hand-raising inhibits the flow of conversation and makes the group leader the recipient of all speech.

The teacher must also decide whether to choose the leader and recorder for the discussion group or have the students do so. In the beginning it might be better if the teacher exercises that judgment. But the roles should be rotated on successive days. During the course of the discussion, the teacher needs to verify that the discussion leader is encouraging all members of the group to speak. The discussion leader and recorder should be evaluated by the group in an inoffensive manner at the end of the session. During the evaluation session the teacher solicits ideas from the total group for encouraging all members of the group to contribute. This serves the dual purpose of teaching leadership responsibility to the discussion leaders and participation responsibility to everyone.

Verifying Meanings

Before students are sent off to their discussion group, it is wise to make sure that they understand what they are to discuss or accomplish. Then the teacher should verify that they comprehend the meanings involved in what they are to do. For example, Mary Hogan demonstrated what a magnet could do and had the children talk about it before she sent them off to their problem-solving lesson in Chapter 5. In this way she prepared them for the group discovery session. It is important, also, that students understand the role of using evidence during a discussion. Students should learn the value of backing-up their comments with concrete data.

Another aspect of verifying meanings has to do with *establishing the focus.* Children as well as adults tend to digress from the chosen topic. The best way to deal with this tendency is to be sure that a discussion focus has been set and is understood. You can accomplish this by providing the discussion group(s) with a set of questions. The questions should be open-ended, providing many alternatives in terms of the discussion. There ought to be enough questions so when you join the group to observe and listen to the discussion you are able to ask, "What question are you discussing now?" Of course, certain questions may cultivate enough discussion, making others unnecessary. Questions will be discussed later in this chapter.

Refocusing

When you visit a discussion group, you may find that the discussion disregards the problem focus and needs **refocusing.** Perhaps the students have misunderstood the meanings, or perhaps they have just strayed from the topic. When this occurs, it is the teacher's job to ask a question or make a statement that will bring the students back to the original topic. If Mary Hogan had found that the students were not discussing the rule for magnets when she toured the problem-solving groups, she would have asked, "Did you find out what magnets pull?" Or she might have said, "Do you remember that we were to find out what a magnet can and cannot do? After finding out what a magnet can pull, can you tell us how these items are alike?"

Hogan also anticipated that some of the groups might complete the assignment earlier than others. As she visited the groups she was prepared to change the focus and extend the experiment by suggesting an additional experiment for the students to per-

form. The same anticipatory act is necessary even if groups are just talking. Some groups get to the heart of the matter quickly, and they may need to consider the topic in greater depth or to move on to a new topic.

Clarifying and Valuing

Many children have been taught that what they say is unimportant and what adults contribute is to be valued. As a result, children tend not to listen well to their peers. They anticipate that the adult will repeat what their peer has said, so why should they bother listening to a classmate? When students reiterate what others have said, it means that they have not been listening. The way to deal with this is to say to the repeater, "Roberto already told us about that. Roberto, will you explain to William what you told us before?"

Another typical problem occurs when students do not understand a classmate's comments. They may just sit there without speaking, or they may ask the teacher, "What did Billy mean?" The trick is to get Billy to explain his meaning rather than have the teacher clarify it. Since students become accustomed to the teacher explaining what has been discussed, they may not focus in and listen to their classmates. To solve this problem, the teacher asks the original speaker, "Billy, will you tell us what you meant by . . .?" When the teacher habitually handles the problem in this manner, students begin to ask questions of their peers rather than of the teacher.

Supportive Classroom Climate

We have already discussed the seating arrangement and structural climate of the classroom. There is another type of atmosphere that the teacher must create if the discussion is to be successful. This has to do with the development of an attitude that supports all student contributions, even if they are not terribly helpful at the moment. The teacher must be so objective during a discussion that the students will not be able to discern either approval or disapproval of their comments.

This does not mean, however, that conceptual errors are allowed. When an error in logic or an error involving a specific fact occurs, the teacher should ask the student to clarify the meaning. The teacher should also solicit corrections or additional statements from other students by asking them questions. "Boys and girls, what do you think about that?" "Does everyone agree?"

"Who has a different idea?" "Do we have any evidence that this is so?" This process must be handled sensitively so students do not hesitate to make comments because they fear they will make mistakes.

When a student makes an error or irrelevant comment, the teacher must ensure that the child making the comment is not attacked by peers. Once again, the supportive climate and encouragement of the teacher are important.

Extending Thinking

The teacher needs to be constantly alert to ways to extend and broaden patterns of thinking. The following questions may be useful for this purpose:

- Ask the students to review the major points already discussed, or summarize what has been said yourself.
- After the summary ask, "What do we still need to consider?"
- If there has been conflict over definitions or values expressed, ask the class if Billy and Susie meant the same things when they discussed communication.
- Remind students that they have already discussed several means of communication. Then ask, "Are there some things we have forgotten?" or "How else might we think about this?"

Evaluation

At the end of the discussion, there should be a final summary of what has been discussed and concluded, the main ideas, and the areas of conflict. During the evaluation, help students understand what has been accomplished. Students should learn that a discussion will always be evaluated in two ways: in terms of the content and in terms of the discussion process. They should also learn that no one will dwell on personal behaviors during the evaluation.

If group observers are used, this is the time they would give their report. Both group evaluation and self-evaluation may be used at the end of the discussion period.

QUESTIONING TECHNIQUES

PURPOSES OF QUESTIONING

Appropriate use of questioning can be the most effective teaching technique teachers use. Questions can be used for the following purposes:

- Motivate and guide students' study
- Orient students to problems and make them aware of values
- Teach students to process information
- Facilitate analysis and evaluation

Questions initiate and guide most class discussions. Research indicates that teachers use questions for both assessment and motivation. In recent years there has been a great deal of debate about teachers' classroom questions. Teachers' questions are generally categorized as either factual or higher cognitive. In the 1970s and 1980s, researchers had conflicting views about the value of teachers' questions. Interpretations of the research during the 1970s suggested that teachers should ask fact questions for recitation during skill instruction. However, using newer statistical measures, researchers in the 1980s reinterpreted the evidence and decided that when teachers ask higher-level questions during instruction, student achievement increases. Reviewing the conflicting interpretations, Gall (1989) concluded:

- When teaching basic skills to young disadvantaged students, teachers should emphasize low-cognitive questions, but include some higher level questions to help children develop thinking skills.
- When teaching average- and high-ability students, teachers should emphasize higher cognitive questions to develop independent thinking.

In general, it has been found that higher cognitive questions are more effective in helping students learn.

Research on questioning as a teaching behavior provides some guidance about how to use this method most effectively. Questions should accomplish the following:

- Stimulate thinking
- Be formulated so that they are precise and concise
- Be appropriate to the purpose of the lesson
- Accommodate the students who are to answer them

The following sections explore some of these characteristics of good questions.

Stimulating Thinking

An interesting, thought-provoking question motivates the learner to do the following:

- Pay greater attention
- Reflect on new ideas
- Consider new avenues for thought
- Suggest analysis or synthesis rather than a factual recall of previously learned information

A good question triggers past experiences and knowledge and motivates new thought.

Precision

A good question is clear, precise, and concise. The question should tell students how to frame their response. Too often teachers ask an ambiguous or vague question and then are surprised at the variety of responses. For example, if the teacher wants to know whether or not the students read an article on the front page of the newspaper that is relevant to what they are studying, the question should not be, "Did you see the newspaper this morning?" The class was studying *expansionism*, so the teacher could have asked, "The front page of the newspaper this morning had an article on expansionism. Who was involved?" or, "Why was expansionism in the news this morning?"

Purposeful Focus

Plan questions so they are appropriate to the purpose of the lesson. If the lesson is a problem-solving activity, then the questions must stimulate inquiry. If the purpose is factual recall, then ask mastery questions. Suppose that your students have just returned from a field trip. To focus their thinking about the experience, you might ask the following questions:

• What did you observe?
• What similarities and differences among the incidents did you note?
• Why did these incidents occur?

Since purposeful questioning is often sequenced, the questions are preplanned rather than off the cuff. However, even though the lesson has been planned to focus on specifics, the teacher should be flexible enough to change the questions if the students' inquiry moves in a purposeful and fruitful direction.

Clustering Questions

Effective teachers use both convergent and divergent questions. *Convergent* questions involve asking students to recall basic facts and actions; these questions usually call for one best answer. *Divergent* questions involve students in abstractions, reflections, and beliefs; they usually require analysis, synthesis, evaluation, judgment, and characterization.

Sequencing of questions depends on the teacher's purpose. For example, a common sequence is to begin with the recall of specific facts, and then lead to questions that elicit reasoning and hypotheses. Another sequence may begin with an open, divergent question to stimulate student involvement and then narrow to deductive thinking and problem solving. The important point is that questions need to be planned.

In Adazzio's comprehension lesson earlier in the chapter, we saw a sequence develop through the questions. The first two questions she asked motivated the lesson and called for divergent responses in order to elicit student involvement and many responses:

1. How do you think the little girl feels as she sees all her family's belongings packed in crates and duffel bags?
2. What do you think happened to Japanese-American stores and businesses that were sealed and padlocked by the government?

Next Adazzio asked narrow, factual questions to verify student comprehension:

3. What actions did the United States government take against Japanese-Americans during World War II? (Main idea)
4. In what ways were civil rights denied to the Japanese-Americans? (Summarization)

To elicit higher-level thinking, Adazzio's next question called for analysis of the facts and evaluation of the outcomes:

5. What were the effects of the internment on the lives of Japanese-Americans? (Transforming reading into students' own words)

Adazzio concluded with a question to evoke both prediction and a value judgment:

6. Do you think this could happen today? Why or why not?

Note that without the sequence of questions, the last question might be considered simple convergent thought process, but clustered with the prior questions, it becomes divergent and thought provoking.

Meeting Students' Needs

Research on questioning and on learning styles indicates that instruction should be differentiated to meet students' needs. Research indicating that disadvantaged students do better with lower-level questions

---

Can you develop a different question sequence for Adazzio's lesson?

has already been noted. However, some middle-class students who do not tolerate a highly structured environment may do better with open-ended questions. Questions should be adapted to the group of students with whom you are working.

TYPES OF QUESTIONS

During the 1960s, Taba and associates developed a system for programming cognitive processes through the sequencing of questions. The questions are used to stimulate the students to process information. The strategy is based on the idea that students need input of content in order to be ready to respond to the questions that are asked. Three cognitive tasks are taught to the students: concept formation, interpretation of data, and application of principles. Each cognitive task requires specific questions.

Cognitive Task I

To facilitate concept formation, the teacher stimulates students to list, group, and categorize items using common characteristics. The questions include the following from Taba (1967, p. 92):

- What did you see? hear? note?
- What belongs together? On what criterion?
- How would you call these groups? What belongs under what?

Cognitive Task II

The interpretation of data is taught by asking students (Taba, p. 101):

- What did you notice? see? find?
- Why did so-and-so happen?
- What does this means? What would you conclude?

Cognitive Task III

The application of principles is sequenced through the following questions (Taba, p. 109):

- What would happen if . . .?
- Why do you think this would happen?
- What would it take for so-and-so to be generally true or probably true?

These cognitive tasks will be expanded in the discussion of inquiry and problem solving in Chapter 7.

In Mary Hogan's science unit about rocks, she adapted the Taba strategy to teach her students that rocks differ in shapes, colors, and textures, and that natural forces cause rocks to change. She asked the following questions:

Questions	Responses
Describe these rocks. (What do you see?)	Students described color, shape.
Describe how the rocks feel.	Smooth, rough, slippery, jagged
How could we arrange these rocks in groups?	Color, shape, texture
Why do you think these rocks are not the same?	Rocks break. Different types of rocks feel different and look different. Something happens to the rocks to make them different.
What are some things that might affect the rocks? What else?	Sun, heat, cold, water, wind, plants, snow
What would happen if the rocks were exposed for many years to ice? Or sun? Or water?	Natural forces (ice, sun, and water) affect the color, shape, and texture of the rocks.

COMMON SENSE ABOUT ASKING QUESTIONS

Reviews of research on types of questions and levels of questions have concluded that learning gains can be correlated with the questions that are asked in the classroom. We know a great deal about the use of questions. The following sections cover some typical questions asked by teachers and some common-sense ideas and advice gleaned from the many research studies.

How Can Teachers Involve Students in Discussion?

Several factors are important. First ask questions to motivate the discussion in a nonthreatening manner. Questions that are interesting and asked in a conversational voice get the best attention from students. Then after calling on a student, wait for the response; do not scare the student off. After the student responds, let your eyes observe other students; let them know if you want them to contribute. Call on additional students, without repeating the question; encourage other students to respond by asking, "Anyone else want to comment?" "Who can add to this?" "Well, boys and girls, what else?" Provide feedback through noncommittal, simple responses, such as "OK," "Good," "Interesting thought," "Hmmm."

The process of eliciting additional students to respond to questions is called *redirection*. Only higher cognitive questions can be redirected since fact questions typically have only one answer.

What Happens When Teachers Call on a Specific Student Before Asking a Question?

By naming the student who is to respond, the teacher encourages all other students to stop listening. Thus, it becomes necessary to regenerate interest through a follow-up elicitation because the class has been effectively inhibited from participation.

However, there are exceptions that merit consideration. If you note that Johnny and Matilda are not paying attention or are misbehaving, it may be profitable to call on one of them and serve notice that you are aware of their inattention and that you will not tolerate it. This lets the inattentive students realize that they had better tune in, and it tells the rest of the class that you are monitoring participation.

There is another situation that may call for naming the student ahead of time. If there is a very shy student in class who rarely contributes to the discussion, sometimes this student will respond if given extra time to prepare. Decision making, along with an extra measure of common sense, is needed before deciding whether to focus on a specific student or to ask the question of the whole group.

What Types of Questions Should Teachers Ask?

The answer is all types. It is important to provide a variety of thinking experiences. Students' interest in answering questions may depend on learning styles and social class background factors. The age of the students may also be a factor. Nevertheless, students need practice in answering a variety of question types, not just those we think are better for them. Also remember that reflective questions are dependent on prerequisite knowledge. One of the best ways to determine students' readiness to answer a reflective question is to sequence the questions beginning with a factual one.

What Happens When Teachers Use Leading Questions?

"Isn't it true that . . .?" The problem with the leading question is that it is insincere. Students sometimes become hostile because they recognize that they have not been asked a real question. Another problem is that students do not pay attention to the leading ques-

tion, and so good listening habits are not reinforced. (In addition, leading questions are frequently used in discipline situations, often with a sarcastic tone of voice: "You do want to go to lunch today, don't you?")

What Happens When Teachers Repeat Students' Comments?

If students know that the teacher will repeat every student response, they do not need to listen to their peers—just to the teacher. Recall the discussion about interaction patterns during a class discussion presented earlier in this chapter. Students tend to talk to the teacher rather than to their classmates; repeating students' comments reinforces this behavior.

But—another exception—sometimes, particularly with young children, a correct response needs to be vigorously emphasized and reinforced immediately. This occurs most frequently during skill instruction. Under this circumstance you may need to repeat the student's comment in a complete sentence. However, it is critical to acknowledge that the student gave the correct answer, but that it is so important, you are repeating it.

Under What Circumstances Should Teachers Cue Students?

Recall the research about wait-time (Rowe, 1974), which indicated that teachers should wait about five seconds for a response. Rowe's research (1969) also pointed out that teachers are less likely to wait for the low achiever than for the higher achiever. Research also reveals that teachers are more likely to cue students whom they anticipate know the answer rather than students they anticipate do not know the answer. What this means, in terms of questioning technique, is that teachers must automatically wait an equal amount of time for both low- and high-achievers to respond, and provide specific content clues to all students who fail to respond after sufficient wait-time.

Another device for eliciting greater response and reflective thought is to use the probe. Probing questions are follow-up questions and are designed to encourage elaboration. A probing question represents a special type of cue. For example, you ask the class, "Why did England send ships to the South Atlantic Ocean when Argentina took over the Falkland Islands?" A student responds that the Falkland Islands belong to England. Now ask the responding student, "Under what circumstances do you believe a country will act aggressively?" This question is intended as a cue to the student to

Research Readings

Rowe (1974) found that student participation, interaction, and involvement increased when the teachers waited three to five seconds before soliciting another response or before providing additional clues. Teacher silence after calling on a student is an extremely important teaching technique to increase involvement and creativeness.

extend his or her thinking in a particular direction. Both the student and the content should be considered before a teacher decides to probe.

Why Should Yes/No Questions Be Avoided?

The yes/no question usually wastes time. Ask the question you really want the student to answer. For example, the questions in this section could have been written as yes/no questions. (Should yes/no questions be asked? Should teachers repeat students' comments?) The problem is that a yes/no response is insufficient, and the teacher has to ask a follow-up question in order to get any information out of the student. Another problem is that the yes/no response tells the teacher very little about a student's thinking, and thus cannot be used to diagnose needs.

STUDENTS' QUESTIONS AND CLASSROOM MANAGEMENT

The questions students ask provide a great deal of insight about the organization and management of the classroom and the effectiveness of instruction. For example, if students ask many procedural questions, it becomes obvious that the teacher has not clearly explained classroom procedures to the students. (Or the students have not had the opportunity to have input into planning classroom procedures.)

When students ask what appear to be very elementary instructional questions, they are telling the teacher they do not understand the instructions or that the lesson is too difficult for them. Students who ask questions to receive assurance from the teacher

What are some ways to help students ask better questions?

that they are proceeding correctly probably lack self-confidence, or they have experienced a great deal of teacher wrath in the past and are presently fearful.

It can be a frustrating experience when teachers have to manage many time-consuming and often pointless questions. For this reason, the teacher must analyze why students' needs are not being met and what kinds of questions are legitimate. Teachers receiving many classroom management (procedural) questions should ask:

- Have the students helped to plan, and do they understand class standards? Do they know what to do when they need paper, when they may sharpen a pencil, when they may get a drink or go to the bathroom, what to do when finished?
- Do they know where to work? Do they know what resources are available to them?
- What should they do if they really need assistance? May they work with a classmate?
- What responsibilities may students assume for their own goal setting?

What kinds of questions should be cultivated in the classroom? Cover questions dealing with the extension of an instructional task, questions that broaden the area of study, and questions that lend depth to the study. Students will ask these kinds of questions when they are really motivated by instruction and when they feel that their teacher respects them and wants them to take some responsibility for personal learning. In addition, it is important for teachers to model appropriate questioning behavior.

Students' Responses

Language usage is the school's *raison d'être*, and teachers need to develop students' speech. Listen to what students have to say and reinforce it through respect. This means that nonevaluative comments ("OK," "All right," "Interesting") need to be made along with teacher questioning to elicit clarifying responses from students. Teachers may need to use cues and probing questions to facilitate students' replies.

SUMMARY

Direct Instruction

1. Direct instruction is an expository teaching strategy that is teacher-directed and controlled and typically used with a large group of students.

2. Direct instruction has an academic focus that relates new learning to students' existing knowledge through teacher presentation and student practice.
3. Teacher questioning to verify students' understanding and three practices are essential in using the model: structured, guided, and independent practice.
4. Direct instruction is inappropriate for inquiry, creative tasks, and problem solving.
5. Students with an external locus of control do better with direct instruction than do students with an internal locus of control.

Comprehension Model

6. To verify students' understanding during reading and content instruction, teachers ask students to summarize, identify the main idea, explain in their own words, apply, and predict.

Advance Organizer Model

7. The advance organizer is an expository teaching model derived from the work of David Ausubel.
8. Teachers use the advance organizer model to assist students organize and integrate new knowledge.

Discussion Strategies

9. Authentic discussions are purposeful and involve sharing ideas, thoughts, and feelings.
10. Both discussion skills and discussion manners need to be taught and practiced.
11. To improve group discussions, evaluation must occur after each session.

Questioning Techniques

12. Teachers' questions initiate and guide most class discussions.
13. Teachers use questions for assessment and motivation.
14. Questions should stimulate thinking, be precise, appropriate to purpose, and accommodate students.
15. Questions need to be preplanned and clustered.

DISCUSSION QUESTIONS AND APPLICATION EXERCISES

1. Prepare a skill lesson using the direct instruction model. Identify the factual questions you will ask students during structured practice.
2. Plan a lesson that relies on reading. Use the comprehension model to design your questions.
3. Make a list of open-ended questions you would use to encourage participation in a large group discussion.
4. Make a list of classroom atmosphere elements that contribute to a good discussion.
5. Record the questions students ask during either the morning or the afternoon. Categorize the purposes for the questions using the following:
   • To extend thinking
   • To obtain permission
   • To clarify tasks
   • To clarify procedures
   What do the questions tell you about your teaching?
6. For a three- to five-day period, record the time you spend with low-, average-, and high-achieving students in your classroom.
7. Select content for a lesson and plan a series of questions. Think about clustering the questions to achieve content depth and higher level thinking.
8. Evaluate your students' small group discussion skills. Look for participation, attentiveness, expression of beliefs, opinions, new ideas, listening to each other, responding directly to each other, and engagement to task and content.
9. Use Mary Hogan's music lesson and identify the three phases of the advance organizer teaching model that she used.
10. How would you arrange your classroom for a discussion? Draw a diagram to illustrate your plan.

CHAPTER

7

Inquiry, Problem Solving, Constructivism, and Students as Researchers

Inquiry teaching has a long, distinguished history. In this chapter you will examine the historical perspective of inquiry and reflective thinking, along with examples of the process. The new buzz word in teaching, "constructivism," also is explained. Three teaching models are demonstrated through classroom teaching episodes; these are group investigation, concept attainment, and backward problem solving. You will learn the importance of the classroom environment for facilitating inquiry and how that environment affects learning, motivation, satisfaction and student involvement. The chapter concludes with case study methodology and a number of research skills to help students think like researchers.

After you study this chapter, you should be able to accomplish the following:

1. Describe inquiry learning.
2. Discuss the importance of inquiry learning.
3. Identify skills needed for inquiry and problem solving.
4. Identify the teacher tasks for inquiry teaching.
5. Using the exercise in the chapter, practice inquiry teaching tasks.
6. Explain how constructivism fits with inquiry experiences.
7. Identify the phases of the group investigation teaching model.
8. Develop a lesson using group investigation.
9. Identify the phases of the concept attainment teaching model.
10. Develop a lesson using concept attainment.
11. Compare group investigation and concept attainment with expository teaching strategies.
12. Demonstrate backward problem solving.
13. Suggest ways to evaluate students' problem-solving skills.
14. Identify and define research skills.
15. Plan questions and means to involve students in individual, small group, or whole class research.
16. Plan a case study and gather appropriate materials.

Professional Lexicon

backward problem solving   A motivating inquiry strategy that helps the teacher assess students' thinking processes and engages students in divergent thinking.

case study approach   An inquiry strategy that provides for thorough investigation of a single event, institution, decision, issue, or individual, and allows the teacher to reduce data to facilitate analysis.

concept attainment   An inquiry strategy designed to help students gain specific concepts by comparing and contrasting attributes; this strategy encourages students' use of metacognition.

constructivism   An approach to teaching and learning that acknowledges that information can be transmitted but understanding is dependent upon the learner (see Chapter 2).

group investigation   An inquiry-oriented cooperative learning strategy that requires interaction, discussion, planning, compromise, negotiation, and research processes.

inquiry   The process of examining and checking ideas, beliefs, and knowledge with data to develop meaning and theory.

reflective thinking   The process of using evidence; the active, persistent, and careful consideration of beliefs and knowledge.

structured interview   A research situation in which questions are predetermined and never differ during multiple interviews.

WHAT IS INQUIRY?

Most educational writers define **inquiry** in terms of the processes involved to resolve uncertainty. While the use of the term is relatively new in educational history, it can be traced to the terms *reflective thinking* and *critical thinking* as used by John Dewey. Dewey (1933, p. 9) defined **reflective thinking** as follows:

> Active, persistent, and careful consideration of any belief or supposed form of knowledge in the light of the grounds that support it and the further conclusions to which it tends.

Dewey analyzed the thinking process and differentiated between thinking and reflective thinking. He stated that thinking begins when the individual is aware of an indeterminate situation or a feeling of perplexity. A common thread runs through reflective thinking. There is consecutiveness of thought, a chaining effect that aims at a conclusion, and an inquiry into beliefs. The difference between thinking and reflective thinking is the ability of the individual to sustain the act while seeking a solution and being critical of the evidence unearthed during the process. The reflective individual subjects the belief and the evidence to reason. The nature of the problem determines the goal to be sought, and the goal determines the process.

Dewey identified five steps in reflective thinking that have served as a basis for all later research into the act of problem solving (1933, p. 107). They also formed the basis for his theory of reflective thinking. Dewey's five steps are as follows:

1. Considering suggestions, in which the mind leaps forward to a possible solution.
2. An intellectualization of the difficulty or perplexity that has been felt (directly experienced) into a problem to be solved, a question for which the answer must be sought.
3. The use of one suggestion after another as a leading idea, or hypothesis, to initiate and guide observation and other operations in collection of factual material.
4. The mental elaboration of the idea or supposition as an idea of supposition (reasoning, in the sense in which reasoning is a part, not the whole, of inference).
5. Testing the hypothesis by overt or imaginative action.

Hullfish and Smith (1961) also differentiated between thinking and reflective activity. Guided by Dewey's theoretical work, these authors found that the major distinction between thinking and reflection is that the latter is purposeful thought, directed and controlled. Thinking consists of three interrelated elements: sentiency, memory, and imagination. An appropriate and controlled balance of these three elements constitutes reflective thinking. Hullfish and Smith described the reflective situation as consisting of the following aspects:

1. The individual recognizes or is aware of a problem situation.
2. The individual acts to clarify the situation, physically or mentally.
3. If-then type thinking occurs: the individual hypothesizes, tests the ideas, and modifies them.
4. The individual makes a decision; action is taken as a result of the previous testing and verification.

Bayles (1960) added to the theory of the reflective process by clarifying the way in which a conclusion can be accepted as final. Bayles described the *principle of adequacy* and the *principle of harmony* (p. 87). The principle of adequacy occurs when the reflector is confident that he or she has obtained all the available information needed to study the problem satisfactorily. The principle of harmony occurs when the reflector interprets the data and reaches a conclusion that is in harmony with all available data. Bayles also used the term *problem solving* and equated it with the term *reflective thinking*. Massialas and Cox (1966, p. 90) identified reflective thinking as both means and end of classroom method. They defined it as

> the process of identifying problems of fact and value, assessing them in view of the assumptions in which they are grounded, and subjecting them to proof in terms of certain criteria.

They distinguished three types of generalizations used in reflective thinking: causal, correlative, and explanatory. Causal generalizations are discovered only after a careful investigation reveals a consequential relationship between two sets of phenomena. The use of data to describe a relationship in which a particular situation is an example is done through explanatory generalizations.

Suchman (1966) described inquiry as learning that is meaningful and intrinsically rewarding to the learner. During inquiry the learner attempts to close the gap between beliefs and observations. The learner uses data to organize observations and account for discrepant events. The learner is motivated by a desire for closure (the need to know and understand) and the desire to satisfy curiosity.

Suchman stated the following axioms about scientific inquiry:

- Inquiry is a back-and-forth process between theorizing and data gathering.
- Theories are checked by comparing them to the data.
- All language in a theory is described precisely and meaningfully.
- Limitations are stated for all theories.
- Theories must be consistent to their structure.
- Theories are derived inductively.
- Scientific theories can never be absolutely true.

Suchman called attention to the inductive thought processes involved in stating a theory and proposing hypotheses. However, as students search for evidence and apply and test the gathered data, they are engaging in deductive thought processes.

WHAT DOES AN INQUIRER DO?

The following story can serve as a mini-example of inquiry, providing insight into what an inquirer does during the process of inquiry.

I was startled by the sound of the puppy barking. Slowly I opened my eyes. "Was she barking or crying? I wonder what time it is?

"Only ten minutes after 5:00 A.M. Why is she up so early? Is she ill? I wonder if she is developing a new habit—waking up earlier each day. Seems to me she woke up at about 6:00 A.M. yesterday. Maybe that's it. Still, 5:00 is not 6:00; something must be wrong with her.

"Well, I'd better get up and find out. OK, puppy, what's wrong? You look perfectly fine. You don't appear to be sick. Let's go outside. Hurry up, so we can both go back to sleep. Strange, it looks too bright outside for 5:00 A.M. OK, pup, back to sleep.

"Hey, she's still barking. Sounds like her stomach is telling her it's breakfast time. I wonder what the other clocks in the house say? Hmm. They agree with the bedroom clock.

"Ah ha! I hear the rest of the family. Maybe it's later than I thought. If our electricity went out, the clocks would all be wrong. I'd better start breakfast.

"The microwave clock is blinking. That's it! I'll call Time and verify. Yep. It's 6:20 A.M. Our electricity must have been out for an hour."

Inquiry in the classroom is concerned with more important problems than whether or not the electricity stopped or a puppy has awakened earlier than usual, but just the same this little problem-solving episode provides a description of the inquiry process. To analyze it, review what happened:

The dog barked earlier than usual. Is it really extra early, or is there another reason for the puppy's barking?

Discrepant event/fact problem	1. The clock is correct; the puppy is developing a new habit.
	2. The puppy is ill.
	3. The clock is wrong; the electricity stopped.
Evidence data gathering	a. Puppy looks fine; appears in good health.
	b. The morning appears to be extraordinarily bright for 5:00 A.M.
	c. Puppy continues to bark as if expecting breakfast.
	d. Others in family are awakening; must be time to get up.
	e. Other electric clocks in house read the same way.
	f. Microwave clock is blinking. (It is a digital clock.)
Tentative conclusion	Clocks in house are wrong. (To verify, time is called.)
Conclusion	Electricity stopped. Clocks did not run for an hour during the night.

Since this type of inquiry occurs may times a day, you need to think about why inquiry is important and what value students derive from planned inquiry experiences.

WHY IS INQUIRY IMPORTANT?

Bruner (1966) characterized the learner who is oriented toward *discovery learning* and the benefits derived from it:

- He or she is intellectually more effective. Discovery is made because the individual expects that there is something to be found out. The expectation motivates the search, and the learner persists in the search for relatedness. Thinking exhibits connectedness; questions are cycled, and the learner organizes and summarizes.

- The learner is governed by intrinsic motivation. The individual is more interested in learning that *something is true* than learning *about something*.
- The learner is heuristically inclined. The individual makes discoveries by practicing problem solving. Problem-solving skills improve through repeated experiences with inquiry.
- The learner preserves information through superior organization. The individual organizes useful information into a personal cognitive structure, thereby maximizing its retrieval.

Discovery learning, according to Bruner, is the process of using one's own intellect to gain knowledge by discovering concepts and organizing them into a structure that is personally meaningful. During the act of discovery, the student tests and verifies relationships. The student may be discovering knowledge that is new to him or her, but not necessarily knowledge that is unknown to others. During discovery the learner is actively using his or her mind. The student is totally involved in the learning experience.

INQUIRY SKILLS AND REFLECTIVE THINKING

Dewey considered reflective thinking a "better way of thinking" (1933, p. 3); Osterman considered reflectiveness as "mindful consideration" (1990, p. 134). Reflectiveness is described in different ways, but most researchers agree that it involves reconsideration of the uncertain for the purpose of gaining insight. The process requires seeking patterns and varied perspectives, considering alternatives, and attending to possible solutions.

As you have probably noted, inquiry learning is a common-sense way of making decisions using the scientific method. Inquiry begins inductively as the student becomes aware of a problem, but as the process continues the student uses deductive processes. Although in practice inquiry is not necessarily a precise process, generally the students proceed through the following stages:

1. Problem Definition
   - Students recognize a problem or puzzlement.
   - Students narrow and limit the problem to make it meaningful and manageable by asking questions.
   - Students attempt to define key aspects of the problem.
2. Hypothesizing
   - Students begin to generalize about the problem and discuss ideas as possible solutions to the problem.
   - Students continue to define terms and state hypotheses.
3. Exploration
   - Students plan and decide what evidence is needed.
   - Students search for evidence to support the tentative solution using observation, field trips, library resources, experiments, interviews, case studies, role-playing, original documents, etc.
   - Students gather data on the basis of relevance to the hypotheses.
4. Data Analysis
   - Students evaluate data noting objectivity, reliability, source, and bias.
   - Data are contrasted; similarities and differences are noted.
   - Trends and sequences are noted.
   - Students summarize the data.
   - Students interpret the data.
5. Reaching a Conclusion
   - Students accept, reject, or modify the hypotheses.
   - The hypotheses are restated, if necessary.
   - Students generalize and suggest ways to test the generalization in new situations.

Our mini-example of inquiry has all the necessary components: feeling perplexed, hypothesizing, exploration, data analysis, and conclusion. However, because it is such a simplistic example there was not any evidence of data being examined for truth or summarized. For example, it was stated that the "puppy looks fine" and does not "appear to be sick." These are subjective observations. They are acceptable if their limitations are understood. The fact that the day appears to be especially bright for 5:00 A.M. is an observation based on experience of observing the daylight at that hour. Like most observations, it is subjective, but it still offers valuable evidence. The rest of the data are more factually based, although they may be subject to error. These are the fine points of inquiry that a teacher needs to communicate to students so they become efficient problem solvers. Let us look at the teacher tasks during inquiry.

TEACHER TASKS FOR INQUIRY TEACHING

CHOOSING APPROPRIATE PROBLEMS FOR STUDY

In planning topics for inquiry, the teacher is confronted with three elements: selecting a problem that provides mileage in terms of content, choosing a problem that is of interest to the students, and formulating a provocative question. Providing mileage in the content means selecting problems that have depth, provide appropriate research skill usage, and fit grade-level goals and objectives. The problem you select should be useful in meeting the content needs, provide for the development of inquiry skills, and enable sequential learning of concepts. It is important to remember that the inquiry problem must be significant enough that there is information provided to students as well as questions that motivate skill development.

It is obvious that the topic must be of interest to students. Inquiry problems that do not appeal to students will not be successful. If students do not perceive that a problem exists, or if it is irrelevant to them, or if it is inappropriate to their developmental level, then they will not be motivated to inquire. Not only must the teacher choose carefully, but it is critical to present the problem in a way that creates controversy and real interest. Choose a problem that is closely related to student experiences and concerns instead of a contrived problem that you might select only because of its suitability for inquiry. The teacher must be the judge and consider student involvement, skill needs, content needs, and the transfer of learning potential.

Inquiry questions are problems stated in question form. Formulating an inquiry-oriented question is a very important task. Every question you ask in the classroom should have a purpose. In a sense, there are no bad questions, but the challenge is to ask a question that will facilitate the thinking appropriate for the task. An inquiry-oriented question should motivate inquiry, assist the students in defining the problem, and suggest possible hypotheses.

Consider the following two questions:

1. What is a "Mom and Pop" grocery store?
2. Why are there more supermarkets in modern cities than "Mom and Pop" grocery stores?

Question 1 is really a subquestion of question 2. Obviously, students will need to define the "Mom and Pop" grocery store; however, this question is not formulated to inspire inquiry, define the problem, or sug-

gest hypotheses. The second graders who were asked question 2 defined the problem and suggested the following hypotheses for investigation:

Problem	Hypotheses
Markets in modern cities tend to be larger today than during past times.	1. Modern equipment is too expensive for small grocery stores. 2. Small groceries are not profitable. 3. People prefer "one-stop" shopping.

DEFINING THE PROBLEM

Karen Adazzio began a safety unit for her seventh graders with the question, "What is the relationship between age and auto safety?" The students had difficulty defining the word *relationship*. To help them decide what the problem was about, she asked, "How many of you believe that teen-agers have more accidents than their parents?" The students (of course!) were incensed at the idea that teen-age drivers might cause more accidents than adult drivers, and they began to justify their belief that teens were good drivers. ("They have faster reflexes." "They take driver training and driver education." "They are more alert.")

Finally, she assured the students that their reasons were plausible, but they would have to investigate to find out if they were accurate. "Who can tell us, very precisely, what it is we need to find out?"

The students thought about it and finally came up with the following problem for investigation: Certain age groups have better driving records than other groups and are less likely to have auto accidents.

Next Adazzio asked the students to suggest hypotheses for investigation, and they decided on the following three hypotheses:

1. Senior citizens have fewer accidents than other age groups.
2. Teenagers have more accidents than other age groups.
3. People who cause auto accidents pay more for their insurance.

To help the students define the problem and consider areas for investigation, Adazzio found it necessary to narrow the focus for the students. She accomplished this by asking the follow-up question about teen-age drivers. Whenever students are unable to open up the investigation and specify the problem, the teacher must probe and facilitate problem definition by narrowing the focus.

DATA BASE

Sources for information are so important in inquiry methodology that most teachers consider the adequacy of their materials and resources first before making a decision about an inquiry problem. The second-grade teacher who posed the question about supermarkets had to consider how students would find out why the size of markets had changed in recent years. The teacher's data sources for students may include field-trip observations, social studies textbooks, resource people, pictures, maps, charts, tables, and informational data written by the teacher. Sometimes students generate data sources in the form of interviews, questionnaires, or case studies. Dramatizations or simulations may also be used as data sources.

Students need contrasting content if they are to learn to process information. Practice with such content will teach them to categorize facts, ideas, or events; evaluate information for interpretive purposes; and develop their own generalizations about why something is true or why something usually happens. As students collect data, the teacher asks questions to help them compare and contrast the data and make inferences based on their information.

CREATING AN INQUIRY-ORIENTED ENVIRONMENT

Both the physical and social environment must encourage students to develop inquiry skills. Students are affected by the physical setting and the context of instruction. Through the arrangement of the classroom, planned strategies, modeling, and choice of materials, the teacher guides students to interact with each other and with the environment and motivates them to engage in discovery learning. Students' needs and life experiences should be considered both in the choice of inquiry problems and in the materials arranged for use.

An inquiry-oriented classroom is characterized by its ability to sustain reflection. Students and teacher do not hurry to closure, but discussions do have a direct focus. In the reflective discussion the teacher's questions tend to act as a springboard for the discussion rather than focusing on a right answer. The questions probe instead of elicit.

Teaching Hints: Planning Inquiry Learning

Assume you read a newspaper article that reported that the California state assembly passed a measure that could send graffiti taggers to prison. The assembly wants to elevate graffiti violations from misdemeanors to felonies. Currently felony convictions occur only when the property damage is over $5,000. The assembly bill would send taggers to state prison when clean-up costs exceed $400.

1. Write an inquiry question to motivate student interest using the article about graffiti taggers.
2. State the problem as you would expect your students to state it.
3. Write a hypothesis that you anticipate your students would propose.
4. Identify sources for gathering data.
5. How will you have students organize their data? (What will students produce?)
6. How will you evaluate students' inquiry skills?

The reflective classroom uses hypotheses as its discussion focus and relies on factual material to support the hypotheses. Factual recall is not valued, but facts are used to support or reject a hypothesis.

Time is another aspect of the inquiry-oriented classroom that is used differently than in a more traditional environment. Since the teacher is not rushing to cover specific material in the reflective classroom, the class has time to participate in democratic processes. The act of clarification is important to inquiry. Students need to communicate and search for a consensus of meaning; thus the reflective teacher does not watch the clock.

During the planning process the teacher must decide whether the environment should be interdependent or unilateral. The social climate should promote social development, and if properly conducted, the class environment promotes independence and the ability to establish meaningful relationships with others.

In an inquiry-oriented classroom the teacher assumes a less prominent position and attempts to guide students to resources of knowledge. The teacher's central purpose is to arouse interest and raise questions so students will inquire and learn to draw upon their own experiences. In addition, teachers should help students to perceive discrepancies in their information. The climate of the classroom allows students

---

What types of behaviors do teachers demonstrate when using inquiry methodology.

---

to gain self-confidence and to direct their own study and thinking.

GUIDANCE AND OBJECTIVITY

The teacher's primary role during inquiry revolves around raising questions. Preplanning a question strategy and preparation of materials enable the teacher to direct students' hypothesizing and guide them to appropriate materials to facilitate their thinking. While students are gathering data, the teacher continuously challenges and prods them to explore new alternatives. Student inferences and conjectures are encouraged. Students will need to be reminded of the temporal quality of knowledge and that authority cannot be trusted as omniscient. The teacher needs to be alert to stimulate the students' search for evidence and remind students to challenge an accepted hypothesis.

Taba (1967a) contended that thinking can be taught by identifying cognitive skills and devising strategies to give the learner the opportunity to practice each particular cognitive skill. Taba identified the task of questioning as vital to the teaching of cognitive skills. Questions should be structured by the teacher to accomplish the following:

- Guide the students' search
- Raise the level of thought
- Focus on content
- Program the study as to sequence and transitions

Taba (p. 48) commented on the merits of this approach:

> Elements of teaching strategy such as appropriate focusing, pacing, and sequencing wide involvement made considerable difference in the amount of productive thought a class can generate, as well as fostering complex and abstract thought by students who are usually considered incapable of it.

Using Taba's three strategies (discussed in Chapter 6) encourages inductive thinking. For this reason the three strategies together are considered to be an inquiry model. (The model was discussed in Chapter 6 because it demonstrates strategic sequenced questions.)

In summary, the teacher's major tasks in using inquiry methodology are to stimulate the use of inquiry processes by students, to guide students' choice of materials, and to arrange an appropriate environment

Teacher Research

Buckmaster (1994) studied her seventh-grade students in a Future Problem Solving class. Students worked in groups of four to solve futuristic problems. To lessen competitive behaviors and improve interpersonal relationships, she implemented activities designed to promote cooperation. She taught the students empathetic listening, negotiation skills, and cooperative structures.

She concluded that the majority of the students felt positive about themselves and their accomplishments. There was evidence of increased student understanding of self and others.

and climate for inquiry. The teacher manages participation, provides cues and feedback, reinforces appropriate behaviors, and directs both formative and summative evaluation of inquiry learning. Now let's take a look at what inquiry instruction is like in different subject fields.

AN EXAMPLE OF INQUIRY INSTRUCTION USING GROUP INVESTIGATION

Although the main components of inquiry instruction are the same, remember that varied purposes will change the way in which it is accomplished. Scientific data gathering usually occurs through experimentation and record keeping. In physical education, discovery may be facilitated through physical movement. In music, discovery learning may focus on the use of instruments or on listening experiences.

ART AND SOCIAL STUDIES

Let's go back to Greg Thomas's fifth-grade classroom. His students are studying U.S. history, and Thomas is integrating art experiences with the social studies. He asks his students, "What does the art of the early New England colonists tell us about their cultural beliefs?"

On the edge of the chalkboard, Thomas has displayed photographs of artifacts and paintings from different periods of U.S. and European history. The students begin to react to the pictures and the question. One outspoken student comments that he doesn't think the New England colonists produced much art, and therefore there would be little to study. Others react differently by asking whether they would study only paintings or whether sculpture and architecture could be included too. Another group of students appears to doubt that it is possible to detect cultural beliefs by studying art or artifacts.

After the students have had sufficient time to react, Thomas calls attention to the different opinions expressed by the group:

- Very little art was produced by the New England colonists.
- The study should be broad and include handicrafts, architecture, and other artwork.
- Students doubt that the study of art could determine cultural beliefs.

Thomas asks the students if they can suggest a way to reformulate his original question into a problem for them to study. After several minutes, they agree on the following problem: Using different types of art forms, can we recognize a people's beliefs?

The problem as stated is slightly different than what Greg Thomas had anticipated, but it still enables the students to study much of what he has preplanned. Next he asks them to decide how to go about the study.

As the students suggest ideas for the investigation, Thomas writes them down on the board. This is their list:

- Look at handcrafted objects from the colonial period
- Look at artists' pictures
- Compare artists' pictures in New England with paintings by other artists from other places and other periods
- Examine tools made during colonial days
- Look at the architecture of the period
- Study furniture produced during the colonial period
- Research information about the New England colonists
- Use slides and filmstrips (Thomas told the students he had some.)
- Study clothing from the colonial period

The students decide to draw much of what they observed to have a record of their research.

Some of the students begin to express preferences in terms of what they want to do. Not all of the students want to record their information with pictures;

some students will take notes instead. The students choose their work groups and plan who will do what in their small groups. The study will take two weeks and will include a visit to the art museum. Several of the students express an interest in making tools and chairs identical to those produced during the colonial period.

At the beginning of each work period, Thomas tells the students where each group should work in the classroom and how much time they have to work. At the end of each work period, Thomas asks the groups to report their progress. Each group reports how they had gone about their study during the period, what they had accomplished, problems they had or anticipated, and plans for the next work period.

Each day when Thomas evaluated with the students he asked for a substantive report of progress and a report on how well the group worked together. In this way he kept the students on task and improved their cooperative group work skills. On consecutive days, prior to each work session, Thomas recycled the study by asking the students, "What are you going to do today?" and "What materials do you need to use?"

At the end of the first week, Thomas suggested to the students that they might need to make a large chart to record the findings from each group. They decided that at the end of the following week each group would make an oral presentation, and then they would discuss the pertinent information in order to analyze the data.

They analyzed the following data:

- A list of furniture used in most colonial homes
- A sketchbook of furnishings
- A sketchbook of dress styles
- Notes about the New England work ethic
- Replicated tools and several pieces of furniture (chairs, stools)

The group studying colonial furniture used a data retrieval chart similar to Figure 7.1, and they continued to fill in the blanks spaces as they found more information. To organize data, students made charts and graphs similar to Figure 7.2 and Figure 7.3.

The students could use additional materials including:

- Sketches of household utensils
- Notes about individual artists' pictures
- Pictures of churches
- Notes about colonial recreation in New England
- Notes about religious interests

What types of behaviors do students demonstrate during inquiry?

Figure 7.1   Comparison of Colonial and European Furniture

	Materials Used	Purpose	Looks	Handmade or Manufactured
CHAIRS				
Colonial	Wood—mahogany	Dining, reading	Straight-backed, simple, hard	Handmade
European	Wood/fabric	Relaxing, dining, reading	Ornate, soft	Manufactured
SOFAS				
Colonial				
European				
TABLES				
Colonial				
European				
CHESTS				
Colonial				
European				

Figure 7.2   Graph Showing Percentages of Handcrafted and Manufactured Products During Colonial Days

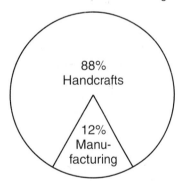

Figure 7.3   Histogram of Daily Activities of New England Colonists

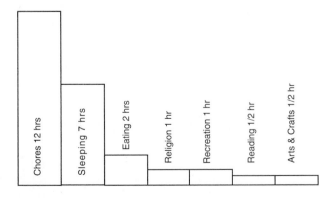

The class discussion focused on the data and what they had learned. Thomas initiated the discussion by asking, "What do we know about the way of life of the colonists who lived in New England?"

He followed this question by asking the students to "compare the art forms and styles of the New England colonists with other periods in American history." During the course of the discussion, the students even compared the furniture of the colonial period with the furniture produced in Europe (Figure 7.1).

WHAT DID THE STUDENTS LEARN?

Using their data, the students decided that they could say the following about the New England colonists with a fair amount of confidence:

- They appeared to be a grave type of people.
- They struggled and worked hard.
- Their art was practical, functional, and symmetrical.
- The language they used was plain and correct.
- Their household utensils and furniture were plain, simple, and functional.
- The artists sometimes were house painters and performed other needed chores like painting signs and making decorations for coffins.
- They used their churches for social gatherings and the church buildings were designed to accommodate people; they were functional.
- Their clothes were practical, not fancy.

Examine Greg Thomas's questions and identify the purpose of each. How would you initiate the discussion after the students' group investigation?

Greg Thomas was pleased with what the students had learned. He asked them if they were ready to draw a final conclusion about the question he had asked them and their statement about the problem to be investigated. The students responded that they had learned a great deal about the colonists by studying their art, and that in fact they really had discussed the colonists' cultural beliefs (see Table 7.1). The answer to the question posed by the students as to whether it was possible to recognize people's beliefs by studying their art forms was affirmative. Students concluded that art provided a visual record of culture.

It is important to note that significant problems for students' research lead naturally to interdisciplinary content. Thomas, through his choice of a motivating situation, deftly integrated content from several social sciences, art, and language arts.

The episode that took place in Greg Thomas's classroom conformed to what Joyce and Weil (1996) described as the **group investigation model.** Thomas's strategy with his students included six phases of inquiry:

Phase 1: Thomas posed the question and encouraged the students to react to the question.

Phase 2: Thomas identified the different opinions about the question and asked the students to suggest the problem to investigate.

Phase 3: Thomas asked the students to suggest ideas for the investigation. Students chose what they wanted to do, organized into groups, and decided on tasks.

Phase 4: Students gathered data independently and in their group situation. Thomas asked for formative evaluations after each work period.

Phase 5: Students gave reports and shared data.

Phase 6: Students concluded by reexamining their original question and problem.

CLASSROOM MANAGEMENT

During group investigation the teacher's role is to facilitate inquiry and problem solving. The teacher must motivate the students, set the stage for the group work, provide the necessary resources, and provide ongoing guidance.

Group students heterogeneously or homogeneously, depending on the nature of the work task. Students are most typically grouped heterogeneously for this strategy.

Verify that students understand what they are to do in their groups before you dismiss them for group work. It is important to plan where each group will work and dismiss each group to its workplace, group by group, so bedlam does not occur as students carry chairs and work materials. Let groups know how much time they have to carry out their work task, and identify a means to get attention during the work period (switch off lights, ring a bell, hold up hand, etc.).

Table 7.1   Activities of New England Colonists

Sleeping	7 hours
Chores	12 hours
Recreation	1 hour
Eating	2 hours
Religion	1 hour
Reading	½ hour
Arts and Crafts	½ hour

Teaching Hints: Group Investigation

You can use group investigation at all grade levels and for all subjects. Students need to be able to sit next to each other and talk quietly together. They can sit on the floor, on chairs, or at desks. This teaching strategy facilitates cooperative inquiry, cooperative planning and projects, and group discussion. Review the six phases of group investigation:

1. Begin with a problem or a situation that is puzzling to the students. The strategy works best when students are motivated to solve the problem or explain the situation.
2. Provide time for students to think out loud about the problem or situation.
3. Organize the students in groups, clarify what each group is to do, set time limits, decide where each group is to work, and redefine the problem.
4. Allow time for group work.
5. Evaluate the group product and the group process. What did the group accomplish? How well did the group members work together? This is the most important phase in the strategy if students are going to improve their group process skills and learn democratic processes.
6. If the group work has not been completed, then phase six—the recycling stage—occurs. The teacher lets the students know when they will work again.

Hands-on activities provide opportunity for inquiry experience and help to balance textbook assignments.

Monitor group work by walking around and listening in as each group plans, discusses, or carries out the work task. If a group is off-task because they do not understand, help them by refocusing their attention on what they are to accomplish. If their confusion indicates general class uncertainty, stop the whole class and clarify the problem. If the problem is behavioral, you may have to change the group members or stop the whole class and ask, "How can we help this group work together?" Then discuss group work roles and rules.

Students improve group process skills only through repeated opportunities to practice. Therefore, it is essential to evaluate progress (Phase 5). It is often a good idea to assign, or have groups decide on, specific work roles. The roles of group leader and group recorder carry important responsibilities. Specialization of work tasks within the group also creates group responsibility. Each member of the group may have to research something specific to contribute to the group report.

CONSTRUCTIVISM: WHAT IS IT?

As teachers we can transmit information to students, but we do not know what students are learning until they do something with the information. According to Lemlech and Hertzog (1995):

Why is constructivism considered an inquiry approach?

Constructivist learning theory is an approach to teaching and learning which acknowledges that information can be transmitted but understanding must be constructed.

Constructivism and inquiry go hand in hand; they are two parts of the same coin.

The teacher assesses what students know, and with this knowledge of the learner, the teacher plans new experiences and knowledge to be gained by the student. Constructivist teaching uses the student's prior knowledge as a building block to integrate new understandings with prior learnings. To accomplish this, the teacher plans active experiences to involve students in explorations, theory building, and experimentation so that students can generate and organize data, and communicate with others. As the learner gains new knowledge, previously held beliefs and ideas may change as new interpretations are made.

As in inquiry/problem-solving experiences, the student is challenged to engage in activity that requires higher level thinking and reflective processes. Ultimately the student must apply the new knowledge to *produce* a product that demonstrates his or her understanding.

Translated into a teaching model, constructivism has four phases:

Phase 1: A puzzling question or problem is introduced.
Phase 2: The learner explores, talks about the problem, and uses his or her own ideas to create and test understanding.

Phase 3: The learner explains what has happened and what has been learned.

Phase 4: The learner demonstrates the ability to apply new knowledge through social participation, in actions related to the classroom, the community, and/or communicated in projects, discussion, and appreciation.

CONSTRUCTIVISM IN GREG THOMAS'S CLASSROOM

The rain had just ceased and the students were pleased to be released from the classroom for time on the playground. Thomas had assigned team games and he wandered among the four groups of students observing them as they played. Several students had just noticed a rainbow in the sky, and they were busy showing it to each other. Thomas listened to their talk.

Back in the classroom Thomas questioned the students about the rainbow. "What do you know about rainbows?"

Responses included the following:

- Visible after a rain
- Possible to make a rainbow
- Many different colors
- Colors called a spectrum
- Something called white light
- White and black are not considered colors

Phase 1

Thomas then asked the students what they would like to know. This time they responded with a number of questions:

- What are the colors of the spectrum?
- Are they always the same?
- Why are black and white not colors?
- How do you combine colors of the spectrum?
- What happens when colors are combined?
- How do colors look in the shade? in the sun? in dim light? in bright light?

Thomas complimented the students on their questions and told them that tomorrow he would bring in some materials to let them experiment. In the meantime he took them outside again and used a garden hose to spray water upward. In this way he recreated a rainbow for the students to see. Back in the classroom he told them to write down their personal observations for discussion tomorrow.

Phase 2

The next day Thomas had a variety of equipment for the students to use. The students selected materials and questions and were told to develop new questions that interested them. In small groups, with Thomas providing assistance when asked, the students used prisms, magnifying instruments, mirrors, white cardboard, shoe boxes, and colored papers. Thomas told the students to jot down what question(s) they were investigating, what materials they used, and how they went about their experiment.

Phase 3

After two activity periods for experimentation, the students recorded their findings and how their findings were meaningful to them. Some of the things the students learned included the following:

- The black paper did not seem to reflect color.
- They saw seven colors in the spectrum. The colors seemed to always be in the same order. (You can make a rainbow using the prism and the sun's rays.)
- The white paper reflected color. (It's better to wear white when it's hot outside.) White is a combination of colors. Black has no color; black absorbs colors.
- You can make the rainbow disappear with a magnifying glass by moving it back and forth.

Phase 4

Thomas asked the students how they could use what they learned or if they knew of any evidence of its use. They responded: "It's better to wear white when it's hot outside and black when it is cold!" "In Florida many of the houses have white rooftops to reflect the heat." "Light colors look grey when there isn't much light; scenery looks different when it is dim outside."

Once again, as the students talked, Thomas recorded what they seemed to understand so that he could plan his next steps to help them learn more about light and color.

THE CONCEPT ATTAINMENT MODEL OF TEACHING

The **concept attainment** model of teaching is an inquiry strategy used to help students gain specific concepts by comparing and contrasting examples that have specific characteristics (attributes) with examples that do not contain the characteristics. Joyce and Weil (1996) developed the teaching model; it is derived from the work of Bruner, who studied the ways in which people categorize, form, and gain concepts. The concept attainment model provides a means for teachers to analyze the ways students form concepts and help them become more efficient.

Let us visit Mary Hogan's second-grade classroom, where she is using this strategy. Hogan writes some words on the board, and as she writes she asks the students to see if they can guess what she is thinking about.

foot (yes)
picture (no)
horse (yes)
plane (yes)
dog (no)

"The yeses give you clues about what I am thinking," hints Hogan.

The students raise their hands and begin to guess. "Are you thinking about animals?" "No, she can't be thinking about animals because the plane is marked yes and the dog is a no." The students continue their questions and responses to each other, and then Hogan offers to make another list to help them.

car
train
telephone
books
wagon

"Now," asks Hogan, "which words should be followed by a yes, and which should get a no?"

The students become excited. Many talk out without raising their hands, and Hogan does not try to restrain them. Finally Hogan says, "Let's do this together. What should I put next to the word car?" The students respond, "Yes." "How about train?" "Yes," answers James. "What about telephone?" "That is a no and so is books." "You're doing just fine," says Hogan, "but I wonder if you know what to put after wagon?" The students are quiet, and then Bill raises his hand and says, "I think it gets a yes."

Hogan smiles. "You've done very well. Can you tell me what I have been thinking about?"

After several minutes, Jed asks, "Does it have something to do with walking and riding?" (Hogan smiles but does not respond.) Jana asks whether she is thinking about ways people travel.

"You are very close, Jana. Suppose everyone thinks about some additional yeses and noes. Perhaps that would help everyone know what I am thinking about."

The students begin to contribute ideas: "Raft is a yes." "Boat is a yes." "Camel is a no." "Submarine is a yes." "Taxi is a yes." "Radio is a no." "TV is a no."

"OK, you have done very well. Are you thinking about what Jana said? Could anyone be more specific? Can you think of a big word that has to do with travel?"

"I can, Miss Hogan, is it transportation?"

"Excellent, Beth. Congratulations, boys and girls. Now can you tell me what you were thinking about while you were guessing the meaning of my yeses and noes?"

"Well, I looked at all the yeses and tried to see how they were alike."

"Gee, I started with the noes and compared them to the yeses."

"I didn't understand about the word foot and that confused me."

"I got stuck on the word wagon."

"Jana, what made you think about travel?" asks Hogan.

"I guess I just put all the yeses together and thought about how they all had something to do with traveling. After you said travel, I began to think how foot, horse, and wagon were related. At first I had a hard time because I couldn't understand why horse was yes and dog was no!"

"Well, boys and girls, you certainly have done a good job. Now why do you suppose I wanted you to think about transportation?"

Mary Hogan's class is studying about cities, and she has used the concept attainment model to introduce the concept of transportation as a characteristic of cities.

At the end of her teaching unit, Hogan again uses this model to help students integrate what they had learned. Let's visit Hogan's classroom four weeks later.

On the board is the following list:

apartments (yes)
farms (no)
subways (yes)
silo (no)
bus (yes)
recreation (yes)

"OK, boys and girls, see if you can guess what I am thinking."

The students begin to talk to each other: transportation (nah), housing (no!); maybe both! Hogan makes another list:

banks
people with many skills
tractors

fields of grain
factories
services

Now the students really begin to buzz. "Let's do the yeses and noes."

"What should banks be?" ("Yes," respond the students.)

"How about people with many skills?" ("Yes.")

"Tractors?" (A chorus of noes greets her.)

"Fields of grain?" ("Nooo.")

"Factories?" ("Yes, we know it.")

"Services?" ("No." "Wait, it's a yes!")

"All right, if you are so positive, give me a list of yeses and noes before you tell me what I am thinking about."

The students' yes list includes museums, opera, tall buildings, doctors, engineers, firefighters, postal workers, and shopkeepers. Their no list includes agriculture, farm animals, farmer, and farmhouse.

"What was I thinking about?" asks Hogan.

"Cities?" asks Jamie.

"All about cities," comments Mark.

"The characteristics of cities," says Jana. And the rest of the class nods, content that they have the right concept.

"Tell me what you thought about while you were guessing," says Hogan.

Once again the students describe their thinking processes. Several students comment how listening to the ideas of others had helped them gain the concept. One student comments that services gave the answer away. Another explains that she went back and thought about people with varied skills and that had put her on the right track.

The concept attainment model of teaching helps students think inductively. Instead of starting with an abstract concept and then providing examples of the concept, the teacher begins with the examples and has the students develop meaning using the exemplars. Cognitive psychologists believe that the best way to learn a concept is through examples. It is just as important to have negative examples as it is to have positive ones because students cannot recognize essential attributes unless they have negative characteristics to compare and contrast.

The concept attainment model has several phases:

Phase 1: The teacher presents positive and negative examples of the concept.

Phase 2: The students compare attributes of positive and negative examples. Students freely discuss their ideas. (They are hypothesizing.)

Phase 3: The teacher neither confirms nor denies hypotheses; writes additional list on board but does not label entries either yes or no.

Phase 4: Students are asked to identify the additional examples as positive or negative based on their prior hypotheses.

Phase 5: Students once again discuss their hypotheses and are asked to state them.

Phase 6: The teacher confirms ideas—or provides help—and names the concept.

Phase 7: Students generate additional examples of positive and negative exemplars as requested by the teacher.

Phase 8: The teacher asks students to describe their thinking during the hypothesizing stage.

TEACHING HINTS

The concept attainment model is used to introduce abstract concepts to students by beginning with familiar examples and moving to the less familiar concept. For example, before teaching about the American revolutionary war, Greg Thomas may need to introduce the concept of revolution and verify that his students understand the concept.

The model is also useful to help students synthesize material that they have already studied. Mary Hogan's use of the model led to the class identifying the characteristics of cities (people with varied skills, recreation, transportation, and services, and commerce) that they had researched in small groups.

The concept attainment model can be used at any grade level (using pictures in kindergarten) to teach selected concepts, initiate units of study, and help students assimilate information. The most important phase of the model occurs when students identify their thinking processes. By doing this, students who are less efficient in hypothesizing learn strategies from the more proficient students. The concept attainment model helps students improve their thinking strategies.

CLASSROOM MANAGEMENT

The concept attainment model is effective with the whole class seated together. It can, of course, also be used with small groups. Since the teacher controls the pace of instruction during this strategy, there is moderate structure. A free discussion encourages student ideas and hypothesizing. Students learn to add on to the thinking process of their peers. This makes the strategy fun and improves the thinking process. Shy students should be encouraged to try out their ideas aloud. The teacher should help students analyze their thinking strategies.

The concept attainment model is dependent on teacher planning. Exemplars need to be carefully selected and sequenced to cue students' thinking. The teacher is responsible for recording examples, prompting students, and providing additional data.

BACKWARD PROBLEM SOLVING

Backward problem solving is a fun way to capture students' interest and get them involved in an inquiry activity. It also provides an ongoing means to observe students' thinking processes in context. Let's see how it works by visiting in Karen Adazzio's classroom.

Concern about the Los Angeles riots in spring 1992 led to a variety of classroom lessons in both elementary and secondary classrooms. School districts across the country were urged to provide means for students to express their feelings about what happened.

Adazzio began the discussion by asking her students, "Could the Los Angeles riots have occurred here?" The students' response was overwhelmingly "Yes."

"Tell me," said Adazzio, "what you consider to be the most pressing issues that precipitated the rioting."

Adazzio recorded the students' list of items on the chalkboard:

- Prejudice against African-Americans
- Tension between African-Americans and Koreans and other groups
- People out of work
- Homelessness
- Hunger
- The Rodney King beating
- Kids don't like school; schools aren't relevant for inner-city kids
- Parents aren't home, kids have no place to go, and nobody cares about them
- Gangs used the King verdict to take advantage and loot guns and other weapons

---

In what ways do inquiry approaches address the problems of teaching students with diverse abilities and learning styles?

That's quite a list," said Adazzio; "Let's focus just on the needs of young people. What would be an ideal situation, so that teenagers would not be involved in riots?"

Ideally, the students decided, there would be school programs that involved parents and kids, programs relevant to the needs of growing teens, and programs that would make sure kids would be successful and feel good about themselves.

"OK," said Adazzio, "Let's assume that is our desired solution; let's just focus on *Relevant School Programs and Student Success.* What would it take to make it happen?"

Adazzio placed the goal inside a large circle (Figure 7.4). "What are the big ideas that are involved in making school programs relevant and ensuring student success?" From this the students identified four components:

1. A caring environment
2. Ending racial divisions
3. Vocational and college preparatory program choices for students
4. Opportunity to earn money while attending school

At this point in the lesson, Adazzio divided the students into small groups. Each group selected one of the four components to develop fully. (What would a school program look like if it provided choices for students?) (What do you consider to be a "caring environment" in the school setting?)

HOW DOES BACKWARD PROBLEM SOLVING WORK?

The strategy assumes that everyone knows the resolution to the problem; but what is not known are the enabling tasks. For example, every teacher wants students to engage in critical thinking (Figure 7.5); but what is not known is how to align curriculum and instructional process to ensure that students practice critical-thinking skills.

The purpose of backward problem solving is to think about divergent means to accomplish a goal and to recognize that for most goals, there is not one best way to realize success. The model is open-ended and encourages creative ideas. It is appropriate for whole class or small group activity.

The phases of backward problem solving include:

Phase 1: Motivation and recognition of a problem situation.
Phase 2: Identification and acceptance of the desired goal/solution.

Figure 7.4 Backward Problem Solving Example

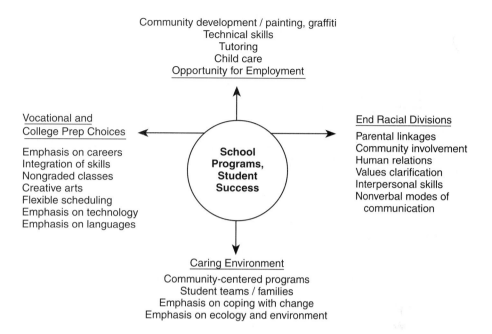

Community development / painting, graffiti
Technical skills
Tutoring
Child care
Opportunity for Employment

Vocational and
College Prep Choices

Emphasis on careers
Integration of skills
Nongraded classes
Creative arts
Flexible scheduling
Emphasis on technology
Emphasis on languages

School Programs, Student Success

End Racial Divisions

Parental linkages
Community involvement
Human relations
Values clarification
Interpersonal skills
Nonverbal modes of communication

Caring Environment

Community-centered programs
Student teams / families
Emphasis on coping with change
Emphasis on ecology and environment

Phase 3: Exploration of diverse means to make the solution take place. This phase may be informal brainstorming or actual research.

Phase 4: The model may end at Phase 3 or be recycled to include exploration and in-depth study of the different facets of the enabling mechanisms identified in Phase 3.

HOW CAN ALL STUDENTS ENGAGE IN INQUIRY?

Diverse interests and abilities need to be accommodated in most classroom situations. Much of the time there is a wide range of thinking ability in elementary and middle school classrooms. Inquiry teaching develops intellectual skills by providing opportunities for students to observe, identify, and hypothesize about problems; to gather and classify data; to analyze, compare, and contrast information; to interpret and verify data; and to come to a conclusion concerning the problem. Most students can accomplish these tasks by using a variety of learning experiences and activities.

Inquiry encourages active thinking and seeking rather than rote memorization; appropriately chosen problems enable students to work at their own ability level. It is important to remember that students are not discovering new knowledge; they are only discovering

Figure 7.5 How to Develop Critical-Thinking Skills

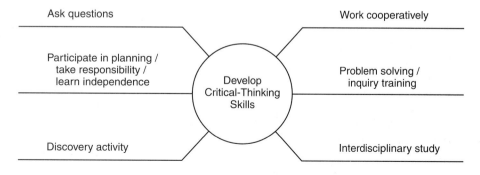

Ask questions

Work cooperatively

Participate in planning /
take responsibility /
learn independence

Problem solving /
inquiry training

Develop Critical-Thinking Skills

Discovery activity

Interdisciplinary study

Prerequisites:
• Models of teaching that foster critical thinking
• Develop risk-taking learning environments
• Questioning techniques
• Interdisciplinary unit planning

Research Findings:
Teaching for Creative Thinking

Sternberg and Lubart (1995) demonstrated teaching for creative thinking by experimenting with a group of children aged 9 and 10 who had a wide range of socioeconomic backgrounds and abilities. Using whole group discussion, in the context of teaching about psychology, students were asked to share something about human behavior that intrigued them. The children were actually defining problems. After a fairly long wait-time, the students actively participated in naming problems that puzzled them. Students were asked to select one problem for investigation. They then designed a research experiment to investigate their problem and considered the risks and obstacles. The researchers concluded that teaching for thinking motivates students intrinsically and improves their creative skills.

what they themselves do not know. This may mean that the low-ability child requires concrete materials and needs to learn by doing, but regardless of ability, the child can engage profitably and successfully in inquiry-related activities. Gega (1990, p. 33), in discussing open-ended activities for inquiry teaching, commented:

> It is this potential for multiple possibilities that sets off an open-ended activity from a close-ended one. Open-ended activities often provide two functions: (1) chances for pupils to discover new examples of an object or event, and (2) chances for them to discover the conditions that might change an object or event in some way.

Teachers can create the desire to think and set the proper conditions for thinking. They can help students to develop curiosity, sensitivity, and habits of subjecting ideas to the test of rationality in order to cultivate the method of inquiry. We will now look at a variety of inquiry and research skill activities.

STUDENTS AS RESEARCHERS

OBSERVATION SKILLS

To discuss the skills used by elementary and middle school students—as researchers—we will visit a colleague of Mary Hogan, Sara Garcia, a third-grade teacher. The students just finished a session with the

YMCA leader of the Feelin' Good program. The leader challenged them by stating that on her next visit the class would check their fitness progress by performing some physical fitness tests.

As the students go out to lunch, Sara Garcia heard them discussing whether girls are more flexible than boys and questioning each other about the fitness tests. During the lunch hour the students got into an argument. Some of the children were performing bent knee sit-ups while others watched. The observers claimed that the children doing the sit-ups were cheating and not performing the exercise correctly. The teacher on yard duty had to stop the activity because of the heat of the argument. The yard teacher reported the situation to Garcia.

Garcia asked the students to explain the problem during the afternoon class session. The discussion focused on whether or not the children performing the exercise had performed it correctly. Observers' reports differed. Garcia decided to use the incident to accomplish several purposes: improve understanding of physical fitness, teach research skills, improve playground behavior, and integrate several subject fields.

On the following day Garcia showed a movie in which children were demonstrating exercises. In the discussion that followed, Garcia helped to clarify and emphasize the following ideas:

- All individuals need a daily fitness program.
- Children and adults should exercise.
- Playing games will not necessarily keep children fit.
- Both girls and boys have the same physiological capacity to be flexible.
- Children are not necessarily more flexible than adults.

Many of the students were surprised that all age groups need exercise and that girls are not more flexible than boys. The students' interest provided Garcia with the lead-in she was looking for, and she asked the students if they would like to become researchers to find out what others believe about fitness and exercise. The students agreed, and immediately one class member asked if they were going to conduct a survey. Garcia responded that they could do that, but first she wanted to talk about the problem they had on the playground.

Garcia asked the students if they understood why some of the observers disagreed with each other about whether the performers were exercising correctly. The children did not understand why there was disagreement, so Garcia asked several students to demonstrate sit-ups. Then she asked several students to describe what they saw. Once again the reports differed slightly.

Now Garcia said, "All right, suppose that we said that when doing a sit-up you must roll up into a sitting position and keep your elbows extended straight from your ears." She had the students demonstrate the sit-up once again. Then she asked the observers for their report. This time the observers agreed about what they saw. "Why did the observers agree this time?" Garcia asked the students. After some discussion, the students realized that this time the observers were all looking for the same behavior. They were using the same criteria to describe what they saw.

Using this procedure, Garcia helped her students realize why they had been arguing on the playground. Then she said, "Now that you understand why you had a problem, let's trace the sequence of events that led up to the yard teacher disciplining you."

Garcia had the students list the events in the order that they happened. With the list on the chalkboard, Garcia explained to the students that each event was caused by the preceding event: that in fact there was a pattern of causes. Then the class talked about underlying causes of behavior, such as emotions. As a result of the discussion, the students understood that each event was an effect of the prior event and that each had caused the final effect of the discipline.

When Garcia felt comfortable about her students' understanding of their own behavior, she suggested that they begin thinking about their research. She told them, "These are some things we need to know in order to begin our research. We need to know about data and observation." Garcia began a discussion of data and observation with the class, giving them the following explanations:

Data: The word *data* means information; data are evidence. The researcher collects data about a specific problem under investigation. Data can be collected by seeing and listening to people, by asking people for information as in an interview, and by asking people for a written report as in a questionnaire.

Observation: Although people may supposedly see or hear the same event, observations differ. This occurs because some people are more perceptive than others, people differ about what they have observed, and sometimes people disagree about why something happened.

To improve observation and make observations valid, people must observe specific aspects of behavior.

To ensure that observations are reliable, several observers must observe independently, and they must agree about what they are seeing or hearing. For example, since the observers in Garcia's class had disagreed about the playground performance of the students doing the sit-ups, Garcia set a standard for skill performance. The next time the observers watched the sit-ups, they were all looking for the same skill performance using specific criteria. This ensured that the observations would be valid. To ensure reliability, Garcia used several observers. If the independent observers agreed about what they were observing, the observations would be considered reliable.

On successive days, Garcia and her students formalized their research. Using observation skills, interviews, and questionnaires, the third graders gathered and organized data and analyzed the results.

INTERVIEWS AND QUESTIONNAIRES

ADVANTAGES AND DISADVANTAGES OF THE INTERVIEW TECHNIQUE

There are advantages and disadvantages to both the interview and the questionnaire. Generally, the interview is a more personal way of obtaining information. Face-to-face contact enables questions to be open ended and determined by the nature of the interaction. The respondent and the interviewer have greater leeway in answering questions and in asking them. During the interview, the interviewer must make a number of decisions. For example, the interviewer must decide when to probe with a follow-up question and when to change the sequence of questions.

The interviewer also must be careful that the interview situation is objective. Facial expression and voice tone can communicate interviewer bias, thereby affecting the information provided by the respondent. Sometimes the sequence of questions and even the type of question asked can communicate bias. For example, if the interviewer asks a leading question (Isn't it true that . . .?), the respondent may interpret the question as biased or may consider it presumptuous. Yes/no questions should generally be avoided during an interview situation because they do not exploit the advantage of the personal, face-to-face nature of the interview. Exceptions to this will be discussed.

Another advantage to the interview situation is the opportunity for the interviewer to detect respondent hesitancy, uncertainty, shyness, and bias. However, to do this the interviewer must be experienced and know what to look for.

It is difficult to organize the interview for analysis. A system must be devised so the interview can be preserved for later analysis. One solution is to tape-record the interview. Tape recording may be done only with permission from the respondent. Very capable interviewers can write down the respondent's answers, but this technique is difficult for elementary and middle school students.

SPECIAL SKILLS AND PROBLEMS

Students need to practice two special skills in the classroom before they begin interviewing. These are the ability to make the respondent feel at ease and willing to be interviewed and the ability to restrain personal comments and expressions so interviewer bias is not apparent to the respondent.

Courtesy to the person being interviewed is another aspect of the interview situation that teachers should discuss with young students. The interviewer must remember that the respondent is performing service by permitting the interview. The interviewer should introduce himself or herself, explain the purpose of the interview, and thank the interviewee for taking time to respond. Young students should be made aware of the fact that sometimes adults do not like to be interviewed by youngsters. The result is frequently more positive if students interview in teams.

INTERVIEWING TECHNIQUES

Structured Interview

Lippitt, Fox, and Schaible (1969) recommend a **structured interview** situation for young researchers. The questions never differ; they are predetermined and asked exactly as planned, usually in a precise order. Sometimes the respondent is even asked to choose a response from a list of possible answers. Lippitt, Fox, and Schaible recommend the structured interview because interviewing is quite difficult to do well and students need to be prepared. They suggest—even with preset questions—that the students practice on each other in the classroom before the interview. Their experience has been that the practice period ensures that more data will be collected during the actual interview situation.

Questionnaires

The questionnaire is an example of a measuring instrument. It is more objective than the interview and can be mailed to respondents. Questions should be short and precise. Avoid vague words, and take care that each question requires just one response. Inexperienced questioners tend to ask more than one question at a time. It is a good idea to try the questionnaire with a select audience of friends before sending it out. Create a pilot study to determine if the questions ask what the class thinks they are asking. Although it is possible to ask open ended questions on a questionnaire, they are more difficult to score and interpret. Some questionnaires are designed to provide objective measures with forced-choice answers, and some questions are open ended so that the respondent may add whatever he or she pleases.

Distribution and Sampling

It is important to decide how to distribute the questionnaire. Since postage can be expensive, this may be a major decision. Typically students decide to hand deliver their questionnaires to the respondents, mailing only those questionnaires that are going out of town.

Teach the students simple sampling concepts. For example, they can learn that one of the first things the social scientist must do is decide what group of people to study. Then, since it is usually impossible to survey everyone in the group, the scientist chooses a limited number of people. The people chosen are called the sample. In choosing the sample, the scientist tries to make sure that the chosen group is representative of the total group so it will be possible to make statements about the total group after completing the study. Sometimes scientists make mistakes and choose a biased sample that does not represent the group to be studied. When this occurs the scientist cannot generalize accurately about the total population. For example, a second-grade class wanted to find out if children in the second grade liked dogs. Since they could not ask all second graders, they chose a sample to question. After they finished their study, they discovered that almost all of the children in their sample owned dogs. As a consequence they had what is called a biased sample, or in other words, a group that was not representative of the total group of second graders.

Choosing the Format for Questions

There are four possible formats for questions in the questionnaire and interview. *Forced-choice* questions require the respondent to choose among alternatives, such as yes/no, always/never, many/few, or often/sometimes/rarely.

A second type is the *scale* question. This asks the respondent to rate an event, trait, or behavior. For example:

I like dogs—

Very much   Much   A little bit   Not much

A third type is the *ranking* question. In this question the respondent is asked to arrange events, behaviors, or traits in the order of preference or importance. Ranking items is more difficult for the respondent than answering forced-choice or scale questions. For example:

Rank the following vegetables in the order that you like them. Number 5 indicates the vegetable that you like the most; number 1 the vegetable that you like least.

_____ Carrots   _____ Celery
_____ String beans   _____ Broccoli
_____ Radishes

The fourth question type is the *open-ended* question, which permits the respondent to say or write anything he or she wants. The open-ended question is the easiest to write, but the hardest to score. However, a great deal of information can be gathered when time is taken to use the open-ended question. For example:

What do you enjoy most about teaching?

USING THE INFORMATION FROM INTERVIEWS AND QUESTIONNAIRES

Before Sara Garcia set her class to work writing questions, she decided that they had better have some idea how data are analyzed. She knew that this information might influence their decisions about the kinds of questions to ask.

Organizing the Data

Forced-choice questions can be tabulated and then analyzed in terms of percentage of persons responding or the frequency of the response (see Table 7.2). A similar type of worksheet can be designed for scale-type questions (see Table 7.3).

Table 7.2 Tally of Responses to the Statement: All Individuals Need a Daily Fitness Program

	3rd Graders	6th Graders	Adults	Total
Yes	20	15	35 (50%)	70
No	10	10	20 (21%)	40
No Response	5	10	15 (21%)	30
Total	35	35	70 (100%)	140

Students can be taught different ways to categorize the information. Questions that ask the respondent to rank the items can be tallied as shown in Table 7.4. Researchers need to decide on criteria to develop categories in order to analyze open-ended questions. For example, if respondents were asked, "What do you like about exercise?" their responses might be as follows:

"It makes me feel good."   "I think it is important
"Nothing."   to do."
"I like sweating."   No response.

To organize this information, the researcher would probably establish positive, negative, neutral, and no-response categories. Then the researcher would need to provide examples of each category to guide the organization of the data. "It makes me feel good" and "I like sweating" would be examples of positive responses. "Nothing" could be interpreted as a negative response. "I think it is important to do" would be a neutral statement. Sara Garcia's third graders would have difficulty interpreting open-ended responses; capable fifth- and sixth-grade students could probably manage it quite well.

Table 7.3 Tally of Responses to the Statement: I Like Exercise

	Boys	Girls	Men	Women	Total
Very Much	15	10	25	20	70
Much	10	5	1	0	16
Little Bit	2	10	0	5	15
Not Much	3	3	4	5	15
No Response	0	2	0	0	2
Total	30	30	30	30	120

Table 7.4 Tally and Ranking of Responese to the Statement: I Like Vegetables

Points	Carrots	Beans	Radishes	Celery	Broccoli
5	20	8	1	15	2
4	10	10	4	10	5
3	5	5	5	10	20
2	3	10	5	2	10
1	2	7	25	3	3
Total	163	122	71	152	113
Rank	1	3	5	2	4

Note: The tally was multiplied by the number of points the respondent gave it.

Analyzing the Data

Sara Garcia assisted the students in developing the following questionnaire that included scale-type responses:

1. Do you think it is important for children to exercise regularly?
2. Do you think it is important for adults to exercise regularly?
3. Do you think aerobic workouts are important?
4. Do you think exercise can make people feel better?
5. Do you think it is important to stretch before you exercise vigorously?

The students were also going to use the same questions in an interview situation, with the interviewer asking one additional question: Do you think exercise is fun?

After the students tabulated their data, Garcia gave them several ways to present the results. She arranged the students into five groups, and each group was told

Figure 7.6 Bar Graph: Do You Think Exercise is Important?

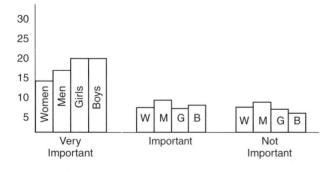

Figure 7.7 Pie Graphs

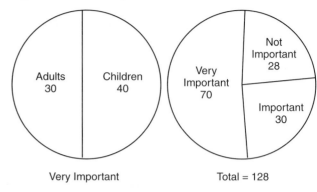

Very Important   Total = 128

to decide how to communicate the results to others. Each group worked with just one of the questions. Their choices included a pie graph, bar graph, table, or chart (Figure 7.6 and Figure 7.7). The students had data for boys, girls, men, and women. They were told that they could sum the data or find ways to present the data for each of the four groups. They had to decide how to communicate the importance of the response. The results as communicated by one of Sara Garcia's groups appears in Table 7.5. Her third graders may need help with the concept of *tally* as a mark and a means to count.

Drawing Conclusions

During the summative evaluation, Garcia's students concluded:

- Children have better understanding of the importance of exercise than adults.
- Males appreciate the value of exercise more than females.
- Adult females were more willing to be interviewed than adult males.
- Adult males were more willing to fill out a questionnaire.

Table 7.5 Tally of Responses to the Question: Do You Think Exercise Can Make People Feel Better?

	Very Important	Important	Not Important
Males	38	18	14
Females	32	12	14
Total	70	30	28

- Deciding on the questions to ask and their form was the hardest research task.
- Choosing their sample was important.
- They felt shy when doing an interview.
- It was fun!

WHAT DID THE STUDENTS LEARN?

Sara Garcia used the research study to integrate subject fields, utilizing interdisciplinary concepts. She was also concerned about her students' social behavior on the playground. Subject by subject, here is a summary of what she accomplished:

Language Arts

Reading: The students read questions, charts, graphs, and the questionnaire. They learned to classify data by sex and to use a scale. They arranged information in sequence.

Oral Language: Students participated in group and class discussions, practiced interviewing, practiced courtesy during interviewing, listened to others, asked questions, and expressed ideas.

Spelling: Students spelled special words related to the research study, such as *male, female, sample, questionnaire, observations, interview,* and *survey.*

Writing: Students wrote questions using capitals and question marks.

Mathematics

The students learned to tally their data. The students performed addition using two-digit numbers; performed column addition; subtracted two-digit numbers; multiplied two-digit numbers; and collected, organized, and interpreted data using charts, tables, and bar graphs.

Science, Social Studies, Thinking Skills

Students used their senses to collect and process data. They developed and used a classification system. They participated in inquiry, identifying a problem and forming questions. They planned an investigation; recorded and organized data; prepared and interpreted graphic material; analyzed, evaluated, and interpreted data; and summarized and communicated their investigation to others.

Social Participation

The students demonstrated curiosity, concern about others, willingness to share data and ideas with others, cooperation with others, participation in group tasks, and acceptance of responsibility to distribute and collect data.

Health and Physical Education

Students shared information about physical activities. They considered the relationship of activity to cardiovascular health, recognized the importance of exercise, and shared negative and positive feelings. They performed exercise activities, explained basic ideas about exercise, discussed physical fitness, and participated in fitness testing.

INDIVIDUALIZING RESEARCH PROBLEMS

Research problems provide means to differentiate instruction. Gifted students, in particular, may need opportunities to learn on their own. Frequently there are a number of students in the classroom who will benefit from working independently, and the research project provides a challenging means to structure content, processes, and product to meet individual needs.

Research projects also can be differentiated for small groups of students by providing different problems at varying levels of difficulty and appealing to diverse interests.

CASE STUDIES

WHAT IS A CASE STUDY?

A *case study* is a thorough investigation of a single event, institution, decision, issue, or individual. Case studies are typically used in business, medicine, law, social work, and therapy. Materials for case studies may include personal records, histories, diaries, graphs, and stories—in fact, a variety of data. Although the data may be varied, it is typically relevant only to the single situation for which it was gathered or prepared. The data should allow systematic analysis. Practice with case study analysis helps students gain insight into similar types of problems or situations. Thinking is usually inductive in nature during the case study.

The **case study approach** enables the teacher to reduce the amount of data to a manageable size to facilitate analysis. For example, suppose a teacher wanted students to understand our legal system and the way in which the Supreme Court makes decisions. Instead of asking students to research everything about the Court and the decisions the Court makes, the teacher provides data, or has students gather the data, about a single Supreme Court decision. Once the data is collected and studied, the students may even role-play the case in order to gain greater insight. The principle illustrated by the case should demonstrate a basic concept that is applicable to similar problems, or in the case of the Supreme Court, it should illustrate the decision-making process of the Court, and how the Court relates to a democratic society.

You can select case studies about real or fictional issues and problems. The studies may be open ended, involved, or quite simple. Whatever you select should be motivating and provide an adequate data base in terms of factual information. The open- ended case requires that students make the final judgment about the outcome or at least suggest possible alternatives.

TYPES OF CASE STUDIES

Newmann and Oliver (1967) identified seven basic types of cases:

1. *Story:* The story may be fictional or about authentic events. Literature or history books are appropriate, or the teacher may write an episode or dialogue for study. The story has a plot and characters.

2. *Vignette:* This type of case is similar to the story, but shorter, and with no plot.

3. *Journalistic Historical Narrative:* A newspaper account of an event is appropriate. The situation may provide an eyewitness account of what happened, or it may be an hour-by-hour description. This type of case could be about a group or an institution rather than about individuals.

4. *Documents:* Primary resource materials are appropriate for this type of case study. Public records of court trials, hearings, and council reports as well as diaries, letters, and speeches are suitable for analysis.

5. *Research Data:* Experimental studies and survey data or statistical data are appropriate. Census reports can be used for inductive generalizations.

6. *Text:* Text material that describes general phenomena and trends or provides specific information about people may be chosen, if the knowledge appears to be objective.

7. *Interpretive Essay:* The selected essay discusses an abstract issue and provides an explanation or an interpretive conclusion. In contrast to the text, which presents an objective description, the essay is subjective and interpretive. The reader of the essay is supposed to be sophisticated and critical.

EXAMPLES OF THE USE OF CASE STUDIES

Language Arts

Greg Thomas used the case study method to accomplish both language arts and social studies objectives. He chose the following resources:

- *West from Home*—Letters of Laura Ingalls Wilder
- *A Gathering of Days*—A fictional New England girl's journal, 1830–32
- *The Endless Steppe*—The story of a girl in exile

The Wilder book, composed of letters from Laura Wilder to her husband, provides historical background and information about San Francisco in 1915. *A Gathering of Days*, by Joan Blos, is a fictional work written in the form of a journal. It is about the rigorous life on a New Hampshire farm in 1830. *The Endless Steppe* is a personal account by Esther Haytzig of her experiences as a girl in exile in Siberia. The story takes place during World War II.

The teacher's goals were as follows:

- To develop an appreciation of authorship
- To differentiate purpose, structure, and style of fiction and nonfiction
- To recognize that personal letters, journals, and diaries are documents—primary resources-and provide a form of autobiography
- To authenticate historical information and background information by reading literature

The student's assignment was to read the selected portion of the book and be prepared to discuss the following questions:

- How does the writer know what really happened?
- What reasons might the writer have for being prejudiced or for exaggerating?
- When did the writer or main character live?
- What event did the writer or main character participate in?
- What decisions did the writer or main character make?
- How would circumstances have been different if the story were told by a male?
- If you were faced with similar conflicts, what decisions would you make?
- How are you like or different from the author or main character?

Art Education

An eighth-grade teacher had students study specific artists to develop an understanding of the contribution of artists and to help students realize that art changes in time as a consequence of development, interests, and values. Groups were formed in the classroom, and each group was given a different case history and examples of one artist's work. From the case history, each group was to respond to the following question: What is art as exemplified by van Gogh, Picasso, Dali, Degas, or Toulouse-Lautrec? Each group was to characterize the artist in its case study.

Teaching Tasks During Case Studies

Is the Case Study Approach Appropriate?

In choosing a teaching strategy a teacher must ask: Which approach will facilitate the accomplishment of my objectives? Case studies are appropriate as a teaching strategy when the amount of data about a given problem, situation, or person is so abundant that it would be difficult for students to choose and examine just the pertinent information. When this occurs the case study approach enables the teacher to reduce the data, thereby limiting the investigation.

Case studies are also valuable when the students cannot research the data because of the complexity of the issues or the reading levels of the students. In this instance the teacher may find that it is advantageous to write the case study to fit the students' reading levels.

Case studies are suitable when the situation calls for an open-ended role that makes students decide what the decision ought to be.

Once you have decided that the case study is the right approach and fits the purposes of the lesson, it is time to select the appropriate materials or write your own.

Selecting Materials for a Case Study

The first consideration in choosing case study materials is whether the students will be able to read and comprehend the selected data. You must consider both the concept load and the vocabulary level. If students do not have the specialized skills needed to read charts, tables, graphs, or maps, then include a skill lesson first.

Organizational considerations also affect the choice of the materials. How will students be grouped for instruction? If students are to work in small groups during the intake portion of the lesson, have you prepared or obtained enough materials? Can one member of each small group be the reader for the other group members?

Since media presentations are the easiest to use with young children, survey films, slides, or tapes. You can record information to use in listening centers. Tapes are advantageous because students can repeat them as often as necessary to obtain needed details.

There is a wide variety of commercial publications available for case study use. In addition, newspapers, textbooks, and literature selections provide a wealth of suitable data. Once you become adept at rewriting materials for your own students, you will find that social studies, science, and health textbooks are a fine source of information.

Motivating the Study and Organizing Study Tasks

As in other inquiry activities, if the proposed case study is not of interest to the students, they will not be motivated to perform the necessary analytic tasks. Therefore, it is important that the teacher determine the relevancy of the assignment before sending students off to study. Once again formulation of the inquiry question is an important teacher task.

Another critical teacher task is deciding how students should organize the data. Suppose the case study involves reading about student misbehavior in the Boston school system. The data include charts on federal aid, maintenance and supply costs, and personnel costs. Facts include information about curriculum, students' difficulties, and class distractions. Since the case study will be evaluated during a whole class discussion, how should students prepare for the discussion? Consider the case study inquiry sequence in Figure 7.8.

Debrief Using Discussion Strategy

Guiding the discussion at the end of the case study is the most important teacher task. During this stage of the study the teacher, through questions, facilitates the following:

- A recap of the definition of key terms. The teacher or a capable student should record the discussion on the chalkboard.
- Clarification of the facts. The teacher asks, "What do we know?" and "How do we know that what we know is reliable?"
- Clarification of issues and conflicting values. "What was involved?"
- Whole class participation in the discussion. "What do you think?" "What else happened?" "Who can add to that?"

Figure 7.8 Case Study Inquiry Sequence

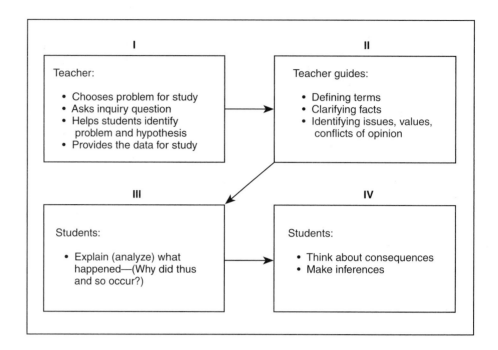

- Students' explanation of why the events occurred. "Why did the Boston school system dismiss 710 tenured teachers?" "Why did the students protest?" For the final discussion, this step is where teacher efforts should be maximized.
- Suggestions for solution. "How can the case be resolved?" "What are the alternatives?" Once again, create a list for students to see.
- Consideration of implications or consequences for each of the alternatives. "If thus and so occurs, what will be the consequences?" "If we were to manipulate this, what would be affected?" "If you were the main character, what decision would you make?" And finally, "How would this solution apply to similar problems?"

LEARNING TASKS DURING CASE STUDIES

Unlike other inquiry strategies, students are frequently presented with the problem, the hypothesis, and the data during case studies. This means that student inquiry begins with data analysis.

During case study analysis, students perform the following tasks:

- Students read, observe, or consume the given information in some other way. Their task is to evaluate the information by differentiating between facts and opinions. They must evaluate objectivity, reliability, and source of information.
- Students judge the adequacy of their information. If sets of data are available, they must contrast the information, noting similarities and differences.
- They note changes in the data.
- They conclude data analysis with summarization and interpretation.
- Through discussion, students share meanings and interpretations.
- Through *auding* (listening attentively), students evaluate others' perspectives.
- Through participation, students share inquiry responsibility.
- Students analyze cause-and-effect relationships to reach a conclusion.
- Students select, from alternatives, the best solution to a problem.
- Students make predictions concerning the outcome of a particular solution or course of action.
- Students make choices based on possible consequences.

EVALUATING PROBLEM-SOLVING SKILLS

It is just as important to evaluate the way in which you, the teacher, accomplish inquiry-oriented teaching as it is to evaluate the students' problem-solving skills. In fact, the two components (teaching and learning) cannot be separated; one is related to the other. The purpose and choice for inquiry, the materials, and the conditions in the classroom all affect what the students do and what they say.

Chapter 15 includes a checklist for evaluating students' critical-thinking and inquiry skills. Other checklists are provided in Chapter 11. Another way to go about evaluating students' skills is to give them an inquiry test problem and then present the following questions:

- Ask students to write a statement of the problem.
- Ask students to select appropriate sources for data.
- Ask students to suggest ways to gather data.
- Ask students how they would organize data for analysis.

Note that the above list does not include the final step, concluding. Practically the only way you, the teacher, can evaluate students' ability to form an appropriate conclusion is to provide them with specific data in the form of observed or supposed facts. Then you can ask the students to make an inference about the data in terms of whether it is sufficient for making a conclusion. Or you can give them a number of conclusions and ask them to choose a conclusion that is logical and, beyond doubt, based on the information given.

Of course, the prime way to evaluate students' skills is to examine the products of inquiry. What students produce while involved in inquiry activities and the discussions that follow the inquiry provide the most meaningful information about students' performance.

SUMMARY

Inquiry

1. The inquiry approach can be traced to John Dewey.
2. Dewey linked inquiry, reflective thinking, and critical thinking.
3. Inquiry processes require the consideration of data, search for evidence, and inductive thought processes.
4. Inquiry teaching requires choosing appropriate problems for study, consideration of the adequacy of materials and resources, creating an appropriate classroom environment, and providing guidance and objectivity.

Group Investigation

5. Group investigation uses six phases of inquiry.
6. Evaluation of group investigation requires assessing substantive accomplishment(s) and group process skills.

Constructivism

7. Constructivism is an inquiry learning approach that requires students to be actively involved in integrating new knowledge with prior knowledge.

Concept Attainment

8. Concept attainment is an inquiry approach used to help students gain specific concepts by comparing and contrasting attributes.

Backward Problem solving

9. Backward problem solving is an inquiry approach that encourages students' divergent thinking.

Students as Researchers

10. Students can be taught to engage in research activity using observation skills, gathering data, interviewing, and developing questionnaires.
11. As researchers, students learn to write appropriate questions, use sampling techniques, and organize and analyze data.
12. Research activities facilitate the integration of skills and content.

Case Studies

13. The case study approach is a means to reduce data to facilitate an intensive study of a single problem, situation, or person.

DISCUSSION QUESTIONS AND APPLICATION EXERCISES

1. Use the information about the seventh-grade classroom studying the relationship between age and auto safety to plan an inquiry problem:
   - Write a different inquiry question.
   - Suggest sources for data.
   - Pretend that students have obtained data about auto safety and write a sequence of questions to help students interpret and apply their data.
2. Choose an article out of the daily newspaper and plan a lesson using group investigation.

3. Think about the example of the fifth-grade students who studied colonial art in order to learn about the New England colonists' cultural beliefs. Plan a concept attainment lesson to teach the concept of culture.

4. Why is it important to distinguish between *activity* and *inquiry?*

5. Which of the following statements would make good inquiry lessons in the classroom?
   - There are fewer farms today than 50 years ago, but U.S. farmers grow more food today than they did 50 years ago.
   - Changes in life-style affect language usage.
   - Most students dislike mathematics.
   - People do not work hard anymore.

   (If you chose the first two, you are right. The second two statements would be extremely difficult to research. They are too broad and need clarification.) Suggest data for students to analyze to study the first two statements.

6. Use the following inquiry example to design an investigation:
   - *Inquiry Question/Problem* How do the members of your methods class feel about using inquiry methodology?
   - *Sources of Data*
   - *Gathering Data*
   - *Organizing Data*
   - *Conclusion*

7. Practice backward problem solving. Identify a teaching/learning problem in your own classroom. What would you like to see happen? (Identify the ideal solution.) Now describe enabling tasks to make the ideal a reality.

8. Use the Taba questioning sequence given in this chapter to design an inquiry lesson.

9. Field research should be planned jointly by teacher and students. However, to practice the skills discussed in this chapter, design a questionnaire for your students. Choose one of the following topics to investigate:
   - Number of languages spoken by families at your school
   - Frequency of moving from one community to another
   - Beliefs about sex role differences (make a list of beliefs such as cleanliness, play differences, traits, etc.)
   - Jobs performed by children
   - Number of hours of television viewing and number of hours of homework

   What question type will you use? How will the data be organized? How will you analyze the data?

10. If you were to use the mini-example about the puppy in this chapter with your students, how would you demonstrate (a) that cause precedes effect in time and (b) multiple causation?

11. Plan a lesson using the four phases of the constructivist approach to learning.

12. In what ways do inquiry-oriented activities make students take responsibility for their own learning?

8

Role-Playing, Games, and Simulations

Role-playing, games, and simulations are considered inquiry teaching strategies because they are all open ended, and even though games and simulations have rules, students control the action. All three strategies involve students in problem solving and are used to help students express personal values and practice decision making. Because values are expressed so freely in these strategies, students develop sensitivity to the feelings and viewpoints of their classmates.

In this chapter you will learn about two different types of role-playing procedures. The procedure you choose will affect classroom management, teacher and student behavior. You also can expect slight differences in outcomes.

After you study this chapter, you should be able to accomplish the following:

1. Identify the purpose of and skills required for role-playing.
2. Identify and explain the nine-step procedure for role-playing.
3. Compare caucus group role-playing with basic role-playing procedures.
4. Suggest ways to use role-playing in the classroom.
5. Identify the purpose and use of simulations in the classroom.
6. Discuss the value of simulations and gaming.
7. Design a simulation or board game using guidelines suggested in this chapter.
8. Identify what teachers can learn about students' learning progress during role-playing and gaming.
9. Compare the teacher task requirements during role-playing, gaming, case study, and inquiry problem solving.

THE PURPOSE OF ROLE-PLAYING

Role-playing is a problem-solving method for arriving at a decision that involves diverse interests and values. Similar to gaming and simulations (which will be explained later in this chapter), role-playing uses a symbolic model. Procedures utilized in role-playing progress through problem definition, delineation of alternatives for action, exploration of consequences, and decision making (Shaftel and Shaftel, 1967).

Skill requirements for effective role-playing include listening, oral language and discussion skills, and inquiry problem-solving skills. During role-play, students must focus on the data or issues in the problem situation. Participants explore alternatives by making tentative decisions and through role-play enactment they experience the consequences. Successive enactments of the role-play facilitate the choice of a final decision or conclusion.

Role-playing is primarily used for teaching citizenship responsibilities and for group counseling. It provides opportunities for students to study human behavior. Joyce and Weil (1996, p. 56) stated that during the process of role-playing:

> students (1) explore their feelings, (2) gain insights into their attitudes, values, and perceptions, (3) develop their problem-solving skills and attitudes, and (4) explore subject matter in varied ways.

Role theory involves the way in which individuals view themselves and others and is specifically concerned with the individual's needs and expectations. Social psychologists have used role theory to study the behavior of the individual in a group and the behavior

---

Professional Lexicon

role-playing   A teaching strategy that uses the sociologic concept of *role* to allow individuals to explore feelings, values, interrelationships, and social problems.

simulations   A procedure that lets individuals simplify and explore social problems using a game format that requires the players to learn concepts and skills and accept responsibility for their actions.

of a group as it responds to the individual. Role theory can be used to study the structure of the individual or society. Some researchers have used the teaching strategy of role-playing to study the effect of dramatization, involvement, and group influence on attitude change as a result of role-playing participation. Educators have used role-playing to facilitate learner involvement and interaction in the process of decision making.

Shaftel and Shaftel (1967, p. 47) stated that role-playing helps students step out of their "culture shell" and become more "open" to the experiences of others. Students learn to explore their own values and personal consequences. Students choose in the light of consequences and discover causal relationships; as students interact, they may become sensitive to others. Role-playing enables students to attack problems in a feeling-thinking-acting sequence.

ROLE-PLAYING METHODS

In Greg Thomas's fifth-grade classroom, the students are listening to a story about a very poor Mexican family.

The father owns his own farm, but in recent years there has not been enough water for the crops, and as a result the farm has not been profitable. The family owes money to local residents, including the owner of a grocery store and a doctor.

The mother of the family has been helping her husband on the farm. There are two children in the family, a boy who is ten and a girl who is eight. Both attend school.

Recently the father's parents came to live with the family. The grandfather has not been well and cannot work. The grandmother is healthy, but she does not adjust well to change.

The father of the family has heard that there are work opportunities in California. He knows he could sell his farm to pay his debts.

Should the family move to California? Each member of the family has his or her own thoughts about the move:

- *Father* He favors the move, but he is concerned about his parents' and family's adjustment. No one in the family speaks English. He is confident that he can find a job in agriculture.
- *Mother* She has heard that the jobs in agriculture are poor paying and seasonal. She is afraid that the family will not be able to manage in California. She

doesn't want her husband to be a migrant worker and work on his knees picking strawberries and tomatoes. She knows that she will be lonesome for her home in Mexico.

- *Son* He wonders if he will have to quit school and help to support the family. He likes school.
- *Daughter* She thinks it will be a grand adventure. She is excited about learning English, but she is worried about leaving her friends.
- *Grandfather* He does not want to be a burden on the family. He hopes that he can find work, too; but he knows that he cannot work in the fields.
- *Grandmother* She does not want to go to the United States. She has heard that the Mexican immigrants are not treated well in the United States.

What should the family do? According to Shaftel and Shaftel, after presenting the motivation, the teacher should select role-players. While the role-players think about their roles and plan their enactment, the teacher talks to the rest of the class, suggesting that they think about each of the roles and how they would feel if they were members of the family. Thomas asks the students to think about questions such as "What would you do if you were the father or the son or another family member?" "How are immigrant groups treated?"

With the class prepared to listen to the role-play, the role-players arrange themselves in the front of the room in a semicircle. Thomas suggests to the role-players that the father begin the enactment by trying to convince the other family members how important the move would be for the family's welfare.

After about five minutes, it is clear that the students have concluded their enactment, and Thomas turns to the class and suggests that they discuss what happened. The discussion and evaluation focus on the family problems identified by the role-players and on how it feels to have to leave your friends and move to a new country (or school).

Next Thomas asks whether there are other solutions to the family's problems. Perhaps the whole family should not emigrate at once to California. This idea was suggested by one of the class members. Thomas suggests that the class explore this alternative, and he chooses new role-players.

Together the new role-players discuss their ideas and prepare for their enactment. After the second

What should a teacher observe during role-playing?

enactment the class once again discusses the role interpretations. If new ideas are presented or new interpretations suggested, there can be further enactments with new role-players. If the students have exhausted their solutions, the concluding discussions should attempt to relate the role-playing experience to personal experiences of the class. For example, Thomas might ask, "Has anyone you know had an experience similar to that of the members of this fictitious family?" Or "Is this a problem that could happen to people today?" Thomas may lead the discussion to a study of the problems experienced by immigrant groups in the United States either historically or in contemporary times.

BASIC ROLE-PLAY PROCEDURES*

The actual role-playing procedures used by Greg Thomas were as follows:

1. *Setting the motivation.* Shaftel and Shaftel call this the warm-up period. It serves to acquaint the class with the problem. The teacher may read the problem or tell it to the class, or the students may see a film or listen to a tape recording of a problem situation. If it is a story, it may be open ended, or incomplete. Older students may read the problem or motivating story. In initiating the problem, the teacher may comment to the students that the incident they are to listen to is similar in nature to a problem they have been having.

2. *Selecting the players.* In selecting the first round of role-players it is important to choose students who are involved in the problem or the behaviors of the characters. Students who identify with the characters, or students who ought to identify with the roles, make the best actors for the first round. An initial exploratory discussion usually reveals those students who are concerned about the issues or characters. After the first enactment, the discussion and evaluation should provide clues for selecting additional players.

3. *Setting the stage.* Working together as a group or with the teacher, the role-players talk about their roles in order to decide how to begin the role-play. Sometimes an individual may need to be encouraged to pursue certain ideas to see what will happen.

4. *Preparing the audience.* While the role-players are settling down, the teacher needs to remind the rest

of the class to listen. The students may be expected to evaluate the authenticity of the enactment. It is usually a good idea to suggest purposeful things for observation and listening.

5. *The enactment.* It is important to remember that the role-players are ad-libbing. Their performance will not be perfect, nor should it be. The presentation should be as spontaneous and natural as possible.

6. *Discussion and evaluation.* The enactment should be evaluated for authenticity, not for theatrics or dramatics. (Would the grandfather really say that or feel that way?) The discussion should focus on the consequences of the solution, or the consequence of certain behaviors. Discuss alternate ideas, and as students express ideas for different solutions or behaviors, choose new players.

7. *A reenactment.* The same players may ask to try it again with a new solution. Typically, however, you should choose a new cast of role-players to carry the action one step further or try it a different way.

8. *Further discussion and evaluation.* Whenever there is a new enactment, follow it with an evaluative discussion focusing on the behavior of the new role-players and their solution.

9. *Generalizing.* When the enactments are concluded, the discussion should help students gain insight into similar problems and situations. Be careful during both the role-play and the discussions that students do not focus on each other. The students may recognize their own problems or personalities in the situations, but you should guard their feelings carefully. The role-play period should be a time of great sensitivity to the feelings of others.

ROLE-PLAYING USING A CAUCUS GROUP

Research by Lemlech (1970) revealed higher participant involvement in role-playing when caucus groups were used. This procedure alleviates the typical classroom management problems because it lessens the "on-stage" feature of the basic role-playing procedures. Using the caucus group plan, the class is divided into small groups. Each group is assigned one role to portray (father, mother, grandmother, and so on). The procedures are as follows:

1. *Teacher sets motivation.* (Same as in basic procedures.)

2. *Students divide* into groups. Arrange the grouping to ensure that the groups are balanced or that a weak student will not be taken advantage of by an aggressive one. Or students may be grouped with thought

*Adapted from F. Shaftel and G. Shaftel, *Role-Playing for Social Values* (Englewood Cliffs, NJ: Prentice Hall, 1967), pp. 74–83.

about their particular interests. Assign a role or issue to each group.

3. *Group discussion.* Groups plan their characterization or their consensus viewpoint about an issue or problem.

4. *Groups choose spokesperson.* Each group decides who will be the group representative for the role-play. The group coaches the role-player.

5. *The enactment.* The spokesperson may improvise or use group ideas during the role-play.

6. *Discussion and evaluation.* The whole class participates as a group to discuss and evaluate the enactment as in the basic procedures.

7. *Group meetings.* Students once again meet in groups to offer advice to their spokesperson based on the prior discussion and evaluation. Groups are encouraged to choose a new spokesperson.

8. *New role-play enactment.* Based on the discussion and the group meetings, the new role-play should develop alternative solutions and new characterizations.

9. *Discussion and generalizing.* The class discusses decisions, conclusions, and applications, or they may decide that further enactments are necessary.

There are two differences between basic and caucus group role-play. Using the caucus group, students feel that there is no audience. Since they all participate in group caucus, there is less tendency to giggle or feel embarrassed during the enactment. Students tend to feel responsible and involved in what happens. The role-players perform with greater freedom because they have a greater sense of personal safety and they have a back-up group ready to provide substantive and moral assistance.

The second major difference between the two procedures is that in caucus group role-play, the students, rather than the teacher, choose the performers. However, it is important that the teacher observe carefully during the selection stage to ensure that a student does not get railroaded into being the group spokesperson. This can also be a problem during the basic type of role-play if students are allowed to call out and suggest that friends play a role. Frequently this problem is accompanied by snickering and gestures.

Ideas, characterization, and perspective are preplanned (procedure 3) prior to the enactments in both the basic and caucus group role-plays, but the actual dialogue that will occur is never preplanned. The role-play performance is always a personal statement by the role-player. This attribute is what makes role-playing a value-laden teaching strategy.

USES OF ROLE-PLAY IN THE CLASSROOM

MORAL EDUCATION

Role-playing implementing the basic procedures can be used for moral education. The reader is urged to review the discussion of moral development in Chapter 4 and look ahead to the teaching strategy of Galbraith and Jones (1975) in Chapter 13.

Arbuthnot and Faust (1981) identified four basic principles of moral education:

1. Teachers should facilitate the development of moral education from a lower stage of development to a higher stage of development.
2. Moral development is provoked when the individual experiences cognitive conflict or disequilibrium.
3. Teachers must devise ways to facilitate self-discovery of higher-stage reasoning.
4. Students should not be forced to participate in any phase of moral education. Individuals have the right to choose a personal value system or belief without harassment.

Moral education procedures often use small discussion groups as well as role-playing. The groups are similar in nature to the caucus groups discussed earlier.

OTHER TYPES OF ROLE-PLAYS

Sara Garcia's third graders practiced being interviewers by using role-playing during language arts. In a class discussion they decided on some interviewing rules:

- Introduce yourself and tell the purpose of the interview.
- Be friendly.
- Ask the questions just as we decided upon them.
- Listen to the responses.
- Ask additional questions if the response is not clear.
- Thank the respondent for the interview.

Garcia decided that the practice sessions would benefit all the students. She asked the students to choose partners. Each pair was to practice and take turns being interviewer and respondent. As the students practiced, Garcia walked around the room listening. After the students reversed roles, Garcia chose several pairs of students to demonstrate the interview situation to the rest of the class.

Mary Hogan's second-grade classroom is experiencing a typical primary-grade problem: tattling. Almost every day, several of the children come in from recess or lunch and complain about others not obeying playground rules. Hogan has tried to listen to both sides of the story and to both participants; she has even tried the deaf-ear approach, although she knows that is not wise. She has lectured the class about tattling. Since none of these approaches has solved the problem, she decides to try role-playing. This is the story she told her students:

Instead of joining the game, Mabel watched the other children playing. When recess was over, Mabel went straight to Mr. Clark, her teacher, and told him that the students had not been following the rules for sockball.

Mr. Clark asked the other children how their game went, and they responded, "Just fine."

At lunch time none of the children would let Mabel play. Once again, she went to Mr. Clark and complained about her classmates, but Mr. Clark ignored her.

The next day during recess, Mabel went to the teacher on yard duty and told her, "Randy pushed me and tore my dress. My mother will punish me when I get home, and it's not my fault." The teacher on yard duty inspected Mabel's dress and promptly went to discuss the matter with Randy.

Hogan asked the children these questions:

- What do you think happened?
- Why do you think Mabel has problems with the other children?
- If you were Mr. Clark or the yard teacher, how would you handle this situation?

The students role-played the story, and after several enactments they concluded:

- Mr. Clark should have been a better listener.
- Mabel was a tattletale because she wanted attention.
- Mabel needed some friends, but she did not know how to be friendly.
- Mabel probably tore her dress herself.
- Randy would get in trouble because the yard teacher would not believe him.
- Mabel's classmates should make an effort to be friends with Mabel and include her in their games.
- Mabel would feel guilty if Randy got in trouble. She should apologize to Randy.

Why is role-playing considered an interactive technique?

USING ROLE-PLAYING FOR DIAGNOSTIC PURPOSES

Role-playing sometimes reveals more information than teachers really want to know about their students! As children act out, they reveal their own feelings. Antisocial tendencies may be revealed in the solutions that students suggest or dramatize. The child who has problems responding to adults or who has difficulties with younger children may reveal aggressiveness, punitiveness, or other insecurities.

Role-playing may help students relieve tensions, lessen insecure feelings, and develop greater sensitivity to others. However, carefully consider whatever the child reveals. Teachers generally are not counselors or psychologists; role-playing may be used to improve social interaction in the classroom, but it should not be used for individual guidance purposes. If you suspect that a student has personal problems, enlist the aid of colleagues trained for that purpose, call in parents, or search out social help agencies.

GETTING STARTED WITH ROLE-PLAYING

CLASSROOM ENVIRONMENT

For role-playing to be successful, the classroom must be psychologically open and permissive. Students need to feel free and secure that their ideas will not be summarily rejected. They must feel safe to express their feelings. The atmosphere of the classroom must indicate mutual respect. The teacher needs to be both responsive and respectful so students have a model to imitate. Students must know that, at least during role-playing, they may express personal feelings even when those feelings are antisocial.

Shaftel and Shaftel (1967, p. 90) pointed out that role-playing should not be used to coerce students into predetermined behavior.

> [The teacher] is concerned with creating an openness to experience in which all known behavior can be examined, explored for consequences, and pondered on.
>
> The teacher facilitates the open exploration of life situations under the assumption that all possible alternatives are available for examination.

TEACHER BEHAVIOR

The purpose of the role-playing session determines much of the teacher's behavior. For example, the third graders who were practicing interviewing needed to focus on ways to communicate friendliness, state the purpose of the interview, and then get on with it. Sara Garcia instructed the students to think about an opening statement that communicates who you are, why you need the respondent's help, and appreciation for assistance. Garcia was using role-playing to teach specific language skills.

If the purpose of the session is problem solving, then the teacher must ask questions that encourage students to focus on the definition of the problem, information, and values. As further enactments are performed, the teacher may ask questions to probe different alternatives. During the discussions the teacher focuses on possible consequences.

Greg Thomas will probably use the immigrant family role-play as an initial study of what happens to new groups in the United States. Additional role-play sessions will be more subject-matter–oriented, and Thomas will probably begin them by helping students recall how the Mexican family felt about coming to the United States. Actual sessions may be more time-oriented for a specific historical period and focus on important issues.

Whatever the purpose of the role-play session, there are two basic behaviors that facilitate leading role-playing: a supportive teacher attitude and an accepting manner. Students should perceive that during role-playing it is all right to express feelings that are normally kept under control, and all suggestions will be listened to and allowed to be explored—even those that sound impractical or antisocial.

GAMES AND SIMULATIONS

DIFFERENCES BETWEEN GAMES AND SIMULATIONS

A **simulation,** like the case study presented in Chapter 7, has a limited and controlled data base. The simulation is a model designed to represent physical or social processes in an abstracted fashion for the purposes of analysis. A *game* is a simulation, but a simulation does not have to be a game. Neither represents total reality. Games are contrived so there will be an aspect of competition and there will be winners and losers. Simulations usually have competition, but they are based on the social process that is to be modeled. A simulation does not necessarily have a winner. Social simulations are designed primarily to teach concepts and skills of negotiation, bargaining, cooperation, and compromise.

Role-playing is an aspect of most simulations, but during a simulation the process of role-playing differs from what has been described earlier in this chapter. During a simulation, students assume roles in order to carry out the decisions and actions of specific individuals involved in the social process that is to be studied. For example, in the simulation game Legislation, students assume the roles of congressional representatives.

Most educational games use game boards. The best example is Monopoly®, created during the 1930s. Monopoly is a miniaturized model of an economy in which the players buy and sell property. The game presents a limited version of reality combined with make-believe. Winning is a combination of luck and decision making. When players lose, they can account for it by blaming their luck, and when players win,

---

Teaching Hints: Leading Role-Playing

- Limit your own expectations. Do not expect that your first, or your students' first role-playing session will be a model situation. If you achieve involvement, consider yourself successful. Accept that students' involvement may be characterized by a noisier session than anticipated.
- Expect students to be self-conscious during their first sessions.
- Encourage students to focus on problems, characterizations, feelings, and solutions, not on silly or self-conscious behavior.
- Evaluate the realism of the enactment, not the acting ability of the students.
- Stop the enactment as soon as you are aware that students have expressed what they feel, know, or want to express. Initial enactments may be fewer than five minutes long.
- Discuss after the enactment. Expect these discussions to be longer than the enactment. Extend thinking through the discussion.
- Encourage more children to participate in role-playing rather than using the same actors.
- Ensure that additional enactments are action-oriented and should explore feelings, issues, and consequences in greater depth.
- Remember that students will not always get to the generalization stage. This takes practice for both you and the students.

Games provide a means for students to relieve tensions and express themselves.

they can credit intelligent decision making! Both simulation games and educational games provide a safe environment for problem solving, role-playing, and decision making. The individual may always say, "I am playing a role," and in this way the ego is always spared.

The terms *simulation games*, *educational games*, and *simulations* are used interchangeably in this chapter to describe interactive game approaches.

PURPOSES AND USES OF SIMULATIONS IN THE CLASSROOM

Motivation

Simulations may be used either to introduce a new unit or to culminate a unit of study. Simulations are motivating to most students, perhaps because they are dramatic and have an element of suspense. It is possible for students to participate in most simulations without prior knowledge of the content; however, prior knowledge may enhance the performance of the player or participant. This is why the simulation makes a good initial activity as well as an appropriate evaluative activity. Simulations may also be used developmentally during a unit of study.

Participation

The stimulating nature of simulations seems to compel involvement rather than passive attention. Game players experience a sense of control over their envi-

ronment. Their actions are directly related to consequences. They influence what happens. If a poor decision leads to an unhappy consequence, the game player can change his or her strategy. Participation in simulations requires mastering skills in negotiation, bargaining, planning, and decision making.

Feedback

The relationship between actions and consequences is readily apparent during gaming. Feedback is immediate. Monopoly players who spend all of their assets buying hotels for their property will soon discover the consequences of the savings depletion when they land on an opponent's property and cannot pay the rent. Role-players in the game Ghetto learn quickly the consequences of being an unskilled laborer. Unlike most paper-and-pencil activities, in which students wait for reinforcement, simulation activities provide immediate input.

Goals

Simulations typically have clearly defined goals and constraints. Participants know when and under what conditions a game will end. Once again the motivation to get to the end of the game or to closure helps to sustain interest. In Ghetto, where each round represents a year in the life of ghetto residents, students typically ask, "How many rounds will we play?" The leader's response to that question affects the participants' game strategy. Both having a time limit and playing until you have winners influence short- and long-range goals and overall game strategy.

Interaction

Simulation activities necessitate students' interaction, and social interaction is often the major purpose for choosing simulations as a instructional strategy. Group-satisfying behaviors are taught as students work rationally with others in a team situation. Communication skills are enhanced as students bargain, debate, and consult with each other. Peer interaction during simulations results in a more natural classroom atmosphere.

Relevance

The acting-out element of a simulation creates a more realistic environment as students are forced to deal with social situations, issues, and problems—even when the simulation represents and focuses on a historical theme.

Open-Endedness

Even though there are rules and frequently winners and losers, simulations are inherently open ended. Students accept that games represent the real world and, as such, have no predetermined end. The game may focus on a process or a problem, but the end of the game cannot be known in advance. There are no correct answers to a simulation. Perhaps it is the open-ended element of the game that makes it so motivating to students. (The teacher cannot control the outcome!)

Ego-Satisfying Behaviors

Since students feel that they can control what happens during the simulation, they also feel more secure and self-confident. All students participate in the simulation, so everyone has an equal opportunity to shine. Superior academic achievement does not guarantee who will be a winner during gaming. Imaginative solutions, luck, and social skills may prove to be more important during the simulation than verbal skills and reading achievement. Simulation activities provide different leadership and participant roles than typical classroom activities. As a consequence, different leaders may emerge during the simulation than during basic skills instruction. With the opportunity for different classroom roles, students develop optimism, status, self-respect, and self-confidence.

What do you think a teacher should try to accomplish during a simulation debriefing session?

Differentiation of Instruction

Students do not feel that they are being graded during gaming activities, although in fact there are many ways for teachers to evaluate social and academic progress during these activities. Grading pressures are relieved during simulation activities because students can participate at various levels without hindering others. The superior student may enjoy the flexibility of the game and the opportunity to explore different ideas in an open environment, while the slower academic student gains from peer interaction and can take part at an appropriate personal level. Goals and constraints can be devised to accommodate the diversity of the students in the classroom.

WHAT DO STUDENTS LEARN DURING GAMING?

Social Skills

Since everyone is participating in an active fashion, the shy student does not feel observed and tends to communicate more freely with peers. The aggressive student is forced to modify interaction habits as new peer relationships develop during the game. Most simulations are dependent on peer interaction, and students are compelled to share their ideas with others. Social skill development occurs as students are forced to obey game rules and work with classmates for the benefit of group or team goals.

Knowledge Goals

Every game or simulation requires basic information or a data base. Whether the game is about legislation or the environment, factual information is important in order to participate. Students acquire facts in a variety of ways during a game, and teachers should expect students to recognize the basic concepts and information upon which the game is predicated.

Valuing

Role-playing develops empathy for others as students assume a variety of roles and attempt to play them realistically. Role-playing also requires listening to others' viewpoints; this develops sensitivity to different value positions. Judging the effectiveness of your own and others' strategies occurs continuously during gaming.

Students need to make judgments about bargains, negotiations, biases, or promises. They learn to evaluate their own interests and the interests of others.

Problem Solving

Gaming and simulations are problem-solving techniques. Gaming has been used by the military to solve tactical and research problems; the business community uses games for training and planning problems. During simulations, students often solve problems instinctively, and after the game is over, strategies can be analyzed to help improve students' problem-solving ability in other situations.

CHOOSING GAMES AND SIMULATIONS

Games teach a wide variety of skills, including problem solving and decision making. Games are even used to reinforce specific skills. The teacher may select a game to fit the desired objectives. The choice should be appropriate to the interests and abilities of students and the aims of the curriculum. Games should also be chosen based on the time allotted for the activity. Some simulations may take several class periods, and others can be completed during an hour or less of class time.

Commercial games can be found in stores specializing in instructional materials.

DESIGNING A SIMULATION OR BOARD GAME

Some teachers like to create their own simulations or board games for use in the classroom. Use the following design procedure to create your own game:

1. Specify the grade level of the students who are to play the game. Include special needs and interests.
2. Identify objectives and areas of the curriculum where you will use the game.
3. Decide whether there will be a game board or whether it will be a simulation.
4. Decide whether the game will be for an entire class or for small groups of students.
5. Set the situation and conditions. Do you need equipment?
6. Determine the goal. Will there be scoring? Will there be winners and losers? How will students know when the game is completed?

7. Decide on rules and constraints that will affect behavior. Establish a time limit so students can plan their strategies and will know when the game is over.

A Sample Game

The game School Council was designed using the guidelines above. The following lists include the information used to create and set up the game and the rules to play it.

Design Procedure

1. It is for students in grades 5–8.
2. It can be used as a language arts or social studies learning experience.
3. Objectives include the development of social interaction skills.
4. It is a simulation and is planned for an entire class.
5. The students are to be divided into five groups. Each group will need the following materials: a Voting Record form, the Group and Council Rules, and the Group Information sheet. Groups may also need pencil and paper for group note taking. During the School Council meeting, a table and chairs will be needed in the front of the classroom.
6. The game is concluded when the School Council makes a decision concerning each proposal. Estimated time is one to two class periods.

The Issues

1. Should some students have special privileges?
   - The computer club wants access to the computer lab during recesses and lunch time.
   - Eighth graders believe they shouldn't have to ask for a hall pass when they need to go to the bathroom.
   - Presently only the seventh and eighth graders have access to the softball fields; fifth and sixth graders feel they too should be able to play softball at lunch time.
2. Should the snack bar sell soft drinks and candy?
   - Most of the students believe it should, but the parent group wants only healthy snacks sold at school. The problem is that no one seems to agree about what is considered healthy.
3. Should sixth graders be allowed to attend the school dances?
   - There are mixed feelings about this. Some sixth graders don't care; most believe they should be allowed to attend. The parent group is undecided. Teachers have not expressed an opinion.

Group Rules

1. Choose one person to be your representative on the School Council.
2. Choose a recorder to transcribe your ideas.
3. Choose one person to be in charge of the Voting Record form.
4. Identify the problem(s) that concerns your group.
5. Identify the other issues you might use to bargain with other groups.
6. Identify reasons why others may not favor your proposal.
7. Plan the best way to convince other groups to support your views.
8. Bargain with other groups in order to obtain support for your proposal.
9. Coach your Council Representative.
10. Predict how the Council will vote on the issues.

School Council Rules

1. Choose a Council President to keep order. The president may introduce the issues but the representatives need to present their viewpoint on each issue.
2. Representatives may ask to speak to their group (constituency) at any time. Adjourn the council meeting while this occurs.
3. Listen to each proposal. You may ask the representative questions to clarify the issues.
4. Discuss each proposal. Decide how each proposal impacts the other proposals.
5. You may agree with the proposal, modify it, or reject it. Vote on each proposal.
6. The Council President may vote.

Group Information

1. Group I represents students in the computer club. They want to be able to use the computer lab during free time. They believe that club members are responsible individuals and do not need adult supervision. The members of Group I have no real interest in the other issues. (They could be used as bargaining chips.)
2. Group II represents sixth-grade students. Most of the sixth-grade students believe that they should be allowed to take part in school dances and other activities that have been reserved for seventh and eighth graders. They care about access to the softball field and support the soft drink and candy issue. They do not care about the computer issue and they are passive about the hall pass situation.

3. Group III represents eighth-grade students. They would like the school dances to be reserved for students in the seventh and eighth grades. This group supports the snack bar selling soft drinks and candy. They care very much about the hall pass issue; they feel it is embarrassing to ask the teacher for permission to go to the bathroom, and believe that eighth graders will not abuse the privilege.

4. Group IV represents the school's parent group. They are not keen on allowing sixth graders to attend school dances, and do not want the snack stand to sell sweets. They do not have a great interest in the other issues.

5. Group V represents teachers at the school. They don't care about the snack bar issue and have no opinion about the softball field or the school dance issue. The teachers are willing to support the use of the computer lab during free time by the computer club, but they are unwilling to provide supervision during recess and lunch time.

 Teaching Hints:
Using the *School Council* Simulation

1. Circulate among the groups.
2. Remind groups to identify the issues involved.
3. Ask probing questions if the groups have failed to identify the problem:
   - How do you feel about special privileges for some students based on age or interests?
   - What would your friends think about a teacher denying a bathroom pass?
   - What are your ideas about whether teachers should be asked to work during the lunch hour?
4. Remind students to negotiate with other groups and use the issues they do not feel strongly about to bargain for what they do want.
5. Give the students time limits for their group discussions.
6. Encourage the Council to discuss the issues before voting.
7. Encourage the Council to speak out so everyone can hear.
8. Debrief. Discuss bargaining and compromising. Find out if groups honored their promises. Discuss why political promises are sometimes not honored. Discuss good rules and bad rules and what should be done when a rule is no longer appropriate. Ask students if they successfully predicted how the Council would vote.

Find out what issues are important to the students at your school. Perform the School Council simulation another time using issues identified by the students.

TEACHER'S ROLE DURING GAMING

Preparation is the first teacher task for gaming. The best preparation is to pilot test your materials. Find some good-natured friends to play the game with you before using it with students. If this is impossible, see that you are thoroughly familiar with the rules and the goals. If the game requires materials or equipment, prepare them in advance. Be sure that you have budgeted enough time to play the game so you will not spoil it by stopping the game prematurely.

Prepare the class for participation. Choose your role-players and provide instructions in the form of rules or constraints. Be certain that students understand the purpose and goals of the activity. Communicate how much time has been budgeted for the activity.

Observe carefully and *circulate* during the game or role-play. Remember that first-time gaming experiences are apt to be a bit noisy, but this does not mean that students should be out of control. Maintain your role as a guide and facilitator during the action; remember that students will be learning from each other, rather than from you. However, if role-players ask advice, it is perfectly proper to provide suggestions.

Take plenty of time to *debrief* and *discuss*. Ask probing questions about the students' gaming experience. If students have ideas about how to improve the game or role-play, allow them to try out their ideas or redesign the game. Discuss the art of negotiation and the reasons for compromising. Discuss how the gaming experience relates to real-life experiences.

EVALUATION OF ROLE-PLAYING AND GAMING

Observation of students during simulation activities should provide information about students' understanding of concepts and skills, critical thinking and decision making, sensitivity to others, awareness of fate and of consequences, and self-concept.

During evaluative discussions it is possible to gain insight about students' competencies to analyze processes, apply the simulation to other situations, compare and contrast the role-play situation to real-life activities, summarize and make judgments about problems and decisions, and restructure the activity.

SUMMARY

Purpose of Role-Playing

1. Role-playing is a problem-solving strategy that helps students confront social issues.
2. Role-playing facilitates learner involvement and interaction in the process of decision making.
3. Role-playing can be used to teach citizenship responsibilities and for group counseling.

Role-Playing Methods

4. Role-playing involves nine steps: setting motivation, selecting players, setting the stage, preparing the audience, enacting the role-play, discussion and evaluation, reenactment, further discussion and evaluation, and generalizing about the problem or situation.
5. Caucus group role-playing groups students for the enactment in order to lessen student embarrassment and feeling of being "on stage."

Moral Education

6. Role-playing can be used for moral development and education.

Diagnosis

7. Teachers can use role-playing to help them assess students' social problems.

Simulations

8. Simulations, like case studies, use a controlled data base to involve students in an intensive social study.
9. Simulations are highly motivating because they are dramatic and suspenseful.
10. During simulations and gaming, students develop social skills and recognize values, learn new concepts, and engage in problem solving.

DISCUSSION QUESTIONS AND APPLICATION EXERCISES

1. Design a simulation using the guidelines in this chapter.
2. Observe students participating in group activities. Cite ways in which students cooperated with each other, accepted responsibility, and demonstrated rationality and respectfulness. List examples of inhibiting factors that affected group behavior.

3. What are some affective behaviors that relate to the development of self-concept and self-identity? Make a list including examples such as students voluntarily share successes and failures; students voluntarily assist others in cooperative work or play activities.

4. Identify some core values that could be taught using role-playing, such as honesty or fairness.

5. Suppose a parent criticized your use of games in the classroom; prepare a response entitled "Why We Play Games at School."

C H A P T E R

9

Curriculum Planning: The Teaching Unit

This chapter begins by identifying and defining key curriculum concepts. Then you will look at a teaching unit using those concepts. Procedures for curriculum development are explained using a step-by-step process. An alternate model for curriculum development also is presented with suggestions for the reader to try both "systems." The chapter emphasizes the importance of a match between the teacher's goals and the learning activities because if students do not actively experience what teachers have in mind in their day-to-day lessons, then the teaching unit does not accurately depict what students are learning.

After you study this chapter, you should be able to accomplish the following:

1. Differentiate the characteristics of three types of units.
2. Write an example of a *theme* and a *generalization*.
3. Write several "big ideas" for use as a content outline in a subject of your choice.
4. Write key questions to demonstrate the teaching-learning process you would follow in your teaching unit.
5. Select learning experiences to fit your content and key questions and that demonstrate a variety of instructional processes and activities.
6. Demonstrate through selected learning experiences how you will evaluate what students are learning.
7. Use webbing as a means to develop a teaching unit.
8. Explain why it is important to *integrate* subject fields and skill instruction.

WHAT IS UNIT TEACHING?

A *unit* is a plan that organizes ideas and knowledge into a meaningful structure for teaching purposes. Basic **concepts** within a subject field or across subject fields are selected to achieve specific purposes. The content of the unit facilitates communication. Without content there is very little students can communicate about for expression and reception purposes. The unit should provide integrative experiences to satisfy students' needs and to develop understandings, values, and skills.

TYPES OF UNITS

Single Subject and Broad Field Units

Units can be developed for most subjects: science (such as biology and astronomy), music, art, health, mathematics, and history. When a unit is intended for a single subject field only, content is usually prestruc-

---

Professional Lexicon

balance   Achievement of equity among subject fields and learning processes in a curriculum plan.

concepts   The big ideas, the significant content of a subject field.

continuity   Reiteration of significant content at different levels to achieve depth in conceptual understanding.

curriculum consonance   The balance of elements in the curriculum to ensure that learning experiences are appropriate and support goals.

generalization   Concept or idea that demonstrates understanding and provides direction for content and learning experiences to explain the theme of a teaching unit.

integration   The linking of subject fields and learning processes to facilitate learning by assisting the learner to see relationships.

interdisciplinary content   Concepts from different subject fields (disciplines) used to demonstrate learning through different lenses.

---

resource unit   A unit developed by a committee for the purpose of providing direction and assistance to classroom teachers.

scope   The breadth of a teaching unit or a curriculum; how much of what is covered in a unit.

sequence   The order of content in a teaching unit.

teaching unit   The plan that is to be implemented in the classroom and that represents the instructional curriculum.

themes   Unit-organizing concepts used to represent the big ideas, overarching concepts, unifying constructs, or underlying assumptions.

webbing   A pictorial means to demonstrate the connecting of ideas for a teaching unit (a spider web).

---

tured for the single discipline, and it is considered *discipline-oriented*. There is relatively little thought given to meeting the needs of a specific group of students.

But units can be designed to teach content from a *broad field*, such as social studies, life sciences, and health education. (Review the organizing patterns described in Chapter 3.) These units are typically organized around a theme and are relatively open ended so that students can have input and the teacher can change activities to meet students' interests and needs.

Resource Units

Resource units are often developed at the district level by a committee of teachers or subject field specialists. The purpose of the resource unit is to provide a great deal of information on possible ways to teach a specific topic. It is not planned with any specific group of students in mind. The resource unit includes learning activities, resource materials, and evaluation methods, as well as lists of objectives and questions.

Teaching Unit

The **teaching unit** differs from the resource unit in degree of specificity: It is focused and planned for a particular group of students and is formulated to teach a limited number of concepts, skills, and values. Before developing a teaching unit, the teacher may make use of a resource unit.

The teaching unit ensures that there is a purpose to the day-to-day lessons. It represents long-range planning for teaching the curriculum. Unit activities should include a broad range of processes and experiences, such as problem solving, research skill activities, language development, and dramatic activities. All of the instructional strategies discussed in Part II of this text can be used in unit teaching.

The teaching unit often is initiated by an inquiry question to stimulate students' thinking and obtain their input about what they would like to know. The inquiry question(s) helps the teacher assess students' preknowledge about the theme and facilitates the planning process.

Single subject units are often planned long in advance of when students will be taught the subject. The thematic unit is typically planned and focused on specific students; therefore, it is ongoing.

CURRICULUM CONCEPTS

When designing a unit, the curriculum developer considers a number of organizing elements that affect the function of the unit, the choice of content, and the length of time the class will focus on the unit.

The **scope** of the unit determines whether the unit will provide broad coverage or in-depth understandings. In a sense, it tells you "how much of what" to teach.

The **sequence** of the unit determines the linear organization of content. Some units may be organized chronologically, as from early times to modern times. Some subject matter may be organized from simple to complex; other material may be arranged from whole to parts or parts to whole. Some curriculum developers believe that one should introduce abstract information first to provide an organizing structure, then concrete information to facilitate integration of content. Other criteria for sequence may have to do with beliefs about the need for a logical development of a field or survey coverage before in-depth knowledge. Much depends upon how you believe individuals learn best.

Continuity has to do with articulation of content from one level to another. For example, Dewey believed that content should be reintroduced at different

Research Readings

The Junior Achievement Program provides K–6 students with a business and economics program. Using sequentially integrated themes, students learn a variety of concepts and skills through hands-on activities that help them apply what they learn to new situations. The themes include: Ourselves, Our Families, Our Community, Our City, Our Region, Our Nation, and Our World (Van Scotter, Van Dusen, and Worthen, 1996).

Research Findings: Who Decides What to Teach?

Klein, Tye, and Wright (1979) conceptualized five perspectives of curriculum:

- The *ideal* curriculum represents the scholar's perspective of what ought to be taught.
- The *formal* curriculum represents the expectations of policy makers concerned about what is taught in the schools.
- The *instructional* curriculum represents the teacher's attitudes, values, and beliefs about what should be taught in the classroom.
- The *operational* curriculum demonstrates the curriculum that the teacher implements in the classroom.
- The *experiential* curriculum is what students actually experience in the classroom.

times in consideration of the students' maturity. Each time the students experience the content it should provide them greater depth in conceptual understanding so that they continue to extend and expand meanings. Another common example of this is the social studies curriculum where students are introduced to U.S. history and political processes in grade 5 and reintroduced in grade 8 and grade 11. Each time the content is extended and expanded further.

Integration determines whether or not one focuses on a single subject discipline or tries to link subject fields and learning processes. Integration helps the learner see relationships in time, space, actions, concepts, problems, and judgments. Integration often makes what is to be learned more relevant for the learner by reaching out into the learner's personal experience and using a societal context for learning. Integration may mean erasing subject field barriers and teaching both content and skills as they are needed. Instead of the clock controlling when something is taught, the teacher decides, based on students' needs, when and what to teach. An example of integration can be seen in the lesson on outlining that Greg Thomas did during social studies instruction in Chapter 6.

Overarching organizing **themes** provide another means to structure and integrate the curriculum. By selecting an overarching theme, teachers can help students see the common thread that runs through different subject fields and disciplines. The theme of change may tie changes in historical periods of time with literary fiction from different periods of time. Change may depict environmental changes, technological changes, and evolutionary changes. Teaching

to a theme is essential for helping students develop a meaningful picture to connect fields of study.

Interdisciplinary content deals with concepts that are derived from different disciplines. Sometimes the content from more than one subject field is integrated, and sometimes it is studied so that the learner is made aware of how each of the disciplines structures similar knowledge. For example, the concept of *role* in political science may have to do with a function or office assumed by an individual (such as the president). In dramatics, *role* relates to the part one is playing, and in sociology, *role* may determine one's status and degree of power.

Balance, in curriculum terms, means the degree to which teachers pay attention to equity among the subject fields and the learning processes. Are social studies and science relegated to 30 minutes at the end of the day twice a week, or are those subjects given the same

Teaching Hints: Choosing a Theme

Before selecting a theme for your teaching unit, it is important to think about the most significant ideas from the discipline(s), then choose the theme that fits.

Students' own questions can be used to plan a purposeful unit of study.

attention and time as language arts? When we talk about learning processes, balance has to do with whether students are asked to *consume* (*listen passively*) most of the school day *or* learning processes are balanced so that students *produce* through learning experiences designed to make them construct their own meanings.

PLANNING A TEACHING UNIT

Greg Thomas wanted to plan a teaching unit that would have as its major focus the social studies. He wanted to integrate other subject fields and include interdisciplinary concepts from several of the disciplines. The unit was for his fifth-grade students who were quite diverse in their capabilities. Recall from Part I that Thomas believes students should be actively engaged in learning activities, and his concern about the environment affects his selection of learning experiences.

GOALS

Thomas planned to include the following overall goals:

- Develop students' research skills
- Develop students' problem-solving capabilities
- Provide opportunities for applying basic skills

Before you read Greg Thomas's teaching unit, write several goals you would like to accomplish in your own classroom. Review Thomas's goals and decide what activities he needs to plan in order to accomplish them. What activities will you need for your goals?

- Provide opportunities for social participation that include leadership and group member responsibilities

He intended to plan specific topics in each subject field, relating the topics to an overall theme. He would write his objectives into his learning experiences because in that way he would develop each subject field systematically. As an experienced teacher, Thomas was able to meld his knowledge of what his students know (and don't know), his knowledge of subject matter and appropriate content, and his knowledge of instructional processes (Figure 9.1).

THEME

Greg Thomas selected *change* as his theme. Because the concept of change is so broad and can be used in

Figure 9.1 Teachers' Preknowledge

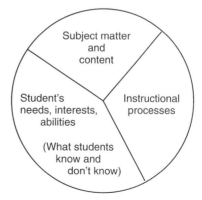

so many ways, he wrote a **generalization** to give meaning to the concept of change as he would be using it:

> Relations to the natural environment and human relationships change as people alter conditions of living and seek to meet basic needs.

Next he began to identify the topics he would focus on in each subject field. The topics helped him select content. In social studies he started off with two topics:

1. Expansion and Development of the West and Southwest
2. Interaction of Cultures and Diversity of Peoples

CONTENT

Using texts and looking at the resources available to him and his students, Thomas made a list of the content he would feature. In addition, he made decisions about how to sequence the content. For Topics 1 and 2, Thomas selected the following content:

The Big Ideas—Content Outline

1. Beginning during the "fabulous" 1840s, the people of the United States considered it a mission and duty to seek territorial expansion.
2. The environment and conditions of living in a region affect human behavior.
3. The needs and interest of people differ; events and actions motivate antagonistic behavior.
4. Industrialization affected people's independence and way of life.
5. Conflict, cooperation, and competition occur when cultures meet.

Thinking about his particular class of students, Thomas studied his content to determine what special meanings his fifth graders needed. He made a list of the social science concepts that he needed to teach. These included *migration, Manifest Destiny, environment, adaptation, culture, conflict, interaction,* and possibly the concept of *change.* He knew that he would have to identify similar concepts in each subject field in order to integrate the study.

KEY QUESTIONS

Next Thomas framed some *key questions* to focus his choice of learning experiences. Using each concept

Teaching Hints: *Ideas For Generalizations*

- Social groups organize themselves to meet the needs of their members. (Order)
- The interaction of culture and environment results in distinctive patterns of behavior. (Patterns of Change)
- Rules represent social values; people make rules to set norms of conduct. (Order)
- Group living necessitates cooperation in and between groups to maintain an orderly, physical, social, cultural environment. (Interactions, Order)
- Living things are interdependent with one another and their environment. (Interdependence)
- Changes in the physical environment affect life in that environment. (Change)
- Our physical and social environments reflect both change and stability. (Change, Stability)
- Political and economic systems interact and affect ways of life. (Systems and Interactions)
- Culture changes occur as a consequence of time, place, and distance. (Culture, Change)
- Learning is essential to human development and is a lifelong experience. (Growth, Change)
- People are unique in their cultural adaptations and social organization. (Adaptation, Change, Culture, Systems, Order)
- Evolution is evident through patterns, processes, mechanisms, and history. (Patterns of Change, Evolution)
- Change can be identified. It can be cyclical, irregular, or exhibit a trend. (Change, Patterns)

and his big ideas, he wrote a tentative list of target or key questions.

Migration

1. What motivated people of the United States to leave their established communities and seek new territories?

Environment and Adaptation

2. How did the western United States and the Southwest come to be the way they are?
3. In the new territories, how did people meet their basic needs?
4. In what ways did the environment of the United States change?
5. In what regions did people settle?

6. How did the ways in which people satisfied their basic needs differ in the Northeast, South, and West?

Culture and Interaction

7. What different experiences did people have in the various regions of the United States?
8. How did these different experiences affect ways of life?
9. What did different cultures borrow from each other?
10. How did different cultural groups feel about land rights, land ownership, farming, education, and family life?
11. How did territorial expansion affect the Native Americans?

Conflict

12. In what ways did the needs and interests of people in the various regions of the United States differ?
13. What disagreements did people in the Northeast, South, and West have?
14. How did the varied needs and interests affect behavior?
15. What events and actions motivated antagonistic behavior?
16. How were Mexicans and Native Americans treated by the expansionists?
17. How have new immigrant groups been treated historically?

Change

18. How did technology affect people's independence?
19. How were workers affected? How were industrial leaders affected?
20. How did the expansion of rail lines affect people's opportunities?
21. In what ways did cities change?

LEARNING EXPERIENCES (ACTIVITIES)

Thomas's next task was to select appropriate *learning experiences* to achieve objectives, stimulate thinking, and appeal to students' natural interests. The integration or linking of several subject fields through his choice of activities was a major consideration.

Thomas used both his concepts and his key questions to help him select learning experiences. The

questions served as trigger points to help him focus students' experiences.

Migration

1. Study map and globe of United States: Identify topographic and climatic differences. (advance organizer lesson)
2. Use large floor map of United States: Identify and attach mountains, rivers, and trails; discuss direction that rivers flow, elevation; compute distances between existing communities; compute time differences between existing communities.
3. Read and listen to stories about frontier settlers, fur traders, explorers, ranchers, Native American leaders, community leaders, and pioneers.
4. Use group investigation to inquire why different groups emigrated from established communities to new regions.
5. Role-play pioneer groups.
6. Present concept attainment lesson using concept of *Manifest Destiny*.

Environment and Adaptation

7. Use group investigation to inquire how regional differences affect basic needs: use of trees, seeds, fruits, animals, fish (the natural environment); farming methods.
8. Visit museum to see artifacts of the nineteenth century.
9. Construct tools and objects used by pioneer settlers: clothing, looms, wagons, flatboats, candles, soap.
10. Problem solving: How does environment (regional differences) contribute to differences in ways of life?
11. Dramatic play: Act out life activities of different settlers.

Culture and Interaction

12. Present concept attainment lesson using concept of culture.
13. Use group investigation to research ways of life of different Native American groups: Sioux, Cheyenne, Plains, Chumash, Huron, Iroquois; Native American policy, agency system, relocation policy.
14. Role-play cultural conflict between pioneer groups and Native Americans.
15. Use group investigation to research regional differences in beliefs about land ownership, land rights,

education, farming, ranching, growth, expansion. (In what ways did groups agree, disagree? How did settlers and Native Americans differ? How did ranchers and farmers differ? How did Eastern settlers and Mexicans in the West differ?)

16. Problem solving: cultural borrowing. What did each group contribute to others?

Conflict

17. Discuss needs and interests of people in Northeast, South, Southwest, and West; relate differences to environmental adaptation and culture.
18. Research agriculture in the South, trading and manufacturing in the Northeast, beginning of the railroads.
19. Compare regional differences: Why did Southerners think that trading and manufacturing were suitable only for the lower class?
20. Read about and discuss the slave experience. Use simulation Slave Auction.
21. Research using group investigation the polarization of sectional attitudes concerning equality. How were different groups treated? (Mexicans, Chinese, Native Americans, African-Americans) What were attitudes about the Fugitive Slave Law, Dred Scott Decision, Nat Turner Rebellion, Missouri Compromise, John Brown, Kansas-Nebraska Act?

Change

22. Make a time line of events and actions leading to industrialization and Civil War. (advance organizer lesson)
23. Trace development of railroads using maps and time periods.
24. Relate industrialization to immigration.
25. Problem solving: How did technology affect regional life? (conditions of employment, organization of work, attitudes of business leaders, where people lived, the lives of children)
26. Trace the growth of cities. Hypothesize about what influenced size, expansion, diminution.

INTERDISCIPLINARY CONNECTIONS

Many of Thomas's activities utilized other subject fields, thereby integrating students' learning; but in addition, he made some specific plans for interdisciplinary connections. In brief, these included the following lists of key questions and activities.

Literature Topic

Literary works can reflect people, places, and historical events.

Key Questions

1. What does literature tell us about the lives of early pioneers and the Native Americans and others affected by the nation's expansion?
2. What motivates people to explore or migrate?
3. What character traits did early immigrants demonstrate?
4. How are we like and different from the early pioneers?

Learning Experiences/Activities

1. Read from the following selection of books:
   Getting There: Frontier Travel Without Power by S. Hilton
   Grasshopper Summer by A. Turner
   Sing Down the Moon by S. O'Dell
   Sarah, Plain and Tall by P. MacLachlan
2. Through pictures, graphics, and writing, identify the attributes of the pioneers you have read about and how the lives of others were affected by the Westward expansion.
3. Write tall tale stories typical of pioneer days.
4. Develop a class book of tall tales.
5. Read original stories to younger children at school. Construct pop-out books for younger children.

Science Topic

Living things share the environment; people affect the ecosystem.

Teaching Hints: Developing a Teaching Unit

- Select significant key ideas for content; develop them in depth. (Balance breadth and depth.)
- Organize content sequentially with powerful learning experiences.
- Provide time for students to use and apply knowledge to make it their own.
- Feature learning experiences that require problem solving or acts of creation.
- Help students relate what they are learning to day-to-day life experiences.
- Make the classroom a democratic learning environment.

Key Questions

1. What are the meanings of *environment?*
2. How is our way of life reflective of our environment?
3. In what ways do people affect the natural environment?
4. In what ways do people influence the life cycles of animals?

Learning Experiences/Activities

1. Use group investigation to research endangered species. (How do people upset the balance of nature?) Read about the desert wood rat and the effect of urban development; read about the ferret and how ranchers killed off prairie dogs which were the main source of food for the ferret.
2. Experiment with plants. (What do all plants need?)
3. Observe and chart the life cycles of specific plants and animals.
4. Explore the Internet for information on the natural environment, national wildlife, and climate change.
5. Use group investigation to research food webs and food chains.
6. Present concept attainment lesson about environment. Distinguish between natural and manmade environment.
7. Problem solving: relationship between predator-prey cycles, population cycles, plant succession cycles.

Art Topic

Art is a visual record of culture and history.

Key Questions

1. What can we learn about our ways of life by studying the art of people? What do objects tell us about periods of history?
2. What will future people say about our culture by studying our art and artifacts?
3. If we were to make a visual record of our community, what would it tell future citizens about what we value?

Learning Experiences/Activities

1. Present concept attainment lesson about images. Describe feelings of early pioneers.
2. Paint images for crowded, itchy, scared, angry, cluttered, curious, and gleeful.
3. Explore the Internet using Art Exploration, Art History Information, Art History Server, and Arts Resources (Library of Congress) to read about and see pictures painted during and of the colonial period of American history.
4. Study light images and construct a pinhole camera.
5. Walk around the community; take pictures; paint pictures. Write captions for the pictures.
6. Mural project: pioneer faces, immigrant experiences.

REVIEW OF THE CURRICULUM DEVELOPMENT PLAN

The planning process begins with the teacher's tacit knowledge of the students' needs, interests, and abilities. In addition, before an actual teaching unit can be developed, the teacher needs to have knowledge of the subject matter (content) and knowledge of instructional processes (refer back to Figure 9.1).

The first real task is the identification of the *theme* and the intended focus of the unit. This can be done by developing a *generalization* to give meaning to the theme. The theme serves as the organizing thread to integrate learning.

Topics in each subject field can be identified, and this is followed by selecting the *big ideas* (content) for the unit(s).

To help focus the teaching-learning process, *key questions* are used to provide continuity, scope, and sequence. The questions can be further sequenced by identifying the conceptual focus.

Learning experiences are selected and organized using the key questions, providing significant activities to develop the desired knowledge, skills, and attitudes. Figure 9.2 outlines the curriculum development process, and Figure 9.3 provides a form to plan teaching units using this process.

OBSERVATIONS ABOUT THOMAS'S TEACHING UNIT

Historical chronology is not of major importance in the unit in the sense that Thomas does not intend to proceed decade by decade. This limitation is sensible

**Point to Ponder:
An Application Exercise**

A third-grade teacher decided on the following topic for a social studies unit: *Meeting Basic Needs of Living Harmoniously in Social Groups.* What would be an appropriate theme? What generalization would provide meaning for the theme? Write several focusing questions and learning experiences.

Figure 9.2 Lemlech Curriculum Development Process

Teachers need to begin with preknowledge of students' needs, interests, and abilities, knowledge of subject matter content; and knowledge of instructional processes.

1. Select an overarching theme.
2. Give meaning to the theme through a generalization to describe the theme.
3. Identify topics in each subject field.
4. Establish goals or objectives.
5. Identify the big ideas (content) in each subject field.
6. Write key questions to structure teaching and learning (continuity, scope, sequence).
7. Select learning experiences/activities. Consider integration of knowledge, skills, attitudes, and interdiscipline connections. Evaluation experiences may be specifically planned or based on the actual experiences. Product and/or performance may be judged.

because it is obviously impossible to include all of history. However, this does not mean that Thomas will not teach time in relation to history. Each period of history can be connected through the use of time lines in the classroom and by relating significant events to other events that students recall.

Thomas selected a limited number of concepts to develop in depth. There are others that he could have selected, but his choices do give him mileage and enable him to integrate subject fields. He is wise in not trying to teach "everything you always wanted to know about U. S. history" to fifth graders.

Although the activities are numbered, the numbers do not mean that each experience takes only one day. Some will continue beyond one class period (construc-

tion, mural, story writing, science experiments). Some activities may also repeat the following day. The evaluation of an activity like dramatic play might reveal the need for repeated experience to clarify concepts. The many research activities may also take more than one class period. Very likely, this unit will consume about six weeks of the semester.

Integration occurs through a variety of experiences. For example, the students will need measurement skills (and metrics) to accomplish their construction. Through their studies in science (living things share the environment, people affect the ecosystem) they will learn about modification and adaptation to the environment. Other subjects will be integrated through experiences in dance, music, and art. Literature will contribute to historical

Figure 9.3 Unit Planning Form

Theme:

    Generalization(s):

    Subject Field Topics:

    Goals/Objectives:

    Big Ideas (Content):

    Focusing Questions:

Learning Experiences/Activities:
    1.
    2.
    3.
    4.
    5.
    6.
    7.

Students' own questions can be used to plan a purposeful unit of study.

chronology and provide insight about the lives of both pioneer people and those displaced by the expansion period of history. The unit planning form in Figure 9.3 provides a model for planning an integrated teaching unit.

ANOTHER CURRICULUM DEVELOPMENT PLAN: WEBBING

The **webbing** plan helps the curriculum developer see connections in the process of selecting content and suggests means to integrate subject fields. It is a non-linear system and graphically depicts patterns and relationships. Mary Hogan used the process to develop a teaching unit using the theme of order, as shown in Figure 9.4.

Hogan based the theme of order on the following generalization:

Group living necessitates cooperation with and between individuals and groups to maintain an orderly physical, social, and cultural environment.

Each of the spokes on the diagram suggested content areas for learning experiences and for the integration of subject fields. For example, from the spoke labeled

Figure 9.4 Curriculum Development: Webbing

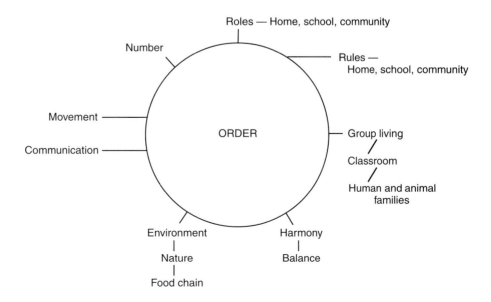

Research Readings

Kids Around Town (KAT) engages K–12 students in curriculum focused on what their government is doing. Using an endless array of topics and approaches the students choose what to study based on what is happening in their community.

Third graders in Pocono, Pennsylvania, studied land use because their favorite play areas were being turned into housing developments.

Fifth graders studied bicycle safety, and then wrote and presented proposals to the city council to require the use of helmets.

The program emphasizes the use of multiple information sources (not textbooks) and social participation. The teacher's role is that of a co-investigator, a coach, and a facilitator.

The KAT model includes seven interdisciplinary procedures:

1. Students are introduced to local government.
2. Students select a local issue or problem to explore.
3. Students study the problem by researching the issues (interviewing, reading, writing letters, and taking notes).
4. Students analyze their data, distinguishing between facts and opinions and checking their evidence.
5. Students propose solutions based on research and analysis.
6. Students participate in social actions by writing letters, presenting proposals, and performing social services.
7. Students' learning is assessed. Using students' social applications, interactions, journals, portfolios, and self-assessment, learning is evaluated (Rappoport and Kletzien, 1996).

The webbing plan can be introduced with an inquiry question. Students' ideas are then elicited and incorporated into the webbing plan. By drawing the circle on the chalkboard, students can help identify the spokes. The following ideas for themes can be used to develop a teaching unit.

Ideas For Themes

Change	Conflict	Identities
Energy	Evolution	Justice
Interactions	Interdependence	Structure
Order	Patterns	Systems
Patterns of Change	Stability	
Systems and Interactions	Conflict Resolution	

CURRICULUM CONSONANCE

By observing the work assignments of students and the experiences they are engaging in, the teacher's objectives should be clear. For example, Greg Thomas said that one of his goals was to have students develop research skills; therefore, students should be engaging in activities that enable them to develop those skills. In looking at the proposed learning experiences and activities for Thomas's unit, we note a number of group investigation lessons and lessons specifically labeled "research" that require students to use multiple sources of information.

Curriculum consonance means that teaching objectives (goals) and instructional processes are mutually supportive. Another way of describing it is to say that goals and processes match or are in alignment. It is quite useless to expect students to develop skills that are not supported in the classroom through appropriate practice opportunities.

Evaluation procedures also need to be consonant with instructional goals and processes. If the goal is the development of research skills, then students should achieve a product based on the use of those skills. If students are to be tested on their understanding of a particular set of events, then the facts related to those events must be specifically taught. You cannot assume that students will remember and apply information and ideas or skills unless they have had the opportunity to practice them in a variety of situations.

Consonance is dependent upon appropriate materials and resources, as well as the instructional processes. If the practice/application materials are not

environment, Hogan planned for the study of plant and animal life, balance of nature, natural order, and cyclical patterns.

The idea of *harmony* could be developed in music, art, and nature as well as through interactions in the classroom.

Group living would be a means to help students develop understandings about basic needs. Both rules and roles would be developed through group membership in the family, school, and classroom. Health and physical education could be tied into the need for social rules and safety for group living.

suitable to the learning experience or task, then consonance will not be achieved.

SUMMARY

Unit Teaching

1. The unit is a means to organize ideas and knowledge into a meaningful structure.
2. Units may be constructed for a single subject field (discipline) or across subject fields.
3. When units are broad-based, they are interdisciplinary.
4. Resource units are developed at the district level by committees of teachers or subject field specialists.
5. The teaching unit represents long-term planning for the curriculum.

Curriculum Concepts

6. Curriculum concepts are part of the professional lexicon for teachers. These include scope, sequence, continuity, integration themes, generalizations, interdisciplinary content, and balance.

Planning a Unit

7. Teachers must determine goals, select an organizing theme, identify content, and select learning experiences when planning a teaching unit.

Webbing

8. Using a nonlinear system, the curriculum planner sees the connections among content threads.

Curriculum Consonance

9. Teaching objectives (goals) and instructional processes need to be planned so that they are mutually supportive.

DISCUSSION QUESTIONS AND APPLICATION EXERCISES

1. Select a resource unit from a school district professional library or a university library and develop a teaching unit for your students. Choose learning experiences to integrate subject fields. Search the Internet for resource information for your students.
2. Visit an elementary or middle school classroom and interview the teacher. Ask about the goals of the teaching unit and compare the goals with students' activities to determine consonance.
3. Select a social science concept and define it using different perspectives from the social sciences.
4. It is important for students of all ages and grade levels to have opportunities to engage in problem solving and research. What materials might be used for primary children (grades K–2) so that they can do research?
5. How does a teacher decide what to teach?
6. Identify a goal you consider important for students to attain. What will you teach and what experience will students have to achieve the goal?
7. Select a theme and write a generalization to give meaning and direction for the development of a teaching unit.
8. Develop your own system to plan a teaching unit.
9. Plan a talk to parents to explain the significance of thematic teaching.

Resources for Learning:
Technology in the Classroom

The first section of this chapter is about how technology changes the classroom setting, helps to integrate the curriculum, and provides new dimensions for student learning. As you read the first part of the chapter think about how technology changes the role of the teacher, how it allows the teacher to focus more on student learning, and finally how technology can help students transform their understandings and apply knowledge in different ways. The second half of the chapter considers the variety of learning materials available to classroom teachers, procedures for the evaluation of learning materials, and the classroom environment in which they are used.

After you study this chapter, you should be able to accomplish the following:

1. Identify several ways that technology has changed the role of teachers.
2. Explain why technology helps teachers focus on student learning.
3. Compare hypermedia systems with webbing as webbing is used for curriculum development.
4. Discuss why a goal of technology is to help students transform and apply new knowledge.
5. Describe several ways teachers can use distance education.
6. Evaluate software for classroom use at a specific grade level using the appraisal form in this chapter.
7. Evaluate a textbook series using the guidelines in this chapter.
8. Design learning centers using the guidelines in the chapter.
9. Plan a lesson using technology and a model of teaching.
10. Discuss how to improve the use of pictures in the classroom.

Professional Lexicon

CD/ROM Acronym for Compact Disc/Read Only Memory; information recorded on a compact disc is accessed using hardware connected to a computer or audio system.

distance education A way to expand learning opportunities for students separated from the teacher in time or space.

hardware Audio-visual equipment used to access media such as computer software, films, or tapes.

hypermedia Involving both hardware and software that may provide access to audio, text, and visual information; the composition of the data is nonsequential. Hypermedia systems can be used to link documents into webs.

media Message systems that communicate information to the user.

multimedia Involving a variety of communication systems that may be used sequentially or simultaneously.

multimodality materials Teaching aids that enhance instruction by appealing to several senses (visual, tactile, auditory).

realia Concrete objects, models, or specimens used to demonstrate concepts and to enhance students' experiences through visual and tactile opportunities.

software Computer program information stored on disks or tapes; also may refer to audio-visual materials.

technology Both the hardware (equipment) and the software (programs, materials) used to enhance learning.

TECHNOLOGY IN SCHOOLS

THE TRADITIONAL ROLE OF TECHNOLOGY

Traditionally when teachers or the public talked about the use of **technology** in schools, they were referring to the availability of **hardware.** Schools that were "technologically advanced" boasted about the equipment they had available for teachers' use, such as filmstrip machines, 16mm projectors, audiocassette recorders and players, televisions, and videocassette players and recorders. In more recent years the desirable equipment includes laser disc systems, computers, and CD/ROM players.

Teachers were required to "check out" equipment from the supply room or office, or they abided by a school schedule that moved the equipment from one room to the next. In either case access to the hardware for teaching purposes was severely limited. Limited use of equipment also defined the use of the actual films, videos, and computer software programs. Planned use was out of the question. The materials rarely were appropriate to the subject being taught at the time teachers had the equipment and seldom fit the students who were to passively experience them.

As a consequence equipment tended to be used as an add-on sponge activity when teachers failed to plan instruction or when they needed a break. Many teachers today are only vaguely familiar with more contemporary equipment (computers, videocassette players, laser disc systems), and **software** (**CD/ROM** programs, videodiscs) and as a result do not plan for their use.

During the 1970s and early 1980s, educational television and computer use were sharply defined by behavioral psychologists who used the technology to produce programmed materials for drill and the practice of skills. Teachers who rejected this philosophy also rejected the use of the equipment. The traditional role of both the computer and educational television was to transmit information to the learner who was expected to consume. The teacher had little role in the determination of content or its delivery.

POSTMODERN ROLE OF TECHNOLOGY

Hooper and Rieber (1995, p. 254) distinguish between "product" and "idea" technology. Product technology is the term used to identify the range of equipment and software that can be used in schools. Idea technologies represent the understandings (concepts) that the user gains as a result of using the products. For ex-

Research Application

Computers should be "regarded as an essential element in an educational approach that focuses on gathering information (and on learning how to transform it into new knowledge), on the changing role of teacher-as-facilitator, on the involvement of children in experiential learning, and on the expanded world of lifelong learning." (Morton, 1996, p. 419)

ample, if the data for a case study were part of a software program on the computer, the use of the data would comprise the experiences to be gained by students. This use of the computer fits the philosophic orientations of our three fictitious teachers.

The traditional role of technology focused on expository instruction and behavioral drill and practice of skills. For teachers this meant they needed to know how to use the equipment, and how to control its use in the classroom. In the postmodern classroom, teachers must be much more sophisticated. *Knowing how* is the antecedent phase. Let us now look at how products and ideas change the role of the teacher.

THE CHANGING ROLE OF THE TEACHER

Hooper and Rieber (1995, p. 253) identify five phases of teacher and student use of technology:

Phase 1: Familiarization This is the "how-to" phase in which the teacher learns to use the equipment. Typically this occurs in the college classroom or as part of a workshop experience.

Phase 2: Utilization In this phase the teacher has the equipment in the classroom or schedules its use and uses the equipment and suggested software or media program at a very basic level.

Phase 3: Integration In the third phase the teacher makes the technology an integral piece in the curriculum plan. It may be part of a group activity; it may be critical to the planned lesson. If it were not working or not available, the lesson would fail.

Phase 4: Reorientation This phase demonstrates the change in the instructional and philosophic perspective of the teacher; it is closely oriented to cognitive and social reconstruction philosophic beliefs and applies constructivism in the classroom. The focus is now on the learner and how the learner can use technology for research and creative efforts. The teacher is less concerned about his or her own use of technology, but more concerned with how technology can improve students' understanding by providing multiple perspectives and applications.

Phase 5: Evolution In a sense, this is the recycling phase. It is demonstrated by the teacher's openness to new ideas, ability to use new methodologies in technology productively, and to encourage students to develop interesting and productive applications.

TEACHERS' PLANNING

Just as new textbooks required that teachers familiarize themselves with the content and perspective of the new series, planning for teaching with technology requires that the teacher be familiar with the ideas and concepts presented via computer software, laser disc, or other **media.** Lessons need to be designed for multiple means of information. Teachers need to arrange stations in the classroom and allot time for work.

Planning Content

What will each source of information contribute to the content picture? How will the content differ? Note that in Greg Thomas's teaching unit (Chapter 9), he had the students using the Internet to study art and the environment. In the past the teacher often relied on a single textbook as the information source. Presently the teacher needs to be aware of what is on the Learning Channel®, the Discovery Channel®, what is available on videodiscs as well as the Internet.

What prior experiences will students need in order to use the media? How will students' pre-experiences be used advantageously? How will students' engagement be affected? What will students need to do in order to produce and verify learning? What content problems and access problems will students confront?

Grouping

Will students work in small cooperative groups? As individuals? In pairs? How will grouping affect the environment of the classroom (noise, space, furniture, monitoring)? Student access to computers is limited in most classrooms. In many schools the ratio of students to computers is 14 to 1 (Mehlinger, 1996). Thus

it is clear that teachers need to consider grouping in the planning of the curriculum.

Strategies

The use of multiple sources of information allows the teacher greater flexibility to select teaching strategies. For example, in using group investigation, the teacher can assign one group to computers, another group may use videocassettes, still other groups could search texts and filmstrips. Classrooms with telephone access can use interactive technology for video and audio communication.

To take advantage of multiple sources of information, it is important for the teacher to use teaching strategies like the advance organizer so that students are adequately prepared to gather data and restructure that data for their own use.

Most important for students is the ability to work collaboratively. (Collaborative skills need to be taught.) Not only do students need to share machines and documents, but what they produce is frequently collaborative. To use data bases intelligently, students need imagination for seeking and searching, and the ability to learn from each other.

Time

Access to the Internet may require more flexible use of time. Teacher planning needs to consider that it may not be possible to define subject fields within strict

---

How does computer use foster student responsibility for their own learning?

Research Findings: Technology and Education

Interactive Educational Systems Design, Inc. reviewed 133 studies on educational technology from 1990 to 1994. They concluded:

1. Technology has positive effects on student attitudes.
2. Technology has a positive impact on students' achievement.
3. Technology makes instruction more student-centered, encourages cooperative learning, and stimulates teacher-student interaction.
4. Effectiveness of technology is influenced by the student population, the instructional design, the teacher's role, student grouping, and students' access to technology (Mehlinger, 1996, p. 405).

boundaries. However, since integration of subject fields is greater and easier, time can be accommodated through the planning of content themes that include subject field strands and skills teaching as needed.

Evaluation

Evaluating what students have learned includes not only what students produce, but the changes in student behavior, and the process of learning. Before evaluating the product that students have produced, it is important to talk to them about their thinking process. For example, the students in Greg Thomas' classroom began on the Internet with one art source. How did they travel the Internet road? How many sources did they study? What led them from one to the next? (It may be valuable to have students keep a journal to record their thinking and seeking process.)

Since technology encourages cooperative learning, what did students learn from each other? How well did they work together? What was each student responsible to do? How did they make decisions about the use of data?

Finally the teacher needs to examine the actual work of the students. How did the students use their data? What did they produce? In what ways do student applications demonstrate the student's integration of subject fields? Have students demonstrated writing skills? Research skills? Creativity? Spatial intelligence? (Go back to Chapter 4 and look at Gardner's multiple intelligences.)

Summarizing Teachers' Changing Role

Effective use of technology by teachers requires that teachers act as guides and facilitators. More than ever before, teachers need to know about students' experiences and prior knowledge in order to select appropriate resources for students to use. Materials (software, laser discs, videos) need to build on students' personal knowledge and serve as a bridge to new understandings.

In one classroom, the students were experimenting with building electromagnets. The students thought they had never seen one at work, but the teacher brought out the laser disc program "Windows on Science" and showed construction workers using a large crane to pick up automobiles in a wrecking yard. The teacher had to be cognizant of what students were familiar with and what was depicted in the laser disc program.

The teacher's new role requires greater management efforts:

- Managing the classroom environment to accommodate spatial needs for equipment and grouping
- Managing time to accommodate interactive needs, networking, e-mail, and getting on the Internet
- Managing multiple resources, requiring that teachers are knowledgeable about the quality of information that each resource offers

The teacher's new role requires the blending of many resources with the environment of the classroom and students' needs. Planning the curriculum is becoming more complex and more interesting.

FOCUS ON STUDENT LEARNING

What do students need to learn to use the new technologies? How do the new technologies make learning more powerful and more significant? These are the questions that teachers need to ask themselves as they plan the curriculum.

Multiple Perspectives

Students must learn to *value* obtaining content information from different sources and often with conflicting viewpoints. Too long has the school promoted the "one best answer" to problems. When students work on open-ended problems that relate to experiences in their own community, they can gain appreciation for the interdisciplinary meanings of concepts in different subject fields. For example, a news report about gasoline prices escalating across the country might prompt a classroom investigation. Students could begin with an open-ended problem concerning gasoline consumption and summer travel, then study supply and demand concepts in economics, political relationships with the Middle East, geographic problems that affect why some regions of the United States have higher gasoline prices than in other regions. The linking of content increases its conceptual impact and builds depth of understanding.

Collaborative Learning

Students need to share equipment, but for learning purposes that is an asset. Listening to others' ideas and viewpoints broadens and enriches your own. Students

---

Should schools have computer labs instead of placing computers in each classroom? How does the computer lab change the role of the teacher and the focus on student learning?

learn to "piggyback" on each other's thoughts, and together, they learn to use different search engines and share thought processes as they seek information. Students who are more adept at research can help prompt others and learn from their own transformation of ideas to others.

Hypermedia

Students are using **hypermedia.** Similar to the webbing concept for curriculum development, hypermedia allows the user to access and link information to fit his or her own thinking style. Hypermedia describe hardware and software used to access nonsequential programs that are interactive and can combine text, graphics, video, and audio. The purpose of hypermedia software is to create an environment in which the user can seek out information without a required or systematic predetermined structure or sequence. This characteristic makes the software particularly meaningful and attractive to students because they build their own relationships and content becomes represented in multiple ways.

Authentic Performance

Instead of one-dimensional term papers and reports, students may author **multimedia** projects using hypermedia systems. They may be handing in to the teacher computer diskettes that combine graphics, sound, and text. By harnessing technology to "prove" their own understandings, students can integrate their skills and approach problems from an interdisciplinary perspective.

The computer offers an endless array of opportunities for student learning. Students working in small groups may participate in simulations that require them to make choices and decisions. Also, students may develop their own simulations for others to use.

One caution is evident. Though students profit from cooperative relationships as they work, the work groups must be carefully monitored to verify each student's responsibilities and ability (access) to contribute to "group think."

Technology has the potential to adapt to students' instructional needs. Accurate assessments of students' knowledge and their prior experiences allow the teacher to choose relevant and appropriate experiences in the microworld environment.

RESOURCES FOR PROBLEM SOLVING

"The Adventures of Jasper Woodbury" is a video series developed at Vanderbilt University for upper elementary and middle school students. Jasper Woodbury, a fictional character, and his teen-age friends are involved in real-life complicated mathematical problems. Each problem is equivalent to a 15-step story problem. Students perform math problems involving meaningful situations, such as computing how many residents of a town would take part in a recycling project and what pickup service would cost.

Computers help make learning fun but not as much fun as watching the photographer.

There are several advantages to the video productions:

- They are more motivating than the flat textbook.
- They can present more information than a textbook can.
- A video can be repeated so that students can search for more clues and additional information.

The Jasper series keeps the students actively engaged. Not only must they collect data while watching the video, but when it is over, they must use that data to solve minor problems that lead up to their major inquiry problem.

Another problem-solving multimedia project is "The Voyage of the *Mimi*" developed by the Bank Street College of Education. The package contains videos, print materials, and computer materials for studying science and mathematics. The video is typically used to present the context of the problem. It is the story of a fictional crew aboard the *Mimi* who are engaged in a scientific study of humpback whales. The viewers see the scientists at work solving actual problems. The computer materials involve students in interactive situations through games and simulations. The print materials provide a text version of the video story and worksheets for students to use. The advantage of the *Mimi* package is that the teacher can choose the entry point for students based on their needs and classroom time. The materials are particularly valuable for enrichment purposes and can be used by individuals or groups of students.

DISTANCE LEARNING

Distance education has the potential to connect learners and teachers who are far apart through telecommunications. Distance learning can provide an organized instructional program using technological media for learners who are separated from the teacher. It is not intended to replace teachers, but rather to expand learning opportunities for students.

The Star Schools program funded by the U.S. Department of Education provides instruction via satellite in German, Japanese, mathematics, and science. The programs in mathematics and science allow for some interaction by providing time during the telecast for students to call in and contribute information that is then made part of the telecast. The telecasts motivate learning, present an inquiry problem, then provide time for students in the distance classrooms to experiment and contribute data. After several calls from students are accepted the program continues. These programs provide a service to schools where teachers lack the expertise in subject fields. This has been particularly true for rural schools where the teaching faculty is small and responsible for multigrades and multidisciplines.

The Galaxy Classroom, another distance learning project, is supported by Hughes Electronics, the National Science Foundation, and other private foundations. The project provides science and language arts curricula in English and Spanish through DIRECTV® television programming. Teaching materials, professional development, and student interactivity are accessed through fax and e-mail. The curricula program also includes hands-on science kits, literature books, and student magazines.

There are increasing opportunities for teachers to join the ranks of distance learning teachers. Continuing education for teachers is still another use of distance education that is implemented in many parts of the country. Working with the TEAMS project that provides mathematics and science programs funded by the Star Schools, the author developed a preservice program for prospective teachers studying constructivist distance learning.

Although the developers of many distance learning programs believe that the programs are best used when offered, more frequently they are used by videotaping the original telecast and then time-shifting for convenience. In doing this, however, the teachers miss out on the opportunity to have their students interact with the television teacher. It is likely that in the near future, students viewing these programs will interact with each other and their distance education teacher using the Internet instead of calling in during the telecast.

SELECTING SOFTWARE

It is as important to review the software students will use as it is the textbooks used in the classroom. An appraisal checklist has been designed by this aughor to help you critique computer software (Figure 10.1).

In addition to the use of the checklist, software programs should be appraised with the following considerations:

- Does the program match students' experiential base?
- Does the program add to the depth of the curriculum?

- Is the program sequenced appropriately and/or can students establish their own sequence?
- Is the program easy to use?
- Are there multiple entry points or must students follow the sequence in order to progress through the program?

- Should there be accompanying materials? If so, are these available?
- Will use of the program make learning (more) understandable? (Would students be better off reading a book? Talking to others? Listening to the teacher?)

Figure 10.1 Evaluating Software

Title _____

Subject Field _____

Publisher _____

Equipment Needs _____

Cost _____

Purpose

    Practice Skills ☐

    Tutorial ☐

    Simulation ☐

    Inquiry/Problem Solving ☐

Target Audience

    K–2 ☐   3–5 ☐   6–8 ☐

Content

_____ Accurate

_____ Appropriate to subject field

_____ Appropriate to target audience

_____ Appropriate to purpose

_____ Free of sexual, ethnic, and religious bias

Presentation (check)	High	Medium	Low
Exhibits clarity of directions	☐	☐	☐
Maintains interest	☐	☐	☐
Promotes interaction	☐	☐	☐
Provides opportunity for user input	☐	☐	☐
Allows pacing to be controlled by user	☐	☐	☐
Provides feedback and reinforcement	☐	☐	☐
Fosters creativity	☐	☐	☐
Fosters problem solving	☐	☐	☐
Enhances integration of experience	☐	☐	☐

Comments

    Content _____

    _____

    Presentation _____

    _____

Recommend for Purchase (Yes/No) _____

USING RESOURCES TO DIFFERENTIATE THE CURRICULUM

Though all students need to study life science, they do not need to all use the same materials. There should be multiple means to gather information, to study, and to achieve a common goal. Resources in the classroom involving texts, films, computers, hands-on materials, exhibits, and experiments can all provide the means to differentiate students' experiences and activities. Some students need information at more complex or superficial levels. Some students crave greater depth for some topics; others need material that is inventive.

One advantage to differentiating instructional materials and students' learning experiences is that each student or group of students can contribute unique information, insight, and productions to the total group. Another advantage is that it makes the learning experience personal for each student. Since students are so diverse in interest and ability, providing different resources enables each individual to be challenged.

EVALUATING RESOURCES FOR LEARNING

Since teachers program the use of instructional materials throughout the school day, it is important that they be involved in the evaluation of the materials. To evaluate instructional materials teachers are confronted with two basic tasks. First teachers need to find out what is available for use at the price they or the school district can afford. The second task is to evaluate the materials for appropriateness and quality.

Appropriateness has to do with whether the materials fit a specific group of students. For example, materials appropriate for fifth graders achieving at grade level and living in a rural area of Montana may not necessarily be appropriate for fifth graders working below grade level in New York City. Quality is determined by using sets of criteria that apply to specific school curriculum objectives and priorities. Let us explore these two tasks and see how they can be accomplished.

Mary Hogan was assigned the task of setting up the screening and evaluation process for choosing one or more new reading, science, and social studies textbooks for her school. The following are the procedures she devised:

Procedures

1. Discuss evaluation process with teachers and school advisory group.

Teacher Research

Eleventh and twelfth grade students in a film class had difficulty identifying stereotypes in film that concerned other peoples' age, race, class, or gender. Baker (1996) concluded that students were better able (and more accustomed) to interpret meaning from literature than from film.

2. Develop criteria or use existing criteria developed by others.
3. Identify textbooks and software to be screened.
4. Set up committees for preliminary screening.
5. Set up committees for substantive evaluation.
6. Choose a small group to analyze results and make decisions.

Hogan was aware that many of her colleagues considered the choice of textbooks to be both a professional right and a responsibility; however, parents and community interest groups believed that they should be consulted about the textbooks children used. To resolve this situation, Hogan decided to go to the school advisory group. This group represented teachers, administrators, and the school community.

Community representatives on the school advisory committee affirmed their interest in the textbook selection process and communicated their concern that textbooks depict a multicultural society and be devoid of racism and gender bias.

In meeting with the teachers, Hogan learned that the school faculty shared the community's concern about the textbooks, and the teachers expressed their willingness to work on joint committees to review the texts.

THE EVALUATION PROCESS

Hogan set up a joint meeting of teachers from different grade levels and members of the school advisory group. They shared several California State Department Curriculum Frameworks that identified criteria for evaluating texts and media.

The teachers particularly liked the suggestion in the Science Framework that criteria be weighted by content (50 percent), presentation (25 percent), and pedagogy (25 percent).

- *Content* would be reviewed for accuracy, thematic treatment, depth, and emphasis.

- *Presentation* would be evaluated for language accessibility to students, interest of prose, use of appropriate conceptual terms, nondogmatic presentation, openness to controversy and inquiry, and relevance.
- *Pedagogy* would be viewed in terms of linkage to real experiences and problem solving, cultural diversity, creativity, and integration of experience.

IDENTIFYING TEXTBOOKS AND MEDIA RESOURCES

The first major task was to identify materials to evaluate. Hogan and several members of the committee began to gather the names of publishers of reading, science, and social studies texts. They then called these publishers and requested review materials.

PRELIMINARY SCREENING

A preliminary screening committee consisting of several faculty members, chosen by the teachers, and several community representatives, selected by the advisory committee, was to begin the screening process. The group evaluated the texts by sampling the content and looking at pictures, print, and format. The screening committee evaluated the following:

- The portrayal of minority persons, places, and culture
- The expression of diversity
- Content related to minority groups
- Stereotyping portrayals
- Diverse opinions and values
- Interrelationships among groups
- Religious bias
- Gender bias (pictures, roles, language)

Preliminary screening committee members responded either "yes" or "no" for each item. Each member of the committee was required to write comments about each textbook that they did not recommend for a complete review.

After the initial screening process, the texts that passed were forwarded to a group of teachers considered expert in each subject field. These professionals would be responsible for the final review.

EVALUATING READING AND LITERATURE TEXTBOOKS

The faculty members assigned to the final review of the reading textbooks developed criteria statements to use for their evaluation. They identified the following categories and items:

1. Target audience
   Low achiever
   Bilingual
   Urban
   Average achiever
   Bicultural
   Suburban
   High achiever
   Majority culture
   Rural
2. Instructional approach
   Basal
   Whole language
   Literature
   Language experience
   Programmed
   Linguistic
   Other
3. Skill development (The series provides for . . .)
   Structural analysis
   Word recognition
   Phonic analysis
   Literal comprehension
   Critical reading
   Creative reading
   Functional reading
   Vocabulary development (word forms)
4. Program development (The series fosters . . .)
   Oral language
   Interrelation of the four language arts components
   Positive self-concept
   Critical reading
   Appreciation of diversity
   Variety of literary forms
   Vocabulary development
5. Presentation (Yes/No)
   Print is clear, readable, and of proper size
   Pictures facilitate understanding and enjoyment
   Headings are motivating
   Layout is interesting
6. Teacher's manual (The manual provides . . .)
   Goals and objectives
   Explanations of content
   Instructional approach suggestions
   Question format
   Student activity suggestions

Evaluation suggestions
Reference suggestions

The reading panel also decided to use a rating scale from 1 to 3 on each item, with 3 reflecting a high score and 1 reflecting a low score.

EVALUATING SOCIAL STUDIES AND SCIENCE TEXTBOOKS

The social studies and science panels used the same rating scale as the reading panel, but their analyses of the textbooks were based on the following criteria:

1. Target audience
   Urban
   Suburban
   Rural
   High achiever
   Average achiever
   Low achiever
   Multiethnic population
   Other: _____
2. Presentation (Yes/No)
   Organizing questions structure content
   Subheads differentiate major and minor ideas and provide organizing structure
   Pictures serve to illustrate concepts
   Readability accurately identified
3. Content program—Social Studies (Yes/No)
   Major concepts clearly identified
   Examples of concepts clear and understandable
   Social science disciplines interrelated
   Suggested student activities facilitate understanding of concepts
   Suggested student activities provide for individual differences
   Content fosters understanding of others
   Content fosters positive self-concept
   Content fosters democratic ideals and values
   Content examines experiences of ethnic groups
   Content includes social problems of ethnic groups
   Content program—Science (Yes/No)
   Represents current knowledge
   Uses themes to integrate and organize information
   Provides deep discussion of topics and concepts
   Stresses scientific inquiry and how we know what we know
   Content open to inquiry

4. Skills and pedagogy (Yes/No)
   Selected content and pedagogy help students develop these skills:
   Observe and make categories
   Use maps, charts, tables, and graphs
   Use a variety of reference materials
   Respond to questions at varied levels of thinking
   Find and process information
   Examine value conflicts
   Make value judgments
   Make decisions
   Differentiate among facts, interpretations, and opinions
   Make inferences
5. Teacher's manual (The manual provides . . .)
   Goals and objectives
   Explanation of conceptual approach
   Instructional strategy suggestions
   Suggestions for levels of questions
   Suggestions for student activities for varied interests and abilities
   Performance evaluation suggestions
   Material, media, and multi-reference suggestions

EFFECTIVE UTILIZATION OF RESOURCES FOR LEARNING

GUIDELINES FOR SELECTING LEARNING MATERIALS

Purposeful Learning Materials

Select materials on the basis of the purpose to be accomplished. Will the materials help students learn? How will conceptual understanding be enhanced or skills developed and strengthened using the learning materials? How will diverse interests, abilities, attitudes, and appreciations be provided for by using the learning materials? These are the questions that teachers must ask before selecting instructional aids.

Concrete Learning Materials

Students learn best when experiences are real and concrete. If direct and real experiences cannot be provided, will the learning resources expand students' understanding and experiences? Learning resources should expand the students' world beyond the classroom.

Challenging Learning Materials

The world outside the classroom is often more motivating for students than the world within the classroom.

Opportunities to select learning materials and activities motivate student learning.

Educational technology provides a means for teachers to "turn students on," but the materials must be appropriate to the maturity of the students. The materials should stimulate thinking by helping students to focus on important ideas, problems, or questions.

Diverse Learning Materials

Eating oatmeal seven days a week for breakfast would be boring. Select different types of educational materials to appeal to varied interests and learning modalities. Materials should be attractive and utilized to enhance the classroom environment.

Students' Understanding of Learning Materials

The purpose and use of the materials should be understood by the students. Students' readiness for the materials should be considered. In choosing films, television programs, reference materials, and software, it is important that students have the necessary knowledge and skills to use the experience productively. Students should understand why they are asked to view a program or use maps, globes, or kits. In using models, kits, or other contrived experiences, it is important to ensure that students know how to use the materials appropriately.

Preparation of Learning Materials

Carefully prepare learning materials for lesson integration and application. Anticipate the need for learning materials prior to the lesson; select the materials before class time. After use, evaluate materials in terms of the suggested guidelines. For example, did the mate-

rials enhance the lesson? Were students motivated? Did students understand how to use the materials?

IMPROVING THE USE OF LEARNING MATERIALS

As discussed earlier in the chapter, all learning materials should be used to integrate lesson elements and provide application opportunities for students.

REALIA AND KITS

Real objects, models, or specimens provide concrete experiences for students during instruction. When these real things are available, they should be used to demonstrate concepts or enhance students' experiences. They should be used in conjunction with reading materials or other learning experiences such as field trips or pictures. When possible, the **realia** should be in their natural setting.

Using a prism to separate colors in sunlight is a more effective lesson than simply reading about the sun's rays. Seeing and touching a powder horn made in colonial times is more meaningful than hearing about it or seeing a picture of it. Having students make a telegraph, rather than watch someone else make one or listen to someone lecture about telegraphs, will increase understanding and learning of concepts.

DEMONSTRATIONS AND EXHIBITS

The reason making a telegraph is more valuable than seeing one has to do with the nature of personal involvement. Making the telegraph requires that students understand the purpose of the telegraph and that they make plans for reproducing one. Students ask questions, clarify, and solve problems instead of being passive learners. But sometimes it is not possible for students to be totally involved in a project. Then a demonstration or an exhibit of the desired concepts may be appropriate. To alleviate the shortcomings of a demonstration, consider the following plans:

- Be certain that students understand the purpose of the demonstration or exhibit.
- Plan each step of the demonstration so it is sequenced in a logical manner.
- Keep the demonstration simple and uncluttered; avoid too many purposes and ideas.
- Motivate the demonstration and ask questions periodically to ensure that students grasp the ideas and do not lose interest.
- Be sure that all students can see and hear.
- Keep the demonstration short to avoid the wiggles.
- Foster students' questions and students' clarifications.
- Plan evaluative questions and follow-up activities to reinforce the demonstrated concepts.

FILMS AND SOUND FILMSTRIPS

Sometimes audio-visual aids are used in the same way that a babysitter is used—to hold the fort while the adult takes a breather! When this occurs in the classroom, however, teachers are communicating to students that the films are unimportant and not to be taken seriously. Audio-visual materials are too important to be used in a careless manner.

Use audio-visual aids in many of the same ways you use a textbook. Effective use requires that teachers preview materials and select them because they are pertinent to what is being studied.

- Preview films and record concepts and vocabulary that may be difficult for the students. Introduce the concepts and new vocabulary before the viewing and listening experience.
- Be aware of any ideas or events that may cause a value conflict for the students. Plan to discuss these ideas or events after the experience.
- Note discrepancies related to historical time periods. If the film is particularly old but still useful, prepare students for what they are to view; help them to be good observers, not silly watchers.
- Introduce the film, motivate students to observe specifics, and set the stage for viewing.

- Evaluate the film utilizing the concepts presented and the vocabulary. Discuss significant behavior viewed in the film. Remember to discuss what was fun or especially enjoyable about the film.

Keep in mind that films do not always have to be viewed from start to end without stopping. Sometimes a film can be used most advantageously by turning it off at a propitious moment to discuss and project what might happen or what has already occurred. Films can also be used without sound to see if students can infer from actions what is happening. Another advantage to films is that they can be reversed to go back to an important concept and study it again. The most important point about films and sound resources is that the teacher should be in control of the experience and utilize it fully as a learning resource.

VIDEOTAPES, RADIO, TELEVISION, AND RECORDINGS

Once again it is important to select carefully only those experiences that are relevant to the students. These resources are particularly motivating because it is possible to use them at the precise moment when something is happening outside the classroom that is appropriate for reinforcing a particular lesson goal. They can also be used by prerecording important events and utilizing them at the "teachable moment." Use these types of media with the following suggestions:

- Introduce key ideas; prepare students for viewing and listening.
- When possible, use in conjunction with the teaching of note taking. Introduce note-taking categories and prepare students with questions about the episode.
- Utilize follow-up activities to reinforce or evaluate the session. If students have taken notes, provide them with feedback and an opportunity to share their notes.
- Evaluate the session just as you would evaluate other experiences. Note students' development of critical listening and viewing skills.

PICTURES

Although pictures are less motivating than films and realia, they are utilized more frequently than any other resource. It is often said that one picture is worth a thousand words; perhaps so, but pictures can be misunderstood or misinterpreted by children unless they are taught to read their meanings. A painting or a photograph reflects the artist's view of the world, and students will have a different perception from that of the artist. Students need to learn how to study an art print or enjoy an artistic creation. Pictures cannot be thrust upon them, any more than can films or recordings.

Use pictures to motivate a study or to introduce key ideas. The trick is to get students to focus on the picture and help them observe, then to make inferences or interpretations based on the picture. Let us suppose that some sixth-grade students are using a textbook that depicts Samoan people—girls, men, and boys. The teacher could proceed in the following way:

1. What do we see in these pictures? (people, food, tools, huts, things that grow)
2. Describe the things you see. (Have the students systematically describe the people—girls, boys, men—and their clothing, tools, and other things in the pictures.)
3. Describe what the girls are doing. Continue with the boys and men. (The older girls are combing the hair of the younger girls. The men are cutting and preparing what looks like food; the boys are watching.)
4. What ideas and values are the Samoan girls learning? Samoan boys? (to help one another; to learn how to perform certain skills, etc.)
5. Do we learn from one another? How? What are some examples?
6. In what ways is it advantageous for older children to teach younger children? In what ways is it a disadvantage?

Note that the questions proceeded through specific thinking stages:

1. The students were asked to collect data by observing the content of the pictures.
2. The students sorted through the data, describing each item specifically. This could have been accompanied with the teacher working at the chalkboard and helping students classify the items: people, behavior, tools, clothing.
3. Students generalized and made inferences from the data. Here the students were asked to study the behavior of the people and decide what the younger girls were learning from the older girls and what the boys were learning from the men.
4. Finally the students were asked to predict the advantages and disadvantages of learning from older children and from others.

Students who are poor readers may read pictures better than their more advantaged classmates.

In learning to read pictures, students should think about what kind of picture it is (photo, map, advertisement) and why it was selected by the author, the teacher, or the photographer. In using social studies textbooks, students should think about why the author of the textbook chose certain pictures and did not personally take the pictures for the textbook. This train of thought should lead to a discussion of author bias and photographer or artist bias. Students can be led to think about what might be missing from the picture or why this particular scene was selected.

Pictures should be used to provide information about basic human activities as well as feelings, human relations, and problem situations. When students give reports, they can be encouraged to select appropriate pictures to accompany their oral and written presentations. When pictures are used on bulletin boards for creative simulation and for research, they should be selected carefully:

- Select pictures to convey specific ideas. Avoid distorted and ambiguous pictures or pictures that present misconceptions unless that is the focus of the lesson. Choose clear and vivid pictures.
- Select groups of pictures to demonstrate contrast or continuity.
- Arrange pictures artistically; avoid cluttering the classroom.
- If you use pictures on the bulletin board, utilize appropriate questions or captions with them.
- Mount pictures (on bulletin boards) so the background does not detract from the picture or cause the viewer to focus on the mounting instead of the picture.
- Utilize pictures for discussion purposes either with the whole class or with small groups of students.
- If you use pictures as a research resource, classify them by topics or problems and mount them so students can use them productively.
- Constantly update your picture file collection. Utilize governmental sources, friends, commercial publications, travel agencies, business corporations, embassies, and chambers of commerce.

TEXTBOOKS AND OTHER PRINT MATERIALS

Print materials are used for a variety of purposes in the classroom. During reading instruction, the textbook guides skill and vocabulary development. Sometimes printed materials are used to identify issues, topics, or problems for study. In addition, textbooks are used to confirm or contradict hypotheses after a discussion or during research. Print materials may be used to obtain information or as a source for conflicting points of view, for meanings, for data, and (heaven forbid!) for enjoyment. This list is not conclusive.

In some classrooms the textbook is used as the dominant tool and may in fact be more important than the teacher because it is used in a lock-step manner to teach the subject. But in most classrooms today printed materials are used judiciously as a resource tool to accompany other resources. They are used *with* the teaching program (instead of being the teaching program). School district and teacher philosophy can often be interpreted from the way in which textbooks are used in the classroom. In some schools and classrooms there is an absence of textbooks—or at least up-to-date textbooks. In other classrooms there are too many books and not enough other resources.

To utilize the textbook or other printed materials effectively, the following practices are suggested:

- Preview the material the students are to read. Introduce new vocabulary; help students understand abstract concepts by providing time to act out the concepts or to generate examples.
- Give students guiding questions to program their reading. Help them to structure what they need to read. Provide a purpose for reading and be sure that students understand the purpose.
- Verify that students have the necessary skills to read the material. If students are to read graphs, make sure they understand how to do so. Teach the necessary skills at the time of need. Verify that students know how to use the glossary, indexes, and appendices; provide immediate practice.
- Teach students how to read for different purposes and explain how different material requires different skills and speeds of reading. Teach skimming and scanning skills.
- Evaluate reading and study skills by asking students questions to verify that they can recall details and sequences of events, comprehend meanings, generalize, and make inferences based on the material.

Use a variety of printed materials, particularly for students who have reading problems. Newspapers, magazines, and cartoons provide a wealth of material for students. Prod poor readers to bring in or draw cartoons and write their own scripts. In utilizing printed materials, suggest to poor readers that they develop questions about the material based on the pictures.

Too often, social studies and science books tend to be out of date. Teachers need to practice a number of techniques to update their written sources of information for students. Textbooks can be supplemented with visuals such as pictures, cartoons, charts, or graphs. These materials are available from newspapers, magazines, and census data and other governmental sources.

Out-of-date material can also be used as springboard lessons. For example, if a reading or social studies book included the price of food and clothing 20 years ago, it would be interesting to have students compare those prices with recent prices for those items. The students might even make time lines based on the change in prices for key items. Nutrition and health concerns change almost daily; textbooks are inevitably out of date, but this fact could be a fine stimulus to a study about changing health practices. Stereotyped information and pictures, particularly about sex roles for women and men, can be compared to up-to-date roles in the community.

When textbooks are misused, it is usually because they are allowed to determine the scope and sequence of study. This is the teacher's fault—not the fault of the author or the publisher. Modern textbooks attempt to meet varied needs for enrichment, diagnostic material, and activities. It is up to the teacher to select books to correspond to needs and to use them wisely.

THE CLASSROOM TEACHER AS RESOURCE DEVELOPER

Quite frequently teachers discover that the learning materials they make themselves are more popular with the students and achieve better results than commercially produced materials. This happens for several reasons:

- You know your objectives better than a publisher, and your materials are created to meet specific instructional purposes.
- You know your students and their interests and ability levels, and so the materials fit.
- Your students appreciate your time, effort, and interest and respond accordingly.

INSTRUCTIONAL DECISIONS

Before developing learning materials for the classroom, there are several decisions to make:

- What do you need to teach? (concepts, skills, attitudes, values)
- How much time is available?
- How do you want to organize students for learning? (reading groups, heterogeneous groups, individualized, whole class)
- What teaching strategy do you want to use? (reading, artifact kits, case study, role playing, computer, learning centers)

Once you make these decisions, develop the materials, duplicate them for use, and go ahead and try them! The advantage to classroom-developed learning materials is that they are easy to revise.

The classroom teacher is responsible for the development of a variety of learning materials in almost all of the subject fields. While basal reading textbooks and mathematics textbooks are usually adequate for students' use, it is rare for workbooks to be appropriate for all students. As a consequence, most teachers create their own reinforcement activities. In addition, skill games for reading and mathematics are developed to correspond to the needs of specific students. Resource materials are also necessary in language, science, health, and social studies. In these fields it is unusual for commercially prepared learning materials to be available in adequate supply.

RESOURCE INFORMATION FOR STUDENTS' RESEARCH

Most elementary and middle school classrooms have a wide range of ability levels, so reading materials must accommodate individual differences. For many school districts it is financially impossible to provide adequate text materials. Writing resource information for students at several reading levels is a professional challenge. However, the classroom teacher can accomplish the task more skillfully than a publisher because the teacher knows precisely what vocabulary students can read. The following guidelines are suggested to facilitate the writing of resource information:

- Identify the concept you want to communicate, and write it as simply as possible.
- Use the students' reading vocabulary and personal experiences as a starting point.

- Provide an example of the concept.
- When preparing material for several reading levels, provide more complex information for more accomplished readers.
- To ensure that each reading level will have something unique to contribute to a discussion, provide something unusual in each selection.

DESIGNING LEARNING CENTERS

Examples of learning centers will be provided in Part III of this textbook. When you study the centers in Part III, you will note how similar their design is to a lesson plan for teaching. Each center has an objective for which it was designed, and the objective states what students are supposed to achieve. There is a list of the materials needed for the activity at the center. The means for evaluation either by teacher, students, or teacher and students together is stated. The procedures were written to tell you, the reader, how to proceed to develop a similar learning center. However, since you will design your own learning centers, the steps will be somewhat different because you are not concerned with telling others how to build a center. The following steps are suggested to design a learning center:

- Identify the objective of the center.
- Identify the activity to accomplish the objective.
- List the materials that will be needed.
- Decide how the activity will be evaluated.

You can design a center to meet the needs of all of the students in the classroom or just those with special needs. If the center is to accommodate all of the students, then it is important to have multilevel activities to accomplish the objective. Also, since students have different learning styles, it is advantageous to accumulate **multimodality materials.**

A system for *accountability* involving record keeping by students enables you to monitor student progress in an efficient manner. You need to know who has used the center, who needs to use the center, and whether or not the students accomplished the objective of the center.

It is important to estimate *how long* it takes students to complete learning center tasks. If one center takes more time than another, or if other students are waiting to use the center, adjustments need to be anticipated and communicated to students.

There are a number of management considerations that facilitate center design and use:

- Locate centers in areas of the classroom where they will not impede the traffic patterns.
- Display center materials to motivate the center's use.
- Anticipate material needs at the center, including receptacles for waste materials.
- Name or number the centers so that you can talk about them with students without misunderstanding.
- Explain the purpose of each center with the students before sending them to the center for work.
- Develop a time schedule for the use of each center and communicate the schedule to the students.
- Monitor students' work at the center to verify that students' work techniques are appropriate.
- Develop a system whereby students can obtain assistance or communicate the need for assistance while working at the center.
- Provide differentiated tasks at the center to accommodate low and high achievers.
- Communicate to students where to place completed work.
- Provide for a cleanup system with students so the center is ready for others to use.

SHOPPING AT THE TEACHER MARKETPLACE

Teacher stores have become commonplace, and many of these education stores even have mail-order catalogs designed to entice the most hesitant buyer. Keep in mind the rules for selecting learning materials when you visit these establishments because it is so easy to be attracted to materials designed to make life easy for the classroom teacher.

"Buyer Beware" signs should be posted on most of the materials designed for seatwork activities. Another trade name for these activities is busy work! These items rarely pass the criteria set for content, presentation, pedagogy, target audience, and desired skill levels.

However, some materials are well worth buying. These include picture sets for bulletin boards, particularly those that depict environments your students will not recognize. Urban, inner-city students will be fascinated by pictures of the rain forest, small towns in Nova Scotia, a statue of Hans Christian Andersen, or life in South Africa. Realia, for culture studies, are always worth collecting as are manipulatives for science, social studies, mathematics, music, and art. Don't for-

get boxes or file cases to store these items. Story books, laboratory materials, and some audio-visual materials provide tangible benefits for students' learning experiences. The important thing to remember is to use the same discretion in the teacher store that you use at school when evaluating resources.

USING MATERIALS AND RESOURCES FOR INQUIRY TEACHING

As you evaluate materials for instruction, keep in mind when and how those materials are used. For example, if students are to work in small groups for a group investigation, then they must have materials that are written in an interesting prose style. Written materials do not necessarily have to be precisely at the students' reading level, but close enough so that context clues and pictures will provide needed information. For multitext research, performed without direct teacher assistance, students should have a variety of materials. It is also important that the different groups have dissimilar materials so that each group can contribute unique information.

Materials for inquiry/problem-solving activities need to grab the students' interest and foster curiosity. But this does not mean that the materials need to be costly or necessarily unusual. For example, providing students with 4d nails, copper wire, sandpaper, and dry cells to make electromagnets and then leaving students to experiment how to make the magnet more or less powerful makes a fine inquiry activity that costs very little.

Perhaps the most important point to remember about inquiry activities and resource materials has to do with the way you present the materials and the questions you ask. The commonest materials can be made into the most challenging activities through open-ended questions and activities. Consider the difference between these two questions:

1. How would you go about making a magnet?
2. Can you make a magnet by rubbing a nail with a bar magnet?

THE PHYSICAL ENVIRONMENT OF THE CLASSROOM

The "stuff" teachers choose for the classroom environment sets the stage for how students feel in the classroom and the ways in which they participate. Attractively designed bulletin boards with thought-provoking questions stimulate student interest and reflection. Learning and interest centers with manipulatives encourage students to explore, invent, and become involved in learning. Students' work samples in the classroom acknowledge that the classroom belongs to children, not just the ruling adult.

The classroom environment reveals a great deal about the teacher's professionalism, management style, and teaching style. The environment also reveals what teachers believe about the ways students learn. Consider the following questions.

Questions About the Classroom Environment

1. Should bulletin boards be changed frequently?
2. Should bulletin boards and exhibits relate to what students are studying, the teaching unit, for example?
3. Should the environment of the classroom encourage students to learn using multimodalities?
4. Should students be encouraged to move about the classroom and use media and centers?
5. Should free time be a part of every school day so that students select their own learning materials?
6. Is it OK to display materials from the ceiling, on window sills, and on cupboards?
7. Should all students see their work samples displayed in the classroom with no teacher value judgments attached?
8. Should students' work products reflect partner and small group displays as well as independent work?
9. Does the environment of the classroom reflect a balanced curriculum?
10. Is the classroom environment attractive, pleasing to the eye, provocative to the mind, and conducive to work activities?

SUMMARY

Technology in Schools

1. Traditionally technology was used in schools as an add-on activity.
2. *Product technology* is a term used to identify both equipment and software.
3. *Idea technology* represents the understandings the user gains as a consequence of using the products.

Changing Role of Teacher

4. Using technology in the classroom helps teachers act as guides and facilitators in the learning process.

5. Teachers need preknowledge of students' experiential background in order to select appropriate resources for learning.
6. The teacher's new role requires greater management efforts.

Focus on Student Learning

7. Students must learn to value multiple perspectives when obtaining content information from media.
8. Students need to practice collaborative behaviors.
9. Using hypermedia, students can access and link information to fit their own thinking style.
10. Students can use hypermedia systems to author multimedia projects.
11. Technology has the potential to adapt to students' instructional needs.

Distance Learning

12. Distance education does not replace teachers, but it does expand learning opportunities for students.
13. Most distance education programs are videotaped for use at convenient times.

Using Resources to Differentiate the Curriculum

14. Resources in the classroom can all provide means to differentiate students' experiences and activities.
15. Differentiating the resources students use ensures that all students can contribute unique information, insight, and productions to facilitate the learning of their classmates.

Evaluating Resources For Learning

16. All learning materials should be evaluated for appropriateness and quality.
17. Texts and media should be evaluated for content accuracy, depth, and emphasis.
18. Resources should be evaluated for race, class, and gender bias.

Effective Utilization of Resources

19. Select learning materials on the basis of the purpose to be accomplished.
20. When possible, learning materials should be concrete and challenging.
21. Select diverse learning materials.
22. Learning materials should be carefully prepared for lesson integration and application.

Classroom Teacher as Resource Developer

23. Teachers often achieve better results with the learning materials they make themselves.

24. Learning centers provide another means for teachers to differentiate experiences in the classroom.

Materials and Resources for Inquiry

25. By asking open-ended questions and providing for creative applications, most learning materials can be used for inquiry experiences.

The Physical Environment of the Classroom

26. The classroom environment reveals a great deal about the teacher's professionalism, management style, and teaching style.

DISCUSSION QUESTIONS AND APPLICATION EXERCISES

1. If you had $200 to spend on resources for the classroom, what would you buy?

2. Select a series of textbooks and a software program and evaluate them using the criteria and guidelines in this chapter.
3. Use the steps provided in this chapter to design learning centers in several different subject fields.
4. Choose a selection of reading, social studies, and health textbooks and evaluate only the picture material in them. Determine whether there are gender biases and stereotypes.
5. Develop a multimedia presentation for students, parents, or colleagues.
6. Plan a group investigation lesson using a variety of technologies.
7. Collect pictures and make charts and graphs to support a lesson of your choice in science or social studies.

Strategies for Assessing, Evaluating, and Communicating Learning Progress

In this chapter you will learn about a number of ways to describe, evaluate, and communicate students' learning progress. The chapter emphasizes the improvement of the learning process through continuous assessment related to ongoing purposes and long-range goals. Assessment data can be attained in a variety of forms including work samples, observation and interviews, checklists and rating scales, tests, and projects. Whenever possible the learner should take part in designing rubrics to be used as criteria for evaluating performance.

Feedback is necessary for the improvement of performance. Grades and test scores provide no feedback and can lead to misinterpretation of the purpose of evaluation. Teacher-student conferences provide a means to share mutual goals, provide information, explore thinking, and teach self-evaluation. Both the one-on-one parent-teacher conference and the three-way student-parent-teacher conferences are explained in the chapter as means to communicate progress and assist students develop responsibility for their own learning progress.

After you study this chapter, you should be able to accomplish the following:

1. Define formative and summative evaluation.
2. Identify what a teacher must do to evaluate students' learning progress.
3. Discuss the meaning of valid test items.
4. Identify problems related to testing students.
5. List types of tests and the purpose of each.
6. Write an example of a test question for an essay examination.
7. Write several multichoice test items.
8. Develop a checklist to be used as rubrics to evaluate a project.
9. Provide examples of performance assessment in different subject fields and differentiate between performance assessment and authentic performance assessment.
10. Explain the purposes for using portfolios.
11. Identify ways to use the concept of exhibition.
12. Explain the use of a social matrix or sociogram.
13. Observe a student in an elementary or middle school classroom and prepare an anecdotal record.
14. Discuss teachers' professional responsibility to communicate learning progress to students and parents.
15. Identify and explain techniques for communicating progress.

Professional Lexicon

anecdotal record   An informal record maintained by the teacher to study specific behavior exhibited by a student.

assessment   A process of gathering data utilizing a variety of factors about student performance.

authentic assessment   The process of using students' work projects to make decisions about their progress.

content validity   The idea that test items must be true to the actual content taught and the learning activity experienced by the students.

criterion-referenced evaluation   Evaluation of student performance based on a specific criterion for performance.

formative evaluation   An on-going evaluation of what students know and need to know to facilitate the teacher's planning process.

performance assessment   Student assessment based on a demonstration of knowledge and skills in a variety of activities and contexts.

portfolio   A visual record (folder), maintained by the student, to display peak experiences (work activities, projects, and the on-going process of writing) and learning progress.

rubrics   Criteria statements, designed by the teacher and/or students, used to evaluate performance.

sociogram   A graphic technique to organize data that depict social relationships in the classroom.

summative evaluation   Measurement of what students have learned at the end of an instructional sequence or unit.

EVALUATION

Dear Mr. Thomas:

Yesterday my son William told me he was getting a "C" in science. William's father works for the Jet Propulsion Lab; he specializes in astrothermodynamics. Mr. Chan spends a great deal of time with William teaching him important scientific facts. Since it is obvious that William takes after his father, we know that he is gifted in science. My husband and I would like you to explain how its possible for a gifted science student like William to receive a "C." Please call us and set an appointment for a conference.

Sincerely yours,
Mrs. Theodore Chan

Dear Mrs. Chan:

I will be pleased to meet with you and Mr. Chan regarding William's progress this semester. I would like to take the opportunity to share his learning progress in several subject fields during the conference. Will Thursday, May 28 at 3:30 P.M. be satisfactory?

Yours sincerely,
Greg Thomas

Mrs. Chan does not sound irate, but the tone of her letter certainly indicates that she is displeased with William's grade in science. Greg Thomas will need to explain:

- That scientific giftedness probably is not hereditary(!)
- How students are graded in his class
- How teachers find out what students have learned
- How William is progressing in other subject fields

Before Greg Thomas has his conference with the Chans, he may want to think about the evaluation process so he is prepared to answer questions about how he arrives at specific grades for students. Thomas uses evaluation to improve learning, to improve teaching, and to provide feedback for curriculum de-

sign. Evaluation is a continuous, cooperative, and comprehensive process. Students are often evaluated before teaching a unit of study or a cluster of skills in order to assess individual and group needs. During teaching, evaluative measures are used to determine how well students and teacher are proceeding toward instructional goals. This is called **formative evaluation.** Evaluation at the conclusion of an instructional unit is called **summative evaluation,** and Thomas uses it to assess overall performance.

To evaluate students' learning progress, it is necessary to identify what students are expected to learn and measure how well students perform what is expected. The teacher knows the purpose of instruction and evaluates to find out if the purpose was accomplished.

When teachers write behavioral objectives for instruction, they are translating teaching purpose into a standard for performance. The following is an example of a teaching objective:

> Students will compare and contrast the life-style of people living in Arctic areas with that of people living in temperate zones.

During instruction, the learning activity should be designed to accomplish the objective. For example, perhaps students will view a film that depicts both Arctic and temperate climatic regions. After the film the students will discuss similarities and differences in life-style related to the social and physical environment. Ultimately these students could be expected to respond to a test question that asks them to identify several ways in which the life-style of people living in an Arctic area differs from the life-style of people living in a temperate zone.

In designing test items, teachers must be careful to write *valid* items. The test questions must be a representative measure of what was actually taught. If the students' learning activity was an inquiry activity in which they observed, researched, and discussed the ways in which the physical and social environment affects people, their evaluative activity should also be inquiry-oriented. It is important that objectives, learning experiences, and evaluative activity match. One cannot expect students to learn through an inquiry strategy and perform in an objective manner. Both teaching strategy and evaluation must correspond.

TESTING PROBLEMS

Teachers frequently have a number of concerns about testing elementary students. In the academic subject fields, when students do poorly on a test, it is difficult to know whether their performance is a consequence of not knowing the subject matter or not being able to read the test. Teachers need to exercise care that they are not testing reading skills when they want to evaluate academic content.

Another problem encountered by teachers occurs when young students appear to be sick during a test. These students may be afflicted with what school nurses frequently call *school stomach*. This affliction is a response to the pressure that testing exerts on students and sometimes results in a fear of peer competition. In extreme circumstances students have been known to fear school attendance.

A third related problem has to do with students' inexperience in test taking. Unaccustomed to performing when required to do so, some students do poorly on a test just because they lack experience or do not recognize the importance of personal effort during the testing situation.

Formal paper-and-pencil tests place still another constraint on teachers. Since students' ability to write involved responses is limited, most elementary tests need to be objective. Although essay examinations can be designed so they are open ended and more appropriate for elementary students, the students' lack of verbal facilities limits their use.

Test bias is also a concern of teachers. Bias occurs when the content of the test penalizes students for lack of experiences that may be a consequence of race, gender, or social class or when the test items use language that is blatantly stereotypic.

Some examples: If a test problem given to a group of U. S. students required knowledge of the sport of rugby, the U. S. students might feel that the test was biased against them because they were unfamiliar with this sport. If boys in the class were exposed to rugby, but the girls were not, then the item could be construed as gender biased.

If collaborative problem solving were to be tested by a researcher who was interested in comparing the performance of individuals versus group problem solving, but the group tested had no experience working collaboratively, then the test item would be both invalid and biased.

TYPES OF TESTS

ACHIEVEMENT TESTS

Achievement tests are used to find out what students have learned and what they need to learn. Many school systems use standardized achievement tests so they can compare how well their students do compared with the performance of other students across the nation. Standardized achievement tests are norm-referenced; the performance of students in California can be compared with that of students in Maine. Suppose William in Greg Thomas's classroom got 75 on a science achievement test. Greg Thomas could compare William's performance as a fifth grader with other fifth graders elsewhere.

Norm-referenced evaluation is always used to compare the results with an established norm. However, sometimes norm-referenced evaluation is deceiving. In subject fields such as social studies or science, the test is dependent on the student's reading skills; thus conceptual attainment may not be measured. If the established norms do not represent minority populations—as many do not—then the test may be related to sociocultural factors and not fair to or indicative of the ability of a minority student. Another problem with standardized achievement tests is that they tend to measure low-level objectives because these objectives are easier to prepare on a test instrument.

CRITERION-REFERENCED EVALUATION

It is often desirable to know how well a student can perform a specific skill or deal with specific concepts. When teachers need this information, they focus the test on individual performance of a designated task or a specific behavior. The criterion for performance is the desired behavior (or task). **Criterion-referenced evaluation** is used for diagnostic purposes and, as such, is appropriate for use prior to instruction, during instruction (formative evaluation), or at the conclusion of instruction (summative evaluation). If the criterion for performance is used to determine whether or not students should be taught the next successive skill, then it can be said that students do not proceed until they have mastered a specific task. This is characteristic of mastery learning. Using *performance assessment* for evaluation purposes will be described later in the chapter.

TEACHER-MADE TESTS

The vast majority of tests given in classrooms are pencil-and-paper examinations designed by teachers to meet specific instructional purposes. As mentioned earlier, the teacher's main task in developing test items is to ensure the **content validity** of each item. Valid test questions correspond with what has been taught and the way in which it was taught. Teachers must also exercise care that questions are clearly stated. If students do not understand the question or if there are several interpretations of the question, then clarity of purpose has not been achieved. Test items must be appropriate for the students taking the test. Sometimes good test questions are not appropriate to age group or sensible in terms of what the responder must do. For example, asking students to name the presidents of the United States in order of their presidency is an inappropriate question because the objective is inappropriate.

Essay and Objective Tests

Teachers typically write two types of tests: essay and objective tests. There are advantages and disadvantages of each. Essay tests take less time to prepare, but they take more time to read and evaluate. The essay examination is also more difficult to grade because the teacher must decide on criteria for evaluation. Essay responses tend to be open ended, with each response differing; this is the reason essay responses are considered subjective. Rubin (1980, p. 446) suggests the use of essay examination under the following circumstances:

- The class is small and the test will not be reused.
- Written expression is being encouraged.
- Attitudes are being explored.
- The teacher is more adept as a critical reader than as a writer of objective test items.
- The teacher has more time to read the exam than to write it.

Essay tests enable students to respond in depth, whereas objective exams tend to be more comprehensive. An essay examination requires that the student spend time planning what to write and thinking about ways to express the response. The planning and the writing time use up the bulk of the test time. The objective test requires that the student spend time reading and thinking. Ellis (1995, p. 220) made the following suggestions for writing essay examinations for students:

- Focus on the main idea rather than specifics.
- Elicit higher-level thinking from students.
- Try to make questions clear and unambiguous.

Sample essay question: Make a list of safety rules to be used when experimenting with chemicals. Explain why each rule is important.

Discussion: This question is specific in delineating what kinds of rules students are to write. It is open ended in that it does not tell students how many to write; the only constraint is that the rules be important. The question should let the teacher assess how much students know about chemicals because if the rules are inappropriate the teacher will be able to judge learning.

Sample essay question: Identify the two emotions described in Robert Frost's poem "Fire and Ice." Which emotion does he consider more significant? Do you agree with Frost? Why or why not?

Discussion: The question is specific in directing students' thinking to the purpose of the poem. Students' comprehension can be quickly assessed. By allowing students to respond with a personal opinion, the teacher has added the open-ended dimension.

True/False Tests

True/false tests are easy to grade, and it is possible to include many questions on a test, thereby increasing the comprehensiveness of the examination. Since many elementary students lack the ability to write essay responses, an objective test gives these students the opportunity to demonstrate their understanding of what was taught. A disadvantage associated with the objective test is the tendency to write low-level questions. Also the test may not match the teaching strategy, if inquiry or problem solving was used.

Sample true/false question: Rocks are moved from place to place by water and ice.

Discussion: This is a good question because it is clear rather than ambiguous, it expresses only one idea, and the question is totally true. (It is not half true and half false.)

Similar to the true/false test, yes/no statements are ideal for lower-grade students. In the examples below, students would be instructed to circle the right answer.

- Members of the family depend on each other.
  Yes   No
- In some families fathers work at home and mothers work away from home.
  Yes   No
- Boys and girls should always perform different types of jobs in the family.
  Yes   No
- Some families depend on children to work.
  Yes   No

Multiple Choice Tests

Multiple choice tests are difficult to write because the choices must be reasonable and similarly written. Students are instructed to choose the best answer in multiple choice questions such as the following examples:

1. If you were ill, who would you talk to?

   (Primary)
      a. Someone who had the same illness.
      b. A friend who understands health problems.
      c. A doctor in the community.

2. Division of labor means

   (Middle/Upper Grades)
      a. Each person performs as many jobs as is possible.
      b. Each person performs a specific task to produce a specific commodity.
      c. Each person performs a job as a skilled or nonskilled laborer.

3. Which of these should you consult to find out how to make enchiladas?

   (Middle Grades)
      a. A recipe written by someone who speaks Spanish.
      b. A recipe written by a nutrition specialist.
      c. A recipe written by someone who has lived in Mexico.
      d. A recipe written by the author of a Mexican cookbook.

4. Reading books is

   (Middle Grades)
      a. A lot of fun.
      b. Sometimes interesting.
      c. Sometimes dull.
      d. Very dull.

Please note that these four questions would never appear on the same test together! Question 4 could be used, along with additional questions, to diagnose students' interest in school and school-related tasks.

INFORMAL STRATEGIES FOR EVALUATING GROWTH

CHECKLISTS AND RATING SCALES

Informal strategies can be used by students or teachers for evaluating skills, specific behaviors, interests, and concepts. The checklist or rating scale utilizes descriptive statements such as "Listens attentively to story," or "Recognizes and uses antonyms," or "Seeks appropriate assistance or guidance." The evaluator checks or rates the item, either numerically or descriptively. By utilizing the checklist at regular intervals throughout the semester, the teacher and the students have a record of learning progress.

This chapter provides examples of different types of checklists or rating systems. The statements included are not necessarily more appropriate for evaluation than other descriptive lists; they are intended for illustration purposes.

Let us suppose that Mary Hogan wants to create a checklist to verify that her second graders are learning the enabling skills for sentence processing. Figure 11.1 lists the items of concern.

Greg Thomas was concerned about his students' dictionary and reference skills. He decided to construct

Figure 11.1   Sentence Processing

Skills	STUDENTS' NAMES			
	Gene	Betty	Sam	Mabel
Demonstrates Understanding of Word Order	+	✓	✓	✓
Identifies a Simple Sentence	+	✓	✓	✓
Uses Modifiers to Expand a Simple Sentence	+	✓	✓	✓
Uses Transformation to Manipulate Sentences	✓	✓	−	✓
Unscrambles Simple Sentences	+	+	✓	✓
Retells a Story in Sequence	+	+	+	−

Code: + ✓ −

Figure 11.2 Dictionary and Reference Skills

Skills	STUDENTS' NAMES			
	William	Everett	Tina	Jen
Alphabetizes Letters and Words by First Letter	+			
Second Letter	+			
Third Letter	✓			
Uses Guide Words to Locate Information	✓			
Uses Dictionary Keys	✓			
Demonstrates Use of Phonemic Respellings	+			
Uses and Interprets Diacritical Markings	+			
Selects Appropriate Meaning of a Word	✓			
Uses Stressed and Unstressed Syllables	✓			
Uses Tables of Contents	✓			
Uses Index	✓			
Locates, Identifies, and Uses Reference Sources	✓			

Code: + ✓ –

Figure 11.3 Critical Thinking

Skills	Student's Names	Total
Identifies Ideas from Different Resources		
Classifies Information by Fact and Opinion		
Sequences Ideas/Events		
Uses Chronology		
Defines Concepts		
Locates Relevant Data		
Uses Evidence to State Generalizations		
Applies Generalizations to New Situations		
Makes Inferences Based on Data		
Identifies Cause-and-Effect Relationships		
Judges Reliability of Information		
Makes Judgment Based on Consequences		

Code: 1 = Poor, 3 = Average, 5 = Superior

a checklist to verify students' progress. The checklist he created is shown in Figure 11.2.

There are literally hundreds of items that could be included on a critical thinking checklist. These skill items would relate to reading as well as thinking. The checklist in Figure 11.3 is illustrative of typical items considered to be critical thinking.

Figure 11.3 could be used diagnostically to determine group teaching needs. For example, it would be possible to total the scores of the children on each skill. Those skills in which most of the class had low scores would identify areas to teach. Assume that in a class of 30 children, the total group score for *Uses Chronology* was 58 out of an anticipated average of 90 points; obviously the class needs help with this skill.

When using an individualized reading approach, individual student records are extremely important to identify the mastery of reading skills. As the teacher confers with the child about his or her reading perfor-

mance, the teacher may want to make note of specific comprehension skills (Figure 11.4).

Figure 11.4 Comprehension—Individualized Reading Program

Skills	Students' Names
Identifies Main Idea	
Identifies Cause and Effect	
Explains Emotional Reactions	
Predicts Story Outcome	
Uses Pictures/Written Material to Make Inferences	
Identifies Fact, Make-Believe, Opinion	
Distinguishes Between Relevant and Irrelevant Information	
Discusses Story in Personal Terms	

Code: Awareness = A, Mastery = M

Figure 11.5   Map Reading

Reads and Interprets the Following Maps:	Students' Names
Climate	
Demographic	
Historical	
Physical	
Political	
Product	
Relief	
Transportation	
Vegetation	

Code: Awareness = A, Mastery = M

The mastery of skill items is often more important than how well the skill is performed. For example, at the fifth-grade level it is important to find out how many students can read and interpret different types of maps. Either students can do it or they cannot; thus it is the mastery of the skill that the teacher is concerned about. Figure 11.5 provides a checklist example for map reading.

A kindergarten teacher was concerned about the performance of locomotor movements. In order to keep track of the students, the teacher used a checklist and recorded either Yes or No beside the movement (Figure 11.6). It is important to remember to date the records so progress can be verified.

This same teacher noted that many of the students had difficulty remembering the songs that were taught.

Figure 11.6   Demonstrates Locomotor Skills

Movements	Students' Names
Walk	
Run	
Jump	
Skip	
Hop	
Gallop	

Code: Yes or No

Figure 11.7   Singing

Skill	Students' Names
Sings Rhythmic Patterns	
Sings Short Song	
Sings Songs with Syncopated Rhythm	
Sings in Minor Mode	
Sings Songs Changing Meters	
Sings with Variety of Tone Qualities	
Sings Expressively	

Code: Accurately/Appropriately = A
Inaccurately/Inappropriately = 1

The teacher decided to record information about each student and the student's singing skills. Figure 11.7 is a checklist that the teacher used.

Knowledge components can also be identified on a checklist for recording students' progress. Figure 11.8 and Figure 11.9 identify illustrative art and music concepts.

Figure 11.8   Art Heritage Concepts

Concepts	Students' Names
Identifies Several American Painters, Sculptors, and Architects	
Relates the Purposes of Art to Different Historical Time Periods	
Recognizes Similarities and Differences Among Art Objects	
Uses Art Resource Materials to Obtain Information	
Discusses Field Trips to Galleries and Museums	
Identifies the Various Uses of Art	
Identifies Career Options for Artists	

Code: 1 = Poor; 3 = Average; 5 = Superior

Figure 11.9 Music Concepts

Concepts	Students' Names
Identifies:	
Staff Notation	
Scale Patterns	
Rhythmic Notation	
Math Relationship	
Familiar Song from Notation	
Chord Pattern	
Sharps and Flats	
Natural Symbol	
Names of Tones	
Repeat Signs	

Code: 1 = Poor; 3 = Average; 5 = Superior

Figure 11.10 Whole Class Discussion Skills

How Many . . . ?
   Participate
   Utilize Facts
   Utilize Relevant Ideas
   Listen to Others
   Use Evidence to Present Ideas
   Use Ideas of Others to Present Own Information
   Challenge Ideas of Others
   Refute Ideas Using Evidence
   State Main Point in Summation

Code: Few; Many

GROUP WORK EVALUATION

To improve both teaching and learning, teachers find that class discussions need to be evaluated for participation, interaction, listening, relevance, and synthesis.

The checklist in Figure 11.10 can be used at the conclusion of (or during) a whole class discussion. Greg Thomas decided to tape-record a discussion session and play it back for his students. The students then critiqued their own discussion using the checklist shown in Figure 11.10. They realized that one of their main problems was that they did not listen to the contributions of other speakers. As a consequence, there was unnecessary repetition. With the teacher's help they came to realize that they needed to prepare for a discussion with notes and evidence so they could challenge each other's facts. They decided to take turns at the end of a discussion to practice making summative statements.

To improve small group work students can be asked to evaluate their work sessions together. The open-style checklist shown in Figure 11.11 suggests that students write in their comments. Sometimes a planning form such as the one in Figure 11.12 facilitates group work.

When students participate in group work or simulations and gaming, their social participation skills should be evaluated. The checklist in Figure 11.13 is appropriate after use of the simulation School Council (Chapter 8).

Demonstration of subject matter skills in a small group encourages students to ask questions.

Figure 11.11   Formative Evaluation of Small Group Process Skills

	Good/Poor
Our Planning/Discussion Was . . .	
We Made the Following Agreements/ Plans . . .	
We Accomplished . . .	
Our Pans Were Spoiled by . . .	
We Need to . . .	
We Anticipate the Following Material Needs . . .	
We Need Assistance to . . .	
We Do Not Need Assistance Because . . .	

Figure 11.12   Small Group Planning Form

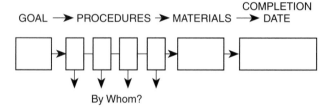

GOAL ➝ PROCEDURES ➝ MATERIALS ➝ COMPLETION DATE

By Whom?

SELF-EVALUATION

Just as good teachers evaluate themselves, students should be encouraged to appraise the development of work skills, social skills, and academic skills. Self-actualization is dependent on accurate self-appraisal. Teachers must carefully guide students in their self-evaluation because sometimes students are extremely hard on themselves. Students should be taught that some skill development is individualistic and dependent on growth characteristics; however, social skills and work study skills may depend on personal effort.

Student Accountability

Students can be held accountable for their performance when

- They know what their assignment is.
- They know how to accomplish it.
- They have the necessary work materials.

Classroom problems typically result when students are unclear about the purpose of the assignment, how

Figure 11.13   Social Participation Skills

Particpates and Cooperates with Others
Observes and Shares Observation
Listens to Others
Expresses Own Viewpoint
Plans with Others
Assists Others
Accepts Personal Responsibility
Carries Out Group Tasks, Plans, and Actions
Shares Efforts
Concludes Tasks
Identifies Agreements or Disagreements
Interprets Agreements or Disagreements
Facilitates Cooperation
Bargains and Negotiates

to use the resources, or when the assignment is due. A number of records can be designed to help students keep track of their responsibilities and to self-evaluate in terms of "How am I doing?" Figure 11.14 shows an example of a contract a student can use to keep track of accomplishments.

After group work or learning center participation, the "I Learned" record (Figure 11.15) is useful. Figure 11.16 and Figure 11.17 are examples of evaluations students can complete after participating in a specific learning activity.

To evaluate work habits, Figure 11.18 can be used with a yes/no response, or it can be made open ended so students write in their responses. Figure 11.19 is an example of a form students can use to give their own impression of the day's activities.

Scheduling Group Work

When there are many work groups in the classroom, it is often difficult for both students and teacher to remember who is to work where—and when. Different types of assignment charts can be devised to keep stu-

Figure 11.14   Student Contract

Today is _____	Name: _____
I Will Do This:	I Accomplished This:
1.	
2.	
3.	
4.	

Figure 11.15   I Learned . . .

Name _____

1. I learned . . .
2. I am excited about . . .
3. I am disinterested in . . .
4. I feel good about . . .
5. I was surprised . . .

Figure 11.16   Learning Activity Evaluation

Mathematics

I really learned a lot today. _____
I learned a little bit today. _____
I did not learn much today. _____
This happened because _____

Figure 11.17   Learning Activity Evaluation

Mathematics

I really needed help today. _____
I needed a little bit of help today. _____
I did not need help today. _____
This happened because _____

Figure 11.18   Work-Study Skills—Self-Evaluation

Did I . . .	Yes	No
1. Plan my work?		
2. Understand my assignments?		
3. Begin to work immediately?		
4. Need help?		
5. Help others?		
6. Enjoy my task?		
7. Work quietly?		
8. Feel satisfied with what I accomplished?		
9. Complete my assignment?		
10. Clean up?		

Figure 11.19   Class Activities

Class activities were . . .

___ 1. Very interesting today
___ 2. A little bit interesting today
___ 3. Not interesting today

Figure 11.20   Work Assignments (Centers and Groups)

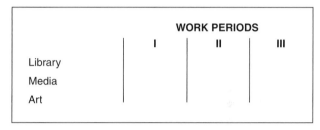

Centers	M	T	W	T	F
Science	Green				
Music		Green			
Research			Green		
Media				Green	
Skill					Green

Figure 11.21   Work Assignments—Pocket Chart

	WORK PERIODS		
	I	II	III
Library			
Media			
Art			

dents on target. Figure 11.20 is illustrative of a work assignment chart. In a pocket chart such as the one shown in Figure 11.21, students' names are on cards that are placed in a pocket designating the appropriate center and work period.

Sometimes teachers use sign-in sheets at each center. In that way the teachers can verify who worked at the center at a given time and day. In addition, there should be one box for finished work and another one for unfinished work available at each work center.

OBTAINING INFORMATION ABOUT THE CLASSROOM ENVIRONMENT

Finding out how students feel about others in the classroom, about their relationships with others, and about their studies provides the teacher with information that assists in planning learning experiences. Frequent assessment of the learning environment communicates to students that a teacher cares how students feel and has respect for them.

For very young children it is possible to obtain an accurate measure of their feelings by asking them a question and having them respond by checking the appropriate facial expression. Use five faces, with the face on the far left reflecting a positively happy, smiling person. The face on the extreme right would reflect a negative, unhappy person, and the faces in between would be at a varying stages of emotional reaction from positive to negative.

Students with a positive self-concept typically have several friendships in the classroom and enjoy their classroom and school work. Good academic work appears to be related to a healthy mental attitude about the self and one's relationship to others. When teachers can help students relate to several others in the classroom, the school situation is perceived more favorably. For this reason it is valuable to measure social relations in the classroom. Simple questionnaires can be devised to obtain the information. With very young children, it is possible to interview each child and obtain the information orally. Another system is to provide each child with a list of classmates. Each class member will have a number in front of his or her name, and in responding to the questions the child can refer to the classmate's number rather than write the whole name. The following types of questions can be used to generate information about social relationships:

- Which students in this class are always willing to help others?

There is no magic number of suggested names that students should write, but three seems to be indicative of students' feelings about others. Figure 11.22 shows a sample questionnaire.

- Which students in this class do you like to work with most often?

When students are responding to these questions, it is important to assure them that there are no right or wrong answers.

- Which students in this class do you not want to work with?
- Who can always be counted on to help in class?
- Who always gets their work done?

Figure 11.22   Questionnaire to Evaluate Social Relations in the Classroom

Which students in this class are always willing to help others?
1.
2.
3.

It is natural for students to have negative feelings about some of their classmates, and it certainly is valuable for the teacher to know which students cannot work together; however, good judgment is advised before using too many questions that ask for negative judgments about peers. Information derived from questions (Which student do you like to work with? or Who would you most like to sit next to?) can be used to develop a matrix or sociogram of social relationships. Armed with this information, teachers can try to improve relationships among students by helping the isolates and rejected students develop patterns of behavior that can be respected by peers.

DEVELOPING A SOCIAL MATRIX

Let us pretend that in a classroom of 25 students the teacher asked the question, "Which students do you like to work with?" A matrix like the one shown in Table 11.1 is constructed in the following way:

- Each student has a number from 1 to 25.
- The top of the matrix is numbered and the side of the matrix is numbered.
- Each time a student is named positively the student receives a + in the square *under* his or her number in the *row* of the person doing the choosing. The left column indicates the choosers, and the top row indicates the chosen.

Analysis of the data in Table 11.1 reveals that students numbered 4 and 24 are isolates and student number 19 was chosen by only one person. However, there are several mutual choices in the class: students 1 and 3, 6 and 7, 5 and 10, 6 and 13, 20 and 2. These students appear to have mutual good feelings about each other. The matrix also reveals that students choose widely among their classmates. In some classrooms you will find several stars and many students who are not recognized at all by others. In this classroom, that does not appear to be the case. The teacher should be able to use the established friendship choices to help students 4, 19, and 24. Note that this matrix does not reflect differences among first, second, and third choices; however, a matrix could be designed to do so.

DEVELOPING A SOCIOGRAM

A **sociogram** is another way to organize data to detect social relationships. A sociogram is dramatic because

Table 11.1 Matrix Social Relations

Choosers \ Chosen	1	2	3	4	5	6	7	8	9	10	11	12	13	14	15	16	17	18	19	20	21	22	23	24	25
1			+				+				+														
2															+					+					+
3	+								+			+													
4		+				+												+							
5										+					+						+				
6						+	+						+												
7							+						+				+								
8						+										+		+							
9		+										+									+				
10						+																	+		+
11		+														+						+			
12	+																+						+		
13						+			+			+													
14														+						+			+		
15	+		+			+																			
16	+									+				+											
17							+											+							
18	+					+					+														
19																				+	+				+
20		+						+	+																
21							+		+		+														
22			+																						
23	+					+	+														+				+
24		+					+						+												
25																					+	+	+		
Total	6	4	3	0	8	5	4	2	2	3	2	3	3	2	2	2	2	2	1	3	5	3	3	0	4

it represents pictorially the social relations or social distances in the classroom. When making a sociogram it is often interesting to depict boys and girls in different ways so one can see instantly whether there is a split between the boys and girls or in the structure of the interaction.

Figure 11.23 exhibits a sociogram for a group of 15 students. It is easy to see that Bill is popular with both boys and girls. Fara, Evelyn, and Dick are isolates. The sociogram is usually used to designate one or two choices, whereas the matrix can represent as many as desired. Colored ink or different types of lines can be used in the sociogram to differentiate between the choices.

In evaluating the relationships in the classroom, it may be worthwhile to determine whether choices would be different if the questions were phrased to make students differentiate between work partners and friendship partners. Would students choose the same individuals to work with as they would to play with? Or they might also be asked, "Who would you most want to be tutored by?"

Sociometric devices should be used periodically to determine whether there are changes in students' attitudes and values about others in the classroom. Information is incomplete if the teacher does not follow up several weeks or months later to determine whether changes have occurred.

ANECDOTAL RECORDS

The **anecdotal record** is an informal technique used to study specific behavior exhibited by a student when that behavior appears to be discrepant or problem causing. The anecdote describes the specific event and

Figure 11.23   Sociogram

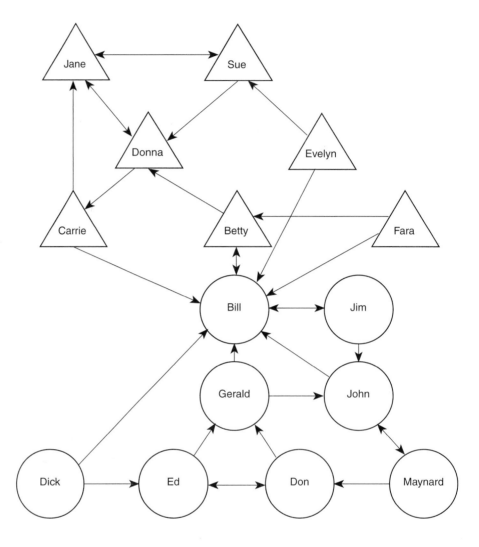

behavior as objectively as possible. If the anecdote contains an interpretation or evaluation by the observer, it is separated from the description. The purpose of the anecdote is to preserve information about the discrepant behavior so it can be analyzed by the parent, teacher, or another professional. Sometimes the anecdote also contains the observer's suggestions or prescription for treatment. Figure 11.24 demonstrates the technique.

The anecdotal record is dependent on the teacher's observation skills. Any interpretation of an observation record must be based on the observed facts. General observations of students' work skills or of teachers performing instructional techniques should be purpose oriented. The observer should be looking for specific behavior and have criteria to use in order to recognize the behavior. A review of the checklists in

this chapter will reveal that each was designed to gather data about specific behaviors, skills, or attitudes. Teacher observation is a valid evaluative technique for both formative and summative purposes.

PERFORMANCE ASSESSMENT

Performance assessment is not a new concept. In *My Pedagogic Creed* (pp. 11–12), John Dewey advocated observing the child's "expressive or constructive activities" to assess what the student is learning and as a medium to develop meaning. In discussing teaching method, Dewey (1929, pp. 11–12) said

> The law for presenting and treating material is the law implicit with the child's own nature . . . the active side precedes the passive in the development of the child nature; expression comes before conscious impression.

Figure 11.24 Anecdotal Record: Shirley Barry

	Observation (What Happened?)	Interpretation (Why Did It Happen?)	Prescription (Planned Action!)
Mon., Mar. 10	Complained of a headache during math; did not finish work; was excused to see nurse.		
Tues., Mar. 11	Same time; same complaint; same effect	Hm-m-m-m. I will talk to nurse.	
Tues., 3 P.M.	No temperature; vivacious; fine after rest (nurse's report).		Conference with student.
Wed., Mar. 12	Same time; same complaint plus stomach ache. (Suggested she rest in classroom.)	Must be having problems with math; no apparent interaction problems with peers.	Conference: Helped her with math, but she did not need the assistance.
Thurs., Mar. 13	Same problem: different time!	Nothing to do with math. Home problems?	Call mother. Set up conference.
Fri., Mar. 14	Conference: Mother revealed that parents are separating. Shirley needs counseling. Mother recognizes problem and says she will alert father to Shirley's security needs. (Hope that next week will be better!)		

William Kilpatrick advocated the use of *projects* for students as an exhibit of what the student has learned. In fact, schools of the nineteenth century typically used the student's work output as a measure of his or her success.

DEFINITIONS

Most of us are more comfortable with an idea when we can define it. **Assessment** is not a single element but rather a process to gather data utilizing a variety of factors to gain information about student performance. The information that is gained might be called the *evidence*. Using all of the evidence, the teacher can then make a judgment or *evaluation*.

Assessment is considered a *naturalistic* means to gather data—natural, because it occurs in the classroom using the real experiences (and activities) of students as they go about performing tasks and, as Dewey would say, constructing meaning. **Authentic assessment** is another means to express the focus on real-world activities using the experiential base of students. Let us look at some of the ways teachers gather evidence about what students are learning.

SELECTING APPROPRIATE STRATEGIES FOR PERFORMANCE ASSESSMENT

Review Greg Thomas's teaching unit in Chapter 9. Note the following activities: small group work, independent and small group problem-solving and research activity, oral discussions, construction, role-plays, and dramatic play. Each of these experiences provides the opportunity for Thomas to assess how his students are performing. Greg Thomas gathers data using the following means:

- *Observation* of students' independent and group work
- *Projects* produced by the student (reports, experiments)
- *Artifacts* (construction projects, artwork, displays, science inventions/demonstrations)
- Individual teacher-student *conferences*
- Oral *participation* in discussions
- Teacher-made *tests*

Note that many of the activities occur over a fairly long period of time (experiments, reports). These tasks require not only content knowledge and the ability to sustain the activity, but transformation through application and interpretation. In conjunction with the

Research Findings: Performance Assessment

Popham (1995, pp. 142–143) identifies three factors that have influenced the use of performance assessment:

1. Dissatisfaction with selected-response tests because these tests focus on low-level responses instead of higher order thinking skills
2. The influence of cognitive psychology because experts believe that cognitive tasks require both content knowledge and procedural knowledge and procedural knowledge can only be accessed through performance projects
3. The sometimes harmful instructional impact of conventional tests because of the influence of tests on the teaching curriculum

Teacher Research

To encourage students' responsibility for editing their own writing, Scheideman (1995, pp. 99–117) had her fifth graders design "quality-writing" checklists. The students decided on the significant components of a story and the attributes of creative writing. The students then used their own lists to revise and change their stories. She concluded that the students grew as writers, thinkers, and editors.

planned learning experiences that will yield data for Thomas, he will also rely on student's *portfolios* and *exhibitions*.

Some data, such as projects, artifacts, and tests, are easy to accumulate and preserve over the course of a semester. Other evidence such as observation data needs to be consciously gathered, recorded, and preserved. The data include many of the informal strategies suggested in this chapter: checklists, anecdotal records, sociograms, students' own evaluations, and journal writings.

What is really important in assessing students' performance is the variety, scope, and breadth of evidence that is used to judge how students are progressing. Though it may be perfectly obvious, data need to be collected in all subject fields and in all settings. This means that teachers in departmentalized schools must share data in order to help each other understand the needs of students. This was one of the prime reasons why middle school restructuring was initiated. In Karen Adazzio's school, the teachers meet in *house meetings* in order to share information about the students that will facilitate planning the curriculum.

ASSESSING HANDS-ON EXPERIENCES

Mary Hogan was teaching mathematics and gave the students ice cream sticks to manipulate. Hogan observed the students move the sticks on their desktops as she directed them to work problems. She noted that several students, when asked to create the problem of

5 + 4, counted out the sticks one by one. When asked to reverse the problem so that it was 4 + 5, they put all the sticks together and begin counting one by one all over again. It was clear to her that these students lacked the concept of reversibility.

If students are asked to find out how to increase the strength of an electromagnet, the teacher might observe the alternatives they try, the care or inconsistency of their tests, and accuracy of their results and conclusions. In addition, the students could be asked to document their experiments so that others can learn from them. The documentation should then be studied for clarity and accuracy.

PORTFOLIOS AND EXHIBITIONS

Portfolios and exhibitions provide visual records of progress. At the University of Southern California, student teachers develop portfolios to demonstrate their teaching prowess. The **portfolio** is used when applying for a teaching position. Specimens for the portfolios are carefully considered.

Similarly, in the classroom, a student's portfolio should represent a choice of peak experiences. Not everything should be put in the portfolio. Students should be asked to consider what the portfolio says about their performance. (What story does it tell?) In addition, students need to consider how the portfolio should be arranged. Portfolios may be kept in several subject fields or integrated, like the curriculum.

What Should Portfolios Contain?

Portfolios can contain the following types of items:

- Creative representations (stories, poems, artwork)
- Process development (writing process: drafts, revisions, and final edited version, each dated)

- Experiments and problems that are self-evaluated and teacher-evaluated
- Reports (individual and group-based)
- Journals, logs, and records of investigations

There should be a table of contents for the portfolio and a preface by the author describing the items. Assessments by the author, teacher, or classmates may appear with the different displays. Some students may prefer to make an audio tape that describes and assesses the various items.

How Should Portfolios Be Evaluated?

Adams and Hamm (1992) and Lemlech (1995) suggest the following means to evaluate the content of portfolios:

- Evidence of critical and creative thinking
- Appropriateness of selected display items, variety of items
- Organization of displayed data
- Patterns in processes and in the way assignments were completed
- Evidence of understanding
- Use of intellectual tools (inquiry) and subject field skills
- Use of technology (computers, calculators, video, audio)
- Understanding of democratic values, social responsibility for the social studies
- Research skills (location skills, note taking, use of the Internet, applications, final report)
- Logical developmental processes such as in the writing process and the search process for research
- Integrative self-assessment

EVALUATION: SOME CONCLUDING REMARKS

Teachers should use a variety of techniques to obtain information about students' learning progress. Effective planning and instruction are dependent on meaningful evaluation. Thus far in this chapter a variety of techniques, both formal and informal, have been presented. Evaluative means are to some extent dependent on students' ages and capabilities as well as the interest and philosophy of the teacher. It is up to the classroom teacher to choose evaluative measures that fit teaching style and students' needs. Performance assessment tells us what students can do, not what they cannot do. The teacher's job is to link learning to assessment.

Research Applications

Baker (1994) explores the implications of equity decisions related to performance assessments. Using *meaningfulness* as a criterion, performance tasks must be motivating to the subject students and the content and purpose understandable to them. Using *linguistic appropriateness* as a criterion, the tasks must be comprehendible and the subject students must have the language competency to transform the task(s) to convey their own meanings.

TECHNIQUES FOR COMMUNICATING CHANGE

FEEDBACK AND CHANGE

Providing students with appropriate feedback concerning performance is an important teaching function. Rosenshine and Stevens (1986, p. 385) identify four types of student responses that require teacher feedback:

1. The student responds correctly, quickly, and firmly. The teacher should acknowledge the student response ("right," "good," "yes," "right on") without disturbing the momentum of the lesson.

2. The student responds correctly, but hesitantly, indicating that the student is unsure or lacks confidence. The teacher should emphasize the correctness of the response. It may also be a good idea to go back and review the process of instruction because other students may also be hesitant about what has been taught.

3. The student responds incorrectly and carelessly. The teacher should not overreact, but should correct the response quickly and go on without spoiling the momentum of the lesson or triggering a classroom management incident.

4. The student responds incorrectly because of lack of knowledge of the facts or the process. In this instance it is important to cue the student in some way to guide him or her to the correct response. If this does not work or it appears that the student's problem is more serious, reteach the process or information to those students who appear to be confused.

Feedback is necessary for the improvement of performance. However, low and high achievers often react differently to teacher feedback. According to Good and

Brophy (1986), poor achievers are often unable to make appropriate use of teacher feedback. In a critical review of research on evaluation and motivation, Sears (1977) cautioned that there is much we do not know about the role of motivation on young learners or low-ability students and that not enough attention has been given to the effect of self-evaluation. Obviously, students perceive and are affected by evaluation in different ways; some students are motivated by challenge, and others need an instructional program that guarantees success. Teachers need to understand their students' responses to success and failure, and perhaps their own motivational patterns as well. Teachers who are discouraged by students' failure will react differently than teachers who perceive failure as a challenge to improve performance.

The communication of learning progress is an extremely important and difficult professional responsibility. Teachers perform this task in as many different ways as they do that of obtaining information about achievement. Block (1977) advised teachers to sequence teaching strategies to gradually increase levels of success. Dweck (1977) suggested that teachers try to change students' causal beliefs so they understand that success is achieved through effort. For some students, programs that guarantee success do not provide the appropriate challenge; for these students, Maehr and Sjogren (1971) suggested independent study so personal effort can be perceived. Keislar (1977, p. 60)

Research Findings:
Cooperative Learning

Johnson and Johnson (1996, p. 29), based on research findings, identify four benefits of cooperative learning as compared with competitive and individualistic learning situations:

1. Higher achievement when problem solving and creativity are required
2. More positive relationships among students and between students and faculty among all ethnic and cultural and social backgrounds
3. Self-esteem, self-efficacy, social competency, coping skills, and general psychological health are enhanced by working with classmates cooperatively
4. Frequent use of cooperative groups promotes a positive student perception of the classroom environment for academic study and personal growth

---

warned that misunderstandings were likely between parent and teacher "if teachers attribute student success to their good teaching and student failure to the student's lack of effort or ability, while the parent assumes just the opposite."

THE TEACHER-STUDENT INTERVIEW OR CONFERENCE

Teacher-student interviews or conferences should be carefully planned to accomplish specific purposes. The conference can be used to gather information about the student's progress and to communicate information to the student concerning achievement. During the interview, the teacher should assess the student's performance in terms of the child's own ability and personal growth and in terms of a criterion considered appropriate for the student. The conference enables the teacher to recognize the student's accomplishments privately; thus the student does not derive satisfaction at the expense of others, nor does the student feel that he or she suffers by comparison to others. The teacher needs to exercise judgment concerning what is to be communicated to the student. Consider the long-range effects of positive versus negative criticism.

The conference provides an opportunity to help the student reflect and self-evaluate. A checklist may

Teacher-student conferences provide a means to share mutual goals, explore thinking, and teach self-evaluation.

be used at this time. During the conference, the teacher can help students select portfolio items and edit their work. The teacher can also determine whether students expressed themselves clearly in writing by listening to them describe their thoughts.

The conference provides a marvelous opportunity for a one-on-one discussion. All subject fields can benefit from the conference as a means to communicate performance accomplishments and provide appropriate feedback.

RUBRICS

Rubrics are criteria statements. When the rubric is well designed, both students and teacher know what the expectations for performance should be. The rubric is a means to focus in on performance. It helps teachers be precise in using criteria for evaluating students' work.

The rubric may be as simple as a checklist or it may be complex and provide a number of different elements of performance. For example, in a research project, the rubric may identify the following criteria: number of research sources, alternative ideas, organization, writing composition, and bibliography. The rubric may specify a scale (1–5) for evaluating each dimension.

Designing the rubric helps both teachers and students. It can be used for professional education to facilitate the examination of the curriculum. Students, too, can develop classroom rubrics. For example, a research rubric like the one described above can be designed by the students to evaluate their own research projects.

During the teacher-student conference, the rubric can be used to help students improve their work because it provides a means to talk about the student's performance in very concrete language.

DIARIES AND LOGS

Students can be asked to keep a diary or a log of their personal activities, accomplishments, tasks, and behavior. The written record can be examined in terms of accomplishments and goals. The diary or log is a fine assessment instrument to facilitate self-evaluation. It can be shared with others if the student so desires, or it can be used in the teacher-student conference. Let primary children dictate their logs and illustrate their activities.

Figure 11.25 Shirley Barry's Math Test Scores

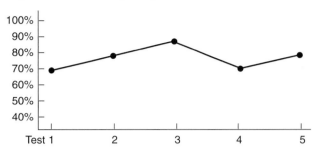

GRAPHIC TECHNIQUES

Another way to encourage students to self-evaluate their progress is to teach them how to record their accomplishments using a bar graph or broken-line graph (see Figures 11.25 and 11.26). These records are particularly appropriate to help students keep track of their spelling achievement, math achievement, completed homework assignments, or decreasing frequency of teacher admonishments. Once again, these graphic techniques can be discussed during the teacher-student conference or shared with parents.

GRADING

Grading establishes labels for specific categories (A, B, C, D, F); each category has specific characteristics. In determining grades, the teacher must decide whether the student fits the characteristics of a particular category. If C is the average or satisfactory category then the teacher must decide on the criteria to be considered average or satisfactory in each subject or skill being graded. Whereas feedback provides information

Figure 11.26 Teacher "Reminders" (Shirley Barry)

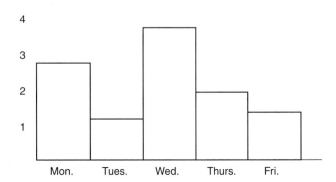

for the student to use to improve performance, grading actually provides no useful information. Knowing that you received a C in science does not tell you how to improve your performance. Nor does it tell you, or anyone else, what you really have learned. Dependent on the criteria that were used, or the group to whom you are being compared, the grade only tells you that the teacher considers you "satisfactory."

A typical problem during grading has to do with the composition of the class population. Suppose that Greg Thomas believes that school grades should reflect the normal bell curve, but his fifth graders happen to be unusually bright. Their math tests reflect a narrow range of scores from 85 to 100. Using the normal curve would mean that a student with a score of 85 could conceivably receive a D or F on the math test. If, on the other hand, the class composition was primarily low-ability students, then a score of 85 might be an A if the range turned out to be 60 to 85. Thus, it is important to remember that the normal curve should not be applied to grade abnormal groups.

Although teachers try to be objective about grading, there are many subjective elements. Teachers usually tell students that homework assignments, class participation, neatness of work, and effort are all considered when assigning a grade. But these elements allow for a great deal of subjectivity, and students and parents are well aware of the selective nature of some of the evidence. Grading can never be totally fair; as a consequence, many schools prefer parent-teacher conferences or the use of descriptive, criterion-referenced evaluation instead of the traditional report card.

When criterion-referenced evaluation is used, parents receive a list of competencies with information about how their child is performing relative to the list of specific skills or competencies. For example, for the sixth grade there may be a list of 20 reading skills that have been identified as essential by the school or school district. Perhaps 15 of the 20 skills have been verified in terms of the child's progress; the remaining skills are still beyond the competence of the student. In this way the parents know precisely what skills the child is capable of performing.

PARENT-TEACHER CONFERENCES

The conference is a time to gather information and to share information. This means that teacher and parent are talking with (not at) each other and listening to each other. As the teacher attempts to establish rapport with the parent at the beginning of the conference, it is important to let the parent know that the teacher is the child's advocate. (Remember that the parent ought to be the child's advocate.) Sometimes parents have preconceived ideas about the conference based on their own childhood memories. For this reason, it is a good idea to be sure that the parent is at ease before focusing on the purpose of the conference.

GUIDELINES

Whether the conference represents a planned or unplanned happening, it is important to remember that conferences involve the expression of personal feelings, ideas, and judgments. It is as essential for the teacher to listen as it is for the parent.

Basic conference components are the same whether the conference has been planned or is unplanned. Suggested guidelines for conferences are as follows:

1. Greet parent(s) and establish rapport through a sharing of interest. Try to put the parent at ease. Sit next to or across from each other. Do not put the teacher's desk between you.

2. Establish the purpose for the conference. If you requested the conference, tell the parent about the problem or the reason for the request. If the parent requested the conference, ask the parent to "tell me about your concern." (If the conference was called to solve a behavior problem, focus on the problem but be sure to avoid judgmental comments such as "Cecil is a weasel!" or "Howard is a coward!" Remember, you are an advocate for the child!)

3. Bring evidence of the students' work to the conference, and share the data with the parent. Interpret test scores and progress for the parent. Remember that you are the expert.

4. Answer parent's questions; listen to parent's observations.

5. Discuss your instructional approach. Present ways to help the student and discuss anticipated progress.

6. Ask for parental suggestions; remember that the parent knows the child better than you do.

7. Establish joint goals for the future. Set a time for a follow-up conference, if necessary.

8. Summarize the conference. Ask the parent, "Do you have any questions you want to ask?" Then state your concept of the conference's accomplishments.

For example:

"We have both agreed that we are concerned about Jed's progress in math."

"I intend to..."

"It is my understanding that you and Mr. E. will monitor Jed's homework."

"Our plan is to . . ."

"We will keep in touch about . . ."

9. Thank the parent for attending.

STUDENT-PARENT-TEACHER CONFERENCE

Perhaps one of the most effective means to communicate with parents about students' progress is to make students responsible for the conference. The portfolio provides the ideal mechanism. Early in the semester students should be made aware of their responsibility to select exhibits of their work for documentation.

At the conference the student talks to the parent, explaining each item in the portfolio. The student needs to explain to the parent the rubrics involved in the various exhibits.

"The criteria (or the rubric) for this assignment was . . ."
The student should be encouraged to discuss why she/he selected particular items for the portfolio.
"I am proud of this because . . ."
"If I were to do this assignment again, I think I would fix . . ."
"To begin with, I didn't understand, but now . . ."
"This isn't perfect, but I did learn . . ."

The three-way conference provides interesting insights in the way students and parents communicate, and it allows students to take charge of their own learning.

Data for the Conference

It is essential to accumulate evidence of the student's work for the parent to examine. This may be done through portfolios or other more traditional means. When Greg Thomas has a conference with the Chans, he will need to show them their son's work. The following evidence can be assembled for the conference:

- Results of daily activities: work papers (follow-up materials in reading and math), independent projects, work accomplished at learning centers (social studies, science, art projects, experiments)
- Checklists of skills and social participation (Greg Thomas shows the Chans the Critical Thinking Checklist)

- Observational data by teacher or others
- Test results from both teacher-made tests and achievement tests
- Data generated by the student in the form of self-evaluative evidence (exhibit or portfolio)

Post Conference

After the conference, record information about agreements and decisions. Note any follow-up plans. If there is a need for other professional assistance, arrange for the appropriate personnel to consult on the case. Record the data and make note of the evidence that was shared with the parent(s). Many teachers find it advantageous to keep a journal that is dated and can be used to refresh the memory of the conference or other happenings. It is very important to assess accomplishments derived through the conference and to carry out professional commitments.

SUMMARY

Evaluation

1. Evaluation should be a continuous, cooperative, and comprehensive process.
2. To evaluate learning progress, it is necessary to identify what students were expected to learn and to measure how well students performed what was expected.
3. Learning activities need to be selected to match the instructional objective.

Testing Problems

4. Teachers need to be certain that when students have problems with a test it is not a consequence of inability to read the test.
5. Some test problems are related to inexperience in test-taking and sometimes fear of the testing situation.
6. Test bias occurs when the content of the test penalizes students for lack of experiences that may be a consequence of race, gender, or social class.

Types of Tests

7. Standardized achievement tests are norm referenced.
8. Criterion-referenced tests tell teachers how well an individual performs a specific task or behavior as measured against a criterion.

9. Teacher-made tests are usually paper and pencil tests designed to test specific instructional purposes.
10. Essay tests are usually designed to be open ended and encourage written expression and depth responses.
11. Objective tests are close ended and generally do not require high–level thinking necessary for inquiry or problem solving.

Informal Strategies For Evaluating Growth

12. Checklists and rating scales can be used by both teachers and students to evaluate skills, specific behaviors, interests, and concepts.
13. The social matrix and the sociogram provide means to study social relationships in the classroom.
14. The anecdotal record is an informal technique used to study specific behavior problems.

Performance Assessment

15. Assessment is a process that utilizes a variety of factors for gathering data about performance.
16. Authentic assessment focuses on real-life experiences and activities.
17. Variety, scope, and breadth of evidence need to be used to judge students' progress.

Portfolios and Exhibitions

18. Portfolios and exhibitions provide visual records of progress.
19. Portfolios may demonstrate creative experiences, process development, experiments, reports, and journal records.

Communicating Change

20. Feedback is necessary for the improvement of performance.
21. Communication of learning progress is an important and difficult professional responsibility.

Teacher-Student Conference

22. Teachers need to assess a student's performance in terms of his/her ability and potential growth.
23. The conference provides opportunity for the student to reflect and self-evaluate.
24. Both teacher and student benefit from one-on-one discussion.

Rubrics

25. Rubrics are criteria statements that tell both students and teacher what the expectations are for performance.
26. Both teacher and students can design the rubrics.

Diaries, Logs, and Journals

27. Diaries, logs, and journals can be used to study change over a fairly long period of time.
28. Written records provide a means for students to self-evaluate.
29. Graphic techniques can be used by students to evaluate their own performance.

Grading

30. Grading is a labeling device to describe performance, but it does not tell the student how to improve performance.
31. Grading does not communicate useful information to parents, students, or other teachers.

Parent-Teacher Conference

32. The conference is a means for both teacher and parent to gather information and share information about the child.
33. Both teacher and parent should be the child's advocate, and discuss accordingly.

Student-Parent-Teacher Conference

34. The three-way conference is one of the most effective means to communicate about students' progress.
35. The student should play the major role at the conference, exhibiting his/her work and explaining it to the parent.

Post Conference

36. It is important that teachers record and maintain vital information about agreements and decisions made at conferences.

DISCUSSION QUESTIONS AND APPLICATION EXERCISES

1. Make a list of activities that demonstrate integration of subject fields and could be exhibited to show how much students have learned.

2. Develop an objective test using science concepts. Choose any grade level.

3. Choose a specific skill and design a criterion-referenced test to find out if students can perform the skill.

4. Formative evaluation means that a teacher checks on how things are progressing during an instructional episode. What are some ways that you can find out if students are learning what you want them to learn?

5. Summative evaluation occurs at the end of instruction. What are some ways to determine what students have learned at the end of an instructional period? Why are summative evaluation and grading closely related?

6. Select a subject field and create an authentic problem-solving activity for performance assessment. Identify the rubrics that will be used.

7. With one or more others, role-play a parent conference for the following purposes: to communicate learning progress; to respond to a concern or complaint; and to communicate behavioral problems.

8. Plan a presentation for parents to explain the purpose of performance assessment, the use of rubrics, and portfolio assessment.

PART III

UNDERSTANDING THE CURRICULUM

The six chapters in Part III focus on major content experiences provided by elementary and middle schools. The content areas by themselves are not the curriculum. The *curriculum* can be defined as all the experiences the school provides for students. This encompasses learning experiences and activities, procedures, and resources planned for students.

Each chapter defines the content field and identifies goals, concepts, programs, teaching approaches, ways to evaluate growth, and relevant issues, such as performance assessment. Integration of the content area with other content fields is discussed in each of the chapters. Suggestions for inclusion and classroom management are included, with specific applications for the content field in most of the chapters of Part III. Ideas for learning centers in each content area are provided.

A few states have curricula frameworks that provide teachers with a basic structure for the scope and sequence of instruction. The framework helps teachers elect appropriate instructional experiences and instructional materials. Some chapters cite the California State Framework. This should be used as a springboard for discussion of the content field and as a basis for comparison with your local or state guidelines.

National curriculum standards have been developed in some of the disciplines. When appropriate these standards are referred to in the relevant chapter; however, they have not been universally accepted by all educators or by every state. When reading standards, you should consider how the standard(s) affects the overall curriculum design and student performance expectations.

12

Teaching English Language Arts

This chapter emphasizes the interrelationship of the language arts. Reading and writing are considered parallel processes, one focusing on comprehension and the other on composing. Both are enhanced by prior knowledge and experience. The chapter emphasizes a constructivist approach to teaching language arts and provides several teaching episodes to demonstrate language arts lessons. Spelling, handwriting, punctuation, and capitalization are considered the writer's tools and they are discussed from that perspective.

Included in the chapter are suggestions for helping students with limited English proficiency (LEP), related research, sheltered English strategies, and helping the nonstandard English speaker. The chapter concludes with a section on portfolio assessment and ideas for learning centers.

After you study this chapter, you should be able to accomplish the following:

1. Identify the language arts components.
2. Explain how the language arts are interrelated.
3. Discuss the importance of language and explain why language changes.
4. Cite factors that affect language development.
5. Contrast traditional language arts programs and the whole language approach.
6. Discuss reading and writing as parallel processes.
7. Identify ways in which reading and writing are taught.
8. Explain why and how cooperative, heterogeneous groups are used for teaching language arts.
9. Suggest ways to facilitate mainstreaming during language arts.
10. Suggest ways to assist the nonstandard speaker of English and the student with limited English proficiency.
11. Create a language arts learning center.
12. Discuss ways to use performance assessment in language arts.

Eagerly the first graders talked about where they would go if they had their very own flying machines. The oral language lesson had been motivated by the reading of the children's book *Me and My Flying Machine* by Mercer Mayer. After sufficient time had been devoted to the oral lesson, the teacher directed the students' attention to the collage-type materials set up on several tables in the classroom. The oral lesson was to be followed by an art experience in which the students would make their own flying machines. The teacher explained that each student was to make a flying machine on a piece of colored paper, which would then be used as the cover to his or her very own creative writing book. Collage materials for the lesson included Popsicle™ sticks, colored pieces of plastic, propellers, string, straws, rubber bands, and small blocks of wood. Over the course of several weeks the students would be reading about flight, performing

---

Professional Lexicon

morpheme A word unit that combines phonemes into a pattern.

nonstandard English Any dialect of English governed by its own rules and language complexities.

phonemes Sound symbols.

primary language Native language, first language of an individual.

sheltered English instruction A strategy to help the LEP student understand content in the second language.

experiments, drawing pictures, and writing stories about where they would go and what they would do in their flying machines.

The teacher demonstrated the interrelatedness of the various language arts and the way in which language arts can be integrated with other subject fields.

WHAT ARE THE LANGUAGE ARTS?

The purpose of language is communication. Language is a tool we use to express ourselves. Through speaking or writing we convey ideas and feelings; the reception of those thoughts occurs through listening or reading. The children in the episode about the flying machine listened to a story first; then they had the opportunity to speak and practice oral language skills. Next they will write about their ideas, and finally they will read their own thoughts and the thoughts of others.

Communication between two individuals means that those individuals are sharing ideas, feelings, and information. The language arts curriculum can be defined as those activities that occur throughout the school day in which communication happens through reception (listening and reading) and expression (speaking and writing).

THE LANGUAGE ARTS ARE INTERRELATED

The receptive and expressive language arts are interrelated. Success in reading and writing are dependent on an adequate oral foundation. For this reason most early childhood classrooms and primary classrooms stress oral language skills. Teachers who hurry to place children in books are often frustrated because they fail to recognize the importance of speaking and listening skills.

During infancy and early childhood, children spend most of their time listening. Since speaking skills are modeled during this period, the quality of the child's models is critical to development. Competence in listening involves decoding speech meanings; the process of speaking involves encoding sounds so they are meaningful. In writing, the individual must encode sounds into graphic symbols; reading involves decoding those graphic symbols to attain meaning.

The children in the preceding oral language lesson were sharing ideas. Their teacher recognized the value of motivational reading to stimulate children's natural curiosity. Because they all had the same experience (listening to the story), their thoughts were meaningful to each other. Communication is the sharing of common meanings for the words that are spoken or written.

WHY IS LANGUAGE IMPORTANT?

We communicate meanings through language. Our meanings are based on our perceptions of reality. When the young child goes home from school and tells mother that the teacher is "mean," the child is probably perceiving the teacher as "mean" based on the *behavior* of the teacher toward the child. We use language to express our conception of, or ideas about, reality, but by the same token we are imprisoned by the language that we use. Language is symbolic; it represents sounds and symbols that are mutually agreed upon as representations of objects and concepts (Anderson and Lapp, 1992).

An example of language as the way in which we see the world is this classic passage from Lewis Carroll's *Through the Looking Glass:*

"I don't know what you mean by 'glory.'" Alice said.

Humpty Dumpty smiled contemptuously, "Of course you don't—till I tell you. I meant there's a nice knock-down argument for you!"

"But 'glory' doesn't mean a 'nice knock-down argument,'" Alice objected.

"When I use a word," Humpty Dumpty said in rather a scornful tone, "it means just what I choose it to mean—neither more nor less."

"The question is," said Alice, "whether you can make words mean so many different things."

"The question is," said Humpty Dumpty, "which is to be master—that's all."

Language is related to personality. Through language the child expresses emotions and thoughts, and as facility is gained, so is self-confidence in the ability to put one's own ideas into words. Social competence is aided by the individual's use of appropriate language. Language also gives us away. The words we choose, the things we say, the way in which we say them, and those things that we do not reveal contribute to the picture we transmit and that others receive.

Language is also used to relieve tension. Psychologists have confirmed that the use of occasional swear words relieves personal stress. When you drop the open pitcher of orange juice on the floor, an expletive may help!

Another purpose of language is the sharing of culture. The literature of our own society and of other societies is available to us and serves to convey information about the human experience. Without language we would have no means to transmit our experience or to profit from the experience of others.

NONVERBAL COMMUNICATION

Teachers need to interpret nonverbal behavior. All individuals communicate nonverbally, and some nonverbal communication is culturally related. Nervousness is often conveyed by handwriting mannerisms, excessive movement, fidgeting, or drumming with the fingertips. Anger may be expressed by the clenched fist, the shaking of the index finger, pounding on the table, glaring eyes, or rigid body posture.

Studies of classroom life by sociolinguists reveal that various classroom activities have specific nonverbal participation patterns (Brooks and Woolfolk, 1987, p. 54). For example, when introducing a new concept to students, the teacher expects students to respond by looking attentively at the teacher. If this response does not occur, the teacher may believe that the inattentive students are uncooperative. Brooks and Woolfolk point out that nonverbal behavior will cause different teacher reactions depending on the classroom activity. A walk to the pencil sharpener during seatwork will usually draw a different response than pencil sharpening during a teacher presentation.

Misunderstanding occurs in the classroom when teachers are unable to read nonverbal signs. Almost classic in the stories of the urban school are the incidents related to attention. Teachers are accustomed to students looking directly at them when they are talking. But Mexican-American, Native American, and African-American children rarely direct their eyes at an adult. In these cultures it is considered impolite to look directly at another person. However, in these same cultures, when an individual is angry, he or she will look directly into the eyes of the person causing the anger. If teachers are unaware of these cultural characteristics, there can be management problems in the classroom.

Body language is very expressive. During a role-play situation, the author observed a student's disdain for a statement made by the person next to her. This individual turned completely around in her seat so her back was to the person she wished to isolate.

Certain physical movements are culturally related. Some Japanese people still bow as a form of greeting. The touchdown dance of football players provides another example of expressive body language related to male culture. Teen-agers will often do a special handshake to indicate club membership. Nonlinguistic body movements (kinesics) while speaking are also expressive and typical of many European peoples.

Teachers frequently use nonverbal communication to control behavior in the classroom. A raised eyebrow or a finger to the lips can be a very effective means to forestall misbehavior, and a commiserating look or a smile of encouragement may be successful in motivating students to continue work or to try harder.

FACTORS AFFECTING LANGUAGE DEVELOPMENT

Individual differences need to be considered in the development of the language arts program. Language development is affected by the individual's cognitive and affective development, experience, intellectual ability, attitude, motivation, and culture. Readiness for the language arts may also be affected by sex differences, although many of these differences have been culturally induced. Readiness for reading is affected by maturity; research indicates that girls mature earlier than boys. The child who can sit still longer can usually listen more efficiently, and listening skills are positively related to success in learning to read. Verbal ability favors girls at young ages; young females are more skillful at expressing themselves than young males.

Language or dialect differences also affect success in the language arts. School English or standard English may cause communication problems for children accustomed to speaking a dialect that is different from the standard structure. Dialect differences are often a result of geography; where a person has lived affects speech sound, expressions, and usage.

When the **primary** (home) **language** is different from English, children may have a great deal of difficulty—even if they are working in a bilingual program. The sounds of English are different from the sounds of other languages, and the ear needs to be trained to hear the appropriate sounds. Aural development in a language needs to precede the development of reading and writing skills. This is another reason why it may be important that children begin formal instruction in their primary language. Teachers must remember that in adulthood social competence—the ability to speak standard English—and economic success are closely related.

The child's first language models are in the home. Socioeconomic class, cultural priorities, and the number of siblings in the family affect the encouragement and reinforcement the child receives. Parents encourage the development of language by modeling language and by listening attentively to the child's speech. Children who do not have language models will be at a disadvantage in school. Differences in child rearing related to socioeconomic status should be reviewed; these differences will affect success in the language arts.

Heath (1986, p. 148) discusses the sociocultural contexts of language development and notes that schools expect students to have learned the following before beginning school experience:

- To describe, label, and provided information about objects and events
- To remember in detail past happenings and be able to share them
- To listen to and follow directions from oral sources
- To interact (politely) with others using language
- To request information from others who may not be peers
- To use language appropriately to talk about personal experiences and to integrate new information into life experiences

Heath believes that only students who can perform these language functions are ready for successful experiences with the language arts curriculum. Teachers need to be language sensitive and provide opportunities for students to develop these common language uses if students are deficient.

LITERACY PROGRAMS

Traditional programs for primary students seem to take the perspective that the teacher and the curriculum determine when and what students should learn to read and write. This behavioristic, linear view of literacy instruction makes the assumption that students are passive and come to school without an understanding of language. Traditional programs bound by the basal reader progress from a very controlled vocabulary and syntax to more complex text materials and syntax. Program developers assume that the child must use materials in sequence in order to progress. In such a program, teachers often withhold writing instruction until students are viewed as ready.

Another view of literacy instruction assumes that students come to school with an understanding of language and the purposes of written language. This perspective is based on cognitive and phenomenological

psychology. Instead of the program defining when and what the student learns, teachers look to the student's prior experiences to determine the learning sequence. This view of literacy instruction allows the teacher to make professional decisions about what to teach and when and how to teach it. The whole language approach to reading instruction assumes that students are active learners and learn language in a natural way.

CHARACTERISTICS OF A CONSTRUCTIVIST APPROACH TO LANGUAGE ARTS

Since humans learn language without formal instruction, many language experts believe that the best approach to language development is through natural social processes in the classroom. Advocates of a constructivist approach to language development suggest that language processes (speaking, listening, reading, and writing) be integrated so a full range of processes are used in all subject fields. Skills are to be taught as they are needed in relationship to the content. Both teaching and learning become more real and natural (Goodman, 1986). Relevance and involvement characterize the curriculum. Experiences and activities are selected on the basis of their interest and usefulness to students. Students are involved because experiences are participatory. Whenever possible, students make real choices concerning the processes they use (Goodman, 1986).

HOW ARE THE LANGUAGE ARTS TAUGHT?

Language itself has no natural content. Thus, when teachers provide language arts instruction, they must use content from subject fields, such as science and social studies. Skills must be taught as they are needed. It is for this reason that *whole language* programs attempt to explore reading and writing in a natural way. In most school districts teachers rely on the following to facilitate the teaching of language arts:

- Core literary works identified by a school or district to provide common cultural experience
- Use of language arts to interrelate curriculum fields; skill instruction applied to all curricula—whole language programs may be utilized
- Informal use of language in all subject fields
- District-developed goals for each language arts component

- District or state recommendations for the allocation of time devoted to language arts instruction
- Basal reading textbooks for print material
- Magazines, newspapers, schedules, and game and model directions
- Content field textbooks

INTEGRATION OF EXPERIENCE AND CURRICULUM

To integrate the child's experiences and facilitate language learning, teachers need to draw upon the child's cultural life. If a child has no one to relate to—in the textbooks, peer group, or teacher model—interest in learning will be nil. The teacher's task is to find ways to enable each child to contribute information, stories, and interests and build these elements into the language arts program.

Integration of experience also has another meaning. In the elementary school, subject fields are *melded*, even though we still talk about teaching science, math, and history. Students learn more efficiently if experiences fit and build upon each other rather than if the experiences are compartmentalized. Since language is used in all of the subject fields, language is taught throughout the school day. Students need to learn the special language of math *(subtrahend, minuend, difference)* and the special language of social studies *(interdependence, migration, democracy)*. Although we may schedule a time for creative writing, we teach writing skills in every subject. Reading can be taught while using the social studies textbook, reading cartoons in a magazine, playing games, or watching filmstrips.

When students interview others as part of their social studies lesson, they are accomplishing both language objectives and social studies objectives. When students describe a science experiment, they may be reasoning deductively for science, but once again they are also languaging and learning to write records. The use of data-gathering tools in the disciplines work naturally to integrate those subject fields with the language arts. In Chapter 7, Greg Thomas's fifth graders were investigating the cultural beliefs of the New England colonists. The students observed colonial art work to determine the colonists' cultural beliefs. To perform their tasks they had to share and communicate information, they had to read texts, and they had to write a report. Thomas was integrating instruction in language arts, social studies, and art education.

In Chapter 7 there was another example in Sara Garcia's classroom. Garcia's students were studying the importance of exercising regularly. Review what the students learned, and you will find the integration of language arts, mathematics, science, social studies, health, and physical education.

Integration is achieved through the use of unit teaching with the unit related to the overall curriculum theme. Units allow content fields to be integrated in meaningful ways. The integrated unit of study is a characteristic of whole language teaching.

Relevance and *involvement* characterize the curriculum. Experiences and activities are selected on the basis of their interest and usefulness to students. Students are involved because experiences are participatory. Whenever possible, students make real choices concerning the processes they use (Goodman, 1986).

Learning centers are primarily focused on conceptional learning. Language processes are featured and integrated. Rarely are skills isolated in the centers. The centers fit the ongoing unit(s) of the whole program.

Materials for instruction include a wide range of resources. Both fiction and nonfiction books are used. Workbooks and programmed materials do not drive the program. The word fit is extremely important when considering learning materials. The materials need to be appropriate to the unit and to the students. Materials should be interesting and challenging.

Heterogeneous grouping is used most of the time. As we saw in Greg Thomas's classroom (Chapter 7), students may be grouped because of interest in a topic, task, or problem. Students may also be placed in a cooperative work group, as Sara Garcia did for writing personal letters (Chapter 7). Although heterogeneous grouping is typical of the whole language classroom, students may also be grouped as special needs arise. The important point is that *grouping is purposeful and changes as the purpose changes*. The following element will illustrate this.

Differentiation of instruction means to recognize individual needs and to provide instruction based on those needs or variations. Individualization does not necessarily mean that teaching becomes a one-to-one situation in the classroom. In practical terms it usually means that students are grouped in small clusters to improve instruction.

Our fictional second-grade teacher Mary Hogan detected from individual conferences that some of her students were having difficulty sequencing events in the stories they were reading. She decided to have 10 of her students read a story out of a reader. Then Hogan suggested that they play the Sequence Game.

She asked the child at one end of the semicircle to begin to retell the story orally. Each child, in turn, was to add the next event in the story. As the story progressed around the semicircle, it was apparent that three of the students were unable to recall events in the order that they had occurred in the story.

When the game (and story) was concluded, Hogan told the students to continue reading in their own self-selected story books. The three children who had difficulty with the activity were asked to remain in the reading circle. Hogan told another story to these three students. This time she used flannel board pictures of the story, asked the three children to take turns arranging the pictures on the flannel board in the order that they had occurred in the story, *and* she used words that expressed the sequence of time *(before, then, next, after)*. Using the tangible pictures and understanding the language concepts, the three children were now successful. Since they now understood what was expected of them, Hogan had the students return to their own reading.

FEATURES OF EFFECTIVE LANGUAGE ARTS PROGRAMS

The use of language in the classroom must be the primary concern of teachers. Through language we express our feelings and ideas and discover what others have expressed. Language facilitates access to knowledge and helps students prepare for a fulfilling life. Effective language arts programs emphasize an oral language program with activities to help students develop fluency in language. The program should encourage all students to express themselves. The oral language program should be integrated with reading and writing.

Research Findings: Language Learning Opportunities

Arreaga-Mayer and Perdomo-Rivera (1996) studied both regular and English as a Second Language classes to determine language learning opportunities provided to at-risk students. The researchers discovered that in both environments teachers rarely focused on language development activities. Emphasis was on whole class instruction and individual seatwork.

There should be an emphasis on the enjoyment of *literature*. Literacy should go beyond mechanical ability. Students can gain important societal values by being exposed to significant literary works as they read about value conflicts and dilemmas faced by others.

There also needs to be an emphasis on *thinking processes* versus a narrow skill-based program. Students should read meaningful contents from literary works and from the content fields.

A *writing program* should help students create, revise, edit, and share their ideas and feelings. Just as students should gain fluency in speaking, they should also be fluent in the use of language to express themselves through writing.

The total school program should develop students' *pride* in their correct use of the conventions: spelling, punctuation, capitalization, and handwriting.

Personalizing Instruction

Mary Hogan let her students know that she cared about them. By personalizing the lesson, Hogan communicated that three of the students needed "teacher" time. Students in Hogan's classroom learned to be unselfish because they were accustomed to receiving the attention of the teacher when they had special needs.

Decision Making

Another element important to the differentiation of instruction is the idea of personal choice. There ought to be occasions during the school day when students may choose how to learn. Mary Hogan accomplished this with the design of optional learning centers. Since objectives can be accomplished in a variety of ways, Hogan arranged an array of learning experiences, all related to the same objective. Students had to make decisions about how they would meet the objective.

Hogan was not an indulgent teacher, and she did not believe that learning experiences should be unstructured; however, she recognized the advantage of student decision making, and whenever possible she provided opportunities for student choice.

Peer Tutoring

By teaching students to accept responsibility to help others, teachers can extend the concept of individualization in the classroom. The pairing of students must be done with a great deal of insight so a reciprocal relationship exists between tutor and tutee, each recognizing the advantage of the helping relationship. The primary advantage of peer tutoring is that individual rates for learning can be accommodated. Peer tutoring for mainstreamed students is a meaningful way to provide individualized assistance. (See the discussion of mainstreaming in this chapter.)

By acting as tutor, students learn to program instruction step by step for a friend; in so doing they become proficient themselves. However, teachers must be careful to monitor the instructional process to verify that instruction is modeled appropriately; if the step-by-step plans of the tutor are not correct, then the teacher must take time to develop the process for the tutor.

An expectation in peer tutoring is that every student will have the opportunity to be both tutor and tutee. In the normal course of events this should happen as students become proficient in evaluating their own skills to determine whether they can give assistance or need to receive help. Once again, teachers need to monitor individual proficiency and ensure that every student has the opportunity to play both roles.

INTERACTIVE INSTRUCTION

Communication involves more than one person. We talk with others, and we write for others. Although reading and writing may be solo activities, we pursue them so others may take advantage of what we know, so we may learn from others, and so we may enjoy literature and dramatics. Although sometimes teachers rue the fact that students can talk, in actuality speech only improves through practice with others. Speech practice must be planned just as reading skill development is planned.

Since students do not view peers as authority figures, they often learn more from peers than they do from teachers. Picture second graders stretched out on the floor as an example of the contagious nature of reading in groups. At first just one student will curl up on the rug with a library book; soon other readers will arrive, arranging themselves in comfortable positions on the floor!

Plan for Interaction

Interactive language experiences need to be planned. By grouping students or allowing them to work in a partner situation, students will stimulate each other to accomplish routine chores, homework, or projects they would never accomplish working alone. Since language

activities are basically skill activities, they need to be practiced. The teacher's role is to choose activities that are worthwhile and provide appropriate practice opportunities. For example, if students need practice in oral communication, the teacher needs to choose activities that will allow students to do the following:

- Hold conversations and discussions
- Give informal and formal talks or reports
- Participate in dramatic activities
- Participate in choral recitations

If students need practice in written communication, the teacher can choose among the following activities:

- Write notes, reports, outlines
- Write letters
- Write stories and plays
- Write summaries
- Write advertisements and publicity
- Write diaries, descriptions, histories

The rationale for interactive instruction is consistent with research reported in Chapter 4, that more student participation and effort leads to more active learning behavior. Oral communication has two components: listening and speaking. Since both need to be practiced, group work is essential. Active learning behavior can be translated into active engaged time in academic tasks.

READING INSTRUCTION

Greg Thomas began the reading period by picking up the book *Old Yeller* by Fred Gipson (1956). The students instantly became quiet. Thomas had begun the book several days earlier, and the students were thoroughly engrossed with the story about the big, ugly, yellow dog who came to live with Travis and his mother and brother.

After about 10 minutes of reading aloud to the students, Thomas wrote the following on the chalkboard:

- determination (yes)
- pluck (yes)
- cowardice (no)
- guts (yes)
- faint-hearted (no)

Next Thomas turned to the students and asked, "What do you think I'm thinking about?"

Several students asked if he was thinking about Old Yeller. Thomas smiled and began to write another list on the board.

- bravery ( )
- fearfulness ( )
- valor ( )
- timidity ( )

"How should I label these words? Yes or no?" The students responded appropriately.

"Can you tell me what I'm thinking about?" asked Thomas.

The students immediately began to talk about the dog, Old Yeller, and how he had demonstrated courage and bravery in the story in so many different ways. Thomas confirmed that he was thinking about the concept of courage.

Next Thomas asked the students about their feelings and emotions as they listened to the story. He asked them how they thought Travis felt about his dog. He encouraged the children to talk about their own pets and ways animals demonstrate courage. ("What are some examples of courageous acts?" "What do you consider cowardly acts?") In this way he made the students consider positive and negative examples of the concept *courage.*

"What were you thinking about when I put the first list on the board?" asked Thomas.

The students responded: "I thought about my own dog." "I knew you were thinking about Old Yeller." "I wasn't sure what 'pluck' meant, but then when I saw the word 'guts' I got the idea." "The second list really helped me."

Next Thomas asked, "What makes a person act bravely? Do you think all people are brave?"

The students expressed different opinions. Then Thomas said he had two very special books in the classroom for them to read over the next several days: *Snow Treasure* by Marie McSwigan (1942) and *Three Without Fear* by Robert C. Du Soe (1947). Both books, he told them, were about children. "How do these children feel, and how do they act? See if you can find sentences that describe the character of the children in the story. Try to decide if these stories could really have happened. Compare the characters in these stories with the characters in *Old Yeller.*" (Thomas turned and wrote the assignment on the chalkboard.)

The students selected their books, and Thomas then divided them into small groups of four. The stu-

dents sat together and helped each other, if needed. Thomas also encouraged the students to stop now and then to discuss different passages that revealed the emotions and characters of the persons in the stories.

As the students read, Thomas observed them. Sometimes he would discuss a particular passage with a student. After about 30 minutes, Thomas stopped the class and began a discussion. He asked them if their stories were real. The class then talked about realistic fiction. Thomas had several children select and read aloud short passages from their books to demonstrate emotions and characters. He told them that the story about the Norwegian children in *Snow Treasure* actually did happen. He explained that the book was an example of historical fiction. He helped them recall other historical fiction books they had read or listened to, such as a book about Abe Lincoln. He asked the students to compare realistic fiction and historical fiction.

Then the class discussed characterization. Finally Thomas asked the students to once again think about synonyms and antonyms for courage.

The next day Thomas would have the students continue their reading, and in their small groups he would ask them to:

- Write a short paragraph to tell others the plot of the story.
- Describe the locale of the story.

He would also sit with different groups and have them read aloud so he could see if they were reading meaningfully and understanding what they were reading.

Now let's look at the components of Thomas's reading lesson.

- Whole group listening (Thomas read aloud.)
- Whole group concept attainment lesson (courage)
- Whole class discussion of Old Yeller using concept of courage
- Small group reading using a class assignment to focus the reading on character and mood/feeling/tone
- Teacher monitoring—diagnosing, providing assistance as needed
- Whole class discussion about the books focused on assignment—some oral reading to prove understanding

The time block used by Thomas was about 70 minutes. Very likely he would follow up the reading period with spelling, using words from the literature period.

Anderson and Lapp (1992) identify four types of literary analyses that children can perform:

1. *Analysis of character:* Using inference from story, students identify what characters value, inferred actions, and feelings.
2. *Analysis of setting:* How does setting affect actions and characterization?
3. *Analysis of mood/feeling/tone:* What was the author's intent? Is the book serious? Humorous? Historical? Realistic? Fanciful? What gives the author away?
4. *Analysis of story pattern:* What is the plot? Who is narrating the story? Is there a special theme—purpose?

Tompkins and Hoskisson (1995) suggest that students can learn how the plot is developed by authors by studying four components:

1. A problem
2. Roadblocks
3. The high point
4. The solution

They also suggest a very simple means for students to begin the analysis through the clustering of happenings at the beginning (introduction) of the story, the middle (development) and the end (resolution). Using a web approach the authors create three spokes; each spoke is marked—beginning, middle, end. Then the events are clustered around each of the three spokes.

WHY IS READING IMPORTANT?

Reading instruction or the lack of instruction is purposeful. Throughout the world literacy skills typically have been used to accomplish national purposes. Reading ability is important because it contributes to societal and individual goals. Economic competence is directly related to the ability to use written information for vocational training, technical applications, professional development, and personal interests. Reading contributes to thinking ability and stimulates the individual to create, critique, and develop intellectually. It is an extremely important aspect of life. People read for a variety of reasons: to obtain information, to solve problems, for personal satisfaction, for recreation, to satisfy curiosity, and to protect their safety, health, and interests.

WHAT IS READING?

Reading is a comprehension activity. It is a receptive form of communication. Listening, which is also a receptive form of communication and a comprehension activity, requires the listener to translate speech into thought. In reading, the reader must decode print into speech and decode speech into thought. Thus the reader must perform two different activities simultaneously (Moffett and Wagner, 1983). Reading is difficult because it is dependent on visual processing as well as comprehension. Researchers do not know how the reader joins the two functions.

In the teaching of reading, teachers are teaching the communication process. Reading instruction is dependent on oral language proficiency and experiential background, along with the self-confidence and motivation of the beginning reader. To understand reading as a communication process, the beginning reader must take an active role in the learning process and be willing to take risks.

To learn to read, the beginner must discriminate between letters that often look alike. Therefore, it is important that the reader discover the critical attributes that discriminate between these letters. It is almost impossible for a teacher to tell students what to look for in order to discriminate between various letters, such as *b* and *d*. The student must be sophisticated enough to know what distinctive features to look for.

Smith (1978) differentiated between learning to read and fluent reading. The beginning reader must first learn to discriminate the critical features and translate them into an identification system of letters and then into a given word name. The fluent reader discriminates the critical features and moves immediately to the word name or word category. Since the beginning reader must learn to identify words and store them in a memory bank in order to make sense out of what is being read, the process of making sense is often tedious. It is for this reason that the beginning reader must be motivated to learn to read and have the necessary self-confidence to proceed with a trying task. Reading materials for the beginning reader should use short predictable sentences so the memory system is not burdened unnecessarily. Beginning reading is more difficult than fluent reading because in learning to read one must identify words before attaining meaning; the fluent reader obtains meaning directly from the visual features.

In explaining the reading process, Smith, a psycholinguist, states that immediate word identification and comprehension are accomplished by the fluent reader by using the skill of redundancy or alternative sources of information. The skilled reader reduces the number of letters or word possibilities that could exist in a given context. The reader relates the possibilities to the frequency of use of words in a specific sequence, on prior knowledge, or to the words surrounding the key word.

A frequent controversy in the teaching of reading has to do with whether a meaning approach or a skills approach is more effective for the beginning reader. Those who favor the skills approach usually advocate an emphasis on phonics, claiming that phonics instruction speeds up the word identification process for the beginner. Psycholinguists contend, however, that the skill focus tends to fractionate the reading process, thereby interfering with comprehension (Carroll, 1978).

APPROACHES TO READING INSTRUCTION

Silent Reading

Silent reading has a variety of purposes. It is usually performed during the teaching of reading when students are asked to read to accomplish a very specific objective. The silent reading time is usually preceded by a short discussion. New vocabulary words are presented during an oral discussion, and then the teacher asks the students to read in order to clarify, predict, understand, or determine sequence.

Oral Reading

After a passage has been read silently, the teacher may ask students to read the same passage orally. During oral reading the teacher verifies understanding by the way the passage is read. Expression, intonation, and rhythm are practiced during oral reading. Sometimes the oral reading is used as the evidence to prove or verify what the students were looking for in their silent reading. Listening to others read and following the text as others read are also objectives for the oral reading session.

Work/Study

One of the most advantageous ways to teach reading skills occurs when reading is the tool for obtaining information, such as reading maps, charts, or graphs, and for problem solving. As students progress through school, work/study reading becomes more important and more closely tied to school success. The ability to read within different subject fields and for a variety of purposes needs to be taught and practiced throughout the school day. During work/study reading time, students should be taught to do the following:

- Adjust speed of reading to purpose and subject
- Locate information using a variety of source materials
- Extract and interpret information from a variety of sources (charts, maps, cartoons)
- Compile and organize information using a variety of sources

Recreational Reading

Reading for recreational purposes should be like the frosting on the cake. If students are to develop lifelong interests in reading, their enthusiasm must be cultivated by providing a variety of reading materials to satisfy diverse interests. Students need to have the opportunity to share with others something that they have particularly enjoyed.

Even recreational reading needs to be modeled. If students are not accustomed to observing adults enjoying reading, they will not choose to read. In some classrooms teachers set aside a special time for recreational reading and proceed to model reading. In one classroom where the author visited, the teacher chose a selection and began to chuckle as she read. After about five minutes the teacher asked the class if she could share something funny. The teacher read the amusing passage to the class and then asked the students if there was anyone who would like to share something that he or she had enjoyed. This procedure became a common happening in the classroom, and as a result the students looked forward to their recreational reading period.

 Teaching Hint: Encouraging Reading

Krashen (1996, p. 5) recommends that schools and districts should encourage free voluntary reading.

The most effective bridge from low levels of reading ability and higher levels is free voluntary reading, or pleasure reading.

How Is Reading Taught?

Reading Readiness

Before charts or books are used to teach reading, the teacher's first task is to determine whether or not the child is ready for formal reading instruction. Readiness has different meanings to different people. Some believe that readiness is indicated when the child expresses the interest or desire to read. However, interest and motivation are not the prime determiners of readiness.

Physical factors such as the ability to discriminate visual differences and the ability to hear likenesses and differences affect learning to read. Eye-hand coordination affects reading. Understanding directions and differentiation of right from left are important because print is directional; the child who has difficulty with directions will have similar problems in learning to read.

Children unable to follow instructions or with poor memory retention or attention spans will not have the mental maturity needed for reading. Social and emotional factors also affect learning to read. The child who cannot sit still, lacks self-confidence, or cannot work cooperatively with others may have difficulty during reading.

Experiential factors may affect success in reading. Awareness of environmental signs is an example of the background experience needed by children learning to read. If the child does not perceive the difference between a stop sign and a school crossing sign, he or she is not ready to read. The child with limited concepts and information will have difficulty understanding reading textbooks.

The assessment of readiness for language arts is an important teacher task. If the teacher judges that the student lacks readiness for instruction, then it is the teacher's responsibility to create learning experiences to develop readiness systematically in those areas in which the student lacks the prerequisite capacities. The student may need activities to develop visual or auditory discrimination, work habits, vocabulary, or concepts. It is also important that the teacher plan a conference with parents to prepare them to assist in the process.

The teacher's prime responsibility is for the classroom itself. The environment should encourage literacy: use pictures, open-ended questions, objects to manipulate and talk about, book jackets, or pop-up books. Literally everything you can think of to encourage talk and interest in reading and writing is fair game to create a literate environment.

Phonemic Awareness

The 26 letters of the alphabet represent about 44 *phonemes*. Children need to learn to identify (name) the letters. By the time the child enters kindergarten, most can recognize the letters in their own names. However, if the child does not associate the letters with appropriate reading and writing experiences, the letter names will not facilitate learning to read.

Because the phonemes represent over 500 spellings, phonetic analysis will facilitate the reading process only about half of the time. As a consequence the complicated rules concerning phonetic analysis often confuse more than they enhance learning to read. The word *cat* is often used as an example to help children develop phonemic awareness. Yet the letter *c* represents three different sounds: *k* as in cat, *s* as in circus, and paired with an *h* it has a *ch* sound as in church. Primary teachers cannot depend on phonics as a sole means for teaching reading yet it is an important strategy for teaching reading.

Experience Charts

Ricardo, a first grader, brought his hamster to school. It was in a cage, and the teacher asked all of the children to sit on the rug in the front of the room so Ricardo could tell about his hamster. But Ricardo was too shy, so the teacher said to the class, "Boys and girls, why don't you ask Ricardo questions about his hamster?"

The children asked questions and learned that the hamster's name was Pepe, that the hamster was gentle and clean, and that he ate lettuce, carrots, cabbage, and peanuts. The teacher added to the information by explaining to the students that hamsters needed to be kept in metal cages because they were able to gnaw their way out of a wooden cage. After talking and watching the hamster for several minutes, the teacher suggested that the class compose a story about Ricardo's hamster. The students readily agreed, and the story was written on the chalk board.

Teacher: Who came to school today?
Student: Pepe came to school today.

How can a teacher determine if a child is ready to read?

Teacher: Who is Pepe?
Student: Pepe is a hamster.
Teacher: What do hamsters eat?
Student: Hamsters eat lettuce, carrots, cabbage, and peanuts.
Teacher: What else do we know about hamsters?
Student: Hamsters are gentle and clean.

The story written on the board was ready for the students to read.

Pepe came to school today.
Pepe is a hamster.
Hamsters eat lettuce, carrots, cabbage, and peanuts.
Hamsters are gentle and clean.

The children took turns reading the story. If they had difficulty, the teacher would prompt them with the original questions that motivated the story. ("What else do we know about hamsters?") Since the children had just experienced the story, they were able to read it easily.

The teacher rewrote the story on a piece of tagboard and hung it on a chart rack for use during reading and science throughout the semester. The teacher also placed a picture drawn by the students (she could have used a picture from a magazine) on the experience chart to help the students recall "Pepe, the Hamster."

Literature-Based Approach

The California State Department of Education *English-Language Arts Framework* (1987, pp. 6–7) contains the following discussion of the use of literature in reading instruction:

> If the end of English-language arts programs is developing a literate, thinking society, then surely the means to that end must be devising for students meaningful encounters with the most effective sources of human expression. In its capacity to move the human spirit in any age, to involve students and motivate learning with its appeal to universal feelings and needs, and to elevate common experiences to uncommon meaning, the language of great, classic literature speaks most eloquently to readers and writers.

Simply stated, the purpose of a literature approach to the teaching of reading is to develop students' appreciation and enjoyment of a variety of literature. Through literature students learn about cultures and societal values. For this reason it is important that students experience the literature of all cultural groups. Literature, as advocated in the California State Frame-

work, can be the basis and integrating core of the total language arts program. Thomas's lesson on *Old Yeller* is an example of how all the components are taught through the use of literature.

Content Field Instruction

Since the language of content field textbooks often poses a problem to elementary students, these textbooks have a great deal of value for reading instruction. The main purpose of the content field text is to convey information, but since the vocabulary may represent conceptual understanding in an academic discipline, students may have difficulty obtaining meaning. Therefore, it is essential that the teacher introduce the specialized vocabulary and verify conceptual understanding before students attempt to read.

In her science unit about rocks, Mary Hogan intended to use content field textbooks for reading instruction one or two days per week. In this way she would teach reading meaningfully and help the students gain information in an academic discipline. Her students had explored the texture of rocks and had talked about how rocks felt and about their varied colors. Now she wanted them to learn how rocks are made and how they change.

Hogan had copies of the Holmes et al. (1979) text *Gateways to Science*, Level 3, which had a chapter about rocks that she considered useful. She had her students find the correct page and look at the illustration of the Grand Canyon. She asked them if they knew how rocks were formed. During the discussion, Hogan asked the students what they would like to know about rocks. She wrote their questions on the board. Then she introduced the key vocabulary used in the chapter. She used the rock samples in the classroom for concrete examples. Her teaching strategy was direct instruction (review Chapter 6). After reading the textbook material, the students worked in cooperative heterogeneous groups to answer their own questions from the reading. The lesson ended with the groups sharing their responses.

Language Experience Approach

The language experience approach to reading instruction is based on the idea that what you can think and say, you can read. For example, the students who wrote the experience story about the hamster will be able to read that story because they just composed it. The story can be used for reading instruction with a group of students or with an individual child. The students in that first-grade classroom could be asked to draw pictures about Pepe, the hamster, and then write personal stories about him.

The students' stories could be taped or dictated to an aide. The aide (or teacher) will type the story for the student, who will then practice reading it aloud. Teachers need to exercise care that in the typing process they do not change a student's story to make it perfect.

The language experience approach is quite motivating for students since they are reading about their own experiences. This approach has been particularly successful with urban students and students with reading problems because the approach is more meaningful and based on the student's own vocabulary and interests. The major advantage of the language experience approach is that it integrates all of the language arts components. Teachers who utilize the language experience approach usually consider themselves *whole language teachers.*

Kinesthetic Approach

This approach uses the language experience approach to reading. Each child has a dictionary box for use during story writing. During the writing period, the teacher circulates around the room. When a student raises his or her hand asking for assistance with a word, the teacher comes over and writes the requested word on a slip of paper. The child traces the word with the index finger and then turns the slip of paper over and writes the word from memory (if the child cannot do so, the word is retraced). Next the word is used in the story. After using the word, the student files the word in the dictionary box for future use.

Reading is taught by using the student's own stories. Spelling is based on the personal words in the student's dictionary box. All of the language components are integrated using the student's experience stories.

Individualized Approach

Another particularly motivating approach to reading instruction is an individualized reading strategy. By providing for a wide range of choices and interests and having many books on hand, the teacher enables the students to self-select what they want to read. This approach assumes that students will naturally select what they are able to read. However, this is not always true, and teachers do need to provide some guidance to students in the selection of an appropriate book.

Veatch (1959) suggests the "rule of thumb" approach. Students are told to scan a page in their chosen book. For each word that they cannot read they are to raise one finger, beginning with the little finger. If they get to the thumb while on the same page, then the book is too difficult and another book should be chosen.

In the individualized approach, the teacher meets with each student individually to check comprehension and skill needs. Skill instruction is usually taught in a small group as the teacher identifies common learning needs. Students progress at their own rate; they do not have to cover any specific number of books. Since they choose their own books, interest is usually high. Students will read individually two or three days per week, confer with the teacher at least once during the week, and have a skill lesson at least once a week.

Teachers differ greatly in the ways in which the individualized approach is implemented. Some teachers individualize every day; others use literature books as a group activity and/or basal reading texts in conjunction with an individualized program.

Record keeping is the most important aspect of the individualized approach. Each child keeps a personal record of what he or she has read plus comments about what he liked or didn't like about the books. The teacher keeps notes of their conferences. The child's reading folder could be turned into a reading/writing portfolio with the student creating his or her own stories.

Basal Reader Approach

Many teachers use the basal reader approach for the following reasons:

- A great variety of text series is available.
- The texts provide for a sequential development of vocabulary and skills.
- The teacher manuals provide assistance in the organization of the reading program.
- The manuals guide the teacher in framing key questions to motivate reading and provide assistance in the assessment of skills and the evaluation of skill mastery.

Because of their ease of use, basal readers are appreciated by teachers. However, the basal text should not be considered the only way in which reading instruction is to be provided in the classroom. The basal reader approach may be combined with any other system.

The basal reader approach has been criticized because authors tend to write for a typical student. As a consequence, the text may be unappealing to minority youngsters, rural students, or other special interest groups. Critics also note that the carefully controlled vocabulary typical of the basal text often causes the writing pattern to be stilted.

WHICH APPROACH IS BEST?

Research has failed to demonstrate which approach to the teaching of reading is superior or more efficient than the others. Rarely does a classroom teacher use a pure form of one specific approach. Most teachers use aspects of several approaches or a combination of approaches in the course of a week. In many classrooms literature is the basis for instruction at least two days per week, content field instruction occurs one or two days per week, and the basal reader is used one or two days per week. Teachers who consider themselves constructivist teachers allow language to permeate the curriculum throughout the school day.

ACTIVITIES TO ENCOURAGE READING

To encourage reading in the classroom and to facilitate the understanding of printed materials, the following activities are suggested:

Reading to Students

By listening to good readers, students develop their own interest in reading. When a teacher reads an adventure story to students and needs to continue the story over several days, it is not uncommon for students to ask if they may borrow the book and read it on their own. By modeling oral reading techniques, teachers teach pronunciation, intonation, punctuation, enthusiasm, and the fun of reading.

Storytelling

Telling a story without a book is a marvelous art that captures the imagination and stimulates interest in stories. After telling the story it is important to ask students: What did you like? What was the plot? How did the story begin? End? Which character did you like best? Why?

Telling the story using a flannel board or puppets or other objects increases the interest in the story.

Readers' Theater

Readers' theater is a technique for having students assume the part of a character in a story. The students read the story precisely as it is, creating the mood and characterization through their voices and expressions. The narrator's part may be read by the teacher or a student. Readers' theater is appropriate at all grade levels.

Listening Centers

A listening library in the classroom provides for the individualization needed by students and allows the teacher to create diverse listening experiences. For example, the teacher may even purchase tapes in a variety of dialects and styles to enrich students' listening experiences (Moffett and Wagner, 1983). Tapes can also be used in conjunction with library books. Students often enjoy reading a story as they listen to it. By listening to a story read well, students improve their own oral reading technique.

Recreational Reading

A supplemental library in the classroom with books that cater to students' diverse interests and reading levels serves to reinforce the reading habit. Many teachers create informal areas of the room to encourage students to relax with a book. Beanbag cushions, large pillows, or a thick rug appeal to young students.

Oral Reading

Silent reading is improved when students have the opportunity to perform orally and listen to themselves read. Oral reading can be performed in the small reading group after silent reading. Sometimes it is a good idea to allow students to rehearse what they are

Teacher Research

Stachoviak (1996) used writing experiences to help kindergarten children learn letter names and sounds. She introduced writing by telling the children that drawing pictures was one way to tell a story; another way was through print. Using ideas from Writers' Workshop, the children wrote stories and shared them with each other. Inventive spelling was used. Stachoviak taught key words. The children became confident in their writing skills and learned the letter names.

going to read orally. Each student can practice with a partner who offers suggestions for improving the oral reading performance.

Writers' Workshop Stories

Students enjoy sharing their own stories with their classmates. The authors can read their stories aloud and ask friends to read them aloud. The students' "published" books can be used for silent recreational reading.

ORGANIZING THE READING PROGRAM

CLASSROOM ENVIRONMENT AND CLASSROOM MANAGEMENT

The learning environment of the classroom affects students' ability to attend to instruction. A classroom that is too warm may make students lethargic. A room that is noisy may affect concentration. A classroom that is cluttered with distracting displays may make it difficult for students to settle down and study. Space, temperature, ventilation, aromas, orderliness, and light may influence learning and students' adjustment to instruction.

The arrangement of furniture and the placement of materials are important considerations in preparing to manage reading instruction. For example, the teacher must decide where instruction will take place. Will the students move their chairs to a designated place for instruction, or will the teacher move from group to group? If the teacher moves, will students be seated throughout the school day in their designated reading group? If the students move, there needs to be a space in the classroom large enough to accommodate the materials for reading group instruction. Young students need a flannel board, charts, and other motivating devices; a chalkboard will probably be needed for all age groups.

The arrangement of learning centers, if they are used, must be considered in the overall planning of the reading program. Accessibility of the learning stations and availability of electrical outlets, if needed, should be preplanned.

The location of books, pencils, paper, and workbooks should be considered to be certain that students can avail themselves of these materials as needed. A typical classroom management consideration is whether or not students should sharpen pencils during reading instruction. If pencil sharpening is distracting during reading, then what alternative decisions will be needed to provide for emergency situations?

Appropriate utilization of time is a major consideration in the reading program. The minutes used for organizational or procedural purposes as children change places for group instruction can detract measurably from the achievement of reading goals. For this reason, movement patterns and classroom rules should be jointly decided and agreed upon by teacher and students. Care must be taken to provide for the physical movement needs of primary children. Perhaps there should be a place in the classroom where restless energy can be expended. A place in the classroom to stretch out or curl up may be necessary for restless students.

GROUPING PATTERNS

Cooperative Groups

Group investigation is an example of cooperative group work. There is a great deal of evidence that students' self-esteem increases when they work in small cooperative groups based on special interests, problems, or tasks. Students working in such groups also achieve higher academic performance and develop a positive attitude about school. Cooperative grouping improves intergroup relations and facilitates ethnic and cultural understanding. By grouping students heterogeneously, students learn to use language with their peers and take responsibility for helping their peers learn. Cooperative groups are particularly effective for teaching out of content textbooks and for teaching literature.

A variety of methods exists for using cooperative groups. (Research on grouping has been cited in Chapter 3.) Group investigation is one strategy (see Chapter 7). Another strategy, particularly effective in reading and mathematics, is to make team (group) members responsible for each other's learning. Called *Student Teams Achievement Decisions* (STAD; Slavin, 1983), this strategy involves team members who help each other and quiz each other. The group has not finished its task(s) until it is certain that all its members understand what it was they were to learn. Slavin recommends that a quiz be given when the teams believe they have completed their learning task(s). Teammates may not help each other on the quiz. A team score is computed based upon how much each student's performance has improved from his or her previous quiz score.

Another cooperative learning strategy is the *Jigsaw* method, first designed by Aronson (1978) and refined by Slavin, in which group members are each assigned an individual task that contributes to the whole group task or problem. This strategy, particularly effective in social studies or science work, is similar to group investigation. Jigsaw could be used quite effectively in a literature investigation in which each group member is responsible for finding particular evidence of characterization, author's purpose, or effect of setting.

Skill Grouping

Should reading skills be taught? Yes, but they should be taught as they are needed in the integrated language arts program. Skills are not taught in isolation.

Grouping students for skill instruction is a means to individualize the reading program to meet special needs as they arise. Typically, students are flexibly grouped for a limited period of time when a skill need arises. An effective reading lesson can be provided to several students at the same time if student needs and skills are matched.

Teacher observation, informal assessment, or students' questions can be used to facilitate the grouping of students for skill instruction. The advantage of doing this on occasion is that direct instruction can be provided in an area of need, and students who are proficient in the skill are not bored with unnecessary instruction.

WRITING INSTRUCTION

Writing may be the most difficult language arts component to develop. Students typically have a large listening vocabulary but a much smaller speaking vocabulary. The child is dependent on the speaking vocabulary for written expression. For this reason, the speaking component should be emphasized. Students who do not use correct sentence patterns or expanded sentences in speech will have difficulty in writing.

Writing involves both composition and transcription. Composition represents selecting and ordering words into a logical pattern for self-expression. To compose effectively, students need to understand the relationship of words to thoughts. Composition is not dependent on transcription; one can compose a story by orally recording it. When the kindergarten child tells the story of his or her picture, oral composition is occurring. When the story is transcribed on paper, the

Research Findings: Skill Teaching

Teaching students skills when needed helps make texts more comprehensible. However, skill teaching should *not* be the focal point of the reading program because:

- The grammatical system of English is too complex.
- Phonics rules are too complicated, have too many exceptions, and frequently are not useful.
- There are too many vocabulary words for students to learn; vocabulary knowledge is acquired most reliably by seeing a new word used in the context of a story (Krashen, 1996, pp. 9–14).

student is transforming speech into graphic symbols. It is the transcription process that is sometimes difficult for the student because it involves using a pencil or crayon and writing legibly. Moffett and Wagner (1983) note that written speech differs from oral speech: When writing down a composition, the individual can revise thoughts, whereas oral composition requires recalling and retelling.

For some time now, both educators and the public have been concerned that we are producing nonwriters as a consequence of assignments that require multiple choice selections, short answers, and worksheet responses. Perhaps an even more critical problem is what Graves and Stuart (1985, p. 31) describe as component exercises, which "squeeze writing out of the school day and convince children that reading and writing are a bore." Graves and Stuart contend that students' self-confidence is eroded because of an over emphasis on skills—an insistence on perfect sentences, spelling, grammar, and handwriting—right from the start.

Kucer and Rhodes (1986) state that reading and writing are parallel techniques that need to be taught as "meaning-making" processes. This is the whole language perspective. Students should be helped to use their background knowledge and experiences, as well as contextual cues, to communicate meaning. Kucer and Rhodes demonstrate that proficient readers and writers are aware that meanings are structured in a coherent way. Whereas the less proficient reader-writer focuses on individual words and spelling, the skillful reader-writer perceives how things fit together.

HOW IS WRITING TAUGHT?

The purposes of the writing program include the following:

1. The development of functional writing to communicate ideas
2. The development of creative writing to express thoughts
3. Skill development in the mechanics of writing

These three purposes are developed through student activities such as journal writing, letter writing, creative writing, informational writing, record keeping, note taking, outlining, research, and proofreading. Reading and writing should be taught together; what you write, you read. (The processes are separated in this text for presentation purposes only.)

The writing process has five basic phases: prewriting, drafting, responding and revising, editing, and sharing.

Prewriting

During this phase the classroom should provide an environment that stimulates ideas and provides opportunities for students to interact and talk informally with each other about their ideas. Sometimes a motivating story, film, picture, or activity may provide the seed to stimulate creativity and composition.

Drafting

This is the first phase of composing on paper. The writer is confronted with the task of deciding, What do I want to say? The writing program should help students develop *fluency*, the ability to use appropriate language with relative ease. The writer should be concerned with writing down what Kucer and Rhodes (1986) called "chunks" of meaning. Concerns should not be focused on form, grammar, handwriting, or spelling.

Responding

This is an optional phase that may be done in conjunction with the revision stage. In this phase the young writer may share what is written with one or more others to gain perspective and additional ideas. Graves (1987) advocates a low-keyed and nonevaluative writing conference to help students talk about their writing. (The teacher should sit next to the student, not across from the student.) The teacher or a classmate merely asks, "How goes it?" The trick is to wait for a response. The writer should share what he or she has written, communicating the essence of the piece and its direction. The teacher or classmate should ultimately ask, "Do you need any help?" Help, if needed, should be in the form of ideas, scope, and sequence—not form.

Revising

In this phase the writer uses the suggestions gained in the conference or from sharing with others. It is time to rethink, rearrange, change, and refine the composition. From the sharing phase, the writer learned whether or not he or she had communicated meaning. Now the writer attempts to achieve greater clarity, emphasis, and wholeness.

Editing

The editing phase of the writing process includes the appreciation of form and the writing conventions. Here the writer examines spelling, punctuation, grammar, accuracy of information, syntax, and precision of word usage. It is often helpful for young writers to have a checklist to go over during the editing stage.

Sharing

This final phase is the icing on the cake. Classroom activities may include sharing the final product by reading it aloud with an audience, publishing the writing as a book, a bookmaking activity, class books, and creating magazines with collections of stories from several students.

Writing Activities

Writing is taught in an integrated fashion throughout the school day utilizing a variety of activities, including descriptive, creative, factual/informative, and expository writing.

Letter Writing

To enable students to recognize the importance of letter writing, personal letters and business letters should be an integral part of the writing program. Many occasions can be used to generate a letter-writing session. For example, if there is to be a school open house, students can write personal invitations to their families and friends; if a classmate is ill, students can write friendly letters. If special information is needed, students can write business letters requesting information or materials and then follow up with a thank-you note.

Teaching Hint: The Card Strategy

Kucer and Rhodes (1986, pp. 190-191) propose an interesting strategy to facilitate the writing process. Their *card strategy* has seven steps:

1. Students are given several small pieces of paper (3-by-5-inch cards would be perfect) to write down ideas for potential writing topics. Students are encouraged to talk to others to obtain ideas.
2. Students select the topic they believe has the greatest interest or potential. They save their other ideas for future use.
3. Students begin to generate ideas related to the selected topic. Each idea is written on a separate piece of paper or card. The ideas may simply be one word that suggests meaning, or a phrase, or a sentence. The idea should generate a chunk of meaning. Students should again be given an opportunity to share their idea cards with one or more others. Small groups of three students work well.
4. Now students select the idea cards they want to use and set aside the cards they are not certain are useful.
5. The students sequence the cards for use in the composition.
6. To provide more opportunity to think about the organization of the composition, each student shuffles the cards and hands them to a partner who arranges them in the order he or she think is appropriate. The partner shares his or her reasons for ordering them, and the prospective author may discuss the sequence originally conceived. This step helps students realize that ideas may be organized in a variety of ways. If desired, students may reach out to still another partner and ask for organizing ideas.
7. Using the cards as a guide, the students write their compositions. By this time the students should be aware that the cards may be flexibly utilized and are intended to suggest areas of meaning to be featured in the text.

Kucer and Rhodes suggest that the card strategy be used for a variety of writing purposes to show students that writing purpose affects the generation and structure of meaning.

The purpose of the letter, the form, punctuation, and capitalization—even the way in which a letter is folded—should be taught at the moment of need rather than as a special language lesson. Students need to learn sensitivity to the timing of letters, appropriate greetings and closings, and the amount of detail a letter should contain.

Creative Writing

Creative writing may involve writing about personal experiences or feelings or make-believe. Poems, rhymes, and stories are all appropriate. All writing that is individually derived is creative. During creative writing teachers should allow students to attend to the content of their work; they should not spoil the creative effort by insisting on correct form. When creating, students should use any words they desire, without concern for correct spelling. If students ask for assistance, the teacher can provide it by writing the desired word on a slip of paper for the student's dictionary word box or by writing the word directly into a dictionary notebook maintained by each student.

At the start of this chapter there was an example of an oral language lesson that began with literature, followed by class discussion, an art lesson, and ultimately creative writing. The students in the example have their own writing books in which they will write imaginatively about themselves and a flying machine. The creative writing will occur periodically over several weeks. After a student completes a story, the teacher will correct it. The corrections will be talked about between teacher and student. The students will not be asked to change their stories to adhere to the teacher's form; but as the students continue to write new stories in their creative writing book, their stories will naturally reflect what they have learned about punctuation, capitalization, and word usage.

Since motivation is extremely important to initiate creative writing, the first-grade teacher, whose students will be writing creatively over a period of time, will need to remotivate each time the students are to write about their flying machines. Part of the time he or she will have individual children read their stories to the class; the students will serve to motivate each other.

Writing Workshop is another way to encourage creative writing. Using this approach, each student maintains a writing folder to file stories that are in process or completed. The student may also keep a writing notebook to jot down ideas, experiences, and feelings for later use in stories. Students may meet in small writing groups to share ideas and help each other. The Kucer and Rhodes strategy works well in the small writing group. The teacher acts as a facilitator and responds to students' needs during the workshop session.

I believe that the Writing Workshop *process* is an effective means to encourage creative writing, but I caution teachers not to use the writing notebook to encourage students to write about their personal problems and/or use the workshop as a therapeutic healing device.

Note Taking

Note taking begins at the personal level to meet the needs of the individual. The notes may be used for studying purposes or, eventually, to write a report or to communicate orally to others. Young students rarely know how to take notes. The skills involved in note taking have much to do with the act of studying. For example, the note taker needs to know the following:

- Purpose/importance of the assignment or task
- Background knowledge
- Organization of the materials to be used

The significance of note taking for preserving information for future reference, or for evaluating print or nonprint information, or as a basis for future outlining, needs to be communicated to students. If students are to take notes in order to study for an examination, then the students will also need to know whether the examination will be essay, multiple choice, or true/false. If students are to use the notes for an oral report, the notes will be different than if they are to be used as evidence citations during a discussion. The purpose and the importance of the assignment must be communicated to students.

Note-taking skill may be dependent on prior knowledge and information about the topic to be researched. When Greg Thomas's students researched architecture and furniture produced during the colonial period (Chapter 7), they had to have some background experience recognizing early American furniture and architecture. The students in the furniture group also had to know that their notes would be used to develop a retrieval chart about colonial and European furniture. This knowledge would influence their research and the type of notes they would preserve.

Note taking is influenced by the nature of the materials to be used. An art history book may be organized in a different way than a science or health textbook. Students need to be alerted to the author's use of headings or questions as an organizing structure. If students are to take notes about slides they have viewed or if they are to take notes during an interview situation, they will need to have a way to judge what is important to record.

In helping students develop note-taking skills, it is important to communicate that note taking is a personal aid to learning and, as such, requires each person to develop an individual notation style.

Outlining

Students need to learn the purpose and structure of an outline. The skills identified by Taba for developing note-taking competence are useful to help students make the discriminations necessary for organizing information into an outline. Rubin (1980) identified readiness skills for outlining. Kindergarten students learn to group items that belong together, such as scissors, doll clothes, paints, and puzzles. At the first-grade level, students may be able to separate items, discriminating between real and make-believe, foods to be cooked and foods that can be eaten raw, or warm weather clothing and cold weather clothing. At the second-grade level students continue grouping activities but are able to make finer discriminations among items. For example, the second grader may be able to identify the different compositions of rocks or different classifications of plants. Third graders become even more sophisticated and learn to classify ideas in a more organized fashion. The third grader may categorize using several different headings and become fairly adept at developing a table of contents for stories and pictures.

Formal structural rules for outlining can be introduced in the fourth grade. However, once again, the outline should be related to the area of study and taught when outlining will be useful to the students.

Informational Writing

Informational writing includes the writing of reports, personal experiences, and news articles. This type of writing may communicate information or personal feelings. Students need to learn how to organize a report to make it interesting, and they need to adhere to a specific form. The development of the form may be decided by the teacher, or guidelines for the report may be developed by the class. Unlike creative writing, informational writing demands that spelling and punctuation receive prominent attention. A class or school newspaper is a particularly motivating way to teach informational writing. Since a newspaper has so many different types of stories, students have the opportunity to choose special interests and styles.

Writing Descriptions and Observations.

Students need a great deal of practice communicating information about events that have happened. Remembering and reporting objectively (who was involved, what was involved, where it occurred, and the length of time of the event) are difficult tasks. Yet every time there is a problem in the schoolroom or out on the playground, teachers ask students: "What happened?" "Who did what to whom and why?"

Strategies for teaching objective writing can be practiced by assigning students to be reporters, historians, judges, or scientists. School or classroom newspapers or magazines are popular ruses to develop observational skills. Other useful activities for practicing these skills include writing up science health experiments, making a procedural accounting of how to make something, or giving a report of what happened in Room 28 yesterday with students asked to stress accuracy and objectivity.

Sharing descriptions with others is valuable for broadening students' perspective. As in the note-taking strategy, if students have the opportunity to share their observations in a small group of others who have witnessed the same event or activity, they will be surprised by the differences in their observations. Differences in choice of vocabulary, phrasing, use of descriptive words, length of sentences, and types of comparisons can be shared. These differences, however, are not evaluated in terms of *good* and *bad* or *correct* and *incorrect*.

Record Keeping

A variety of activities throughout the school day provide opportunities to learn this type of writing. A small group planning session requires a group recorder. This person takes the minutes of the meeting by recording the plans. Individual, group, or class science experiments require a different type of record keeping. In some classrooms, students take turns writing the daily news on the chalkboard. Writing individual or class diaries provides another type of experience in record keeping. First graders may just begin to record facts or experiences, whereas fourth graders may be expected to record information in outlines. Through record keeping, students learn the value of accuracy, a sense of

Research Findings: Writing Behavior

Graves (1975, p. 235) researched students' writing behavior and concluded the following:

- Informal environments and unstructured assignments motivate students to write more and in greater length than specific assignments in a formal environment.
- When students are required to write in a formal classroom environment, girls will do better than boys; in informal environments, boys will write at greater length than girls.
- Assigned writing restricts the range, content, and amount of writing produced by both boys and girls.

time, continuity, cause and effect, and the need for attention to detail. Records should always be written in the students' own words rather than in adult language.

Research

The style of writing used in research papers is similar to the writing of informational papers. The main difference involves the skills that are taught. First graders may begin to learn research skills by filing words in a dictionary box. Third graders may be expected to use picture dictionaries, a table of contents, and an index to locate information. Fifth graders can be taught to make and use bibliographies, utilize several sources of information, write questions about what they want to research, and take notes to answer the questions they have developed.

Proofreading

Proofreading skills need to be modeled as well as taught. Few adults know how to edit their own work, so it is not surprising that students seldom reread their own reports or compositions for the purpose of self-editing. Teachers can model proofreading by acknowledging to students, "Just a minute, let me reread this," or the teacher may say to students, after recording something on the chalkboard, "Does this say what we wanted it to say? Do the sentences fit together?"

Students can be asked to help develop proofreading criteria. For example, students might develop criteria to call attention to punctuation, capitalization, topic sentences, paragraphing, and conclusions. Or perhaps the criteria will suggest rereading to determine whether the story has a good title, an exciting beginning, and a good climax.

MECHANICS OF WRITING

Composition skills include capitalization and punctuation, sentence processing and paragraphing, spelling, and handwriting. These skills are best taught in a meaningful situation rather than as isolated lessons. During the primary grades the teacher provides independent help while circulating and observing the students at work. By the middle grades, students can edit their own work.

Punctuation and Capitalization

As a general rule, the young child will tend to over-punctuate and overcapitalize. The relationship between punctuation and speech needs to be demonstrated to the students. By the end of second grade most students recognize the need to end sentences with a punctuation mark, begin sentences with a capital letter, and capitalize the personal pronoun *I*. By the end of the middle grades most students have mastered the use of capitalizations in abbreviations, in the first word of greetings, in topics in an outline, and in the first word of a direct quotation. Commas used in a series, in writing the date, and between city and state have typically been mastered by the end of fourth grade.

Sentence-Processing Skills

In the primary grades sentence-processing skills begin with students demonstrating understanding of word order in a sentence by unscrambling simple sentences. Sentence transformations begin in the second grade, and the ability to expand a simple sentence is typically mastered by the end of the primary grades. Independent writing of simple sentences is usually mastered by the third grade. Simple paragraph writing occurs during the middle grades.

Word Usage

Selecting and using nouns, pronouns, verbs, and adjectives are typically mastered by the end of the third grade. Students can recognize the use of synonyms, antonyms, and homonyms during the middle grades.

Style

It is extremely difficult for an elementary student to develop writing style until composition skills have

been mastered. Sentence structure, logic, and clarity come first; however, teachers need to exercise care that, in their editing and assisting zeal, they not discourage students from expressing themselves in unique ways. Sometimes students want to use slang in order to express their individuality. To some extent this tendency can be curbed by demonstrating to students the temporal quality of slang terms and the meaninglessness of words when they are no longer commonly understood. When students learn to use figurative language, development of writing style appears. During the middle grades students begin to use metaphors and similes. The frequency of writing and the encouragement provided to students facilitate the development of style in writing.

SPELLING INSTRUCTION

Students have the opportunity to learn and to use spelling words whenever they are expressing themselves in written form. The spelling program should be integrated with the language arts program and taught along with reading and writing. Spelling is considered a writer's tool. A planned spelling period is usually provided by the time students are in the second grade. At that point in time students have typically learned to spell 90 to 95 percent of the words they use correctly. Anderson and Lapp (1992, p. 189) identify four skills needed for correct spelling:

1. Understand the relationship between phonemes and graphemes (sounds and letters)
2. Understand consonant vowel patterns
3. Recognize sound variations of vowels and consonants
4. Utilize the dictionary for spelling and pronunciation purposes

Teacher Research

Scheideman (1995) encouraged her students to create quality-writing checklists. (See the discussion of rubrics in Chapter 11.) While doing so, the students identified the key components of a story and the attributes of creative writing. The students then used their own checklists to edit and revise their stories. Scheideman reports that the students developed as writers, thinkers, and editors.

The classroom environment can be used to facilitate good spelling habits. When spelling becomes a natural part of the writing program and is viewed as a courtesy to readers, children are more apt to develop the dictionary habit to perfect their own writing. The California *English-Language Arts Framework* (1987, p. 45) suggests the following guidelines for the spelling program:

- The program should develop understanding of letter sound regularity to patterns and to meaning-based units.
- Students should self-correct pretests, and words should be selected from students' own compositions.
- Instruction should parallel student development in grades K–3, evolving from invented spellings, to experimentation with rules and patterns, to real knowledge.
- In grades 3–6 students should learn to compare words, discover patterns and relationships, and use semantic and structural analogy strategies.
- In grades 6–9, emphasis should be placed on building a lexical base.

During the spelling period teachers typically use methods and techniques that include observing the word to be studied, hearing it, saying it, defining it in the student's own words, and practicing it by using it in writing. Students should *not* be given a list of rules and exceptions to memorize, nor asked to spell unknown words, nor given meaningless dictionary exercises. Games such as Scrabble® for Juniors, Anagrams, and Spelling Lotto are popular with elementary and middle school students. Many games (crossword puzzles, word wheels) can be created by the teacher to encourage students to use the dictionary and to study spelling words.

HANDWRITING INSTRUCTION

Like spelling, handwriting is viewed as a writer's tool, and is best practiced during actual writing activities. The purposes for teaching handwriting include the following:

- The development of legible and fluent manuscript and cursive writing
- The development of pride in neatness and correctness of writing

Handwriting is taught beginning in the first grade, but its mastery is dependent on the maturity of the individual student. School districts vary as to when they suggest beginning cursive instruction; the transition from manuscript to cursive writing is customarily accomplished in the third grade. Many students are not ready for cursive writing at the start of third grade.

Readiness for handwriting is determined by eye-hand coordination and the ability to differentiate the forms of letters. The use of manipulative materials facilitates readiness for handwriting. These experiences may include the use of clay, tempera, finger paint, and physical activities involving motor skills.

LISTENING INSTRUCTION

Students are requested to listen more than 50 percent of the school day. A listener has no control over the tempo of speech. If school language is different from home language, listening problems are compounded. Listening is considered the basis for the other language arts components. The child who hears *bus* for *boss* obviously is not going to understand what has been said. Similarly the student who hears *git* for *get* may not be able to read or write the word *get*. Discrimination of sounds is critical to learning language and to communication in general.

Listening requires decoding what is heard. We hear sound symbols. These sound symbols are called **phonemes.** When phonemes are combined into a pattern, the phonemes become a word unit, or **morpheme.** Morphemes are combined to form a sentence. If the individual does not discriminate among phonemes, then it will be impossible for that individual to interpret what has been said. We know that students differ in their auditory discrimination and that auditory discrimination is subject to the maturation process. Frequently students do not mature in the development of this skill until they are about eight years old. There is a positive relationship between poor auditory discrimination and reading. The student who does not hear well will not learn to read well.

PURPOSES FOR LISTENING

Tompkins and Hoskisson (1995) identify five purposes for listening. These are

1. *Discriminative listening:* This involves distinguishing among sounds (city sounds versus jungle sounds) and distinguishing among messages. The former is important for young students; the latter is important for older students.

2. *Efferent listening:* This means listening with understanding. Auding is listening with comprehension. Very little instruction is provided to help students listen efferently. Note taking during a lecture or film requires use of this skill.
3. *Critical listening:* After listening to a message, the listener evaluates what he or she has heard. This occurs while listening to a debate, commercial, or political speech.
4. *Aesthetic listening:* We go to a concert to enjoy the sounds. We listen to children giggling and respond pleasurably. In the classroom, students listen to a story and beg the teacher to continue.
5. *Therapeutic listening:* We listen and offer empathy. A student has a problem on the playground and friends listen sympathetically.

ACTIVITIES TO DEVELOP LISTENING SKILLS

The following list of activities can be used effectively in the classroom to develop students' listening skills:

- Oral games. Simon Says or Follow the Leader are two possibilities. Students should take turns being the leader.
- Musical instruments. Have students repeat rhythm patterns. Use rhythm sticks, drums, or oatmeal boxes.
- Nonsense sentences. Recite nonsense sentences and have students listen and correct them. Example: "Drink a Jennie wants."
- Listening to a tape. Students pantomime what they hear.
- Recitation of rhymes and poems. The teacher recites a familiar rhyme or poem and students fill in the missing line.
- Listening to a story and observing pictures of the story. Students identify what was not in the story; students arrange pictures in sequence of the story; students retell the story in their own words.
- Recording of city sounds, country sounds, animal sounds. Students identify what they hear.
- Dance. Students dance the Hokey Pokey.
- Listening to a story. Students express emotion, telling how they would feel if they were the characters in the story.
- Listening to words. Students count the syllables they hear.
- Listening to sentences. Students listen for a new word and then they name it and use it in a new sentence.

- Listening to sentences. Students listen to present and past tense sentences and identify the differences in meaning.
- Taping a discussion. Students critique their own discussion; criteria and guidelines should be used (see Chapters 6 and 11).

Additional suggestions for using and relating listening skills will be found in the other approaches to the language arts components.

ORAL LANGUAGE DEVELOPMENT

Oral language is really the result of learning by doing. Speech is generated from the experience of listening. Although speech is a natural development, it is affected by the substance of the child's environment. An only child can be expected to have advanced language development. The language development pattern is qualitatively affected by the child's enriched experiences. Oral language also reflects the child's emotional and social adjustment. Children who lack adult contact and love fail to extend the quality of their language.

The puppet theater helps kindergarten children develop oral language.

Do middle school teachers need to be concerned about their students' oral language development? Why?

Studies of school-age children indicate that in most cases children's oral language growth increases around the five- to six-year-old level and once again when the child reaches 10 to 12 years old. During the years in between (grades 2–5), growth appears to be much slower. Although the developmental sequence of syntactic structures appears to be consistent among children, the ages where it occurs is inconsistent.

To encourage speaking and listening, the following activities are suggested:

- Dramatics. Students can make up plays and participate in role-plays and dramatic representation.
- Art experiences. Students can participate in art activities and then describe the experience to others.
- Small group interaction. Students can work together to plan a project or resolve a conflict.
- Interviewing. Students can interview peers or others. They can tape the interviews and play them back for classmates.
- Storytelling. Students can listen to or read a story and then retell the story to others.
- Puppetry. Students can make hand puppets and use them for dramatics.
- Singing. Students can sing current favorites and rewrite the words.
- Choral verse. Students can participate in group speech activities.
- Touch and tell. Students can describe what they feel: hot, cold, soft, rough, smooth, sandy.
- Listen and tell. Students can listen to strange sounds and then describe them.

LIMITED-ENGLISH-PROFICIENCY STUDENTS (LEP)

Children learn language naturally and unconsciously through imitation, experience in the family environment, and practice. When students come to school knowing a language other than English, they need to *acquire* English and they need to *learn* English. Krashen and Terrell (1983) distinguish between acquisition and learning.

Acquisition happens naturally, similar to first language acquisition. Students gain language through informal means by communicating with peers or playing games.

Language learning is a formal process. Students learn about language. They learn explicitly. They receive direct instruction in language.

Most important is that the student understands the meaning of instruction. Krashen and Terrell call this "comprehensible input." They believe that speaking fluency emerges after competence through comprehending input and is not essential to language acquisition.

To help the student with limited English speaking skills, the teacher needs to provide a language-rich environment that provides many opportunities to engage in communicative activities. The second language learner often finds that the primary language and the second language collide, causing interference with oral language learning and with reading in the second language. It is for this reason that many teachers believe it is wise to delay reading instruction until the LEP student has acquired a substantial speaking vocabulary. The language experience approach to reading instruction has been found useful for helping the LEP student make the transition from reading in the primary language to reading English (McCormick, 1995).

SHELTERED ENGLISH

Sheltered English instruction, also called content-based second language instruction, is one means of helping students understand and acquire language. In using this technique, the teacher speaks slowly and uses simple, predictable sentence forms. Concrete objects and visuals are used to clearly relate the subject to everyday life experiences. Facial and body expressions and gestures enhance the delivery. Explanations or instructions should be repeated and summarized.

Cooperative work groups with group membership adjustment so that there are language-proficient students working with limited-English-proficiency students are fine means of providing support for students acquiring language.

Repetition of key concepts so that vocabulary is reinforced helps students acquire language. Verification of students' understanding can be done by asking students to repeat instructions and to practice by telling others.

Students should be given opportunity to talk about their own experiences and encouraged to use props similar to what the teacher uses. This will assist students who are having difficulty understanding the language

Teaching Hints:
Sheltered English Strategy

- Speak slowly but naturally.
- Use simple and predictable sentence patterns.
- Use visuals; concrete objects for key concepts.
- Use facial and body expression; use gestures.
- Relate information to students' experiences.
- Repeat; summarize.
- Ask student(s) to restate in their own words.

minority student, as well as the teacher. It also provides a means for the limited-English-proficiency-student to express him/herself when some of the words are unknown.

NONSTANDARD ENGLISH

It is especially important in the teaching of language arts that teachers demonstrate to students their acceptance of all languages and language differences. There is no conclusive evidence that speaking **nonstandard English** has any effect on learning to read or learning to spell. Cultural gaps between school and community appear to be responsible for most learning problems. Moffett and Wagner (1983) observed that speakers of nonstandard pronunciation automatically adjust for dialectical differences in pronunciation, grammar, and vocabulary.

Research indicates that both nonstandard dialects and standard English have language rules and complexities. Nonstandard speakers are able to communicate just as well as the standard English speaker. The dialect speaker is not language deficient—just different (McCormick, 1995).

The nonstandard English speaker understands standard English, enjoys television, and understands print. During reading instruction it is important to differentiate between reading errors due to miscues and reading errors due to the student's expression of the nonstandard dialect that does not affect meaning. Reading problems are not caused by speaking a nonstandard dialect.

The nonstandard English speaker needs to appreciate the *value* of speaking standard English and *recognize* when nonstandard English is spoken versus standard English. When the student writes or speaks

using the nonstandard form, teachers can tell or demonstrate, *sensitively*, that there is another way to express that sentence and it is. . . .

EVALUATING GROWTH

Language arts growth can be evaluated by means of actual learning activities (performance assessment) as well as through standardized tests (see Chapter 11). Although it is not possible to know how well students are listening or how much students comprehend when they are reading, it is possible to evaluate growth when students produce a product. Receptive growth can be measured by expressive acts. When students discuss, dramatize, or use written materials to produce something, comprehension can be evaluated. If students need to interpret written directions while working in a learning center, their comprehension is assessed.

Informal teacher-made tests, observation of students' learning behaviors, learning activity products, and standardized tests should all be used to identify students' levels of ability. Once ability levels are assessed, it is the teacher's task to diagnose any learning problems and design instruction to facilitate the learning process. Students should also be involved in the evaluative process. It is important for students to be aware of their own strengths and weaknesses. However, it is also important that they not be overwhelmed by failures. Particularly in the area of reading, it is significant to confer with the student and develop goals jointly for future progress. Kucer (1988) suggests the use of a checklist (Figure 12.1) to evaluate students' progress using basic reading and writing processes.

PORTFOLIO ASSESSMENT

The student portfolio provides a fine means to assess the progress students make in their writing. Beginning with the prewriting ideas and then the written draft, revision process, and final edited version, the student can self-evaluate and discuss his/her progress with others. The portfolio can be used to exhibit the many types of writing the student performs: creative, informational, report, or diary.

Students' writing can be evaluated, also, in terms of content (relevancy, clarity, originality, and interest) and form (organization, style, punctuation, capitalization,

Figure 12.1   Evaluation of Basic Reading and Writing Processes

Student's Name: _____   Grade: _____   Age: _____   Evaluator: _____

Reading Processes	Yes	Somewhat	No	Writing Processes	Yes	Somewhat	No
1a. Generates and organizes major ideas or concepts				1b. Generates and organizes major ideas or concepts			
2a. Develops and supports major ideas orconcepts with detailsand particulars				2b. Expands, extends, or elaborates on major ideas or concepts			
3a. Integrates meaning into a logical and coherent whole				3b. Integrates meaning into a logical and coherent whole			
4a. Uses a variety of linguistics cues—textual, semantic, syntactic, graphophonic				4b. Uses a variety of linguistic cues—textual, semantic, syntactic, graphophonic			
5a. Uses a variety of text aids—pictures, charts, graphs, subheadings, etc.				5b. Uses a variety of text aids—pictures, charts, graphs, subheadings, etc.			
6a. Uses relevant background knowledge				6b. Uses relevant background knowledge			
7a. Makes meaningful predictions based on what has been previously read				7b. Predicts/plans upcoming meanings based on what has been previously written			
8a. Revises—rereads, reads on, or rethinks—when meaning is lost or when purposes/ intentions or the needs of the audience are not met				8b. Revises when meaning is lost or when purpose/intentions or the needs of the audience are not met			
9a. Generates inferences or goes beyond the information given				9b. Uses writing to explore ideas and to discover new meanings			
10a. Reflects on, and responds and reacts to, what is being read				10b. Reflects on, and responds and reacts to, what is being written			
11a. Uses reading for a variety of purposes and functions				11b. Uses writing for a variety of purposes and functions			
12a. Varies the manner in which texts are read based on different purposes, intentions, and audiences				12b. Varies the manner in which texts are written based on different purposes, intentions, and audiences			
13a. Takes risks				13b. Takes risks			
14a. Understands meaning of sentences as read				14b. Writes meaningful sentences			
				15b. Revises conventions—spelling, punctuation, capitalization, penmanship, etc.—after meaning and purposes/intentions are met			

Source: Kucer, *First Annual USC Teacher Education Conference* (April 1988).

word usage, legibility, and appropriateness). Specific writing skills, such as the ability to write a business or personal letter, a journal, and a research report can be evaluated. When possible, encourage students to develop their own rubrics to self-evaluate growth.

THE INCLUSIVE CLASSROOM

Typically, elementary and middle school classrooms have a wide range of ability levels, from gifted to slow. The addition of students with physical or learning disabilities can also be expected in most classrooms. Mainstreamed children customarily are provided with individualized instruction in language arts; however, appropriate instruction can occur in the regular classroom provided the individualized educational program has been developed with instructional materials and supportive services available to student and teacher.

An advantage to regular classroom placement is the availability of peer tutors. Working with a partner, mainstreamed children can practice reading and oral language skills. Proper reinforcement with peer tutors can have a positive effect on motivation and interest.

Research on direct instruction is applicable to the teaching of academic skills to students with disabilities. Review and the following sections in the text:

- *The Inclusive Classroom* and *Individualized Educational Program* in Chapter 1
- *Direct Instruction* in Chapter 6

LEARNING CENTERS

Learning Centers in the language arts are used as an integral part of the instructional program. The centers facilitate reinforcement of skill development and offer opportunities to explore creative aspects of subject matter and to individualize and expand instruction. The centers presented in this section should be used as points of departure. Let your own creativity be your guide.

Figurative Language Center
Language Arts, Social Studies—Upper Grades

Objectives: To improve comprehension of word meanings, appreciation of language, use of figurative language, and development of cooperative work skills

Materials: An envelope or box to contain the figurative expressions; a direction card

Evaluation: Observation and discussion

Procedures:

1. Direction card explains that students are to take turns choosing an expression from the box or envelope. Each student pantomimes an expression while the other members of the group try to guess the expression.
2. Expressions may include the following:
   - arm of the law
   - on the face of it
   - put on the dog
   - eye of the storm

Language arts learning centers provide a means to differentiate instruction for students.

- cat got your tongue
- out of the woods
- horsing around
- leg of the journey
- paint the town red
- jumped on her high horse
- check bounced
- into the frying pan

To Simplify: Students may work with a partner to pantomime the expression.

To Extend: Students may write their own expressions and hand them out for others to act out.

Listening Center

Language Arts—Lower Grades

Objectives: To improve listening skills; to sequence pictures related to a specific story

Materials: Story record, flannel board pictures

Procedures:

1. Students listen to a familiar story.
2. Students take turns retelling the story using the flannel board pictures.
3. Students self-evaluate by turning pictures over and checking the number sequence.

To Extend: Familiar routines are identified on the tape. Students take turns sequentially dramatizing these routines.

Examples: Making breakfast, getting ready for school, bike riding, painting a picture, making ice cream, making tortillas

Category Center

Language Arts, Art—Lower Grades

Objective: To categorize objects in order to improve comprehension

Materials: Picture file, scissors, paste, paper

Evaluation: Students share pictures and identify category and objects

Procedures:

1. Students sort pictures by categories such as pets, fruits, animals, toys, transportation, vegetables, clothing, or shelter.
2. Students cut out pictures and make a collage to demonstrate one selected category.

Comic Strip Center

Language Arts—Middle and Upper Grades

Objectives: To improve creative writing and expand writing skills.

Evaluation: Students share composed comic strips

Materials: Variety of comic strips with the dialogue eliminated, pencils

Procedures:

1. Students choose a comic strip and compose and insert the conversation in the appropriate spaces.

To Extend: Students may draw and write their own comic strips.

To Simplify: Students may work with a partner to compose the dialogue.

Information Center

Language Arts, Science, Social Studies, or Health— Middle and Upper Grades

Objective: To improve informational writing skills

Materials: Taped stories, paper and pencils

Evaluation: Students share stories with others

Procedures:

1. Students listen to an incident and take notes.
2. Students write a news report of the story identifying the following:
   - Who is involved?
   - What happened?
   - How did it happen?
   - What were the results?

To Extend: More than one incident can be used; students may dramatize the story; students may take the roles of reporter and interviewees.

To Simplify: Students write stories with a partner. Less complicated taped incidents may be used.

Critical Reading

Reading—Upper Grades

Objective: To improve critical reading skills identifying adjectives, facts, and opinions

Materials: Commercial product boxes or advertising pages from newspapers and magazines

Evaluation: Group evaluation, class discussion

Procedures:

1. Products or advertisements are displayed at the center.
2. Students write out the descriptive advertising slogans, adjectives, and gimmicks used by the advertiser.
3. Students compare their answers with each other.

To Extend:

1. Students write their own advertising slogans for products.
2. Students identify the target audience for the product and the advertising.

To Simplify:
1. Limit the quantity of products.
2. Simplify the advertising to be read (write your own).

SUMMARY

Language Arts as a Broad Field

1. Language arts encompasses both the receptive and the expressive aspects of language.
2. The purpose of language is communication; through language we communicate meaning.
3. Language is related to the individual's personality and culture.
4. All individuals communicate nonverbally.

Factors Affecting Language Development

5. Language development is affected by cognitive and affective development, experience, intellectual ability, attitude, motivation, and culture.
6. Readiness for reading is affected by maturity.
7. Language or dialect differences affect success in the language arts.

Literacy Programs

8. Students come to school with an understanding of language and the purposes of written language.
9. The whole language approach assumes that students are active learners and learn language in a natural way.

Characteristics of a Constructivist Approach to Language Arts

10. The curriculum is characterized by integration, relevance, and involvement of students.
11. Learning centers are often featured in the classroom.
12. Materials for instruction include a wide range of resources.
13. Heterogeneous grouping is used to provide purposeful and differentiated instruction.

Integration of Experience

14. Primary language or dialect is a factor in language development and affects school success.
15. To facilitate language learning, teachers need to draw upon the child's cultural life.
16. Students learn more efficiently if experiences fit and build upon each other.

17. Integration is achieved through the design of curriculum themes.
18. Integrated teaching is a characteristic of a constructivist language approach.

Features of Effective Programs

19. There should be an emphasis on literature, thinking processes versus a skills-based program, a writing program, decision making by students, peer tutoring, and personalization of instruction.

Plan for Interaction

20. Students learn to write for others to read.
21. Students are grouped for peer interaction in communicative activities.

Reading Instruction

22. Reading literature and integrating skill instruction as needed by students should characterize the reading program.
23. Students should analyze literary works by studying character, setting, mood/feeling, story pattern (plot).
24. Reading ability contributes to the accomplishment of societal and individual goals and is related to economic competence and technical/professional development.
25. Reading is a receptive form of communication and a comprehension activity.
26. The beginning reader must learn to discriminate critical features and translate them into an identification system of letters and then into a word name.
27. Word identification and comprehension require the skill of redundancy or alternative sources of information.

Approaches to Reading Instruction

28. Reading instruction usually encompasses silent reading, oral reading, work/study reading, and recreational reading.
29. Reading-readiness activities characterize early instruction of children.
30. Experiential factors affect the child's success in learning to read.
31. Phonics cannot be the sole means for teaching reading, but it is an important strategy.
32. Use of experience charts dictated by children and then read by them is an important-learning-to read strategy.

33. The purpose of a literature approach is to develop students' appreciation and enjoyment of a variety of literature.
34. Content field texts are valuable as sources of reading material.
35. The language experience approach to reading instruction is based on the idea that what you can think and say, you can read.
36. The kinesthetic approach is taught using the students' own stories.
37. The individualized approach motivates the student to self-select reading material from a wide range of choices.
38. Basal reader texts provide sequential development of vocabulary and skills.
39. Basal readers are criticized because they are often unappealing to minority students, rural students, and other special interest groups.
40. Students are encouraged to read through story reading, storytelling, readers' theater, listening centers, and recreational reading.

Writing Instruction

41. Writing involves composition and transcription.
42. Writing may be the most difficult language arts component.
43. There are three purposes of the writing program: functional writing, creative writing, and skill development in the mechanics of writing.
44. The writing process includes prewriting, drafting, responding, revising, editing, and sharing.

Writing Activities

45. Writing should be integrated throughout the school day and encompasses letter writing, creative writing, note taking, outlining, informational writing, writing observations and descriptions, record keeping, research, and proofreading.
46. Mechanics of writing include capitalization, punctuation, sentence processing, paragraphing, spelling, and handwriting.
47. Mechanics of writing are best taught in meaningful situations rather than as isolated skills.

Listening Instruction

48. Students are asked to listen more than 50 percent of the school day.
49. There are listening levels; from high to low, these include auding, listening, and hearing.

50. Purposes for listening include discriminative listening, comprehension, critical listening, appreciative, and therapeutic listening.
51. A variety of activities develop listening skills. These include oral games, music, stories, nonsense sounds, dancing, poem recitation, and discussion.

Oral Language Development

52. Language development is qualitatively affected by the child's experiences.
53. The classroom environment can be used to foster oral language development.
54. Oral language activities include dramatics, art experiences, small group interaction, interviewing, storytelling, puppetry, singing, and listening and telling.

Limited-English-Proficiency Students

55. Students need to acquire English vocabulary and need to learn English. Acquisition is a natural process; learning is a formal process.
56. It is most important that students understand the meaning of instruction. This is called comprehensible input.
57. A language-rich environment facilitates acquiring English and provides opportunities for communicative activities.
58. The language experience approach to reading instruction is particularly effective with LEP students.
59. The teacher's use of Sheltered English helps the LEP student understand content in the second language.

Nonstandard English

60. Nonstandard English is a dialect governed by language rules and language complexities.
61. Nonstandard speakers are not language deficient.
62. Nonstandard speakers understand English in television programs and print.
63. The nonstandard speaker needs to appreciate the value of speaking standard English and recognize the differences between standard and nonstandard forms of English.

Evaluation

64. Performance assessments, standard tests, and informal teacher tests can be used to evaluate learning.
65. Receptive growth can be measured by expressive acts.

66. Portfolio assessment can be used to assess students' writing progress.
67. Oral language should be evaluated for speech defects, articulation, and ability to converse with others.
68. Listening is evaluated through expressive means.

Inclusive Classroom

69. Students with physical or learning disabilities can be expected in most classrooms.
70. Mainstreamed students can work advantageously with a peer tutor.
71. Most frequently the mainstreamed student is provided with an individualized educational program.

DISCUSSION QUESTIONS AND APPLICATION EXERCISES

1. Visit a kindergarten, primary, or preschool classroom and listen to the students. See if you can identify Heath's language functions in their speech. What experiences would you suggest to help them prepare for school language?
2. Plan a field trip for a group of students at the primary, middle grade, or upper grade level. Identify the new words that the experience could provide.
3. Design a learning center that integrates several subject fields. Use the learning centers in this chapter as a guide.
4. Observe a group of students participating in block work or dramatic play. Describe your observation and explain what value the experience had for the participating children.
5. In what ways are language and culture related? (What does a teacher need to know?)
6. Identify classroom activities to expand language uses.
7. Why is it important for teachers to be language sensitive?
8. One of your students has had a great deal of difficulty learning to read. You have just discovered that the student owns a camera and has taken a number of pictures of the neighborhood. How could you use this advantageously to teach reading?
9. Suggest activities to improve middle school students' skills in writing reports and motivating ideas for creative writing.
10. Write questions to be used as an advance organizer to help students in grades 5–8 develop critical reading skills.

C H A P T E R

13

Social Experiences:
The Nature of the Social Studies

The purpose of the social studies curriculum is to provide essential knowledge, skills, and values for citizenship participation in our democratic society. Beginning in the primary years, students learn about the history and culture of the United States and the world; they study geography, government, economic theories, social institutions, global relationships, and intergroup and interpersonal relationships. Beliefs in our democratic society are developed through an understanding of due process, equal protection, and civic participation. Skill competencies depend on systematic practice. Study skills, critical thinking, and social participation are essential and contribute to the major purposes of education in the Unites States.

This chapter presents a wide range of content and teaching approaches applicable for social studies teaching. The overriding concern is that teachers prepare students for participation in the democratic system and for problem solving in an increasingly diverse, interdependent, and complex world.

After you study this chapter, you should be able to accomplish the following:

1. Explain why the field of social studies is considered a basic subject.
2. Identify what students are expected to learn in the social studies.
3. Describe three perspectives or conflicts related to social studies instruction.
4. List the typical grade-level topical sequence for social studies instruction in the United States.
5. Identify several themes for the social studies.
6. Identify and describe several strategies for teaching social studies.
7. Identify resources for teaching social studies.
8. Name three categories of social studies skills and suggest classroom activities to develop each skill category.
9. Identify ways to use authentic assessment in the social studies.
10. Create a learning center or a learning packet for social studies.
11. Discuss ways to use technology and other resources for inquiry teaching of social studies.

Professional Lexicon

arranged environment   A classroom environment that uses realia, pictures, and print materials to motivate students' interest in a teaching unit.

citizenship transmission   An approach to teaching social studies that focuses on our cultural heritage; a traditional textbook study.

culmination   Activity at the end of a teaching unit to finalize the unit and determine what students have learned.

development activities   The activities that make up the body of the teaching unit; the learning experiences between the initiation and the culmination.

initiation   An experience at the beginning of the teaching unit to provoke student interest and enthusiasm.

reflective inquiry approach   An approach that teaches students how to think, how to process

information in order to make informed decisions, and how to participate effectively in groups.

semantic maps   A webbing technique to help students construct and link categories of information.

social sciences   *Social studies* is the umbrella term used to describe teaching the seven social sciences: history, geography, political science, economics, psychology, anthropology, and sociology.

social science approach   This approach teaches concepts, generalizations, and processes used by social scientists.

social studies   The umbrella term used to describe teaching the social sciences integrated for pedagogical purposes; the integration of experience and knowledge concerning human experience.

WHY DO WE TEACH SOCIAL STUDIES?

Social studies can be the most exciting and challenging subject field in the curriculum. It is also one of the most important subjects taught to students. The child comes to school relatively unsocialized. Group experiences are usually limited to the family, the nursery school (if the child attended), or the neighborhood. Learning how to work in a group and use group process skills are developmental processes. The interaction that occurs when working in a peer group is different from what occurs in the family group. The assumption of a group role cannot be learned unless one experiences social organization. Interaction in groups requires understanding and adherence to group norms, roles, and social control.

Children come to school knowing very little about people in their own society or elsewhere. They are to some degree ignorant of U.S. social institutions, customs, and values. Although there are diverse people and cultures in the United States, the nation shares a common mainstream culture. This culture has to do with our economic system, our political and judicial systems, and our heritage. United States citizens should be able to speak English and should be educated to participate in the social, economic, and political life of our country. Participation in the mainstream culture can be considered a basic need if one is to live in the United States. Social studies is the subject field responsible for the achievement of this goal.

Mehlinger (1977), a social studies educator, expressed concern that many people in the United States did not appreciate U.S. democracy and the meaning of citizenship. He wrote (p. iii):

> When did the status of citizen fall from grace? At what point in our history did people cease to be proud of being a citizen? It was not always so. At one time people believed that to be a citizen of a republic was a special blessing. In contrast, subjects were to be pitied because they had no opportunity to govern themselves or to determine the rules by which they lived. Who debased the concept of citizenship? What events led many Americans to conclude that being a citizen was no longer a honor and a privilege?

Parents teach certain behaviors that they value in family life—the family always gathers together for Sunday night dinner, or celebrates birthdays together, or plans vacations or holiday observances together. Society also has values that are shared. Loyalty, unity, respect for others' rights, responsibility to vote, innocence until proved guilty—these are but a few of the general values that are shared in our society.

Teachers are responsible for teaching the country's values. If we, the teachers, do not teach about our culture and our values, our country will not have a future. Students are taught about the Bill of Rights and about our branches of government so they understand and appreciate U.S. democracy. We use the symbol of the flag and the "Star-Spangled Banner" to promote group unity; we enjoy a school holiday on Presidents' Day; but before we do, we teach students about our country's accomplishments. Students learn about rights and responsibilities in their daily participation in classroom life.

Why do we teach social studies? Through the teaching of social studies we prepare students to participate in a democratic society. We facilitate the development of humane, rational, and understanding individuals who will preserve and continue our society. We recognize that to be effective citizens there are specific skills, knowledge, values, and attitudes necessary for social participation. It is the role of the school to foster civic virtue and a sense of citizenship. These goals direct the social studies program.

The National Council for the Social Studies, the professional organization of teachers, and university faculty who care about social studies teaching, identified program goals for powerful social studies teaching. These include:

- Fostering individual and cultural identity along with understanding of the forces that hold society together or pull it apart
- Observing and participating in the school and community
- Addressing critical issues and the world as it is
- Preparing students to make decisions based on democratic principles
- Leading to citizen participation in public affairs

WHAT ARE STUDENTS EXPECTED TO LEARN?

Although there is considerable disagreement about what content to select for the teaching of social studies and about how to teach social studies, most educators accept that the overarching goal of social studies is *citizenship education*. Barr, Barth, and Shermis (1977, p. 69) defined the social studies as "an integration of experience and knowledge concerning human relations for the purpose of citizenship education." To achieve this goal, objectives must be developed to accomplish the following:

- Provide *knowledge* about human experiences in the past, present, and future
- Develop *skills* to process information
- Develop appropriate *values* and *beliefs*
- Provide opportunities for *social participation*

We can see that Barr's "integration of experiences and knowledge" really means knowledge from the social sciences—history, geography, economics, political science, anthropology, sociology, and psychology. Barr's definition is specific in detailing the primary goal of the social studies.

An analysis of conflicting perceptions about what should be taught in the social studies and how to go about teaching the subject provided Barr and his coauthors with three basic traditions in the social studies (Table 13.1). To some extent the history of the teaching of social studies can be traced by using the three traditions.

CITIZENSHIP TRANSMISSION (CULTURAL HERITAGE APPROACH)

Every nation of the world is faced with the need to develop cultural unity. In our own country this need was perceived soon after the revolutionary war. Our early citizens were concerned that future generations should know about our history and that young citizens be taught patriotism. This traditional conception of **citizenship transmission** is dependent on the adult's passing on the cultural heritage to the youth. This seems to necessitate that the adult transmitter be a strong and partisan teacher. The method of teaching is primarily inculcation. The teacher has a clear idea of what a good, loyal citizen is and attempts to transmit this idea. Although this conception of the social studies was more pervasive during our early history, it is still a viable concept today.

The content in the classroom of a teacher who believes in citizenship transmission is a combination of the *hidden curriculum* and the textbook or state-prepared curriculum guide. The teacher frequently exhorts students to share, take turns, sit up tall, and "close your lips when a visitor comes into the classroom to talk to teacher." These socializing techniques constitute the hidden curriculum; the textbook and the teacher's own beliefs, mainstream values, norms, obedience to laws, social participation, and perception of

the ideal society together make up the content of social studies. The central goal of citizenship transmission is the focal point and serves to organize the curriculum.

SOCIAL SCIENCE APPROACH

The fifth-grade students returned to their classroom after recess and found a number of display centers. There were pictures of pioneers, pioneer homes, and the interior of a pioneer cabin. There were several wall maps illustrating the Oregon and Santa Fe trails and other pioneer routes west. There was a filmstrip about soapmaking. There were exhibits of a covered wagon, a loom and spindle, a flintlock rifle, and pioneer clothes. There were personal letters obviously written by family members who had traveled westward and a diary written by a young pioneer girl.

The classroom buzzed as the students excitedly wandered about looking at the centers. The teacher watched and listened. After a while the teacher went to the chalkboard and wrote two sets of questions. On one side of the chalkboard he wrote these questions:

- What happened to the pioneers as they moved westward?
- How did the pioneers travel westward?
- Why did the pioneers move westward?

On the other side of the chalkboard he wrote these questions:

- What are primary sources of information?
- What are secondary sources of information?
- How does a historian determine what happened?

The students returned to their seats. Many looked puzzled. The teacher acknowledged their puzzlement by asking several students, "What's the matter?"

"Why are these things on display?" and "What are we going to study?" were the questions that the students asked. The teacher responded, "We are going to pretend that we are historians. Who can tell me, what is a primary source of information?"

The teacher will teach about social science inquiry, and using a westward movement unit of study, the students will learn about human behavior during the early nineteenth century as the American pioneers moved westward. When social studies is taught from the perspective of a social scientist, it is expected that students will come to understand human experience by learning the kinds of problems studied by social scientists and the assumptions and techniques used in

Table 13.1 The Three Social Studies Traditions

Social Studies Taught as Citizenship Transmission	Social Studies Taught as Social Science	Social Studies Taught as Reflective Inquiry
Purpose—Citizenship is best promoted by inculcating right values as a framework for making decisions.	Citizenship is best promoted by decision making based on mastery of social science concepts, processes, and problems.	Citizenship is best promoted through a process of inquiry in which knowledge is derived from what citizens need to know to make decisions and solve problems.
Method—Transmission: Transmission of concepts and values by such techniques as textbook, recitation, lecture, question-and-answer sessions, and structured problem-solving exercises.	Discovery: Each of the social sciences has its own method of gathering and verifying knowledge. Students should discover and apply the method that is appropriate to each social science.	Reflective inquiry: Decision making is structured and disciplined through a reflective inquiry process that aims at identifying problems and responding to conflicts by means of testing insights.
Content—Content is selected by an authority interpreted by the teacher and has the function of illustrating values, beliefs, and attitudes.	Proper content is the structure, concepts, problems, and processes of both the separate and the integrated social science disciplines.	Analysis of individual citizen's values yields needs and interests that in turn form the basis for student self-selection of problems. Problems, therefore, constitute the content for reflection.

Source: Robert D. Barr et al., *Defining the Social Studies* (NCSS, Bulletin No. 51, 1977), p. 67.

the **social sciences.** Students learn to ask intelligent questions similar to those the historian or the sociologist, or perhaps the political scientist, might ask. In this way students learn to reason and to become effective citizens.

The **social science approach,** although rooted in early historical practices before 1900, became particularly meaningful during the 1960s through the work of the Social Science Education Consortium and the varied social science projects funded by the National Science Foundation. Many contemporary textbook series reflect the social science orientation. The changing emphases of the social science disciplines are reflected in the questions that social scientists ask and in the expansion of social studies to include some of the newer disciplines, such as social psychology and anthropology. This approach to social studies teaching was stimulated by the post-Sputnik concerns of the 1960s.

REFLECTIVE INQUIRY APPROACH

Both the social science perspective of social studies and the reflective inquiry perspective expect students to make intelligent decisions. In the social science tradition, the teacher chooses what the student will study and sets the stage for inquiry. However, when social studies is taught using the **reflective inquiry approach,** the teacher expects the students to choose

what to study. The major difference between the social science tradition and reflective inquiry is that in the latter the problem selected may be more relevant to the students. Also it is usually more personal in its focus. The reflective inquiry teacher will try to spotlight several problems that have potential for puzzlement, for a conflict in values, or for social implications. The teacher also needs to consider sources for data concerning the nature of these problems.

In a reflective inquiry classroom, the teacher might bring in a newspaper story for the students to read. An example would be a story about Vietnamese fishermen who were physically attacked by U.S. fishers and the Ku Klux Klan. All three groups lived in Galveston, Texas. The Vietnamese were recent immigrants, and fishing was their way of life in Vietnam. They utilized the same fishing techniques in Galveston Bay as they had in Vietnam, and they fished seven days a week. The U.S. fishermen only fished five days a week, and their techniques were slightly different. The Americans believed that the Vietnamese were guilty of poaching and accused them of taking unfair advantage by fishing seven days of the week.

The teacher using this story would first have the students read the story and then ask the students if they saw a problem. If the students acknowledge that there is a problem, the teacher would ask them to hypothesize about how to study the problem. In the example given, the students might hypothesize that there is a conflict of values. The next step would be to have the students define all aspects of the problem, such as what is meant by the term *values.*

Next the students would suggest ways to study the problem. During the study stage the students would gather facts and evidence to support or refute the hypothesis. Finally the students would come to a decision about the social implications of the problem or how the problem could be resolved.

The teacher's purpose in this classroom is to help students understand that all individuals are motivated by personal needs, interests, and values. As citizens we have to make rational and informed decisions. Reflective inquiry teaches inquiry skills and helps students make choices and deliberate decisions.

WHAT IS SOCIAL STUDIES?

The three approaches to teaching social studies provide information about what some professional educators believe students should learn in the social studies. The conflict about the question *What is social studies?* is concerned with several issues:

- Should social studies be solely responsible for the development of citizenship goals?
- What content in social studies is of most worth?
- What method(s) should be used to teach the social studies?

The three approaches presented can be summarized as follows:

1. *Cultural heritage approach to content.* This approach teaches knowledge and understanding about the past; inspirational heroes and heroines are often selected as focuses; patriotism is emphasized; traditional textbooks are selected for use. Content should cultivate citizenship and loyalty.
2. *Social science approach to content.* This approach teaches concepts, generalizations, and processes used by social scientists; student-centered teaching techniques are utilized. Citizenship goals are achieved through a better understanding of the world.
3. *Reflective inquiry approach to content.* This approach teaches students how to think, how to process information in order to make informed decisions, and how to participate effectively in groups. Content is considered relatively unimportant; it is se-

lected on the basis of mileage. The selected content should provide sufficient data for students to practice problem-solving and group participation skills.

Although the three traditions in social studies education express philosophic orientations to content selection and methods of teaching, teachers do not necessarily choose one approach and exclusively adhere to it in the classroom. It is more likely that teachers utilize a little bit of this approach and a little bit of that approach!

SELECTING AND ORGANIZING CONTENT

Whenever curriculum experts discuss what makes up the curriculum, they are discussing the *scope* of the curriculum pattern; when experts discuss the order or grade level of the pattern, they are referring to the *sequence.* Surprisingly, there is very little variation in the United States from school to school as to what is taught in the social studies.

Expanding communities is the name given to the most typical pattern found in elementary schools. The pattern developed as a response to the developmental needs and interests of young children. Figure 13.1 represents the approach, illustrating the widening perspective and sequence of social studies as students move away from their own egocentric world to study human behavior in far-off places.

The intent of the curriculum design is to introduce students, through inquiry, to social science generalizations underlying each of the communities of which the student is a member. Beyond sequence considerations, Hanna (1963) organized the scope of the program into categories of basic human activities. Two dimensions coordinated the design. The expanding communities represented the sequence, and the basic human activities the scope. Figure 13.1 illustrates the two dimensions.

The expanding communities design was often interpreted too narrowly by teachers and social scientists. Since the advent of television, students view people in remote areas of the world, travels in space, and behavior that may be less than exemplary. As a consequence, teachers may need to incorporate conceptual content and skills related to controversial problems, societal issues, or student concerns.

Many states adopt their own guidelines to provide a basis for determining the scope and sequence of the social studies program. The California State Board of

Figure 13.1 Expanding Communities

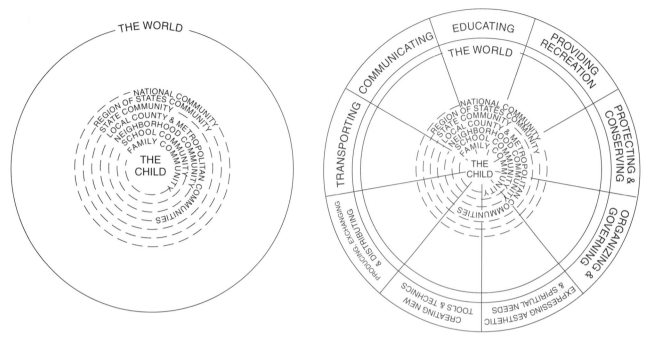

Source: Paul R. Hanna, "Revising the Social Studies: What is needed?" *Social Education,* 27:4 April 1963, p.193.

Education adopted the *History-Social Science Framework for California Public Schools* (1988) in order to provide guidelines and recommendations for teachers and publishers of materials and curriculum developers. The framework is intended as a policy statement and as a guide for designing curricula and courses of study. It also serves as a base from which criteria for instructional materials can be developed. Each grade level in the California Framework has specific recommendations for a major setting or topic, and then a number of subtopics are recommended. The major topics in the California History-Social Science Framework (1988) appear below:

- Kindergarten—Learning and Working Now and Long Ago
- Grade 1—A Child's Place in Time and Space
- Grade 2—People Who Make a Difference
- Grade 3—Continuity and Change
- Grade 4—California: A Changing State
- Grade 5—United States History and Geography; Making a New Nation
- Grade 6—World History and Geography: Ancient Civilization
- Grade 7—World History and Geography: Medieval and Early Modern Times

- Grade 8—United States History and Geography: Growth and Conflict

The Spiral Curriculum, conceived by Taba (1967b), is another approach to the selection and organization of content in the social studies. Basic concepts are structured in such a way that they are used at different levels of abstraction dependent on the age and ability of the students. For example, the concept of diversity could be taught at increasing levels of complexity by first introducing the concept in kindergarten when students study *working together* and continuing to grade 8 when students study the content about regional development in the West, Northeast, and South.

Hartoonian and Laughlin (1989) believe that local curriculum committees and teachers should decide what is taught at the various grade levels in social studies. They view social studies as an integrative subject field responsible for maintaining our cultural heritage and improving self and society. They propose 10

How does the focus of the Spiral Curriculum differ from the focus of the expanding environments curriculum?

*In what ways do the Hartoonian and Laughlin
scope and sequence adhere to the expanding
horizon content approach?*

broad themes to guide decision making in the selection of social studies topics:

1. Cultural Heritage
2. Global Perspective
3. Politics/Economics
4. Tradition and Change
5. Social History
6. Spatial Relationships
7. Social Contracts
8. Technology
9. Peace/Interdependence
10. Citizenship

Hartoonian and Laughlin recommend grade-level clusters with a content focus that is planned around the 10 broad themes:

- Grades K–2—My Orientation to the World
- Grades 3–5—Expanding My World Horizons
- Grades 6–8—Viewing the World from Different Perspectives
- Grades 9–12—Assuming Full Citizenship in a Changing World

Standards for teaching social studies were developed by the National Council for the Social Studies (NCSS) in 1994. (Standards have been developed in the different social science disciplines also. These other standards are not presented here.) The purposes of the NCSS standards (*Curriculum Standards for Social Studies Expectations of Excellence*, 1994, p. 13) are as follows:

- To serve as a framework for the K–12 program
- To serve as a guide for curriculum decisions
- To provide examples of classroom practice to guide teachers in designing instruction

The NCSS identified 10 themes to serve as organizing strands for the social studies curriculum:

1. Culture
2. Time, Continuity, and Change
3. People, Places, and Environments

4. Individual Development and Identity
5. Individuals, Groups, and Institutions
6. Power, Authority, and Governance
7. Production, Distribution, and Consumption
8. Science, Technology, and Society
9. Global Connections
10. Civic Ideals and Practices

The topics are intended to be interrelated. For example, in order to study culture, the students need to have an understanding of many of the other topics. In order to get the flavor of the standards, the topic of *culture* and several of the examples given for curriculum development are presented below.

Performance expectations for elementary grades include the following:

- Explore and describe similarities and differences in the ways groups, societies, and cultures address similar human needs and concerns
- Describe ways in which language, stories, folktales, music, and artistic creations serve as expressions of culture and influence behavior of people living in a particular culture
- Give examples and describe the importance of cultural unity and diversity within and across groups

Using the same topic, the performance expectations for middle grades include:

- Compare similarities and differences in the ways groups, societies, and cultures meet human needs and concerns
- Explain and give examples of how language, literature, the arts, architecture, other artifacts, traditions, beliefs, values, and behaviors contribute to the development and transmission of culture
- Articulate the implications of cultural diversity, as well as cohesion, within and across groups

DIVERSITY OF TOPICS AND PROGRAMS

As you have probably realized by now, the social studies curriculum encompasses almost everything that society is concerned about—multicultural educa-

*In what ways do the Hartoonian and Laughlin scope and
sequence attend to the social, emotional, and physical
growth of elementary and middle school students?*

tion, environmental education, career education, technology, consumer education, global education, law education, and moral education. The teacher is continually faced with making choices about what to include in the relatively short period of time devoted to social studies. Let us take a brief look at several of the modest proposals for some of these topics.

Law Education

Elementary and middle school students need to understand the nature and function of law. The purpose is not to make junior lawyers of the students, nor is it to teach specific laws. The purpose of a law-related unit is to help students understand how laws affect all citizens. Law-related education has great potential to teach critical thinking skills. Nine specific critical-thinking skills can be taught through law-related education (Rogers, 1991):

1. Judging a statement from the premises. Laws are viewed as rules that define behavior and relationships.
2. Judging whether something is an assumption. Rules of evidence are used to help foster this skill.
3. Judging whether an observation statement is reliable. Is the observer credible? Were conditions for observation reliable? Is there a record of observation? Is the observation based on an inference?
4. Judging whether a simple generalization is warranted. Statements are classified to see whether they fit into a larger structure of knowledge. Are the instances biased? Are there counterinstances?
5. Judging whether a hypothesis is warranted. Are there supporting data? Are the data reliable? Can data be explained satisfactorily by a system of knowledge? Are data consistent? Are data testable?
6. Judging whether a theory is warranted. Is there a relationship between concepts and parts of the theory that explain the theory? Does the theory explain the evidence? Is the theory testable?
7. Judging whether an argument depends on ambiguity. Do arguments rely on ambiguity?
8. Judging whether a statement is too vague or too specific. Do statements provide guidance? Are they too vague or too specific?
9. Judging whether an alleged authority is reliable. Does the authority have a credible reputation? Is the authority an expert? Is the authority objective (no self-interest)? Have appropriate procedures been followed?

Which NCSS theme encompasses law education?

To clarify the purpose of laws, students should engage in research, debates, role-plays, mock trials, or simulations. Field trips and neighborhood walks make it possible for students to observe the use of laws in their daily lives. For example, on a walk around the school community students could observe the following:

- The use of street signs to assure orderliness
- The observance of traffic regulations by pedestrians and motor vehicles
- Rules that protect the environment
- Rules that regulate businesses
- Rules that regulate residential and commercial land use

Controversial topics can be introduced to students in law–related lessons to stimulate critical thinking, improve interpersonal communication skills, and help students resolve conflicts. In the mock trial, students can play the roles of plaintiff, defendant, and judge. If the mock trial is performed several times the judges can compare their decisions. The role players can share how they felt as plaintiff and defendant.

McBee (1996) notes that students are well acquainted with controversy in their homes, on the street, and in school, but lack formal training on how

Research Readings

Angell (1991) reviewed the theory and research on democratic climates in elementary classrooms. She used the theories of Dewey; Dreikurs, Grunwald, and Pepper; and Kohlberg, which suggested classroom environments to achieve democratic citizenship through the following:

- Peer interaction in cooperative activities
- Free expression
- Respect for diverse opinions
- Student participation in democratic decision making

She found a relationship between the aforementioned conditions of the classroom and the development of positive sociopolitical attitudes, higher levels of moral reasoning, prosocial behavior, and a sense of community.

to resolve conflict situations. Confronting controversy and making it a part of the contemporary social studies curriculum helps make school relevant, meaningful, and motivating.

Career Education

Career education programs in elementary and middle schools focus on the world of work. Their purpose is to acquaint young students with the diverse occupations that are available as career choices. The program's primary aim is to develop awareness of occupations that may be beyond the child's immediate experiences. The special skills and training required by different occupations make up the substance of the unit. Teachers who choose to develop career education programs must take particular care to avoid sex-role stereotyping.

Multicultural/Multiethnic Education

Investigation of multicultural/multiethnic education reveals great divergence in program implementation. Some teachers design a program about our multicultural heritage; others tend to focus on specific ethnic groups. Certainly the goal of multicultural education is to help students appreciate the contributions of all the people who are a part of our cultural life. This end can be achieved most effectively in a total, integrated social studies program rather than in a fragmented program called *multicultural*.

The infusion of multicultural content is both an equity issue and an issue of integrity. By presenting only the mainstream perspective of academic knowledge, students fail to learn about their own culture and others; they fail to recognize that knowledge reflects human interests and social relationships. For example, most social studies textbooks fail to mention African-American and feminine pioneers. (The westward movement has been described primarily through the eyes of white men, usually described as *rugged individualists*.)

Textbooks today still fail to give adequate treatment, dignity, and respect to varied perspectives and multiple interpretations of history. Suppose that students used social studies texts written in the late 1950s and early 1960s to learn about the Montgomery bus boycott and compared them to Rosa Parks's statements about the boycott. Still another means to gain an understanding of historical interpretation would be to ask the students to write their own perspective of

"How would you feel if you were Rosa Parks and you were expected to give up your bus seat?"

Moral Education

The work of developmental psychologist Lawrence Kohlberg has been influential in motivating interest in moral education programs. (Review the discussion on stages of moral development in Chapter 4.) Kohlberg believed that children need to be confronted with moral dilemmas in order to improve their moral reasoning. Teaching strategies designed to help students perceive that there is not necessarily one best answer to moral dilemmas generally follow this pattern:

1. Presentation of the dilemma (Whole class listens to or reads the dilemma)
2. Opportunity for students to think aloud; consideration of "What's the problem?" (Whole class discussion)
3. Reasoning: Why did it happen? What should be the response to this dilemma? (What will happen now, as a consequence of the dilemma?) (Small group discussions)

The teacher's role during moral education strategies is that of a facilitator, encouraging discussion and helping students learn to reason. Dilemmas appropriate for elementary and middle school students may focus on values that young students are concerned about such as the following:

Honesty	Friendship
Loyalty	Justice
Courage	Respect

HOW IS SOCIAL STUDIES ORGANIZED FOR INSTRUCTION?

The organization of related and sequenced segments of work is described as a *unit of study*. Teaching units in the social studies may be as short as a week or as long as a semester. The selection of a unit of work is related to an overall theme. It should conform to school district or state framework guidelines and is designed to meet the needs and interests of a specific group of students.

The social studies unit should be planned so as to integrate subject fields. The content for the unit focuses on social science concepts. It is through the concepts that interdisciplinary ideas are interrelated. The theme provides the overarching structure to integrate the curriculum. Illustrative themes and topics were identified earlier in the chapter. The actual unit-planning process was outlined in Chapter 9. Examples were provided in Chapters 7 and 9. The following is a list of concepts typically taught in elementary and middle school classrooms:

acculturation	interdependence
adaptation	justice
artifacts	land use
assimilation	law
behavior	migration
change	motivation
citizenship	multiple causation
communication	needs and wants
community	norms
competition	power and authority
conflict	privacy
cooperation	property
culture	resources
diversity	roles
emigrant	rules
enculturation	scarcity
environment	social control
family	socialization
freedom	space
government	supply and demand
groups	technology
immigrant	time
interaction	

HOW IS SOCIAL STUDIES TAUGHT?

Strategies for teaching are diverse and numerous. They range from reading and discussion to construction, dramatics, projects, and role-playing. There is emphasis on critical thinking and analytic skills; reading and research are featured. Values and human relations skills are often taught through games and simulations. Interviewing and case studies are used. Arts and crafts, music, and dancing are all integrated in the social studies. Many of the aforementioned techniques were described in Part II of this text.

Social studies teaching uses all of the teaching models described in Chapters 6 through 8: direct instruction, concept attainment, advance organizer, backward problem solving, and group investigation. The special cooperative learning strategies described in Chapter 12 are appropriate for teaching social studies. A combination of teaching models is often needed during the social studies lesson. For example, a teacher might begin a lesson with concept attainment to ensure that students understand a key concept and then utilize group investigation. Or the teacher might begin a lesson using direct instruction while reading out of a social studies textbook, proceed to role-playing, and then culminate with concept attainment to verify that students understand a specific concept.

The teaching unit is vital to good social studies teaching. Not only are the key concepts and big ideas identified in the unit, but planning ways to integrate other subject fields in social studies is critical to effective instruction. Greg Thomas's discussion about historical literature (Chapter 12) could be utilized by selecting historical fiction relevant to his social studies teaching unit. Using trade books to teach social studies is another very successful strategy, particularly for middle school students.

The classroom environment is very important to the teaching of social studies. (Note the research by Angell in this chapter.) The latitude of social studies activities and experiences is so great that an **arranged environment** needs to be considered. The environment for social studies is not only for motivation but to provoke inquiry or serve as a resource for learning.

In a social studies teaching unit, strategies are planned to initiate, develop, and culminate the unit. An **initiation** may be simple or complex. Thomas could have initiated the unit presented in Chapter 9 by having the students use the floor map and "walk across the United States." This beginning would be provocative and motivate interest.

At the beginning of the section about the social science approach to social studies is a description of an arranged environment. The arranged environment is a more elaborate way to develop students' interests in the teaching unit. The purpose of the initiation is to motivate inquiry and to provide a fruitful way to find out what students know and what they need to learn. This helps the teacher plan successive lessons and indicates whether or not the planned teaching unit is appropriate or needs to be fixed.

Developmental activities are all those experiences that move the unit from beginning to end. If students' interest lags during the course of the unit, the teacher may have to find a way to initiate new interest.

The **culmination** serves as a means to evaluate what has been learned and to end the unit. Thomas ended his unit with the production of a class mural. Sometimes dramatic play is an appropriate means to culminate a social studies unit. The production of a play, a mural, or a project provides a fine way to let parents know what their children are learning in the social studies. These activities serve as authentic assessment techniques. In addition, they provide means to integrate a number of subject fields.

READING IN SOCIAL STUDIES

During social studies, teachers have the opportunity to develop a variety of reading skills: location skills, reading for details and specific facts, skimming, note taking, proofreading reports and projects, choosing reading selections to fit specific historical time periods, and reading historical fiction. These skills can be taught more efficiently using subject field textbooks and materials than using basal readers. However, the reading of subject field materials presents special problems.

Frequently the organization pattern of social studies, science, or other subject field texts uses too few questions and subheads. Major and minor content focuses cannot be differentiated by immature readers. As a consequence, young readers cannot make sense of what they are reading, and they quickly lose interest.

Preplanning by the teacher can counteract this problem. Using the advance organizer teaching model to introduce and prepare students for the reading assignment will alleviate the problem. (Don't forget to evaluate the lesson utilizing the organizer so students integrate what they have learned.) By providing task instructions to facilitate structuring of the material and by helping students to frame questions about what they are to read, a content outline will emerge, and students will then have the necessary insight and motivation to read.

Another problem has to do with the concept load. Students cannot easily define words like *interdependence*, *culture*, and *change*, and as a result they do not understand what they are reading. The remedy is the same as that in reading instruction.

By prescanning the selection to be read and noting the concepts that students will not understand, the teacher can give examples to the students and then allow them to generate their own examples of the concept. The use of the concept attainment teaching model will be useful for this purpose.

Old textbooks can be updated with new pictures (maps, graphs, cartoons, charts, and photos) and with new information. However, sometimes it is valuable to use old and new information and pictures side by side; by doing this, teachers can help students make comparisons and develop interpretive skills.

USE OF PICTURES

In lower grade classrooms many teachers develop picture files related to their teaching unit. These files are not for bulletin board use, but rather for students' research activities. Pictures can be used to facilitate the development of the following social studies skills:

- Gathering data
- Grouping data
- Comparing and contrasting
- Forming generalizations
- Making inferences
- Making predictions

However, it would be a mistake to believe that students can use pictures without guidance. Young primary children will certainly need help. Even older students may have difficulty developing categories. To group data it is necessary to develop classifications for sorting. As students get better at classifying data, they will learn to develop their own categories.

Sometimes pictures disagree with each other. Paintings of early revolutionary battles that appeared in English and U.S. history textbooks are remarkably different. These pictures, now available, can be used for students to form generalizations or to make inferences based on the data. This lesson is most interesting if the students are not told the source of the data.

Older students enjoy cartoons and they can be introduced to the political cartoon. Students can be asked to interpret the picture and the words (if there

Teaching Hints:
Local History Lessons

While studying local history, Kirman (1995) recommends that teachers take photographs of local areas to compare with older pictures of the same sites. Old pictures can be obtained from government archives, museums, and historical societies. Students should be asked to observe change over time, examine the impact of technology, evaluate city planning, judge environmental impact of early decisions, and suggest alternate land use.

are words). The cartoon can be used to trigger historical research. For example:

What motivated the cartoonist?
What event is the cartoonist telling us about?
What is the cartoonist's message?
Why did this happen?

SMALL GROUP RESEARCH

Small group research is a very effective teaching strategy in the social studies classroom. Students should be grouped heterogeneously. Let us suppose that in Mary Hogan's second-grade classroom the children are studying about cities. Hogan has arranged the students heterogeneously into five groups, and each group is to study a different city in order to answer the question *Why do people live in cities?*

The students are using the following types of materials:

- Group A is using a social studies textbook about Japan to learn about Tokyo.
- Group B is viewing a filmstrip about London.
- Group C is using teacher-written information about New York City.
- Group D is using a picture file developed by the teacher after her visit to Honolulu.
- Group E is using some chart material, with the teacher assisting them as they read about Atlanta.

Hogan knows that it is important for all students to contribute to a class discussion. For this to happen,

Teaching Hints:
Small Group Interaction

It is important that all students are perceived as academically competent, contributing participants of the group. Cohen and Lotan (1995) recommend some teacher behaviors to support this perception:

> Before assigning students to group work, discuss the components of the problem they are to solve and the skills needed by group members in order to contribute to the group task. For example, "Your group will need to read the task card and follow directions, precisely." "Your group will need someone . . . who has spatial understanding, visual thinking, imagination, reasoning ability." Then assign students to the group, mentioning the strength of each individual and how you believe each can contribute.

In this way the teacher can help to modify academic status inequalities often perceived by students.

the students need unique information. If all groups used the same material, there would be limited contributions during the discussion, and these contributions would be made by a chosen few.

Hogan chose to study five cities because she wanted the students to be able to generalize about the following:

In what ways are all cities similar?
In what ways are cities different?

This was a personal teaching decision, not a decision that was absolutely necessary.

Collaborative work projects foster application of concepts and experience.

Using Group Investigation

Suppose Mary Hogan had asked the students to plan a city. This lesson would probably follow the preceding lesson. She would group the students heterogeneously, remind them to choose a group leader and a recorder, and then designate places for the groups to work.

The students would begin their task by reviewing what each student knew about the characteristics of cities. If they needed to verify their information, they would be responsible for finding the resources in the classroom. Their work would be enriched because they had been in different groups and used different resources for the previous lesson; their work would also be enriched by their own diversity. Since at least one student in each group could read well, the children would not have a reading problem.

Data Retrieval

For Mary Hogan's students to get to the point where they can make generalizations about the nature of cities, there had to be a system to amass the data that each group brought to the class discussion about the question *Why do people live in cities?* Hogan's system was to write the pertinent information on the chalkboard and then to guide the students to develop categories and accumulate the data for later use. With her students, she developed a data retrieval chart (Figure 13.2).

Semantic Maps

Semantic maps (Figure 13.3) allow students to visualize information and see how things fit together.

> **Why did Hogan group the students instead of having the whole class read the same material? Why did she use five different cities?**

They are another way for students to learn to conceptualize and to compile information for application and integration. In Mary Hogan's group investigation lesson on why people live in cities, the groups could have been asked to develop a semantic map depicting the characteristics of cities. The semantic map could have the question *What are the characteristics of cities?* in the middle of a sheet of paper. From this focal point the students would draw arrows illustrating the characteristics. Each set of characteristics would be captioned with a concept about the characteristics of cities. For example, the captions might be *Workers, Manufacturing, Commerce, Services,* and *Transportation.*

USING PROJECTS TO TEACH SOCIAL STUDIES

The project method of teaching originated with the work of William Heard Kilpatrick, who used projects as a means to unify the curriculum and as a means to involve students in meaningful activities. Kilpatrick's idea of the project corresponded to our concept of a thematic unit.

Projects may be used to unify and integrate a curriculum unit or as a single activity within a unit. Projects may be conceived for students to work on individually or as group projects. An individual project may involve a report about an individual or a particular event. Group projects usually require many different skills and involve several individuals or the

---

Figure 13.2 Data Retrieval Chart

	Tokyo	London	Honolulu	New York	Atlanta
Types of Housing	Apartments Houses			Apartments Townhouses Houses	
Types of Work					
Types of Services		Police Health Fire Schools			
Types of Recreation					
Types of Transportation				Subways Bus Taxi Auto	

Figure 13.3 An Example of a Semantic Map

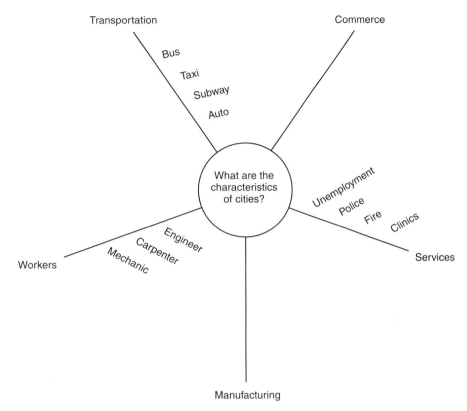

whole class. (Review Sara Garcia's class research project in Chapter 7.)

Projects are constructivist in nature because they require that students generate their own knowledge through an experience. Garcia's students had to interview, develop questionnaires, record data, and come to conclusions. Students can be involved in community projects (promoting safety, organizing a cleanup, writing to the city council, collecting food and clothing for the homeless) or they can study a problem and apply what they learn (overcrowding in the cafeteria, dismal halls, double–parking in front of school, raising funds through a school carnival, putting on a science fair).

Projects can be focused on historical problems that require extensive research. For example, suppose students are studying about the Civil War period. They might be asked to investigate what the slaves did during the war period: Where did they live? How did they get along? Did they join the Union army? Or they might investigate the Underground Railroad: Who escaped? Who helped the slaves? What risks did people take in order to help? (This question provides a good topic for a moral dilemma: Would you have been willing to take the risk of helping the slaves?)

Projects such as these may require that students read historical fiction, create maps of the period, dramatize events, write plays (and produce them), and construct dioramas and murals. Projects provide an interesting and highly motivating means to involve students in interdisciplinary studies.

TEACHING SOCIAL STUDIES SKILLS

Study skills, critical thinking skills, and social participation skills are taught in the social studies. Many subskills can be identified for each of these skill areas.

Study skills are those skills that have to do with acquiring information: locating the information, organizing it, interpreting it, and communicating what has been learned. They are best taught at the propitious moment. For example, when students encounter a graph that they cannot read, the teacher might say, "Just a moment, boys and girls, some of us may have a difficult time reading this graph. Let's all put our pencils down and look up here while I explain how to read a graph."

Study skill needs in the social studies should also be anticipated. If students will be required to gather

Teaching Hints:
Using the World Wide Web

Risinger (1996) writes that the Civil War commands more attention from teachers and historians than any other event in U.S. history. He recommends the Library of Congress Web site to download holographs of two versions of Lincoln's "Gettysburg Address." He also recommends the American Civil War home page.

Gettysburg Address:
http://lcweb.loc.gov/exhibits/G.Address/ga.html
American Civil War Home Page
http://cobweb.utcc.utk.edu/~hoemann/cwarhp.html
United States Civil War Center
http://www.cwc.lsu.edu/index.htm

   Below are several more Web sites related to the Civil War. The addresses were all current when this book was written, but the Internet is a dynamic resource that is constantly changing. New sites appear daily, and old sites disappear or move to new addresses. If you cannot find one of the sites listed, you can search for Web pages on any subject by using search engines and site directories provided with most Internet services.

http://jefferson.village.virginia.edu/vshadow2./
   Archives from two communities on opposite sides during the Civil War
http;://www.access.digex.net/~bdboyle/cw.html
   Information, documents, and archive access
http://www.erols.com/kfraser
   Confederate songs and poetry describing life during the Civil War
http://rs6.loc.gov/cwphome.html
   Photographs of the Civil War from the Library of Congress collection

information from a variety of sources, then they will need research competencies in order to locate information in textbooks, encyclopedias, and other reference materials. Because these competencies are critical to many subject fields, they may be taught during social studies or during reading.

Critical thinking skills, like all other skills, need to be practiced. They include both convergent and divergent thinking. The development of critical thinking skills in social studies include the following abilities:

* Compare and contrast ideas, happenings, objects, or periods of time
* Set criteria to group data

* Formulate appropriate questions
* Use evidence to make inferences
* Formulate hypotheses
* Detect bias, stereotyping, ethnocentricity
* Make decisions and judgments

Social participation is another important skill area in the social studies and is considered a major social studies goal. Literature on social participation indicates that students should be involved in group decision-making activities that necessitate the following (Lemlech, 1976, p. 45):

* Cooperation with others
* Observing and sharing observations with others
* Listening to others' viewpoints
* Planning individual and group research or projects in school and community
* Voluntarily assisting others; accepting assistance from others
* Accepting responsibility and recognizing the need to act
* Identifying and interpreting group agreements and disagreements
* Using persuasion to influence others
* Negotiating and bargaining to influence intergroup action

Activities that emphasize social participation help the elementary and middle school student become aware of how people participate in rational decision making, how social change occurred in the past, and how social change will occur in the future.

Social participation strategies are action oriented; they utilize both small and large group participation. Content typically springs from students' personal experiences in the neighborhood and at school. The newspaper, the student council, and the playground are good sources of information for choosing relevant problems for student investigation.

Point to Ponder:
If You Were the Teacher

A new family moved into a house across from school. One of the children is a student in your class. During their first week in the new neighborhood, their trees were papered and a swastika was painted on the driveway. As the teacher, how could you use this event in a positive way in a social participation strategy?

RESOURCES FOR TEACHING SOCIAL STUDIES

Resources for teaching social studies are almost too numerous to mention. Nonprint materials include pictures, films, tapes, television, realia, records, resource persons, and places. Print materials include textbooks, trade books, newspapers, and the Internet.

Obtaining and utilizing resources require anticipation of classroom needs. This is an important management prerequisite for successful social studies teaching. Since it is fairly easy to anticipate what your social studies unit will be, advanced planning of resources is not as difficult as it might seem. For example, the teaching of a unit on the community can include some slides or photos taken by the teacher of the immediate neighborhood. Magazine pictures can be collected. Software programs may be borrowed from the library. Travel agencies and large corporations are often willing to supply teachers with pictures. Groups like the dairy council or the meat industry welcome teachers' requests. Many teachers utilize their vacation travels to take pictures of places that will be useful in teaching social studies.

Great care needs to be exercised in selecting people to serve as resource guides. Although it is not difficult to identify individuals who have specialized knowledge, the problem is to ascertain whether the individual is able to communicate that knowledge to children. Before finalizing your commitment to an individual, it is a good idea to provide the person with a guide of what to expect in terms of students' questions and in terms of what you want the person to communicate.

Field trips should also be preplanned. The teacher should know what students will see and what they will do on a field trip. The best way to assess this is to take the trip yourself before you take the students. Before the field trip, students should be programmed with questions about what to observe. A walking trip through the neighborhood can be a valuable experience, but only if students are directed to observe some specifics.

Realia can be collected bit by bit and purchased when funds allow. Quite often friends have special objects such as tapestries, knickknacks, or items from personal travel experiences that they are willing to share. Realia can often be borrowed from teacher resource centers. For example, in Los Angeles the Museum of Natural History has a teachers' resource center, from which teachers may borrow all types of realia (including taxidermic animals), slides, and pictures.

Records, tapes, and films can usually be ordered from the school district or county school offices. Many large libraries allow teachers to borrow media, but orders have to be placed well in advance of need.

Print materials include books, maps, graphs, charts, newspapers, *My Weekly Reader, News Ranger,* and printouts of information from the Internet. (Reading during the social studies is discussed in the section *How Are Social Studies Taught?*) When considering the use of textbooks in the social studies it is important to remember that grade-level designations are not necessarily pertinent. It is possible to do a community study at almost any grade level, and it is possible to study other societies at many grade levels. Social studies books should be shared rather than designated for a particular classroom and stored on a closet shelf. For preparation purposes the teacher needs to survey what is available at the school and what is useful for teacher resource purposes and for students' resource needs.

FINDING OUT WHAT STUDENTS KNOW—AND DON'T KNOW

Teachers need to diagnose what a child knows (knowledge) and what a child can do (skills), as well as students' learning characteristics, attitudes about learning and working with others, and ability to work cooperatively with others.

Greg Thomas needs to know whether his students understand the concept of *adaptation*. One of the easiest ways for Thomas to find out is to ask his students the meaning of adaptation. If his students can define it *and provide examples both of what the concept is and what it is not*, then Thomas may feel relatively confident that the concept of adaptation can be used by the students as a tool to study human behavior. Although it is fairly simple to write a paper-and-pencil test to find out what students know, it may not be necessary for diagnostic purposes.

The ability to use study skills is easily diagnosed. If students are able to extract and interpret information from charts, tables, pictures, or cartoons, then the teacher can be confident that students have mastered a certain level of competence. On the other hand, if students are unable to utilize reference materials to locate information, then the teacher knows that reference skills need to be taught.

Critical thinking skills can be similarly diagnosed. Given evidence about certain events, students are asked to suggest probable conclusions. If they cannot do so, then they have not mastered that skill. Skill diagnosis should be systematically performed by the teacher. This can best be done with the use of checklists. Chapter 11 provides examples for use in the social studies.

Interpersonal or social participation skills, such as listening and respecting other's opinions or recognizing one's own and others' biases, can be diagnosed by observing students. During a class or small group discussion, the teacher is able to observe the way students work with their peers. The observation of students at lunch or on the playground also reveals a great deal about social participation skills.

CLASSROOM MANAGEMENT

Classroom management during social studies is no different than during reading or math in the sense that the teacher still needs to perform planning, organizing, anticipating, arranging, and monitoring tasks. However, certain aspects of classroom management may be more significant when teaching a subject field like social studies. For example, if students are to use a variety of instructional materials (books, media, pictures, computers, and the like) and use them in different places in the classroom because of grouping arrangements, then all of the classroom management components assume greater importance. The teacher needs to anticipate what learning materials students will need, where these materials will be used, how students will be grouped, and how evaluation will be handled. Monitoring behavior and learning needs become crucial to the success of the lesson.

The teaching episode in this chapter about the fifth-grade students observing the arranged environment provides an example to analyze for classroom management problems. The episode does not answer the following questions:

- Why did the students not misbehave as they wandered about observing the artifacts and instructional materials?
- How did the teacher get the students to their seats?
- How did the teacher get attention so that a discussion could take place?

These are the kinds of questions a teacher would have to ask before attempting this strategy. The episode lets us know what the teacher did not do; now let us think about what must have really happened.

- The teacher had many items on display, and they were distributed around the room so students would not crowd as they looked at the materials.
- The students were allowed to touch the materials. Since children need to touch what they are looking at (so do adults), any admonishment not to do so would only create a problem.
- The teacher provided enough time to satiate interest; the students had no need to beg for more time.
- The teacher began to write on the chalkboard. This signaled the students that it was time to return to their seats. (The teacher had observed the students carefully and knew they had observed for a sufficient amount of time.)
- Probably the students were accustomed to nonverbal suggestions; the teacher may have gestured or made some expression of the need to begin the discussion.

The trick to social studies classroom management is the anticipation component. The teacher needs to think out the following:

- Where students will work
- What resource tools will be needed
- How the lesson will be motivated
- How much time will be needed
- What problems might be anticipated
- How evaluation will be accomplished

EVALUATING SOCIAL STUDIES GROWTH

Social studies growth can be measured by standardized tests. However, standardized tests have a number of limitations. These include the following:

- The test may be testing reading ability instead of subject matter content.
- The test is often used to label students' ability levels instead of to diagnose skill deficiencies.
- The norms established for standardized tests often do not represent minority populations.
- Low-level objectives are easier to measure; therefore, what the test measures may not be of great importance.
- Standardized tests may not reflect what the classroom teacher taught. The diverse nature of what is taught in social studies makes it a difficult subject to test with a standardized battery.

Growth can be measured by teacher-made tests. These tests are often more reliable because the test can be designed to measure what was actually taught.

AUTHENTIC ASSESSMENT

Authentic assessment using what students actually produce in order to learn may be the best means to assess what students know. Suppose that Karen Adazzio wants to test her students' social science skills and whether her students understand that all social groups have a purpose, a means to make decisions, and that these decisions affect group interaction and the overall structure of the group. She could ask her students to give an oral report or write a written report that includes the following information:

- Investigate two social groups (at school or out of school) and identify the purpose of the group
- Interview at least three members of each group
- Ask each person the same questions (include the questions in your report and use follow-up questions, if needed)
- Describe how the group is organized
- Describe the decision-making process for the group
- Identify ways in which group members support each other
- Discuss what happens if members do not agree with each other
- Make a note of differences in opinion
- Decide whether or not the group serves its purpose and provide evidence to support your conclusion

Note that this type of assessment crosses subject matter lines because students need to use a variety of skills. In addition, the test is related to precisely what the students are studying. It is context bound.

LEARNING CENTERS IN SOCIAL STUDIES

The learning center provides a means to enrich and expand social studies teaching. The center technique can be used to reinforce skills, teach concepts, and differentiate instruction to accommodate learning-style needs. The center may be planned for use by an individual or for small group work.

The Direction Game

Social Studies, Mathematics—Lower Grades

Objective: To reinforce spatial directions (north, south, east, west).
Materials: Game board constructed of tagboard, 20 pictures, spinner, playing pieces
Evaluation: Cooperative play, recognition of directions

Procedures:
1. Construct a square game board of tagboard with 120 squares.
2. Collect 20 small pictures of places in the neighborhood (gas station, stores, fire station, homes) to place on twenty squares.
3. In the center of the gameboard designate a square for START.
4. Write a rules card.
   - Place the pictures on the game board. Space them around the board.
   - Take turns to spin the spinner. Tell the other players the direction you will move your playing piece.
   - If you land on a picture, you may take it.
   - The person who has the most pictures wins the game.

New Business

Social Studies, Language Arts—Upper Grades

Objectives: To reinforce reference skills, decision making, social participation
Materials: Task card, fictional Yellow Pages, want ads, map of a city, books about how to study a community, pictures of businesses in a fictional city
Evaluation: Group evaluation of social participation skills (see Chapter 11). Provide time for group sharing of decisions after all groups have used the center. Provide an evaluation card with a list of possible choices if desired
Procedure:
1. Write task card instructions:
   - If you were to start a new business in the fictional city of Abercrombie, what would it be? List the steps your group will follow to make the decisions.
   - Choose a recorder and a group leader.
   - Decide what each person will do to gather data.
To Simplify: Use easier materials; control the data.
To Extend: Increase the data to be used.

Choose a Role

Social Studies, Language Arts—All Grade Levels

Objectives: To reinforce communication skills, data-gathering skills, comprehension skills
Evaluation: Class discussion after center has been used about the importance of insightful questions and the authenticity of role playing

Procedures:

1. Write role card instructions:
   - Choose a role.
   - Study the role using pictures, books, information sheets, audio tapes.
   - Play the role when you are interviewed.
2. Write interviewer card instructions:
   - Write questions for an interview.
   - Play the role of an interviewer.
   - Guess the role of the person you are interviewing.
3. Develop roles related to a historic time period (pioneer in colonial America, surveyor, shipbuilder, mill owner, pirate) or to careers in contemporary society such as community helpers for primary children.
4. After students play the role of the interviewer and the interviewee, they should exchange task cards with a new role chosen and with the new interviewer writing new questions to ask.

Beliefs

Social Studies, Science, Health, Language Arts—Grades 5–8

Objectives: Students will categorize concept attributes. Students will develop problem-solving, decision-making, and research skills.

Materials: Text materials, pictures, media

Evaluation: Use of evidence to prove or disprove hypotheses

Procedures:

1. Students are given text and pictures related to patterns of behavior, customs, beliefs of specific groups of people or beliefs/practices of society; for example, beliefs about AIDS. These beliefs may be associated with cultural ideas or scientific or environmental beliefs.
2. Included in the learning packet is a retrieval chart.
3. Students are to write several hypotheses about the behavior and/or beliefs.
4. Hypotheses are to be supported with evidence from the written material or the pictures.

Characteristics of Learning Centers in Social Studies

- Learning centers in social studies integrate fields of study. The Direction Game uses social studies and counting skills in mathematics.

- The learning centers are social. While it is true that a center can be used to individualize instruction and that it is possible to design a learning contract for a student using a center, the purposes of the centers proposed here involve goals related to social studies. These centers are for two or more students, and they promote interaction, communication, and decision making.
- The center provides an element of fun and satisfaction. The use of the center should be different from typical classroom activities.
- The center is arranged to attract and motivate the students. Materials do not have to be elaborate, but they can be colorful and appealing. The center can utilize bulletin board space, or a special area can be designed to create the illusion of privacy.
- The center is purposeful and meaningful. Gimmicks are not needed. The activities should be designed to accomplish specific learning objectives.

LEARNING PACKETS

Learning packets are sometimes called *learning modules* or *instructional modules.* They are most typically used in upper elementary grades and middle school. Their primary purpose is to individualize instruction. Similar to the learning center, they often integrate fields of study. The author believes they should provide both fun and satisfaction. Learning packets in the social studies are not intended as a programmed, behavioral approach to teaching; instead, they provide a means to differentiate content, processes, and what students produce. Though packets are often used by a single student, they can be used in pairs or for small groups of students.

Most of the learning center examples can be organized into learning packets.

MULTITEXT READING AND USING THE INTERNET

The use of more than one textbook to study the content of social studies is characteristic of most classrooms. Perhaps the custom originated because many school districts failed to buy enough textbooks for each child to have a copy. However, when studying historical events it is much more valuable to read what different authors have to say in order to detect bias and to compare the authors' interest in the event. Another good reason for using more than one social studies textbook is that most students cannot read at the same level. By utilizing more than one textbook, it is much easier to find print material appropriate to students' ability levels. Since the social studies book is a resource, each text is a little bit different; by utilizing more than one textbook the students learn research methods.

Mary Hogan's small group research strategy demonstrated the appropriate method for using more than one research tool. Obviously Hogan could not find enough textbooks to satisfy her students' needs or she was concerned about accommodating different learning modalities. Multitext reading is a fine approach to adapt textbook reading to ability levels and to teach research skills, but it does not respond to learning-style differences.

The Internet provides still another means to diversify and enrich the input for students. Newspapers can be read using the Internet. (Review the Risinger teaching hint in this chapter.) Internet Yellow Pages can be used by students to find out the addresses they need for their research studies. However, the students may need a skill lesson to learn how to use Yellow Pages for finding information. Though use of the computer is appealing to many students, its use needs to be supervised and carefully guided.

SUMMARY

Why Teach Social Studies?

1. Through social studies students learn group process skills, and about U.S. institutions, customs, and values.
2. Social studies prepares students for citizenship responsibilities.

What Students Learn in Social Studies

3. Students learn about human experiences in the past, present, and future.
4. Students develop skills, values, and beliefs, and learn how to participate in a democratic society.

Citizenship Transmission Approach to Social Studies Teaching

5. Textbook study of history predominates in this approach to social studies teaching.
6. Socializing techniques are used to teach mainstream values, obedience to laws, social participation, and perception of the ideal society.

Social Science Approach to Social Studies Teaching

7. Emphases are on all of the social science disciplines.
8. Students are expected to learn about human experience by studying problems as social scientists might do so.
9. Students learn to ask intelligent questions and engage in inquiry.

Reflective Approach to Social Studies Teaching

10. Students choose what to study with opportunities to select relevant, contemporary problems.
11. Students engage in inquiry and utilize problem-solving procedures.
12. Students make decisions about social implications of problems and proposed solutions.

Selection and Organization of Social Studies Content

13. The expanding communities pattern is based on students' developmental needs and interests.
14. The Spiral Curriculum builds on expanding communities and teaches concepts at increasing levels of complexity and abstraction.
15. The National Council for the Social Studies recommends that content be selected using 10 organizing strands.
16. The strands should be interrelated for integrative and interdisciplinary curriculum.
17. Social studies encompasses diverse topics and programs such as global education, law education, environmental education, moral education, and multicultural education.
18. Social studies is organized for instruction through the teaching of social science concepts.

How Social Studies Is Taught

19. A teaching unit organizes the concepts and learning experiences for teaching social studies.
20. The unit is planned to motivate student interest through an initiating activity.
21. The body of the unit is made up of developmental activities.
22. Culminating activities serve to evaluate what was learned.
23. Small- and/or large-scale projects may be used as learning experiences for the body of the unit.
24. The construction of semantic maps helps students link information and integrate knowledge.

25. Learning centers and learning packets provide means to enrich and expand social studies teaching.
26. Learning experiences are diverse and include constructivist activities, print, and nonprint experiences.

Resources for Teaching

27. Resources include pictures, films, tapes, games, field trips, television, realia, records, and people. Print materials include printouts of material found on the Internet, texts, trade books, newspapers, and magazines.

Assessing What Students Know

28. Student knowledge can be determined through formal (tests) and informal (projects) means.
29. Observation of students' group work reveals their social participation skills and critical thinking skills.
30. Authentic assessment is valuable in social studies and crosses subject field lines as students develop reports and projects.

DISCUSSION QUESTIONS AND APPLICATION EXERCISES

1. Design a social studies learning center or a learning packet to differentiate instruction for gifted students in your classroom.
2. You are to deliver a talk to parents about the social studies at "Back-to-School" night. What will you tell parents about how the social studies curriculum facilitates the transfer of what is learned in school to the out-of-school lives of students?
3. Your students are studying the concept of *culture*. Develop a data retrieval chart using the components of culture.
4. Privacy is a basic value in a democratic society. Develop a rule-making activity focused on privacy needs. Decide how to divide the class into groups so each group will develop its own rule. Decide how to motivate the activity and how to evaluate the rules generated by the groups.
5. Develop a list of ideas on how primary and middle grade students can participate in their community and how upper grade and middle school students can participate in school, city, or state affairs.
6. Identify a motivating activity to initiate a study of global problems; identify a culminating activity for the same unit that can be used for authentic assessment.
7. Design a research lesson that requires a group of students to use the Internet and integrates subject fields.

14

Mathematics Education

This chapter examines how children learn mathematics concepts and links it to the Piagetian stages of development. Eight content strands and unifying ideas for structuring the mathematics program are identified along with the 13 standards advocated by the National Council of Teachers of Mathematics (NCTM).

The chapter includes the four components of problem solving and describes teaching episodes to demonstrate the process. Discovery and constructivist learning are contrasted with a traditional orientation to teaching mathematics. Both small group cooperative learning and whole class discussion during mathematics are examined, along with research studies concerning cooperative learning during mathematics.

The importance of concrete instructional materials is emphasized including the use of the calculator and computer. The special issues that receive attention in the chapter include gender, race, class, and culture; inclusion suggestions; performance assessment; reporting to parents; and mathematics learning centers.

After you study this chapter, you should be able to accomplish the following:

1. Identify two purposes of the mathematics program.
2. Explain why the use of concrete materials is important to the development of mathematical ideas.
3. Give an example of the Piagetian concepts of reversibility and transitivity.
4. Identify content strands in mathematics.
5. Write several objectives for each content strand.
6. Describe the sequence of mathematics instruction in a lower grade classroom.
7. Explain why mathematics specialists advocate discovery learning.
8. Discuss the conflict between behavioral and developmental psychologists related to math content and method.
9. Make a list of instructional materials available for use in the math program.
10. Suggest ways to use calculators and computers in the classroom.
11. Discuss the problems concerning gender, race, class, and culture related to mathematics achievement.
12. Identify planning considerations for teaching mainstreamed students in math.
13. Identify ways to evaluate progress in mathematics.
14. Create a math learning center to reinforce a math concept.

Professional Lexicon

automatize   To perform mathematics skills (procedures) effortlessly.

cardinal numbers   Numbers such as one (1), two (2), and so on, that indicate quantity but not order.

conceptual knowledge   The understanding of concepts, relations, and patterns to make sense of mathematics.

functions   Relationships among quantities and how they can be made explicit without dependence on symbolic example.

ordinal numbers   Numbers that indicate order or position in a series, such as first, second, or third.

procedural knowledge   Knowing how to use symbols and rules to do mathematics.

relations   The associations that are made as objects are counted or compared or related in some way with other objects or pairs.

reversibility   A Piagetian concept applicable to the preoperational level student who may not realize that a number is not affected by the ordering process.

transitivity   A Piagetian concept applicable to the individual who can or cannot coordinate a series of relations using physical objects ("This stick is longer than . . .").

LEARNING MATHEMATICS— WHAT ARE THE GOALS OF INSTRUCTION?

Jana was walking along the beach in Carpinteria, California, when she saw a gigantic footprint in the sand. "Look at the size of that footprint," she said to her friend Enrique.

Enrique was stunned. "My goodness," he said, "how tall do you think that person is?"

"Whoever it was, must be a giant," said Jana. "How can we figure out the height of the person who made this footprint?"

A sound mathematics program emphasizes problem solving, logical structuring of mathematical ideas, the functional application of mathematics content to real-world applications, integration of mathematical topics, use of manipulatives and technology, collaboration among students, and communication about mathematics. These program components are part of the new standards set by The National Council of Teachers of Mathematics (NCTM).

Through the study of mathematics, students learn to work with and communicate quantitative relationships. Mathematics can help students solve real-life problems by providing them with an abstract model for analysis. The study of geometrical and numerical ideas should encourage the solution of practical problems and contribute to students' personal satisfaction.

The mathematics program should focus on logical reasoning and independence of thought rather than on the production of correct answers. Learning experiences need to progress from the concrete to the abstract with an emphasis on real-world problems to generate students' interest. The mathematics program should provide an understanding and appreciation for mathematics concepts, structure, and terminology.

HOW DO CHILDREN LEARN MATHEMATICS CONCEPTS?

Problems like the one at the beginning of this chapter typify the changing curriculum in mathematics. The standards have helped to shift the emphasis of mathematics programs from the memorization of formulas and algorithms to reasoning processes.

The student's ability to use proportional reasoning is tested by the opening problem, and the student could be asked to prepare a report describing his or her thinking process. The teacher could draw a footprint on the chalkboard or display one on the bulletin

Figure 14.1

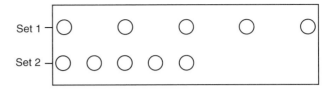

board. The student's ability to communicate effectively through the presentation explaining the thinking process, ideas, graphs, formulas, and calculations would all be considered in the assessment.

The ability to think logically affects the learning of mathematics concepts. Copeland (1982) linked Piagetian stages of development with mathematics learning. At the preoperational level the students uses sensory impressions when confronted with the question, *Are there more objects in one set than in the other, or are the sets the same?* See Figure 14.1.

At this level of development, the student would respond that there are more objects in the first set than in the second. The critical element is the spacing of the two rows. Only by making the two rows of equal length will the student believe that the two sets are equal. Not until the concrete operational stage will the child recognize that the number is *conserved* or *invariant* and that the arrangement of the set does not affect the number of objects.

Primary teachers need to know that even though the primary student counts the number of objects in each set, the student may believe that the spaced row of objects has more objects than the set that is not spread out.

Students are ready for formal abstract level mathematics at approximately 11 years of age, when the child can think at the formal operational level. However, Copeland cautioned that most 11- or 12-year-old children still need experiences with concrete materials to understand many mathematical ideas.

The concepts of **reversibility** and **transitivity** are useful to understand how children learn mathematics concepts. At the preoperational level students do not realize that number is not affected by the ordering process. Students will count objects from left to right and right to left before discovering that the set is the same from both directions. Not until students are six or seven years of age, at the concrete operational level of thought, will they understand the logic of reversibility.

Transitivity refers to the ability of the individual to coordinate a series of relations using physical objects. For example, if students have several sticks of varying length, they can indicate which stick is longest, shortest, longer than, and shorter than. They are aware that there is a relationship among the sticks making one stick longer than the preceding stick but shorter than the successive stick.

According to Piaget (1969), physical and logico-mathematical experiences with objects are significant foundations for the development of deductive thought. Concrete activities with objects should begin during the nursery school years. The use of **cardinal numbers** (one, two, how many) and **ordinal numbers** (first, second) begins during the preschool years. Activities during both the preschool and primary school years should focus on matching objects using one-to-one correspondence in order to determine which group has more or fewer or as many objects. Number names (one, two) can be associated with the matching activity along with practice in reading and writing numerals.

Experiences with logical thinking should begin with concrete activities. Children will not learn seriation through observation; they must have the opportunity to order objects from large to small or tall to short. Varied experiences are necessary for logical thought development.

Experiences with geometry should focus on exploration of shapes, the development of spatial sense, and recognizing geometry in the classroom and home. Students should be encouraged to construct their own objects and figures using a variety of materials.

Measurement ideas should be developed through activities of sorting and comparing lengths, mass, volume, area, and time. Children should be encouraged to verbalize about what they perceive ("This stick is shorter than or longer than. . . ."). Opportunities need to be provided for students to develop concepts of conservation and transitivity of length.

Mathematical ideas are dependent on discovering and creating patterns and classifying and comparing physical objects. Students lacking these experiences during the preschool years will need direct experiences during the primary school program. The primary program should be characterized by informal and exploratory experiences (Figure 14.2). Observation of students as they work with physical objects should reveal whether or not they can compare and classify objects and whether they understand symmetry and balance. The primary child should be en-

couraged to verbalize about experiences involving numbers and to ask questions about activities. Many primary teachers find that cooking experiences develop vocabulary and natural interest in mathematics; for this reason it is a favored primary activity.

CONTENT OF MATHEMATICS PROGRAMS

HOW ARE MATHEMATICS PROGRAMS STRUCTURED?

The mathematics program has typically been organized into major content strands. The *Mathematics Framework for California Public Schools* (1992) has identified eight strands, with an overarching emphasis on problem-solving applications for all of the strands. These are as follows:

1. Functions
2. Algebra
3. Geometry
4. Statistics and Probability
5. Discrete Mathematics
6. Measurement
7. Number
8. Logic and Language

The strands are intended to provide a means to balance content of the mathematics program. It is not intended that a strand be designated at a particular grade level. The strands are to be integrated with each other and run throughout the program. Some strands need to be used in conjunction with other strands.

Figure 14.2 Comparing Volume

At the concrete operational level of thought, the student will recognize that if two glasses contain an equal amount of water, when water from one glass is poured into a tall, skinny glass, the amount of water will not change.

Functions

The **functions** strand explores relationships among quantities and the way in which they can be made explicit without dependence on symbolic example. **Relations** are the associations that are made as objects are counted or compared or related in some way with other objects or pairs. Verbalization in mathematics allows students to talk about sets, numbers, pairs, collections, and sequencing. Functions are taught to elementary students when they study number facts.

Algebra

This strand is used in the context of problems and situations in the other strands. Algebra describes problem situations. It represents the language of variables, operations, and symbol manipulation. Algebra needs to be taught with and as an extension of the functions strand.

Geometry

Through geometry students link mathematics to space and form. Geometric concepts of line, point, plane, and three-dimensional space are developed. Once again manipulative objects are used for investigation, exploration, and discovery. Awareness of geometry in the environment is encouraged by utilizing art forms from business and industry, from nature, and from cultural experiences. Major topics include geometric figures, reasoning/logical thinking, coordinate geometry, and measuring geometric figures.

Statistics and Probability

Appreciation of human achievement and a healthy skepticism of capital T-type truths necessitate understanding, interpreting, and analyzing data that affect our everyday life. Statistics involves collecting, organizing, and interpreting data, as well as making inferences from data. Experiences beginning in the kindergarten should involve gathering, organizing, and analyzing data. (Examples are provided in Chapter 7). Topics include collection, organization, and representation of data; interpretation of data; counting techniques; and probability. Problems in science, health, physical education, and social studies provide good content experiences for student to use in the collection, organization, and representation of data.

Discrete Mathematics

This strand focuses on discrete objects or entities. Here students learn principles for counting discrete objects, basic set theory, discrete structures, recurrence relations, and the analysis of algorithms.

Measurement

Measurement is considered a key strand because understanding of measurement permeates our daily lives. Simple measurement tools are used to develop concepts of measuring distance, capacity, and the passage of time. Topics include arbitrary units of measure, standard units of measure, the approximate nature of measurement, and estimation in measurement.

The purpose of arbitrary units of measure as instructional content is to encourage students to measure with differing units in order to discover the need to compare objects using common properties and accepted units of measure. Techniques of measurement used during the arbitrary units are utilized when students recognize the need for standard units. As students use measuring tools, the concepts of approximation and estimation are taught. The development of the "educated guess" skill needs to be expounded as students practice measurement using measurement tools and observation skills.

Number

This strand emphasizes number systems and how they are used. Techniques for computing are taught. Experiences include counting and comparison activities using concrete sets of objects. Basic addition and multiplication facts are presented. Manipulative materials are used to motivate the development of computational algorithms. To develop students' abilities to work with abstract symbols, informal experiences are provided with physical models. Suggested activities include building with blocks, sorting objects of different shapes and sizes, sorting and classifying objects, fitting objects into each other, arranging objects by size and shape, experimenting with balance, recognizing positional relationships and symmetry, and discovering patterns.

Logic and Language

The strand focuses on logical reasoning processes and the ability to communicate them. During the primary grades, the teaching of logical thinking is informal; beyond the third grade, students learn to be precise. Logical thinking is supposed to be a natural outcome of mathematics instruction. Topics in this strand include patterns in mathematics and formal and informal reasoning. Mathematical patterns are taught through problem-solving activities. For example, the teacher might write the following on the board:

$$3...7...11...15...?$$

Students are asked to guess the next numeral and explain the basis for their decision. Discussion focuses on the recognition of a pattern. Students should be encouraged to recognize patterns in music, nature, and history. Formal and informal thinking occurs as students are encouraged to use and explain terms such as *if, then, and, all, some,* and *sometimes.* Students should be helped to see the value of using language precisely.

UNIFYING IDEAS

The California *Mathematics Framework* (1992) uses the term *unifying idea* to denote content that ties several subjects and mathematical strands together. Suggested unifying ideas for the K–4 grades include the following:

- *Quantifying:* How tall? How many? How much?
- *Finding, making, and describing patterns:* Patterns help students make sense of underlying structures of things, situations, and experiences. Patterns are used in prediction.

Teacher Research

Piper (1993) asked the following research question: *How does broadening the mathematics curriculum beyond computation skills and the textbook affect the attitudes of sixth grade heterogeneous math groups?* To collect data, Piper used math interviews, observations by other teachers, student participation during class time, videotaping, and journals that she and the students kept. Her study resulted in more problem-solving activities, cooperative learning strategies, and better connections to other curriculum areas and real–life situations. She found that the group work motivated the students and they preferred working with a partner or with a small group. Overall she realized that her own enthusiasm and confidence grew as she collected data and that her feelings about math learning were contagious.

- *Representing quantities and shapes:* This idea links students' experiences with mathematics; it helps students remember experiences and communicate about them.

For grades 5–8, the following unifying ideas are suggested:

- *Proportional relationships:* Students explore proportional reasoning (see the problem at the beginning of the chapter). Students study ratio, rate, per proportional parts, slope, similarity, scale relationships, linear functions, and probability.
- *Multiple representations:* Ways to exhibit problems and reasoning are emphasized. Students are encouraged to use sketches, orthogonal and isometric views of objects, diagrams, tables, frequency distributions, charts, graphs (including the computer for graphic displays), and spreadsheets.
- *Patterns and generalization:* This features situations that can be analyzed for pattern relationships, observations, and generalizations. The focus is on variable expression, similarity, different kinds of symmetry, systematic patterns, and ideas from probability.

PROBLEM SOLVING

Problem solving is viewed as an important aspect of the mathematics program. There are four components to problem solving/application skills:

1. Formulating the problem
2. Analyzing the problem
3. Finding the solution
4. Interpreting the solution

Formulating the Problem

How many times were you asked as a student, "What do you think is the problem?" How frequently do you ask your own students to identify the problem situation? Both the recognition of existing problems or perplexing situations and the statement of the problem in a form that can be studied require practice and special skills. The formulation of mathematical problems is similar to writing sentences. Both require precision, organization, and divergent thinking.

Analyzing the Problem

Students need to be taught to plan a strategy for attacking the problem. Quite frequently students are overwhelmed by a problem and cannot understand how to sort out the important information. A number of tactics can be taught to students, but the most critical aspect of problem analysis is the planning process, and it must be emphasized that the same tactics will not work in all situations. For this reason it is valuable to have students share their strategies so poor problem solvers will perceive that there are many ways to go about the task. Some suggested tactics to be taught to students are the following:

- Guess and observe the results; if it works, you don't have to go any further.
- Draw or graph the problem and see if that helps you to understand the relationships involved in the problem.
- Sort out similar and dissimilar elements.
- Identify known and unknown information.
- Identify the operations involved; translate the information using mathematical symbols and notation.
- Act out the problem.
- Construct or use physical objects to represent the problem.
- State the problem in your own words.

Finding the Solution

A variety of skills is needed to find the solutions to problems. It is important that students realize that some problems may have more than one solution or perhaps no solution. It is at this stage of problem solving that students should perceive the value of anticipating the results by using estimation. In addition to the typical operational skills needed, students may also need self-confidence to take risks and attempt to solve problems in new and imaginative ways.

Interpreting the Solution

This problem-solving component should say to the student, "So what?" If the solution is meaningless and the answer does not provide insight, then there was no purpose to the exercise. In interpreting the solution, the student needs to consider the original problem in order to judge the validity of the solution. The problem and the solution should consider the following questions:

- Was the answer reasonable? Expected?
- Was the strategy appropriate?
- Were all the facts considered?
- Is the solution accurate?
- Can the strategy be used with other problems?

- If some of the number components were changed, how would it affect the answer?

CHOOSING APPROPRIATE PROBLEMS FOR APPLICATIONS

In a second-grade classroom the children wanted to celebrate the end of the semester by going out to lunch together. The teacher channeled their interest in order to teach problem solving. The teacher wrote this question on the board: *Should we celebrate the end of the semester by going out to lunch, or should we make lunch for the entire class at school?*

Formulating the Problem

To formulate the problem the teacher guided consideration of these questions: Does it cost more to eat out at a restaurant than it does to make a lunch at school? Which restaurant would they select? How would the children get to the restaurant? Does what they choose to eat make a difference? Could all of the children afford to eat out?

Analyzing the Problem

After the students tentatively decided that perhaps they could walk to a neighborhood Mexican restaurant and that they would choose to eat quesadillas (tortillas with cheese), they realized that now their problem was to compare the cost of eating out with making the same lunch at school.

Finding the Solution

The teacher encouraged the children to guess how much it would cost to eat quesadillas at the restaurant and how much it would cost to buy flour tortillas, cheese, and vegetable shortening at the market. The students soon realized that they had no idea how many tortillas come in a package; nor did they know the price of cheese, shortening, and tortillas. To find the solution the students decided to walk to the market and price their ingredients and to call the restaurant and ask the price of eating the quesadillas there. After they had all of their information, they knew they would have to add the costs and compare eating out with making the lunch.

Interpreting the Solution

The teacher was well aware that the second graders would not be able to perform the addition necessary to work out the cost for an entire class; however, by breaking the cost down for the students so they could compare the cost of one lunch at the restaurant with making the same lunch, the students were able to make a judgment. Their evaluative discussion focused on the following:

• Were their guesses accurate about the cost of eating out and making the same lunch?
• Is it cheaper to eat out or eat in?
• How would it make a difference if they had selected a variety of lunches at the restaurant to compare with the prepared lunch at school?
• Why does the same meal cost more at a restaurant than at home?

Problem-solving investigations need to be meaningful to students and encourage a range of problem-solving strategies. The selected problem should motivate the development of skills and improve students' decision making. Good problems integrate subject fields and encourage investigations that expand students' knowledge, skills, and values.

NCTM STANDARDS

KINDERGARTEN THROUGH GRADE 4

Thirteen standards were identified by the National Council for Teachers of Mathematics (NCTM, 1989). These appear below with a sample excerpted goal for each standard. It is suggested that readers review the complete standards and goals set by NCTM.

1. *Mathematics as Problem Solving.* Use problem-solving approaches to investigate and understand mathematical content.
2. *Mathematics as Communication.* Realize that representing, discussing, reading, writing, and listening to mathematics are a vital part of learning and using mathematics.
3. *Mathematics as Reasoning.* Draw logical conclusions about mathematics.
4. *Mathematical Connections.* Link conceptual and procedural knowledge.
5. *Estimation.* Determine the reasonableness of results.
6. *Number Sense and Numeration.* Understand the numeration system by relating counting, grouping, and place-value concepts.
7. *Concepts of Whole Number Operations.* Develop operation sense.

8. *Whole Number Computation.* Model, explain, and develop reasonable proficiency with basic facts and algorithms.
9. *Geometry and Spatial Sense.* Describe, model, draw, and classify shapes.
10. *Measurement.* Make and use measurements in problem and everyday situations.
11. *Statistics and Probability.* Collect, organize, and describe data.
12. *Fractions and Decimals.* Develop concepts of fractions, mixed numbers, and decimals.
13. *Patterns and Relationships.* Recognize, describe, extend, and create a wide variety of patterns.

GRADES 5 THROUGH 8

A selected excerpted goal is given for each standard. Again the reader is urged to review the document in its entirety.

1. *Mathematics as Problem Solving.* Use problem-solving approaches to investigate and understand mathematical content.
2. *Mathematics as Communication.* Model situations using oral, written, concrete, pictorial, graphical, and algebraic methods.
3. *Mathematics as Reasoning.* Recognize and apply deductive and inductive reasoning.
4. *Mathematical Connections.* Explore problems and describe results using graphical, numerical, physical, algebraic, and verbal mathematical models or representations.
5. *Number and Number Relationships.* Develop number sense for whole numbers, fractions, decimals, integers, and rational numbers.
6. *Number Systems and Number Theory.* Understand and appreciate the need for numbers beyond the whole numbers.
7. *Computation and Estimation.* Compute with whole numbers, fractions, decimals, integers, and rational numbers.
8. *Patterns and Functions.* Describe, extend, analyze, and create a wide variety of patterns.
9. *Algebra.* Investigate inequalities and nonlinear equations informally.
10. *Statistics.* Systematically collect, organize, and describe data.
11. *Probability.* Model situations by devising and carrying out experiments or probabilities.

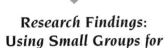

**Research Findings:
Using Small Groups for
Mathematics Instruction**

Mulryan (1995) studied the attending and participating behavior of 48 fifth- and sixth-grade students when they worked in cooperative small groups and in the whole class setting during math. She found the following:

- Students spent more quality time on–task in the small groups than they did in the whole class setting.
- Students participated more actively in the small group than in the whole class setting.
- Boys exhibited more initiating behavior than girls in the small groups.
- Low achievers were more passive than high achievers in the small groups.

12. *Geometry.* Identify, describe, compare, and classify geometric figures.
13. *Measurement.* Estimate, make, and use measurements to describe and compare phenomena.

HOW IS MATHEMATICS TAUGHT?

In a first-grade classroom the students were seated in a group in front of the flannel board. Their teacher, Jed Benson, was telling them a story using five flannel airplanes. He explained, "These airplanes belong to the daring Navy pilots known as the Blue Angels. These pilots often fly their planes in formation like this." (Benson demonstrated on the flannel board.)

"Let's count the airplanes together. (One, two, . . .) Now let's see if we can tell some stories about the numeral *5* using the airplanes."

Benson arranged the airplanes to tell the story of the numerals *2* and *3*. He called on the students to verbalize about what they were seeing. Then he called on different students to arrange the airplanes into the various subsets of five. When the students seemed confident with this activity, Benson passed out counting sticks to each student and sent them to their tables. He told them to arrange the sticks in a straight line in front of them and to count them. ("How many do you have?") After verifying that the students recog-

nized that they had five sticks, he said: "Let's see if you can group your sticks to tell the story of 5 with subsets of 3 + 2. Now do 2 + 3."

As the students worked, Benson observed their manipulation of the sticks. In making the transition from 3 + 2 to 2 + 3, Benson watched to see if the students reversed the arrangement of the sticks or had to count each stick individually. If a student had to count the sticks in order to make the transition, Benson knew immediately that the student did not understand the relationship of subsets to the original set of five and probably lacked the concept of reversibility.

After the manipulative experience, Benson went to the chalkboard and presented the information visually again, this time using dots. Then he presented it using numerals (1, 2, 3, 4, 5) and symbols (+, =). Following the visual representation, he passed out practice sheets for the students to use. Students were encouraged to use their counting sticks to help them as they worked with the abstract numerals on the practice sheet.

Benson's lesson had the following components:

- Motivating visual story of the numeral *5;* verbalization
- Concrete manipulative experience using counting sticks
- Visual presentation using numerals
- Reinforcement of the manipulative and visual experiences with abstract numerals

During each stage of work, Benson had monitored the students' performance and provided both positive and negative feedback.

Instruction in mathematics is enhanced by the use of objects or pictures. Elementary students learn best when they work with real objects and realistic problems. It is more effective to introduce new concepts and skills with a concrete referent than with paper-and-pencil exercises. Benson's teaching sequence was appropriate; he began with a concrete experience that appealed to the students' senses. He provided objects for manipulation. He then moved to the visualization stage and concluded with the abstract symbol stage of representative mathematical ideas. In addition, he provided appropriate dialogue to connect each stage. In the following episode a teacher introduces fractions using a physical object.

In Greg Thomas's fifth-grade classroom the children were asked to bring egg cartons to school. Thomas provided the students with dry beans. He asked the students to fill one half of the carton with beans and leave the other half empty. Then he had the students compare the different ways in which their classmates arranged the beans in order to fill one half of the carton. The lesson continued with directions for the students to represent one-third, one-fourth, two-thirds, and three-fourths.

Throughout the lesson, Thomas had the students compare their arrangements and talk about the number of ways each fraction could be depicted. As the students improved, Thomas had students go to the chalkboard and use symbols to represent the part to whole relationship as fractions.

On successive days, to extend ideas, Thomas had the students use Cuisenaire rods and sets of tangram pieces. Finally the students were asked to bring in some simple cooking recipes to help reinforce the applications of fractions. These activities precede formal abstract work with fractional numbers. Thomas was aware that it was not until about the age of 10 that students could use an operation approach to study fractional numbers.

DISCOVERY AND CONSTRUCTIVIST LEARNING

Mathematics specialists advocate learning by discovery with a constructivist perspective. Traditional teaching of mathematics required a **procedural knowledge** orientation in which students learned "how to." They learned to plug in a formula and perform an operation based on having learned certain rules. For example, the young student learned to add 18 + 3 without understanding the concept of place value or a base 10 numeration system.

In contrast, discovery and constructivist learning requires **conceptual knowledge** of a physical action or a mind picture that can be talked about, written about, reflected on, and ultimately translated to the abstract level. Logicomathematical knowledge is internal to the student rather than external.

Discovering patterns is much more difficult for students than writing answers. The former involves the process of thinking and requires that the student discover which particular pattern will apply to a specific situation. Discovery learning is enhanced by peer interaction. Communication between student and teacher and among students encourages students to share a variety of ways to solve problems, express inventive thinking, and obtain creative results.

Motivation is an important element in mathematics teaching. Problems should be selected by the teacher to foster discovery learning. Students need to feel that the problem is relevant and interesting as well as challenging.

The process of discovery may involve the use of unsophisticated (rudimentary) procedures. As students direct their own learning they will apply familiar procedures until they are ready to speculate about or

Constructivist learning is facilitated by physical action and manipulation of concrete objects.

guess a new pattern or a new way to approach the problem. Discovery occurs in the form of applying the discovered generalization.

Active learning is another way of describing constructivist learning. It may involve working with and transforming physical objects in order to learn through real experience what happens when, for example, you transfer a liquid from one vessel to another or manipulate clay from one shape to another.

Active learning also means involvement in group discussions and verbal clashes with classmates over which solution is right. The group discussion should focus on the thinking process so students are forced to clarify why they believe their solution is correct. An encounter about mathematical ideas can be as important as a discussion carried out in science or social studies.

The teacher's role during discovery and constructivist teaching is to ask questions, encourage students to make guesses, focus the search when needed, and select appropriate situations and experiences to apply the new ideas.

Now let's take another look at the giant's footstep in the sand.* Suppose Jana and Enrique want to solve this problem, and they bring it to the attention of their teacher, Karen Adazzio. She proceeds to draw several giant footprints on butcher paper and asks Jana and Enrique to present the problem to the class. Adazzio then divides the class into five teams and gives each team a drawing. She writes the following questions on the board:

1. How can you find out the height of the giant?
2. What ideas does your group have to solve the problem? (Describe each idea.)
3. Was each idea based on an underlying assumption? Explain the assumption for each of the possible solutions.
4. Did you test each idea? Describe your procedures for each idea that was tested. What math processes were used?
5. What worked? What did not work? Why?
6. Draw a picture of how you solved the problem.
7. Is the group satisfied with its solution? Explain why the group thinks its solution is accurate. If some members of the group are unsure of the accuracy, explain why.

Adazzio gives each group several sheets of paper with key headings on them:

1. Idea #__; Assumption: __; Description of Idea:
2. Testing Procedures for Idea #__; Math Processes:
3. We solved the problem using these procedures and processes:
4. We are satisfied with our solution because:
5. We are dissatisfied with our solution because:

REPETITION, REINFORCEMENT, AND APPLICATION

In the general public and within the math community there has been a great deal of controversy concerning traditional methods of teaching math and the curricular reform policies for teaching math. Teachers need to be cognizant of the dialogue and research in mathematics education concerning these practices and make and communicate decisions related to the following questions:

- Does drill and practice teach procedural knowledge *or* facilitate conceptual understanding? (What purpose should be served?)
- To what extent should drill and practice be used for the correction of errors?
- In what ways does drill and practice affect motivation?
- To what extent does drill and practice facilitate the application of concepts to new and varied situations?

THE AIMS PROGRAM

Activities Integrating Mathematics and Science (AIMS) is a program for effective instructional integration of mathematics and science in grades K–9. Originally funded by the National Science Foundation for grades 5–9, the program was so successful that it is now an established permanent program funded by the nonprofit AIMS Education Foundation. AIMS activities provide students with experiences in four learning environments:

1. Interaction with the real world through hands-on activities
2. Design, construction, and use of appropriate data records
3. Utilization of graphic/pictorial representations to display data
4. Engagement in the higher-order thinking processes of hypothesizing, inferring, and generalizing

---

*Problem and suggestions contributed by Judith Hillen of Fresno Pacific College.

The program provides staff development for teachers and monthly newsletters for continuing instructional support. The giant's footstep lesson in this chapter is an example of an AIMS discovery problem.

SUMMARY OF HOW TO TEACH MATHEMATICS

Mathematics instruction should develop both an understanding of numbers and number systems and the skills for using numbers to solve problems. In general, instruction should correspond with the following sequence:

1. Manipulations of physical objects (concrete experiences)
2. Visualization of the number problem (drawings)
3. Communication/discussion of the problem
4. Abstract representation using number symbols

GROUPING AND WHOLE CLASS DISCUSSION OF MATH

COOPERATIVE GROUPS

A number of math learning activities can be performed in small heterogeneous groups. Small groups enable students to express themselves easily and share problem-solving approaches. The small group helps students feel more comfortable about questioning how to solve problems. It also facilitates the exploration phase of problem solving. Students who are more able can explain problems in "kid's language," thereby facilitating understanding for the student who is less able. More positive attitudes about mathematics appear to develop when students interact with each other and with instructional materials in the small group.

WHOLE CLASS DISCUSSION

Class discussion during problem solving helps students become better and more efficient problem solvers. By questioning how students solved or approached the solution of a problem, students learn to verbalize the problem-solving phase. Since students do this in different ways, less efficient students learn problem-solving strategies by hearing the step-by-step approach of problem solvers who are more able.

Teachers' questions during the class discussion can stimulate student thinking and reasoning. Too often students attempt to implement a procedure for problem solving without understanding the concepts involved. It is important to give students time to respond

Research Findings: Cooperative Small Groups

Webb and Farivar (1994) studied urban middle school seventh graders in their mathematics classes. The ethnic composition of students was 55 percent Latino, 26 percent white, 15 percent African-American, 2 percent Asian-American, and 1 percent Middle Eastern. The students were unaccustomed to cooperative group work. Students in the experimental group received instruction in how to work in cooperative groups, communication skills, and ways to help others learn mathematics. The comparison group received similar instruction except they did not learn how to help others. The investigators found that improving students' ability to help others in cooperative small groups had significant positive effects on behavior and learning outcomes. Most particularly, the results were favorable for the Latino and African-American students.

Teacher Research

Melton (1996), a fourth-grade teacher in Madison, Wisconsin, wanted to know how working with partners of students' own selection would affect the students' math performance. The ethnic composition of the classroom was African-American, European-American, Hmong, and Latino. Melton focused the collection of data on the African-American students. She used a Cognitively Guided Instructional curriculum. She found that partner mathematics and a flexible classroom organization benefitted her students by promoting the following:

- Teamwork
- Active learning
- Self-confidence
- General understanding

Her research indicated that this was because the students had to explain their work both orally and in writing. The students also demonstrated greater risk–taking behavior.

and think through the solution of a problem, to determine why an approach did or did not work, and to develop alternative approaches and methods for solving a problem.

INSTRUCTIONAL MATERIALS FOR TEACHING CONCRETELY

There are a variety of instructional materials available for use in the mathematics program. These learning aids enrich the climate of the classroom, arouse students' interest, and encourage experimentation.

TYPES OF MATERIALS

Materials are needed for counting, sorting, comparing relations, measuring, and practice purposes. Most of the materials are relatively inexpensive or can be made by the teacher.

Size Relations

Objects such as wooden blocks, buttons, nails, wooden rods (Cuisenaire), string and ribbons, or rulers can be used to help students observe size relations. Students may be asked to determine Which is longer? Which is shorter? Which is wider? Which is smaller than . . .? Which is taller?

Mass Relations

Students estimate and measure ounces, pounds, grams, and kilograms. The measurements can be performed using a balance scale. Suggested materials for measuring mass include beans, marbles, stones, coins, buttons, and sand.

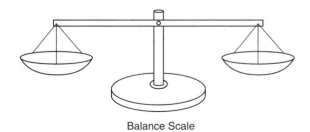
Balance Scale

Volume Relations

Containers of various shapes and sizes need to be available in the classroom so students can experiment with volume relations. Students should measure ca-

pacity using cups, pints, and quarts, as well as milliliters and liters.

Time Relations

To explore time relations students will need to use model clocks, a sundial, and a calendar. Many teachers like to make clocks from paper plates; the hands can be made of chipboard and attached with a brass brad. Teacher-made sundials for use outside are usually adequate for demonstration purposes.

Temperature

Both Fahrenheit and Celsius thermometers should be provided for students to learn to measure temperature.

Counting

For counting and learning place value, the following materials are recommended: ice cream sticks, beans, straws, counting frames, an abacus, a soroban, small wooden blocks, coins, a place-value chart, and a number chart. An abacus can be made with a coathanger wire, a wooden frame, and counting beads. First used by the ancient Romans, Chinese, and Japanese, and still used in banks and businesses in the Orient, the abacus, or soroban, is used to teach place value. Contests in Japan between individuals skilled in the use of the soroban and other individuals using calculators have demonstrated that the soroban can be used more rapidly than a calculator.

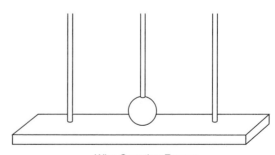
Wire Counting Frames

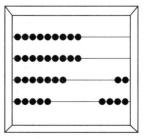
Abacus/Soroban

OTHER CONCRETE INSTRUCTIONAL MATERIALS

The pocket chart that is used so frequently in reading is also useful in mathematics. The pocket chart is labeled for place-value use in mathematics.

Hundreds	Tens	Ones
▮▮▮	▮▮▮▮▮	▮▮▮▮▮▮▮
▮▮	▮▮▮▮▮▮	▮▮▮▮▮▮▮

Pocket Chart

The number chart (0–100) is displayed in most primary classrooms. It is used to help students identify numerals, learn to write number symbols, discover patterns in the base 10 system of numeration, and perform addition and subtraction.

0	1	2	3	4	5	6	7	8	9
10	11	12	13	14	15	16	17	18	19
20	21	22	23	24	25	26	27	28	29
30	31	32	33	34	35	36	37	38	39
40	41	42	43	44	45	46	47	48	49
50	51	52	53	54	55	56	57	58	59
60	61	62	63	64	65	66	67	68	69
70	71	72	73	74	75	76	77	78	79
80	81	82	83	84	85	86	87	88	89
90	91	92	93	94	95	96	97	98	99
100									

Number Chart

The number continuum is a useful semiconcrete tool in the classroom. All that is needed is heavy tagor chipboard on which is drawn a straight line with points and arrows pointed in both directions to convey the number continuum. It is a good idea not to write the numerals on the number line. When the number line is displayed on the chalk ledge, numerals can be written in at designated points. The number line can also be used on the classroom floor.

Commercially made rods of varied lengths and colors are functional in the primary classroom. Students learn quickly that if they want to make 6, the

11   12   13

Number Continuum

6-rod will be as long as two 3-rods or the 2-rod plus the 4-rod.

Dienes blocks or place-value blocks help students perform subtraction. The blocks allow students to visualize the exchanging of hundreds, tens, and ones.

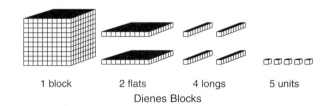

| 1 block | 2 flats | 4 longs | 5 units |

Dienes Blocks

Students enjoy using puzzle cards to practice their basic facts. These can be made out of chipboard or out of wood for long-standing use. The cards should have pictures or dots for counting, along with the abstract numerals.

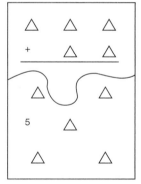

Puzzle Card

Geoboards, used to explore geometric figures, shapes, and relations, can be made or purchased commercially. A square piece of wood is used, with nails spaced one inch apart, vertically and horizontally. By stretching rubber bands around some of the nails, students study geometric concepts, relations, and measurement.

Dominoes can be used for sorting and learning number facts.

Rummy-type games are popular in the lower grades and the cards are easy to make from tagboard. More challenging rummy–type games using tiles require students to process numbers in a variety of ways. (The Rummikub® tile game for ages 8 to adult is an example.)

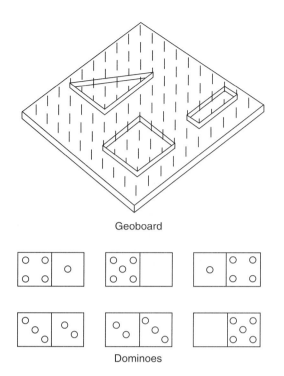

Geoboard

Dominoes

These games can be used for middle school students. Games and puzzles are ideal for helping students **automatize** procedures.

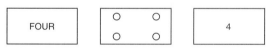

Rummy-type Cards

Game materials for practice and drill purposes can be bought or made. Useful items include number cards, lotto- or bingo-styled games, dominoes, Old Maid, or Fish. The game Battleship® has been popular in middle

	1	2	3	4	5	6	7	8	9	10
A										
B										
C										
D										
E										
F										
G										
H										
I										
J										

Battleship® Grid

Manipulative experiences facilitate comparison and classification of geometric figures.

grade classrooms to help students use a number grid. The ocean grid in Battleship teaches coordinate graphing and location skills as students graph and plot the opponent's ships through a series of hits and misses.

CALCULATORS AND COMPUTERS IN THE CLASSROOM

Calculators and computers affect not only *how* mathematics is taught in classrooms, but *what* is taught. Handheld calculators can be used in a variety of ways; the calculator allows students of all ages to experiment with mathematical ideas. The calculator motivates exploration of place value. It is also useful for the investigation of concepts and problems that would be too difficult for students if they had to do it on their own with pencil and paper.

The calculator allows students to extend their thinking in creative ways and makes computation less tedious. Students can use calculators to study real-world problems such as budgeting, marketing, and balancing a checkbook.

The calculator can also be used during the trial-and-error stage of problem solving to enable students to project and estimate a possible problem solution. Students will gain insight into the problem-solving process that would not be possible without the calculator.

Copeland (1982) cautioned that students should be introduced to the basic operations using physical objects prior to learning to use a calculator; however, the calculator can be used as a recorder of what the students have experienced. Calculators can be used in primary grade classrooms, but their use is more typical in grades 4–8.

To use the calculator productively, the students needs to know what operations are necessary to perform in a given problem. The calculator only helps the student speed up the computation step. Since the student needs to plug in the operation(s), it is important that teachers require students to think through the correct operation or sequence of operations. In mathematics education the computer has been used successfully to assist in instruction (Computer Assisted Instruction—CAI) and manage instruction (Computer Managed Instruction—CMI).

CAI has been used for drill and practice programs and computer programming. However, while most math experts agree that drill and practice on the computer may help automatize procedural learning, it will not help students learn to think conceptually about mathematics. Holmes (1995) comments that automatization should be an objective of the mathematics teacher *after* the students have the conceptual knowledge that underlies a procedure.

SPECIAL CONSIDERATIONS: GENDER, RACE, CLASS, AND CULTURE

Careers in the twenty-first century will require greater numerate capabilities. It is estimated that by the year 2000 one out of every five people in the United States will use computers. Yet current practices in classrooms often discourage female students, minority students, and low-income males from higher-level studies in mathematics. Teachers tend to give majority male students more time and attention than female students, minority students, and low-income students receive during mathematics. Sometimes this teacher behavior is unconscious, yet it still persists.

Suggestions to teachers have been made in several categories. The following are some suggested ideas

adapted from the *Mathematics Framework for California Public Schools* (1992):

- Demonstrate math concepts using contexts and representations from other cultures (using money, for example).
- Take advantage of staff development opportunities to expand understanding of students from other cultures.
- Provide equal quality time to all students. Verify that you are doing so through peer observation and/or videotape.
- Group students heterogeneously for problem solving.
- Encourage family assistance and student collegial work groups after school hours.
- Obtain assistance for students through community mentors who share the same culture and language.
- Plan appropriate support activities for students and verify that students are receiving assistance as needed.

From the review of research concerned with gender-related differences in mathematics education, it is apparent that fewer females enroll in higher-level mathematics courses that are prerequisite to, or will prepare them for, advanced careers in technology and the professions, and fewer females and minority students are encouraged by their teachers to enroll in higher-level mathematics courses. Gender, race, class, and cultural differences must be eliminated, and can be if teachers will make a conscious effort to encourage the target groups to engage in problem-solving activities, demonstrate the usefulness of mathematics, and verify that all students receive quality support.

INCLUSION

Although skill instruction for exceptional children frequently occurs in special education classrooms, students with special learning problems and disabilities can benefit from mathematics instruction in the regular classroom. Instructional planning for the mainstreamed student should focus on the following considerations:

Learning Style

- For the kinesthetic learner, provide more manipulative aids than is typically done. Be sure that students have counting sticks and other aids for computation tasks.
- For the auditory learner, record math facts on a cassette; record skill activities.

- For the visual learner, utilize individual chalkboards for students to write and draw on; suggest that students draw problems; use the Language Master for math facts.

Motivation

- Choose situations that are relevant to the mainstreamed child to motivate skill development.
- Explain the practical use of the skill (calculating gasoline consumption, identifying health risks).
- Vary activities to increase interest.
- Reinforce strengths; do not dwell upon deficiencies.
- Program instruction in short segments so that the student does not sit too long.
- Allow the child to work with a friend who will be of assistance.
- Reinforce positive accomplishments with realistic praise.

Instruction

- Diagnose needs carefully. Identify the precise need or error to be corrected.
- Determine the missing link in the chain of understanding. Reteach using concrete materials.
- Verify understanding verbally. Provide appropriate practice.
- Group students heterogeneously; mainstreamed students profit from group experiences. (They need opportunities to listen to others solve problems.)
- Utilize math learning centers for reinforcement activities.

Instructional Materials

- Clarify instructions and verify that students understand instructional tasks.
- Be certain that materials are clear and understandable. Some students may need large print.
- Verify that students can read the instructional materials and understand the math operations and processes.
- Avoid burdening the student with too many problems or assignments at one time.

Time

- Monitor the amount of time the child is working to ensure that activities are varied, movement needs are provided for, and length of assignment is reasonable, individualized, and motivating.

EVALUATION OF LEARNING

Progress in mathematics learning can be evaluated by teacher observation, performance assessment, teacher-made tests, standardized tests, and conferences between students and teacher. As Benson observed his students manipulating the ice cream sticks, he was able to detect which children had not attained the concept of reversibility. Students' interest and enthusiasm for working with math concepts can usually be detected through observation. Observation of students as they work is usually the first step in evaluation of growth. For example, if a student appears to be confused, the teacher can then engage the student in a discussion: "Show me how you found the answer." "How do you know that you should multiply first?" "Explain the pattern to me."

Teacher-made tests can focus on math vocabulary, the identification of processes, estimation, explaining problems, or performing computation. The tests can be completion, multiple choice, or matching. It is important that the mathematics test is not a test of reading skills. Teacher-made tests in math have greater content validity than formal standardized tests because teachers know what they have taught. The tests can be designed to gather information about the concepts and skills taught and practiced during the mathematics program.

The test can be a creative endeavor with pictures for young children and symbolic information for the more mature students. With young children, care needs to be exercised that they can read and understand the directions.

PERFORMANCE ASSESSMENT

Mathematical power as described by the California *Mathematics Framework* involves four dimensions: thinking, mathematical ideas, tools and techniques, and communication. Performance assessment utilizes rubrics (standards). The rubric must be commonly shared by teacher and student, and it must exist in the four dimensions. Some rubrics may prescribe exactly what needs to be present; others may be more open ended and state what needs to be accomplished.

Review the giant footstep problem. The teacher, Karen Adazzio, provided specific tasks to engage her students in thinking processes and mathematical ideas, the need to use math tools, and the opportunity to communicate both in the group and in what was expected of the group in terms of output. These tasks could have been accompanied by a rubric jointly agreed upon by teacher and students which would define expectations of the task specifying for students what would be conceived as "really well done" or "acceptable" performance, and "suggestions for improvement."

The goal of performance assessment is to examine what students produce rather than to focus on the students themselves. Teachers can use portfolios of student work, direct observation, conference talk between student and teacher, and group work. It is important that students participate in the assessment process and learn to explain their thinking.

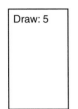 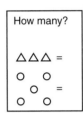 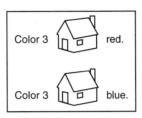

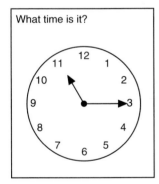 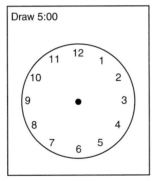

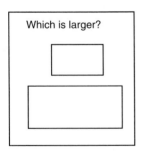 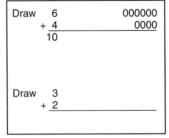

REPORTING TO PARENTS

In reporting progress to parents, it is important to remember that the isolated mathematics test is meaningless unless it is accompanied by an explanation of the concept that was taught. If all the parent sees is a test

sheet that informs him or her of a score (5 out of 12), the parent will focus on the number of correct answers instead of gaining a perspective on what the child understands. Communication about a student's progress in mathematics is best achieved through a parent-teacher conference rather than through test papers.

Performance assessment provides a more meaningful way to let parents know how their child is doing. When students become accustomed to describing their thinking process, they can talk about their work and explain to parents what they were trying to accomplish. The three-way conference enables students to participate in communicating to parents about their mathematical power.

LEARNING CENTERS

Learning centers in mathematics are used to reinforce math concepts, individualize instruction, and provide for special needs. Center use can be an integral part of the instructional program.

Estimation

Mathematics—Lower Grades

Objectives: To practice estimation; to compare mass

Materials: Two-pan balance scale, small objects (rocks, erasers, blocks) *Note:* To the scientist a balance scale measures mass and a spring scale measures weight.

Evaluation: Observation of mass, discussion, self-evaluation

Procedures:

1. Student(s) arrange objects from light to heavy or heavy to light on the table top.
2. Items are measured and compared with original guesses.
3. Objects are rearranged on table top to see if original estimation was incorrect.

Which Container Holds a Cup? Pint? Quart? Liter?

Mathematics—Lower and Middle Grades

Objectives: To compare containers of different size and shape; to use standard and metric units; to estimate volume.

Materials: Plastic containers of different sizes and shapes, sand, plastic drop cloth or newspapers, large spoon or scoop, measuring units

Evaluation: Observation, discussion, self-evaluation
Procedures:

1. Table and surrounding floor area are protected with the drop cloth or newspapers.
2. Students should be encouraged to guess and record how much each container will hold before measuring.
3. Students use standard measuring units to fill plastic containers with sand in order to determine how much each container holds.
4. Containers are compared and estimation validated.

Congruent Figures

Mathematics—Upper Grades

Objectives: To identify and draw congruent figures and line segments
Materials: Rulers, paper, pencils, task cards, examples for self-evaluation
Evaluation: Self-evaluation with peers
Procedures:

1. Set of task cards explains what students are to do. *Example:* Draw two congruent geometric figures. Draw two geometric figures that are not congruent. Draw the radius and diameter of a circle. Label each. Draw and label an angle, ray, line segment, isosceles triangle, parallelogram, trapezoid.
2. Compare your drawings with examples at center.

Congruent Figures

Mathematics—Lower Grades

Objectives: To identify and draw geometric figures
Materials: Crayons, paper, examples of different sizes and shapes, ruler
Evaluation: Teacher observation, self-evaluation
Procedures:

1. Find three objects (in the center) that are rectangles. Draw them.
2. Find three objects that are circles and draw them.
3. Find three objects that are triangles and draw them.
4. Draw two squares that are different sizes.

Problem Solving

Mathematics—Middle and Upper Grades

Objectives: To identify problem components; practice problem solving; develop the ability to generate data; participate in peer discussion of problem components and processes

Materials: Problems, box, paper and pencil, guide card
Evaluation: Answer sheet; discussion of processes, patterns, and probability
Procedures:

1. Prepare a guide card to remind students how to solve problems. The guide card should ask:

   What do you need to find out?
   What facts are given?
   What ideas do you have?
   What processes do you need to use?

2. Students may choose the problems from a special shoe box or "fish" for the problems.
3. Students should first identify the information, draw the problem, and/or use manipulative materials.
4. Explain the problem and how you would solve it.

Illustrative Problems for Problem-Solving Learning Center

1. Pretend that you have $300 for a vacation. Travel will cost you 1/4 of your total; food will cost you 1/5 of the total; accommodations will cost 1/3 of the total. How much will you have left for entertainment and gifts?

2. Make a chart of class absences for the month of October. See how many ways you can illustrate the information. Table 14.1 shows a sample chart. Were there more boys or girls absent during October? Did absences increase or decrease during October? What reasons might account for this? Which day of the

Table 14.1 Class Absences for Month of October

	Week 1		Week 2	
	Girls	*Boys*	*Girls*	*Boys*
Monday	2	3	3	4
Tuesday	2	2	1	2
Wednesday	2	1	0	0
Thursday	3	2	1	2
Friday	3	3	1	2
	Week 3		Week 4	
	Girls	*Boys*	*Girls*	*Boys*
Monday	3	4	3	5
Tuesday	3	4	3	4
Wednesday	0	1	2	2
Thursday	2	3	3	1
Friday	3	3	4	2

week had the most absences? The least? What reasons might account for this? Is this pattern typical of other classrooms at school?

3. In a fourth-grade classroom, seven children had birthdays in the month of December; fourteen children had birthdays during the months of January, February, and March; five children had birthdays in April; four children had birthdays in May; and two children had birthdays in June. None of the children had birthdays during the summer or fall months. Was this distribution of birthdays unusual? How could you find out? In this problem, students should be encouraged to organize the data, suggest ways to detect a pattern, interpret the solution. Is this pattern of birthdays typical of other fourth-grade classrooms? Fifth-grade? Sixth-grade?

Weather Chart

Mathematics, Science—Upper Grades, Middle Grades

Objectives: To observe, record, and predict weather conditions; to make inferences from graphs, peer interaction, and discussion

Materials: Weather instruments (mercury thermometer, alcohol thermometer, mercury barometer, wind vane, anemometer), pencil and paper, weather charts

Evaluation: Compare predictions and measurements with other students, weather bureau, newspaper

Procedures:
1. Students use weather instruments to observe and measure weather conditions.
2. Students record information (see Figure 14.3).
3. Students make daily predictions of the weather.

Money

Mathematics—Lower Grades

Objectives: To identify value of coins; to find equivalent sets of coins

Materials: Charts, paper and pencil, manipulative coins, task cards

Evaluation: Self-check with charts at the center

Procedures:
1. Task cards should identify a set amount of money that is to be illustrated. *Examples:* Draw all the ways you can make 42¢, 53¢, $1.00.
2. Students use the coins to help them find the answers.
3. Students draw their answers.
4. Students check their answers with prepared charts at the center.

SUMMARY

Goals of Instruction

1. Well-implemented math programs emphasize problem solving, logical structuring of math ideas, and functional application of content.
2. Students should learn to communicate quantitative relationships.

How Children Learn Mathematics Concepts

3. Developmental levels affect the learning of math concepts.
4. Concrete activities with objects contribute to learning math concepts.
5. Experiences with logical thinking should begin with concrete activities.
6. Mathematical ideas are dependent on discovering and creating patterns and classifying and comparing physical objects.

Content of Math Programs

7. Eight strands emphasizing problem–solving applications structure the math program.

Figure 14.3   Weather Record Form for Students to Complete

Weather Record					
Day	**Temperature**	**Air Pressure**	**Wind Direction**	**Wind Velocity**	**Prediction**
Monday					
Tuesday					
Wednesday					
Thursday					
Friday					

8. The National Council of Teacher of Mathematics have identified 13 standards for teaching mathematics.

How Math Is Taught

9. Concrete instructional materials help to teach math concepts.
10. Manipulative experiences and visualization help teach math concepts.
11. Discovery and constructivist learning are advocated to facilitate conceptual understanding.
12. Active learning is another way of describing constructivist learning.
13. Repetition and reinforcement are used to teach some procedures in math and develop automatization.
14. Small heterogeneous groups and whole class discussion contribute to math learning.

Instructional Materials

15. There is a wide range of instructional materials available for use in the mathematics program.
16. Materials are used to motivate student interest and encourage experimentation.
17. Games and puzzles are ideal for helping students automatize procedures.

Gender, Race, Class, and Culture Issues

18. Teachers need to encourage target groups to engage in problem-solving activities, demonstrate the usefulness of math, and verify that all students receive quality support.

Inclusion

19. Instructional planning for the mainstreamed student should focus on the student's learning style, motivation needs, instructional needs, material needs, and time and movement needs.

Evaluation/Assessment

20. Both formal and informal means can be used successfully to evaluate learning progress.

21. Performance assessment should examine what the student produces.

Reporting to Parents

22. Isolated math tests as a reporting device are meaningless to parents.
23. Performance assessment provides a more meaningful way to let parents know how their child is doing.

DISCUSSION QUESTIONS AND APPLICATION EXERCISES

1. Perform conservation tests with different-aged children and describe stages of development.
2. Prepare a speech for a PTA meeting on the value of using concrete materials in mathematics. Explain the use of Cuisenaire rods.
3. Prepare a lesson to teach subtraction that requires renaming tens to ones. Use concrete materials.
4. Plan a mathematics learning center to reinforce the understanding of fractional parts.
5. A student's response is totally irrelevant to the given problem; how will you discover what the student knows and what he or she does not understand?
6. What science, social studies, and health questions could be studied by the second graders who investigated going out to lunch along with the comparison of lunch costs?
7. What subject fields could be integrated with the study of the giant's footprint? Explain how you would do it.
8. Write a problem to engage students in math thinking, math ideas, use of tools and techniques, and communication. Write a scoring rubric for the investigation.
9. Refer to the Webb and Farivar research findings; identify the questions students should learn to ask each other when they are giving help.
10. Suggest several ways to assess students' problem-solving abilities.

C H A P T E R

15

Science Education

The development of science as a way of thinking is of primary importance in the teaching of elementary and middle school students. Greater emphasis on experimentation and inquiry-oriented teaching has made the process of teaching science as important as the content of science.

Science enlarges the student's perspective of the world and its environment. Science experiences are varied and appealing to the natural interests and curiosity of most students.

There are innumerable possibilities for science units; the choice can be based on the interests and maturation level of a specific class of students. Science teaching units typically reflect an interdisciplinary approach, are based on a curriculum theme, and integrate subject fields.

We can help students appreciate scientific principles and the processes of science by modeling a scientific attitude and demonstrating methods of inquiry.

After you study this chapter, you should be able to accomplish the following:

1. Identify purposes for teaching elementary science.
2. Identify the content for elementary science programs.
3. Describe several ways of teaching science.
4. List several national science programs and what these programs emphasize.
5. Make a list of science materials and equipment for classroom use.
6. Identify and discuss ways to evaluate science learning.
7. Create a science learning center emphasizing discovery learning.
8. Explain why mainstreamed students need a hands-on approach to learn science concepts.
9. Identify classroom management considerations when teaching science.

The Wump World was a small world, very much smaller than our world. There were no great oceans, lofty mountains, giant forests, or broad sandy deserts. The Wump World was mostly grassy meadows and clumps of leafy green trees with a few winding rivers and lakes. But it was perfect for the Wumps, who were the only creatures living there.

Mary Hogan continued reading *The Wump World* (Peet, 1970, p. 1) to her students. When she finished, she showed her students several globes with only water and land masses on them. She asked the students, "What covers most of the earth's surface?" In this way Hogan introduced a unit of study on the earth and the environment.

Hogan enjoys teaching science; she feels competent and secure in her science teaching. However, many elementary and middle school teachers feel insecure about

---

Professional Lexicon

constancy   Used to describe something that does not change; other aspects of constancy may be described as stability, steady state, and conservation.

models   Physical (concrete), mathematical, or conceptual objects, patterns or descriptions; refers to the ways things are alike.

open-ended science teaching   An approach that provides opportunities for students' own questions and opportunities for students to expand their inquiry by asking, "What would happen if . . .?"

scale   Differences in magnitudes; the ratio between upper and lower limits of variables. Scale affects the way things work.

systems   Groups made of parts that relate to each other and to the whole. The study of systems involves attention to the connections and interactions among the components and how parts affect the whole.

their science knowledge and their understanding of science concepts. For these teachers it is critical that they study their science books and other materials and learn to use science supplies and equipment. Curriculum guides and professional books on science are also helpful in planning the science program.

Scientific, mathematical, and technological literacy are on center stage in our changing society. If knowledge in these three areas is not the cause of change, it certainly is helping to shape the character of society. School science in elementary and middle schools does not ensure that young people will be budding scientists, mathematicians, or sophisticated technicians; however, by building literacy in these fields, young students will recognize and appreciate how scientific knowledge influences and changes their lives. Two publications by the American Association for the Advancement of Science have led the charge for reform of the curriculum in science, mathematics, and technology education. These are *Science for All Americans* (1990) and *Benchmarks for Science Literacy* (1993).

WHAT ARE THE PURPOSES OF SCIENCE IN THE ELEMENTARY AND MIDDLE SCHOOL?

Science is an essential and fundamental subject within the curriculum. Science provides students with opportunities to do the following:

- Think critically and practice methods of inquiry
- Develop science concepts that facilitate understanding of the biological and physical environment
- Develop appropriate attitudes and skills essential for democratic citizenship

Science offers unique opportunities to interrelate curriculum areas. Language development is facilitated when students have an experiential base to practice reading, writing, listening, and speaking. Science provides relevant situations for the integration of other subject fields, such as social studies and mathematics. The problem-solving skills learned in science and social studies facilitate the development of decision-making capacities that enable students to accept citizenship responsibilities.

Through the study of the natural environment students develop principles, processes, and generalizations of science. As students learn the application of these principles, organized knowledge becomes meaningful.

Why should science be considered a basic subject?

Science teaching is concerned with *content* (facts, concepts, theories, generalizations) and with *process* (observation, measurement, classification, comparison, inference, generalization, theory building).

CONTENT OF SCIENCE PROGRAMS

Both content and process are intertwined in the science program using the content as the subject of the inquiry. The emphasis of the science program is on discovery to develop problem-solving skills and scientific attitudes. Most science units and textbook series focus on three major divisions in the natural sciences:

1. Living things
2. The earth and the universe
3. Matter and energy

Topics related to these scientific fields of study include the following:

Living Things

Organisms
Life cycles
Plants and animals
Human body
Health and disease
Our senses
Fossils
Dinosaurs
Ecology
Environmental issues
Conservation
Recycling
Natural resources
Pollution
Food chains

The Earth and the Universe

Rocks and minerals
Earthquakes and volcanoes
Erosion
The changing earth
Sun and the planets
Stars and the universe
Air and weather
Wind
Sun, air, water

Matter and Energy

Molecules and atoms
Physical and chemical properties
Temperature, heat
Solar energy
Machines
Magnetism and electricity
Sound
Light
Space travel

These topics are taught through the use of *integrative themes.* According to the American Association for the Advancement of Science (AAS) Project 2061, the themes should be areas of major emphasis in the science curricula. The themes provide the overarching structure and major ideas for science inquiry and teaching. *Benchmarks for Science Literacy* states that the themes are ways of thinking rather than theories or discoveries. *Benchmarks* suggests four themes: **systems, models, constancy** and *change,* and **scale.** The *California Science Framework* suggests six themes that include energy, evolution, patterns of change, scale and structure, stability, and systems and interactions. The general focus of each theme is briefly described below.

THEMES FOR SCIENCE INSTRUCTION

Energy

This is the central concept of the physical sciences. Energy links the scientific disciplines of physical sciences, earth sciences, and biological sciences. It is important in the relationships of science, technology, and society.

Evolution

Evolution is change through time. This theme helps to integrate the history of natural things and the study of patterns and processes. Subthemes included in the study of evolution are direction, constraints, and chance.

Patterns of Change

Change through time may be studied through the theme of evolution. In addition, curricula may focus on rates and patterns of change in the natural world. Questions may involve how to control change, how to describe change, and how to predict change. This theme enables the study of trends, cycles, and irregular changes.

**Teaching Hints:
Using the Internet**

The following Web sites provide information and important links to other Internet sites. These addresses on the World Wide Web were current when this text was written; if any are no longer active, try using a search engine to look for other sites on the same subject.

Deserts, Plants, Animals
http://www.unp.ac.za/unp.departments/
    zoo/bglbook.html

Weather
http://www.weatheronline.com
http://www.intellicast.com

Life Cycle
http://www.wp.com/lifecycles

Scale and Structure

Curricula examine the structure of the natural world, the diversity of life, and the structure of matter. The theme is closely aligned with the study of systems and interactions and the effect of structure and function.

Stability

This theme refers to constancy (why systems do not change). In using this theme it is important to study nature so that students recognize that some changes occur but are masked by the constancy of change.

Systems and Interactions

Natural systems such as the solar system, ecosystems, individual organisms, and chemical and physical systems are the foci of study. The interactions of systems are significant areas of focus.

HOW IS SCIENCE TAUGHT?

How students learn science is just as important as what students learn. In the teaching of science, a major objective is to develop students' problem-solving capacities. To do this, learning experiences must be structured to provide students with opportunities to participate in processes of discovery.

For example, in Chapter 5 there was an episode about second-grade students studying magnets. First the children *observed* the teacher using a horseshoe magnet; then they themselves used the magnet. Their problem was to find out what magnets will pull.

As the children *experimented* with different objects that magnets attract, they *discussed* their observations in their small groups. They *hypothesized* in the sense that they tried out different explanations for what they were observing. They continued to experiment until they were satisfied with their *explanations.* The students *classified* their data by grouping their objects into those that were attracted to the magnet and those that were not. With the teacher's assistance they formed a *generalization* about their experiment.

There are a number of problem-solving skills that can be taught during science, but every science lesson will not feature all of these skills. The foregoing explanation is not intended as an all-encompassing list of the processes involved in discovery.

STUDENTS' ATTITUDES

One of the purposes for science is to develop appropriate attitudes and skills essential for a democratic society. A scientific attitude is considered essential in our society. Students will learn to accept the tentativeness of certain evidence; they will be willing to subject their ideas to testing; they will understand that it is okay to change their minds and that hypotheses often need revision.

Gega and Peters (1998) comment that when we talk about scientific attitudes we really mean the development of critical thinking. These authors identify four attitudes considered to be part of scientific literacy: curiosity, inventiveness, critical thinking, and ability to accept uncertainty. These four areas are certainly relevant not only for science, but for other curriculum fields as well. In science teaching, teachers may have opportunities to encourage curiosity and to confront students with interesting problems to stimulate an investigation.

In a sixth-grade classroom the students were disdainful about washing their hands before lunch. Jim's attitude was typical of many of the students: "Phooey, all we've been doing is sitting and writing. Why do we need to wash our hands?"

Teacher: All right. How could we find out if dirty hands make a difference?
Rhoda: What happens to food or to us if our hands are dirty?
Teacher: Why don't we design an experiment to find out?

Working with a friend stimulates learning experiences.

Jim: Well, most of us eat sandwiches; maybe we should preserve one touched by us unclean ones and another one by the cowards who wash up!

Teacher: Well, Jim, I'm not impressed with your terminology, but I think you are on the right track.

Sean: If we preserve a whole sandwich, how will we know whether what happens is a result of dirty hands or natural food spoilage?

Tina: Maybe we should just use bread without anything in between that would spoil.

Rod: Yeah, Tina, that's a good idea. But there's another problem.

Tina: What's that?

Rod: Even the air can contaminate; we still won't know if it's dirt or bacteria in the air.

Bart: We could enclose the bread in some airtight jars.

Jan: Ah, good. Why don't we get two jars with lids and put the bread inside?

Susan: Wouldn't we need to sterilize the jars?

Rod: That's a good idea.

Teacher: Boys and girls, you are doing great. It sounds to me like you have developed a good test to see if dirty hands really make a difference.

The next day the teacher brought bread and jars to class. The students talked about sterilization, and several students were appointed to take the jars to the school cafeteria for sterilization. The students refined their procedures and decided that each slice of bread would be handled by several students. One jar was labeled *Dirty*, and the other *Clean*. Three students were assigned the task of washing with soap, and three were chosen at random to touch the piece of bread to be labeled *Dirty*.

As the week progressed the students were rewarded by being able to record how the presence of mold changed the bread in the jar labeled *Dirty*, while the other piece of bread showed no noticeable change.

This teacher demonstrated confidence in her students. She gave them enough time to think about how the experiment could be designed. She herself modeled a scientific attitude by allowing the students to discover instead of telling them or having them read to find out the answer. As the experiment progressed, the students observed, questioned, and developed general-

Teacher Research

Miller et al. (1995) describe the Botanic Garden Project they implemented with middle school students at the Bluebonnet Applied Learning Academy in Fort Worth, Texas. The teachers designed a curriculum in which they "partnered" with professional botanists. The students used cuttings from the botanic gardens and propagated new plants, created ecosystems, and designed nature trails and an organic garden. The students also served as docents for other students' visits to the Botanic Garden. Students gained in communication skills through interviewing, leading tours, and responding to questions. They produced written reports, field studies, and trail guide maps.

izations. Ultimately the students' curiosity led them to their textbooks to study about mold and bacteria.

OPEN-ENDED TEACHING AND CONSTRUCTIVISM

The teaching of science provides a marvelous opportunity for teachers to release their own and students' creativity. Constructivism in science encourages hands-on activities. By asking questions like, "What would happen if both pieces of bread developed mold simultaneously (heaven forbid) or someone sneezed on the bread as they touched it . . .," new ideas for experimentation are explored.

If the sixth-grade students had not thought about the possibility of bacteria in the air contaminating their experiment, the teacher might have said, "How can we make sure that the only variable affecting the bread is dirt?"

Open-ended science teaching is similar to inquiry teaching, which is discussed in Part II of this text. It is important to identify the ways in which science can be taught most successfully. For this reason, examples of open-ended science teaching will be cited.

Seven fifth-grade students had been working on a time line of great inventions through the ages. When they shared their work with their classmates, the teacher realized the children had little conception of how magnetism was converted to electricity even though they were discussing the inventions of Faraday, Henry, and Oersted.

The next day in class the teacher provided the following materials: dry cells, insulated copper wire, sandpaper, large nails, and paper clips. The students were divided into small groups. Each group had the following problems to solve:

- How do you make an electromagnet?
- What ideas did your group have? Describe how you went about solving the problem. How do you know the electromagnet works? Describe your testing process.
- How do you change the strength of the electromagnet?
- What ideas did your group have? Describe your experiments.

Through experimentation the students learned that an electromagnet is made by winding the wire tightly around the nail and connecting the ends of the wire (which have been stripped of insulation using the sandpaper) to the dry cell. Further experimentation led to the discovery that the strength of the electromagnet was affected by the number of turns of wire on the nail. (More coils of wire increased the strength of the magnet.)

Although this procedure is relatively uncomplicated, many of the students did not realize that the wire had to be stripped at the ends before attaching it to the dry cell; nor did they realize that the amount of wire would affect the outcome. Many had no idea that the dry cell had both negative and positive poles and that both would be required to make the electromagnet. By comparing the electromagnets made by different groups of children, students were encouraged to find out who made the strongest magnet. (A simple way to find this out is to see which magnet picked up the most paper clips!)

The homework assignment for this class was to make a list of ways that electromagnets are used at home. Students were so enthused with their experiments that the teacher presented them with a list of projects they could make to continue their study of electricity. The list included a telegraph system, a lifting crane, a motor, and a crystal radio. The students chose their projects and were divided into project teams for the planning stage. Each student was required to draw a plan and list the specifications for the intended project. The students had a variety of pictures of telegraphs, motors, cranes, and radios. They were able to choose which model they wanted to make.

To make the models the teacher provided wood for the bases, tin from tin cans, nails, copper wire, sandpaper, coat hangers for the station finder on the radio, empty spools of thread, thin sticks, corks, masking tape, different types of clips, tubes from aluminum foil for winding coils, and diodes for the radios.

The projects motivated students to read about electricity and experiment with their projects. For example, students asked the following questions:

- Does it make any difference if you use more than one dry cell? (If two are used, how do you go about it? A connecting wire is needed!)
- Will radio waves pass through different materials? Which ones?
- How can we make our radio louder or softer?
- How do you send messages using the Morse code?
- How does an electromagnet differ from a regular magnet? Do they both pick up the same things?
- How can we make the motors faster? Slower?
- How much weight will our crane pick up?

The students' own questions, rather than the teacher's, became the focus of individual experimentation. Their questions served to expand their interests and open up the study of electricity, and their teacher was able to raise questions about ethical behavior and the relationships of science, technology, and changes in society.

Construction

The students were encouraged to work with a partner during the construction stage. On the first day of construction the teacher demonstrated correct tool safety procedures. These included the use of sawhorses, bench hooks to hold the wood, and the C-clamp. The teacher also explained how to measure using a T-square and a ruler, how to nail two pieces of wood together, and where to store tools when not in use. The students also needed to learn how to use tin snips to cut tin from the cans and how to wind wire evenly for the coils.

Construction is considered a creative and socializing experience. During construction students attempt to create a likeness to the original model. Projects are evaluated for authenticity even though authentic materials may not be used. Projects to be constructed require the following:

- Group planning
- Selection of materials
- Manipulative skills

- Sharing of materials and ideas
- Cooperative problem solving
- Measurement skills
- Experimental attitude
- Continuous evaluation
- Appropriate use of tools and materials
- Research related to use and function

As an activity, construction satisfies students' natural urge to produce something of their own and provides a means to motivate research about the real thing or product. Social and scientific concepts are learned when construction is carried out in a purposeful manner.

LANGUAGE ARTS DURING SCIENCE

Reading is used as a way of teaching science when students need to find out something (research), students need to extend their information and experience, and a substitute for original investigation and experimentation is desired. Reading is a particularly natural means to learn about science. Even though it is considered important for students to inquire on their own and experiment because of the benefit in terms of scientific attitudes, reading materials provide classroom resources that are not available in any other way.

When the students in Mary Hogan's classroom began to discuss the environment, one of the students asked, "What is a desert like?" Hogan, in her best teacherly fashion, responded, "How could we find out?" When the students asked if there were any books in the classroom about deserts, Hogan suggested a number of different resources. She identified the characteristics of the different resources:

- This book shows the author's interest in plants and animals of the desert.
- This book has many pictures of deserts.
- Our own classroom picture file will provide some information about desert sands and rocks.
- This resource may provide some information about the temperature of deserts.

Hogan then directed the students to choose their own resource for research about deserts and plan to have a classroom discussion about deserts in about ten minutes. To facilitate the students' reading, she wrote several questions on the board:

1. What is a desert?
2. Why can some plants live in deserts?
3. What are some desert plants?
4. What animals can live in deserts?
5. What is the name of a place in the desert where water can be found?
6. Why is a camel suited to desert travel?

More advanced students would have used the questions as advance organizers to assist them in their note taking.

Reading and writing during science (or during any other academic subject) should be purposefully directed. Unfamiliar words or concepts should be introduced and explained as needed using the context of the material. Science reading should not be a session where the teacher directs students to "Take out your science book and read Chapter 5."

Reading during science is far more effective when several resources are used. This method provides different viewpoints and perspectives on what is to be investigated, and it provides for individual differences in reading ability and in reading interests. Utilization of different resources also develops students' research and location skills. Teachers can identify the resources available as Hogan did for her second graders, but it is a good idea for students to find the appropriate pages through the use of the table of contents and the index.

DEMONSTRATIONS

Should teachers ever demonstrate an experiment? Certainly they should. There are occasions when it is more appropriate for the teacher to demonstrate a science concept or perform an experiment than to have students perform the experiment. Some experiences are beyond the manipulative skills of students and may in fact be unsafe for students to perform. Under these circumstances it may be wise for the teacher to perform the experiment and have students observe. Sometimes the purpose of a teacher experiment is to motivate new areas of interest or to evaluate students' observation skills, attitudinal growth, and conceptual understanding. Here again a demonstration may be the most efficient means to accomplish the purpose.

GATHERING DATA AND RECORD KEEPING

If students are to improve in their ability to use scientific processes, they need to learn how to gather data and describe their observations in order ultimately to decide why something happened. All kinds of records for writing up experiments can be devised.

Examples of the kinds of questions teachers can use to motivate thinking processes and communication during inquiry can be found in Chapter 14 with the giant footstep questions and in this chapter with the episode involving electromagnetism.

Figure 15.1 is another example. Students should be encouraged to devise their own records for writing up experiments. For young children it is often a good idea to create a large chart to record class observations. Sometimes the data can be recorded using smiles or frowns or other pictorial means to reflect the observation. The emphasis should be on describing what *is*, not what *ought to be*. If an experiment does not come out as teacher and students anticipated, then the discussion should focus on why not. Sometimes an experiment should be duplicated for verification purposes. This too can be explained to children.

FIELD TRIPS

Field trips may be simply a walk through the neighborhood to observe something special or a real excursion that requires planned transportation. Whichever

it is, the field trip must be planned and be an integral part of an ongoing science program. Students should be prepared for the trip with information about what they will see and what they are expected to do. If they are to take notes, this too must be communicated. If specific students or groups of students are to be responsible for particular information, then this should be assigned before the trip commences.

The field trip should be evaluated in terms of "What did we learn that we didn't know before?" "What surprised us?" "What did we verify?" and "What did we enjoy?" It is important to discuss the field trip and accurately record essential information, but it is not necessarily important that the field trip be written up individually by students.

SUMMARY OF HOW TO TEACH SCIENCE

Science teaching utilizes scientific concepts and focuses on the processes used by scientists. Discovery learning is featured because it motivates students' curiosity and interest in scientific subject matter and provides opportunities to practice the skills of observing, measuring,

Figure 15.1 Third-Grade Experiment Record

Problem: Miss Garcia's plant looks sick.

Hypotheses:
1. She did not water enough. (Plants need a lot of water.)
2. She watered too much. (Plants need a little bit of water.)
3. There was not enough sunshine. (Plants need sunlight.)

Materials: New plants

Procedures:
1. Plant #1 will be watered daily and placed on the windowsill.
2. Plant #2 will be watered twice a week and placed on the windowsill.
3. Plant #3 will be watered daily and kept on Miss Garcia's desk.
4. Plant #4 will be watered twice a week and kept on Miss Garcia's desk.

Results (Observations)

	Plant # 1	#2	#3	#4
3rd Day				
5th Day				
8th Day				
11th Day				
15th Day				
Conclusions:				

Table 15.1 Science Activities for Data Collection and Data Evaluation

Discussing	Planning, Reporting, Sharing
Recording	Record Keeping, Listing, Describing
Writing	Fiction, Reports, Information
Constructing	Making Gadgets, Science Equipment, Projects
Expressing	Talking, Singing, Drawing, Painting
Reading	Fiction, Science Information, Reports
Experimenting	Soil, Magnets, Sound, Light. . .
Observing	Animals, Plants, Events, Experiments. . .
Dramatizing	Role-Plays, Plays
Collecting	Pictures, Plants, Rocks. . .

classifying, comparing, generalizing, and theorizing (see Table 15.1).

The teacher's role as a resource person and facilitator is featured in science teaching in contrast to the teacher as an authority figure. Science teaching attempts to develop students' skills in other subject fields such as mathematics, social studies, and language arts. There is an effort to integrate cognitive, affective, and psychomotor behaviors. Learning *how* to learn science is as important as learning the content of science.

HOW IS SCIENCE ORGANIZED FOR TEACHING?

USING A THEME AND PLANNING A TEACHING UNIT

On a rainy day in Seattle, Washington, some first graders entered their classroom and asked their teacher if she had seen the rainbow. She responded, "Yes. Do you know how to make a rainbow?"

The students were perplexed. It had not occurred to them that it was possible to make rainbows. Their teacher took them outside to observe the rainbow once more. This time she asked them to name the colors they observed and the sequence of the colors (violet, blue, green, yellow, orange, red). She asked them to observe the way the colors merged. Once more the teacher asked the students, "How can we make a rainbow? What do we need?"

Observing the rainbow across the sky, the students realized that they needed sunlight and water. The next day the teacher provided jars and suggested that the students take them outside to see if they could make rainbows. With the teacher's assistance, the students soon learned that they would also need mirrors to reflect the sunlight through the water-filled jars. The

Teacher Research

King (1994) studied the effect of teaching fourth and fifth grade children how to question and how to explain ideas in science. She found that when students use questions that guide them to link ideas within a lesson with prior knowledge, they are able to construct more complex knowledge. She developed prompt cards for the students to use with questions, such as the following:

Explain why . . .
Explain how . . .
How are ___ and ___ similar?
How does ___ tie in with ___ that we learned today?

student's interest in and curiosity about light and colors led the teacher to develop a teaching unit that integrated science, art, and mathematics. Some of the science generalizations included the following:

- The earth is warmed by heat from the sun.
- Sunlight is a mixture of many colors.
- Most of the earth is covered by water.
- The sun heats the water.
- Rainbows are made because water changes the direction of the light.
- Some colors change direction more than other colors do.
- Color depends on the light that is reflected.
- Light that is not absorbed is reflected.
- White light is composed of the colors of the rainbow.
- A sundial can be used to tell time.

Science discovery lessons included the following:

- Using magnifying glasses and mirrors
- Making, mixing, and matching colors
- Learning how shadows help us tell time

Using the theme *patterns of change*, the unit developed by this teacher effectively integrated science, mathematics, and art, but as the unit progressed, the teacher realized that health could also be integrated by having the students study the care and use of their eyes. The development of a teaching unit in science is similar to the development of a unit in social studies. Just as a social studies unit can be planned to fit an all-encompassing theme, so can the science teaching unit.

It is important to identify the concepts to be taught and the possible learning experiences. By identifying the activities to achieve the unit objectives, the teacher can anticipate equipment, materials, and resource needs. Culminating activities should also be planned. It is advantageous to use a unit plan in science because it ensures that important concepts rather than trivia are taught, and it provides the teacher with a format to see that there is continuity in the lessons planned.

Although social studies teaching units may be limited to one or two a semester, it is customary in science to have a series of short units progress through the semester. Also, in science it is possible to include many science experiences that have nothing to do with the unit of study. This happens because it is advantageous to include experiences that may arise as a result of students' interests.

SCIENCE TEXTBOOKS

The teacher should be the one to decide what is to be taught during the semester. Science books are not organized to be followed in sequence necessarily. Although the content of the book is organized in unit form, it is up to the teacher to choose the sequence of the units. Most textbooks emphasize discovery learning and suggest appropriate experiments to help children understand the science concepts.

NATIONAL SCIENCE PROGRAMS

Curriculum improvement projects have been developed by scientists and science educators for use in the schools. These projects emphasize the following:

* Inquiry learning
* Sequenced experimentation by students to learn science concepts
* Understanding the underlying science disciplines
* Understanding the environment
* Development of mathematics skills
* Use of technology

Some of the major national projects will be discussed.

"WINDOWS ON SCIENCE"

"Windows on Science" was one of the first videodisc science programs developed. The laser disc K–8 curriculum program integrates reading and writing in the science curriculum with interdisciplinary and cross-disciplinary instruction. Each of the laser discs (there are 15 of them) has hundreds of photographs, diagrams, movie clips, and animations. The visuals are motivating to students and support the suggested lesson plans. Research studies questioned the effectiveness of the program and concluded that "Windows on Science" evoked greater interest in science topics and was equally effective with male and female students and limited-English-proficieny Hispanic students as with English-only students. Information can be obtained from "Windows on Science", Optical Data Corporation, 30 Technology Dr., Warren, NJ 07059.

"THE VOYAGE OF THE MIMI"

This program, described in Chapter 10, is another example of a microcomputer-based laboratory system available for classroom use. The program requires students to analyze, hypothesize, and evaluate as they gather data, explore, and discover. "The Voyage of the *Mimi*" has four learning modules: Maps and Navigation, Whales and Their Environment, Introduction to Computing, and Ecosystems.

NATIONAL SCIENCE PROJECTS, 1960S AND 1970S

Science Curriculum Improvement Study (SCIS)

This project focuses on science concepts concerned with matter, energy, organism, and ecosystem. Twelve units were developed for the project. Teachers using the SCIS materials guide children in their exploration of the science materials and encourage the students to investigate, discuss, and ask questions. The purposes of the project include the development of scientific literacy, investigative experience, and scientific attitudes. The materials designed by SCIS are available from Rand McNally & Company, Chicago, IL.

Conceptually Oriented Program in Elementary Science (COPES)

This project developed a Spiral Curriculum for grades K–6 using five conceptual schemes: the Structural Units of the Universe, Interaction and Change, Conservation of Energy, Degradation of Energy, and the Statistical View of Nature. All five schemes are used concurrently from K–6. The learning activities are designed to help students learn the concepts through active involvement. Skills such as analysis, classification, communication, experimentation, and interpretation are used repeatedly during the activities. The materials are available through the Center for Field Research and School Services at New York University.

Elementary Science Study (ESS) for Grades K–8

The units in this project are designed to promote investigation through construction activities. Schools may select and sequence the ESS science units to develop their own curriculum. The purpose of the activities is to have students develop a sense of satisfaction and confidence that they control a bit of their world by inventing and making something that really works. All of the suggested activities use simple everyday materials. An example is the student book for the Batteries and Bulbs unit, which contains pictures and descriptions of gadgets and projects that can be made by students. The purpose of the book is to interest the student in the wide range and variety of gadgets that can be made using simple tools and scrounged materials. Fifty-six units have been developed for grades K–8 and are available through Delta Education Inc., Box M, Nashua, NH 03061.

Science—A Process Approach II (SAPA II)

SAPA II is a revision of the original project that was developed by the Commission on Science Education of the American Association for the Advancement of Science. The K–6 project focuses on science processes instead of science subject matter; this focus is based on a belief that the scientific method for acquiring knowledge is essential to the education of all students. For this reason students participate in the activities that scientists would perform. Science lessons begin with the process of identifying the problem, proceed with ways to find solutions, and end with a group evaluation to determine whether or not the students have achieved the specified objectives.

Eight basic processes are taught in grades K–3: observing, using space/time relationships, using numbers, measuring, classifying, communicating, predicting, and inferring. In grades 4–6, five additional processes are developed. These integrated processes are formulating hypotheses, controlling variables, interpreting data, defining operationally, and experimenting (Gega, 1991, p. 682). SAPA II is available through Delta Education, Inc., P.O. Box M, Nashua, NH 03061.

Unified Sciences and Mathematics for Elementary Schools (USMES)

Another National Science Foundation project, USMES (grades K–8) was funded to develop interdisciplinary

instructional units in science, mathematics, language arts, and the social studies. Problem-solving processes are featured in the environmental investigations. Materials include a lab manual, background information for teachers and students, a teacher resource book for each of the problems, and a curriculum correlation guide. Information can be obtained from ERIC, Ohio State University, 1200 Chambers Road, Columbus, OH 43312.

These older programs are still useful for involving students in hands-on learning. They also provide "model" programs for you (teachers) to obtain ideas to tailor-make programs for your own students.

MORE SCIENCE TEACHING RESOURCES

Activities for Integrating Mathematics and Science (AIMS)

An overview of this program for grades K–9 was presented in Chapter 14. The program integrates science and mathematics. The rationale is that science encompasses the arts of questioning, investigating, hypothesizing, discovering, and communicating, while mathematics contributes the language that provides clarity, objectivity, and understanding. Essentially, the program encompasses language arts and social studies as well. Activities attend to real-world applications. The integration of mathematics and science appears to benefit both subject areas; student learning is increased through the integration that motivates investigation and participation in hands-on projects. The program provides staff development workshops for teachers, investigations for use with students, books for students, posters, manipulatives, and science-related materials for the experiments. The project also produces a monthly newsletter for teachers. Contact the AIMS Education Foundation, P.O. Box 8120, Fresno, CA 93747, for information.

National Audubon Society Program for Middle School and Junior High School

This project is aimed at helping teachers develop instructional units using discovery-oriented learning, hands-on experimentation, group projects, decision making, and state-of-the-art technology (Palmer and Muscara, 1991). The Audubon program orients teachers to the latest issues in environmental science and suggests innovative uses of video and computer resources. The program is funded by Citibank and has been operating in the District of Columbia Public Schools and in Montgomery County, Maryland. Contact the National Audubon Society, 801 Pennsylvania Ave. SE, Washington, DC 20003, for information.

Lawrence Hall of Science Projects

The Lawrence Hall of Science at the University of California at Berkeley, Berkeley, CA 94720, has produced a number of science projects for classroom use since the 1960s. The programs are targeted for elementary and middle school students. The programs are quite diverse and ongoing. They come complete with kits and teacher guides. Because there are so many, you should contact the developer for information.

Science and Youth Project (SAY)

Ponzio and Fisher (1996) describe the Science and Youth Project that provides early science teaching for prospective teachers at the high school level and introduces constructivist activities to elementary students. The innovative curriculum engages students in hands-on activities and applications for a community service project. Curriculum modules are in both English and Spanish. Curriculum is implemented through a three-step process: exploration, discussion, and application in the form of a community project. Using captivating curriculum titles, the topics are appealing and motivating for elementary students. A description of several of the modules follows:

Beyond Duck, Cover, and Hold. This is about earthquake and disaster preparedness.
What's Bugging You? Pests and responsible pest management is the topic area.
It Came From Planted Earth. This module focuses on agriculture, plant food, and fiber uses.

For information about the project and modules, contact Richard Ponzio, Director of SAY at the University of California, Davis.

MATERIALS AND EQUIPMENT FOR TEACHING SCIENCE

Science materials and equipment should not be a problem for the imaginative teacher. Common, everyday materials and equipment from the immediate environment can be used to enrich the science program. In the ESS project students are urged to use materials typically found around the house, school, or street:

Corks	Glue	Hammers
Tin Cans	Scissors	Emery Boards
String	Rulers	Milk Cartons
Bottles	Springs	Pulleys
Wire	Crates	Screwdrivers
Meters	Switches	Juice Cans
Pipes	Lights	Shoe Boxes
Magnets	Pans	Seeds
Balloons	Vinegar	Baking Soda
Fuses	Nails	Tacks
Measuring Cups	Balance	Spoons, Forks

Students and their parents can also be counted on to help equip the science program. Frequently students can bring many of the materials listed to class.

Iron filings, used frequently when students are studying magnets, can be obtained by sending students to the school sandbox with a magnet and an envelope to store the filings in. The teacher's main problem is to develop science kits for the different investigations or science units. Apple boxes, obtained at the produce department of large markets, make marvelous storage containers for the science materials and equipment.

SCIENCE SPECIALIST TEACHERS

In some elementary schools and most middle schools a science specialist teacher is responsible for the entire school science program. This teacher's classroom is equipped as a science laboratory. The specialist teacher organizes and plans the science teaching units for each grade level. The classroom becomes a science center, and all the materials are stored in this facility. In elementary programs students come to the center two or three times each week with their regular teacher accompanying them. The regular teacher serves as a *team member*, with the science specialist teacher performing the major teaching tasks. Follow-up teaching and reinforcement of science concepts occur in the students' regular classroom. In this way other subject fields are integrated, and the science program is not fragmented and apart from the real life of the children.

In the middle school where science is treated as a separate subject, it is extremely important that the science teacher joins with the language arts (English) and social studies teachers to plan integrated studies.

SCIENCE CENTERS

Some schools set up one classroom as a science center. The center is scheduled for use by the teachers, and each teacher is responsible for keeping the center equipped and ready for the next person's use. The center may also be used by a science club or students with special interest in science activities. The major advantage of a science center is that equipment and materials can be shared by many teachers instead of each teacher being responsible for obtaining personal resources.

RESOURCE PEOPLE

The science program, whether it is taught in the self-contained classroom or in a science classroom, should utilize resource people at school and in the community. The school custodian is probably an expert electrician, plumber, and carpenter; the custodian may be willing to share his or her skills in the classroom and thereby help translate textbook content into real-life problems with practical solutions.

The community itself should provide resource places and people valuable to the science program. Museums, the fire station, industries, the weather bureau, ecology groups, the city engineers' office, and the sanitation department all may be sources of information and sources for classroom consultants. Using community resource people or visiting in the community adds a sense of reality to the study of science.

It is important for teachers to verify that the expert knows how to talk to students. Before turning a resource person loose in the classroom, the teacher should verify what is to be communicated and how it is to be communicated. Young students may not react positively to the parent photographer who wants to lecture about the use of light meters; however, these same children may be very interested in how to build their own camera.

HOW SHOULD SCIENCE LEARNING BE EVALUATED?

Three purposes for science education were presented at the beginning of this chapter:

1. To provide students with opportunities to think critically and practice methods of inquiry

2. To develop science concepts that facilitate understanding of the biological and physical environment
3. To develop appropriate attitudes and skills essential for democratic citizenship

These purposes should be used to guide the evaluation of science learning.

EVALUATION OF CRITICAL THINKING AND METHODS OF INQUIRY

Observation of Students' Performances

Observations of students as they engage in group discussions, experimentation, group work, and individual projects provides information about how well students are progressing in using methods of inquiry. For example, a checklist (Figure 15.2) provides a format for observation of inquiry skills.

Communication

Listening to students as they talk with each other and as they respond to questions and participate in discussions provides evidence of what they know, how they have reasoned, and the care and testing with which they submitted their inner thoughts.

Written Reports and Record Keeping

Earlier in this chapter and in Chapter 14, classroom lessons illustrated the types of reports students can be asked to make while involved in problem solving and experimentation. These reports represent a fine assessment tool to verify students' understanding of scientific processes, critical thinking power, and ability to describe the thinking process. The observation record (Figure 15.1) for the third-grade experiment is another means to verify students' methods of inquiry.

Drawings and Graphing

Students can be asked to draw or make graphs to communicate their understanding of processes, ideas, progress, or solutions. Students may sketch or diagram inventions and understandings. The drawings, along with the written records and reports, can be used for portfolio assessment.

Products

Students can construct what they have been studying. Examples in this chapter included electromag-

Figure 15.2   Critical Thinking, Inquiry Skills Checklist

	Names of Students			
	Malcolm	**Jean**	**Maria**	**Rick**
1. When presented with a problem situation, does the student attempt to identify and define the problem?				
2. Does the student identify relevant information?				
3. Does the student suggest possible solutions or raise questions about cause and effect?				
4. Does the student suggest means to test or find ways to explain the data?				
5. Does the student attempt to gather data, observe, or collect evidence in a variety of ways?				
6. Does the student accurately report/observe the evidence?				
7. Does the student interpret the data accurately?				
8. Does the student recognize the need to validate the experiment/ research?				
9. Does the student attempt to generalize, make inferences, or theorize based on the interpretation?				

nets, crystal radios, and motors. Students can build pinhole cameras, kaleidoscopes, and inventions. Products can be used as apart of a science fair or other type of exhibition.

Suppose that some upper grade students were studying about sounds. Their teacher brought a megaphone to class. To determine whether or not the students could think scientifically, the teacher asked them the following questions on a test:

1. How can we make a megaphone?
2. How is a megaphone used?
3. How can a megaphone help us hear?

The students in this class were expected to identify the materials needed to make a megaphone and to identify how they would go about discovering its use. They were also expected to suggest ways to find out how the megaphone would improve their ability to hear sounds. This type of test measures the application and use of methods of inquiry. It does not focus on facts or scientific concepts.

EVALUATION OF SCIENTIFIC CONCEPTS

If those same upper grade students had made megaphones and discovered their use and determined how a megaphone could be used to help them hear better, their teacher could develop a test to determine whether or not the students understood the concepts associated with sound energy. The test could be short answer,

essay, or multiple choice. In this test the teacher might ask the following questions:

1. Why does a megaphone conserve sound energy? (A megaphone reflects sound in a specific direction.)
2. Explain how a megaphone works. (A megaphone concentrates the sound waves instead of allowing the sound waves to spread out equally in all directions.)
3. Does it make any difference which end of the megaphone you use? Explain. (The large end gathers the sound, the small end magnifies the sound.)

Students can also demonstrate knowledge of scientific concepts by what they say during an evaluative discussion or by what they write when they interpret an experiment. After studying organisms, students should know that living things are interdependent and that organisms may be classified by similarities and differences in characteristics. Concepts such as these should be generated by the students after performing experiments or reading about the adaptation of organisms.

EVALUATION OF STUDENTS' ATTITUDES AND SKILLS FOR A DEMOCRATIC SOCIETY

A scientific attitude describes the individual's skills development and willingness to do the following:

- Be open-minded (unbiased)
- Use reliable sources of information

After performing an experiment, students should write an interpretation and engage in an evaluative discussion.

- Validate information from a variety of sources
- Be curious
- Examine evidence and deliberate
- Interpret on the basis of evidence
- Understand the significance of multiple causation
- Reject superstitions

These behaviors can be evaluated by critically observing students' performance on work tasks, group participation, and the kinds of things that students choose to do or to share. For example, the student who chooses to participate in a science fair, pursues science hobbies, or suggests a class experiment certainly is expressing personal choice and a scientific attitude. A scientific attitude is vital in a democratic society because the individual is more likely to believe in and practice the following:

- Questioning results
- Searching for causal relationships
- Using several resources
- Accepting responsibility
- Critically evaluating own and others' work
- Contributing thoughts and opinions
- Applying scientific methods to a variety of situations

Further discussion of assessment and evaluation procedures can be found in Chapter 11.

LEARNING CENTERS

Science learning centers may be a part of the ongoing science unit or an added dimension used to reinforce skills during reading or mathematics. The centers may be used by a group of students working together or by an individual alone. Following are four experiments that can be used in a science learning center.

Soil Testing
Science, Language Arts—Upper Grades

Objectives: To observe and participate in a simple investigation to determine the composition of soil; to explain how the composition of soil affects the growing of crops

Materials: Blue and red litmus paper, soil samples from different places, paper cups, bottle of water, bottle of limewater, teacher information sheets or science books about soils and farming

Evaluation: Discussion—How does the composition of soil affect the growing of crops? Self-evaluation of experiment using teacher-prepared exhibit of acid, alkaline, neutral litmus paper

Procedures: Task card
1. Place a soil sample in a paper cup. Prepare at least four samples.

2. Add small amount of water to each sample to dampen the soil.
3. Test samples with the litmus paper.
4. After five minutes, remove the litmus papers and observe their color. (Blue litmus paper turns red or pink in an acid soil; red litmus paper turns blue in an alkaline soil. If the paper colors stay the same, then the soil is neutral.)
5. How do your soil samples differ?
6. If one of the soil samples is acid, change it to a neutral condition using the limewater.
7. What difference does the composition of the soil make to a farmer? Read and find out.

Making Magnets

Science, Mathematics—Middle Grades

Objectives: To compare the strength of temporary magnets; to generalize about temporary magnets
Materials: Iron nails, steel pins, steel screwdriver, head of a hammer, iron bolt
Evaluation: Discussion and self-evaluation using teacher-prepared answer sheet
Procedures: Task card
1. Brush the nail with a magnet.
2. Use the nail to pick up the steel pins.

   Find out:
3. How can you make the nail a stronger magnet? (Brush the nail longer.)
4. How do you know when it is stronger? (It will pick up more pins.)
5. Does it matter how you brush the nail with the magnet? (Brushing the nail in one direction makes the nail stronger.)
6. Try the experiment with other objects. Record your results. (It will be more difficult to magnetize steel than iron; however, the students should also discover that once magnetized the steel will retain magnetism longer.)

Life Cycles

Science, Social Studies, Language Arts, Mathematics—Lower Grades

Objectives: Observation of life cycle; sequencing the life cycle in appropriate order
Materials: Tank of tadpoles in different stages of development, garden exhibit in different stages from seed to mature plant, duplicated pictures of the two exhibits, scissors, paste, paper

Evaluation: Students may compare their life-cycle sequence with a teacher-prepared exhibit
Procedures: Students are to observe the two exhibits. Students cut out pictures and paste them in sequential order to illustrate the life cycle of the frog and of a plant.

Visual Arts

Science, Art, Language Arts—All Grade Levels

Objectives: To observe and describe accurately; to improve art skills; to enjoy an aesthetic experience
Materials: Weeds, flowers, leaves, and branches, or fish, insects, and pets; drawing or painting materials
Evaluation: Self-evaluation and group sharing
Procedures:
1. Observe the exhibit.
2. Describe the exhibit.
3. Draw or paint what was observed.

INCLUSION FOR SCIENCE TEACHING

Science teaching, as described in this chapter, emphasizes student participation in discovery learning. Mainstreamed children need a hands-on approach to

Research Findings:
Mainstreamed Students
and Science Instruction

Scruggs and Mastropieri (1994) observed three classrooms of third, fourth, and fifth grade children during science teaching to see whether students with visual, physical, auditory, and learning disabilities were successfully mainstreamed. They identified seven variables that were consistently associated with success:

1. Administrative support
2. Support from special education personnel
3. Accepting classroom atmosphere
4. Appropriate curriculum
5. Effective teaching skills
6. Peer assistance
7. Disability-specific teaching skills.

The researchers concluded that inclusion of these students in the regular classroom did not impede the progress of the students who did not have disabilities.

learning and a great deal of individualization. This makes science ideal for facilitating their acceptance, both personal and by peer mates, into the regular classroom.

Since most science activities are group-oriented, the mainstreamed student can work in a carefully selected small group or be programmed to work individually. The experiences themselves should be of high interest to the student since most students enjoy the study of animals, plants, magnetism, and the solar system. Manipulative experiences tend to be therapeutic, thus increasing the significance and attraction of science. Experimentation is particularly appealing, and the use of the senses in science enhances the study experience.

CLASSROOM MANAGEMENT

Classroom management considerations in science are similar to the concerns expressed about social studies. Anticipatory planning is of greater significance when students are to perform experiments in small groups that are not under the immediate supervision of an adult. The teacher needs to consider student safety, work space, and need for material resources. The modeling aspect of experimentation should also be considered. Suggestions are as follows:

Safety. Before students use science equipment or tools, they should be given specific instruction in their care and use.

Work Space. Before students are dismissed for work, the work space area should be designated, and consideration should be given to providing sufficient work space for each group.

Resources. Equipment, materials, and textbooks should be inventoried to ensure that they are of sufficient quantity to meet study or experiment needs of students.

Modeling. Modeling by the teacher of open-ended, inquiry-oriented learning is important so students recognize that it's okay if an experiment fails, and that most experiments need validation.

SUMMARY

Purposes of Science

1. Purposes include critical thinking and methods of inquiry, development of science concepts, and development of appropriate attitudes and skills.

Content of Science

2. Science teaching intertwines content and process.
3. The emphasis of the science program is the development of problem-solving skills and a scientific attitude.
4. Science programs focus on living things, the earth and universe, and matter and energy.
5. Topics are taught through use of integrative themes.

How Science Is Taught

6. Students should be provided with opportunities to observe, discuss, hypothesize, and explain.
7. Students need to learn to accept the tentativeness of evidence and to subject their ideas to testing.
8. Open-ended teaching and constructivism encourage hands-on activities.
9. Students' own questions may be the focus of individual experimentation.
10. Discovery learning is featured.
11. Students should engage in reading, the use of multimedia, demonstrations, experimentation, record keeping, and field trips.

How Science Is Organized for Teaching

12. Using an orverarching theme, teaching units can be planned to integrate other subject fields and provide opportunity for interdisciplinary lessons.
13. A variety of special curriculum programs and projects are available for classroom use.
14. These special projects have a number of similarities: Students are engaged in discovery processes, gathering and analyzing data, hypothesizing, evaluating, and judging.

Materials and Equipment

15. Common, everyday materials and equipment from the immediate environment can be used in the classroom to teach and enrich the science program.

Specialist Teachers

16. Science specialist teachers may be responsible for much of the science program in some elementary schools. Most middle schools include science teachers.
17. The science specialist needs to join with other teachers to integrate and team the planning of the instructional program.
18. In most communities there are resource people available to assist with the science program.

Evaluation of the Science Program

19. Students' critical-thinking skills and methods of inquiry should be evaluated.
20. Teachers can assess students' progress through observation, communication, drawings, graphing, written reports, experiments, and projects.
21. Attitudes and skills should be assessed by observing students' performance on work tasks, group participation, students' choices for projects, questioning stance, open-mindedness, validation procedures, and deliberation of findings.

Inclusion

22. Mainstreamed children should be engaged in hands-on learning in the regular classroom (as should all children).
23. Group participation and peer assistance and interaction are valuable for use in the inclusive classroom.

Classroom Management

24. Management considerations in science must include safety, work space, use of equipment, and modeling experiences.

DISCUSSION QUESTIONS AND APPLICATION EXERCISES

1. Identify scientific concepts and processes to be taught for a specified group of students. Describe three discovery learning experiences to teach the concepts and processes.
2. Develop several science kits for use in science experiments. List the equipment and materials to be found in each of the kits.
3. Your upper grade students have discovered how to light a bulb using wire and a dry-cell battery. What additional open-ended experimentation could they perform?
4. Your lower grade students are studying plants. Suggest some experiments they could perform to learn about seeds, plant growth, and plant propagation.
5. You have been requested to explain to parents why inquiry teaching is important in the teaching of science. What will you say?
6. Describe an investigation students will perform and the way in which you will require them to communicate their processes and solutions.
7. Draw a webbing concept map with a theme in the center; identify the science content and interdisciplinary connections.

16

Physical and Health Education

Most physical fitness experts recognize that children's fitness has declined in the United States in recent years. Perhaps this is due to inattention to the teaching of physical education. The wellness concept has been suggested to integrate the teaching of health and physical education. The concept encompasses nutrition, physical fitness, stress management, and personal responsibility for a healthy lifestyle.

In this chapter goals, content, and teaching strategies are discussed for both subject fields. Some key ideas presented in the chapter include:

- Physical conditioning activities and good sportsmanship
- Exercise and nutrition
- The development of healthful ways of living
- Self-awareness and self-esteem
- Thematic teaching and the integration of health and physical education with other subjects

After you study this chapter, you should be able to accomplish the following:

1. List the content areas for physical and health education.
2. Define physical fitness and state the purposes of physical and health education.
3. Describe stabilizing, locomotor, and manipulative movements.
4. Suggest classroom activities to foster a positive self-image and explain how play activities foster appropriate social behavior.
5. Discuss ways to develop health education goals.
6. Identify and describe the instructional sequence for teaching both a directed and indirect lesson in physical education.
7. Suggest movements appropriate for warm up, vigorous exercises, and cool down.
8. List equipment appropriate for physical education.
9. Identify ways to evaluate growth in physical and health education.
10. Suggest ways to teach health education.
11. Suggest ways to integrate the teaching of health education with other subjects.
12. Identify classroom management considerations when teaching physical education.

Professional Lexicon

adapted physical education   Individualized ideas and suggestions provided by a physical education specialist to service students with special needs.

biomechanics   The science that studies the effects of both internal and external forces on human body movements.

locomotor movements   Progressive movements that involve changing body position, as in running and walking.

manipulative movements   Activities that involve giving or receiving force to and from objects, as in kicking, striking, and throwing.

stabilizing movements   The most basic human movements that affect balance, posture, and axial movements.

PHYSICAL FITNESS AND WELLNESS

President John Kennedy once commented that we are an "underexercised" nation. We are spectators rather than participants; we tend to ride instead of walk. In recent years there has been an alarming incidence of coronary heart disease among children. Coronary heart disease has been associated with a lack of exercise in the adult population. Physical educators and health service professionals have been concerned that children rarely perform physical activities with high intensity; the heart rate never reaches levels higher than 180 beats per minute.

Physical fitness experts believe that children's fitness has declined through the years. Some of the reasons may be the following:

- There is less emphasis on physical education in the schools.
- Funding for after-school playground activities is almost non-existent.
- The attractiveness of television and computer games has distracted children from outdoor activity.

It appears that in the information age our technological society has decreasing demands for physical exertion, but increasing opportunities for spectator and non-physical recreation such as video games and television sports. In the urban United States children rarely climb trees, play sandlot or street ball, or even walk to school.

The World Health Organization has related good health to physical, social, and mental well-being. The concept of wellness emerged from this idea of the integration of physical fitness, nutrition, and stress management. The wellness concept assumes that individuals are responsible for their personal healthy lifestyle.

HEALTH AND PHYSICAL EDUCATION PROGRAMS

Health and physical education are interrelated and need to be coordinated in order to attain a complete school and community health program. Foundation disciplines for both subjects come from the life sciences, medical sciences, physical sciences, and the social sciences. Content for both subjects includes the following:

Physical Education

Rhythms and dance
Aquatics
Outdoor education
Gymnastics, tumbling
Team sports and individual sports
Movement patterns and skills

Health Education

Personal health
Nutrition
Family health
Consumer and community health
Communicable and chronic diseases
Alcohol, tobacco, and drug education
Environmental health
Safety and accident prevention

Physical and health education programs emphasize the development and maintenance of total body fitness. To medical specialists, fitness means freedom from disease. To social scientists, particularly psychologists, fitness has to do with mental health; physical educators describe fitness in terms of the individual's physical performance. The physical educator determines fitness by testing muscular strength, muscular endurance, flexibility, circulorespiratory endurance, and body weight and composition.

Both subjects are taught as separate lessons and as integrated lessons within other subjects such as language arts, science, and social studies. Incidental learning, unrelated to a particular health or physical education unit, can be provided advantageously. For example, when the first graders were studying about light and color (described in Chapter 15), health instruction focused on the care of the eyes. Health and physical education lessons may come about as a consequence of safety needs, class discussions, and school or community concerns.

GOALS OF PHYSICAL AND HEALTH EDUCATION

PHYSICAL EDUCATION

While the basic purpose of physical education is to provide students with movement experiences, the underlying goal is optimal growth and development consistent with each individual's characteristics, interests, and abilities. Physical education experiences should be of a developmental nature so that students progress competently. Physical education goals as defined by the *Physical Education Framework for California Public Schools* (1994, pp. 6–7) include the following:

1. Movement skills and movement knowledge (Underlying disciplines: motor learning, biomechanics, exercise physiology and health-related physical fitness)

2. Self-image and personal development
(Underlying disciplines: human growth and development, psychology, aesthetics)
3. Social development
(Underlying disciplines: sociology, historical perspectives)

To support the goals, the framework identifies the following skill areas:

- Sensorimotor and perceptual motor
- Locomotor
- Nonlocomotor
- Balance
- Eye-hand coordination
- Eye-foot coordination
- General coordination
- Creative movement

HEALTH EDUCATION

The purpose of health education is to prepare students to accept responsibility for applying health principles in their daily lives and to promote family and community health. Health education should develop positive habits, motivation, and patterns that enhance healthful ways of living. Health education, according to the *Health Framework for California Public Schools* (1994) should develop health literacy by emphasizing lifelong, positive health attitudes and behaviors and the capacity to obtain, interpret, and understand basic health information. The literate person would (pp. 4–5) do the following:

- Accept personal responsibility for lifelong health
- Respect and promote the health of others
- Understand the process of growth and development
- Use health-related information, products, and services

HOW ARE PHYSICAL EDUCATION GOALS DEVELOPED?

The National Association for Sport and Physical Education advocates a daily minimum of 30 minutes of physical education (excluding recess and lunch activities) at the elementary level and increasing time at the middle school level.

MOVEMENT SKILLS AND MOVEMENT KNOWLEDGE

Movement abilities advance in a sequential manner. Gallahue, Werner, and Luedke (1975, p. 6) identified six stages from simple to complex movements:

1. Reflexive behavior—infancy to 1 year
2. Rudimentary movement abilities—0-2 years
3. Fundamental movement patterns—preschool to 7 years
4. General movement skills—8–10 years
5. Specific movement skills—11–13 years
6. Specialized movement skills—14 to adulthood

Children's movement abilities are progressive. Although each phase is distinct, the child may advance through more than one phase at a time. Motor skills may be categorized within three sets of movement activities: stabilizing activities, locomotor activities, and manipulative activities. Students improve in these categories of movement through practice. At school this practice is mediated through the content of physical education (self-testing activities, games and sports, rhythms, and aquatics). As in other subjects of the curriculum, the teacher's task is to sequence learning experiences appropriate to the students' developmental levels. Primary students (K–2) need basic movement experiences for each of the categories of movement; middle and upper grade students need both general and specific movement skills within each category of movement. The physical education program should help students not only enjoy movement for movement's sake, but appreciate the aesthetics of creative movement.

Research Findings: Physical Education

Solmon and Carter (1995) studied 104 kindergarten and first-grade children's perceptions of their physical education class. The students were middle class, 25 percent minority, and equally divided by gender. The researchers observed the students frequently and interviewed students individually. The teacher, a physical education specialist, taught lessons that encompassed a wide range of basic motor skills and movement concepts using equipment, fitness testing, games, stretching, and jogging. The students frequently worked in pairs of male-female. The researchers learned that the students defined physical education as exercise and believed they were learning fitness and health concepts. They perceived that physical education was fun and made them feel good. As a consequence of the grouping practice (male-female), the teacher had inadvertently fostered gender differences.

Stabilizing Activities

Maintenance of stability is considered the most basic of all human movements. Although we may place our body in a variety of positions that may include axial movements and varied postures, the trick is to control equilibrium. Both locomotion and manipulative activities are dependent on stability.

Stabilizing movements are those in which the body maintains balance, changes posture, or engages in axial movements. Stability includes axial movements and postures. Axial movements are those involving the trunk or limbs. Postures are concerned with the maintenance of balance. Examples of axial movements include bending, turning, stretching, and swinging. Examples of postures include standing, rolling, stooping, and dodging.

Each movement may present special problems for an individual because of individual characteristics or abilities. Teachers need to be aware of some of the more typical problems listed below.

- Most individuals need to see a movement performed before they can perform it.
- Lack of flexibility will affect the performance of the movement.
- Concentration on performance is necessary.
- Controlled movements, as opposed to jerky, ballistic-type movements, need to be stressed.
- Speed is difficult to develop, and changing tempo during a performance is difficult for many individuals.
- Maintenance of balance causes difficulty.

Locomotor Activities

Locomotor movements are progressive and involve changing body position relative to fixed points on the ground. Locomotor activities include running, walking, hopping, skipping, jumping, climbing, leaping, galloping, and sliding.

Teachers need to be alert to the following typical locomotor movement problems:

- Students need to be able to alter their performance based on circumstances peculiar to the movement situation. For example, a faster or slower pace by others means that the student must be flexible in order to change the original movement.
- Locomotor activities are often combined with stabilizing or manipulative movements, and this combination may cause difficulty.
- Students sometimes exaggerate arm or leg movements.
- Rhythm needs to be established for most movements.
- Some students have difficulty alternating feet and using both sides of the body; it is difficult for some students to begin a movement with both feet.
- When running, some students tend to land on heels first; some students tend to run on toes only.

Manipulative Activities

Manipulative movements involve giving or receiving force to and from objects. Activities include kicking, striking, throwing, catching, bouncing, rolling, trapping,

Success on playground apparatus requires stabilizing movements.

and volleying. These activities are dependent on loco-motor and stabilizing movements. Manipulative activi-ties combine one or more movements (locomotor and/or stabilizing) and use those movements together with other movements. For example, in throwing an underhand toss, the performer must assume a stable position with one foot ahead of the other, bend slightly, project the ball forward and upward, release the ball, and follow through with arms in the direction of the propelled ball. Manipulative movements are more diffi-cult than stabilizing or locomotor movements and are dependent on the performer's understanding and inte-gration of space, time, force, and flow.

In teaching manipulative movements, the teacher needs to be aware of and anticipate the following problems:

- Students do not develop proper follow-through in movements.
- Students have trouble with timing—the object is released too soon or too late.
- Some students position their feet improperly, tend-ing to place feet together instead of one ahead of the other when throwing or kicking.
- Some students have difficulty shifting their weight as they kick, trap, or throw.
- Lack of coordination of arms and body movement due to poor rhythm causes a problem for some students.
- The failure to maintain balance when throwing or kicking is a typical problem.
- Maintenance of eye contact with target when catch-ing, trapping, or kicking is a common problem.

Appreciation of physical fitness can be enhanced through the study of **biomechanics.** Students can ex-periment with how body movements are influenced by gravity, friction, and the laws of motion.

SELF-IMAGE

The goal of a positive self-concept can be fostered by providing students with opportunities to learn about self and about others, to learn to face adversity, and to overcome problems. Self-image is enhanced through planned experiences and opportunities such as the following:

- Learning about the body and its parts and functions
- Performing physical movements in a successful manner appropriate to individual characteristics, interest, and abilities

- Understanding and accepting personal capabilities and limitations
- Exploring movements
- Experimenting and being physically challenged
- Expressing ideas and emotions through body movement and physical exercise
- Choosing, demonstrating, and satisfying personal skills and recreational interests

Certain customs in elementary classrooms and middle school physical education classes can have a negative effect on the self-concept. Frequently older students are allowed to elect captains and choose teams. The student who is not well coordinated will be the last one to be selected, with the natural psycho-logical consequence to the child's ego. The following paragraphs describe an incident in a fourth-grade classroom where the teacher anticipated the problem and found a way to develop a student's self-concept and promote social behavior.

Drew was considered the best athlete in the fourth grade. The children in his classroom consistently chose him for captain. After the election process, Drew and the other three captains would go through the formality of selecting their teams. If asked, Emma Wellesly, the fourth-grade teacher, could have listed the order in which each child would be chosen, and that was precisely what was troubling her. She knew that Ben would be the last to be selected because out on the playground he was uncoordinated. Ben seemed to be going through a trying period; he did quite well in the classroom, but his ego seemed destroyed when he came in from recess or lunch.

Wellesly decided to delay the selection process until later in the day so she could think about the situ-ation. Sometimes she had the captains use the attend-ance cards and select their teams outside, away from the class, in order to spare hurt feelings; yet as soon as the teams were written on the board, the students would know instinctively who had been chosen first and who had been chosen last.

As she watched the children work on their spelling, she observed that Ben was quizzing Drew. She saw Ben shake his head as Drew made a mistake; she went closer and heard Ben tell Drew a trick for remem-bering the word. Drew nodded and said, "Hmm, I think that will help. Thanks, Ben."

It occurred to Wellesly that the two boys worked well together and seemed to have a genuine friend-ship, yet they were rarely together on the playground because of Drew's physical prowess. Wellesly decided to talk to Drew. She asked him if he had ever wanted to do something and had tried very hard but had failed because he lacked the necessary skills. Drew recalled that he had wanted to ski with his older brother but had been unable to do so. Wellesly then explained how much Ben wanted to do well in sports and that he needed someone to have confidence in him and to assist him.

Drew confided that he really liked Ben and felt sorry for him when he wasn't selected for a team. "Ben helps me a lot in class. Do you think he would really like me to try to help him on the field?" The teacher assured the boy that Ben would be pleased.

Just before lunch Wellesly settled the class, called the captains to the front, and said "Now is the time to choose your teams." When it was Drew's turn to make his first selection, he said, "I want Ben to be on my team." Ben was shocked, but he walked to the front to stand next to Drew, as was the custom. Drew put his arm around Ben's shoulders and whispered, "Who shall I choose next, Ben?"

Physical education offers rare opportunities to develop both self-image and social behavior. Emma Wellesly modeled both humanistic and respectful behavior. Students imitate teacher behavior; in the preceding episode Drew modeled compassion.

SOCIAL BEHAVIOR

Play activities serve to help the child move from egocentric behavior to social behavior. During the primary grade years, students play most cooperatively with a single partner or in a small group. As physical skills improve, students can play in small groups and in teams. Competitive play during the middle grade years is enjoyed by students; however, students should compete with others of similar ability rather than with older students or adults. Successful group behavior occurs when students have opportunities to be both a group leader and a group participant.

Social behavior can be developed by providing opportunities for students to assume leadership responsibility. Students can be scorekeepers, umpires, referees, and play leaders for younger children. They can be in charge of equipment, they can demonstrate and teach specific skills to a friend or a small group of students, and they can be team leaders.

As group members they can demonstrate cooperative behavior and good sportsmanship. They can offer encouragement to others by their own participation

Research Readings

In the context of time management, middle school students should be engaged in a discussion of the importance of exercise (Noddings, 1992).

and by praising others. They can accept responsibility for their own behavior.

RECREATIONAL INTEREST

It is quite natural to develop interest in activities where there is some proficiency and in activities that are particularly enjoyable. Physical education activities can be extremely satisfying to students when a relaxed atmosphere is created for participation. Activities that are paced so students experience a warm up, a period of vigorous exercise, and a cool-down period will usually result in relieving classroom stress and providing students with a feeling of ease and good health.

Teachers can help students identify play areas for afterschool participation (parks, playgrounds, community facilities) and encourage students to suggest appropriate games and sports for afterschool recreation.

HOW ARE HEALTH EDUCATION GOALS DEVELOPED?

School health programs encompass health guidance, health instruction, and the development of a healthful school environment. Health guidance begins with obtaining a health history when the child first enters school. During preschool admission programs, parents should also be given information about immunization rules, vision and hearing screening tests, and school health rules that affect attendance. Health guidance continues throughout the elementary years.

Teacher observation of students should be performed daily. Teachers are often the first to detect signs of illness and signs of child abuse. Teachers along with other members of the school staff (doctors, nurses, principal) should prepare reports and solicit cooperative assistance from other social agencies to ensure the health of the child.

A healthful school environment includes teaching about sanitation; the use of school facilities such as the drinking fountains, the lavatories, and the cafeteria;

and the maintenance of a healthful classroom environment. Students are asked to accept responsibility for the following:

- Opening windows to provide appropriate ventilation
- Controlling lights and window shades to provide for visual health
- Emptying trash
- Placing clothing and lunches in the proper place
- Washing hands before meals and after using the bathroom
- Maintaining the classroom so it is orderly and attractive

Health instruction goals are accomplished by expanding the students' awareness from self to family to others. Development of awareness begins as the student shares his or her own feelings of wellness. The primary-age student is helped to differentiate between health and illness. Knowledge about individual needs for rest, sleep, and relaxation are introduced during the primary grades.

Nutrition and *dental care* are emphasized throughout the grades, and teaching strategies focus on providing students with food choices and consumer information about food nutrients appropriate to their grade level.

Food choices influenced by culture and ethnicity are featured in the health program so students learn to accept and understand other students' likes and dislikes.

Students in grades 5–8 need guidance concerning what to eat before and after athletic events. Energy needs and hydration concepts need to be taught so that students will avoid high-fat and sugar items and instead eat complex carbohydrates for efficient energy, and drink adequate water before physical activity.

Fitness and *cardiovascular health* are developed by teaching about the body and how it works, and that physical activity is related to the increase of pulse and breathing rates. The school nurse along with the classroom teacher may provide fitness counseling and guidance in order to develop positive attitudes about fitness and exercise.

Family and community health problems focus on student responsibility for maintaining personal good health. The value of regular health and dental care is advocated, and the utilization of community health resources is encouraged. Students may be asked to demonstrate ways that the family takes responsibility for good health practices. Laws affecting health practices are studied, and the responsibilities of health agencies are identified.

Heredity and *genetic disorders* are studied during the upper grades. Students learn to differentiate between the effects of environment and heredity on human organisms, and knowledge of the traits that are inherited are studied and contrasted to those traits that are acquired.

Mental and emotional health goals are developed by providing opportunities for students to make decisions and learn to cope with stress and anxiety. Through the realization that a person feels better when feelings of happiness, anger, and frustration are expressed, students learn to analyze the positive and negative aspects of stress.

The health program is responsible for providing instruction about alcohol, drugs, narcotics, and tobacco and for relating the use and misuse of these substances to family and community health. Responsibility of individuals in the prevention of the misuse of these substances is the focus of instruction.

Disease prevention and control are studied during health education. Often community resource people are invited to the school for special programming. The school shares responsibility with the community for providing information about communicable diseases and ways to control such diseases. Through the education of the children, parents can be encouraged to use immunization programs and other preventive measures. Students can also be instructed in self-observation for symptoms of illness, and instruction can focus on microorganisms that cause or affect the spread of communicable diseases.

Environmental studies are integrated with both social studies and science. Students learn about ecological conditions that affect the environment and how a healthful environment affects the quality of life. Water, soil, air, and noise pollution are appropriate areas of study to develop understanding that living things are interdependent with others and the environment. The conservation of human resources along with natural resources may be integrated into a health/science unit to develop understanding that people can control, change, and improve the environment for the benefit of all.

HOW IS PHYSICAL EDUCATION TAUGHT?

PLANNING

Planning physical education instruction should be based on the purposes to be accomplished and the students' characteristics, interests, and abilities. Unit planning for

Teaching Hints: Correlating Physical Education with Other Subject Fields*

While studying ancient Greece, have students research the ancient Olympic games and compare them with the modern Olympics. Students might research the following:

- The origin of the Olympic games
- Who took part in the ancient games
- The ways in which warfare and religion contributed to the early games
- The ways in which the games have changed (Make a timeline to reflect both the years and the changes.)
- How world events have affected the modern games

*Suggestions from the Constitutional Rights Foundation (Summer 1996, 10, 2), 601 South Kingsley Drive, Los Angeles, CA 90005.

instruction is appropriate in physical education just as it is in other subject fields. Themes selected for use in social studies and science are appropriate for inclusion of physical and health education.

Our fictitious Greg Thomas developed weekly plans for physical education (Table 16.1), and whenever possible he correlated his physical education activities with other subject fields. For example, using his theme of change, his students studied the importance of water in land use and human adaptation. He taught his students the Israeli song "Mayim," (which means water) and he also taught them the dance "Mayim," which required learning the grapevine, running step, and hop (Hall, Sweeny, and Esser, 1980, p. 157). He integrated health education by emphasizing how much water the body needs, particularly before participation in competitive sports. Thomas made it a habit to encourage his students to get a drink of water before beginning play activity.

Thomas's students were learning to play softball. The students were organized into four teams. The students knew the rules and were in the second week of a three-week unit on softball. (Mondays and Tuesdays the students were engaged in team sports.) On Monday Thomas worked with teams A and B to practice batting, catching, throwing, and running skills. Team A was in the field. Four students played first and second bases, shortstop, and catcher; the other students positioned themselves in the outfield. Team B was lined up at the batting tee at home base. The students in the field rotated positions, practicing throwing and catching, and the students at home plate each had three turns batting and running to first or second base. To teach more effective base running, Thomas had placed cones on first and second base so the students would try to increase their rate and their efficiency. Thomas stood near first base, coaching the catching, throwing, and batting. He also timed the batter's run to first base.

On Tuesday Thomas provided the same instruction for teams C and D, while teams A and B played an actual game of softball.

On Wednesday the whole class participated in the mechanics of body movement through engagement in exercise relays. Thomas drew three lines on the playground 15, 30, and 45 feet in front of the start/finish line. The teams were in four lines. Each team member performed three exercises: one on the 15-foot mark, another on the 30-foot mark, and the third on the 45-foot mark. The player then ran back to the starting line and tagged the next person on the team. The exercises chosen by Thomas were sit-ups, jumping jacks, and half-knee bends.

On Thursday the students participated in gymnastics and tumbling. Thomas taught individual and partner

Table 16.1   Weekly Schedule for Fifth Grade Physical Education

Monday	Tuesday	Wednesday	Thursday	Friday
Teams A & B Skills Workup:	A & B Softball	Exercise Relays		
Batting			Individual and Partner Stunts:	Square Dancing:
Catching		(Whole Class)	1. Russian Dance	1. All-Amer, Promenade
Throwing			2. Turnover	2. Mayim
Running			3. Rooster Fight	3. Virginia Reel
Teams C & D Softball	C & D Skills Workup	Exercise Relays		

stunts. He borrowed resting mats from the kindergarten rooms for use in this activity. He chose the V-Seat exercise, the Russian Dance, the Rooster Fight, and the Double Bear.

On Friday the students used the auditorium, where Thomas would teach rhythms and dance. The selected dances correlated with the social studies and the science units. Each week Thomas taught one new dance and practiced two familiar routines. He allowed the students to select another dance when time allowed.

Thomas's physical education lesson had four components:

1. A warm-up period
2. An instructional phase
3. An activity phase
4. Discussion of the day's activity

For the *warm up* he worked with the whole class doing simple stretching exercises. During the *instructional phase* he often grouped the students in teams (see Monday's and Tuesday's lessons). The *activity phase* received the bulk of time (usually 20 minutes). *Discussion* occurred when the students were back in the classroom and concerned personal and group problems, good sportsmanship, what students had learned, and relationships to other subject fields.

TEACHER-DIRECTED INSTRUCTION

Mary Hogan's students enjoyed playing sockball and kickball, but Hogan observed that they needed to improve in catching, pitching, and kicking. She planned a skills workup session for half the class on Monday and the other half on Tuesday (see Table 16.2). Before

going out to the playground, Hogan explained to the students where she wanted them to stand while she demonstrated the skills; she wanted to make sure that they would be able to see and hear her. Half the students were assigned to play a game of sockball; the other half would receive the skill instruction. Once out on the playground, Hogan demonstrated correct catching, pitching, and kicking. She emphasized how to hold the hands for catching, how to focus on the ball as it approached, the position of the feet for pitching, and the correct follow-through for kicking. Then she set the students up in groups of four and helped each group establish a drill formation to practice the skills. As the students practiced, Hogan observed them and assisted those students who were having difficulty. Throughout the drill session she encouraged the children to proceed quickly. She praised them and gave them instructions: "Watch the ball"; "Look at the target"; "Extend your fingers"; "Follow through."

Hogan's directed lesson had the following six components:

1. *Warm up.* The whole class did stretching exercises.
2. *Instruction.* Hogan gave the students organization instructions and instructions about skills to be taught.
3. *Demonstration.* Hogan demonstrated the skills to be practiced.
4. *Practice Period.* The students had the opportunity to practice the skills that were demonstrated.
5. *Reinforcement (Evaluation).* As the students practiced, their teacher encouraged them and offered suggestions for the improvement of their performance.

Table 16.2 Weekly Schedule for Third-Grade Physical Education

Monday	Tuesday	Wednesday	Thursday	Friday
One Half Class Apparatus Teach Skip Ring Travel on Horizontal Ladder		One-Half Class Teach Catching, Throwing, and Kicking Skills		
One-Half Class Small Group Skill Games Ishigetigoko Jumping Fancy Duck on the Rock	(Teams reverse Monday's activities)	One-Half Class Play Kickball	(Teams reverse Wednesday's activities)	Rhythms Whole Class

6. *Discussion.* Students were given time to talk about the activity and relate it to other subject fields, co-operative behaviors, good sportsmanship, and what they learned as a consequence of the activity.

During the reinforcement phase Hogan was careful to offer only positive feedback. If she had not been satisfied with the students' performance, then she would have repeated steps 2–4. At the end of the lesson during the discussion she might go back over the skill components to offer additional guidance.

STUDENT EXPLORATION

"How many boys and girls know how to play hopscotch?" (Students respond yea! and nay!) "Good, let's all get up and show each other movements for playing hopscotch."

Greg Thomas observed the students as they jumped on two feet and did some hopping. He noted that many of the students had difficulty landing on two feet simultaneously, and very few could move from the two-footed jump to a one-footed hop.

Thomas chose several students to demonstrate the jump and the hop; then he suggested that all the students try once again. This time he suggested that they jump and then hop on the left foot. Next he had them practice jumping and hopping on the right foot.

After the students had practiced, he asked them which had been easier, the right- or the left-footed hop. The students discussed the movements and decided that much depended on whether they were right- or left-handed. Thomas followed up with a lesson on dominance in their health books.

Children (and adults) learn more effectively when there is an opportunity to experiment (explore) with the movements involved. After experimenting with the movement, the students begin to watch others to see if they can correct their own performance. Thomas observed his students to detect when it would be appropriate to demonstrate the desired skill. He was careful to allow the students to move through the exploration stage and be motivated for a demonstration. His sequence of instruction was as follows:

1. Experimentation (exploration)
2. Observation of others
3. Demonstration by others
4. Practice
5. Evaluation

The advantage of the indirect approach used by Thomas is that it allows students to match their own developmental levels, satisfy their curiosity and creativity; the approach also allows the children to decide upon their own actions. It is less structured than the directed instruction lesson even though Thomas suggested the movements for exploration. Shillingford and Mackin (1991, p. 470) provide another example of indirect teaching; the example is a lesson for second graders. They suggest the use of tennis balls or beanbags and a sequence of developmental challenges that cause children to test themselves.

- Can you throw the ball in the air and catch it?
- How high can you throw the ball and still catch it?
- Can you throw it in the air, clap your hands, and catch the ball?
- Who can throw it in the air, touch the ground, and catch the ball?
- Can you turn one more time than you did yesterday?
- What else can you do between the time you throw the ball in the air and catch it? (p. 470)

SMALL GROUP ACTIVITIES

Dividing students into small groups, squads, or teams in physical education allows greater participation and lessens waiting time for turns. Because a variety of activities can be planned, all of the groups do not need equipment for play. For example, primary students may be grouped so one group is playing on the apparatus, another group is involved in a circle game that requires a ball, and a third group is participating in stunts and skills. The activities can be rotated during the class period or on successive days. The tennis ball/beanbag activity lends itself to this arrangement. The small group strategy allows the teacher to provide individualized instruction to a small group of students who are able to see and hear and respond to the teacher. Instruction to a large group on the playground sometimes involves management problems. Mary Hogan chose small group skill games when she was teaching half her class an apparatus skill.

SKILL INSTRUCTION

Students do not necessarily learn a skill just because they play a game that requires the skill. Skills need to be taught, and they need to be practiced. The movement

> ### Teaching Hints:
> ### Warming Up
>
> Six major muscle groups should be warmed up before vigorous exercise: neck, shoulders, arms, hips, legs, and ankles.

skills described earlier in the chapter are developmental; the student must learn to maintain balance, change direction, adjust to environmental problems. The student's safety may be dependent on the movement skills learned at school.

The teacher's task is to model the desired skill or have it demonstrated by students who perform the skill correctly. When observing students practicing the skill, it is important to observe whether the students are implementing the key elements involved in the skill. A third task is to provide feedback to correct the student's performance or to reinforce correct achievement.

Skill instruction can begin as an exploration lesson or as a direct instructional lesson.

MIDDLE SCHOOL EXPERIENCES

Additional experiences for middle school students should include:

- Exploration and preparation for careers in health and physical education
- Social dancing
- Team handball
- First aid and CPR
- Outdoor education
- Bowling, golf

PHYSICAL EDUCATION INSTRUCTION IN THE CLASSROOM

There are many occasions when it is more propitious to teach physical education inside the classroom. This may be necessitated by inclement weather or by students' need for physical activity. Typically, physical education in the classroom has meant low involvement activities that provide teacher and students with a change from the normal routine, but nothing vigorous enough to elevate the pulse rate. There is nothing wrong with choosing low-intensity activities for the classroom; however, when students sit for several hours during the school day, they will feel more alert and more joyful if they are involved in activities that require muscular strength, endurance, and aerobic exercise.

There are many movements that can be taught inside the classroom to help students relieve tension by stretching, exercising vigorously, and then relaxing to prepare them for academic study. The following suggestions for music, props, space, exercises, and clothing will assist in motivating students for classroom exercises.

SUGGESTIONS FOR CLASSROOM EXERCISE

Music

Themes from the Disney movies are good accompaniment for classroom exercise. The songs from *Dr. Doolittle* are excellent with primary children. Popular songs are fine with older students. Allow students to choose them from TV series and record them on tapes for the exercise period. Have students suggest movements appropriate to the music. Be sure that the music has a good beat. Change the music for the cooldown period to help quiet and relax the students.

Props

The purpose of props is for motivation. The use of chairs or other props enhances the exercise period. Doweling or short ropes can be used to keep the arms straight for bending exercises. Ropes or doweling can be used with a partner for resistance movements. Paddles or wands ar great for attaching strips of cloth; use the paddles with the cloth for swinging exercises or scissor exercises. Books can be used for weights. Use one book in each hand and perform arm lifts.

Space

Obviously an empty classroom or auditorium would be optimal for indoor exercising. However, in the normal classroom students can be arranged in staggered formations around the room. Make sure that they are able to see you model the exercises and that they will not touch another student as they exercise.

> ### Teaching Hints:
> ### Cooling Down
>
> Cooling down is as important as warming up. The cool-down exercises may be the same as the warm-up exercises.

Exercises

Students will always complain that they are tired. Use good judgment as to the number of repetitions for each exercise. Always model the movement to be performed. Encourage smooth movements using the full range of motion. Physical fitness periods should have three distinct stages: warm up, vigorous exercise, and cool down.

Clothing

If the exercise period is to occur on a set day of the week, ask girls to wear pants on that day. However, since one of the objectives for classroom physical education is to relieve tension, you really do not know in advance when you might want to engage in an exercise session. The problem can be solved if girls keep a pair of shorts in the classroom to be put on under skirts for this activity. (Parents readily approve of this idea!)

EQUIPMENT FOR PHYSICAL EDUCATION

The following equipment facilitates the physical education program:

- Balls—six-inch, nine-inch, and thirteen-inch for volleyball, kickball, basketball, football. One for every two students is considered optimal.
- Jump ropes—single, double, and one 20-foot rope for each class
- Beanbags
- Soccer pins
- Hoops
- Mats
- Bats
- Playground apparatus
- Paddles or racquets with balls or birds
- Horseshoes, shuffleboard cues, and discs
- Table tennis equipment
- Tubes, tires, stilts
- Vaulting boxes and horses
- Percussion instruments and records for rhythms and dance, record player, tapes
- Cones

EVALUATING PHYSICAL EDUCATION GROWTH

Evaluation in physical education should be based on individual growth and development. Students should be apprised of their personal progress so they can relate progress to practice and personal goals. Since both the potentials and the abilities of students differ, students should not be compared with each other.

It is important to identify the individual needs and abilities of each student. This may be accomplished through observation, interviews, and physical fitness tests. The following procedures may be used:

1. Observe the student as he or she relates to other students to determine basic needs and interests.
2. Review and analyze the student's health record; review vision and hearing records.
3. Evaluate growth (weight and height) using standard growth charts.
4. Observe the student performing movement activities.
   - Can the student exercise vigorously and recover quickly, or does the student continue to look fatigued?
   - Can the student control body movements?
   - Does the student's performance improve after practice and feedback?
   - Is the student enthusiastic about activity?
   - Does the primary-age child support his or her weight when using the horizontal bar?
   - Can the primary child climb the jungle gym?
   - Does the student share equipment and take turns?
   - Does the student help others or interfere with others?

SELF-ASSESSMENT

Students should be encouraged to self-assess and keep records of their own performance. For example, students could check their heart rate before, during, and after vigorous exercise. Students should establish personal goals and evaluate progress toward the goal(s). Self-assessment helps students accept responsibility for their own wellness.

Middle school students can perform peer assessment by establishing rubrics and then evaluating progress using the criteria.

The National Association for Sports and Physical Education (1992) has defined the physically educated person as one who:

- Has learned skills necessary to perform a variety of physical activities
- Is physically fit
- Participates regularly in physical activity
- Knows the implications of and the benefits from involvement in physical activities
- Values physical activity and its contributions to a healthful life-style

HOW IS HEALTH EDUCATION TAUGHT?

EXPERIMENTATION

Many aspects of health education can be taught through the utilization of the scientific method. The students who developed the experiment for testing the effect of dirt on their hands when handling bread were studying health as well as science. Personal health care studies are often motivated and initiated through science experiments. Upper grade students studying light can construct cameras and microscopes and then go on to the study of the eye. Experiments with food decay, contamination, and growth of bacteria are typical of the studies appropriate for health instruction.

RESEARCH

The use of actual situations for study has a positive effect on health attitudes and habits. In a sixth-grade classroom the teacher initiated a safety unit by asking the students to research safety problems at school. The students analyzed the safety records in the school office and then investigated the areas where accidents were occurring. They observed other students at the bicycle rack area, on the playground, on the stairways, and on the sidewalk in front of school. They watched before school, during recess and lunch, and after school. They studied the frequency of accidents, the location, and the activity. Then they recorded their findings and wrote their conclusions (Figure 16.1). They compared their own study with the school district's study at other schools. Finally the students wrote plays to dramatize the safety problems. Using their own dramatizations, they taught other students at their school about safety.

RESOURCE PEOPLE

Community resource people are valuable assets to the school health program. Health department professionals and fire and police personnel are usually willing to come to school and perform demonstrations or lecture. Hospitals frequently have a list of speakers to assist in health education. Community service organizations sometimes have health specialists who are experienced in working with children. Some organizations have instructional materials available for classroom teaching. The American Heart Association has developed two kits for teaching about the heart and

Teaching Hints:
Avoiding Gender Bias

Words, tone, and directions to students for physical education and health activities should be carefully monitored for gender interpretations.

exercise. The kits contain filmstrips, cassette tapes, and an instructional booklet for the teacher. The materials are in both Spanish and English. One kit is appropriate for lower grades, the other for upper grades.

HEALTH GUIDANCE AND EXAMINATIONS

Students are usually examined several times during their elementary and middle school years by the school nurse or doctor. The examination can be a learning experience if the students know in advance how it will be performed and what will be learned from the examination. Students can study growth charts from health textbooks. They can study problems of being underweight and overweight. Nutrition and food habits can be the focus of a unit. Dental hygiene can be studied in conjunction with the dental examination.

Figure 16.1 School Safety Record

	Frequency			
	K–3		4–6	
Location and Activity	**Boys**	**Girls**	**Boys**	**Girls**
Bicycle Rack Area				
• Fighting				
• Falls				
• Skidding				
Playground				
• Unorganized Activities				
• Fighting				
• Running				
• Apparatus				
Stairway				
• Skipping Steps				
• Pushing				
• Running				
Sidewalk				
• Carrying Too Many Things				
• Watching Others				
• Running				

DEMONSTRATIONS, DISCUSSIONS, TEXTBOOKS, AND SPECIAL PROJECTS

Audio-visual resources, exhibits, and models are useful for demonstrating health concepts. Many materials can be borrowed from community resources, but student-made models and exhibits are most meaningful. Pictures and posters are readily available from health organizations and the National Safety Council.

It is extremely important in health education that the teaching approach be positive, calmly presented, and as objective as possible. Issues in health education may elicit emotional reactions from different segments of the community; thus it is essential that the teacher help students discuss problems in a nonthreatening classroom climate.

Textbooks are available for grades 3–8, and most textbooks integrate science and health concepts. Textbooks should be used for resource purposes. Many of the new texts encourage students to assess their fitness habits and evaluate what they eat and drink.

The Health Activities Project (HAP) developed by the Lawrence Hall of Science at the University of California at Berkeley is an activity-focused health curriculum for grades 5–8. The program is organized into four modules: "Breathing and Fitness," "Sight and Sound," "Heart Fitness," and "Action." The overall goal of the project is to help students understand their own

bodies and develop a sense of control through their ability to effect physical improvement, fitness, and decision making.

EVALUATING HEALTH EDUCATION

Health education should be evaluated in the same ways that growth is assessed in other subject fields. Paper-and-pencil tests may be designed to test health concepts. If students produce projects, models, or dramatizations, then these may be used for evaluation. Attitudes and habits may be observed to see if there is continuous and consistent growth. Since much of the learning in health education should be organized so students engage in inquiry and discover for themselves, the use of scientific methods and attitudes should be evaluated.

Assessment should focus on health literacy:

- Does the student accept responsibility for his or her own health?
- Does the student demonstrate respect for the health of others?
- Does the student understand the process of growth and development?
- Does the student use health-related information to guide the use of products and services?

Whenever possible students should be encouraged to self-assess their own health and physical fitness. They should be encouraged to set goals for physical, emotional, and social behavior and then evaluate their own progress toward those goals.

INTEGRATION OF HEALTH AND PHYSICAL EDUCATION WITH OTHER SUBJECTS

Thematic teaching should predominate. Themes identified earlier in the text should be extended to health and physical education. In addition, physical education experiences can be used to enhance other curriculum fields. For example, the teacher can give auditory directions that require students to remember a sequence of directions and rhythmically produce it. The rhythm can be orchestrated by the teacher. Students might be asked to clap hands overhead, snap fingers, shake fingers, and roll arms. The students could even be asked to remember a set number of repetitions.

Students can listen to records and act out stories or sounds. Kindergarten students can be asked to shape

Teaching Hints: Using the Internet

These sites on the World Wide Web, with addresses current when this text was written, provide interesting information and suggested links for health and physical education.

Nutrition
http://www.olen.com/food/
http://ificinfo.health.org/

Environmental Health
http://www.epa.gov

Safety and Accident Prevention
http://www.firesafe.com
http://www.otis.utc.com/ridingsafely.html
http://www.safewithin.com/

Substance Abuse
http://www.health.org/
http://www.madd.org

their bodies to look like whole numbers. Animal movements are particularly motivating for primary-aged children: to walk like an elephant or cat, to make your back look like that of an angry cat, to walk like a crab (on hands and feet with hands behind you, walking backward).

Mathematics can be enhanced by having students learn to time their skill performances or measure their running distances.

For science, Newton's laws of motion can be taught:

• Bodies in motion tend to stay in motion or bodies at rest tend to stay at rest unless acted upon by some outside force.
• The change in speed when acted upon by an outside force is proportional to the force applied and occurs in the direction of the force; the greater the force, the greater the acceleration.
• For every action there is an equal and opposite reaction. (This can be illustrated by bouncing a ball against a wall or dribbling the ball.)

For social studies integration, teach regional and cultural games and dances. Music and art integration are discussed in Chapter 17. Health education integration has been discussed throughout this chapter.

INCLUSION AND ADAPTED PHYSICAL EDUCATION

Whenever possible students with disabilities should participate in the physical education program. However, participation should be guided and modified when necessary. Some physical problems require temporary accommodations; others need long-range planning and special services.

TEMPORARY SERVICES

When students have accidents and occasional muscular or orthopedic problems, special accommodations need to be arranged. Depending upon the seriousness of the problem students can often participate in a modified physical education program. For example, they may be able to play horseshoes, Ping-Pong,® board games and shuffleboard. (See following paragraph.)

SPECIALLY DESIGNED PROGRAMS

Students with cardiovascular disorders, nutritional problems, postural deviations, temporary physical problems, and hyperactivity may be able to participate in the general physical education program with physician approval. In some cases, however, the physician may prescribe a modified program or individualized program. Modifications may be specified, such as no running, no contact sports, and use of crutches permitted.

MAINSTREAMING

In cases of mental retardation, emotional disorders, and learning disorders, in general, these students can participate in a regular physical education program with classmates.

ADAPTED PHYSICAL EDUCATION

For students with permanent physical disabilities, respiratory disorders, sensory problems, or cerebral palsy, direct designated physical education by a physical education specialist is necessary. The **adapted physical education** program may include assistance from parents and other faculty members and aides.

Students' readiness to participate in physical activities is determined by their developmental level. Students with special problems, whether because of mental retardation or as a consequence of other disabilities, may not be ready to participate in group activities. Because students with disabilities are often overprotected by parents, peers, and teachers, many do not have the necessary motor skills to participate with others. Before these students can be integrated with peers in group activities, they should be allowed to progress using self-testing individual sports activities.

CLASSROOM MANAGEMENT IN PHYSICAL EDUCATION

Classroom management problems occur during physical education because sometimes there is a tendency to let physical education be a game or free-time period for students. As a consequence, teachers do not perform the planning, organizing, monitoring, and anticipatory tasks that they engage in for other subject fields.

This idea of physical education and play time being one and the same is most evident when teachers tell students, "We are not going to have P.E. today, because you have been too noisy," or "You didn't finish your mathematics on time, sooo . . . ," or "We have had so many interruptions today that we need to skip P.E."

All of the above comments should be used as the rationale for why physical education is important every day. If students are noisy, less alert than they should be, or harassed, the need for vigorous exercise is all the more evident.

Typical classroom management problems in physical education relate to decision-making concerns: class organization and grouping, equipment, and instructional approach.

CLASS ORGANIZATION

Whenever teachers need to change the place where an activity occurs, there will be management considerations. Unless a teacher wants the whole class to surge forward to the door at the same time, he or she should not direct students with the comment, "Let's go out to P.E. now." Directions to students should include the following information: Who is to leave the classroom? When are they to leave the classroom? Where are the students to go to participate in the activity? What equipment will they need? Should they walk, run, skip to the destination? These directions should be stated clearly and concisely.

Consideration should also be given to how to get the students back to the classroom. The following decisions need to be made: Should students line up before returning to the classroom? Should they move by groups, games, or all together? Will they go to the bathroom or obtain drinks? (If they do not obtain drinks on the playground, will they want to do so in the classroom?)

INSTRUCTIONAL ARRANGEMENTS

Another organizational problem has to do with instructional arrangements. If skill or game instructions are needed, will they be provided in the classroom or out on the playground or in the gymnasium? Game or rule-type instructions are best handled while students ar sitting at their desks. Sometimes a chalk talk before an activity is helpful. But if students are to observe a demonstration, then it is important to plan how they will stand or sit in order to see and hear. There are several arrangements advocated by physical education specialists for facilitating skill demonstrations. For example:

- *Semicircle.* Students can sit or stand in a halfcircle formation, and the teacher can demonstrate the skill. This arrangement is particularly good if only half the class is involved in the demonstration.

- *Circle.* Teacher or model can demonstrate from the center of the circle. However, if the teacher/model is to give instructions orally, the semicircle is better for talking/listening.
- *Squad/Small Group.* Students stand in short lines by group. This is a good arrangement if students are to practice or give evidence of having attained a skill. The teacher can walk between the groups or stand in a central location to observe performance.
- *Scatter.* If the teacher/model has a megaphone or is standing on a stage, this formation minimizes students' "messing around" tactics. Teachers who use this formation for demonstrations usually assign students to a special spot on the floor. Whenever the teacher calls for a scatter formation, the student moves to the special spot. The scatter formation facilitates students' exploration of movement.

The decision about how to arrange students for demonstrations should also be based on the type of learning situation. Are students to learn via direct instruction, or is the instructional planning based upon student exploration? This decision will need to be made prior to the decision about the type of formation.

GROUPING FOR PLAY ACTIVITIES

A third decision that frequently causes management problems is grouping students for play activities. Should students be grouped by friendship patterns, by size, by ability, or by interest? There are trade-offs involved in each of the choices. Perhaps there should not be one consistent way of grouping students for physical education; instead, it may be a good idea to change the pattern depending on the games, skills, and purpose of the activity. Whichever pattern is chosen, the decision, along with the objective of the lesson, should be shared with the students.

PHYSICAL EDUCATION EQUIPMENT

In some schools activities must be chosen on the basis of the available equipment. Sometimes there is not enough equipment for an entire class of children to participate in the same game activity. Luckily there are many activities that do not require equipment. The trick is to plan ahead, be knowledgeable about your resources, and present the game plan to the students confidently. A typical error of new teachers is to send students out to the playground and forget to give them equipment. What results is confusion out in the yard, with students running around to find the teacher and the keys to the classroom.

Most management problems in physical education can be avoided with unit planning and anticipatory thinking about instructional arrangements, grouping, and equipment needs.

ADOLESCENT PROBLEMS

Health and physical education may provide unique opportunities in the presentation of subject matter for teachers to help students confront very typical problems of early adolescence such as the problems of grooming and personal hygiene. Helping students use common sense in their attire, cleanliness, and healthfulness can be achieved through subject field content. Teachers also need to serve as role models for the students. In addition, it is important for students to recognize others' unique qualities and learn to appreciate classmates who are different.

CONTROVERSIAL ISSUES

CHILD ABUSE AND NEGLECT

Teachers learn to recognize when their students do not look just right. You note symptoms of illness, you can tell when a student is hyper, and you can tell when a student is depressed. You are also, very likely, the first person to recognize when a child has been mistreated. Telltale physical signs and emotional reactions will cue the alert teacher to child abuse or neglect.

It is the teacher's legal responsibility to report instances of child abuse and neglect. The teacher should make this report to the school nurse or the school principal. Most schools have report forms to be filled out for this purpose. Child abuse and neglect have been defined as follows (Section 3 of the Child Abuse Prevention and Treatment Act, P.L. 93-247):

> the physical or mental injury, sexual abuse, negligent treatment, or maltreatment of a child under the age of eighteen by a person who is responsible for the child's welfare under circumstances which indicate that the child's health or welfare is harmed or threatened thereby.

Instruction in the classroom about child abuse and sexual exploitation can occur after parents are notified of the forthcoming lesson(s). Students should be provided with information on sexual abuse and rape.

They should learn to identify ways to seek assistance if abused or threatened. They need to learn how to avoid situations with increased risk, and practice through role-plays how to avoid negative social influences and pressures.

Teachers need also to recognize that they too can be accused of child abuse. Should this occur, one should immediately obtain legal assistance. Emans (1987) points out that both the laws to protect children and the enforcement procedures often deny institutional rights to the child and the person accused of the crime. For as long as this author can remember, teachers have been counseled to never work alone with a student, particularly a student of the opposite sex. This is good advice for all ages.

TEACHING ABOUT DRUGS

It is now recognized that elementary teachers need to begin during the primary grades to develop students' knowledge and understanding about the use and misuse of drugs, narcotics, alcohol, and tobacco. Health and physical education provide great opportunities to accomplish this. There have been a variety of approaches to teaching students about substance abuse, but most have failed. These approaches have included programs that communicated information only, programs based on affective education, and scare-tactic programs using the testimony of former addicts.

What works? The Southwest Regional Laboratory has found that students need to be aware of the immediate consequences of drug use (how drugs affect your breath, your eyes, your ability to concentrate, your mood) versus the long-term effects. Many students wrongly believe that their peers condone the use of drugs; they need to learn that most students of their own age do not use drugs and do not condone drug use.

Students often experiment with drugs because they are under stress. The curriculum should teach students positive ways to relive stress: recreation with friends, exercise, sharing and communicating, developing friendships. Students need to be taught conflict-resolution skills and the process of decision making. They may also need to learn how to develop positive friendships. Finally, they should be give information on the ways peers, family, and the media influence their use of drugs, narcotics, and alcohol.

Jill English of the Southwest Regional Educational Laboratory has found in her work with elementary and high school students that role-playing activities,

Socratic-type questioning, and small group discussions work best to teach about substance abuse. Lecturing, preaching, and moralizing are doomed to failure.*

The first strategy for teachers is to verify that there is an alcohol or drug problem. Keeping a log to document student behavior may be the first step. The next step is to share the log with other knowledgeable people and to determine if the behavior(s) occurs in other classes, other settings. When possible, involve the student's family, and try to determine why the student is using drugs. The most common reason for alcohol and drug abuse among young students is to gain peer acceptance. For this reason students need to learn ways to resist peer pressure. Communicating with the student's family helps to link community services available to respond to drug and alcohol problems.

BLOOD-TRANSMITTED DISEASES

Information about communicable diseases such as sexually transmitted diseases (STDs), including HIV/AIDS and hepatitis B need to be discussed in the health curriculum. Students need to understand that many health-related choices are theirs to make. Many communicable and chronic diseases are the consequences of ignorance and shortsightedness.

Because teaching about communicable and chronic blood-transmitted diseases can have cultural, socioeconomic, genetic, or religious implications, teachers need to be sensitive in the development of curriculum. Before initiating teaching lessons, parents should be notified so that they may withdraw their children from this segment of the health curriculum.

Both students and teachers should exercise care in helping an injured person. A wounded individual should be guided to the health office, but other students and the teacher should not come in direct contact with an injured person who is bleeding. In some school districts, teachers are advised to wear latex gloves when supervising on the playground, and students should be cautioned about touching other students' wounds.

Most educators agree that sexually transmitted disease education needs to be a part of the school curriculum beginning in the elementary grades. Middle school students should be given specific information

on ways to eliminate or reduce the risk of HIV infection. Parents and community members can be invited to work with teachers in preparing the curriculum.

SUMMARY
Physical Fitness and Wellness
1. Children's fitness has declined through the years.
2. Good health is related to physical, social, and mental well-being.

Health and Physical Education Programs
3. The two subjects are interrelated and need to be coordinated.
4. Foundation disciplines include life, medical, physical, and social sciences.
5. Both subjects are taught as separate lessons and as integrated lessons within other subject fields.

Physical Education Goals
6. Goals include movement skills and knowledge, self-image development, and social development.

Health Education Goals
7. The purpose of health education is to develop health literacy.

How Physical Education Goals Are Developed
8. Movement abilities advance sequentially; children's movement abilities are progressive.
9. Motor skills are categorized as stabilizing, locomotor, and manipulative.
10. Positive self-image is fostered through opportunities to learn about self and others and to understand one's own capabilities and limitations.
11. Group participation helps the child develop appropriate social behavior.
12. Recreation involving vigorous exercise helps students relax and relieve tension.

How Health Goals Are Developed
13. School health programs involve personal guidance, instructional activities, and the school environment.
14. The health program should expand the students' awareness from self to family to others.
15. Nutrition and dental care are emphasized through teaching strategies and consumer information.

*The author is indebted to Jill English, Instructional Consultant for the Southwest Regional Educational Laboratory, for assistance with this section.

16. Cultural beliefs and preferences about food are discussed to build appreciation and understanding.
17. Fitness and cardiovascular health are taught in the classroom and on the playground.
18. Fitness counseling is provided by the school nurse and the classroom teacher.
19. The health program includes instruction to build student responsibility for family and community health.
20. Students learn to differentiate between the effects of environment and heredity on human organisms.
21. Disease prevention and control are taught during health instruction.
22. Environmental studies are integrated with social studies and science.

How Physical Education Is Taught

23. Physical education is taught through direct instruction in skills, exploration strategies, teams, and small and large group activities.
24. Many physical activities can occur within the classroom during inclement weather.
25. Vigorous movements in the classroom relieve tension and promote relaxation.

Equipment For Physical Education

26. Equipment includes items for manipulative movements, apparatus for climbing, and instruments for rhythms.

Evaluation of Physical Education Growth

27. Individual assessment should occur by relating practice to individual goals and the individual's health record.
28. It is important that students self-assess by keeping records of their personal performance and taking personal responsibility for their health.

How Health Education Is Taught

29. Similar to science education, health can be taught through use of the scientific method.
30. Students can engage in research studies, such as safety studies and nutrition studies.
31. Many community agencies and health care individuals are available to assist as resource people in the classroom.
32. Health guidance and examinations should be the purview of the school nurse or doctor.

33. Demonstrations, texts, projects, models, and the Internet are available for teaching materials.

Evaluating Health Education

34. Health education should be evaluated in the same ways that other subject fields are assessed.

Integration with Other Subjects

35. Thematic teaching should predominate.
36. Health education can easily be integrated with science, social studies, mathematics, art, and language arts.

Inclusion

37. When possible, students with disabilities should participate in the general physical education program.
38. Temporary services may need to be available for students who have accidents or return from a weakening illness.
39. Individually designed programs may be necessary for some individuals with, for example, cardiovascular disorders.
40. Adapted physical education is designed for students with permanent disabilities.

Classroom Management

41. When physical education is treated as a free period instead of as an instructional period, teachers can have classroom management problems.
42. Typical problems in classroom management relate to grouping, use of equipment, use of space, or the instructional approach.

Controversial Issues

43. Classroom teachers need to be alert to child abuse and neglect.
44. Classroom instruction should discuss abuse and exploitation.
45. Teachers are responsible for teaching about the potential harmfulness of tobacco, alcohol, and drugs.
46. Students need information about blood-transmitted diseases, but before teaching about this topic, teachers should obtain family permission.

DISCUSSION QUESTIONS AND APPLICATION EXERCISES

1. Identify people, animals, things, and emotions that students could dramatize to music.

2. Compare the motor skills of a primary-age student with a physical disability and a normal primary-age student. How were the performances similar? Different?
3. Develop a lesson plan for students that allows them to explore movements.
4. Visit a YMCA or sports club and observe an aerobic exercise workout. Create an aerobic rhythmical sequence for students in grades 5–8.
5. Evaluate the nutritional value of food at fast-food restaurants and plan a lesson for grades 5–8 based on your findings.
6. Prepare a presentation for parents to explain the relationship between coronary heart disease and lack of exercise emphasizing that children, too, can have coronary heart problems.
7. Develop a checklist for evaluating students' track and field skills.
8. Investigate which social agencies will provide health services to elementary and middle school students. Find out how a teacher can obtain help for a student.

17

Arts Education

The importance of education in the arts was recognized by the United States Congress when it created the National Endowment for the Arts in 1965. In recent years Congress has imposed some content restrictions on works of art and prohibited funding of individual arts. However, many citizens and arts and humanities groups recognize the importance of the arts and believe that government should be supportive. Educators have been encouraged to develop special cultural programs for teaching the arts.

The creative arts emphasize the development of aesthetic sensitivity as well as personal and creative expression. Child development concepts are used in the planning of curriculum experiences. Instructional programs should emphasize exploration, drama, movement, production, music and art concepts, recognition of artists and works of art, selection of instructional materials and media, and the development of artistic judgment. The integration of subject fields is encouraged, not only so that students experience a total, balanced school program, but because the arts represent the history of humankind.

After you study this chapter, you should be able to accomplish the following:

1. Identify reasons why it is important to teach the arts.
2. Identify the fundamental purposes of teaching music, art, dance, and drama.
3. Discuss the content of the various arts programs.
4. Suggest classroom activities appropriate for teaching art.
5. Relate art activities to the child's developmental level.
6. Suggest classroom activities appropriate for teaching music.
7. Identify illustrative objectives for teaching music.
8. Make a list of suggestions for teaching visual and performing arts.
9. Summarize trends in the teaching of the arts.
10. Suggest ways to evaluate growth in the creative arts.
11. Identify resources and equipment for teaching the creative arts.
12. Identify several national programs and projects in the arts and the emphasis of each.
13. Suggest ways to integrate the arts with other subjects.
14. Discuss mainstreaming in the arts.

Professional Lexicon

aesthetic judgment   The expression of preferences and appreciation based on understanding of form, content, technique, and purpose.

constituent elements   The rhythm, melody, harmony, and form of music.

eurhythmics   The art of interpreting music by involving the whole body in rhythmic movements.

expressive elements   Music tone qualities, tempo, and dynamics.

IMPORTANCE OF THE CREATIVE ARTS

The arts encompass both the visual and the performing arts: art, music, dance, and drama. Each of the arts is a discipline with aesthetic, perceptual, creative, and intellectual components. Together they contribute to the total development of the individual and increase an individual's ability to communicate with others. The creative arts contribute to the goal of self-realization by helping students to express themselves, to enjoy creative experiences, and to make qualitative judgments.

The visual, aural, and performing arts encourage students to explore their own personal responses to creative experiences. The arts enable students to utilize creative imagination, to see and hear clearly, and to express essential feelings. The emphasis on the senses in the arts motivates consciousness and exploration of aesthetic experiences.

More than other curriculum areas, the aesthetic arts help students to appreciate different cultures and the challenges of a pluralistic society. Through the arts students become receptive to unfamiliar sounds, customs, styles, languages, and preferences. The arts of every culture are valued: none is superior to another; each is distinctive. Hoffer and Hoffer (1987) recommend that the teacher not only point out where the music or art originated from, but also help students investigate distinctive characteristics to find out what makes it different. Students also need to learn about the social and political times during which the work was created. Arts instruction acts as a means to acquire cultural literacy.

The visual and performing arts contribute to and clarify concepts and skills in other subject fields, but it is important, also, to teach each as an essential discipline-based subject field. There needs to be systematic and sequential teaching of the arts as well as an effort to integrate other subject fields with the arts. Elliot Eisner recommends the study of four operations in the arts: art/music production, art/music criticism, art/music history, and aesthetics. These four operations refer to making art, appreciating it, understanding it, and making judgments about it (Brandt, 1988, p. 7).

The arts allow the individual to make a personal statement. Each provides a continuing and lasting record of a people and is a reflection of a society's way of life. Each provides means to analyze society and culture. Universal communication is facilitated through the arts. Aesthetic experiences in the arts involve the mind and the feelings.

PURPOSES OF MUSIC EDUCATION

At the Music Educators National Conference (1990) the following goals were recommended for students in grades K–12:

- Make music, alone and with others
- Improvise and create music
- Use the vocabulary and notation of music
- Respond to music aesthetically, intellectually, and emotionally
- Be acquainted with a wide variety of music, including diverse musical styles and genres
- Understand the role music has played and continues to play in the lives of human beings
- Make aesthetic judgments based on critical listening and analysis
- Develop a commitment to music
- Support the musical life of the community and encourage others to do so
- Continue musical learning independently

The music educators are concerned that music instruction not be viewed as a field for the entertainment of students or that it be viewed for only serious and talented students. All students need music education. However, there have been questions about the emphasis on music performance. Former Education Secretary Bennett advocated study of the historical and cultural roots of music; many music educators believe that it is the music history courses that make students resent music as a field of study. These educators believe that cultural literacy can best be accomplished through study of the music students perform.

PURPOSES OF THE VISUAL ARTS

The basic purposes of the visual arts are to enable students to see clearly, to express feelings, to demonstrate and communicate individuality, and to understand and apply art knowledge.

Art education frequently aims to expose students to art production and art appreciation. Students are to enjoy discovery and be discoverers. The art curriculum should increase sensitivity and heighten perceptual and creative awareness. Art educators want students to integrate thinking, feelings, imagination, and senses in the application of art knowledge to personal experience. Art instruction should help students to perceive visual relationships, produce art, understand the art of others, and judge artistic products.

The *Visual and Performing Arts Framework for California Public Schools* (1989) identifies four instructional components to be developed in all of the arts: visual/tactile perception, creative expression, art heritage, and **aesthetic judgment.** Examples of these components will be given in the area of art education.

VISUAL/TACTILE PERCEPTION

The purpose of this component is to sharpen students' sensory awareness of the world around them. The goal is to maximize seeing, feeling, and understanding of form, color, and texture. Illustrative objectives include the following:

- To identify varying colors, shapes, and textures in natural and manmade forms
- To distinguish color qualities by value and hue as well as identify negative and positive shapes and textures
- To model three-dimensional qualities as indicated by overlapping planes, vertical position, size, and color intensity.

CREATIVE EXPRESSION

The second component is accomplished by providing students with art media to learn skills and express ideas and feelings in visual form. As students partic-

How does an artisan differ from an artist?

ipate in creative exploration, instruction should focus on art concepts and the structure of art.

Students will demonstrate in their drawings techniques of action; continuous line; and imaginative, decorative, or realistic styles. Through artwork they will express their own moods and feelings. Students will use media appropriately (drawing, painting, sculpture, graphics) and create two- and three-dimensional art forms.

ART HERITAGE

Development of art values and understanding of our art heritage is gained as students study works of art and artists of the past and of contemporary times in our own society and in other cultures and societies.

- Students identify similarities and differences among works of art produced by different cultures and societies at different times.
- Students describe the varied uses of the visual arts in modern society.
- Students express the purposes of art as it relates to the celebration of historical events, conveys beliefs and values, and communicates social practices.

AESTHETIC JUDGMENT

Students learn to critique, express preferences, and appreciate works by learning about the visual, intellectual,

Through creative exploration, the student can learn skills that express ideas and feelings.

and philosophic bases for understanding art and for judging the form, content, technique, and purpose of artworks.

- Students describe qualities in visual work: line, color, shape, intensity, value, texture, composition, and contrast.
- Students express preferences in art, comparing sensory qualities, styles, art form, and materials.
- Students critique a work of art, comparing style and function.

ORGANIZATION OF ART EXPERIENCES

The 1947 research of Viktor Lowenfeld, reported in Lowenfeld and Brittain (1987), has been influential in the organization of art experiences for children. Lowenfeld found that there was a progressive pattern to the development of children's drawings. Like Piaget, Lowenfeld noted the egocentric behavior of the young child and observed the changes in children's drawings from representations of the self in early childhood to objective realism in the later elementary years. Although levels of development should not be rigidly interpreted, the stages do provide a guide to the choice of art activities. Growth is continuous for each child; objectives for art lessons will overlap at the skill levels.

Lowenfeld's stages are described by Brittain (Lowenfeld and Brittain, 1987):

- *Scribbling stage.* This stage generally lasts until about age four. During scribbling, the young child makes random marks on paper.
- *Preschematic stage.* Children make their first representational pictures during this stage. Generally this stage lasts from age four through seven.
- *Schematic stage.* From seven to nine years of age, children's drawings symbolize their environment. Typically the drawings are arranged at the bottom of the paper in series fashion: house, tree, flower, person, dog.
- *Dawning realism.* This stage lasts from ages nine to twelve. Drawings symbolize rather than represent objects. During this stage children rarely want to display their work.
- *Pseudonaturalistic.* This stage begins around age 11 or 12. The students are highly critical of their own work. The work is often kept hidden. Human figures are drawn in great detail with awareness of sexual characteristics. Students are interested in cartooning during this stage.

The primary child (K–2) emerging from the scribble stage is spontaneous, usually nonreflective, and not concerned with reality. The young child loves to express drawings and paintings in vivid terms using bright colors. The child works best with large pencils or brushes on extra large paper. Content for the primary child typically relates to the child's self and family.

The following activities are considered appropriate for the K–2 child:

- Students enjoy experimenting with a variety of art materials: paint, felt-tip pens, crayons, clay, tissue, chalk, starch, paste, sand, string, yarn, plastic, beads, and wood.
- Using the materials, students explore, learning to create line, form, color, texture and patterns; students can recognize two- and three-dimensional forms.
- Students enjoy art experiences and can communicate feelings and observations. Students express reactions to verbal and visual impressions.
- Students can make pictures expressing feelings, moods, imagination, stories, music, and physical activity.
- Students make designs using varied art materials. Designs are typically borders; sometimes an overall design is achieved.
- Students make models using clay, wood, and paper.
- Students express appreciation of nature (flowers, rocks, shells, sky, grass, rainbows), order (nature, classroom), appearance (self and others), and artworks (of others and classics).

The middle grade student is sociocentric rather than egocentric and is able to work both independently and cooperatively with others. The student is more oriented to reality and wants to produce art objects that are more truly representative—details are important. The student will describe similarities and differences in shapes and patterns. Color is used more realistically and with more restraint. The concept of space becomes important to the child of this age, and he or she will attempt to express it in landscapes, figures, and total composition. The following activities are considered appropriate:

- Students experiment with ways of using art materials. The student will use the side and point of crayons and chalk. He or she will enjoy using crayon resist and wet chalk. Mixing and blending colors are explored. Using tempera paint, the student enjoys dripping, spraying, and stippling. Greater manipulative abilities allow the student to use watercolors and mix and blend the colors. The child enjoys manipulating clay—punching, pinching, and coiling. The student can use papier-mâché and can cut, tear, fold, fringe, and curl paper.

- Students make pictures of real and imaginative experiences. They enjoy using a variety of art media; can portray essential characteristics of form depicting front, back, above, below; and consider colors, contrast, size, shape, texture, and pattern.
- Students produce three-dimensional models using clay, paper, and wood.
- Students are more aware of design features and enjoy experimenting, making designs for a variety of purposes.
- The middle grade student appreciates collections, art objects, bulletin board arrangements. The student will express enjoyment in selecting and reacting to pictures and art experiences.

Because the upper grade student's motor skills are more controlled, he or she can create more mature art productions. The student can work longer and more intently and is able to work independently. If the student has been exposed to art experiences, the vocabulary will be more developed and art appreciation more sophisticated. The student should be able to compare artists and artworks in relation to sensory qualities, style, and materials. Students at this age are more analytical about what they see and more evaluative about what they like.

The upper grade student can manipulate a wide variety of art materials with greater control and sophistication:

Crayons: Uses side and point, uses pressure to produce light and dark, blends colors, makes transparencies and etchings

Chalk: Blends; uses dry or wet surfaces

Charcoal: Combines with water colors, shades, uses point and side

Clay: Carves and builds by pinching, pulling out, using slab and coil construction

Paper: Curls, fringes, braids, weaves, bends, folds, rolls, twists

Papier-mâché: Enjoys making masks, covering buildings, frames

Tempera paint: Can spray, drip, stipple, spatter; mixes and blends colors

Watercolors: Can combine with other art materials

Art activities for grades 5–8 are almost limitless.

- In making pictures the student can express feelings and reactions and portray people, events, time, weather, and perspective. In using a variety of art media, the student considers composition and color.

- The upper grade student enjoys lettering, both upper- and lower-case.
- Students enjoy producing three-dimensional objects.
- Students consider design in overall patterns and in borders and understand principles of design.
- Students express appreciation of art objects, pictures, and artists. The student can observe line, form, texture, motion, and color; arrange and order objects and collections; consider personal appearance; and visit museums. The student can recognize examples of U.S., Native American, and Mexican art, as well as the work of artists studied in class.

PURPOSES OF DANCE

Dance has been an integral part of the socialization process of many cultures. It is considered the oldest component of the arts. Dance communicates nonverbally through body talk; it is considered an alternative to talk. Dance links movement with feeling and provides for multisensory integration and creative expression; it contributes to historical and cultural heritage, and aesthetic valuing.

Goals identified by the *Visual and Performing Arts Framework for California Public Schools* include the following:

- To develop the student's awareness of the body's communicative potential and capacity for spontaneous movement response
- To increase motor efficiency and kinesthetic sensibility
- To develop the student's ability to express perceptions, feelings, images, and thoughts through dance
- To develop respect for originality in dance
- To develop the student's knowledge and appreciation of our multicultural dance heritage
- To recognize current dance forms and styles and the place of dance in contemporary culture
- To develop sense of involvement in dance expression and positive attitudes toward self, others, and the environment
- To cultivate intellectual bases for making judgments about dance in relation to personal and community values and the environment

Some representative activities for the several goals could include the following:

- Discovering natural movements and describing how the movements feel
- Expressing mood or feeling through movement

- Creating an original dance with a beginning, middle, and end
- Participating in performances and productions
- Exploring heritage and cross-cultural influences on dance forms
- Studying Western culture dance and the evolution of ballet, jazz, tap, and social dance forms

PURPOSES OF DRAMA/THEATER

The California framework identifies the primary goal of teaching drama/theater as the development of the student's imagination and problem-solving and communicative potential. Specific goals include the following:

- To experience dramatic elements, actions, and characterizations
- To develop skills in storytelling, playmaking, and playwriting
- To develop an awareness of the collaborative nature of playmaking
- To develop acting skills for theatrical performance
- To develop an awareness of the collaborative nature of theater and the many skills needed to prepare a finished production
- To develop a knowledge of and appreciation for drama/theater heritage
- To develop a system of aesthetic valuing of drama/theater

    Representative activities might include the following:

- Reacting to imaginary sounds
- Creating rhythms and performing them
- Communicating to others stories of dramatic emotion
- Expressing characterizations in different situations
- Improvising a story line
- Creating a theater event; coordinating media
- Making decisions for theater productions involving space, resources, lighting, script
- Collaborating in a group production
- Making judgments about character, theme, meaning, quality

WHAT SHOULD STUDENTS LEARN IN THE ARTS?

MUSIC EDUCATION

Music instruction is typically organized to teach concepts, process skills, music skills, and attitudes and values through the activities of listening, singing, moving, playing, and reading and writing notation. Concepts are related to **expressive elements** (tone qualities, tempo, and dynamics), to **constituent elements** (rhythm, melody, harmony, and form), and to the structure of music. The process skills interact with the concepts as the teacher asks students to organize data, generalize and make inferences, and apply knowledge. Students develop music skills as they pursue the aforementioned activities. Attitudes and values are developed through the total music experience and are encouraged by motivating students to choose musical experiences and by providing opportunities for decision making.

Illustrative objectives for each of the activities will provide some insight concerning the content of the elementary music period.

Listening

- Students identify a familiar song by listening to its rhythm clapped or beat out.
- Listening to a song or recorded music, students can differentiate major and minor keys.
- Listening to an orchestral number, students can identify instrument families.

Singing

- After listening to a melody, students repeat it with accurate pitch.
- After listening to the rhythm of a melody or after reading the rhythmic notation, students reproduce the number singing the rhythmic pattern accurately.
- Reading notation, students harmonize and sing in two parts.

Moving

- Students demonstrate basic conducting patterns with the hand to lead a melody.
- Using large muscle movements, students represent rhythmic components of a number.
- Students demonstrate the tempo of a number by swaying, stretching, sliding, or rocking.

Playing (Performance)

- Using a variety of percussion instruments, students create rhythm. Using an autoharp, bells, or other instruments, students accompany a song.
- Using instruments, students demonstrate understanding of tempo, dynamics, and tone color.

Reading and Writing Notation

- Given a pattern of melody written in blank notation, students identify a familiar song.
- Reading tempo markings, the students demonstrate understanding by playing or singing a song appropriately.
- Given a staff and appropriate symbols and notes, students write a pattern of melody in blank notation.

ORGANIZATIONAL GUIDELINES FOR TEACHING MUSIC

Musical activities are planned to correspond to the developmental characteristics of elementary-age children just as the art activities are. Land and Vaughan (1978) made the following suggestions for planning musical activities for five- to eight-year-old students:

- Each music lesson should include a variety of experiences chosen from singing, performing, reading notation, composing, and listening.
- There should be opportunity for both individual or small group participation and whole group participation.
- There should be teacher choice and student choice of music.
- The vocabulary of songs should be examined to verify that students will understand the words. If they do not, explanations should be given.
- Music should reflect students' moods and needs for self-image.
- Music concepts are learned best through movement activities.
- Since the young child is imaginative, there should be opportunity for the exploration of movement and dramatization of songs.
- Music should reflect the community and culture of the children.
- Students should be asked to identify simple rhythmic patterns.
- Students should feel successful during the music period.

Activities for grades 4–8 should be planned with the following considerations:

- Increased coordination of the older student allows greater freedom in choosing instruments for them

---

Since primary-age children do not naturally sit still for very long, how can music be used advantageously to promote academic engagement?

---

to play. They enjoy the ukulele, guitar, autoharp, and recorder, along with percussion instruments.
- Developmental differences among children in grades 5–8 are great, so the activities should be varied: square and folk dances; participation using instruments, singing, composing, and listening.
- Greater maturity allows the use of music books and the singing of two- and three-part songs. As boys' voices change, they can sing the lower parts. Students of this age can harmonize by ear.
- In grades 6–8 students enjoy changing the words of popular songs to write their own class songs. They also enjoy performing in musicals and writing dramatizations for performance.
- Students should be given the opportunity to make choices about what they are to perform and correlate other subject fields in their dramatizations. They should be able to create introductions, codas, descants, and other tonal embellishments.
- They are able to understand musical terms and symbols such as *cadence, accent, tempo, rhythm pattern, interval, scale, sharp, flat, clef, tonal pattern, underlying beat, phrase, key signature, p-pp, f-ff, crescendo, retard, minor, major.*

HOW SHOULD THE ARTS BE TAUGHT?

Two lesson plans are used to demonstrate teaching approaches for the aesthetic arts. In both examples, the arts are integrated. However, there is a wide range of appropriate techniques for teaching the four disciplines, and there should be specific teaching in each of the arts. As in physical education, both exploration and direct instruction are appropriate.

IN MARY HOGAN'S CLASSROOM

Mary Hogan's major objective was to teach the concept of rhythmic pattern duration. In addition, she wanted to incorporate movement, and build appreciation of folk music typical of the Caribbean area, South America, and West Africa. She planned to demonstrate to her students that rhythm patterns have long and short sounds and that when a melody uses a rhythm pattern, the words are sung in a long and short rhythmic sound pattern. She chose the calypso song "Tinga Layo."

Hogan's Objectives

1. To recognize and identify rhythmic changes
2. To sing and move to the rhythmic pattern accurately

3. To clap and produce the rhythmic pattern using coconut shells
4. To recognize the rhythmic pattern written in blank notation on the board

Materials

Record player
Record
Four sets of coconut shells

Procedure

Hogan: Yesterday Benny brought in his Harry Belafonte record and we listened to calypso music. Who remembers what impressed us about the calypso music?

(The students respond that it was the rhythm that was unusual and that they had enjoyed it.)

Hogan: Good, I thought you'd remember, and since you enjoyed it so much, I brought another calypso record for you to hear.

(Hogan plays "Tinga Layo" and students listen. Some students nod and seem to know the words.)

Hogan: This time, boys and girls, see if you can clap the rhythm of the song when I give you the signal. (Hogan provides the cue for the rhythm pattern that occurs six times during the song. Then she brings out some coconut shells and claps them together.)

Hogan: What does this sound like?

(The students respond that is sounds like a pony's hoofbeats.)

Hogan: Yes, who would like to play them when we hear the rhythm pattern?

(She chooses four students to participate.)

Hogan: While our friends play the shells, let's have everyone else count the number of times we hear the same pattern.

(After the song, Hogan has the students respond, and several had counted correctly; the pattern was repeated six times.)

Hogan: I'm going to write the notes on the board; see if you can recognize which are short sounds and which are long sounds.

Hogan: Let's see if we can sing the pattern. (She leads them by pointing to the notation on

---

How does Hogan ensure that all of the children are engaged in the lesson?

---

the board. Next she teaches the entire song and asks them to match the words to the rhythm pattern written on the board. She asks them to identify the words that represent the short sounds and those that represent the long sounds.)

Hogan: All right, let's give some other people a chance to perform using the shells. (The children pass them to friends.)

Hogan: While some of us are using the shells, who would like to pretend they are a pony and move to the rhythm of the music? Good. (Hogan chooses several children.) Now, let's have the rest of us cup our hands this way and clap to make the sound of hoofs. (The lesson continues in this way until all of the children have had a turn to use the shells or create movements to the music.)

Hogan: Well, boys and girls, we have done such a good job with "Tinga Layo," let's talk about what the music tells us. . . .

ANALYSIS OF HOGAN'S MUSIC LESSON

Hogan chose the lesson for three reasons:

1. She needed to teach the concept of rhythmic patterns.
2. She wanted to introduce folk music to the children.
3. The lesson fit neatly with the students' prior experience of listening to Belafonte sing calypso music.

She motivated the lesson by having the students recall the previous day's listening experience. To develop the concept she had the students participate in the following activities: listening, singing, movement (clapping) and performing (using the coconut shells), body movement, and reading notation.

Hogan verified understanding of the concept by having the students clap the rhythm, count the number of times the pattern was used, identify the words to fit the pattern, and move in rhythm.

She would follow the lesson on a successive day by having the students use different instruments (bongos, maracas, claves) to accompany the rhythmic pattern and to compose patterns of their own. She intended to have the students gain some understanding of folk music by learning and comparing other folk songs with "Tinga Layo."

Teaching strategies for music should be varied. They may begin with singing, listening, creative movements, or performing. Music may even begin with an inquiry

Research Application

Project FLARE (Fun with Language, Arts, and Reading) in Pasadena, California, pairs classroom teachers and artists to develop interdisciplinary thematic units. The units integrate either social studies or science, use the appropriate grade-level curriculum, and teachers select appropriate literature. The teacher-artist team selects activities based on the particular students' interests. Included in the program are field trips to artists' studios and local art shows. The project is supported by the Armory Center for the Arts, local businesses, the school district, and the California Institute of Technology. Teachers contend that FLARE has had a powerful effect on language for both English speakers and bilingual speakers because of its incorporation of drawing, sketching, and graphic visualization that encourage students to reflect and talk about their creations (Aschbacher, 1996).

lesson. The important point is to sequence lessons so that they relate to each other and fit the developmental needs of the students. Children should have the opportunity to learn music concepts, to enjoy, to feel successful, and to release emotion.

In Greg Thomas's Classroom

Greg Thomas's fifth-grade students were excited about Halloween. He decided to use that stimulation advantageously. He planned an art lesson in which the students would make papier-mâché masks.

Thomas's Objectives:

1. To make three-dimensional masks using the medium of papier-mâché appropriately
2. To work imaginatively to express and communicate personal feelings
3. To work individually and explore the fanciful and the strange
4. To create movements to characterize the masks.

Materials:

Strips of newspaper
Paste
Balloons
Tempera paint and brushes
Scissors, Plastic spray

Procedure:

Thomas: I've been listening to several of you talk about you Halloween plans. I was wondering how many of you like to wear a mask on Halloween? (Many of the students respond affirmatively.)

Thomas: How does it feel to wear a mask?

Linda: I can't breathe when I wear a mask.

Jerry: I like it because it lets me hide and surprise people.

Cora: I like to scare my friends.

Jeff: It makes me feel different—kinda strong.

Thomas: Does wearing a mask change what you see or hear?

Linda: Well, I feel like the character I'm pretending to be.

Thomas: What do you mean?

Linda: If my mask is of a pirate, then I feel like a pirate.

Cora: This year I'm going to be the Greatest American Hero.

Thomas: I thought It would wear this mask when I answer my door this year.

Jeff: Wow! Did you make that mask?

Thomas: Yes, and I thought that perhaps you folks would like to make masks today. (Students respond very positively.)

Thomas: All right. Listen carefully: this is what we are going to do. This is a papier-mâché mask. It is made by pasting strips of paper over a balloon. Then it is decorated to suit the character you want to be. When it is dry, it is sprayed to protect the finish. The last step is cutting the balloon in half and cutting openings for the eyes and other features. It is even possible to add other materials, like yarn or paper, as I did on my mask, to obtain special effects and features.

To plan your masks, you must first think about the medium that you are going to use. How can you use it to convey the mood that you want your character to portray? Remember that you must design your mask to fit your face. Visualize your own face. Do you have a large forehead? Do you need a big space between your hair and your nose or a smaller space? Make a sketch of the way you want your mask to look. When you are satisfied with your plan, begin work with the paper and the balloon.

I'm going to ask our art monitors to set the materials out on each table, but before you begin to work, I want each table to be covered with newspaper so that you don't spill paste on the table top. Now—everyone look over here at the chart rack. If you have a question about the procedures for working with papier-mâché, you may look at this chart. If you have a question that you need to ask of me, raise your hand and I will come over to your table.

Thomas's art lesson took three consecutive days to complete. On the second day the students cut and painted and decorated their masks. On the third day they sprayed them to protect the finish. At the end of the week, Thomas suggested that all the students put on their masks and walk to the auditorium. Thomas carried his own mask with him and asked the students, "How do you think I should act when I wear this mask?"

After students responded, Thomas turned on a special tape of recorded music. He told the students to take their scatter positions on the floor and assume a body posture that would be appropriate for the mask that each student was wearing.

Next the students were asked to create movements that would indicate how each character feels, thinks, and acts. Thomas also brought a number of props for the students to use to help them create their movements and characterizations (adapted from King, 1975).

Thomas will also ask the students to write about their characters as a special creative writing lesson.

ANALYSIS OF THOMAS'S ART LESSON

Thomas was primarily interested in developing creative expression. He motivated this by providing opportunity for the students to talk about how it feels to wear masks. He asked the students to use their imagination, but he also suggested that they plan the design of the mask. He called attention to the spatial organization of the face.

Since every medium poses special problems, Thomas was probably wise in allowing the students to explore the medium instead of giving too much direction

about its use. He carefully provided for individual needs by telling the students to raise their hands if they needed assistance, and he also provided a step-by-step procedural chart for using papier-mâché.

Thomas culminated the mask making in an interesting way. Instead of just talking about and sharing their masks with each other, Thomas had them assume the characterization and portray with movements the mask each was wearing; in this way he incorporated dance and provided opportunity for students to express feelings, images, and thoughts. We can assume that Thomas developed aesthetic judgment as well as creative expression through the art, oral language, and physical movement lessons.

Art is taught through direct instruction to develop art concepts and art skills; art is also taught using discovery approaches that allow students to explore a medium and express feelings and individual perceptions. Strategies should be varied depending on the medium to be used and the concepts to be developed. A great deal of preplanning is necessary for art activities so when the actual lesson is implemented, the teacher is free to observe and express encouragement to children. Although in most subjects the teacher acts as a model for students to observe, during art it is better if students are free to express their own creative nature instead of trying to imitate the teacher.

IMAGE MAKING

Image Making Within the Writing Process is an arts-based literacy program that integrates children's visual imagery and the writing process. The project has been in operation since 1990 and is used by elementary and middle school teachers to inspire illustrating and authoring. Some students begin with the writing process first, and then illustrate; others begin with visual modes of expression and then create stories to fit the pictures.

The Laboratory for Interactive Learning at the University of New Hampshire has studied the image-making program. They compared the writing abilities of project students with a control group and found the following about project students (Olshansky, 1995, pp. 44–47)

- Writing topics were more varied and imaginative.
- Story plots were more fully developed.
- Stories had a beginning, middle, and end.
- Stories were better crafted.
- The authors used more descriptive language.

SUMMARIZING STRATEGIES OF INSTRUCTION IN THE ARTS

Since the 1970s, the trend in teaching the arts has been toward the following:

- Emphasis on discipline-based instruction through use of structural concepts in the disciplines of music, art, theater, and dance
- Emphasis on movement as a unifying component
- Application of stages of development to the selection of aesthetic experiences
- Emphasis on enhancing a positive self-concept and self-actualization
- Utilization of inquiry methodology when appropriate; emphasis on performing, modeling, and discussion
- Emphasis on understanding the philosophic, emotional, sensory, and intellectual bases for making judgments

EVALUATING THE CREATIVE ARTS

As in physical education, evaluation in the creative arts must be measured in terms of the student's own progress and performance. The student's contribution to discussions and the student's enjoyment of the arts provide an index of the student's competencies in art and music.

Musical skills, such as listening, reading, and writing music, creative skills, and performance skills (playing instruments, moving, singing, and conducting), are best evaluated through sensitive observation by the teacher. Students' behavior as they participate in rhythmic activities, singing, or expressing ideas about music are primarily evaluated by direct observation. A music checklist can be constructed to record information about the student. Listening competencies can be evaluated during a discussion that focuses on identifying the mood of a melody, the instruments, rhythmic patterns, or phrasing. The picture of the children writing notation provides another observational method to evaluate whether or not the student can read and write music.

Dance activities can be evaluated by students' enjoyment in movement, observation of form and interpretation, and students' discussion and comments about participation.

Evaluating drama activities is similar to dance experiences. One needs to observe students' ability to imagine, to recall experiences and utilize them, to express characterization, and to communicate through verbal and nonverbal means. Drama also provides a variety of related language arts experiences that can be part of the assessment: writing plays, retelling stories, and improvising story lines.

Both acting and taking part in theater production can be evaluated. In theater production, students can

Art projects help students appreciate the visual arts.

Research Applications

Goldberg (1992) suggests using a variety of means to assess what students know in the arts. Tests and written work may be valid to assess students' knowledge, but she argues that the arts can provide opportunity through genuine artwork for students to explore their understandings and ideas with creative freedom.

learn about and perform directing, stage management, publicity, set design, use of special effects, lighting arrangement, and costume design. Students' appreciation of drama and theater can be assessed as well as their recognition of cultural forms and historical periods and major themes in theater.

Art products should be self-evaluated by the child. The teacher's task is to guide the self-evaluation so students are not too harsh on themselves. The teacher should help the child focus on what is good about the picture or art object by calling attention to the use of the medium, color, spatial organization, design, or whatever else will encourage the student. With success recognized, the teacher can then help the child set some realistic goals for the next project.

Group discussions of artwork should be handled in a similar manner. Each child should be praised in some way—for creativity, ideas, expression of feelings, discoveries about the use of the media, or solutions to problems. Pictures should not be evaluated to choose the best picture. Classroom exhibitions should represent all students' work, not just those appreciated by the teacher.

RESOURCES FOR TEACHING THE ARTS

Resources for teaching music and dance experiences include textbooks, tape recorders, record players, films, slides, and videotapes. Audio-visual aids can enhance the music program, but as in all other subjects, good teaching is the most important element for a good program.

Instruments have great appeal to students. Simple instruments can be made by teacher and students, or they can be purchased. Students enjoy rhythm instruments, percussion, and melody and harmony instruments. Typical rhythm instruments are sticks, triangles, tambourines, castanets, cymbals, bongo and conga drums, claves, maracas, autoharps, and flutelike instruments.

Students enjoy making unusual instruments out of boxes, bottles, metal containers, and cardboard.

Art and materials for theater productions appear to be limited only by a lack of imagination. There are vast choices available to teachers and students. Materials are needed for modeling, lettering, picture-making, painting, crafts, set production, props, and design activities.

Art materials should be well organized for accessibility and for ease in use. Materials may be stored in boxes, shelves, or drawers. Tin cans, five-gallon ice cream containers, plastic pans, and foil pie plates are all useful for holding art tools and materials.

Work areas for art activities include the floor, table tops, easels, and outside patio areas. Newspapers or plastic or oilcloth drop cloths should be available to cover any area that is to be used for work or storage. Large work areas available for groups of students are optimal because students can share tools and materials.

Museums, libraries, galleries, and music and art centers provide marvelous field trip experiences for students. These community resources usually have docents or artists available to discuss what students will see or hear. Local artists and musicians are frequently interested in visiting schools and providing some leadership to young people interested in the arts.

PROGRAMS AND PROJECTS IN THE ARTS

LEARNING THROUGH AN EXPANDED ARTS PROGRAM (LEAP)

Art and music are used in this program to teach basic skills. This arts-oriented program, begun in New York City for gifted and talented students, has been extended successfully to all students, even those who have tested below the 15th percentile (Dean and Gross, 1992).

Professional artists, musicians, and education consultants work with students in grades K–8 (and help to train their teachers) using innovative approaches to teach a variety of ideas in fields far-flung, such as architecture, archaeology, robotics, opera composition, and African storytelling. The LEAP approach uses materials and projects that are interesting to students. The students gain a sense of accomplishment and self-confidence through the completion of creative tasks.

Dean and Gross describe one of the many LEAP programs, Promoting Success. Students in this program make puppets, paint murals, and create their own songs, plays, and dances while learning reading and writing. The project leader uses a storyboard to help students learn sequencing and recall details of a story. After reading a story, the students draw simple figures for their storyboards. The consultant then rereads the story, and students recognize each scene in the story. Students then use their storyboards to retell the story in their own words. If students' sequencing is incorrect, the consultant goes back and rereads that section of the story so that students understand the impact of each idea. In this way students learn to recognize both the main ideas of stories and the consequence of sequencing. Subsequent sessions will focus on making puppets and their characterization using the story elements, students' rereading of the story, and visualization of the scenes through murals.

Other LEAP projects focus on developing math abilities. Musical math appears to reduce students' anxieties and provides a sense of self-confidence. As in the reading and writing program, the math program uses storyboards, murals, puppets, plays, and dances.

EDUCATION FOR AESTHETIC AWARENESS (EAA)

EAA is a process-oriented program for teachers in the Greater Cleveland area. Developed by the Cleveland Area Arts Council, the program is funded by grants from several private foundations and by the National Endowment for the Humanities and the Alliance for Arts Education. EAA's purpose is to build confidence and aesthetic literacy among classroom teachers and art specialists. Selected faculty members study—intensively—ways to teach the arts and to develop a school philosophy for the teaching of the arts. Specifically, the teachers study melody, rhythm, and harmony in music, and line, shape, and texture in painting. In addition to attending class lectures in each art form, the teachers study aesthetic philosophy, building curriculum in the arts, advocacy, use of community arts, and the politics of school change (Robiner, 1980).

ARTS IN EDUCATION

Arts in Education is a concept that was developed in the United States Office of Education's Humanities Division. The concept has been used to encourage school systems, curriculum developers, arts organizations, and teacher preparatory programs to develop sequential, integrated arts programs in the schools. Professional artists participate in the school programs.

Programs have been cooperatively funded by private foundations and the National Endowment for the Arts, National Institute of Education, the National Endowment for the Humanities, and the Office of Education.

The programs are diverse in nature, with different states setting different priorities for the Arts in Education. Magnet programs have been established in several states to attract majority students to inner-city schools with strong arts-related curricula. Other states have assigned state personnel to develop strategies for school improvement with a focus on the arts. Another strategy has been the use of the principle of *networking*. Network members are partners and peers committed to Arts in Education. Professional educators service the network, facilitate program development, and secure community resource personnel to assist in the schools' programs. The chief school administrator is responsible for providing leadership by advocating program development, materials development, and some budgetary support (Fineberg, 1980).

CEMREL

CEMREL is an aesthetic education program developed by the Central Midwestern Regional Educational Laboratory of St. Louis, Missouri (CEMREL, 1971). Classroom kits have been designed to be used by classroom teachers or art specialists. The teacher is able to select the instructional package or kit needed. There are four components to the program:

1. *Introduction to Aesthetic Phenomena.* This component consists of materials related to the physical elements of the arts (light, sound, time, motion, shape).
2. *Elements in the Art Disciplines and the Environment.* Materials in these kits focus on the interaction of elements within the arts.
3. *Process of Transformation.* These kits focus on the process of synthesizing aesthetic and physical elements in a work of art.
4. *People in the Arts.* These kits are designed to develop an appreciation of the artistic process and understanding about artists and their work.

GETTY INSTITUTE FOR EDUCATORS ON THE VISUAL ARTS

The Getty Institute program, in existence since 1983, was designed to help teachers develop discipline-based art education for the classroom. The institute focuses on four instructional approaches: art production, art history, art criticism, and aesthetics. Its program is similar to many state frameworks and to policies advocated by the National Art Education Association. The institute provides summer workshops for teachers to study art curriculums and resource materials. Teachers also observe art demonstration lessons. The institute provides continuing support to the teachers during the school year through regular activities and an information bulletin. Participating teachers become district leaders responsible for in-service activities in their school district.

Greer and Silverman (1988, pp. 10–14) evaluated the Getty Institute program and came to the following conclusions:

- Vast changes have been made in the way teachers teach art.
- The discipline-based approach allows for an identifiable scope and sequence.
- Students are gaining a sense of history as well as developing creative skills through the program.
- The discipline-based approach implemented at the elementary level would also be valuable at the secondary level.

The Getty Institute program has begun to be implemented in many school districts across the country. The discipline-based approach is given a variety of names. For example, in Ohio it is called the Balanced Comprehensive Art Curriculum; it is described as balanced because equitable instructional time and resources are provided in grades K–12 (Tollifson, 1988).

Research Findings: Colors in Nature

Cohen and Gainer (1976, p. 159) studied colors that came from nature. They discovered the following natural pigments:

- Juniper berries make a light brown.
- Walnut shells make a dark reddish-brown.
- Holly berries make purple.
- Sagebrush makes yellow.
- Oak bark makes a purplish-brown.
- Red onion skin makes brown.
- Charcoal makes black and gray.
- Soil makes dark brown and sometimes dark red.

The Ohio program emphasizes art production, art history, art criticism, and art in society.

COMPREHENSIVE ARTS PROGRAM

Developed by the Southwest Regional Laboratory (SWRL), this sequenced basic program for elementary students is research based and classroom verified to provide arts concepts and to encourage independent inquiry.

The art program is designed to develop students' awareness and appreciation of the role of artist, the art critic, and the art historian. The program concentrates on visual analysis, art production, and critical analysis.

Visual Analysis

Students observe and analyze objects and illustrations of objects. For example, during the third block of instruction (each block consists of four units), students observe and analyze imaginary buildings and figures, trees, and animals. They study size differences that are a consequence of distance and proportion.

Production

Students use a variety of art media to create their own work. Examples provided in the program's scope and sequence at the third block include crayon drawing, tempera paint technique, sponge painting, cutting paper on a line, and pulling forms from clay.

Critical Analysis

For this component the students observe and discuss the works of artists and begin to analyze and evaluate artworks using both a cultural and historical context. During block three, the students analyze American, European, and Asian landscape paintings; Japanese screens in the twentieth century; and sculpture.

The program includes a program guide, a critical analysis guide, filmstrips, and assessment materials.

The music program is organized around six basic music concepts: rhythm, melody, harmony, form, tone color, and dynamic level. Awareness, appreciation, and performance tasks enable the students to understand music in terms of its expressive properties. Program components are performance proficiency, criticism proficiency, and composition proficiency.

Performance proficiency encompasses singing, playing instruments, reading standard music notation, and moving to music.

Criticism proficiency includes labeling and describing, analyzing, and evaluating.

Composition proficiency focuses on writing music notation, elaborating existing music, and composing original music.

The program is organized into 16 blocks of instruction. Each unit of the block is organized around one of the six concepts. For example, during the second block, concentrating on rhythm, the students learn double and triple meter, and for notation they learn bar line, sets of two quarter notes, and sets of three quarter notes.

The music program includes a program guide, assessment materials, song tapes, unit tapes, instrument posters, and notation performance cards for the tone bells and the autoharp along with aids for teaching standard music notation.

Both the music program and the art program are available from Phi Delta Kappa, Bloomington, IN 47402.

PROJECT CHART

Initiated by the Rockefeller Foundation, CHART (Collaboratives for Humanities and Arts Teaching) projects work with a local school board, superintendent, community businesses, and cultural interests of a city to fund local artists, historians, museum curators, storytellers, and teachers to develop interdisciplinary curriculum (Renyi, 1994). The interdisciplinary approach usually involves English, social studies, and art coordinated around a theme. The project provides special subject matter knowledge for teachers and the teachers supply pedagogic information.

The project helps to restructure schools by convincing personnel to be innovative in their scheduling to accommodate the new curriculum. For example, at the middle school level, it was necessary to implement block scheduling so that teachers could work with a single block of students.

CHART has been in operation since 1983 and its projects are varied. In Los Angeles the HUMANITAS project is a thematic course of study that spans subject areas and encompasses the cultural and ethnic diversity of the students. In Pittsburgh, the Arts PROPEL program is based on the cognitive importance of the arts and features student exploration through perception, reflection, and production. The program is assessed by having students develop portfolios.

MANHATTANVILLE MUSIC CURRICULUM PROGRAM (MMCP)

MMCP is an inquiry approach to the teaching of music. MMCP curriculum for children ages three through eight is called MMCP Interaction: Early Childhood Music Curriculum; the program for children nine and above is called MMCP Synthesis. Both use a spiral approach to teaching activities that range from simple to complex. Emphasis is on the structure of music (form, tone quality, dynamics, duration, and pitch). Activities begin with student discovery, then progress to invention, and finally involve composition. For example, in the series entitled "Metal Encounters," from the interaction curriculum during the first phase, students explore a variety of sounds using metal sources. Students are encouraged to add to the sounds center with their own metal objects. In the second phase the students contrast sounds from metal objects and discuss sound-producing techniques. During this phase the students identify sounds that are similar to sounds that they recall, such as a ticking clock, a dripping faucet, or a bouncing ball. In the third phase the students practice making sounds and repeating sound patterns. In phase four the students play the game of the Sound Machine. Working in small groups, the students arrange sound patterns so they are satisfying to the group, expressive, and meaningful.

ORFF METHOD

Carl Orff, a German composer, worked with Dorothee Gunther, a movement specialist, to develop a school program that unified dancing and gymnastics. From this experience Orff went on to collect and adapt percussion instruments appropriate for the use of young children. The Orff method for teaching is based on the idea that children are naturally inclined to express themselves with music and with improvisation. The Orff instruments allow children to explore music and sound. Used in elementary schools, the Orff program begins with melodic experiences, encouraging students to improvise, use body movements, sing, and utilize speech sounds and patterns. Favored instruments include the glockenspiel, the metalophone, the six-stringed viola da gamba, and the bordun (a bass two-stringed instrument).

KODALY

Hungarian composer Zoltan Kodaly has influenced music teaching in the United States. Kodaly advocated the use of the John Curwen hand signals that teach syllables (Do, Re, Mi, Fa, So, La, Ti, Do) and recommended that children be taught to read and write music notation. Kodaly emphasized folk singing and believed that singing experiences should begin during the preschool years.

DALCROZE

Eurhythmics involves the whole body in rhythmic movements. Emile Jacques-Dalcroze, a Swiss teacher, developed this system for teaching music. After eurhythmics experiences, students practice singing using solfege. Dalcroze has been influential in the preparation of music teachers.

INTEGRATION OF SUBJECT FIELDS AND LEARNING CENTER IDEAS

ARTS-INTEGRATED SCHOOLS

There is considerable evidence that the integration of arts motivates students and improves their performance in the core subjects as well as the arts. Sautter (1994, p. 434) notes that

> The arts-integrated school challenges students and shows them how to learn through individual art forms and through interdisciplinary, hands-on projects that link them to many areas of knowledge.

Sautter emphasizes that by educating through the arts, thinking skills, imagination, and oral or written expression are enhanced.

Research Findings: Arts Education

The National Arts Education Research Center at New York University studied arts education in the schools and concluded the following (Sautter, 1994):

- Within a variety of settings and with a variety of population groups, the arts have a significant impact on academic achievement.
- The arts are another way of perceiving and another way of knowing.
- The integration of aesthetics, skills, history and theory, and higher-order thinking skills can be applied to learning about the arts and they help students achieve at a greater level in academic areas.

Interdisciplinary learning can be enhanced through the utilization of the arts as unifying strands throughout the school day. Selwyn (1995, p. 9) points out that the study of the arts is the study of history. "Music, visual arts, dance, theater, crafts, writing, and other arts are both artifacts of and a means by which to study a culture."

Listed by subject fields, fusion ideas will be identified. The ideas should also serve as concepts to develop into learning centers.

Social Studies and the Arts

- Use the arts as a visual record of cultural development. Study history through paintings, architecture, sculpture, dance, drama, occupations, fashion, and furniture.
- Study and reproduce artifacts; observe the statues of famous historical figures; create statues and write a dialogue between historical figures.
- Draw historical events. Create a courtroom and role-play a famous trial recreating the events as they occurred. Then recreate the trial with new information.
- Dramatize historical events and plays from different historical periods.
- Contrast handcrafts and manufactured products.
- Draw murals.
- Research occupations, furnishings, fashion, and the like and keep notes through the use of a sketchbook.
- Study the cultural use of silhouettes historically.
- Draw maps.

Social Studies, Music, and Dance

- Use music and dance as records of cultural diversity and development.
- Interpret social, political, and economic change by listening to and singing songs from different historical periods and different cultural groups.
- Study customs, beliefs, and values by listening to and singing folk songs, work songs, religious music, sea chanteys, recreational music, and lullabies.
- Study ethnic and cultural differences by listening to lullabies.
- Trace technological development through music. (How many steamboat and choo-choo songs are written today?)
- Use environmental materials to reproduce early instruments.
- Identify a specific culture or society by studying the instruments used in a musical selection.

- Study cultural groups through their dance customs.
- Perform folk and square dances depicting culture and historical time period.

Science and Art

- Study and draw natural and manmade environment.
- Use a sketchbook to record observations of experiments.
- Draw Darwin's theory of evolution.
- Study and draw landscapes, rainbows, plants, animals, and human anatomy.
- Experiment, study, and draw light and color, warm and cool colors.
- Use natural materials to make colors.
- Use natural materials to make instruments.
- Record (sketch) observations while looking through a magnifying glass, a prism, or a microscope.
- Record the development of inventions.
- Study the human eye and compare it with a camera.

Science and Music

- Find answers to the following questions:
  What causes sound?
  How does temperature affect sound?
  How does the thickness of bars and strings affect tone?
  How does the frequency of vibrations affect pitch?
  How are vibrations made?
  How do sounds differ?
  How does distance affect sound?
  What happens when you use a megaphone or other devices?
  Through what substances will sound travel?
- Compare the range in octaves of the human voice and instruments.
- Listen to and identify environmental sounds.
- Study the human ear; compare it with animals' ears.
- Make instruments out of different materials and compare sounds.

Language Arts, Art, and Drama

- Use artworks, literature, and theater to stimulate creative writing.
- Create murals or cartoons with talking people.
- Use adjectives to describe warm and cool colors, dull and bright colors, and to describe characters and characterizations.
- Do the stage design for a play or musical.
- Draw posters and write slogans.

- Make puppets for dramatics or puppet shows.
- Convey moods and feelings of pictures, stories, and plays.
- Draw or act out a book report.
- Use visual images to communicate.
- Pretend to be a famous human and keep a journal as that person might have written it.
- Write a letter to a friend or a parent from a soldier or sailor during the Korean or Vietnam War.
- See the second and third items in the Social Studies, Music, and Dance list.

Language Arts and Music

- Use music as a stimulus for creative writing.
- Interpret moods and feelings from music.
- Interpret lyrics of songs.
- Compose new lyrics for popular or old familiar songs.
- Describe the style of musical selections (gay, proud, militant).
- Read a play and identify stage sounds that will help the audience interpret the plot or understand the characterization.

Mathematics and Art

- Illustrate math problems involving weight, balance, measurement, or geometry.
- Illustrate the time of day using the sun and appropriate shadows.
- Draw designs; divide using the concept of positive and negative space.
- Draw patterns.
- Use symmetry in design work.
- Plan a board game; divide spaces.

Mathematics and Music

- Identify the pulse or beat of songs.
- Study the speed of sound.
- Measure how sounds differ in decibels.
- Working in groups, use different numbers of beats to get a set distance.

Physical Education, Health, and the Arts

- Study space and form in movement activities.
- Move, identifying positive and negative space.
- Study and draw the human body.
- Study health factors related to appearance. Draw good health posters.

- Study and draw the food groups.
- Paint a salad bar depicting the salad choices.
- Use a sketchbook to record observations of experiments.
- Draw action figures; depict through dance.
- Study artists who specialize in sports pictures.
- Paint a sports picture. Use pantomime to demonstrate a sports event.
- Perform folk games and dances.
- Study body parts involved with making sound.
- Enjoy creative and interpretive dance movements.
- Practice singing a phrase in one breath.
- Study the relationship of exercise and breathing.
- Perform exercises and stretching to music.
- Explore space using music.
- Working in small groups, develop rhythm movement patterns; each group should perform for the other groups.

INCLUSION AND THE ARTS

The arts can be the great classroom equalizer. Students poor in other subject fields may be talented in the arts. Children with physical disabilities frequently perform exceptionally well in music and art. Students with physical or psychological problems may find personal satisfaction in the expression of arts. The arts program can focus on students' abilities rather than their limitations. Most students enjoy using color, space, line, and textures in art, as well as rhythm instruments in music. These experiences allow students to do different things and special things and at the same time keep in contact with their environment.

Although music and art activities can be individualized, in most situations students enjoy participating in group activities. Small work groups for music or art can accommodate individual differences, special abilities, and varied interests. In music, group work could consist of practicing and learning songs using recordings, planning accompaniments, or composing music. In art work, students may be grouped to use different media; some groups may be experimenting; other groups may be extending an art project; or they may be grouped for special instruction.

When grouping is used as an organizational technique during instruction in the arts, it is very important for the teacher to move from group to group to observe students' progress and to provide the guidance needed to encourage skill development. The

mainstreamed student will probably need more guidance and feedback than other students. Motivation and involvement enhance learning in the arts; for this reason, students need both small group work and whole class involvement.

SUMMARY
Importance of the Creative Arts
1. The arts encompass both the visual and the performing arts (music, dance, drama, and art).
2. Visual, aural, and performing arts encourage exploration and creative expression.
3. Aesthetic arts help students appreciate different cultures.
4. Each of the arts provides a continuing and lasting record of human endeavors.

Purposes of Music Education
5. Goals for students include making and creating music, using appropriate vocabulary, appreciating a variety of music, and making aesthetic judgments about music.
6. Music educators advocate that students study cultural literacy through the study of music.

Purposes of the Visual Arts
7. Visual arts should enable students to see clearly, express feelings, demonstrate and communicate individuality, and apply art knowledge.

Visual/Tactile Perception
8. The goal is to maximize seeing, feeling, and understanding of form, color, and texture.

Creative Expression
9. Through artwork students should express their own moods and feelings.

Art Heritage
10. Students need to study works of art and artists of the past and of contemporary times to appreciate their own and others' cultures.

Aesthetic Judgment
11. Students learn to critique and judge artworks based on knowledge and appreciation.

Organization of Art Experiences

12. Art experiences should be based on children's developmental level.
13. Children's drawings often reveal their developmental level.
14. The use of art materials should be based on students' motor skills, perception of space, and manipulative abilities.

Purposes of Dance

15. Participation in dance activities should help students develop body awareness and increase motor efficiency and kinesthetic sensibility.
16. Dance should help students appreciate culture and heritage.

Purposes of Drama/Theater

17. The primary goal should be to develop the student's imagination, communication, and problem-solving abilities.
18. Students should participate in creating theater.

Music Education

19. Music education includes listening, singing, moving, playing, and reading and writing notation.
20. Music concepts are related to expressive elements and constituent elements.

Organization of Music Activities

21. Activities should correspond to the developmental characteristics of the students.
22. As students increase in coordination there are a greater range of instruments that they can learn to play.
23. Participating in music activities relieves tension and helps students relax.

Teaching the Arts

24. Art is taught through direct instruction to develop art concepts and skills.
25. Art is experienced through discovery approaches that encourage students to explore a medium and express feelings and perceptions.

Evaluating the Creative Arts

26. Evaluation in the creative arts should be measured by the student's personal progress and performance.

27. Sensitive observation by the teacher as students participate in the arts can be used to assess progress.

Resources for Teaching the Arts

28. Resources for the arts include texts, tape recorders, instruments, films, slides, video, the Internet, CD/ROMs, art materials, stage equipment, museums, libraries, and galleries.

Programs and Projects

29. Programs and projects in the arts are varied; many use professional artists and musicians.
30. Programs encourage participation in the arts and develop awareness and appreciation.
31. Some of the projects are intended to develop teachers' knowledge and expect teachers to translate what they have learned into appropriate pedagogy for the classroom.

Integration of Subject Fields

32. Interdisciplinary learning is enhanced through the arts as unifying strands.
33. Integration of arts motivates students and improves their performance in academic areas.
34. Education through the arts enhances thinking skills, imagination, and oral and written expression.

DISCUSSION QUESTIONS AND APPLICATION EXERCISES

1. Using the four instructional approaches of aesthetic perception, creative expression, heritage, and aesthetic judgment, develop lessons for teaching music, dance, theater, and art.
2. Develop lessons for integrating the arts with other subject fields.
3. Identify basic supplies for an art center.
4. Explain why arts lessons may be particularly appropriate for students who are considered discipline problems.
5. How could arts programs open the classroom climate and make it more challenging and exciting?
6. What music and art competencies do you believe students should develop in grades K–8?
7. Observe a preadolescent group of students on the playground or in an afterschool activity. Attend specifically to gestures, fashion, movements, and verbal expressions. Record your observations by

categories. Judge how school programs in the arts contribute to what you have observed and how the arts program could relate more meaningfully to these students.

8. Study the drawings of students in grades 1–3. Describe the differences and relate differences to developmental stages as described in this chapter.

9. Select a historical event and create a series of lessons that involve students in literature, theater, art, and music or dance.

PART IV

PROFESSIONAL GROWTH

You are a professional, and you are goal oriented; your behavior is guided both by an understanding of your professional commitment and by your personal needs as a growing, self-actualizing person. You are aware that the future of our society depends on you and other teachers acting responsibly, intelligently, and sensitively to achieve a better tomorrow.

Reform in public education depends on the insight and sagacity of teachers. Expert teachers must accept leadership responsibilities, not only for self-growth, but as a source of advice for colleagues. Teachers need to be courageous and risk takers in the professional domain, otherwise there will be no experimentation, and problems of practice will not be critiqued, challenged, or scrutinized.

18

Professional Development and Teacher Leadership—Personal Responsibilities

The roles and responsibilities of teachers have changed dramatically during the last several years. In this chapter some of the ways that teachers are performing leadership roles are discussed. The hierarchical, bureaucratic governance structure of schools has changed also. Although restructuring of schools does not cause teachers to be leaders, participation beyond the classroom certainly is related to teachers' shared decision making in schools.

New professional roles require that teachers concern themselves with their own professional development. This chapter explains the ways that teachers can self-assess and grow professionally. Teacher portfolios are a means for authentic assessment and many teachers are preparing them to exhibit their professional prowess and excellence.

Teachers' legal rights and responsibilities and students' rights conclude the chapter. Affecting teachers are tenure laws, malpractice and negligence, and copyright laws. These legal issues are discussed along with teacher benefits and salary issues.

After you study this chapter, you should be able to accomplish the following:

1. Identify several ways to continue your own professional education.
2. Explain in what ways teachers' responsibilities have been restructured in some schools.
3. Explain why developing collegiality is necessary for professional development.
4. Identify how clinical supervision can assist the beginning teacher.
5. Identify the purposes of staff development programs.
6. Select personal instructional improvement goals and prioritize them; decide on means to collect data for self-evaluation and a timeline for improvement.
7. Identify one or more professional associations of personal interest.
8. Explain how the copyright law affects teachers in the classroom.
9. Discuss tenure and dismissal procedure affecting teachers.
10. Explain under what circumstances teachers are liable.
11. Identify instructional, supervisory, and assessment responsibilities of teachers.

Professional Lexicon

collegiality   The establishment of a professional relationship for the purpose of service and accommodation through the mutual exchange of perceptions and expertise.

comparative negligence   Negligence in which the teacher is held responsible commensurate to the extent of negligence when both teacher and student are liable for an injury.

continuing contract   A type of employment contract that protects nontenured teachers from summer dismissal; notification of dismissal must occur by a certain date, usually May 1.

contributory negligence   Negligence in which the injured person fails to exercise reasonable self-care.

indefinite contract   A type of employment contract for tenured teachers that is renewed automatically each year without mutual action.

in loco parentis   Literally "in place of the parent"; the ability of teachers to act in a parent's place in school situations.

negligence   Failure to exercise reasonable care and judgement to protect students from injury.

participation rights   The rights of children to participate in decisions that affect their lives and futures.

restructuring   See Professional Lexicon, Chapter 3.

right of protection   The right of children to protection from abuse.

rights of provision   The rights of children to have physical, social, economic, and cultural well-being.

TEACHERS AS PROFESSIONALS AND LEADERS

Three fictional teachers have been introduced in this text; each in his or her own way is considered an expert teacher. Hogan, Thomas, and Adazzio have demonstrated that they care about their students. They have demonstrated their skills in planning and implementing lessons and their ability to assess students' needs, interests, and accomplishments. We will now explore how they demonstrate leadership skills, how they work with colleagues, and how they feel about teaching as a profession.

MARY HOGAN

"Sometimes I get really tired of teaching. Particularly after what feels like a bad day—when there's too much noise and commotion, nobody is listening to me, and time gets away from me. But then, after school I talk to a friend who is also a teacher, and she helps me to think back about the day and figure out what went wrong. I know I do like teaching; I like being able to think about what to teach, how to teach it, and anticipating students' reactions. I really like it when I see that special look in students' eyes that says, 'Hey, that's neat!' and 'I got it!' and then they begin to talk about their own experiences that make it all fit together.

"Because so much of the day is spent talking to children, I really was excited when I was asked to demonstrate teaching models for other teachers. It's fun talking to colleagues about the decisions involved in choosing one model over another. We are going to set up a peer coaching plan, and I look forward to the opportunity to work with other teachers at my school."

GREG THOMAS

"What I like best about teaching is thinking about what will involve the students in real problem solving. I like arranging stuff to create a situation or event for students to explore—and then listening to them wonder. I've never had to worry about students getting out of hand. I like listening to students talk about their ideas together. I don't think you need to set up artificial means so that every student participates; all you need to do is plan challenging experiences. I guess one of the first things I learned as a beginning teacher was to throw out the teacher's manual, look at and listen to the kids, and then reflect on my goals and how to achieve them.

"Two days per month I work with new teachers helping them with classroom management and instructional problems. I am involved in developing a new resource guide for the district for teaching social studies. These activities are very rewarding professionally. I think these activities with other teachers help me, personally, to be a better teacher."

KAREN ADAZZIO

"The other day I was teaching a lesson within a lesson—using Roger Green's story of *King Arthur and His Knights of the Round Table*. The class had recently read the book so it was perfect to use as an organizer for an historical timeline to study the Middle Ages, High Middle Ages, and the Renaissance Reformation. I really had fun with it, but it took a little bit before the kids caught on that the story was to serve as a means to study feudalism, help us connect the historical time period, and study geography. I told my teacher friend Jan about it, and she shared a similar experience where she was `nesting' lessons together and integrating several subject fields. When Jan and I start talking about teaching, we tend to lose track of time. I really learn so much from her during these sessions, and it always makes me realize how fortunate I am to be a teacher. No two days are ever the same. Teaching is constantly challenging.

"When I began talking with several other teachers about teaming and grouping our students, I really felt like I was on a high. Pretty soon we realized that we needed to figure out block scheduling to lock in our students so that the teaming would work. The other teachers asked me to serve as the group leader; I think that really made me feel good—that they would choose me, and I work hard to keep the team on track. We are really committed to improving the instructional program for students, and it's great sharing decisions and designing a new program."

TEACHER DECISION MAKING

All three of the teachers (Hogan, Thomas, Adazzio) demonstrated that they are constantly engaged in making judgments because what they do in their classrooms cannot be routinized. They need to decide throughout the school day what to teach, how best to teach it, how to accommodate diverse learners, how to utilize both theory and pedagogy, and how to meld subject field academic concepts into concepts appropriate for teaching.

Teachers need to know what their students know and what they do not know, and this requires considerable judgment. They need to monitor and supervise their students' learning activities as well as the work activities of aides or others who work in the classroom. They need to set up a learning environment in the classroom that is conducive to what they are teaching, how they teach it, and motivating for the students they teach.

Teachers work cooperatively with other adults, other teachers, health care workers, consultants, and administrators. They relate what they teach to what others are teaching, to school district guidelines, and to the state's formal curriculum. Teachers need to share understandings and assessments with parents.

Teachers exercise considerable authority over the educational program in their classrooms and over the students they teach. The knowledge base for teaching is now recognized as considerable. Porter and Brophy (1988), in synthesizing the research on good teaching, comment that teacher knowledge encompasses knowledge about content, knowledge about pedagogical strategies for teaching the content, and knowledge about the students to be taught (p. 75). They view teachers as semiautonomous professionals.

Sykes (1996) explored the meaning of professionalism and concluded that the classic model of a professional may not apply to teachers; however, the virtues of professionalism do apply to teachers and teaching because teachers have considerable responsibilities requiring knowledge in teaching, use and management of resources, the settings of standards, conferring with others, and organization and management of the school environment.

Teachers have begun to connect with each other, collaborating, sharing in decisions that affect the ways they practice their profession, and shaping the school environment. As a consequence teachers' work has changed to include professional responsibilities beyond the classroom. (See Elmore, Peterson, and McCarthey, 1996.) Some of these responsibilities are listed below.

Teachers' Professional Responsibilities (Beyond the Classroom)

- Consideration of school organizational structures (Adazzio's block scheduling)
- Teacher teaming for instruction
- Collaboration to develop new curricula
- Uses for technology
- Responsibility for faculty retreats and workshops

IMPROVING TEACHING THROUGH RESTRUCTURING SCHOOLS

Elmore, Peterson, and McCarthey (1996), identify three major reasons why school **restructuring** is attempted:

- To provide a means for parents to be involved and influence school decisions
- To provide a means for teachers to improve working conditions, engage in collegial interactions, and work collaboratively with administrators
- To decentralize schools, decrease bureaucratic structures, and increase school-site management and accountability

In the 1990s restructuring has helped to change teaching and learning, changed the ways teachers are prepared for teaching, changed the organization of schools, and changed both teachers' and administrators' interactions and work.

SCHOOL ORGANIZATION

At Karen Adazzio's school, students are now grouped in clusters that are assigned to several teachers for teaching and guidance. In addition, class periods changed to provide larger blocks of time so that teachers can implement thematic units and interdisciplinary instruction. To accomplish this the teachers began to work together planning instruction and at times teaming during instruction. The teachers also assumed responsibility for counseling the students. The process of "restructuring" affected teacher relationships, content of instruction, how students were grouped, the way *time* is structured, school-wide decision making.

TEACHING PROCESSES

Restructuring should affect the ways in which students are taught. Thematic teaching emphasizes the relationships of the different disciplines. Factual information is deemphasized and instead deeper meanings are sought. Use of students' prior knowledge becomes integral to the process because the focus of teaching is on student engagement and participation.

THE TEACHERS

The "egg-crate" structure of the classroom and the isolation of teachers disappears in the restructured school. Teachers have access to each other for planning, collaboration, consultation, and coaching (Lemlech, 1995). Teachers are actively engaged in developing curriculum, selecting resources, and defining assessment processes. Teachers "teach" differently. They are encouraging self-directed learning. They are guiding and facilitating through creating appropriate environments for learning. They are questioning instead of telling.

THE STUDENTS

Students are engaged in "active" learning. This means that students interact frequently in small groups—not just in skill activities—for the purpose of raising questions, experimenting, sharing knowledge, discussing, and using technological resources. Students manipulate objects and data to construct their own understanding. They are expected to explain and demonstrate what they are learning through the products they create (stories, reports, pictures, programs, and projects).

Research Findings:
Effects of Restructuring

Peterson, McCarthey, and Elmore (1996) report on restructuring experiments at three elementary schools. From observations and interviews over a two-year period, the researchers concluded:

- Changes in the ways teachers teach and children learn relate to teachers' beliefs, understandings, and behaviors when focused on specific classroom problems.
- Teachers who perceive themselves as learners and pursue personal learning improve their teaching practices.
- Changing school organizational practices can provide opportunities for teachers to learn new strategies and practices, *but* changing school structures does not cause teacher learning.
- When school faculties share a common purpose and perception of good practice, successful relations among school structure, teaching practice, and student learning occur.

SCHOOLWIDE DECISION MAKING

The involvement of teachers in decision-making and problem-solving teams, teacher networks, and school-to-school networks affects the structural organization of the school. Traditional hierarchical relations fade and the school's organizational structure becomes "flat." Faculty dialogue and support for risk taking affect policy decisions and professional development.

TEACHER REFLECTION

All three of the teachers featured in this text think about teaching. They attempt to understand the following:

- What their students know and are learning
- What worked and why, and what didn't work and why

The reflective teacher constantly *wonders* "If I had tried this or that, would it be better?" "What else would work?" "How could I have . . .?" "What would have happened if . . .?" "This reminds me of the time when . . ."

Researchers have long been aware of the value of reflection on practice. Changes in practice are dependent on thinking about *tradition* (routines you are accustomed to enacting) and consideration of alternatives. Interaction with others and collaboration stimulate the process of reflection. The process of reflection requires that the reflector detach him/herself from the situation or event and *re*consider the happening for the purpose of perceiving alternative actions and interpretations.

Reflective practice can be encouraged through talking to others about actual teaching happenings (Lemlech and Kaplan, 1990), study groups and group discussions (Lewison, 1995), reading and responding to professional literature (Ross, 1989), and teacher-as-researcher projects (Gebhard and Oprandy, 1989).

TEACHERS AS RESEARCHERS

Action research is another way teachers work individually and collaboratively to solve school-based problems. Action research is the name given to research conducted by teachers in their own classrooms or on school grounds. Cochran-Smith and Lytle (1993) define teacher research as "systematic and intentional inquiry carried out by teachers."

In a collaborative mode, teachers jointly identify a problem they feel could be solved by school-based research. They develop the research process together and then conduct the research in their own classrooms. They report their results to each other and modify instructional procedures as needed or design an intervention strategy. The process allows teachers to reflect on their own practice and solve their own problems (Glatthorn, 1987; Lieberman, 1986).

Though many teachers involve themselves in short action research projects in their own classrooms, others seek peer collaboration on an action research agenda. An example of action research that began as an individual project and ultimately became a collaborative project was told to this author by an inner-city fifth-grade teacher. She was curious about the effect on school attendance if she initiated active learning experiences that would be introduced on Monday and concluded on Friday so that students would recognize that if they were absent they would miss out on constructing and experimenting. She found that her students' attendance improved as a consequence.

Now a group of fifth- and sixth-grade teachers at the same school are developing activities with the same intent. On the first day of the project, the students are informed about the purpose of the project and how it will be scheduled. With the help of the office manager, they will compare their attendance pattern prior to the implementation of the project and with last year's attendance figures during the same calendar period.

Teachers need to be active researchers and reflect on practices in their schools and classrooms. Many

 Teacher Research

Sagor (1991) describes Project LEARN (League of Educational Action Researchers in the Northwest), which fosters school improvement through the formation of action research teams of teachers who work collaboratively for an entire school year on a school problem or jointly perceived area of inquiry. For example, middle school math teachers studied what would happen if students were given the opportunity to write about math concepts the day before a test. The teachers found that writing about concepts before examinations improved the acquisition of math ideas.

such studies have been extremely valuable and contributed to knowledge about teaching and to the dialogue about teaching. Projects like LEARN (League of Educational Action Researchers in the Northwest) help teachers understand research techniques. Some teachers have formed partnerships with college professors and are jointly engaged in research practices.

PREPARATION FOR LEADERSHIP: COLLEGIAL RELATIONSHIPS

PRESERVICE PREPARATION

The University of Southern California uses a Collegial Teacher Preparation Program for student teaching. Student teachers are paired for their classroom practice experience. The purpose of the program is to create a bond between partner student teachers to enhance their ability to become professionals and teacher-leaders. The author has defined **collegiality** as *the establishment of a professional relationship for the purpose of service and accommodation through the mutual exchange of perceptions and expertise* (Lemlech and Kaplan, 1990).

Lemlech and Kaplan (1990, 1991) studied the developmental pattern and sequence of collegial relationships among the student teachers (Figure 18.1). They found that collegial relationships progress from a friendly and helping relationship, to the exchange of ideas, and to dialogue about beliefs and knowledge, appreciation of each other's strengths, and ultimately to trust and commitment to each other based upon a feeling of proficiencies and equality.

 Teacher Research Hints

MacGillivray (1995, p. 139) provides six tips for getting teacher research started.

1. Read teacher research studies.
2. Tap into or create a support system—maybe just a buddy down the hall will work.
3. Build a study around something that you have a passion for or a burning curiosity about.
4. Be flexible. Assume adjustments are part of the process.
5. Enlist aid from knowledgeable people around you, other teachers, administrators, and district-level personnel.
6. Make your students co-researchers.

How do teachers prepare for leadership roles?

Figure 18.1   Collegial Development Stages and Characteristics

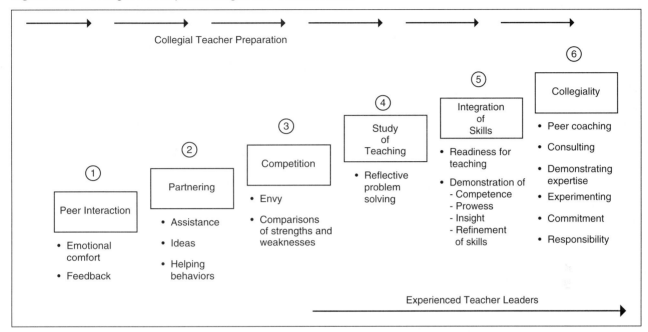

Source: J. K. Lemlech and S. N. Kaplan, "Collegial Preparation, Reflective Practice, and Social Studies Teaching," 1991.

As colleagues, the partner student teachers establish their own identity, recognize each other's expertise, and accept responsibility to provide each other with consultant services. In essence colleagues become coproblem solvers. The collegial relationship generates reflective thinking about teaching processes, enhances the individual's own learning, and promotes problem solving and insight. Lemlech and Kaplan believe that the professionalization of teaching is dependent on the development of expertise in the knowledge base of teaching, teacher empowerment, teacher leadership, and collegial relationships.

Just as the Collegial Preparation Program changed the student teaching program from an apprenticeship model to a collegial model, the program also necessitates changes in the roles and responsibilities of the public school supervising teachers. Hertzog-Foliart and Lemlech (1993) compared traditional supervision with collegial supervision of preservice teachers. They found role changes in three teaching components: *planning*, *lesson enactment*, and *feedback*. Traditionally, the supervising teacher directs "what" the preservice teacher should teach, and then during the lesson "watches" to see that it is enacted; for feedback, the supervising teacher traditionally "tells and critiques."

But in collegial supervision, the supervising teacher becomes part of the "planning team" as the partners and the supervisor engage in the *process* of planning. During the lesson the supervising teacher *guides* partner observation. During feedback time, the supervising teacher guides the *reflective thinking* of the colleagues, models professional dialogue, and facilitates the collegial relationship of the preservice teachers.

The supervising public school teachers in the Collegial Preparation Program become professional partners with the university's coordinators. Leadership roles are profoundly different and affect thinking about professional relationships, curriculum, instructional processes, and the social environment of the school.

TEACHER LEADERSHIP AND EXPERIENCED TEACHERS

Horejs (1996), Lomas (1996), and Stone (1996) studied experienced teachers' leadership at an elementary school, a middle school, and a high school. They asked, *Why do teachers assume leadership roles?* The teacher leaders at these schools all indicated that they were primarily motivated by needs at their schools, the challenges that existed, and a desire to share in decision making to shape school outcomes.

At the elementary level, teacher leaders were engaged in the following activities:

- Grade-level leadership
- Faculty committees
- Curriculum development
- Writing grants
- District office liaison
- Collaborative sharing with other teachers
- Collegial leadership

At the middle school level, teacher leaders were engaged in:

- Collaborative sharing with other teachers
- Collegial leadership
- Staff development
- Mentoring

At the high school level the teacher leaders had even greater responsibilities and the range of activities was greater. These teachers took part in:

- Faculty committees
- Curriculum development
- Writing grants
- Chairing departments
- Implementing technology
- Staff development
- Collegial leadership
- Mentoring
- School improvement and change activities

CONTINUING EDUCATION— PERSONAL DEVELOPMENT

All professionals need to be concerned about keeping abreast of current knowledge and skills in their field of endeavor. For many years medical and dental professionals have been required by state law to attend professional development classes. Accountants are also required to obtain continuing education credits each year. So it is not surprising that the public expects public school teachers to attend continuing education classes in their school districts or on college campuses.

ACCEPTING PERSONAL RESPONSIBILITY FOR PROFESSIONAL DEVELOPMENT

Many individuals prefer to direct their own professional development rather than work in a group situation or under clinical supervision. There is a great deal of evidence that teachers are good learners and can improve their teaching skills and repertoire of instructional strategies. Studies by Bents and Howey (1981) indicate that adults prefer to study in real-life situations, confronting actual problems. Adults are more motivated to learn when personal needs and interest intersect.

Set Personal Goals

To improve personal performance, it is important to set goals that focus on your own planning and teaching behavior rather than on students' behavior or on the improvement of the school's educational program. The following goals are recognized as important to instructional improvement:

- Base learning experiences on significant conceptual content versus selection based on "fun" activities.
- Select learning experiences that are consonant with personal goals. (If critical thinking is a goal, then the activity should engage students in practicing critical-thinking skills.)
- Increase student-to-student interaction versus student-to-teacher-to-student interaction.
- Encourage constructivist thinking.
- Differentiate instruction based on students' needs, interests, and learning styles.
- Improve organizational skills to decrease nonteaching time.
- Integrate subject fields to unify learning.
- Utilize academic fields to teach reading comprehension skills.
- Increase teacher feedback to students during direct instruction.
- Increase flexible grouping of students throughout the school day.
- Increase output activities for students.
- Increase professional reading.
- Apply research findings in the classroom.

Analyze Your Own Performance

It is possible to analyze your own performance to verify what it is you need to improve. Using a tape recorder in the classroom, small episodes of instruction can be recorded for later analysis; or, you may want to ask a student or another teacher to videotape a teaching episode. Before listening to the episode or viewing it, decide on the purpose of your evaluation:

- Do you want to listen to the questions you asked?
- Are you listening for the number of responses and degree of interaction?

- Are you concerned about management skills?
- Is enthusiasm or clarity of instructions what interests you?
- When students work in groups, do you encourage them to ask and give help to each other?

Do not attempt to critique everything. Focus on one or two elements of your teaching style and develop a checklist that will enable you to listen in a purposeful manner.

Another way to help you analyze your performance is to invite a trusted colleague to observe. You and your colleague should develop an observation chart to enable your friend to observe specific elements of instruction.

It is also possible to develop a checklist for older boys and girls to use to give you feedback about teaching. You should design this checklist and be certain the students understand what it is they are to evaluate. It is a good idea to let them know that you are always striving to improve your teaching techniques and that you value their assistance.

Sometimes the areas of performance that need to be improved cannot be detected easily using a tape recorder or feedback from others. For example, suppose you suspect that you are wasting too much teaching time with organizational matters and with classroom management. If this is the case, you may want to develop a list of questions to ask yourself to determine how likely it is that essential teaching time is not being used productively. Miller (1980, p. 164) suggested the following questions about the use of concrete time:

- How much time is spent in academic subject areas?
- How much time is spent in other activities?
- How much time is spent in transitions?
- How much time is spent in maintenance?
- How much time is spent in diagnosing students' needs?
- How much time is spent in feedback activities?

Design a Self-Help Program

After analyzing your performance, decide on your goal and arrange a time line to accomplish your objectives. Consider what you have learned about successful staff development programs and, using that information, model your personal program. For example, to increase you awareness and knowledge about your goal you could decide to do the following:

- Read professional literature
- Attend a professional class
- Talk to a knowledgeable expert

Your next task may be to find another teacher who is an expert in the technique you want to master. Ask your colleague if you may visit his or her classroom during a particular session so you will have an appropriate model. You may need to share your goal and your plan with your principal so provisions can be made to allow you to visit other teachers.

Your third task is to develop a plan for practicing the skill. You will probably have to arrange to have someone observe your performance so you can receive feedback.

Finally, after appropriate practice and feedback, work out a system whereby you utilize the technique consistently in your teaching. Once again, you may want the assistance of a colleague to help you plan instruction utilizing the new skill.

Research Findings: How to Make Learning Interesting

Zahorik (1996) studied how elementary and secondary teachers make learning interesting. The 65 teachers in the study were all enrolled in a graduate course on teaching methods, and their assignment was to write four reflective papers concerning interest:

1. Qualities of a Good Learning Experience
2. An Interesting Activity I Have Used
3. How I Create Interest and What I Do to Avoid Disinterest
4. Subject-Matter Facts and Concepts I Have Found to Be Interesting to Students

To stimulate interest, Zahorik learned that teachers:

- Engage students in hands-on activities
- Personalize the content by linking it to prior knowledge
- Permit students to share ideas and experiences
- Use group tasks
- Use a variety of materials
- Behave with enthusiasm
- Select practical tasks applicable to out-of-school experiences
- Select a wide range of activities

The teachers avoided:

- Sedentary activities
- Unsuitable tasks (inappropriate to the students)
- Artificial tasks that made students distrustful

COOPERATIVE/COLLEGIAL DEVELOPMENT

Many teachers, including this author, find it rewarding to work with one or more colleagues for the purpose of professional growth. Speaking with others about what works and what doesn't helps to clarify teaching theory, personal beliefs, planning, and decision making. It is particularly helpful when colleagues who disagree with each other about methodology work to prove what is appropriate or optimal. Personal experience some years ago with several colleagues emphasized how much fun and interest in the teaching process is generated when you discuss (argue!) with good friends about when to introduce a particular concept, what should come first, appropriate activities and materials, and motivation. Discussions such as these are good medicine for instructional improvement in the classroom.

PEER COACHING

The concept and purpose of peer coaching is often misunderstood. It is *not* intended as a means to remediate poor instructional practices; nor is it intended as a mentoring strategy. Hertzog (1995, p. 164) states that "coaching . . . builds communities of teachers who continuously study their craft, develop shared language and common understandings necessary for collegial study of new knowledge, and provides a structure for the follow-up to learning that is essential for acquiring new skills."

CHARACTERISTICS OF COACHING

Colleague teachers choose to coach each other because they want to master a *new* instructional strategy (new to them); they want to master the use of new instructional materials/resources; or they are *experimenting* with new ideas, grouping, or content.

Joyce and Weil (1996) state that the major purpose of coaching is to implement an innovative method of teaching and determine its effect on various groups of students. Suppose a group of teachers are learning the group investigation model of teaching. One of the teachers demonstrates the model and introduces the theory and research about the model. Next the teachers practice the model with each other. Then several of the teachers decide to try it out in their classrooms. By utilizing a peer coaching process, teachers can work with a partner to observe the implementation of the model. The peer partners observe

Coaching Hints

- Coaching is situation specific to colleague teachers
- Colleagues are learning/practicing new skills, knowledge, and/or strategies
- Colleagues are experimenting
- Coaching is ongoing and continuous
- Teachers have a collegial relationship and coaching is a means for self-help

each other and verify whether the syntax of the model was utilized precisely and accurately. The observer notes how well students worked with the model. Suggestions by the observer to the partner teacher support and provide insight to supplement the teacher's self-appraisal.

Based on workshop and staff development experiences, Lemlech, Hertzog, and Pensavalle recommend the following format for peer coaching:

1. Peer partners share a concern or teaching problem.
2. The concern or problem is delimited so that the consulting partner can focus specifically on the teaching behavior or problem during an observation.
3. The partner consultant observes and takes notes.
4. The notes are shared, and both teachers take part in the analysis.
5. The consulting partner only provides feedback on what was specified. If additional information about teaching is sought, the partner who was observed must ask for it. It is not volunteered.

TEACHERS AS STAFF DEVELOPERS

Staff development is one of the new role responsibilities that teachers are assuming. Collegial relationships free teachers to both acknowledge and accept personal strengths and weaknesses. Teachers should not be ashamed to acknowledge areas in which they are not, and perhaps do not want to be, expert. But many teachers do have areas of expertise, and in these areas they must assume responsibility for leadership.

Teachers are uniquely qualified to lead staff development programs because of their intimate knowledge of the classroom population, the community context, and essential skills. Many of the same skills needed for motivating children are important in staff development programs. For example, the teacher leader needs to be

Teachers are uniquely qualified to lead staff development programs.

enthusiastic, clear about the staff development purposes, able to keep the program participants engaged in the task at hand, select activities appropriate to the goal, and relate the program to classroom implementation.

The teacher leader needs to be skillful in human relations. Acheson and Gall (1992) caution that the use of indirect behaviors such as dealing with feelings, acknowledging, and praising ideas will work better than lecturing, criticizing, or giving directions. These authors also note that teachers expect an instructional leader to discuss their concerns and meet with them individually.

STAFF DEVELOPMENT PROGRAMS

Successful staff development programs typically focus on the following:

- Improvement of specific skills
- Demonstrations and opportunities for practicing new skills and receiving feedback
- Relationship to local school problems
- Curriculum development needs and processes
- Support services

Good teaching is contagious. Successful teachers attract other teachers who want to learn new ideas and techniques. Schoolwide improvement occurs simultaneously as teachers improve.

Improvement of teaching performance happens slowly and developmentally. Most teachers are motivated to improve their instructional performance because they care about their students. Research indicates that paying teachers to participate in staff development programs is not as effective as appealing to teachers' natural motivation to improve abilities and become better at what they do.

Improvement at the school level is dependent on individual teachers. Concerned teachers must be involved in the planning of the improvement process. For schools to improve, teachers must meet together, be aware of the scope of the problem, and be committed to improvement. Teachers are professional experts and must make the decisions about the change process.

As teachers take on the role and responsibility for their own staff development, consideration must be given to the following questions (Lemlech, 1995, p. 204):

- *Who* needs to learn what? (Who else other than the teachers need to "know"—students, parents, library personnel, principal, district personnel?)
- *How* is the new different from the old?
- *What* needs to be learned in order to implement the new?
- *What* support services and resources are affected by the "new"?

Teacher Research

Haskvitz (1995), a middle school social studies teacher, wondered how he could help students integrate what they learned at school into their daily lives. He planned an experiential program focused on community service to accomplish his goal. The students selected to participate in an antigraffiti project. Students researched areas of the world most affected, cost to local communities, and potential solutions (public education, parent and student education, communication). Haskvitz found that his community service project accomplished the following:

- Helped students interact with society
- Improved student learning
- Created a need to learn through problem solving
- Integrated subject fields
- Helped students apply social studies concepts
- Provided a means for students to learn by doing

TEACHER LEADERSHIP

There is considerable evidence that teachers are performing a variety of roles and assuming responsibilities beyond the classroom, unlike those performed in the past by traditional classroom teachers. Classroom teachers have become researchers, mentors, peer coaches, curriculum developers, and staff developers. The new teacher leader is involved structurally in the school, participating in decision-making teams and problem-solving groups, creating standards, writing grants, and serving on personnel committees to screen new teachers.

Teachers are engaged in the study of their profession and involved in experiences as learners, teachers, and leaders. Their activities are full-time, continuous, and interactive. Roles and responsibilities nurture inquiry processes and make teachers more thoughtful and reflective personally and professionally.

PARTNERSHIP MODELS: UNIVERSITY AND SCHOOL DISTRICT

The university–school district partnership model offers teachers another approach to continuing education and teacher leadership. There are a remarkable number of partnership models in existence. Some have informal arrangements; others have formalized

the association and may call themselves Professional Development Schools (PDS).

Informal models may be "favored" schools or cooperating network schools that work with one university teacher education program. The university assigns a cluster of student teachers and a university coordinator to the school. The close relationship and favored status evolves as teachers and university personnel become accustomed to each other and both develop expectations about the relationship which includes relinquishing traditional controls. The teachers participate and lead school-site seminars for the student teachers and interested university faculty, and the university coordinator may help to arrange staff development programs for the participating teachers.

The PDS may be a formalized partnership funded by an outside agency. The funds are often used to release teachers by paying for substitutes to enable the partner teachers to engage in staff development. PDS are usually involved in restructuring activities. The expert teachers at the PDS and the university share

Research Findings: The Renaissance Project

The Renaissance Project is aimed at transforming middle school mathematics. The project provides interesting insight into how to help teachers meet the demands of reform. Teacher leaders active in the reform movement have learned the following (Acquarelli and Mumme, 1996, 478–482):

- To change teaching practices, teachers need to become part of a professional learning community.
- Beliefs about teaching mathematics change as teachers practice new behaviors and subject their beliefs to examination.
- Pedagogy used during staff development time needs to be congruent to the pedagogy expected of teachers in the classroom.
- Classroom experiences should be scrutinized for equity issues; all students, regardless of gender, race, and class, should experience a challenging mathematics curriculum.
- Professional development for teachers needs to be grounded in classroom practices.
- All teachers (beginning and experienced) are capable of rethinking their teaching practices.

responsibility for providing appropriate experiences for the student teachers.

Partnership schools are characterized by the following:

- The continuing education of teachers
- Reflective teachers engaged in site-specific inquiry
- A democratic community with shared school governance
- Collegial relationships among school faculty and between university and school faculty
- A cohort of student teachers educated jointly by the university and the expert teachers
- An environment that supports and nurtures the sharing of expertise

TEACHER CENTERS

Teacher centers were first created in England and Wales. In the United States, teacher centers were first funded in 1978. Their purpose was to give teachers control over their own professional development. Although most centers have university faculty involvement, they were created to move continuing professional education away from the college campus.

Every teacher center has a policy board made up of a majority of teachers, administrators, and university faculty members. The policy board and the center's director supervises the center.

Teacher centers have the potential to provide innovative professional activities for continuing education. Each center is different and provides different services and activities for teachers. Some centers focus on traditional in-service approaches, while others are resource centers and offer minicourses and workshops on alternative approaches to curriculum areas.

In the future, teacher centers may be staffed by teacher specialists in each curriculum area. These teachers may be released by their school district for a set period of time or on a part-time basis. Teachers will be able to visit the center to obtain new curriculum ideas or resource materials. As presently established, the center is responsible for attracting teachers, identifying teacher needs, and providing professional service to teachers.

PROFESSIONAL ASSOCIATIONS CONTRIBUTE TO PROFESSIONAL DEVELOPMENT

Teachers have a wide range of professional group choices available to them for membership. There are professional associations related to almost every subject field. The following organizations provide services to elementary and middle school teachers:

- American Association for Health, Physical Education, and Recreation
- Council for Exceptional Children
- International Reading Association
- National Art Education Association
- National Association for Bilingual Education
- National Association for Gifted Education
- National Association for Research in Science
- National Council for Geographic Education
- National Council for History Education
- National Council for the Social Studies
- National Council of Teachers of English
- National Council of Teachers of Mathematics
- National Music Educators Association
- National Science Teachers Association

Professional development is enhanced by membership in these national groups. Each of the associations offers members periodic journals, newsletters, bulletins, and research information. In addition, they typically hold a national conference that meets over a long weekend. The conference location shifts each year to vary both the local perspective and the travel time. At the conferences teachers take part in committee work, workshops, and discussion groups. Each association brings in noted scholars in the subject field, who report on noteworthy curriculum development, research, and socially significant issues. Frequently the association, in cooperation with a local university, manages compressed classes for teachers interested in unit credit. Publishers' exhibits at these conferences provide teachers with the opportunity to view and critique the latest instructional materials and media related to the subject field.

In recent years the professional associations have assumed the responsibility of providing their members with continuing education. The conference enhances professional life and provides teachers with an enjoyable way to engage in dialogue with other professionals.

Two other national groups need to be recognized for their contribution to the professional advancement of teachers. The National Education Association (NEA) and the American Federation of Teachers (AFT) both provide members with ethical, legal, and political leadership and services. The NEA serves members who primarily live in suburban and rural

Teaching Hints: Using the Internet

"Teachers Helping Teachers" is a site developed by middle school teacher Scott Mandel. Elementary, middle school, and high school teachers send in questions, responses, lessons plans, and suggestions. This Web site provides connections with other areas of interest for teachers planning research or seeking ideas for lessons.

http://www.pacificnet.net/~mandel

Another good resource is the *Educator's World Wide Web Tour Guide* published by Wentworth Worldwide Media, Inc.

areas; AFT members typically live in the large urban areas. The NEA publishes *Today's Education* and the *NEA Reporter*. The AFT publishes *Changing Education* and *The American Teacher*. Both groups furnish members with congressional and political information important for the profession, as well as curriculum and instruction articles, through their journals and newsletters.

LOCAL AND STATE ASSOCIATIONS

Many of the national professional associations have local and state chapters. These smaller groups often have their own newsletter or journal and regional conferences. The local meetings focus on classroom and community problems and function as a collegial support system. Committee and task force participation is encouraged by these groups. Frequently state legislative information on problems are handled by these state associations, and state departments of education will turn to the local chapters for assistance and for information about educational problems and priorities.

PERSONAL DEVELOPMENT THROUGH EXTRACURRICULAR ACTIVITIES

It is as important to grow as a mature and cultured adult as it is to develop as a professional person. It is commonly recognized that "all work and no play" can truly make one a very dull person. The all-work syndrome also contributes to the phenomenon known as *teacher burnout*. Outside interests, activities, and friendships, distinct from professional associations and activities, help the professional person achieve balance.

Teachers join drama groups, political party groups, book clubs, and recreational organizations in order to get away from school and gain a different perspective about community life. Involvement in community affairs and in the cultural life of the community helps teachers develop vital intellectual, social, and emotional capacities. Continuing education encompasses all aspects of human development. Adult growth is dependent on positive relationships with others as well as interaction with one's life work.

TEAM TEACHING: CONTRIBUTION TO PROFESSIONALISM

Team teaching is a way of combining the instructional efforts of two or more teachers in order to use their abilities to best advantage. Teacher aides or assistants may also be included in the teaming arrangement. Teaming can be particularly advantageous at the elementary level because of the diversity of subjects that are taught. For example, if several fourth-grade teachers at a school teamed, each might be a team leader for a different subject of the curriculum. The team leader would accept greater responsibility for planning and teaching in the area of his or her expertise. The other members of the team would serve as assistants during instruction and would help with reinforcement.

Group planning time is critical when working in a team situation. Members of the team need to share plans and objectives and receive feedback about whether a lesson accomplished its purpose. Team teaching provides a system whereby new and inexperienced teachers can learn teaching methodologies from more experienced colleagues and receive feedback about their own teaching performance.

Implementation of teaming is different in each situation. In some schools an experienced teacher is called the *lead teacher* and is responsible for most of the planning. However, the professional reason for teaming should be to refine instructional techniques and provide students with instruction from teachers who are motivated and superior in each subject field. Teaming provides a built-in system for staff development.

Since teachers pool their respective classes in team teaching, this organizational system allows students to be grouped by need rather than by grade. Students move from one group to another depending on the subject and the student's ability. Nongraded teaching teams from primary grades, middle grades, or upper grades are popular in many schools.

Research Findings: Fostering Success

The National Center for Restructuring Education, Schools, and Teaching has studied how alternative organizational structures in schools foster successful outcomes for students. Darling-Hammond (1996) identifies four factors that appear significant for enabling low-income and minority students to succeed:

1. Structures that facilitate teachers knowing students well and staying with them over a relatively long time.
2. Exhibitions of student learning throughout the school that demonstrate what is valued.
3. Groups of teachers working collaboratively in teams to help students learn across disciplines over multiple years.
4. Teachers engaged in structures for shared decision making and discussion about teaching and learning.

In Karen Adazzio's middle school, the students are clustered in what have been called *houses*. Teachers do team teaching in this arrangement for integrating the core subjects. At Adazzio's school the teachers bank time in order to have extra planning time together. Banking time is a means to teach longer several days a week so as to dismiss school earlier on another day to accommodate teachers' planning needs.

WORKING WITH OTHER ADULTS IN THE CLASSROOM

In the 1990s we have seen significant changes in the roles of teachers. The educational program is broader and more versatile than programs designed in past years. Today in many classrooms the teacher is responsible for providing leadership and guidance to other adults working in the classroom. Auxiliary personnel in the classroom may be parent volunteers, senior citizens, paid adults (aides), or teacher assistants (paraprofessionals) who are enrolled in preparatory teacher education courses. The reader may want to review the discussion about assuming professional responsibilities in Chapter 5.

Today's teacher frequently finds that he or she is responsible for leading a diverse teaching team composed of volunteers, aides, cross-age tutors, and special consultants. In this new managerial and leadership role, teachers need to anticipate meaningful non-teaching tasks for the auxiliary personnel. These tasks need to be assigned, explained, guided, and evaluated.

Planning time needs to be arranged with the classroom team, and teachers must be sure that everyone understands the classroom program and desired room standards. Emergency procedures and duties should be communicated. Preparation should be made to keep the auxiliary personnel meaningfully involved; an ongoing system may need to be devised so classroom team members always know what to do next.

Frequently the classroom aide or volunteer is older than the teacher; however, it is the teacher who has the professional expertise. Leadership should be demonstrated by defining and guiding what needs to be accomplished in the classroom. Interpersonal relations should be warm, friendly, but appropriately professional. When working with other adults in the classroom, the teacher should do the following:

- Encourage the exchange of ideas
- Accept feedback
- Ask questions to clarify own and others' understanding
- Act respectfully and encourage trust and respect
- Provide both positive and negative feedback
- Assign meaningful tasks without overloading the aide
- Speak simply and clearly without use of professional jargon
- Exercise care to protect students' confidential records and to withhold personal information about students

In accepting the assistance of auxiliary personnel in the classroom, the teacher needs to keep in mind that the purpose of other adults' help is to individualize instruction. Sometimes in the assignment of work tasks, this is forgotten, and aides are given busywork and clean-up chores exclusively. Although these work tasks may be helpful, the idea of teacher aides is to free the teacher to spend more time with students and provide additional tutoring time for students.

If aides are to tutor students, they will need to understand the nature of the child's learning problem (if there is one) and appropriate methodological techniques for assisting. The classroom teacher is responsible for staff development with the classroom aides to ensure that tutoring tasks are performed correctly. To

Figure 18.2 Assignment Worksheet for Auxillary Personnel

Name: _____ Date: _____

Work Assignments:

1. 9:00 A.M.   Prepare Science Center: magnets, nails, paper, iron filings, cardboard
2. 9:30 A.M.   Listen to Jennifer read a book; assist her as needed
3. 10:00 A.M.   Assist the "wolves" at the computer center
4. 10:30 A.M.   File children's stories in their portfolios
5. 11:00 A.M.   During physical education, supervise Jerry's team on the apparatus
6. 11:45 A.M.   Accompany children to the cafeteria and lunch benches

help the aide develop necessary skills, the teacher may want to suggest paraprofessional classes and observation experiences. The teacher should be constantly alert to opportunities to provide appropriate continuing education for the assistants.

Figure 18.2 provides an example of an assignment sheet prepared by a first-grade classroom teacher for the aide. This teacher duplicated the blank assignment sheet and then filled it in each day with the assigned tasks. The teacher will have to verify that the aide understands the tutoring tasks. Also note that the teacher performs the diagnosis and makses the decisions about what kind of help the student should receive.

ASSESSING TEACHER COMPETENCE

Sadly there are a number of states that have teacher performance evaluation systems that conflict with current knowledge about teaching and learning. For example, in California the required Stull evaluation of teachers focuses on a behavioral lesson plan for direct instruction that ignores constructivist and inquiry approaches. In Florida teachers are downgraded for facilitating student discussion and inclusion of personal experiences (Darling-Hammond, 1995). Policy standards in a number of states pose dilemmas for young teachers who find that these policies are in direct conflict with what they are learning at the university.

NATIONAL CERTIFICATION

The National Board for Professional Teaching Standards (NBPTS), created in 1987 by President Bush, has developed a set of national standards to certify highly accomplished teachers. These standards were developed by respected educators and are being tested across the country. The standards are being implemented in many schools of education for the preparation of new teachers. Many experienced teachers are applying to the National Board for certification using those standards. The standards are organized into five general conceptual expectations about teaching and teacher performance:

1. Teachers are committed to students and their learning.
2. Teachers know the subjects they teach and how to teach those subjects to students.
3. Teachers are responsible for managing and monitoring student learning.
4. Teachers think systematically about their practice and learn from experience.
5. Teachers are members of learning communities.

TEACHER PORTFOLIOS

To demonstrate competence teachers are asked to develop a personal portfolio. In the portfolio they provide evidence of their lessons, student work samples, pictures of their classroom, videos and audio tapes. The portfolios are intended as authentic measures of performance and can be used for national certification.

What Should Portfolios Contain?

At the University of Southern California, student teachers begin the development of personal portfolios during their first student teaching assignment. The students begin with a statement about their teaching philosophy and goals. They take photographs of their bulletin board displays and their learning centers. They include videotapes of their use of teaching models. Long-term planning is demonstrated through the inclusion of an integrated and interdisciplinary unit of study. Both self-assessments and partner critiques of lessons are included in the portfolio. (Student teachers are prepared through the Collegial Preparation Program.) Individual lessons and student work samples that result from the lessons are included, as is the rationale for the lesson(s). The student teachers use their portfolios during exit interviews at the university and when they apply for teaching positions.

Vermont has a state-mandated portfolio program for prospective teachers (Dollase, 1996). The prospective teacher's portfolio must contain the following:

- Lesson plans
- Unit plans
- Evidence of student learning
- Reflective statements from the candidate
- Summative evaluations from student teaching

Teacher education programs in Vermont adopt a theme for their preparation program, and the theme is used as a basis for the portfolio preparation. Dollase's example is Trinity College's *Learning and Teaching: Constructing Meaningful Connections.*

Wolf (1996) suggests that portfolios be organized to include the following:

- Background information (resume, context for teaching, philosophy, and goals)
- Teaching artifacts and reflections (such as suggested above)
- Professional information (activities, recommendations, evaluations)

Reasons to Develop Portfolios

Teachers are developing portfolios for personal satisfaction to demonstrate their teaching excellence, to achieve national certification (or state certification) and to attain teaching bonuses. At the University of Southern California-Norwood Professional Development School, the teachers wanted portfolios to satisfy their own personal expectations for performance and as a means to screen new teachers who wanted to join the PDS. Wolf notes that portfolios ensure that a teacher's evidence of exemplary teaching doesn't disappear.

However, before requiring student teachers or experienced teachers to develop portfolios for assessment purposes, a number of issues need to be addressed. Some of these are as follows:

- Selection of significant items for documentation (What should be considered significant?)
- For elementary teachers, should all subjects be represented in the portfolio?
- How should items be displayed and stored?
- What period of time should the portfolio represent?
- Should the novice teacher develop the portfolio with the advice and assistance of an experienced teacher?

- Should the experienced teacher and/or colleague provide a critique of some of the lessons displayed in the portfolio? Or should the portfolio represent the decisions of only the novice teacher?
- How will the portfolio be evaluated? Should there be identified standards?
- Who will evaluate the portfolio (other teachers, administrators, personnel directors)?

LAW-RELATED ISSUES AFFECTING TEACHERS

TEACHER TENURE

Most states have tenure laws to protect teachers from irresponsible and arbitrary dismissal. Tenure laws specify how teachers gain tenure and under what conditions or circumstances tenured teachers can be dismissed. The purpose of tenure is to provide capable teachers with security so changes in school boards or public reaction to educational issues will not result in teacher dismissal without just cause. Generally grounds for dismissal are described in the state's tenure statute. Most states will dismiss a teacher for immorality, unprofessional conduct, insubordination, and incompetency. Teachers must be dismissed for cause.

Dismissal of tenured teachers cannot occur without specific procedures being followed. These procedures vary among the states. In most states the teacher needs to be informed in writing of the charges filed against him or her prior to the dismissal hearing. After written notice, the teacher is usually given a specified amount of time to prepare for a hearing before the school board. The teacher has the right to have counsel at the hearing. If a teacher is dissatisfied with the results of the hearing, the teacher may take the case before the courts.

Teachers can also lose tenure status by resigning from their school district position. Unless the school board grants a leave of absence, teachers will lose tenure status if they voluntarily absent themselves from their position. Teachers moving from one school district to another within their own state can also lose tenure unless the new school board agrees to tenure status.

Teachers gain tenure by teaching in a school district for a set number of years and following the requirements of the state. Teachers are typically considered to be probationary teachers during the nontenured period. The probationary period varies between two and four years among the states. In some school districts teachers must be evaluated a specified number of times during the probationary period to verify satisfactory performance. In some states the teacher applies to the state for tenure status after serving satisfactorily in a school district; in other states the teacher must be recognized by formal action of the school board before tenure rights are granted.

Some states have **continuing contract** laws. For teachers who have not yet gained tenure, they may expect that a school board will notify them of the expiration of their contract, usually by May 1. If they are not notified of dismissal by that date, they may assume to have a continuing contract. The continuing contract protects nontenured teachers from summer dismissal when it would be difficult to obtain another position.

Tenured teachers have what is called an **indefinite contract.** What this means is that the contract is renewed automatically each year without mutual action by teacher and school board.

SALARIES

Most school districts have a single salary schedule for all teachers. Salaries are differentiated by experience and education. Salaries are adjusted both vertically (for experience) and horizontally (for education). So a teacher with an advanced degree and/or special training will be placed higher on the salary schedule than the teacher without special education.

Some states have a minimum salary law that affects public school teachers. In such cases, the school board may pay teachers higher than the minimum salary, but not lower.

Many states have *collective bargaining* laws. These laws identify the procedures for school boards to negotiate with teacher organizations. The teacher organization with the greatest membership in the school district is typically given the right to represent the teachers of the district for salary and benefit negotiations.

OTHER BENEFITS

Most school districts allow teachers ten full days of sick leave. Some districts allow half days. Generally unused sick days may be accumulated from year to year and in some districts the unused time may be part of a retirement package.

Most districts provide health-care benefits for teachers and the teacher's family. Other benefits include maternity leave, child-care leave, personal business leaves, and sabbatical leaves. Districts differ in terms of benefits paid to teachers for sabbatical leaves.

PROFESSIONAL LIABILITY AND MALPRACTICE

Professional liability occurs as a result of **negligence;** that is, because the teacher did not exercise due care or did not foresee harm. Fischer, Schimmel, and Kelly (1987, p. 57) identify the four conditions necessary for a teacher to be held for damages when a student is injured:

1. The teacher was required to be on duty and protect the student from injury.
2. The teacher failed to exercise due care.
3. The student was injured as a result of the teacher's failure to exercise due care.
4. The student can prove injury as a consequence.

Professional liability increases if students are young and the teacher is expected to be on duty. Negligence charges need to be proved based on lack of supervision and foresight of foreseeable danger. Close supervision is necessary during physical education and when students use special equipment that is dangerous. Whenever students can harm each other during activities and through use of equipment, teachers can be held liable for negligence.

If the injured student failed to exercise reasonable care of him or herself, then the student may be guilty of **contributory negligence.** This can occur only if the student is old enough and has the mental maturity to exercise reasonable care.

Comparative negligence arises in situations in which both the teacher and student are at fault. This typically means that the teacher will be held accountable for some proportion of damages to the extent that the teacher contributed to the injury (McNergney and Herbert, 1995).

Teachers can protect themselves by purchasing insurance. Insurance programs are often sponsored through professional organizations. Both the NEA and AFT have liability insurance programs.

There are public pressure groups anxious to charge school districts with educational malpractice when a student is injured intellectually or psychologically. Such cases are often based on a student's failure to learn. Cases involving student failure to learn would involve many teachers and the school district. There does not appear to be a way for parents to prove liability of a given teacher or school district in such a case.

COPYING MATERIALS FOR THE CLASSROOM

Several years ago an instructional specialist from a small school district proudly told me how she had copied a whole chapter out of one of my textbooks for the teachers in her school district. She anticipated that I would be flattered and pleased. Imagine her surprise when I countered with, "Don't you know that you violated copyright law?"

Copyright law protects literary works from being copied by others either before publication or afterward. Fischer, Schimmel, and Kelly (1987) relate the case of the UCLA professor whose lecture notes were recorded by a student in class, sold to an entrepreneur, copied, and sold to other students. The professor sued the entrepreneur, claiming that his lecture notes were protected by common-law copyright. The court agreed. Common-law copyright protects an author's or artist's creative endeavor before publication; after publication, federal law protects the author or artist.

Teachers often want to use published pictures, articles, or poems in their classrooms. In general, teachers may make a single copy for use in the classroom. Copies for each student can be made under certain conditions. Conditions include tests of brevity, spontaneity, and cumulative effect (Fischer, Schimmel, and Kelly, 1987). Most school districts have guidelines available for teachers to verify what is fair use of an author's work.

IN LOCO PARENTIS

The idea of schools operating **in loco parentis** (in place of parents) means that schools have the power to act as if they were parents from the time students leave home to the time they return home. In recent years this doctrine has been weakened, and courts often rule in favor of First Amendment rights for students versus school rights and authority. The doctrine has also been weakened in the instance of corporal punishment; in some states parents have the right to forbid the use of corporal punishment. In general, decisions about punishment of students is a decision of the local school board.

In elementary schools, in loco parentis often means that teachers perform tasks that a parent would perform. For example, primary teachers may have to tie shoes, button sweaters, or verify that students eat their lunches. The teacher listens and sympathizes.

STUDENTS' RIGHTS

On November 20, 1989, the United Nations General Assembly adopted the Convention on the Rights of the Child. The Convention deals with three kinds of rights, in particular participation rights, provision rights, and protection rights. Edmonds (1992, p. 205–207) defines these rights.

Participation rights mean that children have the right to participate in decisions that affect their lives and futures; they have freedom of expression, freedom of conscience, thought, and religion, freedom of association and assembly, and freedom from government interference in their privacy.

Rights of provision deal with the economic, social, and cultural rights of the individual. For example, rights of provision include the rights to have adequate foods, shelter, health care, and conditions that do not foster conflict or abuse.

The **right of protection** means that the Convention protects children from potential abuse or harm. For example, in Guatemala, a 13-year-old youth was kicked to death by the Guatemalan police in March of 1990. Amnesty International pressured the director of the national police force and ultimately the police officers were sentenced to 15 years in prison. This, of course, was a hollow victory, but it emphasizes the nature of the Covenant.

The challenge for teachers, according to Edmonds (p. 205), is to do the following:

- Learn what human rights are
- Help young people understand their rights
- Examine the problem of universality and global multiculturalism
- Create a classroom and school in which children's rights are achieved

SUMMARY

Teachers as Professional Leaders

1. To engage in appropriate lesson planning, teachers need to know what students know and do not know.
2. Teachers need to share understandings and assessments with parents.
3. Teachers' knowledge encompasses subject field content, pedagogical strategies, and knowledge about students.
4. Teachers make decisions about use of resources, setting standards, organization, and management of the school environment.

Improving Teaching Through Restructuring Schools

5. Restructuring has changed teacher preparation, the organization of schools, and teachers' and administrators' interactions.
6. Restructuring affects the way time is structured, teacher relationships, content of instruction, and schoolwide decision making.

Teacher Reflection

7. Changes in teaching practice are dependent on teachers thinking about traditional practices and consideration of alternative practices.
8. Reflective practice is encouraged through teachers' interactions, study groups, reading professional literature, and teacher-as-researcher projects.

Continuing Education/Personal Development

9. To improve performance, teachers need to set goals that focus on planning and teaching behaviors.
10. The teacher can analyze his or her own performance through video and audio recordings, checklists, and peer coaching.

Cooperative/Collegial Development

11. Peer coaching assists teachers to study teaching, develop shared professional language, and provides a structure for the follow-up of professional learning.
12. Teachers undertake coaching to master new instructional strategies, to implement new resources, and to experiment with new ideas.

Teachers as Staff Developers

13. Due to intimate knowledge of classroom life, teachers are uniquely qualified to be staff developers for colleagues.
14. Successful staff development programs provide demonstrations, help to improve instructional skills, relate to local school problems, serve as a support mechanism, and develop curriculum.
15. Teacher leaders perform many diverse roles including researchers, mentors, peer coaches, and curriculum and staff developers.

Partnership Models

16. University–school district partnerships are quite diverse, but most include a cluster of student teachers and a university coordinator.

17. The models are characterized by continuing education for teachers, reflective teachers, teacher researchers, collegial relationships, and a democratic community.

Professional Associations

18. Professional associations provide staff development services to their members.
19. Associations exist in each subject field and the NEA and AFT service members through salary negotiations, public relations, and communication about current social problems.
20. Each of the associations provide newsletters and journals.
21. Many of the associations have local and state affiliates.

Extracurricular Activities

22. Engagement in cultural and political groups, sports activities, and book clubs help teachers balance work and recreational activities.

Team Teaching

23. Team teaching helps teachers improve instructional skills, utilizes expertise, and helps teachers collaborate professionally.
24. Organizational structures need to be adjusted for team teaching to work.

Working With Other Adults

25. Teachers often have to coordinate the work of noncertificated adults in the classroom.
26. Interpersonal relations need to be friendly, warm, and appropriately professional.
27. Work assignments for classroom aides should support the instructional program and not be composed of busywork tasks or exclusively of clean-up chores.

Assessing Teacher Competence

28. Assessment of teacher competence should include evidence of lesson planning, student work samples, and authentic measures of performance.
29. Many teachers are seeking national certification for personal satisfaction and as a means to demonstrate teaching excellence.
30. Teacher portfolios should contain background information including the teacher's philosophy and goals, teaching artifacts and reflections, and professional information.

Legal Issues Affecting Teachers

31. Tenure laws protect teachers from irresponsible and arbitrary dismissal.
32. Most states grant tenure after a set number of years and satisfactory evaluations during the probationary period.
33. Most school districts provide health-care benefits.
34. Most school districts have a single salary schedule for all teachers.
35. Teacher negligence charges need to be proved based on lack of supervision and foresight of foreseeable danger.
36. Teachers can protect themselves through professional insurance policies.
37. Teachers need to be aware of copyright law that protects literary works from being copied.
38. Schools operate in loco parentis; teachers of young children often perform tasks that a parent would perform.
39. Students have participation rights that enable them to make decisions that affect their lives and futures.
40. The right of protection guards children from harm and potential abuse.

DISCUSSION QUESTIONS AND APPLICATION EXERCISES

1. You are beginning the use of cooperative learning groups in your classroom. How can you model cooperative collegial development for your students to demonstrate adult cooperative learning?
2. Why is it important for beginning teachers to join professional organizations?
3. Identify some instructional areas for improvement. What are some activities that will help you improve your performance?
4. How would you encourage professionalism and continuing education among your peers?
5. Using the information about successful staff development programs in this chapter, suggest some questions to evaluate a staff development workshop.
6. Write a content outline and suggested activities to teach your students about human rights and in particular, children's rights.
7. Name one or more books on the current best-seller list.
8. List the cultural events you have attended in the last month. (Delete movies from your list!)
9. Identify a teaching/learning problem in your classroom. Describe how you could gather research data to provide insight concerning the problem.
10. Describe several successful means you use to "grab" students' interest and participation.
11. Design a self-evaluative checklist similar to Figure 18.3.

Figure 18.3 Self-Evaluative Checklist

Develop your own self-evaluative checklists similar to this one.	Yes	No
I plan my lessons before presenting them.	___	___
I choose instructional materials that are relevant and appropriate for my students.	___	___
My directions are clear and concise.	___	___
My follow-up materials reinforce my lessons. (They are not busywork.)	___	___
I self-edit my handouts to see that they are grammatical and legible.	___	___
I pace my lessons to keep students interested.	___	___
I encourage students to participate.	___	___
I try to talk to each student individually.	___	___
I listen when students want to talk to me.	___	___

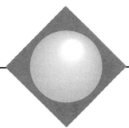

Bibliography

The AAUW Report: How Schools Shortchange Girls. The AAUW Educational Foundation, Wellesley College Center for Research on Women, 1992.

Acheson, K. A., and M. D. Gall. *Techniques in the Clinical Supervision of Teachers: Preservice and Inservice Applications.* 3rd ed. New York: Longman, 1992.

Acquarelli, K., and J. Mumme. "A Renaissance in Mathematics Education Reform." *Phi Delta Kappan* 77 (March 1996): 478–482.

Adams, D. M., and M. E. Hamm. "Portfolio Assessment and Social Studies: Collecting, Selecting, and Reflecting on What Is Significant." *Social Education,* 56 (February 1992): 103–105.

American Association for the Advancement of Science. *Benchmarks for Science Literacy.* New York: Oxford University Press, 1993.

———. *Science for All Americans.* Washington, DC, 1990.

Ames, C., "Achievement Goals and the Classroom Motivational Climate." U.S. Office of Education: Research Grant DEH 023T80023, Office of Special Education and Rehabilitative Services, 1992.

Anderson, P. S., and D. Lapp. *Language Skills in Elementary Education.* 5th ed. New York: Macmillan, 1988, 1992.

Angell, A. V. "Democratic Climates in Elementary School Classrooms: A Review of Theory and Research." *Theory and Research in Social Education,* 19 (Summer 1991): 241–266.

Arbuthnot, J. B., and D. Faust. *Teaching Moral Reasoning: Theory and Practice.* New York: Harper and Row, 1981.

Arlin, M. "Teacher Transition Can Disrupt Time Flow in Classrooms." *American Education Research Journal,* 16 (1979): 42–56.

Armstrong, T. *Multiple Intelligences in the Classroom.* Alexandria, VA: Association for Supervision and Curriculum Development, 1994.

Aronson, E. *The Jigsaw Classroom.* Beverly Hills, CA: Sage Publications, 1978.

Arreaga-Mayer, C., and C. Perdomo-Rivera. "Eco-behavioral Analysis of Instruction for At-risk Language Minority Students." *The Elementary School Journal,* 96 (January 1996): 245–258.

Aschbacher, P. "A Flare for the Arts." *Educational Leadership,* 53 (May 1996): 40–43.

Au, K. *Literacy Instruction in Multicultural Settings.* New York: Harcourt, Brace, Jovanovich, 1993.

Ausubel, D. P. *The Psychology of Meaningful Verbal Learning.* New York: Grune & Stratton, 1963.

Ausubel, D. P., and F. G. Robinson. *School Learning.* New York: Holt, Rinehart and Winston, 1969.

Baker, E. L. "Making Performance Assessment Work: The Road Ahead." *Educational Leadership,* 51 (March 1994): 58–63.

Baker, J. "Analyzing Stereotypes in Media." *Teaching and Change,* 3 (September 1996): 244–259.

Barr, R., J. L. Barth, and D. S. Shermis. "Defining the Social Studies." *National Council for the Social Studies Bulletin,* 51(4) (1977): 387–411.

Bayles, E. *Democratic Educational Theory.* New York: Harper and Row, 1960.

Bents, R. H., and K. R. Howey. "Staff Development—Change in the Individual." In *Staff Development/*

Organization Development, 11–36. Alexandria, VA: Association for Supervision and Curriculum Development, 1981.

Besag, F. P., and J. L. Nelson. *The Foundations of Education: Stasis and Change.* New York: Random House, 1984.

Blatt, M., and L. Kohlberg. "The Effects of Classroom Moral Discussion Upon Children's Level of Moral Judgment." *Journal of Moral Education*, 4 (1974): 129–161.

Block, J. H. "Motivation, Evaluation, and Mastery Learning." *UCLA Educator,* 19 (Winter 1977): 31–36.

Bracey, G. W. "The 5th Bracey Report on the Condition of Public Education." *Phi Delta Kappan,* 77 (October 1995): 149–160.

Brandt, R. "On Discipline-Based Art Education: A Conversation with E. Eisner." *Educational Leadership,* 45 (January 1988): 6–9.

Brett, M. "Teaching Extended Class Periods." *Social Education,* 60 (October 1996): 77–79.

Bronkhurst, A. D. "Cognitive and Motivational Processes in African American and Hispanic Advanced Placement Students." Unpublished doctoral dissertation, University of Southern California, December 1995.

Brooks, W. M., and A. E. Woolfolk. "Effects of Students' Nonverbal Behavior on Teachers." *The Elementary School Journal,* 88 (September 1987): 50–63.

Bruner, J. "The Act of Discovery." In *Readings in Contemporary Psychology in Education,* 1a–15a. C. E. Meyers and R. G. McIntyre, eds. New York: Selected Academic Readings, 1966.

Buckmaster, L. "Effects of Activities that Promote Cooperation Among Seventh Graders in a Future Problem-Solving Classroom." *The Elementary School Journal,* 95 (September 1994): 49–62.

Caine, R., and G. Caine. *Making Connections: Teaching and the Human Brain.* Alexandria, VA: Association for Supervision and Curriculum Development, 1991.

California State Department of Education. *English-Language Arts Framework for California Public Schools, K–12.* Sacramento: California State Department of Education, 1987.

———. *History-Social Science Framework for California Public Schools, K–12.* Sacramento: California State Department of Education, 1988.

———. *Health Framework for California Public Schools, K–12.* Sacramento: California State Department of Education, 1994.

———. *Mathematics Framework for California Public Schools, K–12.* Sacramento: California State Department of Education, 1992.

———. *Physical Education Framework for California Public Schools, K–12.* Sacramento: California State Department of Education, 1994.

———. *Science Framework for California Public Schools, K–12.* Sacramento: California State Department of Education, 1990.

———. *Visual and Performing Arts Framework for California Public Schools, K–12.* Sacramento: California State Department of Education, 1996.

Canter, L. *Assertive Discipline: A Take-Charge Approach for Today's Educator.* Seal Beach, CA: Canter & Associates, 1976.

Carroll, J. B. "Psycholinguistics and the Study and Teaching of Reading." *Aspects of Reading Instruction,* S. Pflaum-Connor, ed., 11–43. Berkeley: McCutchan, 1978.

Carroll, L. *Alice in Wonderland.* Philadelphia: John C. Winston, 1957.

Central Eastern Regional Educational Laboratory (CEMREL): St. Louis, 1971.

Child Abuse Prevention and Treatment Act. P. L.. 93–247 (Section 3).

Clinchy, B. M. "Goals 2000: The Student as Object." *Phi Delta Kappan,* 76 (January 1995): 383–385.

Cochran-Smith, M., and S. L. Lytle, eds. *Inside/Outside: Teacher Research and Knowledge.* New York: Teachers College Press, 1993.

Cohen, D. "New Study Links Lower I.Q. at Age 5 to Poverty." *Education Week,* 1993.

Cohen, E. G., and R. A. Lotan. "Producing Equal-Status Interaction in the Heterogeneous Classroom." *American Educational Research Journal,* 32 (Spring 1995): 99–120.

Cohen, E. P., and R. S. Gainer. *Art: Another Language for Learning.* New York: Citation Press, 1976.

Constitutional Rights Foundation. "Sports and the Law," No. 10 (Summer 1996).

Copeland, R. W. *Mathematics and the Elementary Teacher.* 4th ed. New York: Macmillan, 1982.

Cuban, L. *How Teachers Taught—Constancy and Change in American Classrooms, 1890–1980.* New York: Longman, 1984.

Darling-Hammond, L. "Changing Conceptions of Teaching and Teacher Development." *Teacher Education Quarterly,* 22 (Fall 1995) 9–26.

Cohen, E. P., and R. S. Gainer. *Art: Another Language for Learning.* New York: Citation Press, 1976.

———. "The Right to Learn and the Advancement of Teaching: Research, Policy, and Practice for Democratic Education." *Educational Researcher*, 25 (August/September 1996): 5–17.

Davidman, L., with P. T. Davidman. *Teaching with a Multicultural Perspective*. New York: Longman, 1994.

Dean, J., and I. K. Gross. "Teaching Basic Skills Through Art and Music." *Phi Delta Kappan*, 73 (April 1992): 613–618.

Dembo, M. H. *Applying Educational Psychology*. 5th ed. New York: Longman, 1994.

Dewey, J. *Democracy and Education*. New York: The Free Press, 1916, 1944.

———. *My Pedagogic Creed*. Washington, DC: The Progressive Education Association, 1929. (Originally published by Dewey in 1897.

———. *How We Think*. Boston: D. C. Heath, 1933.

Dollase, R. H. "The Vermont Experiment in State-Mandated Portfolio Program Approval." *Journal of Teacher Education*, 47 (March/April 1996): 85–98.

Dunn, R., and K. Dunn. *Learning Styles: A Practical Approach*. Reston, VA: Reston Publishing, 1978.

Dweck, C. S. "Learned Helplessness and Negative Evaluation." *UCLA Educator*: 19 (Winter 1977): 44–49.

Edmonds, B. C. "The Convention on the Rights of the Child." *Social Education*, 56 (April/May 1992): 205–207.

Eisner, E. W. *The Educational Imagination-On the Design and Evaluation of School Programs*. New York: Macmillan, 1979, 1985.

Eisner, E. "Standards For American Schools: Help or Hindrance?" *Phi Delta Kappan*, 76 (June 1995): 758–764.

Eisner, E. W., and E. Vallance. *Conflicting Conceptions of Curriculum*. Berkeley, CA: McCutchan Publishing Corp., 1974.

Ellis, A. K. *Teaching and Learning Elementary Social Studies*. 5th ed. Boston: Allyn and Bacon, 1995.

Elmore, R. F., P. L. Peterson and S. J. McCarthey. *Restructuring in the Classroom—Teaching, Learning, and School Organization*. San Francisco: Jossey-Bass, 1996.

Emans, R. L. "Abuse in the Name of Protecting Children." *Phi Delta Kappan*, 69 (June 1987): 740–743.

Emmer, E. T., and C. M. Evertson. "Synthesis of Research on Classroom Management." *Educational Leadership*, 38 (January 1981): 342–347.

Evertson, C. M., and C. M. Anderson. "Beginning School" *Educational Horizons*, 57 (1979): 164–168.

Fineberg, C. "Arts in Education-Beyond Rhetoric." *Educational Leadership*, 37 (April 1980): 583–587.

Fischer, L. D. Schimmel and C. Kelly. *Teachers and the Law*, 2nd ed. New York: Longman, 1987.

Flavell, J. J. *The Developmental Psychology of Jean Piaget*. Princeton, NJ: Van Nostrand Reinhold, 1963.

Gall, M. D.. "Synthesis of Research on Teachers' Questioning." In L. W. Anderson ed., *The Effective Teacher*. New York: Random House, 1989: 301–306.

Gallagher, J. J. "Education of Gifted Students—A Civil Rights Issue? *Phi Delta Kappan*, 76 (January 1995): 408–411.

Gallahue, D. L., P. H. Werner and G. Luedke. *A Conceptual Approach to Moving and Learning*. New York: John Wiley and Sons, 1975.

Gardner, H. *Multiple Intelligences—The Theory in Practice*. New York: Basic Books, 1993.

———. "Reflections on Multiple Intelligences: Myths and Messages." *Phi Delta Kappan*. 77 (November, 1995): 200–209.

Gebhard, J. G., and R. Oprandy. *Multiple Activities in Teacher Preparation: Opportunities for Change*. Indiana University of Pennsylvania, Evaluative Report. ERIC Document Reproduction Service No. ED 307 813.

Gega, P. C., and J. Peters. *Science in Elementary Education*, 8th ed.. New York: Prentice Hall, 1998.

Gibbs, N. "The EQ Factor." *Time Magazine*. (October 2, 1995).

Glatthorn, A. A. "Cooperative Professional Development: Peer-Centered Options for Teacher Growth." *Educational Leadership*, 45 (November 1987): 31–35.

Goldberg, M. R. "Expressing and Assessing Understanding Through the Arts." *Phi Delta Kappan*, 73 (April 1992): 619–623.

Good, T. L., and J. E. Brophy. *Educational Psychology*, 3rd ed. New York: Longman, 1986.

Goodman, K. *What's Whole in Whole Language?* Portsmouth, NH: Heinemann Educational Books, 1986.

Gordon, T. *Teacher Effectiveness Training*. New York: Longman, 1974.

Graves, D. H. "An Examination of the Writing Processes of Seven-Year Old Children." *Research in the Teaching of English*. (Winter 1975): 235.

Graves, D. H. *Experiment with Fiction*. Portsmouth, NH: Heinemann, 1987.

Graves, D. H., and V. Stuart. *Write From the Start*. New York: E. P. Dutton, 1985.

Greer, P., and R. H. Silverman. "Making Art Important for Every Child." *Educational Leadership*, 45 (December 1987): 10–14.

Griffin, G. A. "Influences of Shared Decision Making on School and Classroom Activity: Conversations with Five Teachers." *The Elementary School Journal*, 96 (September 1995): 29–46.

Hall, J. T., N. H. Sweeny, and J. H. Esser. *Physical Education in the Elementary Schools*. Santa Monica, CA: Goodyear, 1980.

Hanna, P. "Revising the Social Studies: What Is Needed?" *Social Education*, 27 (April 1965): 190–196.

Hartoonian, H. M., and M. A. Laughlin. "Designing a Scope and Sequence for the 21st Century." *Social Education*, 53 (October 1989): 388–398.

Haskvitz, A. "Community Service in the Classroom and in the Curriculum." *Teaching and Change*, 2 (Winter 1995): 169–184.

Heath, S. B. "Sociocultural Contexts of Language Development." In *Beyond Language: Social and Cultural Factors in Schooling Language Minority Students*, 143–186. Sacramento, CA: California State Department of Education, 1986.

Heinich, R., M. Molenda, J. D. Russell, and S. E. Smaldino. *Instructional Media and Technologies for Learning*. Columbus, OH: Merrill/Prentice Hall, 1996.

Hertzog, H. "The Professional Teacher in a School-University Partnership." In *Becoming a Professional Leader*, J. K. Lemlech, ed. New York: Scholastic, 1995.

Hertzog-Foliart, H., and J. Lemlech. "Linking School and University through Collegial Supervision." *Teacher Education Quarterly*, 20 (Fall 1993): 19–28.

Hertzog, H., and J. K. Lemlech. "Collegial Teacher Preparation: Impact on the Supervising Teacher's Role." Paper presented at Association of Teacher Educators annual meeting, Los Angeles, 1993.

Hoffer, M. L., and C. R. Hoffer. *Music in the Elementary Classroom: Musicianship and Teaching*. New York: Harcourt Brace Jovanovich, 1987.

Holmes, E. E. *New Directions in Elementary School Mathematics Interactive Teaching and Learning*. Englewood Cliffs, NJ: Merrill/ Prentice Hall, 1995.

Hooper, S., and L. P. Rieber. "Teaching, Instruction and Technology." In *Contemporary Issues in Curriculum*, A. C. Ornstein and L. S. Behar, eds. Boston: Allyn and Bacon, 1995.

Horejs, J. "Perceptions and Perspectives of Elementary Teacher Leaders." Unpublished doctoral dissertation, University of Southern California, July 1996.

Horwitz, R. A. "Psychological Effects of the Open Classroom." *Review of Educational Research*, 49 (1979): 71–85.

Howe, H. "Uncle Sam Is in the Classroom!" *Phi Delta Kappan*, 76 (January 1995): 374–377.

Hullfish, G. H., and P. G. Smith. *Reflective Thinking: The Method of Education*. New York: Dodd Mead, 1961.

Johnson, C. *Old-Time Schools and School-Books*. New York: Dover Publications, 1963.

Johnson, D. W., and R. T. Johnson. "The Role of Cooperative Learning in Assessing and Communicating Student Learning." In *Communicating Student Learning*, ASCD Yearbook, 25–46. Alexandria, VA: Association for Supervision and Curriculum Development, 1996.

Joyce, B., and B. Showers. "Improving Inservice Training: The Messages of Research." *Educational Leadership*, 37 (February 1980): 379–385.

Joyce, B., and M. Weil. *Models of Teaching*. 5th Ed. Needham Heights, MA: Allyn & Bacon, 1996.

Keislar, E. R. "The Teacher as Internal Evaluator of Student Performance." *UCLA Educator*, 19 (Winter 1977): 57–62.

Kilpatrick, W. H. *Philosophy of Education*. New York: Macmillan, 1951.

King, A. "Guiding Knowledge Construction in the Classroom: Effects of Teaching Children How to Question and How to Explain." *American Educational Research Journal*, 31 (Summer 1994): 338–368.

King, N. *Giving Form to Feeling*. New York: Drama Book Specialists, 1975.

Kirman, J. M. "Teaching About Local History Using Customized Photographs." *Social Education*, 59 (September 1995): 11–13.

Klein, M. F., K. Tye, and J. E. Wright. "A Study of Schooling: Curriculum." *Phi Delta Kappan*, 61 (December 1979): 244–248.

Kounin, J. S. *Discipline and Group Management in Classrooms*. New York: Holt, Rinehart and Winston, 1970.

Kounin, J. S., and P. H. Doyle. "Degree of Continuity of a Lesson's Signal System and the Task Involvement of Children." *Journal of Educational Psychology*, 67 (1975): 159–164.

Kounin, J. S., and L. W. Sherman. "School Environments as Behavior Settings." *Theory into Practice*, 18 (June 1979): 145–151.

Krashen, S. D. *Every Person a Reader*. Culver City, CA: Language Education Associates, 1996.

Krashen, S. D., and T. D. Terrell. *The Natural Approach*. Englewood Cliffs, NJ: Alemany Press, 1983.

Kucer, S. B. "Authenticity as the Basis for Instruction." *Language Arts*, 68 (November 1991): 532–540.

———. "Evaluation of Basic Reading and Writing Processes." Paper presented at the University of Southern California Teacher Conference, Los Angeles, 1988.

Kucer, S. B., and L. K. Rhodes. "Counterpart Strategies: Fine Tuning Language with Language." *The Reading Teacher*, 40 (2), (November 1986): 186–193.

Land, L. R., and M. A. Vaughn. *Music in Today's Classroom: Creating, Listening, Performing.* 2nd ed. New York: Harcourt Brace Jovanovich, 1978.

Lemlech, J. K. "Affective Involvement in Inquiry Methodology Using Role-Playing in Teacher Education." Unpublished doctoral dissertation, University of Southern California, 1970.

———, ed. *Becoming a Professional Leader.* New York: Scholastic Publishers, 1995.

———. *Classroom Management: Methods and Techniques for Elementary and Secondary Teachers*, 2nd ed. New York: Longman, 1988.

———. "Social Participation Skills in Elementary Classrooms." *Social Studies Review*, 16 (Fall 1976): 43–50.

Lemlech, J. K., and H. Hertzog. "Science Methodologies: Constructivist Distance Learning." Los Angeles: Los Angeles County Office of Education—Teams. Funded by the Connections 2000 Star Schools Project, 1995.

Lemlech, J. K., and S. N. Kaplan. "Collegial Preparation, Reflective Practice, and Social Studies Teaching." Paper presented to College and University Faculty Association of the National Council for the Social Studies annual meeting, Washington, DC, 1991.

———. "Learning to Talk About Teaching: Collegiality in Clinical Teacher Education." *Action in Teacher Education*, 12 (Fall 1990): 13–19.

Lemlech, J. K., and M. B. Marks. *The American Teacher: 1776–1976.* Bloomington, IN: Phi Delta Kappa Educational Foundation, 1976.

Lewison, M. "Taking the Lead from Teachers: Seeking a New Model of Staff Development." In *Becoming a Professional Leader*, J. K. Lemlech ed., New York: Scholastic, pp. 76–114, 1995.

Lieberman, A. "Collaborative Research: Working With, Not Working On." *Educational Leadership*, 43 (February 1986): 28–32.

Lippitt, R., Fox, R., and L. Schaible. *The Teacher's Role in Social Science Investigation.* Chicago: Science Research Associates, 1969.

Litsinger, D. *Social Studies Instruction at the University Elementary School, UCLA.* Berkeley: University of California Press, 1965.

Lomas, A. "Why Do Middle School Teachers Assume Leadership Roles?" Unpublished doctoral dissertation, University of Southern California, July, 1996.

Lowenfeld, V., and W. L. Brittain. *Creative and Mental Growth.* 8th ed. New York: Macmillan, 1987.

MacGillivray, L. "Teacher Research." In *Becoming a Professional Leader*, J. K. Lemlech ed., 117-140. New York: Scholastic, 1995.

Maehr, M. L., and D. D. Sjogren. "Atkinson's Theory of Achievement Motivation: First Step Toward a Theory of Academic Motivation?" *Review of Educational Research*, 41 (1971) 143–161.

Marland, S. P. "Education of the Gifted and Talented. Report to Congress." Washington, DC: U.S. Government Printing Office, 1972.

Massialas, B. G., and B. Cox. *Inquiry in Social Studies.* New York: McGraw-Hill, 1966.

McBee, R. H. "Can Controversial Issues Be Taught in the Early Grades? The Answer Is Yes!" *Social Education*, 60 (September 1996) 38–41.

McCormick, R. *Instructing Students Who Have Literacy Problems.* Englewood Cliffs, NJ: Merrill/Prentice Hall, 1995.

McNergney, R. F., and J. M. Herbert. *Foundations of Education—The Challenge of Professional Practice.* Boston: Allyn and Bacon, 1995.

Mehlinger, H. D. "Foreword." In *Building Rationales for Citizenship Education*, J. P. Shaver, ed., iii. NCSS Bulletin 52, Washington, DC: National Council for the Social Studies, 1977.

———. "School Reform in the Information Age." *Phi Delta Kappan*, 77 (February 1996), 400–407.

Melton, J. A. "Does Math Performance Improve When Students Select Their Own Partners?" *Teaching and Change*, 3 (3) (1996): 244–259.

Mercer, J. "Sociocultural Factors in Labeling Mental Retardates." *Peabody Journal of Education*, 48 (April 1971): 19.

Miller, L. "BTES: Implications for Staff Development." In *Time To Learn*, C. Denham and A. Lieberman, eds., 159–172. Washington, DC: National Institute of Education, U.S. Department of Education, 1980.

Miller, P., K. Shambaugh, C. Robinson, and J. Wimberly. "Applied Learning for Middle Schoolers." *Educational Leadership*, 52 (May 1995): 22–25.

Moffett, J., and B. J. Wagner. *Student Centered Language Arts and Reading, K–13, A Handbook for Teachers.* 3rd ed. Boston: Houghton Mifflin, 1983.

Morton, C. "The Modern Land of Laputa: Where Computers Are Used in Education." *Phi Delta Kappan,* 77 (February 1996): 416–419.

Mulryan, C. M. "Fifth and Sixth Graders' Involvement and Participation in Cooperative Small Groups in Mathematics." *The Elementary School Journal,* 95 (December 1995): 297–310.

Myers, M. "The Shared Structure of Oral and Written Language and the Implications for Teaching Writing, Reading, and Literature." In *The Dynamics of Language Learning,* J. R. Squire, ed., 121–146. Urbana, IL: ERIC Clearinghouse on Reading and Communication Skills, 1983.

National Council for the Social Studies. *Curriculum Standards for Social Studies Expectations of Excellence.* Washington, DC: 1994.

National Council of Teachers of Mathematics. *Curriculum and Evaluation Standards for School Mathematics.* Reston, VA: National Council of Teachers of Mathematics, 1989.

The National Education Goals Report. Washington, DC: U.S. Government Printing Office, 1994.

Nelson, J. L., K. Carlson, and S. B. Palonsky. *Critical Issues in Education.* New York: McGraw-Hill, 1996.

Newmann, F. "On Restructuring Schools: A Conversation with Fred Newmann by R. Brandt. *Educational Leadership,* 53 (November 1995): 71.

Newmann, F., and D. W. Oliver. "Case Study Approaches in Social Studies." *Social Education,* 31 (February 1967): 458–463.

Noddings, N. *The Challenge to Care in Schools—An Alternative Approach to Education.* New York: Teachers College Press, 1992.

———. "A Morally Defensible Mission for Schools in the 21st Century." *Phi Delta Kappan,* 76 (January 1995): 365–368.

Olshansky, B. "Picture This: An Arts-Based Literacy Program." *Educational Leadership,* 53 (September 1995): 44–47.

Ornstein, A. C., and D. U. Levine. *An Introduction to the Foundations of Education,* 3rd ed. Boston: Houghton Mifflin, 1985.

Osterman, K. F. "Reflective Practice, A New Agenda for Education." *Education and Urban Society,* 22 (October 1990): 133–152.

Palmer, C., and C. Muscara. *Educating for the Environment.* Educational Leadership, 48 (April 1991): 65–67.

Peet, B. *The Wump World.* Boston: Houghton Mifflin, 1970.

Petersen, P. L. "Direct Instruction Reconsidered." In *Research on Teaching,* P. L. Petersen and H. J. Walberg, eds. Berkeley, CA: McCutchan.

Peterson, P. L., and T. C. Janicki. "Individual Characteristics and Children's Learning in Large Group and Small Group Approaches." *Journal of Educational Psychology,* 71 (October 1979): 677–687.

Peterson, P. L., S. J. McCarthey, and R. F. Elmore. "Learning from School Restructuring." *American Educational Research Journal,* 33 (Spring 1996): 119–154.

Piaget, J. "How Children Form Mathematical Concepts." In *Mathematics in Elementary Education,* N. J. Vigilante, ed., 135–141. New York: Macmillan, 1969.

Piper, N. H. "Looking at Students' Attitudes About Mathematics." *Teaching and Change,* 1 (Fall 1993): 4–17.

Ponzio, R., and C. Fisher. "Introducing Prospective Teachers to Contemporary Views of Teaching and Learning Science: The Science and Youth Project." In *Educating Teachers For Leadership and Change—Teacher Education Yearbook III,* M. J. O'Hair and S. J. Odell, eds. Thousand Oaks, CA: Corwin Press, 1996.

Popham, W. J. *Classroom Assessment: What Teachers Need to Know.* Boston: Allyn and Bacon, 1995.

Porter, A. C., and J. Brophy. "Synthesis of Research on Good Teaching: Insights from the Work of the Institute for Research on Teaching." *Educational Leadership,* 45 (May 1988): 74–85.

Public Law 94-142, Education for All Handicapped Children Act (November 29, 1975).

Qin, Z., D. W. Johnson, and R. T. Johnson. "Cooperative Versus Competitive Efforts and Problem Solving." *Review of Educational Research,* 65 (Summer 1995): 129–144.

Ramsey, I. "Comparison of First Negro Dialect Speakers' Comprehension of Standard English and Negro Dialect." *Elementary English,* 49 (May 1972): 688–696.

Rappoport, A. L., and S. Kletzien. "Kids Around Town: Civics Lessons Leave Impressions." *Educational Leadership,* 53 (April 1996): 26–29.

Raywid, M. A. "Synthesis of Research Alternative Schools: The State of the Art." *Educational Leadership,* 52 (September 1994): 26–31.

Renyi, J. "The Arts and Humanities in American Education." *Phi Delta Kappan,* 75 (February 1994): 438–437.

Renzulli, J. "What Makes Giftedness? Reexamining a Definition." *Phi Delta Kappan*, 60 (November 1978): 180–184, 261.

Risinger, C. F. "The United States Civil War on the World Wide Web." *Social Education*, 60 (November 1995): 174–175.

Robiner, L. G. "Education for Aesthetic Awareness: A Powerful Process." *Phi Delta Kappan*, 61 (April 1980): 547–548.

Roderick, M. "Research Bulletin." *Phi Delta Kappan*, 15 (December 1995).

Rodgers, F. A. "Using Law-Related Education to Facilitate Students' Learning in Critical thinking." In *Law Related Education and the Preservice Teacher*. C. C. Anderson and D. T. Naylor, eds., 35–40. Washington, DC: American Bar Association, 1991.

Rosenshine, B., and R. Stevens. "Teaching Functions." In *Handbook of Research on Teaching*, 376–391. M. Wittrock, ed. New York: Macmillan, 1986.

Rosenthal, R., and L. Jacobson. *Pygmalion in the Classroom*. New York: Holt, Rinehart and Winston, 1968.

Ross, D. D. "First Steps in Developing a Reflective Approach." *Journal of Teacher Education*, 40 (January/February 1989): 22–30.

Ross, J. A. "Effects of Feedback on Student Behavior in Cooperative Learning Groups in a Grade 7 Math Class." *Elementary School Journal*, 96 (October 1996): 125–143.

Ross, L. Q. *The Education of Hyman Kaplan*. New York: Harcourt, Brace and World, 1937.

Rotter, J. "Generalized Expectancies for Internal Versus External Control of Reinforcement." *Psychological Monographs*, 80 (1966): 609.

Rowe, M. B. "Science, Silence, and Sanctions." *Science and Children*, 6 (1969): 11–13.

———. "Wait-Time and Rewards as Instructional Variables, Their Influence on Language, Logic, and Fate Control: Part One. Wait-Time." *Journal of Research in Science Teaching*, II (1974): 81–94.

Rubin, D. *Teaching Elementary Language Arts*. 2nd ed. New York: Holt, Rinehart and Winston, 1980.

Sagor, R. "What Project LEARN Reveals About Collaborative Action Research." *Educational Leadership*, 48 (March 1991): 6–10.

Sautter, R. C. "An Arts Education School Reform Strategy." *Phi Delta Kappan*, 75 (February 1994): 432–437.

Scheideman, S. N. "Writing Checklists: Empowering Students to Succeed." *Teaching and Change*, 2 (Winter 1995): 99–117.

Schlechty, P. C. *Schools for the 21st Century: Leadership Imperatives for Educational Reform*. San Francisco: Jossey-Bass, 1990.

Scruggs, T. E., and M. A. Mastropieri. "Successful Mainstreaming in Elementary Science Classes: A Qualitative Study of Three Reputational Cases." *American Educational Research Journal*, 31 (Winter 1994): 785–812.

Sears, P. S. "Evaluation and Motivation: A Critical Review." *UCLA Educator*, 19 (Winter 1977): 26–30.

Selwyn, D. *Arts and Humanities in the Social Studies* Bulletin 90. Washington, DC: NCSS Publications, 1995.

Shaftel, F., and G. Shaftel. *Role-Playing for Social Values*. Englewood Cliffs, NJ: Prentice Hall, 1967.

Shanker, A. "Full Inclusion Is Neither Free nor Appropriate." *Educational Leadership*, 52 (January 1995): 18–21.

Shillingford, J. P., and A. S. Mackin. "Enhancing Self-Esteem Through Wellness Programs." *The Elementary School Journal*, 91 (May 1991): 457–466.

Slavin, R. E. *Cooperative Learning*. New York: Longman, 1983.

Smith, F. *Understanding Reading*. 2nd ed. New York: Holt, Rinehart and Winston, 1978.

Solmon, M. A., and J. A. Carter. "Kindergarten and First-Grade Students' Perceptions of Physical Education in One Teacher's Classes. *The Elementary School Journal*, 95 (March/April 1995): 355–366.

Stachoviak, S. "Will Kindergarteners' Writing Experiences Improve Their Learning of Letter Names and Sounds?" *Teaching and Change*, 3 (Spring 1996): 315–324.

Sternberg, R. J., and T. I. Lubart. "Creating Creative Minds." In *Contemporary Issues in Curriculum*, 153–162. A. C. Orenstein and L. S. Behar, eds. Boston: Allyn and Bacon, 1995.

Stipp, D. "The Gender Gap." *Wall Street Journal* (September 11, 1992).

Stone, M. "Cultivating and Supporting High School Teacher Leaders." Unpublished doctoral dissertation, University of Southern California, July 1996.

Streitmatter, J. *Toward Gender Equity in the Classroom—Everyday Teachers' Beliefs and Practices*. New York: State University of New York, 1994.

Stroeher, S. K. "Sixteen Kindergartners' Gender-Related Views of Careers." *The Elementary School Journal*, 95 (September 1994): 95–103.

Suchman, J. R. *Developing Inquiry*. Chicago: Science Research Associates, 1966.

Sykes, G. "Reform of and as Professional Development." *Phi Delta Kappan*, 77 (March 1996): 464–467.

Taba, H. "Implementing Thinking as an Objective in Social Studies." In *Effective Thinking in the Social Studies*, 25–50. J. Fair and F. Shaftel, eds. Washington, DC: National Council for the Social Studies, 1967a.

———. *Teacher's Handbook for Elementary Social Studies*. Palo Alto, CA: Addison Wesley Publishing, 1967b.

Task Force on Standards for Teaching and Learning in the Social Studies. "A Vision of Powerful Teaching and Learning in the Social Studies: Building Social Understanding and Civic Efficacy." *Social Education*, 57 (September 1993): 213–223.

Thorne, B. In "Girls Will Be Girls," M. Lawton. *Education Week* (March 30, 1994): 27.

Tollifson, J. A Balanced Comprehensive Art Curriculum Makes Sense. *Educational Leadership*, 45 (4) (December 1987/January 1988):18–22.

Tompkins, G. E., and K. Hoskisson. *Language Arts Content and Teaching Strategies*. 3rd ed. Englewood Cliffs, NJ: Prentice Hall, 1995.

Tyack, D. *Turning Points in American Educational History*. Waltham, MA: Blaisdell Publishing, 1967.

United States Government. *Statistical Abstract*. Washington, DC: U.S. Government Printing Office, 1995.

Van Scotter, R., L. Van Dusen, and B. Worthen. "Starting Early: Junior Achievement's Elementary School Program." *Educational Leadership*, 53 (May 1996): 33–37.

Veatch, J. *Individualizing Your Reading Program*. New York: G. P. Putnam's Sons, 1959.

Veenman, S. "Cognitive and Noncognitive Effects of Multigrade and Multi-Age Classes: A Best Evidence Synthesis." *Review of Educational Research*, 65 (Winter 1995): 319–382.

Vygotsky, L. *Thought and Language*. Cambridge, MA: Massachusetts Institute of Technology Press, 1962.

Walsh, E. *Schoolmarms: Women in America's Schools*. San Francisco: Caddo Gap Press, 1995.

Wang, M. C., M. C. Reynolds, and H. J. Walberg. "Serving Students at the Margins." *Educational Leadership*, 52 (January 1995): 12–17.

Watts-Warren, B. "Links Between Family Life and Minority Student Achievement: Removing the Blinders." *The International Journal of Social Education*, 9 (Fall/Winter 1994–95): 11–27.

Webb, N. M., and S. Farivar. "Promoting Helping Behavior in Cooperative Small Groups in Middle School Mathematics." *American Educational Research Journal*, 31 (Fall 1994): 369–396.

Weiner, B., ed. *Cognitive Views of Human Motivation*. New York: Academic Press, 1974.

Wolf, K. "Developing an Effective Teaching Portfolio." *Educational Leadership*, 53 (March 1996): 34–37.

Yando, R. M., and J. Kagan. "The Effect of Teacher Tempo on the Child." *Child Development*, 39 (1968): 27.

Zahorik, J. A. "Elementary and Secondary Teachers' Reports of How They Make Learning Interesting." *The Elementary School Journal*, 96 (May 1996): 551–564.

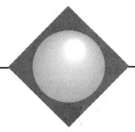

Author Index

Acheson, K. A., 379
Acquarelli, K., 380*
Adams, D. M., 217
American Association of University Women, 8
Ames, C., 66, 67
Anderson, C. M., 78
Anderson, P. S., 229, 236, 248
Angell, A. V., 267
Arbuthnot, J. B., 59, 158
Arlin, M., 78
Armstrong, T., 61
Aronson, E., 243
Arreaga-Mayer, C., 233*
Aschbacher, P., 354*
Au, K., 13*
Ausubel, D.P., 98, 112

Baker, E. L., 217*
Baker, J., 189
Barr, R., 261, 263†
Barth, J. L., 261, 263†
Bayles, E., 127
Besag, F. P., 25
Blatt, M., 60
Block, J. H., 218
Bracey, G. W., 32*
Brandt, R., 347
Brett, M., 46*
Brittain, W. L., 349
Bronkhurst, A.D., 67*

Brooks, W. M., 230
Brophy, J., 372
Brophy, J. E., 218
Bruner, J., 128
Buckmaster, L., 132*

Caine, G., 60
Caine, R., 60
California State Department of Education, 284, 286, 296
Canter, L., 80
Carlson, K., 11, 14, 33
Carroll, J. B., 237
Carter, J. A., 326*
Central Eastern Regional Educational Laboratory, 358
Clinchy, B. McVicker, 5
Cohen, D. ,6
Cohen, E. G., 271*
Cohen, E. P., 359*
Copeland, R., 296
Cox, B., 127
Cuban, L., 32, 32*

Darling-Hammond, L., 383*
Davidman, L., 12*
Davidman, P. T., 12*
Dean, J., 357
Dewey, J., 14, 27, 34, 79, 127, 129, 214
Dollase, R. H., 385
Dunn, K., 62
Dunn, R., 62
Dweck, C. S., 218

* The author's name appears in a boxed element.
† The author's name appears in a footnote.

399

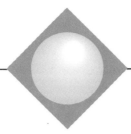

Subject Index

academic feedback, 76, 101
academic focus, 107
academic rationalism, 38, 49
academy, 18, 20
Activities Integrating Mathematics and Science (AIMS) program, 291, 314
adapted physical education, 324, 338
adaptive motivation pattern, 54, 67*
adolescent problems, 340
adults in the classroom, 383–384
advance organizer, 106, 112–113
  and classroom management, 113
aesthetic judgment, 346, 348–349
alternative scheduling, 43
alternative schools, 38, 41–42
American Association for Health, Physical Education, and Recreation, 381
American Association for the Advancement of Science, 305
  Project 2061, 306
American education foundations, 21
American Federation of Teachers, 381
Americanization class, 29*
Americanization through schooling, 11
analysis of teaching episode, 77–78
anecdotal record, 202, 213–214
anticipatory thinking in the classroom, 79
application exercise, 175*
apprentice schools, 18, 20
Arithmetic, 22
arranged environment, 260, 269

* This information appears in a boxed element.

art and music center, 92
arts education, 149, 346–363, 361*
  goals of, 351–352
  inclusion, 363
  programs and projects, 357–361
  resources for, 357
  teaching approaches, 352–356
Arts in Education, 358
arts-integrated schools, 361
assertive discipline. *See* discipline
assessment, 76, 100, 202, 215, 216*
  authentic, 202, 215
  of teacher competence, 384–385
at-risk students, 4, 8, 9–10
attribution, 54
  model of achievement motivation, 66
automatize, 282
autonomous level, 59

backward problem solving, 126, 140–141
balance, 168, 170
Barnard, Henry, 24
beginning of school, planning for, 91–97
  of semester, checklist, 93
behaviorism, 32
behavior, student, 73–74
Benjamin Franklin, 20–21, 22
Bilingual Education Act, 12
bilingualism, 12–13
bilingual programs, 31
biomechanics, 324, 328
Blue-Backed Speller, 22
Bloom, Allan, 33

403

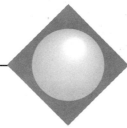

About the Author

Professor Johanna K. Lemlech, University of Southern California, has been a public school teacher in the Los Angeles Unified School District, director of Teacher Education and Student Teaching at the University, and chair of the Department of Curriculum and Instruction. She was awarded the Crocker Professorship from 1992–1996. Her specialties are teacher education, curriculum, instruction, and school leadership. Dr. Lemlech has authored four textbooks for teacher education: *Handbook for Successful Urban Teaching, Classroom Management for Elementary and Secondary Teachers, Becoming a Professional Leader,* and *Curriculum and Instructional Methods for the Elementary and Secondary School.* She was the principal investigator of the USC–Norwood Professional Development School. Dr. Lemlech is currently studying collegial behaviors among student teacher cohorts and leadership activities of experienced teachers.